The Unexplained Mysteries

Pictures Acknowledgements

1061 Bridgeman Art Library/Watts Gallery, Compton; 1062 Whitworth Art Gallery, University of Manchester (T), Sonia Halliday (B); 1063 Sonia Halliday; 1064-65 William MacQuitty; 1066 Robert Estall; 1066-67 BTA; 1067 Country Life (T), Mary Evans Picture Library (B); 1068 Mansell Collection (T), BTA (B); 1069 Mansell Collection (T); 1070 Aldus; 1071 Novosti (T, C), Popperfoto (B); 1072 Natural Science Photos; 1073 Tunnel Cement, Essex; 1074 Michael Holford (T), Ronald Sheridan (B); 1075 Ronald Sheridan; 1076 Mary Evans Picture Library (T), Photoresources (B); 1077 Hutchinson Library (T), Marion Morrison (B); 1078 Psychic News (T), Leslie Flint (B); 1079 Kobal (L, BL), Popperfoto (C. R); 1080 Psychic News (T), Psychic News/London Express (C, B);1081 John Massey Stewart (L), Werner Forman Archive (R); 1082 John Massey Stewart (T), Werner Forman Archive (BL); 1082-3 Topham; 1083 John Massey Stewart (C); 1084 Alan Hutchinson Library (T, C), Australian Information Service (B); 1085 Bridgeman Art Library (T), Robert Estall (B); 1086 Photo Meyer (C), Museum of Fine Arts, Anwerp (TR); 1086-7 Robert Hunt Library ; 1087 Mary Evans Picture Library; 1088 Sheridan Photo Library (TC), Mansell Collection (TR), Press Association (B); 1089 I.W.M.; 1090 Sunday Times/David Bailey (T), Foto EFE (C); 1091 Mary Evans Picture Library (B); 1092 Scala (T), National Council of Tourism in Lebanon (B); 1093 Scala (B); 1094 Bruce Coleman/Leonard Lee Rue III (T), Map by Collins Edwards & Partners/Ed Stewart (B); 1094-5 Bruce Coleman/Jen & Des Barlett (T), Bruce Coleman/Ronald Thompson/Frank W. Lane (B); 1096 Bruce Coleman/Jane Burton (T), Thomas Gilcrease Institute (B); 1097 Ardea Photographics; 1098-1100 Illustration by Iain McCaig; 1099 Map by Richard Burgess (B); IBC Hutchinson Library; 1101 Francis N. Ryan; 1102 Map by Colin Edwards & Partners (T), Colin Godman (B); 1102-3 Colin Godman; 1103 Syndication International; 1104 Francis N. Ryan (T), Colin Godman (B); 1105 Francis N. Ryan; 1106 Werner Forman Archive/British Museum (T), Ashmoleon Museum (B); 1106-7 Aldus Archive/Warburg Institute; 1107 Werner Forman Archive/British Museum; 1108 Mary Evans Picture Library; 1108-9 Mary Evans Picture Library; 1110 Photri (TL), artwork by Studio Briggs (B); 1111 Science Photo Library/NASA (T), Bruce Coleman/J&D, Barlett (C), Bruce Coleman/Allan Power (BC), Bruce Coleman (BR); 1112 Science Photo Library; 1112-3 Science Photo Library/David A. Hardy; 1113 CIC International; 1114 Janet & Colin Bord (T), map by Colin Edwards (B); 1115 Artwork by Ed Stuart (T), artwork by Mike Holland Studio (B); 1116 Thor Heyerdahl; 1117 Michael Holford; 1118 Spectrum; 1120 Picturepoint (B); 1121 Peter Newark's Western Americana; 1122 Mary Evans Picture Library; 1124 Kobal Collection (T), Michael Holford (B); 1125 H. G. Andrade/Playfair Archive; 1126 Michale Holford (TL0, Scala (TR); 1126-7 Michael Baigent; 1128-9 Mary Evans Picture Library; 1130-1 Mary Evans Picture Library/Harley Rutledge; 1131 Artwork by Ed Stuart; 1132 Mary Evans/Harley Rutledge; 1133 Mary Evans/A. Lawson (C), Mary Evans/Probe (B); 1134 BBC Hulton Picture Library (T), European Space Agency (BL), A. J. Clark (BR); 1134-5 Zefa; 1135 Vivien Fifield (B); 1136 Institute of Geological Services (T), New Scientist (C), map by Colin Edwards & Partners (B); 1137 Map by Colin Edwards & Partners; 1138 Psychic News (T), BTA (B); 1139 Psychic News (B); 1140 Psychic News (T), Science Photo Library/Mehau Kulyk (B); 1141 Xinhua News Agency; 1142 Map by Colin Edwards & Partners; 1142-3 Poperfoto; 1143 Xinhua News Agency; 1144 Topham (T), Xinhua News Agency (B); 1145 Topham (L), Xinhua News Agency (R); 1146 Syndication International; 1146-7 Bruce Coleman/Leonard Lee Rue; 1147 Syndication International; 1148 Natural Science Photos/g. Kinns; 1149 Fortean Picture Library; 1150 Alan Hutchinson Library; 1151 Werner Forman Archive/Statens Historika Museum, Stockholm (T), Alan Hutchinson Library (C); 1152 Giraudon (T), Bridgeman Art Library (B); 1153 Michael Holford; 1154-7 Elmar Gruber; 1158 United Nations/Y. Nagata; 1158-9 United International Pictures; 1159 Science Photo Library/Julian Baum; 1160 Bill Chalker/Australian Centre for UFO Studies (B); 1161 Bridgeman Art Library; 1162 Sefton Photo Library (T), National Portrait Gallery London (C); 1162-3 Science Photo Library; 1163 Science Photo Library (T); artwork by Janos Marffy (B); 1164 Bruce Coleman/Masood Qureshi (TL)/Jane Burton (TR)/Hans Reinhard (TC); 1165 Alan Hutchinson/Carlos Freire; 1166 UPI, New York (T, B), Guy Lyon Playfair (C); 1167 Alan Hutchinson Library (T), UPI, New York (B); 1168 Alan Hutchinson Library (T), UPI, New York (B); 1169 British Library; 1170 Cyrus Lee; 1171 S. Ostrander (L), UPI, New York (R); 1172 Cyrus Lee (T), Dr H. Puthoff, Stanford Research Institute (B); 1173 Institute of Geological Sciences (T), Zefa (B); 1174 Institute of Geological Sciences; 1175 Space Frontiers (C), American Meteorite Laboratory (B); 1176 Dale P. Cruikshank; 1177 Arnold Desser/Harry Price Library; 1178 Mary Evans Picture Library (T), Popperfoto (BL); Harry Price Library (BR); 1179 Mary Evans Picture Library (T), Euan Wingfield (B); 1181 Scala; 1182 Mary Evans Picture Library (T), Science Photo Library (B); 1183 Mary Evans Picture Library; 1184 Science Photo Library (T), Michael Holford (B); 1185 Don Davies; 1186 Ronald Sheridan (T), Mary Evans Picture Library (C); 1186-7 Mary Evans Picture Library; 1187 Popperfoto (T), Jean-Loup Charmet (B), 1188 Zefa (T), Michael Holford (B); 1188-9 Jean-Loup Charmet; 1189 Res Features; 1190 Syndication International; 1190-1 Bridgeman Art Library; 1191 Sonia Halliday (C), Lorna Ainger (B); 1192 Parabond Productions; 1193 Associated Press (T), Rex Features (B); 1194 RCHAM of Scotland (T), National Portrait Gallery London (B); 1194-5 RCHAM of Scotland (T), East Lothian Library (C); 1196-7 RCHAM of Scotland; 1198 Foundation for Research on the Nature of Man; 1199 Ed Stuart; 1200 PSI Search; 1201 Mary Evans Picture Library/SPR; 1202 Mary Evans Picture Library/Harry Price Collection; 1203 Bavaria-verlag (L), Psychic News (R); 1204 Mary Evans Picture Library/Sigmund Freud (T); Mary Evans Picture Library/Harry Price Collection (B); 1205 Anita Gregory (T), Roger Viollet (B); 1206 René Dazy (T), BBC Hulton Picture Library (B); 1210 artwork by Studio Briggs; 1211 High Times/artwork by Chris Spollen; 1212 artwork by Studio Briggs (T); Theosophical Publishing Co.; 1213 artwork by Studio Briggs (B); 1214 Peterborough Public Library; 1214-15 BBC Hulton Picture Library; 1215 Stanley Trowers & Partners (T); 1216 BBC Hulton Picture Library (T), illustration by Murray Aikman; 1217 Terry Rice (T), Paul Snelgrove (B); 1218 Mary Evans Picture Library; 1219 Mansell Collection (T), Tony Stone Worlwide (C), Mary Evans Picture Library (B); 1220 Mansell Collection (T), Topham (B); 1221 Photri (T), Ground Saucer Watch (B); 1222-4 Ground Saucer Watch; 1225 EFE; 1226 Fortean Picture Library (TL), National Portrait Gallery, London (TR); 1226-7 Science Photo Library; 1227 Mary Evans Picture Library (T), Tony Craddock/Science Photo Library (B); 1228 Mary Evans Picture Library (T), Mansell Collection (B); 1229 Mary Evans Picture Library; 1230 Sheryl C. Wilson (T), Theodore X. Barber (B); 1230-1 Grandon; 1232 Kobal Collection (T), Mary Evans Picture Library/SPR (B); 1233 John Cutter; 1234 Topham (T), Popperfoto (B); 1235 Popperfoto (TL), Mary Evans Picture Library (TC, B); 1236 Topham (T), Amnsell Collection (B); 1237 Mansell Collection (T), Bruce Coleman/Javier Andrada (B); 1238 Colin Godman; 1239 Colin Godman (T); 1240 Colin Godman (T); 1241 Keystone (T), Louvre (B); 1242 Sotheby's; 1242-3 Kobal Collection; 1243 Kobal Collection (T), Colour Library International (C); 1244 Topham; 1245 A&V Vargo (T), Zefa; 1246 Playfair Archive; 1247 Playfair Archive (T), Guy Lyon Playfair (B); 1248-9 Playfair Archive; 1250 Spectrum; 1250-1 Topham; 1251 Spectrum (TL), Sheridan Photo Library (TR, C); 1252 artwork by Studio Briggs; 2152-3 UPI, New York; 1253 Bruce Coleman/Christian Zuber; 1254 Mary Evans Picture Library (T), Euston films: "The Quatermass Conclusion" (B); 1255 Mary Evans Picture Library; 1256 Associated Press (T), UPI, New York (B); 1257 Janet & Colin Bord; 1258 Rex Features (L); 1259 UPI, New York; 1260 W. C. Reeves (T, C), Culver Pictures (B); 1261 Michael Holford; 1262 Aldus Books/Courtesy Principal, St Hughes College, Oxford (T), Mary Evans Picture Library (B); 1263 map by Ed Stuart (T); 1264 Mansell Collection (C), Mary Evans Picture Library (B); 1265 Michael Holford (T); 1266 Popperfoto ; 1266-7 Robert Hunt Picture Library; 1267 Popperfoto ; 1268 Robert Hunt Picture Library (T), Popperfoto (C); 1269 Robert Hunt Picture Library; 1270 Giraudon; 1271 Lauros-Giraudon (T), Ronald Sheridan (B); 1272 Giraudon (T), Ronald Sheridan (B); 1273 Giraudon (T), C. M. Dixon (C), Werner Forman Archive/British Museum, London (B); 1274 Elmar Gruber; 1275 Elmar Gruber (T), Topham (B); 1276 Elmar Gruber (T), map by Ed Stuart (C); 1277 Rex Features; 1278 artwork by Ed Stuart (T), Science Photo Library (B); 1279 artwork by Studio Briggs (L), Science Photo Library (R); 1280 Photri;1281 Sonia Halliday; 1282 Arnold Desser; 1283 Roger Viollet; 1284 Michael Holford (T), Kobal Collection (B); 1285 Michael Holford; 1286 Mary Evans Picture Library (T), John Cutten (B); 1287 Novosti (T), Mary Evans Picture Library (C, B); 1288 Thomas Gilcreare Institute (T), Joel Finder Collection (C); 289-90 Robert Hunt Picture Library; 1290-1 Daily Telegraph Colour Library; 1292 Jeanie Morrison; 1293 Mary Evans Picture Library; 1294 Mary Evans Picture Library (B); 1295-6 Toby Hogarth; 297 US Air Force/Bryce Bond (B); 1298 Flicks/UPI (T), Science Photo Library/Tony Craddock (B); 1299 Artwork by Hayward Art Group/linework by Studio Briggs (T), Associated Press (B); 1300 Artwork by Ed Stuart/Aviation Week and Space Technology (T), Kobal Collection (B); 1301 UPI, New York; 1302 Map by Colin Edwards & Partners (T), Photri (B); 1303 illustration by Murray Aikman; 1304-5 Fortean Picture Library; 1305 Philip Daly; 1306 Combier (T), French Government Tourist Office (C), Michael Holford (B); 1307 Michael Holford (TR), Ronald Sheridan (C), René Dazy (B); 1308 Jean-Loup Charmet (T), Roger Viollet (C); 1309 BBC Hulton Picture Library (T); 1310 Aldus Books/M. Lethbridge (T), Robert Estall (B); 1311 Roger Mayne (T), Lorna Ainger (B); 1312 Map by Steve Westcott (T), Roger Mayne (C), Bettman Archive (B); 1313 Spectrum Colour Library; 1314 Jeannie Morison (T), Mary Evans Picture Library/Harry Price Collection (B); 1315-7 Mary Evans Picture Library/Harry Price Collection; 1318 Paul Snelgrove; 1319 James Phillips (T), Stephen von Mehesz (B); 1320 Paul Snelgrove (T), Stephen von Mehesz (B): 1321 Illustrated London News Picture Library; 1322-3 A. Cooper Rollinson; 1323 Science Photo Library/NOAA; 1324 A. Cooper Rollinson (T), Science Photo Library/Sally Bensusen (B); 1326 Mary Evans Picture Library; 1326-7 Devonshire Library Services; 1328 Mansell Collection (T), Devonshire Library Services (CL), Mary Evans Picture Library (TL, TR); 1330 Spectrum Colour Library (T), Aldus Books/Mrs Lethbridge (B); 1331 Lorna Ainger; 1332 Roger Mayne (T); 1333 Artwork by Studio Briggs (T), Focus Exeter (CL, CR); 1334 Illustration by Murray Aikman; 1334-5 Philip Daly; 1335 Philip Daly (C), Robert Sheaffer (B); 1336 Maps by Studio Briggs/Courtesy of Betty Hill (T), Betty Hill (B); 1337 Philip Daly; 1338 Mary Evans Picture Library(T), Richard Burgess (B); 1339-40 Mary Evans Picture Library/Harry Price Collection; 1341 Hamlyn Group (CR), Space Frontiers (B); 1342 Hamlyn Group (T), Science Photo Library (C, B); 1343 artwork by Janos Marffy; 1344 UPI, New York (T), Photri (C); 1346 Royal Albert Memorial Museum, Exeter (B); 1346-7 Mary Evans Picture Library; 1347 Devon Library Services (TC), Royal Albert Memorial Museum, Exeter (CR), Southwark Local Studies Library (B); 1348 Mary Evans Picture Library (T), BBC Hulton Picture Library (B); 1350 Routledge & Kegan Paul (T), Robert Estall (B); 1351 Illustration by Richard Burgess (T), Mary Evans Picture Library (B); 1352 artwork by Graham Bingham, Paul Binerley (TL, TR, BL, CBR), Robert Hunt Library (BR), Zefa (CTL, CTR, CBL), Rex Features (B); 1353 Robert Estall; 1354 Jeannie Morrison (T), Richard Burgess (B); 1355 Toby Hogarth (T), Jeannie Morrison (B); 1356-7 Toby Hogarth (T); 1358 Betty Hill (T, C0, Philip Daly (B); 1359 Philip Daly; 1360 Betty Hill;1361 Ronald Sheridan (T), Jean-Loup Charmet (B); 1362 Jean-Loup Charmet (T, C), Sonia Halliday (B); 1362-3 Ronald Sheridan; 1363 Art Directors; 1364 Sonia Halliday (T), Ronald Sheridan (CR); 1365 Giraudon (T), Sonia Halliday (C), Art Directors Library (B); 1366 Mary Evans Picture Library (T), Andrija Puharich (C); 1366-7 Andrija Puharich; 1368 Andrija Puharich (T, C), UPI, New York (CL); 1369 Andrija Puharich; 1370 Jeannie Morrison (T), National Gallery of Scotland (B); 1371 Jeannie Morrison (T); 1372 Kate Robertson; 1374-5 Science Photo Library; 1374-6 artwork by Studio Briggs; 1378 Mary Evans Picture Library (T), Scala (B); 1379 Picturepoint (T), Mansell Collection (B); 1380 Agence Angeli; 1381 Gurdijeff: Making a New World by John Bennett (T), Popperfoto (B); 1382 Gurdijeff & Mansfield by James Moore (T, C); 1382-3 Witness by John Bennett; 1384 John Cutten (C), Witness by John Bennett (B); 1385 Witness by John Bennett; 1387 Scala (T), Map by Colin Edwards & Partners (B); 1388 Jean Loup Charmet (T), Dr John Macrae (C), Spectrum (B); 1389 Werner Forman Archive (T), Michael Holford (CL), Topham (CR); 1390-1 Jean-Loup Charmet; 1392 René Dazy (T), Jean-Lopu Charmet; 1392-3 Jean-Loup Charmet; 1393 Mary Evans Picture Library; 1394 UPI, New York (T), John Massey Stewart (B); 1395 Novosti; 1396 Artwork by Studio Briggs (T), Science Photo Libray/NASA (C), Sovfoto (B); 1397 Topham (B); 1398-9 SPR/Paul Snelgrove; 1401 Robert Harding/Museo de Americo, Madrid; 1402 Universitäts Bibliothek, Heidelberg; 1403 Michael Holford (T), Mansell Collection (B); 1404 Beinecke Rare Book & Manuscript Library, Yale University (T), Map by Colin Edwards & Partners (B); 1418 Michael Holford; 1420 Paul Snelgrove (T), Graham Whitlock (B)

The Unexplained Mysteries

GREENWICH EDITIONS

This edition published in 2000 for
Greenwich Editions
A member of the Chrysalis Group plc
10 Blenheim Court
Brewery Road
London N7 9NT

ISBN 0-86288 306 7

Packaged by De Agostini Rights/MEB-DP

Cover image: Rod Dickinson / Fortean Picture Library

Printed in Czech Republic by Aventinum
60198

THE CASE FOR GOD

DEBATE OVER THE EXISTENCE OF GOD HAS RAGED FOR CENTURIES. HERE, WE SURVEY THE ARGUMENTS OF THE THEOLOGIANS AND THE ATHEISTS, AND ASK WHETHER A BELIEF IN A SUPREME DEITY IS NECESSARILY AT ODDS WITH A SCIENTIFIC VIEW OF THE UNIVERSE

Theists believe that the Universe was created and is sustained by an eternal, omnipresent, omnipotent and invisible God, as illustrated below, in The Sower of the Systems, *by George Frederic Watts. Atheists, however, hold that the Universe was formed by accident and is sustained through the action of eternal, omnipresent, omnipotent and invisible principles – the laws of nature.*

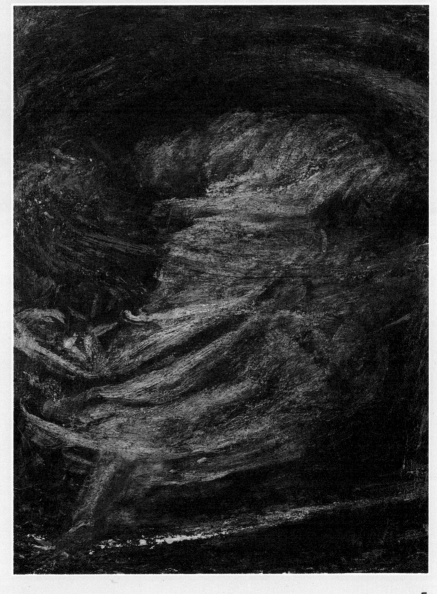

Atheists deny the existence of God. However, this does not mean they have no faith; for, as much as anyone else's philosophy, theirs often implies a belief in an invisible reality underlying the world that we experience with our senses. But for them – in contrast to theists – the ultimate organising principles are thought of as blind, impersonal and unconscious. These principles are also generally considered to be changeless and eternal, and to apply throughout the Universe: nothing can escape them or lie beyond their scope. Moreover, although they influence and control matter, they are not in themselves material. They cannot be crystallised in a test tube, and the mathematical formulae in terms of which they can be expressed are not carved on the planets, nor traced out by rays of light. Indeed, they elude the senses, and can be known only indirectly, through their effects. The most fundamental laws of nature, atheists say, cannot themselves be explained scientifically: they simply have to be accepted as given.

Thus atheistic theory has it that the Universe, and all that lies within it, depends on certain eternal, omnipresent, omnipotent and invisible principles. But how does this theory compare with the idea that the Universe depends on a God, who is also eternal, omnipresent, omnipotent and invisible?

Perhaps the chief difference is that, for the atheist, the laws of our Universe are blind, unconscious and uncreative. By contrast, for the believer in God, the ultimate reality is conscious, creative and alive. Indeed, in the eyes of the believer, the laws of nature share some of the properties of God, precisely because God is the source of these laws.

Atheists usually maintain that their view is simpler and more scientific than the theist view, and regard God as an unnecessary hypothesis. Although, at first sight, this theory has a certain plausibility, on further reflection it turns out to raise more difficulties than it solves. In the first place, if matter is regarded as inanimate, governed only by blind laws and chance, there is no place in the system for consciousness. Even the consciousness of the atheist himself has to be regarded as nothing other than a kind of shadow of electrical and chemical changes inside his brain – a shadowy consciousness that cannot actually do anything or influence actions that are entirely determined by a combination of the laws of physics and chemistry and random events, over which there is no control. This is, of course, a view much at variance with our experience of ourselves as creatures capable of exercising free choice, and to take it seriously requires deep faith in the atheist philosophy.

Atheists also hold that both the evolutionary process and the Universe as a whole are without meaning. But only the most committed seem able to take this gloomy view seriously, since it renders their own lives and theories quite pointless.

There is, too, the problem of the laws of nature – laws on which so-called 'scientific' atheism depends. As we have seen, these are supposedly universal, changeless and omnipresent, as well as immaterial. In fact, they sound more like cosmic ideas than material things, and can be known only as ideas, through scientific theories and mathematical formulae. In the final analysis, it is through these laws that the atheist has to try to account for human consciousness – a difficult task.

What is more, although the laws of nature play such an important part in atheistic philosophy, ironically the theory is not itself scientific, since it can never be proved but accepted only by an act of faith.

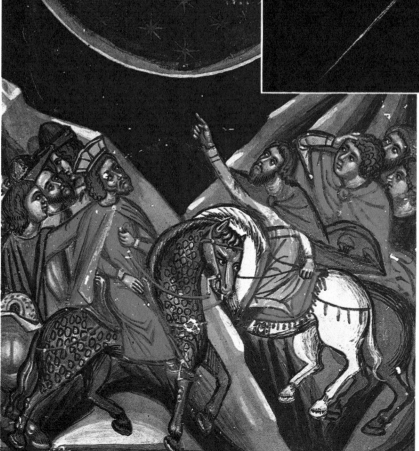

" Science probes and investigates, religion accepts and worships. There is room for both, in different moods... We have learnt even in physics that there are mysterious guiding entities. We call them waves, or we call them PSI. "

Sir Oliver Lodge, My Philosophy

God is depicted creating the Sun and stars, above, in a detail from a 16th-century French stained glass window. Both Eastern and Western religious traditions often portray God creating the world through the power of his Word.

The Ancient of Days, by William Blake (1757-1827), above left, shows the creation of the world with a pair of dividers – the tools of the engineer.

The vision of the Roman emperor Constantine is shown in a Cypriot mural painting of the 15th century, far left. The power of mystic experience has long been recognised but does not in any way constitute proof of the existence of God.

These particular difficulties do not arise, however, if we suppose instead that the Universe arises from the creative activity of a power we might call God. For if God is the conscious source of the Universe, and also contains the Universe, the laws of nature can be seen rather as ideas in the mind of God. This theory suggests that consciousness is present within the Universe, and that it was transferred to living beings arising in the course of the evolutionary process.

If this view is correct, then the consciousness that dwells in Man is the same as the consciousness of God, so it should be possible to experience directly that this is so. Mystics in all religious traditions have testified that it is indeed the case – though sceptics might argue, with some justification, that all mystic experience could be an illusion. The direct insight of mystics has, however, been intuitively recognised as one of ultimate reality, far surpassing ordinary everyday experience. For this reason, it cannot be adequately described to those of us who have not experienced it, just as colours cannot be adequately described to someone who has been blind from birth. This direct revelation or enlightenment lies at the heart of all religions: it is

*In*Focus

THE GOD WITHIN

However convincing religious or mystic visions may be to the person who experiences them, they can never constitute proof of the existence of God. Religion, it seems, will always be a matter of faith rather than of knowledge. Arguments for and against the existence of God are fairly equally weighted, and it can always be argued by the sceptical that religious experience could be illusory.

The Hebrew language, in a curious way, seems to acknowledge this possibility. The Hebrew word for the verb 'to pray' is *hitpalel* – a reflexive verb, literally 'to judge oneself', that seems to emphasize the relevance of subjective religious experience.

the vision of the prophets, seers, enlightened ones, sages and saints, and connects all religious traditions with their divine source. Thus the existence of God is more than just a philosophical theory, and has been supported – although, of course, not proven – by the deepest experiences of men and women throughout the ages.

SUPREME ANALOGIES

But the consciousness of God gave rise to and sustains the Universe, and this consciousness is clearly inconceivably greater than the consciousness of men and women. For this reason, we cannot expect to form any adequate idea of God's nature in terms of our inevitably limited ideas and experience. The best we can do is to use analogies. These vary according to different traditions – but all seem to express a basically similar concept.

A familiar image in Judaic tradition is that of God as a craftsman or potter making a pot. An 18th-century version likened God to a celestial engineer who designed, made and maintains the Universe as if it were a gigantic clockwork mechanism. Certain modern versions, meanwhile, see God as a kind of cosmic computer programmer. One of the problems with these approaches is that they treat matter as existing separately from the consciousness of the maker, suggesting a picture of God imposing his will on a Universe that exists outside him.

Hindu tradition takes a rather different analogy, and sees the Universe as a vast dream of God. Everything around us, as well as ourselves, exists only within the dream of Vishnu, the preserver and protector of the world. When we have dreams, we are merely experiencing dreams within a dream. Thus, the material world has no independent existence separate from the mind of God: matter is not dead and inanimate, but rather a kind of image in the divine mind. If God stops dreaming it, then it will simply vanish. This way of thinking emphasizes that nothing is separate from the being of God, and that God is in all things, providing a valuable and different perspective from the view of God that is predominant in the Judaic tradition. But one possible disadvantage is that it can lead to a view of the physical world as essentially illusory.

A third analogy, found in both Western and Eastern traditions, is based on human speech. By uttering words, we enable what comes into our minds to take on a physical existence as sound, and at the same time to bring about specific effects upon the external world. Some of the most striking examples are provided by the words of command spoken by political rulers, which can cause armies to go to war, cities to be built, or prisoners to be freed. Using this analogy, divine creation can be seen as happening through speech, as God utters words that automatically have specific effects. Thus, for example, we read in the first chapter of *Genesis*: 'And God said, Let there be light and there was light.' God is also seen as the supreme judge and law-giver. His 'words' give rise, on the one hand, to the laws of nature, and on the other, to the moral laws in accordance with which human life should be led, as communicated to Man through divinely inspired prophets and seers – and, for Christians, supremely, in the 'Word made flesh', Jesus Christ.

INVOCATION AND PRAYER

Although this idea of God creating through the power of his speech can easily degenerate into a picture of a remote and mighty emperor sitting on a throne, there is another important implication that can modify this image. If God speaks to Man, then perhaps Man may also speak to God. Indeed, the addressing of God through invocations and prayers plays an important part in most religious traditions.

A further analogy that emphasizes this aspect of communication more strongly, while at the same time avoiding the impression of distance and remoteness created by the image of the all-powerful autocrat, is that of a loving father. The son's being and consciousness are derived from the father, but at the same time the son has a freedom and independence that would not be possible in a lifeless machine made by an engineer. The strength of this analogy is that it emphasizes the possibility of a relationship founded on love between Man and God. Its weakness, however, is that it can easily give rise to misleading images, such as that of a stern, bearded patriarch, or become associated with negative emotional responses in people whose relationships with their all-too-human father have been less than happy.

Many other rather more poetic analogies have been developed within certain cultures. In India, for example, one is based on the play of a child; and God's relationship to the Universe is seen as one of play, or *lila*. In another Hindu image, God is seen as a dancer, Shiva in the form of Nataraja, whose powerful cosmic dance creates the activity and changing patterns of the Universe.

In spite of their many differences, varied images of God – as craftsman, dreamer, ruler, father, playing child and dancer – all have in common the idea of creative conscious activity. But none can possibly give an adequate conception of God, and in all religious traditions it is emphasized that God lies beyond all our powers of imagination and comprehension. For instance, among the Jews, the making

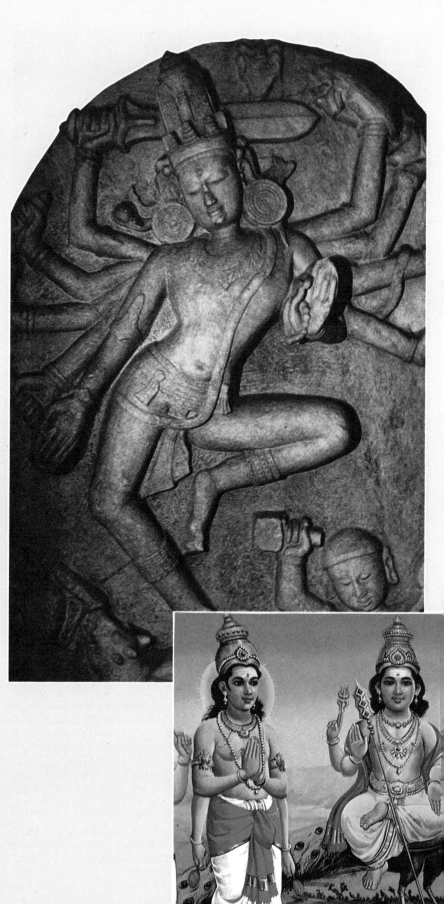

According to Hindu tradition, the cosmic dance of Shiva, left, is seen as creating the ceaseless activity and changing patterns of the Universe.

The Mexican god Chac-Mool, right, is a divine messenger. Sacrifices are placed on the tray that the god carries in his hands; and, when they vanish, they are believed to have been taken away as an offering to the Sun.

The gods of the Hindu pantheon are depicted, below, in a family group that makes them seem more familiar than exalted.

of images or idols of God is prohibited because God can never be adequately represented by any man-made object; and the same prohibition is maintained in Islam. In the Hindu tradition, God's ultimate nature is said to be unknowable: 'not this, not that'. In Taoism, it is said that the 'Tao that can be expressed is not the everlasting Tao. The name that can be named is not the everlasting Name.'

In Buddhism, the absolute is spoken of in terms of what it is not. And in Christian theology, the being of God is recognised as beyond all human conception, the ultimate mystery. Similarly, in Judaism, the true name of God is regarded as too sacred to be spoken. What belief in the existence of God implies is a recognition that the ultimate source of all things is supremely conscious, creative and alive. The atheist, by contrast, believes

that the invisible organizing principles underlying the Universe are essentially unconscious, blind and purposeless. Neither of these beliefs can, it seems, be proved by the limited methods of science; and we cannot rely on the powers of logic. In choosing between them, we have to rely on our own experience and deepest intuitions. If we accept the philosophy of atheism, we may congratulate ourselves on the extent of our intellectual understanding and think that the hypothesis of the existence of God can be disregarded. But if we come to recognize that God exists, then we may well begin to contemplate the unfathomable mystery of life and of creation.

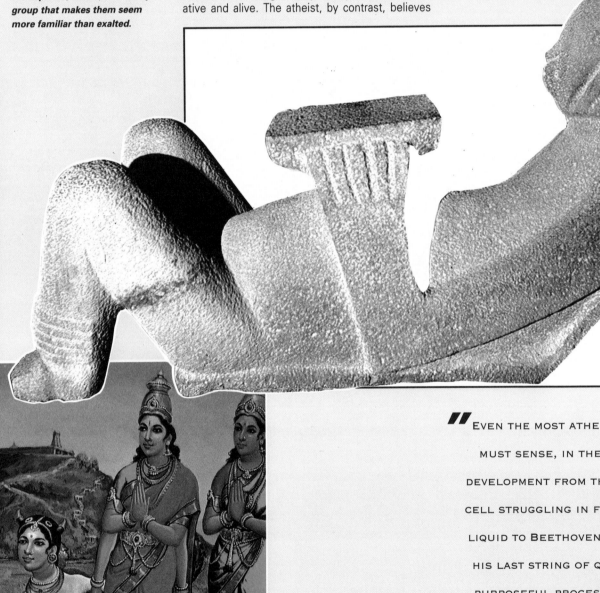

"EVEN THE MOST ATHEISTIC OF US MUST SENSE, IN THE CHAIN OF DEVELOPMENT FROM THOUGHTLESS CELL STRUGGLING IN FEATURELESS LIQUID TO BEETHOVEN COMPOSING HIS LAST STRING OF QUARTETS, A PURPOSEFUL PROCESS IMPLYING SOMETHING MORE MEANINGFUL THEN MERE SPECIES-SURVIVAL."

HILARY EVANS, GODS: SPIRITS: COSMIC GUARDIANS

THE HORROR OF GLAMIS

FOR CENTURIES, GLAMIS CASTLE HAS HAD A REPUTATION AS A PLACE OF STRANGE AND AWFUL HAPPENINGS – EVENTS THAT STRIKE TERROR AT THE HEARTS OF ALL WHO EXPERIENCE THEM

Glamis Castle, picturesque home of the Earl of Strathmore and Kinghorne, below, was a wedding gift from King Robert II upon the marriage of his daughter to Sir John Lyon in the 14th century. From the time that Sir John moved to Glamis, the family seems to have been dogged by misfortune.

The painting of the Third Earl, Patrick, with his children and greyhounds, right, dominates the far wall of the drawing room at Glamis. It is around Patrick that two strange stories revolve.

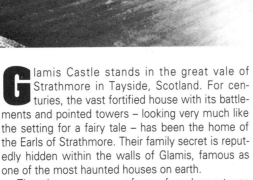

Malcolm II, above, reigned as King of Scotland from 1005 until his death at Glamis in 1034, at the hands of an army of rebels. Tradition holds that he was slain in what is now known as King Malcolm's Room, top right, and that his brutal murder saw the start of the 'horror' at the castle.

Glamis Castle stands in the great vale of Strathmore in Tayside, Scotland. For centuries, the vast fortified house with its battlements and pointed towers – looking very much like the setting for a fairy tale – has been the home of the Earls of Strathmore. Their family secret is reputedly hidden within the walls of Glamis, famous as one of the most haunted houses on earth.

That there was some form of unpleasantness within the castle's walls is an undoubted historical fact. And that the castle is today the centre of a triangle formed by three biblically named villages – Jericho, Zoar, and Pandanaram – may indicate the terror felt by its minions; for, according to a Scottish National Trust guidebook, the men who built and named them 'had at least some knowledge of the Scriptures and regard for the wrath of God'. That wrath, claim locals, was called down on Glamis for the sins of the first dozen or so lairds. In recent times, however, there is little to suggest that life at the castle has been anything other than pleasant and peaceful. While Michael Fergus Bowes-Lyon, the 18th, and present, Earl is well-liked by his tenants, as were his immediate forbears, the conduct of at least one of their ancestors called into being what became known as the 'horror' of Glamis.

It is the obscure nature of the horror that makes accounts of it all the more terrifying. Indeed, no recent Earl has ever spoken of it to an outsider, except in enigmatic terms, and no woman has ever been let in on the secret. It is passed on only to the Strathmore heir on his 21st birthday.

The historical record of horror at Glamis Castle goes back to 1034, when King Malcolm II was cut down by a gang of rebellious subjects armed with claymores, the large broadswords peculiar to Scotland. It was said that every drop of Malcolm's blood seeped from his body into the floorboards, causing a stain that is still pointed out today, in what is called King Malcolm's Room. That the stain was made by Malcolm's blood is disputable, however, for records seem to show that the flooring has since been replaced. Nevertheless, Malcolm's killers added to the death toll of Glamis by trying to escape across a frozen loch: but the ice cracked and they were drowned.

CURSE OF THE CHALICE

The Lyon family inherited Glamis from King Robert II, who gave it to his son-in-law, Sir John Lyon, in 1372. Until then, the Lyon family home had been at Forteviot, where a great chalice, the family 'luck', was kept. Tradition held that if the chalice were removed from Forteviot House, a curse would fall on the family. Despite this, Sir John took the cup with him to Glamis. The curse, though, seems to have had a time lapse: Sir John was indeed killed in a duel, but this did not occur until 1383, and the family misfortunes are usually dated from this time.

The 'poisoned' chalice may well have also influenced events 150 years later when James V had Janet Douglas, Lady Glamis, burned at the stake in Edinburgh on a charge of witchcraft. The castle reverted to the Crown; but after the falsity of the charge was proved, Glamis was restored to her son. The spectre of Lady Glamis – the 'Grey Lady' as she is known – is said regularly to walk the long corridors even today.

It was Patrick, the Third Earl of Strathmore, who made the idea of a Glamis 'curse' widespread in the late 17th century: indeed, to many people he seemed the very embodiment of it. A notorious rake and gambler, he was known in both London and Edinburgh, as well as throughout his home territory, for his drunken debauchery. Facts covering his career and his character are festooned with folklore, but he must have been something of an enigma; for despite his wild ways, he was philanthropic towards his tenants at least. The *Glamis Book of Record*, for instance, details his plans for building a group of lodges on the estate for the use of retired workers. Now known as Kirkwynd Cottages, they were given to the Scottish National Trust by the 16th Earl of Strathmore in 1957, to house the Angus Folk Collection.

Two principal stories endure about Patrick. The first is that he was the father of a deformed child who was kept hidden somewhere in the castle, out of sight of prying eyes. The second is that he played cards with the Devil for his soul – and lost.

The first story is fed by a picture of the Third Earl that now hangs in the drawing room. It shows Patrick seated, wearing a classical bronze breast-plate, and pointing with his left hand towards a distant, romanticised vista of Glamis. Standing at his left knee is a small, strange-looking, green-clad child; to the child's left is an upright young man in scarlet doublet and hose. The three main figures are placed centrally, but two greyhounds in the picture are shown staring steadfastly at a figure, positioned at the Earl's right elbow. Like the Earl, this figure wears a classical breastplate, apparently shaped to the muscles of the torso – but if it is a human torso, it is definitely deformed. The left arm is also strangely foreshortened. Did the artist paint from life – and if so, does the picture show the real 'horror' of Glamis?

DIABOLICAL GAMES

The second story goes like this. Patrick and his friend the Earl of Crawford were playing cards together one Saturday night when a servant reminded them that the Sabbath was approaching. Patrick replied that he would play, Sabbath or no Sabbath, and that the Devil himself might join them for a hand if he so wished. At midnight, accompanied by a roll of thunder, the Devil appeared and told the card-playing Earls that they had forfeited their souls and were therefore doomed to play cards in that room until Judgement Day.

The pact presumably came into operation only after Patrick's death, and there is some evidence that he revelled in the tale. But did he tell it merely as a joke or as some sort of elaborate cover up, in order to scare intruders forever from the castle? If the latter was his intention, it was certainly strikingly successful. In 1957, a servant at the castle, Florence Foster, complained in a newspaper article that she had heard the Earls at their play in the dead of night, 'rattling dice, stamping and swearing. Often I lay in bed and shook with fright,' she said, and resigned rather than risk hearing the phantom gamblers again. The story persists even today of a secret room known only to the Earls themselves, and no one knows for certain which of the hundred-odd rooms at Glamis was used by Patrick for his diabolical game of cards.

Another story tells – with curious precision – of a grey-bearded man, shackled and left to starve in 1486. A later one, probably also dating from before Patrick's time, is gruesome in the extreme. A party of Ogilvies from a neighbouring district came to Glamis and begged protection from their enemies, the Lindsays, who were pursuing them. The Earl of Strathmore led them into a chamber, deep in the castle, and left them there to starve. Unlike the unfortunate grey-bearded man, however, they had each other to eat and began to turn cannibal – some, according to legend, even gnawing the flesh from their own arms.

Lady Elizabeth Bowes-Lyon, below, who was to become Queen Mother, grew up at Glamis. She is said to have felt the presence of what was possibly the 'horror' in the Blue Room.

One or other of these tales may account for a skeletally thin spectre, known as Jack the Runner; and the ghost of a black pageboy, also seen in the castle, seems to date from the 17th or 18th century, when young slaves were imported from the West Indies. A 'white' lady is also said to haunt the castle clock tower, while the grey-bearded man of 1486 appeared, at least once, to two guests simultaneously, one of whom was the wife of the Archbishop of York at the turn of the 20th century. She told how, during her stay at the castle, one of the guests came down to breakfast and mentioned casually that she had been awakened by the banging and hammering of carpenters at 4 a.m. A brief silence followed her remarks, and then Lord Strathmore spoke, assuring her that there were no workmen in the castle. According to another story, as a young girl, Queen Elizabeth, the Queen Mother (daughter of the 14th Earl, Claude George Bowes-Lyon), once had to move out of the Blue Room because her sleep was being disturbed by rappings, thumps, and footsteps.

Fascinating as all these run-of-the-mill ghosts and their distinguished observers are, however, it is

the 'horror' that remains the great mystery of Glamis. All the principal rumours – cannibal Ogilvies notwithstanding – involve a deformed child, born to the family and kept in a secret chamber, who lived, according to 19th-century versions of the story, to a very old age. In view of the portrait openly displayed at Glamis, and always supposing that it is the mysterious child who is actually portrayed, subsequent secrecy seems rather pointless. If Patrick himself was prepared to have his 'secret' portrayed in oils, why should successors have discouraged open discussion of the matter?

UNMENTIONABLE HORROR

Despite the secrecy, at the turn of the 19th century, stories were still flying thick and fast. Claude Bowes-Lyon, the 13th Earl who died in 1904 in his 80th year, seems to have been positively obsessed by the horror, and it is around him that most of the 19th-century stories revolved. It was he, for instance, who told an inquisitive friend: 'If you could guess the nature of the secret, you would go down on your knees and thank God it were not yours.' Claude, too, it was who paid the passage of a workman and his family to Australia, after the workman had inadvertently stumbled upon a 'secret room' at Glamis and been overcome with horror. Claude questioned him, swore the man to secrecy, and bundled him off to the colonies shortly afterwards. To a great extent, the obsession seems to have visited itself upon his son, Claude George, the 14th Earl, who died in 1944.

In the 1920s, a party of young people staying at Glamis decided to track down the 'secret chamber' by hanging a piece of linen out of every window they could find. When they finished, they saw there were several windows that they had not been able to locate from the inside. When the Earl learned what they had done, he flew into an uncharacteristic fury. Unlike his forbears, however, Claude George broke the embargo on the secret by telling it to his estate factor, Gavin Ralston, who subsequently refused to stay overnight at the castle again.

When the 14th Earl's daughter-in-law, the next Lady Strathmore, asked Ralston the secret, Ralston is said to have replied: 'It is lucky that you do not know and can never know it, for if you did, you would not be a happy woman.'

That statement, surely, is the clue to the horror of Glamis. Old Patrick's deformed offspring did not alarm the father because nothing like it had been seen in the family before. Possibly the 'wicked' Earl rather delighted in him. But if the same deformity appeared even once in a later generation, the head of an ancient, noble and hereditary house would certainly have been reluctant to broadcast the fact. Perhaps Claude, 13th Earl of Strathmore, knew of such a second, deformed child in the Bowes-Lyon line, and passed the secret, and the fear of its recurrence, on to his successors?

> **"** IF YOU COULD GUESS THE NATURE OF THE SECRET, YOU WOULD GO DOWN ON YOUR KNEES AND THANK GOD IT WERE NOT YOURS. **"**
>
> **CLAUDE BOWES-LYON**

PERSPECTIVES

THE HAUNTED HIGHLANDS

The Highlands of Scotland abound in tales of ghosts and supernatural incidents. Given the number of castles in the region – and the bloody fighting they must have seen during their long histories – it is not surprising that many are associated with gruesome events. One story concerns Duntrune Castle in Argyll, which in the 17th century was about to be attacked by a chieftan called 'Left-handed Coll'. Before he did so, he sent his piper to do a bit of spying, but the man was discovered and shut up in a turret room. However, he managed to warn his chief by playing *The Piper's Warning to his Master*, whereupon Campbell of Duntrune chopped off both his hands. In recent years, two skeleton hands were found under the kitchen floor, and the piper's ghost and tune is said still to haunt the tower.

Amid the ruins of Dunphail Castle, a few miles south of Forres, in the Grampian region of northern Scotland, visitors have claimed to hear the sounds of battle and to have seen the spectral, severed heads of several men. In a previous century, apparently, the men had escaped from the castle while it was under siege, and then hurled sacks of grain over the wall to starving members of their clan. The men were soon captured and beheaded, and their heads thrown over the walls, accompanied by the chilling cry: 'Here's beef for your bannocks (bread)!'

A young girl's pride, meanwhile, lies behind the haunting of Castle Grant, near Grantown-on-Spey, 20 miles (32 kilometres) south of Forres, in the Highland region. The ghost is believed to be the spirit of a certain Barbara Grant, who has been seen washing her hands in a bedroom in the tower, then rushing across the room to the staircase. It is said that, in the 16th-century, her father had locked her up in the tower because she refused to marry a man he had chosen for her, but whom she did not love. And there, in the tower, she eventually died – only her agitated ghost still supposedly reliving her sad fate.

MAMMOTHS - ALIVE OR DEAD?

WOOLLY MAMMOTHS ARE SUPPOSED TO HAVE DIED OUT THOUSANDS OF YEARS AGO. BUT REPORTS OF SIGHTINGS MADE DURING THIS CENTURY SUGGEST THEY COULD STILL BE ROAMING THE UNEXPLORED VAST FORESTS OF SIBERIA

The artist's impression of the woolly mammoth, below, was made on the basis of discoveries of remains in northern Siberia. The mammoth's habitat was probably midway between the barren tundra of the present-day Arctic and the wooded taiga of slightly more southerly regions. The taiga would give it all the food – and cover – it would need to survive. So could mammoths still be alive in Siberia today?

The mammoth remains found in 1900 at Berezovka, Siberia, provided scientists with a fascinating wealth of new material. Yet one fact remained puzzling: the unswallowed grass and flowers that were found to be in the creature's mouth indicated that it must have met a sudden death – but how?

Rigorous analysis of the creature's stomach contents showed that it contained grasses, mosses and lichens of various kinds, as well as the green branches of such tundra trees as fir and pine. The presence of certain seeds also showed that death had occurred in autumn. The autopsy findings of the geologist seemed to point to one conclusion: that the mammoth had been browsing when it stepped on to thin ice and plunged into a shallow ravine, breaking its leg and pelvis – a fate that Dr Otto Hertz, leader of the expedition, believed had befallen many other mammoths. Thrashing about, it

The perfectly preserved body of a six-month-old mammoth, 'Dima', found in the permafrost at Yakutsk, Siberia, in the summer of 1977, is shown, left, being removed from the ground.

had pulled down tonnes of snow and semi-frozen slush from the sides of the banks, and suffocated. An interesting fact was that parts of the body had undergone the adipocere change – a hardening of the normally semi-liquid body fat into a sort of suet that, once set, remains almost permanent. This condition occurs when a body – whether human or animal – has been immersed in water or buried in a damp environment.

PRIZE SPECIMENS

Since then, a number of other partially preserved carcasses have been found in the permafrost belt. In 1948, for instance, excavations with a high-pressure hose in Alaska uncovered the head and forequarters of a baby mammoth; while an even better specimen than the Berezovka example came to light in the same Siberian district – Yakutsk – when a road was being bulldozed through the area in the summer of 1977. The body excavated seemed to be that of a six-month-old animal and, as its trunk was intact, experts were able to note for the first time the two distinct 'fingers' at the end of this. They were probably used for delicately picking up small objects in the manner of modern elephants, although the lower finger of the mammoth may also have acted as a form of flap used to shut out the cold from the nostrils.

This mammoth had died in a similar way to the one found in 1900, it was conjectured; and, as Hertz pointed out, such deaths must have come regularly to the bulky beasts. But, sceptics still argue, surely not all mammoths could have died in such a way? The 'catastrophist' school of thought maintains that a colossal catastrophe, causing an abrupt change in temperature, froze up the Siberian wastes and thus deprived the mammoth of its food. This theory was first promoted at the beginning of the 19th century by the French naturalist Georges Cuvier, generally regarded as the father of modern palaeontology (study of fossils). The main body of modern science, however, disagrees with catastrophism. One objection is that Cuvier based his hypothesis on an erroneous interpretation of the

Tests showed that 'Dima' – the baby mammoth, seen being examined right *and on display below – probably died by stepping on to thin ice. The carcass was in such excellent condition that two 'fingers' could be clearly seen at the end of the trunk. These had probably been used for picking up small objects, in the manner of elephants, and for shutting off cold air from the nostrils.*

15

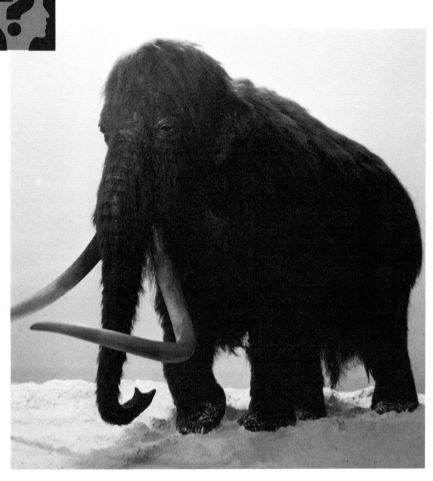

almost certainly used as snow-ploughs to scrape off the top surface of the snow and to expose the lichen and grass below. They could certainly live in extreme cold, with their matted hair, small ears – designed to conserve body temperature, unlike those of their modern cousins in Africa, which disperse it – and fatty humps that, like those of the camel, stored energy. But in a bad winter or frozen spring, browsing animals might not have been able to scratch deep enough for food. If such conditions recurred over decades and perhaps hundreds of years, herds would inevitably dwindle and die.

LOCAL EXTINCTION

Facts back up this idea. Writing in the *Bulletin* of the Geological Society of America in 1898, Robert Bell provided evidence for a similar theory, quoting an event that occurred on Akpatok Island in Ungava Bay, Canada. This large island had always swarmed with reindeer; but one winter, 'when the snow was deeper than usual, rain fell upon it (an almost unprecedented occurrence) and formed a heavy and permanent crust of ice over both the bare ground and the snow, thus preventing the deer from obtaining their food. The consequence was that the whole number perished, and the island has never been re-stocked. If this former great herd had comprised the whole species then living, the reindeer would now be extinct.'

Bell also mentioned the huge number of mammoth bones found clumped together around the shoreline of Siberia, particularly in the mouths of such rivers as the Lena. He pointed out that, in his own time, before the buffalo were all but wiped out by hunters, great herds of them had been known to drown when they attempted to cross frozen rivers on ice that was not strong enough to bear their weight. And, we should remember, the mammoth was much heavier than the buffalo.

All these theories – plus the less convincing one that prehistoric Man hunted certain animals to the point of extinction – may have some bearing on the disappearance of the woolly mammoth. But one tantalising thought remains: are these massive beasts really extinct?

The great forests of Siberia, the *taiga*, extend over 3 million square miles (7,770,000 square kilometres); and, apart from a scattering of nomadic and primitive hunters, they are uninhabited. In 1581, Ermak Timofeyevich, captain of a Cossack

'gaps' of millions of years between fossils found in one rock stratum and those found in an adjoining one. The state of geological knowledge in his day was such that scientists did not realise that volcanic and other upheavals in the Earth's surface could jumble strata in a confusing way. In any case, no such gaps in the fossil record had occurred in Siberia since the decline of the mammoth. Nor, as Hertz showed, had the vegetation changed much since the Berezovka specimen died, apparently in the act of eating buttercups.

The most reasonable explanation for the extinction of the great herds lies not in a sudden temperature change, but in a series of particularly hard winters. The mammoths were migratory animals, wandering slowly south in winter and back north in the spring. Their curious, inward-curving tusks were

The massive bulk of the woolly mammoth, above, is a model based on remains found in the Siberian permafrost.

P E R S P E C T I V E S

A SUDDEN CATASTROPHE?

According to Dr Immanuel Velikovsky, seemingly supernatural events, described in legends throughout the world, are actually accounts of catastrophes caused by the close approach of comets to Earth. Velikovsky cites many examples, including the crumbling of the walls of Jericho in *The Bible*, and the story of Phaethon in Greek mythology, whose solar chariot, we are told, almost crashed into the Earth.

As he claimed in *Worlds in Collision*, the disappearance of the mammoths must also have been the result of one of these cataclysms. The mammoths, he argued, 'did not succumb in the struggle for survival as an unfit product of evolution'. Indeed, many of the best specimens, buried deep in the permafrost, show signs of having died suddenly and – for Velikovsky, an important point – the kind of vegetation

found in mammoth stomachs no longer exists in Siberia. Velikovsky claimed that these facts argue for a sudden cataclysmic change in climate. But the argument is by no means conclusive – particularly as Velikovsky got one of his facts wrong. Plants very similar to those found in the mammoth stomachs *are* to be found in Siberia today – raising the fascinating possibility that mammoths might not be extinct after all.

*In*FOCUS

MAMMOTHS IN BRITAIN

Most of the important discoveries of mammoth remains have been found within the Arctic Circle. But there is at least one discovery of British mammoths on record – that found near Aveley in Essex, in 1964.

The find was made in a clay-pit and comprised two skeletons, lying at almost the same spot, within a foot (30 centimetres) of each other. The lower skeleton was of a straight-tusked elephant – a creature present in Britain during the warm periods between successive cold phases of the Ice Age. The other skeleton, buried in a layer of peat, was of an early form of mammoth, an ancestor of the woolly mammoth. Its curved tusks can be seen in the photograph, *left,* at the top right. One tusk is complete, though broken; the other is only about 6 inches (15 centimetres) long, and worn, pointing to damage during its life. The remains are estimated at between 100,000 and 200,000 years old – a little older than the hippopotamuses that, another find has shown, once roamed the site of London's Trafalgar Square.

band sent into Siberia at the beginning of Russia's conquest of the territory, reported that one of the first things he and his men saw on the east side of the Ural range was 'a large, hairy elephant'. The natives expressed no surprise, and told him that it was known by a name meaning 'mountain of meat'. This was a full century before the Dutch diplomat and explorer Evert Ysbrandt Ides suggested the possibility that the *mamontovakosty,* or 'mammoth ivory', being found in large amounts, came from an elephant-like creature.

GREAT TRACKS

An even more impressive story was reported by a respected French diplomat named Gallon in 1920. He was stationed in Siberia at the time, and one day happened to begin talking to a Russian peasant, a hunter who had spent four years in the *taiga,* shooting bear and wolf. In his second year in the forest, he told Gallon, he found: 'a huge footprint pressed deep into the mud. It must have been about two feet [60 centimetres] across the widest part and about eighteen inches [45 centimetres] the other way... not round but oval. There were four tracks, the tracks of four feet, the first two about twelve feet [4 metres] from the second pair which were a little bigger in size. Then the track suddenly turned east into the forest of middling-sized elms. Where it went in, I saw a huge heap of dung; I had a good look at it and saw it was made up of vegetable matter. Some ten feet [3 metres] up, just where the animal had gone into the forest, I saw a row of broken branches made, I don't doubt, by the monster's enormous head as it forced its way into the place.' The hunter followed the trail and,

some days later, found that another had joined it, just like the first one.

'The wind was in my face, which was good for approaching them without them knowing I was there. All of a sudden, I saw one of the animals quite clearly, and now I must admit I really was afraid. It had stopped among some young saplings. It was a huge elephant with big white tusks, very curved; it was a dark chestnut colour, as far as I could see. It had fairly long hair on the hindquarters, but it seemed shorter in the front. I must say I had no idea there were such big elephants... the second beast was around; I saw it only a few times among the trees. It seemed to be the same size.'

The hunter's gun, though suitable for taking bear, was not, he judged, of heavy enough calibre to take on such monsters. So he crept away and returned to his winter quarters, terrified by what he had seen, and mystified by the sheer bulk of the two beasts.

'Such,' concluded Gallon's report, 'was the tale of this man who was too ignorant to know that what he had just seen were mammoths. And when I told him the name, he did not show the least sign that he understood what I meant.'

No scientist has yet come up with a totally satisfying explanation of why the woolly mammoth should have become extinct. Meanwhile, its staple diet, as revealed in the stomach of the Berezovka mammoth, still flourishes in Siberia. Taking into account Gallon's detailed testimony, as provided by a Russian witness hunting in the *taiga,* there may well be the faint but very real possibility that a few of the hairy giants are still lumbering among the vast and largely unexplored forests of Siberia.

ANCIENT EVIDENCE

THOSE WHO BELIEVE THAT SPACE-BEINGS VISITED EARTH CENTURIES AGO POINT TO THE WONDERS OF THE ANCIENT WORLD AS EVIDENCE FOR EXTRA-TERRESTRIAL ACHIEVEMENT. BUT MIGHT ANCIENT PEOPLES HAVE BEEN CAPABLE OF SUCH ACCOMPLISHMENTS?

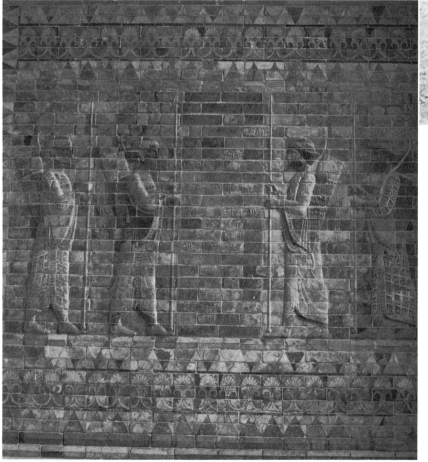

While most archaeological work is concerned with the mundane bric-a-brac and rubbish left by ancient societies, every now and again an object turns up that completely surpasses all previous estimates of an ancient culture's technical skill. During the 1970s, for example, archaeologists working in Bulgaria made an extraordinary series of discoveries about the Neolithic Karanovo culture that flourished there around 4500 BC. The finds date from a time when Man is generally thought to have had little or no knowledge of metallurgy; yet the Karanovo graves revealed a surprising treasure-trove of beautiful, finely made gold and copper jewellery, as well as weapons. Finds such as these are slowly, but continually, forcing archaeologists to re-assess their views of ancient Man's technological abilities.

But it is Egypt that has produced more scientific wonders, often of great antiquity, than any other region. The ancient Egyptians had an advanced knowledge of medicine and surgery: they even used contraceptives of honey and acacia gum (an effective spermicide), and it has been suggested

FOR ALIENS?

that they understood the use of penicillin (an antibiotic produced naturally on moulds). A model wooden glider from Saqqâra, built around 200 BC, also shows at least a basic grasp of the principles of aerodynamics, while the Great Pyramid, built around 2600 BC, amazes even 20th-century Man with its sheer size and architectural perfection.

Many writers, though, have insisted that the Great Pyramid of Cheops at Giza could not be built even with present-day scientific skill and machinery. As Erich von Däniken, for one, stated bluntly in *Chariots of the Gods?*: 'Today, in the twentieth century, no architect could build a copy of the Pyramid of Cheops, even if the technical resources of every continent were at his disposal.' The implication of such a claim is obvious: if we could not build it, how could the ancient Egyptians have done so with what we assume to have been basic technology and simple tools? Did the Egyptians perhaps have 'outside help', from extra-terrestrials?

Von Däniken and other supporters of the 'ancient astronaut' theory draw similar conclusions for many of the architectural wonders of the ancient world. Another puzzling structure often cited is the huge stone complex of Tiahuanaco, near Lake Titicaca in the Andes of Bolivia. Its temples are made of stone blocks weighing up to a hundred tonnes, quarried between 60 and 200 miles (100-300 kilometres) away. How Tiahuanaco was constructed remains a mystery. The file, however, suggests that much of the advanced knowledge we proudly believe is peculiar to our modern world – including sophisticated metallurgy, surgical operations, the use of electricity and the idea of heavier-than-air flight – may have been available hundreds, even thousands of years ago. If we also take into account the myths of the 'gods' who are said to have taught Man so much about both the arts and

The facade of the tomb of Sneferu, left, is dwarfed by the Great Pyramid of Cheops behind it. Erich von Däniken gave the weight of the pyramid as more than 31 million tonnes and said it would have taken ordinary mortals 664 years to build it. In fact, the pyramid weighs about 6 million tonnes; and engineers and archaeologists estimate that it could have been erected well within the 23-year reign of its builder, Cheops.

The Persian frieze showing archers, below left, dating from the sixth century BC, made use of ancient glazing techniques that were lost during the Dark Ages and rediscovered in western Europe only during the Industrial Revolution.

Were the gods worshipped by ancient Man really interplanetary visitors? Marduk, the horned god of agriculture, is shown on a seal, above right, from Mesopotamia that dates from the third century BC. The head of an idol, below, is from Bulgaria, where a very advanced culture existed as long ago as the fifth century BC.

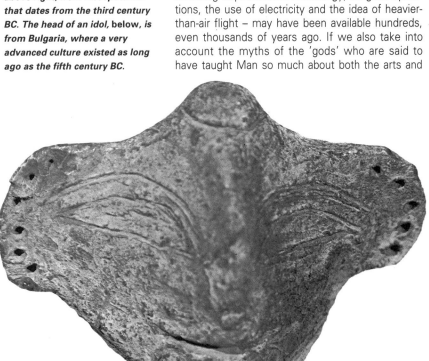

the sciences, then the case for extra-terrestrial intervention in Man's early history almost begins to look plausible.

But is the extra-terrestrial hypothesis really a fair explanation of ancient technological 'anomalies'? Unfortunately, writers like von Däniken too often exaggerate and distort the evidence. In order to show that extra-terrestrial help was needed, for example, von Däniken had to attempt to discredit the Egyptians by implying that they had none of the basic resources necessary for such a massive undertaking as the construction of the Great Pyramid of Cheops.

FALSE IMPRESSION

Almost every stage of von Däniken's argument relies on a misinterpretation of the facts, and the clear evidence that the Egyptians themselves were responsible for the Great Pyramid is ignored or brushed aside. The fact is that the name of Pharaoh Cheops (or Khufu), remembered by the later Egyptians as the cruel taskmaster who had ordered the building of the Great Pyramid, is carved on some of its limestone blocks. The structure is an extraordinary achievement; but the Egyptians were, without doubt, masters of mathematics, architecture, stone-masonry and, above all, organisation. The dozens of other pyramids dotted along the Nile Valley, ranging from a few feet high to little short of the Great Pyramid's 450 feet (137 metres), stand as witnesses to the fact that Egyptians could certainly have built Cheops' pyramid.

Cheops' Great Pyramid and other 'ancient anomalies' can only be deemed extra-terrestrial artefacts at the expense of ancient peoples. By creaming off their greatest achievements as 'proof' of extra-terrestrial intervention, von Däniken creates a false impression that is downright insulting to highly sophisticated ancient cultures such as those of the Egyptians, Mayans, Hindus and Babylonians. As cosmologist Carl Sagan put it: 'Essentially, von Däniken's argument is that our ancestors were too stupid to create the most impressive surviving architectural and artistic works.'

Archaeological evidence, often just shards and fragments, is far too limited to reconstruct the real scope of ancient peoples' skill and knowledge. After all, we would not like our culture and technology to be assessed on the basis of soft-drink bottles, which will far outlast the paper on which are described our educational systems, the thoughts of our philosophers and saints, our medical knowledge and the mathematics and scientific skills that have already flown us to the Moon. Nor would we like to think that an archaeologist of the future would ascribe the remains of a fragmentary radio, preserved by chance conditions, to an alien intelligence. Yet this is how von Däniken treats the evidence that indicates ancient Man may have used surprisingly advanced technology.

A Narrow View

Ancient astronaut theorists, while professing to be free-thinking and far-sighted, are possibly victims of a very narrow view of history that sees our own era as the most important point in time, a focus by which all other historical periods must be evaluated. Indeed, books like *Chariots of the Gods?* ooze enthusiasm for the scientific know-how of the space age. Von Däniken wrote his first books for a public charged with excitement by the success of America's Apollo programme, which culminated in the first manned landing on the Moon in 1969, providing proof that interplanetary travel was more than mere science fiction fantasy. He viewed Man's history solely in terms of a development from 'primitive' ancestors to modern space-age technology; and he zealously sought spacesuits, goggles, lunar modules and the other trappings of space-age technology in ancient art – as if beings capable of crossing the vast distances of interstellar space would be using anything like the crude equipment we used to reach the Moon!

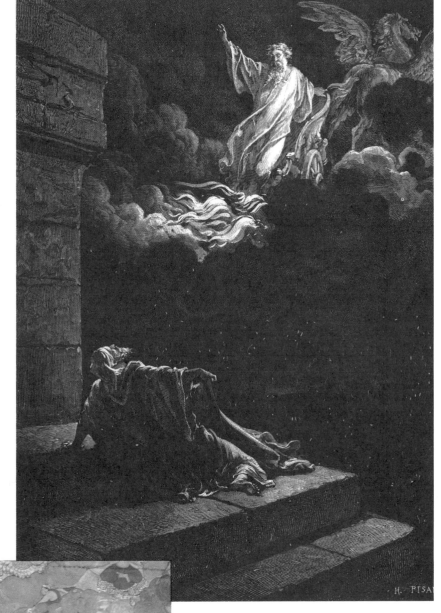

According to the biblical account: 'There appeared a chariot of fire... and Elijah went up by a whirlwind into heaven,' as illustrated above right. Debate continues as to whether the text is to be taken literally or whether it is merely a graphic way of describing death.

Krishna on the bird-god Garuda, right, fights Indra, seated on an elephant. In Hindu legend, Krishna performed miracles, subdued Indra and slew Kamsa, usurper of the throne of Mathura. For 'ancient astronaut' theorists, such legends are pointers to extra-terrestrial beings that visited Earth long ago.

Many skills and techniques that once flourished are now forgotten, and many apparently new discoveries could simply be rediscoveries of knowledge that has faded away or been obliterated by Man-made and natural destruction. We should therefore avoid the all-too-easy mistake of thinking that only scientists of the modern world are capable of advanced technological feats.

The ancient astronaut school's interpretation of mythology fails precisely because of this narrow view of history. It compares myths of flying chariots and helpful gods from heaven with 20th-century concepts of space flight and extra-terrestrial intelligences; and we are asked to leap back in time with the image of the modern astronaut into the world of the Greek and Egyptian gods. But what about the centuries in between? Did the 'space gods' suddenly disappear from Man's mythology? A fact ignored by von Däniken is that they did not. All the motifs in the 'legends of the sons of God' that are used to argue the case for extra-terrestrial intervention in ancient times continue to be found much later, not only in those stories that have been collected by anthropologists, but in the extensive fairy-lore of medieval and post-medieval Europe. They include the appearance of what seem to be supernatural deities in mysterious flying craft, the abduction of mortals to remote worlds, and the superior knowledge of strange visitors, usually benign, who teach selected mortals new skills and arts.

One legend that is often cited by those who make up the ancient astronaut lobby is the North American Indian tale of the adventures of Wampee, which runs as follows:

'Wampee was hunting one day when he came across a circular depression on a clearing of rich grass. Hearing the strains of distant music, he looked up and saw a speck in the sky; the speck drew nearer and nearer, and proved to be a basket, which came to ground on the circle marked on the grass. From it stepped twelve beautiful maidens. When they began to dance, Wampee – overcome with passion – ran into the clearing; but when they saw him they resumed their song and the basket carried them off into the sky. Wampee returned to the clearing frequently, and one day he managed to capture one of the maidens, making her his wife. She bore him a son; but missing her own kind, she built a circular basket and flew away from the earth with her son, never to be seen again.'

Could this myth perhaps be put down to a memory of some ancient extra-terrestrial contact? The resemblance to some of the more bizarre UFO stories of today is striking. In fact, a comparison between those myths that supposedly describe extra-terrestrial visitations, medieval and modern fairy-lore, and the more exotic UFO contact stories, shows that they could well be part and parcel of the same phenomenon. (John Michell has amply demonstrated this point in his book *The Flying Saucer Vision*.) There are certainly people alive today who claim to have 'seen' the fairy world or to have flown in a flying saucer; and while they probably had some kind of experience, we cannot be sure that we can take their stories literally. Yet von Däniken took at face value an ancient myth about a romance between a mortal and a god, offering it as

According to Erich von Däniken, ancient gods – such as Krishna, right – may not only have been ancient extra-terrestrials, they may also have produced a new, perhaps the first, homo sapiens.

'evidence' that aliens genetically manipulated Man's evolution. What is more, while he mentions UFO sightings, von Däniken ignores the bizarre UFO contact stories and the medieval fairy-lore. Yet the myths of 'space gods' that he uses as main evidence have the appearance of ancient UFO contact stories; and medieval fairy-lore could well be a vital 'missing link', bridging the gap between the two kinds of story. Indeed, the 'little green men' of modern UFO mythology are quite possibly the green-clad elves of Celtic folklore.

PRODUCT OF THE MIND?

For many years, it was standard to view the UFO phenomenon simply in terms of extra-terrestrial craft, an interpretation now very much on the wane. While many UFO sightings may indeed be of hardware of some sort, this theory does not explain the contact and close encounter stories, a phenomenon that is probably at least half in the mind. Just as von Däniken saw certain examples of ancient art in terms of spacesuits and lunar modules, so the observer of a 'UFO landing' inevitably interprets the experience through his own cultural filter and 'sees' a fiery chariot, fairy ship or spacecraft, depending on the age in which he lives. Nevertheless, there are too many such stories to doubt that the phenomenon is real in some sense, whether as an entirely psychological occurence or a physical reality that is normally out of our reach. Possibly it borrows from both; but the interpretation – in terms of rocket packs or gossamer wings – is certainly a subjective product of the contactee.

Trying to understand the psychology behind the whole range of stories of Man's contact with 'other beings' demands a less easy, and perhaps less satisfying, approach than the glib 'spaceman' theories of the ancient astronaut school. But it tells us much about the human mind and its attempts to come to terms with the unknown. Rather than force the gods into the strait-jackets of 'ancient astronauts', perhaps we should be using mythology and folklore in order to gain a wider perspective on modern stories of close encounters with 'extra-terrestrials'.

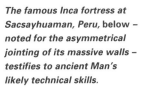

The famous Inca fortress at Sacsayhuaman, Peru, below – noted for the asymmetrical jointing of its massive walls – testifies to ancient Man's likely technical skills.

SPIRITS OF THE STARS

THE VOICES OF CELEBRITIES COULD OFTEN BE HEARD AT SEANCES HELD BY MEDIUM LESLIE FLINT, FOR SHOW BUSINESS PERSONALITIES SEEMED TO FAVOUR HIM AS A CHANNEL FOR DIRECT VOICE COMMUNICATION

L ong after they died, Rudolph Valentino, Lionel Barrymore and Leslie Howard continued to perform before appreciative audiences – not on stage or film, of course, but in the darkened seance room of a London direct voice medium, Leslie Flint. These are but a few of the famous dead – the full list reads like a *Who's Who?* of the arts, with an additional sprinkling from other notable professions – who communicated through Flint during his 42 years as a professional medium.

It has to be said at the outset that claiming spirit contact with the famous usually arouses suspicion. Their lives, likes, and loves are usually public knowledge, and so a gifted impersonator would have no difficulty in posing as a medium and 'communicating' in a voice similar to that of any late celebrity.

But Leslie Flint's spirit visitors were not always famous. Indeed, at the height of his career, many ordinary people were able to pay a fee to sit with him; and some later testified to speaking to their relatives and friends. Flint, in such circumstances, could have known nothing about the dead who returned, and faking their voices and speech mannerisms is therefore seemingly out of the question.

Flint's spirit links with show business stars took him to the United States and to the Hollywood homes of many legendary figures; and the wealth he encountered on those visits was in stark contrast to the poverty he experienced as a child.

Leslie Flint, pictured above, was a professional medium for 42 years, during which time his seances were closely scrutinised by scientists and psychical researchers alike. Many sitters testified that the voices were indeed those of deceased persons, both famous and obscure, personally known to them. Rudolph Valentino, shown as he appeared in The Sheik, *right, proved to be one of the most frequent communicators, though he was a silent star in life. Flint was, in turn, one of Valentino's most ardent fans.*

Flint's parents had parted when he was young, and he was brought up in a Salvation Army home. At an early age, he was credited with the ability to 'see' the dead, but this served only to separate him from other children. When he left school, he had a number of temporary jobs, including one as a grave-digger, but he was soon drawn into a Spiritualist group, and it was here that he first developed his direct voice mediumship.

It took Flint seven years to develop this rare gift, sitting twice a week. At first, he would go into into a deep trance and trumpets were used to amplify the voices of those spirits attempting to communicate with the living. As his powers grew stronger, however, he was able to remain conscious during seances and eventually dispensed with the trumpets. Sitters would assemble in the seance room,

Eminent visitors from the 'other side' making guest appearances at Leslie Flint's seances included Amy Johnson, above right, who reported that there are no aeroplanes in the after-life for her to fly; George Bernard Shaw, above, who continues to write, however; as well as Leslie Howard, above left, and Lionel Barrymore, left, two giants of the screen.

lights would be put out, and voices would address them from thin air. Flint occasionally joined in the conversation.

Rudolph Valentino came into Flint's world at an early stage. Another medium told Flint that a man with the initials R.V. wanted to help him in a psychic way and work through him to help mankind. The spirit then appeared to the medium, dressed as an Arab. Valentino was the only person Flint thought fitted the bill – he had read a book about him as a teenager – but could not understand why the great screen lover should want to help him.

Confirmation soon came from a totally unexpected source. A letter arrived from a German woman, saying that Valentino had communicated at a seance in Munich. Valentino had apparently given Flint's name and address, and had asked the medi-

um to tell Flint that he was trying to make contact. Over a period, the Munich seances also produced further items of information that corroborated statements made by Valentino to Flint through other mediums.

Sometimes Valentino spoke in his native Italian, and on one occasion he made a striking prediction. He said that Flint would visit Hollywood, stay in Valentino's Beverly Hills home and hold seances in his bedroom. Unlikely as this seemed, it all came to pass. Some years later, while visiting Hollywood, Flint was invited to visit a psychical researcher. As soon as Flint was given the address, he realised it was the former home of Rudolph Valentino. What is more, the room in which seances were held was the star's former bedroom.

Leslie Howard, Lionel Barrymore and Mrs Patrick Campbell are other stars who are said to have made an appearance at Flint's seances; and Rupert Brooke and George Bernard Shaw have returned to reveal that they are still writing. Amy Johnson, however, said she is no longer flying: it seems there are no aeroplanes in the spirit world. But they do have pianos, and Frédéric Chopin is still playing and composing, while Shakespeare continues to write plays, 400 years after his works were first performed.

Mahatma Gandi and Cosmo Gordon Lang, former Archbishop of Canterbury, also spoke at length on spiritual matters from their new vantage points in the next world; and Marylin Monroe returned to say she did not commit suicide but died from an accidental overdose of drugs. Queen Victoria sent messages to her last surviving daughter, Princess Louise, and King George V communicated to two members of his household.

Flint has described himself as the most 'tested' medium in Britain and has apparently always been willing to take part in experiments. An early investigator of his direct voice mediumship was Dr Louis Young, who had exposed several doubtful mediums in the United States. He once made Flint fill his mouth with coloured water before a seance started, in order to ensure he could not be throwing his voice. Then the lights were put out. Spirits chattered away as usual.

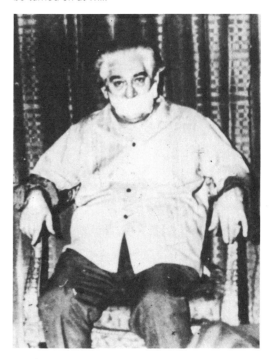

The Rev. C. Drayton Thomas, a member of the council of the Society for Psychical Research (SPR), conducted a more severe test in 1948. He placed a strip of sticking plaster across Flint's mouth and then covered it with a scarf. The medium's hands were also tied to the arms of his chair, and another cord ensured that he could not bend his head down, thus preventing him from loosening the plaster with his hands.

Once again, spirit voices spoke with their usual clarity, often very loudly. This would have been impossible if Flint were faking them. At the end of the seance, the medium was found to be bound and gagged just as he was at the start, and the clergyman had considerable difficulty in removing the sticking plaster without causing pain.

In 1972, the *Sunday Express* science correspondent, Robert Chapman, assisted by Professor William R Bennett, former head of the Department of Electrical Engineering at Columbia University, New York, and Nigel Buckmaster, an SPR member, devised an even more elaborate means of establishing the authenticity of the spirit voices. First, Flint was gagged and bound firmly to his chair. Then he

The Reverend C. Drayton Thomas, top, a member of the Society for Psychical Research, tested Flint in 1948. He was satisfied that, during the test, Flint remained bound and gagged, but the spirit voices were heard clearly throughout.

Leslie Flint's mouth was sealed with sticking plaster, as shown above, in a test conducted by the Sunday Express. To prevent any tampering with the gag, his hands were also restrained, right. The investigators heard the voices, and also saw the ectoplasmic voice box, supposedly responsible for producing them, as it materialised in thin air, just a little way from the medium's head.

was fitted with a throat microphone, designed to show whether he was producing the sounds by ventriloquism. Two television cameras were also used, together with an infra-red detector so that Flint could be observed in the dark.

Yet the voices spoke, and investigators also saw the ectoplasmic voice box, said to be used by spirit communicators, as it formed about two feet (60 centimetres) from the medium's head. 'There could be no question of these voices coming from some hidden tape recorder, furtively switched on by Flint,' Chapman concluded, 'because there was question-and-answer dialogue with the "other side".'

SPIRITS ON TAPE

Many of the voices of celebrated visitors were recorded by researchers, George Woods and Betty Greene, who kept appointments with Flint for more than 15 years, during which they compiled a library of 500 tapes. Oscar Wilde, for instance, said his new existence was quite unlike his earthly life. 'It is no longer a sin here to be human and to be natural.'

Leslie Flint retired in December 1976. The recordings made by Woods and Greene, and by many other sitters, provide a lasting reminder of his mediumship. Despite many glowing tributes, sceptics have found it easy to pick holes in some of the seance conversations. The words and mannerisms of some famous speakers are not always what we would expect.

Flint himself, after all those years of listening to spirit voices in a darkened seance room, continued to find some aspects of his own mediumship puzzling. He could not explain, for example, why some of the voices spoke only in a whisper, whereas others spoke loudly.

One other aspect of Flint's work, often overlooked in articles about him, is worth recording. Very often, sitters would sit and chat for an hour in his seance room and nothing would happen at all. Flint may have been one of the most gifted direct voice mediums of all time, but his powers could not be turned on at will.

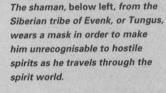

TO HELL AND BACK

THE SHAMAN – MEDICINE MAN, PRIEST AND TRAVELLER IN THE SPIRIT WORLD – IS THE CENTRAL FIGURE OF MANY PRIMITIVE TRIBES. HERE WE EXAMINE HIS RITUALS AND THE ROLE PLAYED BY TRANCE IN HIS ACTIVITIES

The shaman, below left, from the Siberian tribe of Evenk, or Tungus, wears a mask in order to make him unrecognisable to hostile spirits as he travels through the spirit world.

The artefacts, below, belonging to a shaman of the Tlingit Indian tribe, were unearthed in 1970 on Prince of Wales Island, Alaska, USA. They were part of a burial find that comprised four boxes of cedar wood, containing all the tools the shaman needed, including dolls with broken limbs and a mask of a strangled man, for working magic.

'I spent three years living in hell.' These were the words with which a Siberian shaman of the Buriat tribe began recounting the story of his life to the Russian anthropologist A.A. Popov.

The shaman was not speaking figuratively, nor using the kind of exaggerated metaphor that is sometimes used to describe unpleasant experiences. He was claiming that he had, quite literally, spent three years in the underworld in the company of ghosts and evil spirits.

Such claims are by no means unusual among shamans – tribal healers, magicians and mediums. Indeed, shamanistic beliefs flourish in every part of the world where tribal societies still exist – from Siberia to South America, and from Greenland to Indonesia. And while each tribe will have its own gods, its own mythology and its own cosmology, they all share one vital characteristic: the central human actor in every one of them is a shaman, a man or a woman who has personally undergone spiritual experiences that have brought him or her into direct contact with the supernatural.

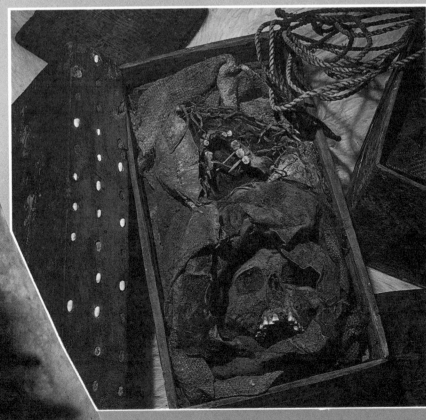

It is usual for these experiences to begin with some personal crisis. Sometimes they even take place entirely within the mind. For example, the future shaman may undergo a long period of moodiness and withdrawal, the sort of personality disorder that Western psychiatrists might diagnose as 'depression'. On other occasions, however, the crisis is brought on by a purely physical event – such as being struck by lightning or falling from a tall tree.

The crisis undergone by the shaman who told Popov that he had 'spent three years in hell' was of the latter variety. He first came into contact with the supernatural, so he averred, while suffering from a severe attack of some feverish disease. From the description that he gave, it appears to have been a violent attack of smallpox.

DIVINE INSTRUCTION

At the most acute stage of his illness, the future shaman fell into a trance of such depth that the members of his tribe took it for death and, on the third day of the entrancement, began to prepare the supposed corpse for burial. While these preparations were taking place, however, the sick man suddenly recovered consciousness and evidently wanted to speak. When he eventually managed to do so, he told his friends that he had been 'in the spirit world' and, while there, had undergone various initiations, receiving from divine beings instruction in healing and other mysterious arts. He was now capable, so he said, of healing the sick, communicating with the gods and guiding the souls of the dead through the unfamiliar territory of the spirit world. In short, following his entrancement, he had now become a fully-fledged shaman.

The long account given by the shaman of his experiences while in trance indicates that the spirit

The painting, far right, comes from the journals of Father Nicolas Point who lived as a Roman Catholic missionary among the Indians of the Rocky Mountains in the United States between 1840 and 1847. Its caption reads: 'One becomes a medicine man only after making a pilgrimage during which he [sic] prays fervently, fasts from four to eight days, and eventually receives a sign from a bear, a red deer, a green ram, or perhaps even from a monster'.

The Evenk wooden fetish figure with blue bead eyes, right, is from Siberia, and represents the person at whom some shamanistic spell is directed.

The thunderbird headdress, below, was used in winter dance rituals by a secret society, and collected in Kwakiuti, Alert Bay, British Columbia, in about 1920. It is thought highly likely that the ecstatic activities that once characterised shamanism survive in the mystical and secret societies still flourishing among North American Indians today.

world he visited apparently has its own time scale, quite different from that of the world of everyday existence. For while the shaman was unconscious for only three earthly days, during that time he seemed to have spent several years, so he said, with gods and demons.

When he became unconscious, so he told Popov, he was carried down into the underworld, where he not only saw souls in torment, but encountered and overcame many malignant demons. Having passed through these afflictions –

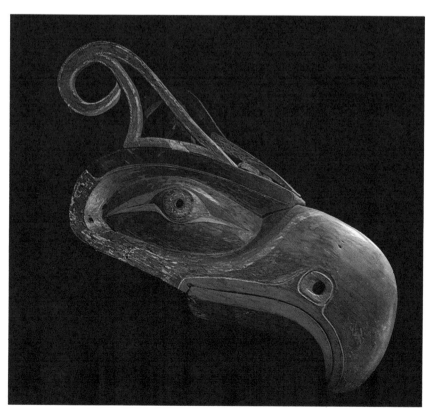

trials that he believed were imposed by the gods in order to test his fitness for the exalted status of shamanship – he was mysteriously transported to a magic island.

On this island stood a birch tree, its roots extending down into hell, its topmost branches winding amid the stars. This tree – which sounds remarkably similar to *Yggdrasil*, the ash tree that supports the Universe, according to Scandinavian mythology – was the property of 'the Lord of the Earth', an awesome being who looked benignly upon the future shaman and gave him a drum that was made from the wood of the wondrous tree. This gift was of great significance, for the use of a magic drum is a central feature in many Siberian shamanistic rituals, performed for healing and other purposes. By giving the entranced man a drum in this way, the god was symbolically conferring shamanship upon him in an act analogous to the

Western European 'tradition of the instruments' – the presentation to a Catholic priest, as part of his ordination, of the cup and paten, or communion plate, with which he will in future carry out the daily celebration of the Mass.

From the island, Popov's informant said that he next travelled to a mountain, where he was killed, chopped in pieces, boiled in a cauldron for three years and, after being supplied with a new head that was forged for him on an anvil by a supernatural blacksmith, brought back to life. The gods then instructed him in healing, mediumship and other magical arts. His initiation into shamanship was now over.

While it would be absurd to believe this shaman's account to be literally true, there is no reason to reach the conclusion that he was obviously lying. Indeed, it seems clear that, during his illness, he subjectively underwent a similar pattern of experiences to those ceremonially undergone by the initiates of almost all formalised religio-magical cults, ranging from the mysteries of the ancient world to the Golden Dawn and other 19th-century occult fraternities.

OUTWARD AND VISIBLE SIGN

In this age-old pattern can be discerned three sharply defined elements. First, the person undergoing initiation into shamanism is subjected to various tests and also comes into contact with either good or evil spirits, or both. Then, he or she is made to suffer a ritual death. Lastly comes a spiritual resurrection to a new and much altered form of existence. In fact, most primitive faiths embody some kind of ritual that gives an outward and visible sign of the inward and spiritual death and resurrection undergone by the shaman while in trance in the course of initiation.

Thus the Buriat tribe of Siberia is known publicly to ratify the status of those recognised as shamans by means of a special ceremony that begins in the shaman's own dwelling place, a Siberian yurt (tent made from felt or skin), which is entered via a crude ladder or rope that is lowered through the central smoke hole.

The shaman's costume, above, is from the Buriat of Siberia, one of whose tribesmen, left, utters incantations to the sound of a drum, the inner surface of which is decorated with a fetish figure. The photograph was taken in the 1930s, but shamanism is now, as then, very much a living tradition in Siberia.

The three pictures seen here show different shamans around the world – a Brazilian shaman communing with the spirit world, right; a Siberut shaman from Indonesia, below; and Australian aborigine shamans taking part in an ecstatic dance, below right.

to their bodies, and to escort the souls of the departed to the afterworld. In the Buriat tribe of Siberia, for example, the shaman can traverse the seven hells to ask favours of the Lord of the Underworld; while the Inuit (Eskimo) shaman sometimes undertakes a spiritual voyage to the bottom of the ocean, to the Mother of the Seals, to ask her for food in time of famine.

The universal pattern of initiation as a shaman is of death followed by rebirth. Generally, the gift of shamanism is passed on through heredity, or may be acquired through an event that is regarded by the community as supernatural. Sometimes, however, a member of the tribe may simply decide to be a shaman, or be elected by his fellows. Shamans of this kind are generally regarded by their tribes as inferior, but in North America it is quite normal for the would-be shaman to set off on a quest for magical powers. Nowhere, however, is the experience of shamanistic ecstasy in trance enough to confirm the initiate as a shaman: he is recognised as such only after a period of instruction, from one or more master-shamans, in the religious traditions of the tribe, and in how to recognise and treat diseases by 'non-magical' means.

*In*FOCUS

CULT FIGURES

The religious phenomenon of shamanism is generally associated with tribes living in Siberia, among whom it was first studied. Indeed, the word 'shaman' is derived from the Siberian Tungus *saman*. But, in fact, shamanism is to be found throughout the world – in strikingly similar forms.

The characteristic ability of shamans the world over is the capacity to leave the body at will – to have out-of-the-body experiences. This enables the shaman to hold discourse with supernatural beings, to heal the sick by returning their errant souls

In an illustration from the late 15th-century Norton's Ordinall, right, an alchemy master and his assistants prepare ingredients for the transmutation of metals. There are some interesting parallels between the death and rebirth rituals of shamanistic initiation and the alchemical process. In alchemy, the base metal, symbolizing the soul of the alchemist, is subjected to various forms of chemical 'degradation' until it darkens in colour, representing death. Only then, through the application of the Philosopher's Stone, can the metal – or the spiritual state of the alchemist – become transmuted into pure gold.

The rite begins when a small, but sturdy, birch tree is uprooted and taken to the yurt. Once there, it is firmly set up inside the dwelling, its roots and lower trunk being buried in the earth beneath the hearth, its trunk rising through the smoke hole immediately above the hearth and its topmost branches soaring high into the air above the yurt. This tree is a material analogue to the magical birch, the property of the Lord of the Earth, from which the mystic drum given to Popov's shaman during trance was made.

After the tree has been correctly positioned, the shaman takes a sword or other weapon in his right hand and, ascending through the smoke hole of the yurt, climbs to the topmost branches of the birch. He thus signifies that he lives in two worlds – the ordinary world of men, symbolised by the yurt, and the spirit world, symbolised by the crown of the tree. From his lofty perch, which signifies that his consciousness has been raised to the level of that of the gods, the shaman solemnly invokes the world of the supernatural and calls upon it to aid him in his healing and other spiritual activities.

TIMBER TEMPLES

Under the guidance of a senior shaman, the candidate is then conducted in solemn procession to a remote and unfrequented wilderness in which a group of birch tree-trunks has been erected to form a traditional circular or elliptical pattern. The use of a similar arrangement of tree-trunks for religio-magical purposes may once have been worldwide. Indeed, there seems little reason to doubt that structures such as Stonehenge and other megalithic monuments were developments of this type of timber 'temple'.

At the birch-tree temple, an animal, usually a goat, is sacrificed, and the orifices of the candidate's head are smeared with its blood. This is a magical action, intended to ensure that the shaman will see and hear with the eyes and ears of the gods and speak with their voices, for the act of sacrifice makes the victim the property of the gods, and every part of its body, but especially the blood, partakes of their divine nature. As far as the shaman is concerned, this blood has become a supernatural substance that will bring all his senses into contact with the spirits.

The shaman in charge of the proceedings then climbs a birch tree, using a 'ladder' of nine notches, symbolising the nine heavens of Siberian mythology and the states of ecstasy supposedly corresponding with them. The candidate follows the master shaman's example and then climbs eight more birch trees. On climbing each tree, the future shaman goes – or at least appears to go – into deeper and deeper trance as he progressively ascends the tree. On each of his returns to Earth, he reverts to normal consciousness. The public ratification of his status as shaman is now over.

Stonehenge, below, the megalithic monument on Salisbury Plain, England, is thought by some to be a development of the shamanistic 'temples' that consisted of birch trees arranged in a circular or elliptical pattern.

HITLER AND THE HOLY LANCE

THE LANCE THAT PIERCED CHRIST'S SIDE AT HIS CRUCIFIXION BECAME A HOLY TALISMAN FOR THE TEUTONIC WARLORDS OF EUROPE. IN THE 20TH CENTURY, IT WAS PLUNDERED BY ADOLF HITLER, WHO KNEW ITS MYSTICAL SIGNIFICANCE ALL TOO WELL, AND LINKED WITH IT HIS DESTINY

I n the streets of Vienna in 1913, a down-and-out former art student tried vainly to make a living by selling postcard-sized watercolours. Occasionally, driven off the streets by cold, he would wander through the corridors of the Hofburg Museum. Here, he was particularly fascinated by a number of valuable pieces known as the Habsburg regalia. Among these, the unprepossessing young vagrant, Adolf Hitler, paid special attention to the Holy Lance – reputed to be the spear that had pierced Christ's side while on the cross.

The legend concerning the Holy Lance takes its origin from *John 19: 33-37*:

'But when they came to Jesus, and saw that he was dead already, they brake not his legs: but one of the soldiers with a spear pierced his side, and forthwith came there out blood and water. And he that saw it bare record, and his record is true: and he knoweth that he saith true, that ye might believe. For these things were done that the scripture should be fulfilled, A bone of him shall not be broken. And again another scripture saith, They shall look on him whom they pierced.'

The verse following this tells how Joseph of Arimathaea gained permission to take the body of Jesus and, helped by Nicodemus, laid it in a tomb on the night of Good Friday.

Other oral and written traditions, beginning with the earliest Christians and continuing to the Middle Ages, depict the rich Jewish philanthropist, Joseph, as obsessed with the artefacts associated with the dead Christ. He is said to have preserved the cross itself, the nails, the crown of thorns, and also the shroud from which Christ rose on the third day. Using clues left by Joseph, Helena – mother of the first Christian emperor, Constantine – was apparently able to rediscover these relics. But even before Christ's death, according to the same traditions, Joseph had begun collecting. After the Last

Supper, he took charge of the cup in which Jesus had consecrated the bread and wine; and after the resurrection, he kept it alongside the spear. Subsequently, the two items became known as the Holy Grail and the Holy Lance, respectively.

Joseph's subsequent travels with the Grail and the Lance are the subject of folk tales and legends that are to be found in almost every country in Europe. In Britain, he is said to have hidden the Grail at Glastonbury. Afterwards, we are told, he thrust his staff into the ground, where it sprouted to become the still-surviving Glastonbury Thorn, which thereafter is known mysteriously to have bloomed only at Christmas-time.

Romantic writers, beginning with the French poet Chrétien de Troyes in about 1180, took up the legend and linked the fate of the Holy Grail and the Holy Lance with the adventures of King Arthur and the Knights of the Round Table, notably with Lancelot, Gawain and Perceval.

Alongside these romantic stories – themselves based on Celtic tradition and scraps of historical fact – there ran a thread of evidence, albeit thin, that the Lance, at least, had survived the centuries, and had somehow been passed down sometimes through good hands, sometimes through unworthy ones. With its ownership, it seems, came a marked degree of power, to be used either for great good or for terrible evil.

At least four 'Holy Lances' existed in Europe during the early part of the present century. Perhaps the best-known was in the keeping of the Vatican, although the Roman Catholic Church seems to have regarded it as no more than a curio. Certainly, no preternatural powers were claimed for it by the papal authorities.

A second lance was kept in Paris, where it had been taken by St Louis in the 13th century, after his return from the Crusades in Palestine.

MIRACULOUS VISION

Another lance, preserved in Cracow, Poland, was merely a copy of the Habsburg lance. The latter probably had the best pedigree of them all. It had been discovered at Antioch, in the Near East, in 1098, during the First Crusade, but mystery – and possibly imagination – obscured the manner of its finding. Crusaders had mounted a successful siege of the city and had taken control, when a more heavily armed band of Saracens turned the tables, shutting up the Crusaders within the walls. After three weeks, water and food were running low and surrender seemed the only course. Then a priest claimed to have had a miraculous vision of the Holy Lance, buried in the church of St Peter. When excavations at the spot revealed the iron spearhead, the Crusaders were filled with a new zeal and rode out to rout their attackers.

Germanic tradition, somewhat at odds with these dates, claimed the Habsburg lance had in fact been carried as a talisman in the ninth century by Charlemagne through 47 victorious campaigns. It had also endowed him with clairvoyant powers. Only when he accidentally dropped it did Charlemagne die.

The lance later passed into the possession of Heinrich (Henry) the Fowler, who founded the royal house of the Saxons and drove the Poles eastwards – a foreshadowing, Hitler may have thought in later years, of his own destiny. After passing through the hands of five Saxon monarchs, it next fell into the possession of the succeeding Hohenstaufens of Swabia. One of the most outstanding of this line was Frederick Barbarossa, born in 1123. Before his death, 67 years later, Barbarossa conquered Italy and drove the Pope himself into exile. Again, Hitler may well have admired the brutal harshness, coupled with a charismatic personality, that led Barbarossa to success. Like Charlemagne, however, Barbarossa made the mistake of dropping the lance as he waded through a stream in Sicily, and he drowned within minutes.

This was the legend of the weapon, now among the Habsburg regalia, which so fascinated the young Hitler. He spent his first visit to the Holy Lance studying its every detail. It was just over a foot (30 centimetres) long, tapering to a slender, leaf-shaped point, and at some time the blade had been grooved to admit a nail – allegedly one of those used in the crucifixion. This had been bound into place with gold wire. The spear had been broken, and the two halves were joined by a sheath of silver, while two gold crosses had been inlaid into the base, near the haft.

The evidence of Hitler's personal fascination with the Habsburg lance rests on the testimony of Dr Walter Johannes Stein, a mathematician,

The blade of the Habsburg spear, far left, is reputed to be the lance that pierced Christ's side while he was on the cross. Because it was a holy relic, the iron blade has been extensively repaired with gold and silver during its long history. It is now bound together with wire and an inscribed 'sleeve'.

In a painting by Rubens, left, a Roman soldier confirms that Christ is dead by plunging a spear into him. According to tradition, it was revealed to the soldier at this moment that Christ was truly the Son of God and the spear acquired enduring magical potency.

Just one face in the crowds of Germans who exulted at the outbreak of the First World War, Adolf Hitler, right, was poverty-stricken and obscure at this stage, but dreaming already of leading the Nordic race to supremacy.

By selling watercolours like the one, below, Hitler scratched a living in Vienna in 1913.

economist and occultist who claimed to have met the future Führer just before the First World War. Stein, a native of Vienna, was born in 1891, the son of a rich barrister. He was to be a polymath and an intellectual adventurer until his death in 1957, taking a first degree in science and a doctorate in psychophysical research at the University of Vienna. He also became expert in archaeology, early Byzantine art and medieval history; and in the First World War, as an officer in the Austrian Army, he was decorated for gallantry.

In 1928, he published an eccentric pamphlet, *World History in the Light of the Holy Grail*, which was circulated in Germany, Holland and Britain. Just five years after that, Reichsführer Heinrich Himmler ordered that he be pressed into service with the Nazi 'Occult Bureau', but Stein escaped to Britain.

The Second World War found him in the guise of a British intelligence agent. After helping the British to obtain the plans for 'Operation Sealion' – Hitler's projected invasion of Britain – he acted as adviser to Winston Churchill on the German leader's occult involvements.

Stein never published his own memoirs; but before his death, he befriended a former Sandhurst commando officer, then a journalist, Trevor Ravenscroft. Using Stein's notices and conversations, Ravenscroft published a book, *Spear of Destiny*, in 1972, which first brought Hitler's fascination with the Habsburg spear to public attention.

But what hold could the Holy Lance, a Christian symbol, have had on the violently anti-Christian, ex-Roman Catholic Adolf Hitler? Already he was given to violent anti-Semitic rantings, and already he was a devout student of Friedrich Nietzsche's Anti-Christ, with its condemnation of Christianity as 'the ultimate Jewish consequence'.

Charlemagne, King of the Franks, above, became Holy Roman Emperor in AD 800. One of the legends that have grown up around him says that he owed his success in war to the Holy Lance.

The triumphal entry of Hitler into Vienna in March 1938 is shown below. One of his first acts was to order the removal to Germany of the Habsburg treasure, which included the Holy Lance.

Part of the answer lay in a medieval occult tradition regarding the history of the Holy Lance. As the *Gospel of John* describes, the Roman soldier who pierced Christ's side had unwittingly fulfilled the *Old Testament* prophecies (that Christ's bones would not be broken). Had he not done as he did, the destiny of Mankind would have been different. According to both Matthew and Mark, the true nature of Christ was revealed to the soldier, said to have been named Gaius Cassius Longinus, at that moment: 'And when the centurion, which stood over against him, saw that he so cried out, and gave up the ghost, he said, Truly this man was the Son of God.' *(Mark 15:39)*

To the mind of the occultist, an instrument used for such momentous purpose would itself become the focus of magical power. As Richard Cavendish puts it, speaking of the Grail and the Lance in his book *King Arthur and the Grail*:

'A thing is not sacred because it is good. It is sacred because it contains mysterious and awesome power. It is as potent for good or evil as a huge charge of electricity. If it is tampered with, however compelling and understandable the motive, the consequences may be catastrophic for entirely innocent people.'

According to Stein, Hitler was fully aware of this concept as early as 1912: indeed, it was through Hitler's obsession with the legend of the Holy

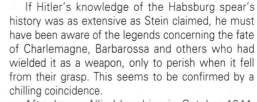

Lance and its power as a 'magic wand' that the two men met. In the summer of 1912, Dr Stein purchased an edition of *Parsival*, a Grail romance by the 13th-century German poet Wolfram von Eschenbach, from an occult bookseller in Vienna. It was full of scribbled marginal commentaries, displaying a combination of occult learning and pathological racism. On the flyleaf, its previous owner had signed his name: Adolf Hitler. Through the bookseller, Stein traced Hitler and spent many hours with him, appalled but fascinated. Although it was to be years before the poverty-stricken postcard painter took his first steps on the road to power, there was already an evil charisma about the man. Through all the tortuous windings of his discourse, one obsession stood out clearly: he had a mystic destiny to fulfil and, according to Stein, the Holy Lance held the key.

Hitler described to Stein how the spear had acquired a special significance for him: 'I slowly became aware of a mighty presence around it, the same awesome presence which I had experienced inwardly on those rare occasions in my life when I had sensed that a great destiny awaited me... a window in the future was opened up to me through which I saw, in a single flash of illumination, a future event by which I knew beyond contradiction that the blood in my veins would one day become the vessel of the Folk-Spirit of my people.'

Hitler never revealed the nature of his 'vision'; but Stein believed that he had seen himself a quarter of a century later, in the Heldenplatz outside the Hofburg Museum, addressing Austrian Nazis and ordinary, bewildered Viennese. There, on 14 March 1938, the German Führer was to announce his annexation of Austria into the German Reich, and to give the order to carry the Habsburg regalia off to Nuremberg, spiritual home of the Nazi movement.

Taking possession of the treasure was a curious priority, in view of the fact that Hitler despised the house of Habsburg as traitors to the Germanic race. Nevertheless, on 13 October, the spear and the other items of the regalia were loaded on to an armoured train with an SS guard and taken across the German border. They were lodged in the hall of St Catherine's Church, where Hitler proposed to set up a Nazi war museum. Stein believed that once Hitler had the Holy Lance in his possession, his latent ambitions for world conquest began to grow and flourish.

> **❝...THERE WAS ALREADY AN EVIL CHARISMA ABOUT THE MAN. THROUGH ALL THE TORTUOUS WINDINGS OF HIS DISCOURSE, ONE OBSESSION STOOD OUT CLEARLY: HE HAD A MYSTIC DESTINY TO FULFIL AND... THE HOLY LANCE HELD THE KEY.❞**

The scene, left, is from Parsifal, Wagner's last opera. Hitler was fascinated by the legend on which the opera is based. Here, the enchantress Kundry, redeemed from a life of evil, dies as Parsifal takes the Holy Grail from its shrine. He holds the Holy Lance, which, having been used to work evil by the black magician Klingsor, is an instrument of blessing in the hands of the virtuous Parsifal.

The Luitpold Arena in Nuremberg, bottom, scene of the Nazis' most spectacular pre-war rallies, saw an informal 'march past' by victorious US soldiers in April 1945, inset. In the ruins of the shattered city, the Holy Lance, with other war booty, was found in a bombproof vault.

If Hitler's knowledge of the Habsburg spear's history was as extensive as Stein claimed, he must have been aware of the legends concerning the fate of Charlemagne, Barbarossa and others who had wielded it as a weapon, only to perish when it fell from their grasp. This seems to be confirmed by a chilling coincidence.

After heavy Allied bombing in October 1944, during which Nuremberg suffered extensive damage, Hitler ordered the spear, along with the rest of the Habsburg regalia, to be buried in a specially constructed vault.

Six months later, the American Seventh Army had surrounded the ancient city, which was defended by 22,000 SS troops, 100 Panzers and 22 regiments of artillery. For four days, the veteran American Thunderbird Division battered at this formidable defence until, on 20 April 1945 – Hitler's 56th birthday – the victorious Stars and Stripes was hoisted over the rubble.

During the next few days, while American troops took on the task of rounding up survivors of the Nazi military and began the long process of interrogating them, Company C of the US Army's Third Military Government Regiment, under the command of Lieutenant William Horn, were detailed to search for the Habsburg treasure. By chance, a shell had made their task easier by blowing away brickwork and revealing the entrance to the vault. After some difficulty with the vault's steel doors, Lieutenant Horn entered the underground chamber and peered through the dusty gloom. There, lying on a bed of faded red velvet, was the fabled spear of Longinus.

However sceptical critics may be about Walter Stein, the occult in general and the Holy Lance legends in particular, it is historical fact that, a few hundred miles away in a bunker in Berlin, Adolf Hitler chose that evening on which to take a pistol and shoot himself.

OF THE MANY MIRACLES ASSOCIATED WITH THE
SAINTS, NONE IS MORE MYSTIFYING THAN THAT
OF INCORRUPTIBILITY – WHEN THEIR BODIES DO
NOT DECOMPOSE AFTER DEATH

THE HOLY INCORRUPTIBLES

A ll over the world, there is an instinctive folk belief that holy saints have the power to defy the physical dissolution of their bodies at death. As St Cyril of Jerusalem summed it up, in the fourth century: 'Even when the soul is gone, power and virtue remain in the bodies of the saints because of the righteous souls which have dwelt in them.' Yet even a casual study of the lives of Christian saints reveals that there are a great many of the holy and virtuous who did not receive this mark of 'divine favour', while a number who did were not beatified or canonised. Some of the truly pious even had a horror of this bizarre perpetuation.

The faithful flock to touch the magnificent reliquary in the cathedral at Goa, in India, top, that holds the body of St Francis Xavier. The great Catholic missionary died in 1552 and was immediately placed in quicklime. Yet his body was not destroyed and, even today, remains astonishingly lifelike.

Priests in Madrid, above, venerate one of St Francis Xavier's well-preserved arms. Frequently, parts of the incorruptibles have been removed – in an act known as 'translation' – to be used as holy relics.

It is said of the dying St Thérèse of Lisieux that, when a novice announced she was sure God would preserve her body from corruption, Thérèse replied: 'Oh no. Not that miracle...' God granted her wish.

There has been remarkably little study of this strange subject, despite the high quality of proof demanded by the Congregation for the Causes of Saints in the process of canonisation. Church records also, themselves, demand serious consideration because exhumations and examinations have nearly always been carried out before many witnesses – including, where possible, doctors and medical specialists. Indeed, it seems astonishing that so well-documented a fact as the incorruption of certain persons should have escaped scientific and medical scrutiny for so long.

Father Herbert Thurston, the subject's first historian (writing in the late 19th century), describes six types of phenomena associated with cases of incorruption (not all of which may occur in the same case). Very often a persistent fragrance is reported, emanating from the body, and an absence of rigor mortis; there may be absence of putrefaction; sometimes, too, there is bleeding (from stigmata or wounds suffered in martyrdom, for example) long after death; in a few cases, the body is felt to be warm long after death: and, more rarely, there is ritualised movement of the limbs that cannot be accounted for by mere contraction of muscles. To this can be added another group of phenomena frequently encountered in cases of incorruption. Often, the secret or long-forgotten burial place of the saint is revealed to his discoverers by a dream or vision. Sometimes, too, their first interment is marked by unusual phenomena, such as the strange lights that played around the grave of St Charbel Makhlouf; and long-dead bodies, or their remaining parts, may exude a fragrant clear oil in great quantities – its origin and composition, a mystery, as in the case of St Walburga who died in AD 779 and from whose bones, to this day, there distils such oil. To this extraordinary exudation, as well as to the physical relics, blood and clothing of the incorruptibles, are attributed great powers of healing, the success of which has been established at many shrines by virtue of a whole catalogue of astonishing medical case histories.

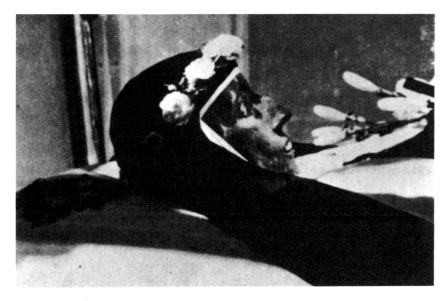

St Teresa Margaret, who died in 1770, is seen above, as she appears today in her glass coffin in Florence, Italy. Although a little dried and discoloured, her body shows no sign of putrefaction. This is all the more remarkable, considering she died of a gangrenous condition, her corpse appearing rigid, swollen and purple just after her death. But, two days later, she had assumed the radiant beauty and fragrance of a true incorruptible.

St Bernadette of Lourdes, below, looks as fresh and lifelike as when she lay dying in 1879. Her face is, however, now covered with a thin layer of wax to prevent discoloration.

The only other work of any note on incorruption is that of a New Orleans housewife, Joan Cruz, who over many years patiently extended the lists of incorrupt saints begun by Father Thurston, by going through all the generally available ecclesiastical biographies.

MECHANICAL EVIDENCE

The Incorruptibles contains 102 such cases approved by the Congregation for the Causes of Saints of the Catholic Church. There may also be a great many others, lying undiscovered in their graves, or whose details are hidden in the secret archives of the Vatican. However, even such a prodigious sweep through the hagiographical literature failed to turn up a study of incorruption by any physician, eminent or otherwise, apart from the statements of those doctors who attended specific post-mortem examinations. The following case is typical. Blessed Maria Anna Ladroni died in Madrid in 1624. One hundred and seven years later, she was examined for the second time by ecclesiastical authorities during the process of her beatification. According to her official biography:

'Not less than eleven professors of medicine and surgery, all of them among the first and most famous in the city and court of Madrid, took part in the proceedings and made deposition as witnesses. They took out their instruments and made some long and deep incisions in the fleshy parts; others laid open the breast, others scrutinised the cavities thus exposed to view, others explored any orifice by which it might have been possible to introduce preservatives against putrefaction. In fact, their united efforts resulted in what was... an absolute dissection of this innocent body... The interior organs, the viscera and the fleshy tissues were all of them entire, sound, moist and resilient. The fluid, which was observed to exude from the body, impregnated all the interior and all the substance of the flesh. The deeper the incisions... the sweeter was the fragrance which was emitted from them...'

One of the astonishing aspects of incorruption is not that it happens at all, but that it frequently happens to bodies under conditions that would encourage the normal processes of disintegration, including those of death caused by disease, and burial in close proximity to other bodies that decomposed normally. Some, like St Charbel, St Catherine of Bologna, and St Pacifico of San Severino, had been consigned to the bare earth without any ill effect, except perhaps some minor distortion by the pressure of the earth. Others 'survived' burial in such damp conditions that their clothes rotted off their intact bodies, as in the case of St Teresa of Avila and St Catherine of Genoa. The coffin of St Catherine of Siena was actually left exposed to the rain for some time before being brought indoors. And when the body of the visionary St Catherine Labouré was exhumed in Paris in 1933, 56 years after her death, it was found to be incorrupt, despite the moisture that had attacked her triple coffin.

INVISIBLE STIGMATA REVEALED

A number of the incorruptibles had been stigmatics during life, and in some cases their mysterious wounds persisted beyond the grave. St Catherine of Siena believed she bore the marks of Christ's Passion invisibly; and on her death, the wounds appeared on her hands, feet and side. When her body was examined and parts detached as separate relics – an act known as a 'translation' – one such mark was still visible on her perfect left foot, 217 years after her death. In the case of Blessed Osanna of Mantua – who died in 1830 and whose intact body is still displayed in the cathedral at

The painting, left, by Il Sodoma, shows the religious ecstasy of the stigmatic St Catherine of Siena. During her life, she believed she bore the invisible marks of Christ's suffering and felt great pain. Only after her death, in 1380, did the marks became clearly visible, remaining so for over 200 years.

One of the most revered of all incorruptibles is the Curé of Ars (a village in France) who died in 1859 and was canonised in 1925. Shortly after his death, he was discovered to be incorrupt and his body was put on public display in the Basilica in Ars, top right. Although his face has been covered with his waxen death mask in order to prevent discoloration, his body is said to remain miraculously preserved, as shown right.

The artist's impression, left, is of St Charbel Makhlouf as he appeared towards the end of his life. The Lebanese hermit died in 1898, at the age of 70. Some months after his death, dazzling lights were seen around his tomb in the cemetery of Annaya. Taking them to be a sign of divine favour, the monks exhumed his body and found it to be completely incorrupt and exuding what appeared to be a mixture of fresh blood and sweat. He was declared a saint in 1977.

Mantua three times a year – her stigmata became even more pronounced than they had been in life; and at the exposition in 1965, her body was described as dried, browned and shrunken, but without any sign of corruption.

Another remarkable case is that of St Charbel Makhlouf, who died at the Hermitage of St Peter and St Paul at the St Maroun monastery in Annaya, Lebanon, in 1898. In accordance with the custom of his order, like many of the incorrupt, he was buried without a coffin. For many weeks, strange lights were seen around his grave – as in the case of St John of the Cross, who died in 1591 and who was seen to be still flexible and moist (but slightly discoloured) at the last public exposition of his body at Segovia, Spain, in 1955. Because of the unusual lights, an exhumation was ordered by the monastery's superiors, and the grave was duly opened 45 days later.

St Charbel's body was perfectly intact, despite the rain and floods that had made the grave a pit of mud and water. The body was washed and reclothed, and placed in a wooden coffin in the monastery chapel. In a short time, an oily liquid – said to be blood and perspiration, and smelling of fresh blood – seeped from its pores, so copiously that the clothing had to be changed twice a week. Many cures were attributed to pieces of the soaked cloth. There the body remained until 1927 when, after a medical examination, it was placed in a wood-lined, zinc coffin, with reports from doctors and witnesses sealed in a zinc tube at its feet, and bricked into the monastery wall. Twenty-three years later, in 1950, pilgrims to the shrine noticed a liquid oozing through the wall, and the tomb was opened. Once again, in the presence of ecclesiastical and medical authorities, St Charbel was found to be completely lifelike and flexible. His partly rotted clothing was soaked in the oily fluid (much of which had solidified in the coffin). The zinc tube was badly corroded, but the saint himself was free of corruption. Every year since, his tomb has been opened and the body carefully examined. Each time, it seems fresh and intact, and the oily exudation, which collects to a depth of about 3 inches (8 centimetres), is drained off for distribution to the ailing.

A number of the early incorruptibles are to be found among English saints, perhaps the most famous being the popular Anglo-Saxon foundress of Ely Monastery, St Etheldreda, who died in AD 679. Sixteen years later, her sister, St Sexburga, who had succeeded her as abbess of Ely, exhumed Etheldreda's remains to entomb them in the church. One of the witnesses, a doctor called Cynefrid – who had removed a tumour from Etheldreda's jaw only three days before she died –

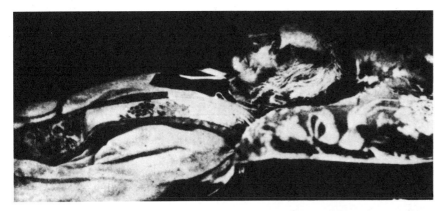

beneath the altar of the basilica dedicated to her name. It was rediscovered during restoration work on the basilica 777 years later. From reliable eyewitness testimony, we know that, on 20 October 1599, the original cypress coffin was found to be in good condition inside a marble sarcophagus. In front of a large crowd, its lid was prized off to reveal St Cecilia's body in her dying position, still totally incorrupt after almost 1,500 years. The body – with the neck wound plainly visible – went on view for a month before its reinstatement beneath the altar in a special casket that was especially commissioned by Pope Clement VIII.

An even stranger case, which defies all the normal expectations, is the martyrdom of the Polish saint, Andrew Bobola, at the hands of the Cossacks in 1657. After a cruel beating, he was dragged by horses from one town to another, partly flayed, and had parts of his face and limbs cruelly torn away before being dispatched by a sabre. He was hastily buried in a churchyard at Pinsk, during a hot summer, in moist ground and in the midst of many other corpses that had decayed normally. Forty years later, his body was discovered intact (apart from his wounds), and the corpse has since been subjected to many medical examinations. In 1917, it was put on exhibition, and seen to be still pliable and well preserved. Five years later, Red Army troops, hearing of the legend of St Andrew's preservation, surrounded the church at Pinsk and

was interviewed by no less a person than the Venerable Bede, who recorded the following statement in the pages of his *Ecclesiastical History*:

'And when, so many years after her bones were to be taken out of the grave, a pavilion being spread over it, all the congregation of brothers were on the one side, and of sisters on the other, and the abbess, with a few, being gone to take up and wash the bones, on a sudden we heard the abbess within loudly cry out... Not long after, they called me in, opening the door of the pavilion, where I found the body of the holy virgin taken out of the grave and laid on a bed, as if it had been asleep.'

To his astonishment, Oynefrid noticed that, in place of the great wound in Etheldreda's jaw, following removal of the tumour, there was now what was described as 'only an extraordinarily slender scar'. Even the clothes in which the abbess was buried still remained intact. Thereafter, St Etheldreda's new resting place became one of the most famous shrines in England, until King Henry VIII ordered that the church should be destroyed and its relics scattered.

BUNGLED EXECUTION

A particularly bizarre example of incorruption is afforded by one of the oldest cases, that of St Cecilia, of a noble Roman family, and martyred in AD 177. An inexperienced executioner bungled her beheading, and she lay for three whole days, dying on the floor of her family home, her hands crossed in prayer, her face to the floor, and her neck half-severed. Her body was dressed in rich robes, and placed in the catacomb of St Callistus in the exact position in which she had died. In AD 822, her secret burial place was revealed in a vision to Pope Pascal I, who arranged placement of her body

A statue of the early Christian martyr St Cecilia of Rome, above, lies over her remains. It is widely believed to be an exact representation of her body as it was found 1500 years after her martyrdom in AD 177. Her beheading had been incomplete (as the neck wound clearly shows), and she was buried in the position in which she had lain dying, for three days. In October 1599, her coffin was opened and her body discovered to be undisturbed and whole.

entered to break open his tomb. After dragging out the body and presumably satisfying their curiosity, they left it lying on the floor. It was taken to Moscow and returned years later, only after a plea by Pope Pius XI. The relic now resides in the Church of St Andrew Bobola in Warsaw.

Many of the incorruptibles met their deaths either by violence or by the usual selection of diseases that afflict more ordinary mortals. The presence of livid wounds (as in the case of St Andrew Bobola) or the bacteriological seeds of putrefaction (as in cancerous conditions such as that suffered by St Etheldreda) should have hastened corruption. But, somehow, these special bodies did not decay in any normal way. Many people might be inclined to dismiss such stories as the product of an intense religious belief, spread by the faithful of a less sceptical age. But incorrupt bodies have been authenticated in our own day, too.

TO THE ENDS OF THE EARTH

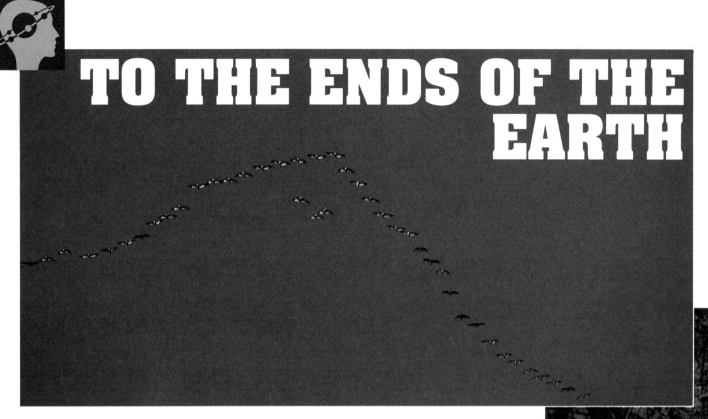

THE PHENOMENON OF MIGRATION IS ONE OF THE MOST MYSTERIOUS OF THE NATURAL WORLD. WHY DO SO MANY ANIMALS EMBARK ON LONG AND PERILOUS JOURNEYS?

In medieval times, people believed that geese hatched from barnacles. This may seem no more than a fanciful fairy tale today, but then it seemed quite logical. After all, migrating geese were to be seen for only a few months in the year – so what was more natural than to suppose that they were part of a normal biological cycle in which goose follows barnacle as flower follows seed?

That this superstition survived, as it did, for hundreds of years is a measure of how difficult the concept of migration was to grasp. In medieval times, after all, few people ever travelled long distances – and so it is hardly surprising that they were unable to imagine that birds could fly across continents to spend parts of the year in lands that, at the time, had not yet been discovered.

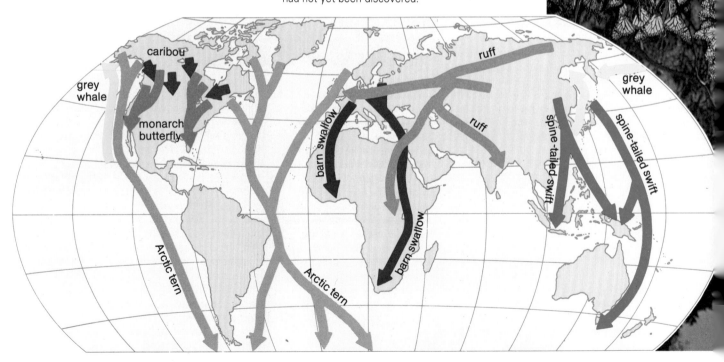

English folklore had it that cuckoos turned into hawks in the autumn, while the Greek philosopher Aristotle believed that robins changed into redstarts – and even claimed to have seen them do it.

Other birds were thought to hibernate. And though today, the sight of swallows perched on branches of trees in the autumn ready to fly away en masse seems incontrovertible evidence of migration, even the great 18th-century English naturalist, Gilbert White, failed to realise what it implied. Like most of his contemporaries, he believed that swallows and house martins spent the winter holed up, safe and warm, in the bottom of ponds.

MOVEMENT EN MASSE

Only since the great advances in transport of the 19th century, the advent of steam ships and trains – and, more recently, of cars and aeroplanes – have we begun to appreciate the quite extraordinary scale on which animals move. And increasing knowledge has brought home just how many animals migrate – not only the familiar ones like eels and swallows, but a whole range of unexpected animals, from bobolinks (songbirds) to butterflies.

All animals, of course, move about their habitat to some extent, and it is fairly arbitrary as to how much of that movement should be classified as migration. But on the whole, scientists prefer to restrict the term to the seasonal movements that many animals make between their breeding areas and separate winter feeding grounds. Thus the swallow, which regularly breeds in Europe and winters in Africa, migrates, while spiders, tossed about hither and thither on the wind, do not.

No single aspect of migration is more astonishing than the immense distances that some animals travel. The record undoubtedly goes to the Arctic tern, which flies an amazing 22,000 miles (36,000 kilometres) from its nesting ground inside the Arctic Circle to the Antarctic, and back, every year. It has been calculated that these sea birds must fly 24 hours a day for 8 months of the year to complete the exhausting round trip.

Perhaps the most familiar migrating creatures are birds – such as the snow and blue geese above *and* above left, *which fly each year from their breeding grounds in northern Canada to the Mississippi delta. But other animals migrate, too. Monarch butterflies follow a similar route southwards in winter, joining up into small bands and eventually into huge swarms, as shown* left, *which completely cover the vegetation when they stop to rest. Salmon also migrate,* right, *returning from the sea, where they live most of the year, to the rivers in which they were born in order to spawn. The map,* far left, *gives an idea of the immense distances covered by animals of all kinds, and of birds (including the ruff, a species of sandpiper), mammals, fish and insects, in their yearly migrations.*

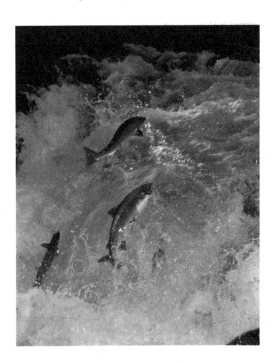

Many other birds fly great distances, too. And some aquatic animals also undertake tremendous trials of endurance. Eels, for instance, regularly swim from the Sargasso Sea in the Atlantic, where they breed, to rivers and streams in Europe; and among larger animals, the hump-backed whale is just one that regularly plies the 5,000 miles (8,000 kilometres) between the tropics and the south polar seas in spring and autumn.

For animals that migrate overland, the distances are reckoned in hundreds of miles rather than thousands. Even so, some of the journeys are very long. Caribou, for example, regularly trudge 600 miles (1,000 kilometres) across the snowy wilderness of northern Canada. They do so in such numbers, and along such precisely determined routes that, in places, their hooves have even worn deep ruts in the underlying rock.

Another astonishing aspect of migration is the sheer number of animals that can be on the move at the same time. In America, for instance, a single swarm of migrating monarch butterflies covered an area of over 150 square miles (400 square kilometres); and in the early 19th century, flocks of migrating passenger pigeons were so dense that they darkened the skies for days.

From Europe come other stories of massed animals on the march. A Norwegian steamer once sailed for 15 minutes through a sea of lemmings; while, in Hungary, a migrating army of millipedes once brought a train to a halt, its wheels spinning on a sludge of squashed bodies. But perhaps the most horrifying incident occurred in South Africa, where 30 miles (50 kilometres) of Atlantic beaches were found to be piled high with washed-up corpses after a herd of migrating springbok had plunged into the sea.

The questions raised by these grisly episodes are some of the most challenging that the natural world has to offer. Indeed, migration itself remains one of the least explained aspects of nature, raising many questions. Why should animals move in such numbers? How do they find their way? Why do they need to travel so far? And how did the strange habit of migration first begin?

*In*Focus THE HOMING INSTINCT

Only rarely do homing pigeons lose their way, like the bird below, *grounded through disorientation.*

The homing ability of pigeons has been investigated more thoroughly than that of any other species. All attempts to explain it in terms of smell, memory of landmarks, and keeping track of the outward journey have failed. Until recently, the most popular theory among scientists was that the birds navigated by the Sun by day, as sailors have done for centuries.

" ONE OUT OF EVERY TWO SWALLOWS DIES ON ITS JOURNEY TO THE SUB-SAHARAN DESERT AND BACK. SO WHY DO THEY BOTHER IN THE FIRST PLACE? "

When Europeans first arrived in North America, bison, such as the herds seen below, *still roamed the plains in their millions, migrating southwards in winter, northwards in summer.*

But conclusive evidence against this theory came as a result of experiments in which the time sense of the pigeons was confused by keeping them in artificial light at night and in darkness by day. To navigate by the Sun, it is necessary to be exposed to regular periods of daylight; yet these pigeons still got home, despite the fact that their internal 'clocks' were inaccurate by hours.

Since several other theories have failed, too, much effort has been devoted in the past few years to trying to show that pigeons navigate using a magnetic sense. But once again, this idea does not really seem to provide a satisfactory answer. For, in another experiment, when magnets were fitted to birds to swamp their ability to detect the Earth's magnetic field, they were still able to get home almost as easily as birds without magnets, despite being initially confused.

Of course, birds are likely to use several senses, not just one, to help keep them on course, and observing the position of the Sun probably plays a part in the process. There is also some evidence that birds that fly at night, like the mallard, use the Moon and stars. And some other migrants use an extremely sensitive sense of smell to help them get home. But these known senses seem unlikely to provide a full explanation: some kind of 'sixth sense', still entirely mysterious, may well be involved.

Today, scientists are devoting considerable effort to answering these questions. This involves not only brain power, but sophisticated equipment. Because biologists are not as mobile as the animals they study, they need binoculars, radar and even aeroplanes to keep track of their quarry. To identify individual animals in a crowd, they rely on radio transmitters, ear tags or markings in luminous paint. Contact lenses made from frosted glass have even been fitted on pigeons to see if they could find their way blind (they could), and planetaria have been built where caged birds can be stood while the heavens are mechanically rotated and the effects on the birds' behaviour observed.

But perhaps the greatest problem for scientists is to discover why animals should wish to migrate in the first place. Migration is, after all, a dangerous business; when an animal leaves the security of its permanent home, it becomes vulnerable to its enemies. One out of every two swallows dies on its journey to the sub-Saharan desert and back. So why do they bother in the first place?

The simple answer – and the one that most biologists will give – is that it must be advantageous to the species as a whole for them to do so. Ever since Charles Darwin first put forward his theory of natural selection, it has become axiomatic that, if a habit or characteristic exists in a species, then it must be good for that species – otherwise it could not have evolved.

But can migration always be seen as an advantage? In many cases the answer is obviously yes – but there are significant exceptions .

One good example is provided by the European barn swallow. Inevitably, the approach of winter means a reduced food supply, and so the swallows migrate. But to find a suitable source of food, in West and South Africa, they have to cross the Sahara, and the Sahara is a dangerous place. So why do so many of them cross it at its widest point?

And again, why do so many swallows fly so far south in winter? Since they stop to rest on their way to South Africa, they must be aware that there are plenty of very habitable countries en route – and, indeed, a few birds do over-winter in them. But many swallows fly on south. Are there really immense advantages to be gained by flying so far – or have swallows just somehow got stuck in an outmoded habit?

Orthodox biologists resort to a rather circular argument to justify the swallow's migratory habits. Since the European swallow population is stationary, they say, the 50 per cent mortality rate during migration is necessary if the biological equilibrium is not to be upset. In other words, they are suggesting that migration is an ingenious device for maintaining the swallow population at a level the English countryside can support.

These scientists apply the same sort of reasoning to animals such as the lemming and the springbok. As we have seen, so many animals die during migration that it is difficult to work out any advantages of the habit. But, according to experts, it is merely another instance of nature knowing best. Lemmings, before they migrate, become both more fertile and more successful at rearing their young. As a result, their population begins to rise – and if, the scientists argue, large numbers of lemmings did not rush headlong into the sea, even more would die of starvation as their habitat became increasingly unable to support them.

And yet this orthodox argument, convincing as it seems at first, does not offer an entirely satisfactory explanation of the mysteries of migration. Could it be that these scientists are wrong, and that factors far subtler than those that merely ensure the 'survival of the fittest' preserve modes of behaviour that seem, at first sight, to confer no possible advantage to the animal species concerned?

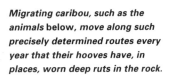

Migrating caribou, such as the animals below, move along such precisely determined routes every year that their hooves have, in places, worn deep ruts in the rock.

CASEBOOK

TWO ELECTRIFYING EXPERIENCES

**IN THE SPACE OF
A WEEK, TWO
COUNTRY LANES
WERE SCENES OF
TERRIFYING CLOSE
ENCOUNTERS.
WERE THEY PART
OF A PLANNED
ATTACK?**

*The blue light in the sky, right,
was seen by motor-cyclist Paul
Green as he approached
Langenhoe Hall, in Essex. It was
emitting a strange, high-pitched
humming noise.*

One of the curiosities of the history of UFOs is clustering activity, in which several incidents occur within a small locality only a few days apart. Sometimes the events are similar; sometimes – as in the following close encounters in south-east England – they appear to be linked only by place and time. But always there is a strange inconclusiveness about them, something that suggests that, if only we could find the missing link, we would understand what it is that those behind the UFO phenomenon are trying to tell us.

The first event occurred on a Sunday morning, 14 September 1965, at about one o'clock. An engineer named Paul Green, aged 29, was riding his motorcycle in a southwardly direction along the B1025 road, which runs between Colchester and West Mersea in Essex. He had been visiting his fiancée, and was now on his way home. The motorcycle was going well, purring along at some 40 miles per hour (70 km/hr).

He had just passed through the village of Langenhoe, and was up to Pete Tye Common, where he overtook a rider on a motor scooter. A minute or so later, he was approaching Langenhoe Hall when he suddenly heard a high-pitched humming noise away to his left – in the east. As the noise became louder, he looked up, expecting to see an approaching aeroplane, but he saw only a small point of blue light that was about 5 miles (8 kilometres) away to the east, approximately over the town of Brightlingsea.

As Paul Green watched the light winking, and then growing brighter and flashing, he realised that it was moving in his direction. Rapidly it became larger, and at the same time the humming that he had become aware of became louder and louder, too. Once the object was over Langenhoe Marsh, Paul became uneasily aware that his motorcycle engine was now coughing and spluttering, and after it had 'missed' several times, it suddenly stopped dead and the lights went off.

At that point, the flashing blue light was just over a mile (just under 2 kilometres) away, to the east of the road. Watching intently, Paul now saw, within the extreme brightness of the light, an enormous object that resembled the upper half of a large spinning top. It was about as big as a gasometer, with a dome on the upper part. Fierce blue flashes of light apparently emanated from inside this dome. By now, the object had stopped moving in Paul's direction and, instead, was descending slowly; at one stage, it tilted its underside towards him. The outer rim of the craft carried a number of round objects spaced equidistantly, so that it gave the impression of what he described as a 'luminous ball-race'.

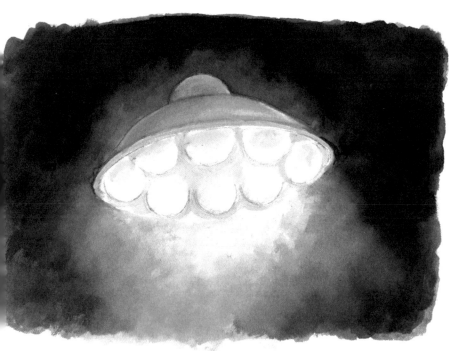

> **"** WATCHING INTENTLY,
> PAUL NOW SAW, WITHIN
> THE EXTREME BRIGHTNESS
> OF THE LIGHT, AN ENORMOUS
> OBJECT THAT RESEMBLED THE
> UPPER HALF OF A LARGE
> SPINNING TOP. IT WAS ABOUT
> AS BIG AS A GASOMETER – WITH
> A DOME ON THE UPPER PART. **"**

When the UFO flew nearer, as seen in the artist's impression above, Paul Green noticed that fierce blue flashes came from inside the dome on top. Under the craft were luminous, ball-like objects.
The map below shows Paul Green's route and the path of the UFO near West Mersea in Essex.

Paul Green dismounted from his motorcycle and took a few involuntary steps towards the object, quickly coming to an unsteady halt. He later said: 'I felt spellbound and unable to move or speak, just as if I had become paralysed. The flashing blue light became so intense that it was painful, and it appeared to fluctuate in rhythm with my heart beat and hit against my chest. I felt myself tingling all over, rather like the electric shock one gets when handling an electrified cattle fence.'

At last the humming died down and the UFO descended towards the farmhouses at Wick. It was about then that the scooter that Paul had overtaken also came coughing and spluttering to a halt. The rider, a young lad in a leather jacket, dismounted and stood looking at the flashing light, as if transfixed. But Paul had no time to speak to him.

Paul reported: 'My head began to throb, and felt as though there were a band tightening around it. With a great effort, I made myself move, and I grasped the bike and tried to start it.' In the end, he managed to push it along, finally achieving a bump-start. He mounted and drove home as quickly as he could. After a short distance, a line of tall hedges hid the 'thing' from him, but he could still see the blue glow in the sky.

It was unfortunate that the witness was so terrified by his encounter and the painful physiological effects that he never thought of speaking to the young man on the scooter, so that a chance of obtaining corroborative evidence was missed.

Paul Green arrived home at 2 a.m., and took the unusual course of awakening his invalid mother – he needed to tell someone of his experience. The next day, his hair and clothes were so charged with static electricity that they crackled continually.

Two weeks after his frightening experience, Paul Green was interviewed for *Flying Saucer Review* by Dr Bernard Finch, one of its regular investigators. Dr Finch was convinced that Paul's story was true, and added that: 'He described symptoms which can only be ascribed to the effects of a very powerful magnetic field on the

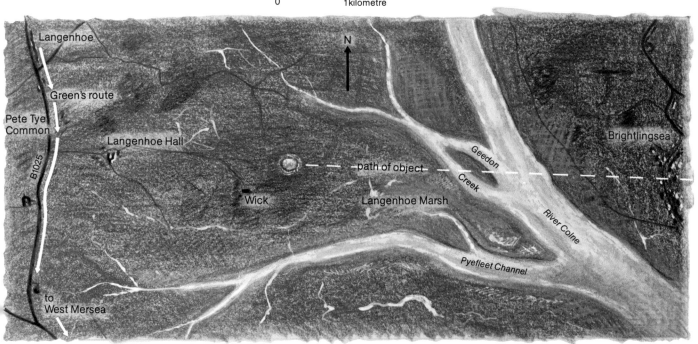

CASEBOOK

human body.' He went on to speculate that, if this field were strong enough, it could produce a kind of light 'as yet unknown to our science'.

There is an interesting postscript to the story. A few days after the incident, Paul was discussing his experience with a friend who lived at nearby Shrub End, some 5 miles (8 kilometres) north-west of Langenhoe. He told Paul that, around the time Paul saw the UFO, he was at home when suddenly his dog started to bark. He opened the door to let the dog out, and saw a large blue light passing rapidly by in the sky directly overhead, travelling towards the north-west.

Six days later, and about 20 miles (30 kilometres) from the scene of the Langenhoe close encounter of the second kind, another strange incident was reported. It may well have been a close encounter of the third kind.

Geoffrey Maskey, aged 25, had stopped his car in a Felixstowe lane known as Walton Avenue. With him were two friends, Michael Johnson and Mavis Fordyce. It was 10.30 p.m. when, without saying a word, Michael suddenly opened his door, got out and disappeared into the night. After a few minutes, the waiting friends heard a high-pitched humming noise.

Mavis was alarmed, and Geoff looked out of the car window to try to spot the source of the noise. He saw a glowing, orange-coloured, oval-shaped object some 6 feet (2 metres) in length, and about 100 feet (30 metres) above the lane. The orange glow lit up everything nearby.

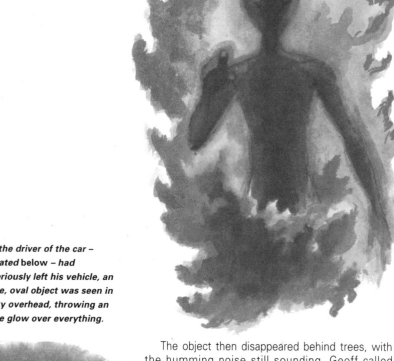

The man in the flames who was seen pointing, illustrated in the sketch right, was supposedly encountered by driver Geoffrey Maskey in Felixstowe, Essex.

After the driver of the car – illustrated below – had mysteriously left his vehicle, an orange, oval object was seen in the sky overhead, throwing an orange glow over everything.

The object then disappeared behind trees, with the humming noise still sounding. Geoff called Michael's name and, when there was no response, reversed along the lane and called again. Suddenly, Michael came stumbling through a hedge, clutching his neck and his eyes. The others thought he was playing a game with them, until he collapsed in the road. Geoff went over to him and found he was unconscious. They got him into the car and took him to Felixstowe Hospital.

Michael regained consciousness at the hospital. The doctor diagnosed severe shock. There were also burn marks on the back of his neck, and a bump below his right ear. As a precaution, Michael was transferred to Ipswich Hospital, and Geoff Maskey was not allowed to see him again until he was discharged, next afternoon. Michael spoke then about a force that seemed to pull him from the car, and of 'a man in the flames pointing at him.'

The remarkable thing was that, if indeed there had been 'a force' capable of pulling a man from a car (or, more likely, a mental compulsion to leave the car), then it was certainly selective; neither Mavis nor Geoff felt its influence in any way.

The *Ipswich Evening Star* reported the incident, alleging that the Felixstowe Hospital doctors spoke jocularly of 'Martians' and seemed to consider the explanation given by Geoff and Mavis a tall story. It was suggested they had mistaken the flame from the local propane gas plant flare-stack for a UFO. This the witnesses denied with vehemence.

Bearing in mind the Langenhoe sighting, it seems likely there was something strange in Felixstowe that night. Its nature, however, remains a mystery.

PSYCHIC DETECTION

THE DISAPPEARANCE OF YOUNG PAT McADAM HAD BAFFLED THE SCOTTISH POLICE. THEN, YEARS AFTER THEY HAD GIVEN UP THE HUNT, AN ENTERPRISING NEWSPAPERMAN BROUGHT IN A PSYCHIC SLEUTH – THE DUTCH CLAIRVOYANT GERARD CROISET

Gerard Croiset, a clairvoyant who often helped the Dutch police in their investigations, is seen below, holding a picture of Pat McAdam, inset, who was 17 when she vanished in 1967.

Pat McAdam, a Scottish teenager, went missing while on a journey home on 19 February 1967. She was one of the 3,000 or so people who disappear in Great Britain every year. Most of these are found again – either dead or alive; but Pat was one of the five per cent who are not. The search for this particular missing girl had one remarkable feature – detective work by the renowned Dutch clairvoyant Gerard Croiset.

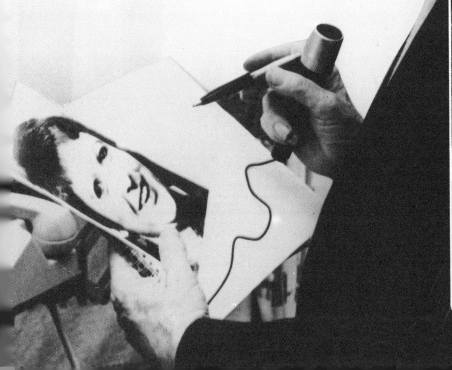

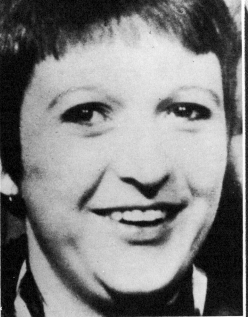

Croiset was introduced to the case by a Dumfries journalist, Frank Ryan of the *Daily Record,* who had covered Pat's disappearance and the police investigation right from the beginning. When, by chance, he was in Holland, he decided to visit Gerard Croiset in Utrecht. This meeting, in 1970, and Croiset's subsequent work with Ryan, form the basis of one of the psychic's most striking cases.

The Dumfries CID had been able to reconstruct Pat McAdam's last recorded movements fairly easily. Pat was 17 years old and worked in a local knitwear factory. She and a friend, Hazel Campbell from nearby Annan, had decided to go to Glasgow on Saturday, 18 February. They took the bus to Gretna and then hitched a lift into Glasgow. The two girls then spent the day shopping. Hazel bought clothes and shoes, and they both bought black patent leather handbags.

Pat and Hazel also met some young people over a drink and went to the Flamingo dance hall. Just before midnight, the girls went to a boy's house where there was a party going on. They stayed there after the party.

Early the next day – Sunday, 19 February – the girls set off for Central Station, where they washed before catching the bus to London Road. There, they did not have to wait long before a lorry stopped to offer them a lift. At about 11.30, the driver pulled into a café at the Star service station at Lesmahagow, 20 miles (32 kilometres) from Glasgow on the A74 road. The girls were hungry and Pat ate a hearty meal, consisting of a hamburger, eggs and beans. Hazel was tired and left to grab some sleep in the cab of the lorry, while the driver and Pat drank whiskies in the café. Later, the three continued their journey south. Hazel dozed, while Pat and the driver chatted together.

At Kirkpatrick Fleming, the lorry swung off the A74 towards Annan, and the girls realised that the driver was leaving his route to take them home. Hazel was dropped outside the Cooperative Stores in Annan just as the town clock showed 2 p.m.

From that moment, no one has heard a word from Pat McAdam.

POLICE DESCRIPTION

On Tuesday, 21 February, Pat's parents, Mary and Matthew McAdam of Lochside Road, Dumfries, went to the police station to report their daughter's disappearance. Pat's description was issued: it read 'Patricia Mary McAdam, born 25.6.49, medium build, fresh complexion, brown eyes, dark hair cut in a "Mia Farrow" style'. The police learned that she had been wearing a purple coat over a black and silver woollen dress that was low-cut and sleeveless. She had black suede shoes, a yellow cardigan, and a green and red headscarf. Mrs McAdam said Hazel had assumed that the lorry had dropped Pat at home before continuing south to Hull, the driver's destination.

The police suspected that Pat may have intended to leave home and would get in touch, sooner or later, with her family. But as time passed, it became clear that Pat had not run away. She was very interested in clothes – yet she left a complete wardrobe behind. She enjoyed a good time – yet she left £47 in cash at home. She did not take her

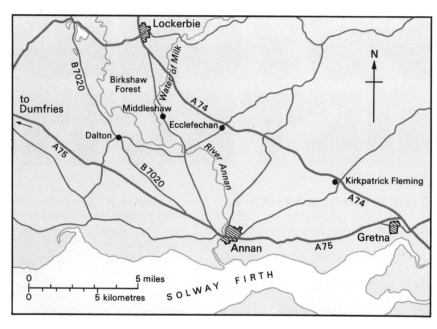

national insurance card and has never applied for a replacement. The police enquiry hinged on tracing the lorry driver. Despite a nationwide appeal, it took three weeks to find him. He claimed that he had dropped Pat on the outskirts of Dumfries, but had no idea what had become of her. Since the driver was the last person known to have seen Pat alive, efforts were concentrated on establishing the lorry's movements after it left Annan. Witnesses came forward, and eventually its route was reconstructed. After setting out on the A75 to Dumfries, the lorry turned off and took the narrow B7020 towards the village of Dalton. The lorry was large – a 26-tonne articulated vehicle. It blocked the narrow lanes, and local people remembered seeing just such a lorry manoeuvring north of Dalton, near Williamwath Bridge. It could have been on its way to the Birkshaw Forest and the A74, leading towards the south. The police continued to appeal for witnesses: 'Will any person who saw a motor lorry on 19th February anywhere in Dumfriesshire

A map of the region of Dumfries and Galloway, in south-western Scotland, where Pat was last seen, is reproduced left. The lorry which gave her a lift set out along the A75 road from Annan towards Dumfries where Pat lived, but turned off on to the B7020.

One of the posters with which the Daily Record flooded Scotland in a bid to get some hint of Pat's fate is shown right.

It was in the High Street in Annan, above, that Hazel Campbell finished her journey and saw her friend Pat for the last time.

The country road near the village of Dalton, left, was the heart of the search area, following reports that a lorry seen near there resembled the one in which Pat took her last ride.

or the adjoining areas, in any unusual circumstances – for instance, stationary in a lay-by or on a quiet country road – please communicate immediately with the police.'

The same day, 17 March, police with tracker dogs combed the undergrowth in the Dalton area but found no clues.

The Regional Crime Squad in Glasgow joined the hunt on 20 March. The *Daily Record* distributed posters and leaflets throughout the country, and the lorry driver faced more interviews with the police. Pat's father expressed fears that something terrible had happened to his daughter, and the police were prepared to accept that it had. The rest of the month saw increased digging in the lonely woodlands and river banks of the search area.

During April, there were responses to the posters but they produced no leads; and despite television appeals by Mrs McAdam, nothing was heard from Pat. Detective-Inspector Cullinan, in charge of the investigation, said he believed the secret of Pat's disappearance lay hidden in the Dalton area. He begged the villagers to rack their brains to recall any odd happenings on that fateful Sunday in February. The Dumfries police force held regular press conferences, an unusual event in missing persons cases, and they dug regularly for Pat's body between Annan and Dumfries.

Frank Ryan, the journalist, had all this in the back of his mind when he happened to find himself in Holland in 1970, three years later. Ryan knew that the Dutch clairvoyant Gerard Croiset had been involved in the hunt for Muriel McKay, a Fleet Street newspaperman's wife who had been kidnapped in 1969. Her body was never found, and it was conjectured that her corpse had possibly been cut up and fed to pigs. Croiset was involved in the case only to the extent that relatives of the missing woman had asked him to help.

DIRECTIONS FROM A PSYCHIC

On 16 February 1970, Frank Ryan arrived in the town of Utrecht to talk to Gerard Croiset at his home at 21 Willem Zwigerstraat, where he had small consulting rooms and an office. Ryan explained that he was interested in a missing girl. He showed Croiset the poster bearing Pat's picture and said she had gone missing three years earlier. Croiset interrupted, not wishing to be told any more. Just two questions, he said, needed answering. Was the girl happy at home? And where was she last seen? Ryan answered and indicated the general area of south-west Scotland on a map that he had brought along. Croiset paused and then said he 'saw' a transport café. This, he explained, had significance in the story. Next, Ryan indicated, with the map, the area between Annan and Dumfries where Hazel had last seen Pat. Concentrating on the area in more detail, Croiset said that he 'saw' a place where there were fir trees and exposed tree roots on the banks of a river. He described vividly how water had undermined the banks. Near there, he said, was a flat bridge over the river, with grey tubular railings. Ryan would find this bridge, he was told, at the foot of a hill. If he crossed the bridge, Croiset continued, he would come to a cottage. The building was now being used for some other purpose than as a residence, for it had advertising

signs on it. Round the cottage would be found a white paling fence.

Croiset rapidly sketched the hilly setting on large sheets of notepaper, which he gave to Ryan. He then instructed Ryan not to publish anything until he had found the site and photographed it. Ryan returned to Dumfries in a state of some excitement and set off with a local photographer, Jack Johnstone, to the search area.

Croiset seemed to have been describing the Williamwath Bridge, near Dalton. But to Ryan's dismay, the bridge, though flat, was not in the setting the Dutchman had described. However, Jack Johnstone recalled that there was a bridge in Middleshaw, about 3 miles (5 kilometres) away. Ryan had not been aware of this, as there had been no reports of the lorry there. However, as they drove towards it, Frank Ryan's hair stood on end.

It was exactly as Croiset had described. The bridge, lying at the foot of a hill, had grey tubular railings. Ryan searched for a particular detail that Croiset had predicted and sketched – bent railings, with a kink in the handrail. In fact, none of the rails was bent, but Johnstone photographed a wire fence attached to the bridge that drooped in exactly the way the Dutchman had pictured. But was it the bridge in Croiset's vision? They looked for other details, and found that the river bank was indeed undermined, and that tree roots were exposed.

There was also a building, carrying advertising signs and surrounded by a white fence, a short distance up the road from the bridge. As Croiset had described, the hills were covered in fir trees.

Ryan decided to tell Mrs McAdam what he was doing. He also explained that Croiset needed to make contact with something belonging to Pat and, borrowing the girl's Bible, set off for Utrecht.

Croiset was delighted when shown the photographs. 'This is what I saw!' he exclaimed. He was very impressed with the accuracy of his vision and was now even more determined to help Ryan.

When handed Pat McAdam's Bible, however, Croiset said bluntly: 'She's dead.' With no hesitation, he told Ryan she had been buried in the area he had 'seen'. The body lay hidden, he said, in a sort of cave made by the tree roots in the river bank. Ryan pressed for more details and Croiset said he would try to 'see' clothing belonging to the girl. Ryan's large-scale map was produced, and Croiset showed him where to look. At a point marked 'Broom Cottage', Ryan would find a car with a wheelbarrow beside it. Later, the interpreter clarified this: he told Ryan that it was, in fact, only part of a car – a wreck with a wheelbarrow leaning against it.

After this detailed briefing, Ryan returned to Dumfries, determined to collect witnesses before his next visit to the area. The bridge that figured so clearly in Croiset's first vision crosses a river called the Water of Milk, west of Middleshaw; the car in the second vision was predicted to be three-quarters-of-a-mile (1 kilometre) downstream. Ryan told his wife and another journalist just what he was hoping to find, and the party set off for Broom Cottage.

ACCURATE PREDICTION

There, in the garden of Broom Cottage, exactly as Croiset had described it, was an old green Ford Popular with no wheels, being used as a henhouse. An old wheelbarrow was leaning against the boot. It was an electrifying experience for the search party. Later, Frank Ryan emphasized that he had never been near Broom Cottage in his life and therefore could not be persuaded that he had managed to transfer, unconsciously, an image of the scene to Croiset. He also felt he now had proof that Gerard Croiset was using some form of power quite beyond the normal .

Ryan wrote up the story for the *Daily Record* and told his friend Detective-Inspector Cullinan exactly what had happened. That night, Sunday, 15 February 1970, Ryan and two detectives returned to the spot to search for clothing. Croiset had been right. The remains of a black dress, parts of a handbag, and a stocking were caught in the undergrowth on the river bank.

These discoveries made front page news, and local people waited impatiently for the police to announce developments. When these came, how-

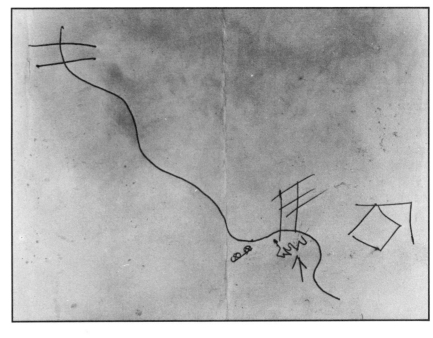

One of Croiset's predictions appears on the map, above, as drawn by him. It shows the Water of Milk; at the top left is the bridge at Middleshaw, and at the bottom right is the house carrying advertising signs. The tangled tree roots in the river bank are arrowed (trees rise above them). Another predicted item was an old car, with a barrow leaning against it (twin circles and crosses to the left of the roots). These objects were later found by journalist Frank Ryan.

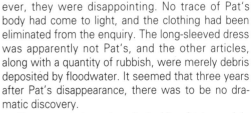

The actual bridge across the Milk at Middleshaw is shown below.

ever, they were disappointing. No trace of Pat's body had come to light, and the clothing had been eliminated from the enquiry. The long-sleeved dress was apparently not Pat's, and the other articles, along with a quantity of rubbish, were merely debris deposited by floodwater. It seemed that three years after Pat's disappearance, there was to be no dramatic discovery.

Ryan now returned again to Utrecht to explain the setbacks. Croiset was a trifle disappointed but explained that, when he was focusing on a scene, he could not be sure that the details he 'saw' would help the police. He was pleased, however, with the new photographs and saw them as encouraging proof that he had indeed received a vision of a place he could never have seen with his own eyes. Far from being discouraged, Croiset proceeded to give Ryan a description of the man that the police should question. He was, he said, aged between 32 and 34, 5 feet 4 inches (1.63 metres) tall and dark-haired, with one ear larger than the other. Croiset claimed to have a mental image of Pat taking a walk with this man before she died. They had strolled near an area where trees had been felled, and her body was nearby, he said.

BUILDING UP A PICTURE

On 19 February, Ryan conducted seven interviews with Croiset, each one adding a little to the picture that the clairvoyant was painting of Pat's last hours. Forestry workers confirmed that there had been felling in recent years, and Mrs McAdam recalled giving Pat £5 to buy a new dress. Croiset was still convinced that the dress found by Ryan was Pat's – not the one she had been wearing but one she had bought. The police, however, had no evidence of Pat having bought a dress in Glasgow: Hazel had bought clothes but, she insisted, Pat had bought only the handbag.

Hopes of finding more clues in the area were dashed by a heavy snowfall, and there were no developments until the end of the month. The *Daily Record* realised that they had a strong story on their hands, and flew Gerard Croiset to Scotland to visit

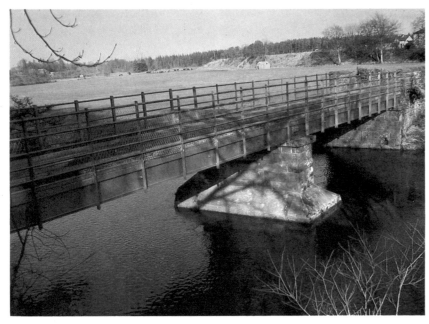

the scenes he had described. Accompanied by the head of the local CID, he spent a day touring the area. He had never been to Scotland before, but was sure of everything he had told Ryan. He was also convinced that Pat had been murdered, and claimed that her body had been dumped in the Water of Milk. After being lodged in tree roots, he said, it had been swept away to sea. If this is true, her body will probably never be found.

TV INVESTIGATION

Five years later, in 1975, a BBC Television team carried out its own investigation into the Pat McAdam case. Interviewed in Utrecht, Croiset was able to recall the case clearly from the notes he had made at the time. He believed there had been a complete triumph for his clairvoyance, as a friend had told him, misleadingly, that the police search had produced a body.

A body had indeed been found in the area, but it was not identified as Pat's. In a routine search, the remains of a woman had been found in a pond. She was in her forties, wore a wedding ring and had coins in her possession dating from after Pat's disappearance.

The fate of Pat has never been established. The person who, as far as is known, saw her last – the lorry driver – did not shed any more light on it. Subsequently, he was sent to prison to serve two concurrent life sentences for offences involving other people: one sentence was for murder, the other for crimes including rape and attempted murder. The judge recommended that he be detained in prison for at least 30 years.

Despite the fact that Pat McAdam was never found, alive or dead, Gerard Croiset maintained that this case stood as one of his most successful, and he clung to this belief until his death in 1980, at the age of 71.

How, then, did Croiset score his 'hits'? Could Frank Ryan unwittingly have transmitted images of the search area to him? All the pertinent facts of the case were in Ryan's mind and Croiset may have 'read' them somehow. Typical Croiset cases are full of images of drowning. In the Netherlands, the

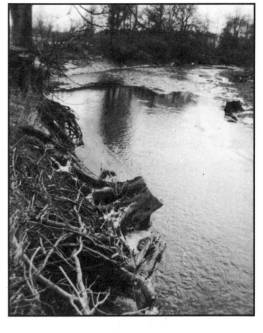

Tangled tree roots, as shown right, exposed on the bank of the Water of Milk, were 'seen' clairvoyantly by Croiset. Here, he said, Pat's body had been caught for a while after having been thrown into the river.

canals claim as many victims as the roads, and most missing persons are eventually found there. Similarly bridges, white-painted wooden fences and tubular railings are to be seen everywhere in the Netherlands. The timber house with the advertising signs at Middleshaw has a Dutch look about it. So could it be that Croiset, using Ryan as a link, seized on these familiar images?

If Pat McAdam's body had been found, the case would have become a classic work of psychic detection. But before rejecting the clairvoyant's successes as pure coincidence, one must pause and calculate the odds against finding a cottage with a particular garden containing an old car with a wheelbarrow leaning against it. That car and barrow are testimony to the accuracy of the strange vision that came to Gerard Croiset, hundreds of miles away in Utrecht. Today, Pat McAdam is still missing and her file at Dumfries CID remains open in the hope that eventually some vital clue will lead to a resolution of the case.

The battered remains of a Ford Popular, below, support a wheelbarrow in the garden of Broom Cottage, exactly as predicted by Gerard Croiset. When Ryan, with two companions, encountered this scene, he became fully convinced of Croiset's powers.

TALKING WITH THE ANGELS

JOHN DEE WAS A RESPECTED ELIZABETHAN MATHEMATICIAN WHO HAD MORE THAN A SCHOLARLY INTEREST IN THE OCCULT. HE EVEN CLAIMED TO HAVE FOUND A WAY OF TALKING TO THE ANGELS AND USING THEIR SECRETS TO DEVELOP 'ENOCHIAN MAGIC'

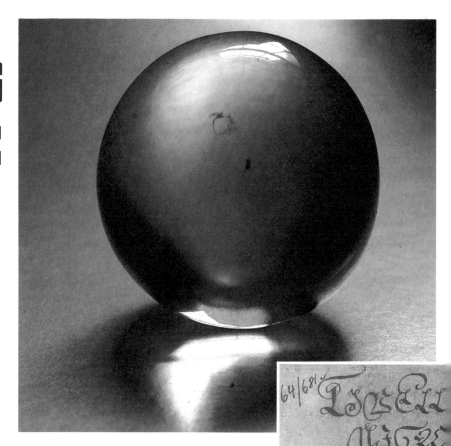

John Dee rates an entry in most standard reference works for his contribution to 16th-century mathematical and navigational knowledge. Yet this same man believed he had learned the secrets of the angels – what goes on in heaven and which angels control various parts of the world, for example. So did he actually communicate with angelic spirits? Or was he the victim of self-delusion and the deception of a cunning medium?

The majority of those who have studied Dee's life and opinions have come to the latter conclusion. The *Biographica Britannica*, for instance, describes him as having been 'extremely credulous, extravagantly vain and a most deluded enthusiast'.

But occultists tend to take a very different view – particularly those inclined to what has been called the 'Western Esoteric Tradition'. This is a synthesis of European astrology, ritual magic, alchemy and other techniques of practical occultism as developed in the late 19th century by S.L. MacGregor Mathers and his associates of the Hermetic Order of the Golden Dawn. It also incorporates some of the principles of Dee's system of 'Enochian magic', based on his presumed mastery of the language of the angels, 'Enochian'. Some believe that Dee did indeed learn the angels' tongue, and therefore argue that Enochian magic is of great significance and value. Unlike other systems, it is not concerned with demons or devils, however; and, because the language is of heavenly origin, it is supposed to enable the magician to control spirits more successfully.

Whether Dee was wise or foolish, an obsessed eccentric or a magus, there can be no doubt of his dedication to scholarship. His library, the printed and manuscript contents of which cost him more than £3,000 (a huge amount at the time), was a

John Dee, left, was known as a scholar and the developer of an intriguing system of magic.

Dee's crystal ball, top left, was used by the mediums through whom he worked.

The next 30 years or so of Dee's life were eventful, exciting, and sometimes perilous. He travelled widely in Europe, lecturing at ancient universities and making friends among the scholars. He also became interested in the 'angelic magic', expounded by Abbot Trithemius in his influential manuscript *Steganographia;* and, in addition, he cast the horoscopes of many of the great men and women of his time.

It was this last activity that, in 1553, during the reign of 'Bloody Mary', brought Dee into danger.

At the time, Queen Mary's half-sister, the Princess Elizabeth, was being held in semi-confinement, since she was suspected of plotting with Protestant malcontents to overthrow the Queen and place herself on the throne. Through one of her ladies-in-waiting, Blanche Parry, the Princess entered into a correspondence with Dee, which eventually resulted in the astrologer showing her Queen Mary's horoscope.

Through the agency of two informers, the links between Dee and Elizabeth were conveyed to the Queen's council. Immediately, the unfortunate astrologer was arrested and thrown into prison. Not only were his astrological researches into the probable duration of Mary's life regarded as near treason, but it was believed likely that he was attempting to murder her by black magic.

Eventually, Dee was cleared of the charge of treason, but he was immediately rearrested on the charge of being a suspected heretic. He gained his final release in 1555.

In 1558, Mary died and Elizabeth came to the throne. Dee enjoyed Elizabeth's favour as her astrological adviser. Indeed, it was he who selected a propitious date for her coronation; and it was he who was called upon for advice when it was suspected that sorcery was being employed against the throne.

CONJUROR OF WICKED SPIRITS

Nevertheless, Dee's life was not entirely happy. He was perpetually short of money, spending most of his income on his library and alchemical experiments; and he was distressed by the continued suspicions of many that he was, to quote his own words, 'a companion of hellhounds, and a caller and conjuror of damned and wicked spirits.'

It is likely that those who regarded Dee in this light would have thought their worst suspicions confirmed if they had known of Dee's experiments in communication with the angels, which he is believed to have begun in October 1581.

The six months before this were troubled ones for Dee. His sleep was much disturbed, his dreams were peculiar, and there were mysterious knockings in his house. But as the Australian philologist and writer on Enochian magic Dr Donald Laycock remarked, it would seem that the spirits wished to contact Dee, rather than the other way round.

Dee worked through mediums, the first being Barnabas Saul who claimed to be able to see angels and other spirits in a magic crystal. But Dee was not satisfied with Saul and dismissed the seer after a few months.

On 8 March 1582, a new medium approached Dee – a certain Edward Kelley, a strange young man whose antecedents were obscure. He was only 27

The wax talisman, top, was made by Edward Kelley, Dee's partner in magic, on directions he received from an angel.

The manuscript, above, was owned by Dee. It gives instructions for invoking Venus in ritual magic.

very large one for the period, and it included works on every subject with which 16th-century scholars concerned themselves. Theology, mathematics, geography, navigation, alchemy, astronomy, astrology and ritual magic – all these areas of study were duly represented.

Dee was born on 13 July 1527 at Mortlake, now a London suburb, but then a pleasant Surrey village. In view of the importance he always attached to astrology, it is interesting to note that, at the hour of his birth, the Sun was in Cancer and the zodiacal sign of Sagittarius was on the horizon. This combination, according to astrological devotees, is favourable for a career based on scholarship and the study of secret sciences.

Such astrological indications were certainly confirmed when, at the age of 15, Dee became an undergraduate at Cambridge and commenced his studies with great intensity. As he himself recorded:

'I was so vehemently bent to studie, that for those years I did inviolably keep this order; only to sleepe four houres every night; to allow to meate and drinke (and some refreshing after) two houres every day; and of the other 18 houres all (except the times of going to and being at divine service) was spent in my studies and learning.'

Dee's efforts received their due reward: in 1546, he was appointed Greek under-reader, a sort of junior professor. He was also made a fellow of the newly founded Trinity College. But even at this early stage of his career, there were whispers that he dabbled in black magic. Some even suspected that an ingenious mechanical beetle, devised by him for use as a special effect in a Greek play, was a creature from hell.

MR

MARY

Dee: As concerning the vision which was presented yesternight (unlooked for) to the sight of Edward Kelley as he sat at supper with me, in my hall, I mean the appearing of the very sea, and many ships thereon, and the cutting of the head of a woman, by a tall black man, what are we to imagine thereof?

Uriel: The one did signify the provision of foreign powers against the welfare of this land: which they shall shortly put into practice. The other, the death of the Queen of Scots: it is not long unto it.

In other words, Uriel – speaking through Kelley in the year 1583 – was specifically prophesying an attempt at the invasion of England by some large fleet, and the execution of Mary Stuart, Queen of Scots. The reference to the executioner as a 'black man', meanwhile, may well have been an indication of the executioner in his black hood.

LANGUAGE OF EDEN

As it turned out, Mary was executed in 1587 and the attempted invasion by the Spanish Armada came in 1588. But little of the information supplied by the angels was as specific as this. Much of it consisted of obscure magical, mathematical and, particularly, linguistic teaching. The language of Enochian was, according to Uriel and his fellows, that originally spoken in the Garden of Eden. Lengthy discourses were dictated to Dee in this tongue – at first sight, gibberish. For instance, *micaolz olprt* means 'mighty light' and *bliors ds odo* means 'comfort which openest'. But sometimes, translations were obligingly provided by the angels. From these, it is clear that Enochian is more than mere strings of syllables. It exhibits traces of syntax and grammar, and has the rudiments of language.

The illustration, right, shows Kelley raising the dead in the churchyard of Walton-le-Dale in Lancashire. Kelley was a man of ill-repute with a shady past, but he won Dee's confidence on the basis of his psychic skills.

The manuscript, far right, is in Dee's own hand and records one of the conversations that took place with the angels.

Two of the most prominent women in Dee's life were Queen Mary, left, and Queen Elizabeth, below left. Mary imprisoned him for showing his horoscope of her to Princess Elizabeth who, when she ascended the throne, made him her astrological adviser.

The Spanish Armada, below, was sent against England in 1588. Five years before, Dee had learned about the invasion in a conversation with the angel Uriel who, as usual, communicated through Kelley.

years old, but his short life seems to have been full of mystery, danger and questionable deeds. He had been a student but had not taken a degree, becoming a notary instead. Accused of forgery in the course of his work, he was said to have had his ears cropped for his offence. He had also supposedly employed ritual magic in the search for buried treasure, had studied alchemy and was in possession of strange elixirs, powders and coded manuscripts. Most sinister of all, he was reputed to practise necromancy, the rite of raising the dead for the purposes of prediction and divination. At first, Dee was suspicious of Kelley, but not for long – for Kelley saw the angel Uriel in Dee's 'shewstone' and was given instructions for the manufacture of a powerful talisman. This convinced Dee of his magical powers.

The association between Dee and Kelley lasted seven years, and the two held hundreds of seances, the first at Mortlake, the last at Cracow in Poland. On the instructions of the angels who spoke through Kelley, the men and their families had wandered thousands of miles up and down Europe.

Records of many of their experiments, carefully compiled by Dee, have survived to the present day, but they are often virtually meaningless to the modern reader who has not made a specialised study of Elizabethan magic and alchemy. They do, however, contain passages that seem to be precognitive.

Take, for example, the following exchange that took place between Dee and the angel Uriel on 5 May 1583:

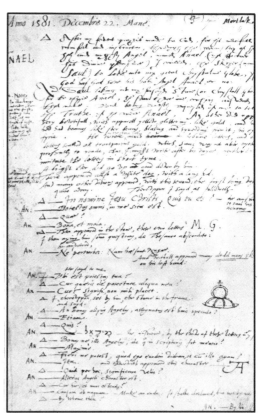

Dr Laycock has carried out a detailed study of Enochian and; in the introduction to his *Complete Enochian Dictionary*, he concludes that its structure and grammar are remarkably similar to those of English. In spite of his scepticism about the language, Dr Laycock is prepared to admit that there may be something in Enochian magic. Indeed, he has remarked:

'I have known well people who have pursued the study of Enochian from the point of view of practical occultism, and who claim that, whatever the origin of the system, it works as practical magic.'

The seance held on 17 April 1587 was the beginning of the end for the Dee-Kelley association. On that day, an angel, calling herself Madimi, gave instructions that the two men should sleep with each other's wives. Dee was deeply disturbed by this prospect, wondering whether it could be devils who were impersonating angels; but the spirits emphatically urged him on: '...In hesitating, you sin... All these things ... are permitted to you.' Dee still hesitated but, on 22 May, gave in and the wife-swapping finally took place.

This event finally placed too much of a strain on the Dee-Kelley relationship, however, and Dee returned to England, giving up all practice of magic. He died in abject poverty in 1608. Kelley preceded him in death, killed abroad in unknown circumstances, in 1595.

What then, of the value of the Enochian magic, the Enochian language, and the other occult teachings conveyed to Dee and Kelley by their supposed angels? No one can be quite sure. But there is a lot to be said for the point of view expressed by Laycock: 'If the true voice of God comes through the shewstone at all, it is certainly as through a glass darkly'.

SEARCH AMONG THE STARS

Huge storm systems swirl in the atmosphere of Jupiter, the largest planet in the solar system, below. The gas giant dwarfs two of its own satellites in this picture taken by a Voyager spacecraft. Planets even larger than Jupiter are known to circle some stars relatively close to the Sun.

ONE DAY, SELF-REPRODUCING ROBOT COLONISTS MAY BE LAUNCHED ON VOYAGES OF GALACTIC EXPLORATION. ALREADY, ASTRONOMERS HAVE BEGUN THE SEARCH FOR INHABITED PLANETS ORBITING THE NEAREST STARS

Even if only a few planets have given rise to civilisations like our own in the past few thousand million years, the whole Galaxy should now be teeming with life, for it seems that only about 10 million years would be needed to colonise it. So where might such intelligent beings be? And if intelligent life has not arisen elsewhere in the Galaxy, then why is our planet so special?

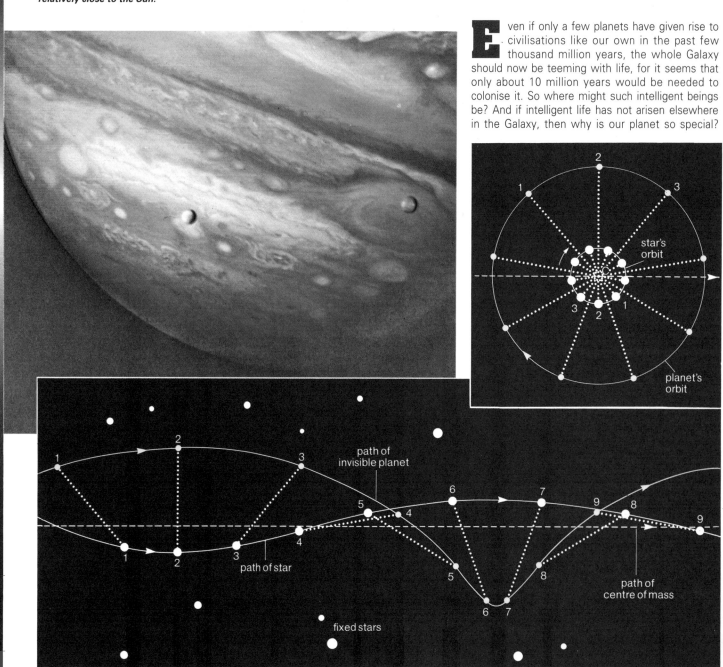

presence. By studying such an oscillation, it could even be possible to determine how many companions are affecting the star's course in this way.

It is by an application of this technique that Barnard's star fell under suspicion of having two planets, each with a mass about equal to that of Jupiter, in almost circular orbits. Other stars, such as 61 Cygni and 70 Ophiuchi, also seem to have 'invisible' companions, each apparently more massive than Jupiter. Until now, planets as small as Earth could not be detected; but modern technical advances make it likely that, if the nearest stars possess such companions, they will soon be detected, especially when large telescopes are put into orbit around the Earth.

The second method of detecting the planets of other stars is to examine the spectrum (the band of colours formed when starlight is broken up into its constituent wavelengths). Fine dark lines ('missing wavelengths') appear in any such spectra, and these shift their position slightly if the star's velocity towards or away from the observer on Earth changes. Such changes of velocity reveal that a star is being pulled by an unseen companion. Once again, advances in the design and construction of large spectrographs may well enable us to detect at least the larger planets that are in orbit about the nearest stars.

Why, among the many millions of Earth-like planets orbiting Sun-like stars at a suitable distance for life to appear, might Earth alone have given rise to an intelligent species capable of asking questions such as these?

We are, today, in a position to address these problems, both scientifically and technologically; and to do so, we need to search for three things – the planets of other stars; evidence that there is life on these planets; and signs of intelligent life.

At present, there are three techniques that might be used to find the planets of other stars. One is to study the movement of a relatively nearby star against the background of the more distant stars. This motion will be a straight line only if the star is unaccompanied. If it has companions, then these bodies will revolve around their joint centre of gravity; and the star will follow a 'wavy' line through space, which would reveal its 'invisible' companions'

If sent into orbit above the Earth's distorting atmosphere, as illustrated above left, telescopes might be able to see extremely faint objects with great clarity – including, perhaps, Earth-sized planets circling nearby stars.

Birds, fish and mammals that have adapted to water look superficially similar – for example, the penguins, left, the shark below left, and the whale below. Earth-like planets might also tend to produce intelligent beings of near-human appearance.

In theory, an unseen planet might reveal its presence by influence on the star to which it belongs. The star and the planet revolve about their common centre of mass, or 'centre of gravity', as shown above left. The numbers indicate the corresponding positions of the two bodies in their respective orbits. In relation to the Earth, the centre of mass follows a straight course through space, as shown left, but the star follows a wavy path, thus betraying the presence of its invisible companion.

The third method of detection is to observe the planets directly through telescopes. This is in many ways like trying to see a firefly near a searchlight, but it may be possible when large space telescopes are in orbit. And if the planets can be photographed and their spectra examined, it may then be possible to look for evidence of life.

To an alien observing Earth from the depths of space, our planet's atmosphere would soon give away the fact that there is likely to be life here. An alien's spectroscope would reveal the presence of an enormous amount of free oxygen, a highly active element, which would quickly combine with other substances unless it were continually being replenished by plant life. And more careful study would reveal traces of methane, which is produced biologically. Our alien might even detect fluorocarbons, the result of leakages from refrigerators and aerosol spray cans. Likewise, if we found such chemical 'signatures' in the spectra of the planets of other stars, we could legitimately deduce that they probably carried life of our type and possibly had technological civilisations, too.

Our Sun is shown, below, as it looks on radio wavelengths. The image was produced by a computer from signals picked up by a radio telescope: the red spots are the areas that emit radio waves most strongly. If the solar system were observed by the radio telescopes of an alien race, the Sun might be far 'outshone' on certain wavelengths by the flood of signals from Earth's transmitting stations.

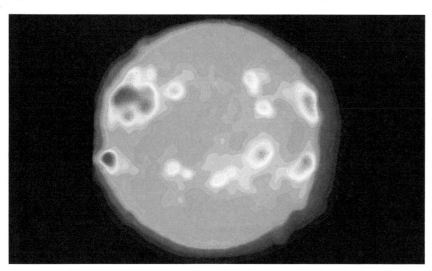

The discovery of life-bearing planets would greatly strengthen the probability that the Galaxy also contained intelligent races. Indeed, the idea that among perhaps millions of life-bearing planets Earth was the only one to produce intelligence would become ridiculous. It is a rule of organic life that, no matter how different the origins of diverse species, environment plays a dominant part in moulding them. The penguin, the dolphin and the shark, for instance, are respectively a bird, a mammal and a fish, whose evolutionary lines diverged millions of years ago. Nevertheless, they are all adapted to the same environment, the oceans.

Again, it has been pointed out that the mammals of North America and the marsupials of South America, genetically distinct and geographically separated from each other, produced their own forms of the sabre-toothed cat, the camel and the hippopotamus. Intelligence has obvious survival value: so it seems reasonable to suppose that, on an Earth-like planet with forms of life based on carbon and water, emerging in environments similar to the Earth's, intelligent species would evolve and perhaps develop a technological civilisation.

There are several possibilities for galactic travel. The artist's impression, right, shows a so-called ramscoop starship. Instead of carrying a large load of fuel, ram-propelled spacecraft would use the hydrogen atoms scattered throughout space. These could, in theory at least, be collected by huge magnetic fields operated by the ship. Here, a damaged ramscoop starship is seen arriving at a planet which has already been colonised.

How, then, might other civilisations gather indisputable evidence of our existence? One way might be to eavesdrop on the use we make of the electromagnetic spectrum. At the present time, our own planet is 'noisy', in that the presence of life on Earth could be readily detected at interstellar distances because of our ultra-powerful military radar systems and television broadcasting stations. We do not need to send out radio signals deliberately designed to draw the attention of other intelligent species. So, if another civilisation had receivers big enough to pick up such signals, it could probably calculate how far Earth is from the Sun, and also the length of our year and our days. It would, however, require much more sensitive receiving apparatus to decipher our actual programme signals, so there are probably few extraterrestrials who would understand our television violence and soap operas.

INTERSTELLAR EAVESDROPPING

There is no doubt that, in the very near future, it should be possible for us, too, to eavesdrop on any civilisations, comparable in technology to our own, on planets orbiting stars out to a distance of some 250 light-years. Within that radius, there are around a million stars.

What is more, if such aliens are already travelling between the stars, using spaceships somewhat more advanced than *Daedalus* – a vehicle designed by the British Interplanetary Society – it should be possible to 'watch' their progress across space. The ships' engines should produce highly energetic radiation in wavelengths ranging from the radio region of the electromagnetic spectrum to the gamma ray region. And the ship's exhaust plume would interact with the galactic magnetic field, generating characteristic radiations. So far, however, we have detected no such signs of interstellar travel.

But alien races might not use radio and television waves to communicate. Perhaps they would even look on these as being as primitive as semaphore – in which case, sending out one or more unmanned probes to other stars might be a

*In*Focus ON THE SAME WAVELENGTH?

Might intelligent beings from other worlds live in such different mental 'universes' from ours that we could not even recognise them as intelligent? Might their senses even be entirely different from ours? Two gold plaques, bearing engraved diagrams, are now speeding through interstellar space on robot *Pioneer* spacecraft. It has been said that they would probably not even be recognised by aliens as a message: if, for instance, such organisms had eyes at all, they might not be sufficiently sensitive to the optical wavelengths. But Carl Sagan, who helped to design the plaques, countered that all planetary atmospheres are likely to be transparent at optical and radio wavelengths, just as the Earth's atmosphere is; and since 'eyes' that form images from radio waves are inconceivable – they would have to be impossibly huge – organisms on such planets would be likely to see the same wavelengths as we see. But could we recognise intelligence in a micro-organism that completed its life cycle in a matter of hours, or in an intelligent nebula that thought and acted on a time-scale of millennia? We would surely find it harder to establish rapport with them than we would with the humanoid extra-terrestrial, *left.*

However, if there are other intelligent life-forms in our Galaxy, they may use physical laws and processes that we are still too primitive to have discovered, and they may therefore communicate by means of which we have no conception. After all, for all but the last hundred years of the countless millennia during which Man has been evolving, he has been unaware of the (natural) radio waves arriving at the Earth's surface from the depths of space. So who knows what else might be reaching us from the stars without our knowledge?

It must be borne in mind that, with our present hardware and techniques of data processing, we have probably only barely dipped a toe into the infinite ocean of space.

THE GALACTIC ZOO

It may well be that primitive forms of life will yet be discovered on other planets in our own solar system. If this happened, we would have to accept that the odds are in favour of life arising on any suitable planet and that there must be many, probably millions, of civilisations in our Galaxy. And if we still could not find any sign of their existence, we should have to ask ourselves why it was so hard to get in touch with them.

Perhaps more advanced civilisations deliberately hide themselves from us: maybe we are quarantined, or even treated as the galactic equivalent of a zoo. Or perhaps we are undergoing a test that must be faced by any intelligent species that acquires the power to destroy itself by war or the greedy exploitation of its planet. If we grow up, rather than blow up, the aliens may then make themselves known to us.

Or it may be that, despite what was said above, life on other planets has taken very different paths from that taken by human beings. The dominant species on other life-bearing planets may be so completely alien to us that no communication between them and ourselves is possible: we may not even be able to recognise such life-forms as intelligent beings – or even living beings! Even on our own planet, we find it difficult to communicate with intelligent fellow mammals, such as the dolphin and the whale.

Nevertheless, there is widespread hope that we are not alone in the Universe and that other intelligent species are sufficiently similar to us that, one day, we may be able communicate with them.

" PERHAPS WE ARE UNDERGOING A TEST THAT MUST BE FACED BY ANY INTELLIGENT SPECIES... IF WE GROW UP, RATHER THAN BLOW UP, THE ALIENS MAY THEN MAKE THEMSELVES KNOWN TO US. **"**

more economical and surer way of searching for planets suitable for life, or even already occupied by intelligent species.

In one version of this idea, the probe explores the vicinity of a star and moves on if it finds nothing of interest. If it comes across a promising planet, however, it goes into orbit about it. If there are signs of life on the planet, the probe may be programmed simply to listen at first for the use of radio by an intelligent species.

Another idea is the 'von Neumann probe', named after a great American computer pioneer who studied the concept of self-replicating machines. The von Neumann machine would be an intelligent robot probe, capable of building duplicates of itself from raw materials mined on planets and asteroids. In theory, one or more such duplicates could be built and sent to other planetary systems in order to carry on the task of exploration and reproduction. Interesting discoveries would then be radioed back to the civilisation that sent out the first probe. But even with probes 'breeding' in this manner, such a search might take something like 10 million years.

Many people therefore argue that Man's quest for intelligent life in the Galaxy should involve a search not only for radio signals but also for von Neumann-like probes orbiting the planets of our own solar system. Even if they had once been here, but had left for some reason, the traces of their manufacturing activities could still exist in abandoned mines on some of the asteroids or satellites of the solar system.

SECRETS OF THE MASTER BUILDERS

HOW WAS IT POSSIBLE FOR PRIMITIVE SOCIETIES TO BUILD STUPENDOUS MONUMENTS SUCH AS STONEHENGE, THE STATUES OF EASTER ISLAND, THE STONE CITIES OF THE ANDES AND THE PYRAMIDS OF ANCIENT EGYPT?

The technical feats that made possible the building of Stonehenge and other megalithic structures of northern Europe are quite stupendous, while claims made by modern writers about the people who built them are no less impressive. The circle of massive arches at Stonehenge dates from around 1750 BC, and is made up of sarsen stones, weighing about 50 tonnes each, brought from the Marlborough Downs about 20 miles (30 kilometres) to the north. One estimate puts the work of construction at 5½ years for 1,500 men.

The site was already ancient when the sarsens were erected. The bluestones, forming a double circle, had been brought to Salisbury Plain from the Prescelly Mountains of South Wales some five centuries previously. Weighing about four tonnes each, 82 of them had been brought on boats or rafts by sea and river, with two overland journeys of a few miles, to their present location.

The feasibility of the journey was established in 1954 when 4-tonne blocks of concrete were transported in exactly the same way over that route. The

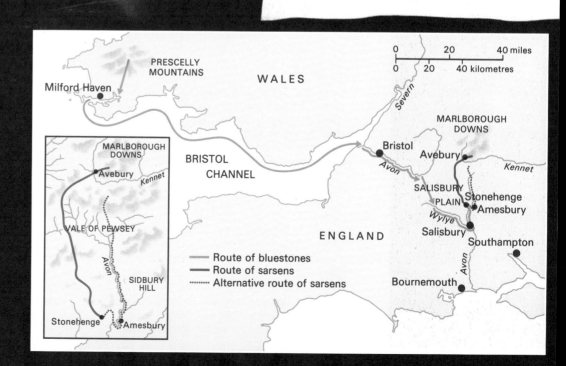

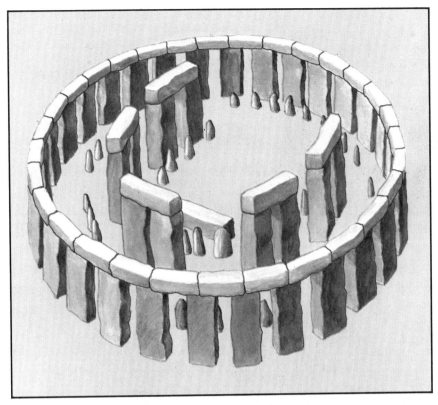

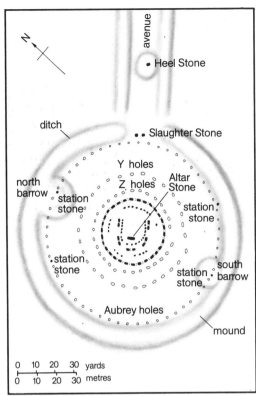

The illustration and ground plan above show how Stonehenge probably originally looked. Routes by which it is thought that the megaliths were brought to the site, shown in the photograph left, are indicated below left. The sketch below shows the raising of the megaliths. First the uprights were levered into place, then the lintels were placed on platforms and gradually edged higher, finally being eased into place.

blocks required 64 men to haul them on sleds and rollers – the largest, the so-called Altar Stone, required 110. Methods by which the standing stones could be set upright, and the lintels lifted on to them, using only Bronze Age tools, have also been worked out.

Stonehenge abounds in mysteries, but these do not lie in the engineering that was employed. Rather, questions remain about the importance of the site – a religious centre from 2500 BC onwards – an importance so great that stones had to be transported hundreds of miles to that particular place. We still do not know either which of the

numerous astronomical alignments that have been found in the structure are genuine and which are merely the result of chance; while the significance of the genuine ones, to which the ancient builders devoted so much attention and skilful labour, also eludes us. Was the positioning of the stones perhaps determined by underground streams and other 'water lines', allegedly detected by dowsers? No one has yet come up with satisfactory answers to these points. As we have seen, the engineering involved is not that mysterious at all, and several explanations have been offered. Indeed, there is one theory that the science of the antediluvians, as it survived at the time of Stonehenge, included a method of overcoming the law of gravity.

According to one school of thought, however, there is danger in attempting to reconstruct methods used by builders in the past – the danger of being too enthusiastic about a favoured technique without rigorous experimental verification, or of jumping to conclusions from unrepresentative, small-scale experiments. Indeed, the Norwegian explorer Thor Heyerdahl may have been guilty of this when he attempted to repeat the achievement of the Easter Island statue-builders.

Easter Island is a remote speck in the Pacific Ocean, the most easterly of the Polynesian islands, and home to numerous giant-headed, legless statues. At least 1,000 of them are known, some still in quarries from which they were never removed, others lying damaged in various places, but most gazing out over the rocky, infertile island. Standing between 12 and 15 feet (4 and 5 metres) high, many weigh as much as 20 tonnes. So how were these 'monsters' moved to their final resting places?

Heyerdahl attempted to answer this question in 1956 by organizing a dozen inhabitants of the island to move a head some distance and erect it. It took them 18 days, but they succeeded in the end.

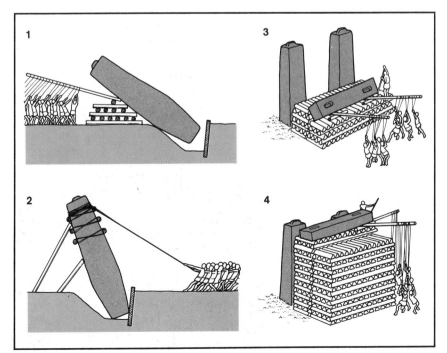

balsa raft the *Kon-Tiki* because he believed the same people sailed westward to establish the statue-building society of Easter Island. Thus, his theory links the supposed near-magical skills of the Easter Islanders with the super-technology that is spoken of in connection with the ruins of Tiahuanaco.

According to Heyerdahl, early colonists used balsa rafts; but he does not credit the possibility of the involvement of ancient spacemen. Erich von Däniken, on the other hand, claims that four-fingered beings, seen in rock pictures at Tiahuanaco, are representations of four-fingered ancestors who arrived from space. Indeed, to end such speculations, it may require some archaeologist to demonstrate the feasibility of conventional explanations by actually organising the transportation of a 100-tonne

Heyerdahl's achievement can justly be criticised in its contribution to solving the mystery of the Easter Island statues, however; for the head that was moved was one of the smaller ones, weighing less than 15 tonnes, and it was shifted only about 100 yards (90 metres) across smooth, sandy ground, with the help of modern ropes. This comparatively simple exercise would therefore seem to bear little relevance to the 4-mile (6.5-kilometre) journey made by the largest of the island's statues, a giant of 80 tonnes. The statues also were undamaged when originally erected, whereas Heyerdahl's team damaged the head of their statue while setting it up.

But neither armchair theorizings nor the small-scale trials of Heyerdahl and others can quite lay to rest a doubt inspired by the awesome statues of Easter Island – the thought that these ancient gods (if that is what they were) 'walked' to their final homes by means not understood by us.

ANDEAN ACHIEVEMENTS

Ingenuity must be stretched even further to imagine means by which the cities and fortresses of the high Andes could have been built. Tiahuanaco lies 13,000 feet (4,000 metres) above sea level, an altitude that taxes the lungs of visitors who are not mountain-dwellers. The city, lying just within the Bolivian border, overlooks Lake Titicaca. Nobody knows exactly when it was built – perhaps between AD 200 and 600, perhaps somewhat later. Its temples are massive, and the blocks from which they are carved are huge, too – some are 100 tonnes in weight. The quarries from which they come have been located, and these are between 60 and 200 miles (100 and 300 kilometres) distant.

We know little about the construction process. Some of the stone, at least, was probably brought across the lake, in the season when its waters were at their highest. But other stones must have come by land: perhaps ramps, lubricated with wet clay, would have been constructed to get the stones over slopes. Maybe huge numbers of slaves, or even freemen, would have been available to drag the blocks to the site.

But unconventional theorists cannot be blamed for dismissing such conjectures and pointing to the legends of the Incas, as told to the Spanish in the 16th century. These stated that Tiahuanaco was built by a white-skinned, bearded race, led by the god Tikki Viracocha. Thor Heyerdahl even named his

Were the Easter Island statues gods that 'walked' to their present sites? Thor Heyerdahl attempted to prove that this was not the case when, in 1956, he persuaded a dozen islanders to move one of the statues from the quarry where it had lain since it was carved, and erect it, as shown top and above. In the end, they succeeded, as shown right, although they damaged the statue in the process. It has been pointed out, however, that this experiment does not prove that this was indeed the way that the statues were raised: Heyerdahl's islanders used modern ropes and – a still more damning fact – the statue they moved was one of the smallest – a mere 15 tonnes, as compared with the 80 or so tonnes of the largest statue. To move a statue five times as heavy would be a formidable task even using modern ropes.

PERSPECTIVES

A HIDDEN NETWORK

The existence of ancient engineering achievements, vast in scale, has sometimes remained unsuspected by archaeologists intent on other matters. The extensive canal system of the Mayas is a case in point. Until the late 1970s, only a few such canals were known. Then a new type of radar, developed to survey the planet Venus, was used to search for Mayan sites. Carried on flights over Central America, the radar revealed networks of lines clustering along rivers and around swamps. Study on the ground confirmed that the features were remains of a canal system.

The canals, used for drainage and irrigation, were built in pairs, the excavated earth being thrown into the space enclosed by each pair to form a raised island, on which crops were grown. The system ensured that the crops received neither too much nor too little water. Indeed, the canals permitted an efficient, high-yielding agriculture that supported a population of over 2 million. The Mayan civilisation flourished for over a thousand years until it suddenly collapsed about AD 900 – perhaps because flood or drought caused the failure of the canal system.

block over 100 miles (160 kilometres) of rough ground, through forests and across river gorges.

The only one of the Seven Wonders of the ancient world that is still standing, the Great Pyramid at Giza, a few miles south-west of Cairo, meanwhile, has been the object of speculation for centuries. It was built in the 26th century BC for the Pharaoh Cheops (or Khufu), and rises 450 feet (137 metres) above the levelled bedrock, its base covering an area of 13 acres (5.2 hectares). It is estimated that the pyramid is made up of 2,500,000 sandstone blocks, weighing about 6.5 million tonnes. When it was first built, the royal tomb sparkled white in the brilliant Egyptian sunlight, for it is known to have been faced with smooth limestone slabs, long since stolen.

So how was the magnificent structure raised? Such writers as René Noorbergen and Erich von Däniken claim that 2.5 million blocks with an average weight of 2.5 tonnes could not have been transported and manipulated into place by 100,000 men (the figure reported by the Greek historian Herodotus) during the 22 years of Cheops' reign. In a flurry of unsupported statistics, Noorbergen concludes that:

'We are speaking of a project that required almost one million people... one-third to one-half the estimated population of all of Egypt around 2700 BC.'

The Great Pyramid at Giza, above, was built 46 centuries ago as a tomb for the Pharaoh Cheops. It is a stupendous feat of science and organisation – but does it provide evidence, as one writer has suggested, that the pyramids date from before the Flood and were built using some form of lost super-technology?

However, there has to be something unreasonable about a calculation that leads to the conclusion that eight man-years are required to cut, transport and position each block in the pyramid – even though this figure includes the workers' families and the soldiers who were allegedly required to police the workers. Noorbergen also makes much of the quantities of timber required for the barges that floated the blocks down the Nile from as far away as Aswan, a distance of 600 miles (960 kilometres), and for the sledges or rollers with which they were dragged into position. He reports that:

'Mathematicians tell us 26 million trees would have been required to fashion the necessary number of sledges and rafts.'

While this is certainly interesting, Noorbergen's arguments are but a thin thread on which to hang, as he does, the claim that the pyramids date from before the Flood and were constructed with a lost super-technology.

Nevertheless, the achievements of ancient builders readily provoke the thought that they may have commanded enormous forces of which we know nothing. On the whole, though, it is more likely that they could call on only those forces that are the common property of the human race – willpower, intelligence and skills born of experience. Against this background, however, certain anomalies stand out – anomalies such as electrical batteries that are 1,500 years old, and metal artefacts in 'impossible' locations in ancient rocks. These remain to intrigue the speculative mind.

> **▚▚** WHEN WE ARE CONFRONTED WITH A BLOCK WITH AN ESTIMATED WEIGHT OF 20,000 TONNES, OUR IMAGINATION, MADE RATHER BLASÉ BY THE TECHNICAL ACHIEVEMENTS OF TODAY, IS GIVEN ITS SEVEREST SHOCK. **▚▚**
>
> **ERICH VON DÄNIKEN,**
>
> **CHARIOTS OF THE GODS**

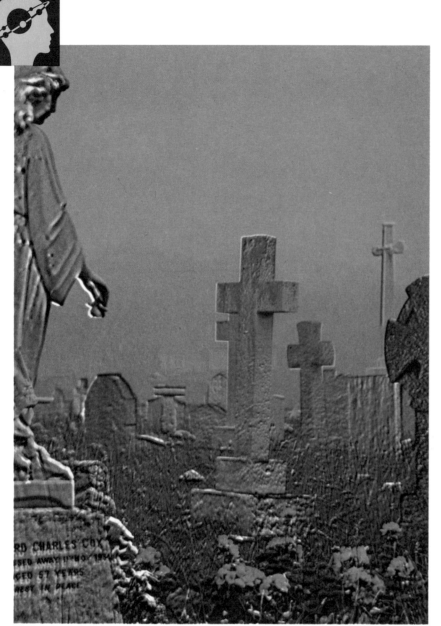

Almost everyone in the Western world is afraid of dying. The fear is so widespread and has such profound effects that the medical profession has coined a word for it: thanatophobia (*Thanatos* is the Greek for 'death').

The fear itself is natural enough – but what exactly are we afraid of? The answer differs greatly from one person to another. One fears the pain and the indignities that terminal illness may bring; another fears divine judgement; someone else, on the contrary, is afraid that there is nothing after death but oblivion; and another is anxious not for himself but for dependents left behind. But to most people, death is simply 'the unknown', too fearful to be contemplated. The result is a taboo on any discussion of the topic.

This conspiracy of silence inevitably adds to the burdens of those who are approaching their death. Today, in developed countries, most terminally-ill patients are sent to hospital – removed from home to endure painful and frequently embarrassing treatment, and finally dying among strangers. They are facing the greatest trauma of their lives, yet all too often no one will even talk with them about their imminent death. Visitors try to maintain the fiction that all will be well; discussing the making of a will is often considered to be in dubious taste; and even if surrounded by people, the dying patient is appallingly isolated.

But a new profession has been created to meet such needs – that of counselling for the dying. One of the most remarkable workers in this field is Dr Elisabeth Kübler-Ross, an American who has been counselling the dying, from tiny children to old people, since the 1960s. But what is probably the most important result of her work is sometimes a source of embarrassment to fellow professionals. In 1974, Dr Kübler-Ross made this uncompromising statement: 'Before I started working with dying patients, I did not believe in life after death. I now believe in it beyond all shadow of a doubt.'

Extraordinary personal experiences have convinced her of this. But before they occurred, what she had seen of the deaths of others sometimes also suggested that they marked the transition to a new life.

COSMIC CONSCIOUSNESS

TERMINALLY ILL PATIENTS HAVE GAINED REASSURANCE FROM A REMARKABLE DOCTOR WHO BELIEVES SHE HAS EXPERIENCED THE PROCESS OF DYING AND THEREFORE NOW HAS NO FEAR OF DEATH

Figures of angels and the symbol of the cross, found in profusion in every Christian graveyard as above, express a profound hope for a life beyond the grave – a hope that goes hand in hand with a deep fear of death. Yet some who have been on the very brink of dying claim to know that there is an afterlife.

Dr Kübler-Ross has observed that there are five stages that a terminally ill person can go through – though he or she may not reach the last stage before death comes. The first is denial, accompanied by avoidance of others: 'It can't happen to me – and I won't talk to anyone.' This is followed by anger: 'Why me? Why not someone older, less well-educated, less useful?' The third stage is bargaining: 'If I do as I'm told, you will make me better won't you?' Then comes depression: 'I really am dying – me, dying!' Finally, comes acceptance.

It is at this last stage that nurses often report the patient's behaviour changing drastically. He may

hear voices or see visions of dead friends and relatives who, seemingly, have come to escort him into a new existence. (Such hallucinations have been dubbed 'take-away visions' by thanatologist Dr Raymond Moody.) The patient may also speak of recurring images of tunnels, lights, and feelings of peace, like those occurring during out-of-the-body experiences.

THE HAPPINESS BEYOND

In her work, Dr Kübler-Ross has encountered many such cases. She has also spoken with many patients who had clinically 'died' but who were subsequently resuscitated. Their stories of leaving the body and experiencing great happiness, even excitement, are remarkably consistent. Few wanted to 'come back', and usually only out of a sense of responsibility for a loved one who was left behind. Most significantly, almost everyone who had experienced a short period of 'death' had no fear of dying finally. As one doctor who resuscitated a woman patient remarked: 'I have worked with people many times to get them to accept their death; but this was the first time I have ever had to get someone to accept *life*.'

Of course, not everyone dies peacefully, without pain or distress. In many people, the will to live is very strong and results in a battle, as in the case of Wallace Abel. In 1975, he found himself in the Scottsdale Memorial Hospital in Arizona, USA, suffering from a heart attack. During his stay, his heart stopped twice, and both times he was resuscitated. Recalling the second occasion, he said:

'Suddenly there was a tugging at my midsection. A transparent figure of me was struggling to leave my body. I recognised it immediately, but my body seemed to refuse to let [it] go... My image struggled, twisted, pulled. Suddenly, I realised I was witnessing my own struggle for life.'

Not all thanatologists believe that these 'near death' experiences are valid evidence of some kind of life beyond the death of the body. Another American, Dr Russell Noyes, a psychiatrist at the University of Iowa Medical School, studied the stories of 114 resuscitated patients – which included accounts of out-of-the-body experiences, floating sensations, freedom from pain and a sense of joy. He concluded that such experiences merely represent 'depersonalisation', an 'emergency mechanism', or sort of reflex action, which is genetically programmed to help us over the greatest trauma of our lives, that of death. Noyes does not believe that any of the tales of the dying are anything more than hallucinations.

RELIVING DEATH

The strength of Kübler-Ross' conviction, however, rests – as we have said – on her own amazing personal experiences. In the early 1970s, after a tiring day in which she had counselled several dying patients, Dr Kübler-Ross lay down to rest. Suddenly, she had the experience of leaving her body. She learned later that someone checked her pulse and respiration at this time and thought she was dead.

When Kübler-Ross 'returned' to her body, she felt that she had discovered that consciousness can leave the body under certain circumstances in life – and presumably does so at death, permanently. What is more, she felt that she now knew what it was like to die. But an even stranger and far more traumatic experience was to follow, transforming her whole outlook on life – and especially death. One night, she was finding it difficult to sleep when suddenly:

'I had one of the most incredible experiences of my life... I went through every single death of every single one of my thousand patients. And I mean the physical pain, the... agony, the screaming for help. The pain was beyond description. There was no

A soul joyfully and trustingly leaves its body escorted by angels, in William Blake's picture, below. People near death often see beings – usually deceased loved ones – who have apparently come to act as guides into the next stage of existence.

The souls of the dying in a 19th-century New York hospital are depicted, left, as seen by the clairvoyant Andrew Jackson Davis, the 'seer of Poughkeepsie'. Davis claimed to be able to see into the world of spirits, which he called 'Summerland'. But departure from life could be blighted by the grim conditions of the hospitals of the time. Problems exist today, too, since even a patient surrounded by medical staff, as below, may be intolerably lonely.

time to think and no time for anything except that, twice, I caught a breath, like between two labour pains. I was able to catch my breath for a split second and I pleaded – I guess with God – for a shoulder to lean on, for one human shoulder, and I visualized a man's shoulder that I could put my head on.

'And a thunderous voice came: "You shall not be given". Those words. And then I went back to my agony and doubling up in bed. But I was awake, it wasn't a dream. I was reliving every single death of every one of my dying patients.'

Again the voice thundered: 'You shall not be given'. Gasping for breath, she raged at it: 'I have helped so many and now no one will help me.' But at that moment, the realisation came to her that she must do it alone, that no one can do it for her. And in place of the unimaginable suffering came 'the most incredible rebirth experience'. She described it as follows:

'Everywhere I looked in the room – my legs, the closet, the window – everything started to vibrate into a million molecules. Everything vibrated at this incredible speed... Behind was a sunrise, the brightest light you can imagine... the light was full and open, like the whole sun was there... the vibrations stopped, and the million molecules, including me... fell into one piece... and I was part of that one. And I finally thought: "I'm okay, because I'm part of all this".'

She began to see every pebble, leaf and bird – everything that is – as being part of a whole 'alive universe', seemingly experiencing what the mystics have termed 'cosmic consciousness'. In some way, too, the experience gave her insight into the continuity of all things, including the spirit before and after death.

However, this dreadful, yet enlightening, experience was not to be the final paranormal event in her life. Some time later, as she sat in her office in a hospital in Chicago, a former patient of hers walked in to thank her personally for all she had done and to encourage her to continue in her good work. Kübler-Ross recognised Mrs Schwartz instantly, and thought she must be hallucinating. Mrs Schwartz was dead. Then the doctor's scientific training asserted itself: she presented the apparition with a pen and paper and asked her to write a note, dated and signed. Mrs Schwartz duly did so and went away. The handwriting has since been compared by experts with that of the dead woman and vouched for as hers.

VOICE FROM BEYOND

On a further occasion, Kübler-Ross tape-recorded the voice of another deceased patient, Willie. As she put it:

'I understand that this is very far out, and I don't want people to be less sceptical. I am sceptical myself. The scientist in me needed Mrs Schwartz to sign a paper, though I knew she was in my office. And I needed a tape recording of Willie's voice. I still listen to it and think it's one big, incredible dream. I am still filled with this incredible sense of awe and miracle.'

An acknowledged pioneer in the growing field of thanatology, Dr Kübler-Ross has written a major work, *On Death and Dying*. It is, in many respects, essential reading for doctors, nurses, social workers and others who are continually faced with the problems of coping with terminally ill patients. Yet her certainty about the afterlife, her out-of-the-body experiences and her descriptions of cosmic consciousness have proved a shocking embarrassment to many members of the medical profession. Her work is freely quoted, and her vast practical experience drawn on, but very few students care to discuss her spiritual discoveries. The dying patient who is lucky enough to be counselled by Dr Kübler-Ross may well never hear her speak of an afterlife unless she is specifically asked to do so. But to her five stages in the process of dying, she has now, privately, added a sixth: the afterlife.

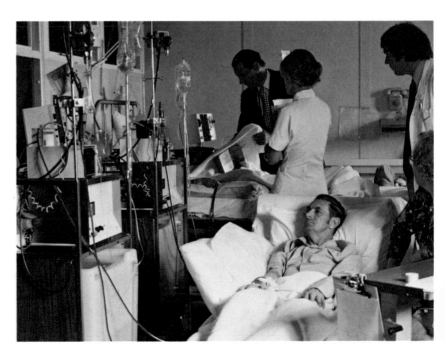

THE BELL WITCH STRIKES

THE MOST SAVAGE AND RELENTLESS POLTERGEIST ON RECORD MUST SURELY BE THE 'BELL WITCH', WHOSE SYSTEMATIC PERSECUTION OF THE BELL FAMILY OF TENNESSEE, USA, IN THE EARLY 19TH CENTURY, STOPPED ONLY AT MURDER

In the illustration below, slaves on a cotton plantation – similar to the one owned by the Bell family – practise a voodoo ceremony. The Bells may have been influenced by such an atmosphere of belief in the paranormal.

It has become almost axiomatic that ghosts do no physical harm to those who experience them. Indeed, apparitions are frequently reported as being solid and 'normal'; and it is only when they walk away through the wall or disappear as if 'switched off' that the observer realises what he has seen and becomes alarmed. Even the rumbustious poltergeist – whose activities include such apparently dangerous acts as throwing stones, smashing glass and crockery, and starting fires – causes little or no bodily damage to its victims.

But there is one well-attested case of a supernatural power, which not only seems to have killed its victim but apparently set out to do so with deliberate intent – the so-called 'Bell Witch'. The late Dr Nandor Fodor, a Freudian psychiatrist and pioneer of modern psychophysical research, called the case 'America's greatest ghost story'; but if his conclusions are correct, it must also rank as one of the world's most bizarre murder mysteries.

The malevolent power that laid siege to the homestead of John Bell and his family in Robertson County, Tennessee, USA, during the year 1817 lay totally outside the experience of that rural but rich community. A century and a quarter had elapsed since America's only serious outbreak of witchcraft mania died down at Salem, Massachusetts; while the Fox sisters of Hydesville, New York, founding daughters of modern Spiritualism, lay more than 30 years in the future. The term 'poltergeist' was in fact unknown at the time.

The Bells and their neighbours were Bible-belt Christians with a streak of superstition that paralleled that of their slaves: both black and white consulted a village 'wise woman' named Kate Batt. It was natural that they should call their trouble by an old name. As Dr Fodor put it:

'The "Witch", as the haunter was called, serves well as a descriptive term... modern poltergeists, no matter how much mischief and destruction they wreak, stop short of murder. The Bell Witch did not, and it only ceased its activities after the death by poisoning of John Bell, the head of the household,

The Puritans, above, are seen arresting a 'witch' during the infamous outbreak of witchcraft mania at Salem, Massachusetts, in 1692, when 30 people were accused of sorcery and 19 of them hanged. Although most American rural areas, like those in Europe, had their 'wise women' and natural psychics, from the end of the Salem trials to 1817, when the Bell Witch first made itself known, paranormality in the United States had not been a burning issue. But then – literally, as far as the Bell family was concerned – all hell broke loose.

whom it tortured and persecuted with a fury of unrelenting savagery.'

The phenomena began in 1817 and petered out in the late spring of 1821, some months after the death of John Bell, although they did reoccur briefly seven years later, apparently to fulfil a promise to one of the dead man's sons. During its reign, the Witch also attracted hordes of ghost hunters, most of them anxious to prove it a hoax. But these all met, according to contemporary records, with 'egregious defeat'.

Richard Williams Bell, a younger son of the family, wrote an account of the phenomena, entitled *Our Family Trouble*, in 1846, when he was 36 years old; and although he was only 10 when the Witch ceased its activity, his account tied in with later, more detailed records. One of these, published in 1867 by a Clarksville newspaper editor, M.V. Ingram, included interviews with all surviving members of the family and contemporary witnesses, as well as the testimony of the author, who had himself witnessed the outbreak as a child. Another was a document by John Bell Jr, as related to his son, Dr Joel Thomas Bell. The definitive version was given in 1934 by Dr Charles Bailey Bell, son of Dr Joel, who lectured on neurosurgery at the University of Nashville's Medical Department, was a consultant at Nashville City Hospital, and a prominent member of several national medical bodies. As a young medical student in 1888, Dr Charles Bell had interviewed his great aunt Elizabeth 'Betsy' Bell about her recollections: then 83, she had in her

youth been at the centre of the phenomena – and perhaps even an unwitting murderer.

John Bell was a prosperous cotton plantation owner, well-liked and respected by his neighbours and friends, among them General Andrew Jackson, who was to become seventh President of the United States and a witness to the Witch's activities. John and his wife, Luce, lived in a large, two-storey house with their nine children. Their domestic servants and plantation hands were black slaves; but – as far as was possible under such conditions – the Bell children mingled with the hands on terms of easy familiarity and friendliness. One of the most outgoing was Betsy Bell, a robust and apparently contented 12-year-old.

DISTURBING THE PEACE

The manifestations began in the form of knocks and raps on the walls and windows of the house. These increased in power and volume so that, by the end of the year, they were literally shaking the building to its foundations. Gnawing, scratching and flapping sounds alternated with the rattle of invisible stones on the roof, the clattering of what sounded like heavy chains on the floor, and half-human gulping, choking and 'lip smacking' noises.

Then, one day, the force displayed its strength, pulling Richard Bell's hair so violently that it lifted him clear of his bed. He felt 'that the top of his head had been taken off .... Immediately, Joel yelled out in great fright, and next Elizabeth was screaming in her room, and after that something was continually pulling at her hair after she retired to bed.'

Up to this point, the family had kept their curious troubles to themselves, but now they let a close friend and neighbour, James Johnson, into their secret. After witnessing the phenomena for himself, Johnson concluded that some intelligence lay behind them. He performed a brief exorcism, and this did seem to silence the Bell house for a while.

But the Witch returned – and with renewed vigour, slapping Betsy's cheeks until they were crimson and pulling her hair until she screamed with pain.

John Bell and James Johnson now called in more neighbours to form an investigating committee, partly to keep the tormented Betsy company, and partly to induce the Witch to speak.

Betsy spent a night away from home; but the 'trouble followed her with the same severity, disturbing the family where she went as it did at home, nor were we any wise relieved', according to a later account given by Richard Bell. Indeed, the committee itself seems to have done more harm than good. In fact, the development of the Witch's voice seems to have come about under the urgings of the committee. At first, it was low and inarticulate – a thin, whistling sound – but gradually it turned into a weak faltering whisper and, towards the end of its career, it became loud and raucous. Unlike the other physical phenomena, which took place only after dark – although usually in lamplit rooms – the voice could be heard both day and night, and came from any direction. And as the voice grew in strength, so did the Witch's violence.

'The blows were heard distinctly, like the open palm of a heavy hand, while the sting was keenly felt,' we are told; and they were rained indiscriminately on anyone who happened to be around, but particularly on Betsy Bell and her father, John.

From the beginning, the force had seemed to centre on Betsy; and as the voice developed, so the formerly robust girl began to suffer fainting fits and breathing difficulties that lasted up to half-an-hour at a time. During these attacks, the Witch remained silent; but as soon as Betsy had recovered, it would begin to talk again. The obvious conclusion was that, somehow, Betsy was producing sounds by ventriloquism; but a doctor who visited the house laid his hands over her mouth at the time the voice was heard, and soon satisfied himself that she was in no way connected with these noises.

VOICED OBSCENITIES

When the voice first developed, its utterances tended to be of a pious nature. It could reproduce, word for word, for instance, the Sunday sermons of the two local parsons, imitating their tones exactly. It sang beautifully, and recited tracts from *The Bible*. Unfortunately, however, this was only a temporary phase. The voice soon began uttering obscenities, which were particularly distressing to a Bible-belt family. It also alarmed them by claiming to be 'Old Kate Batt's witch'.

The Witch's ability to produce disgusting odours was also demonstrated on several occasions, once to local witness William Porter when the Witch got into bed with him and twisted his bedclothes off him 'just like a boy would roll himself in a quilt'. Porter leaped out of bed and picked up the roll of bedclothes, intending to throw them into the fire. He said: 'I discovered it was very weighty and smelled awful. I had not got halfway across the room before the luggage got so heavy and became so offensive that I was compelled to drop it on the floor and rush out of doors for a breath of fresh air. The odour... was the most offensive stench I ever smelled... absolutely stifling.'

Once Porter had recovered, however, he came back into the room and shook out the bedclothes, only to find the mysterious extra weight had vanished – and that the stink had evaporated.

Like many other poltergeists, the Witch also produced apports. During Luce Bell's Bible study meetings, it took to dropping fresh fruit, as if from nowhere, on to the table or into the laps of those present; and once, on Betsy's birthday, it produced a large basket of oranges, bananas, grapes and nuts, claiming: 'These came from the West Indies. I brought them myself.'

But perhaps more in keeping with the Witch's real nature was the scatological prank it played on Betsy Bell, when a local quack doctor offered her a potion to rid her of the power that tormented her. It was an unpleasant mixture, and the quack warned her that it would make her very ill. A copious evacuation of the stomach followed, the Witch roaring with laughter at the surprise of the household when Betsy's vomit and excrement were found to be full of pins and needles. Richard Bell wrote:

They were real brass pins and needles. Mother kept them as long as she lived. I have seen the pins and needles myself. As a matter of course, Betsy could not have lived with such a conglomeration in her stomach, and the only solution to the matter

In FOCUS

WITCH ON THE WAGON

When Andrew Jackson (1767-1845), seventh president of the United States, was a general in the army he took a wagon, pulled by a team of army horses, to visit his old friend John Bell. To his horror and surprise, he was treated to a startling demonstration of the Bell Witch's superhuman physical strength.

Jackson drove up to the house, the wagon suddenly ground to a halt, despite the enormous efforts of the driver and horses, straining at the traces. Unable to find any natural cause for the stoppage, the general cried: 'By the eternal boys! It is the Witch!'

At this point, a sharp, metallic voice – apparently coming from the nearby bushes – said: 'All right, general, let the wagon move.' And the wagon started to roll forward once again, towards the house. The Bell Witch, it seemed, had wanted to prove its abilities to the visitors.

was that the Witch dropped the pins and needles in the excrement unobserved.'

As time went on, the Witch ceased its physical attacks on Betsy, but began instead to torment her emotionally. She had become engaged in her early teens to a local man, Joshua Gardner, to whom, apparently, everyone in the family and neighbourhood thought she was ideally suited. But from the moment it developed the power of speech, the Witch derided Joshua and advised against the match whispering: 'Please Betsy Bell, don't have Joshua Gardner, please Betsy Bell, don't marry Joshua Gardner.' Eventually, it grew sharper in its remonstrations, making embarrassing revelations

Hollywood's expression of paranormal violence is depicted in a scene from the film The Omen, *above. The disruption occasioned by real-life poltergeists is often more psychological than physical, but the Bell Witch attacked its victims on all fronts – socially, psychologically and physically.*

about the young couple's relationship in front of friends, and promising that Betsy would never know a moment's peace if she married Joshua. Eventually, hysterical and in despair, she returned his engagement ring.

THREATS MADE GOOD

But behind all these developments lay the Witch's implacable hatred for John Bell, head of the family. From the start, the Witch had sworn that it would torment Old Jack Bell to the end of his life – and it made good its threat.

On 19 December 1820, John Bell was discovered in his bed in a deep stupor and could not be roused. His son, John, went to the medicine cabinet; but instead of the prescribed medicine, he found 'a smokey looking vial, which was about one-third full of dark-coloured liquid'.

The doctor arrived in time to hear the Witch crowing: 'It's useless for you to try and relieve Old Jack – I have got him this time; he will never get up from that bed again.' Asked about the strange medicine, it said: 'I put it there, and gave Old Jack a big dose out of it last night while he was fast asleep, which fixed him.'

Neither the doctor, nor any member of the household, could explain the presence of the mystery bottle, but a rather arbitrary test was made of its contents: the doctor dunked a straw into the mixture and wiped it on to the tongue of the Bells' pet cat. 'The cat jumped and whirled over a few times, stretched out, kicked, and died very quickly,' according to a contemporary account.

The doctor's next action would be unforgivable today, and even in his own time would have drawn suspicion had he done it in Europe; but his scientific

Witch vanished for good, pausing only to say that it would return again in 'one hundred years and seven' to a descendant. As Dr Fodor remarked, this doubtful honour should have fallen to Dr Charles Bailey Bell; but the year of 1935 came and went, and the Bell Witch failed to keep its tryst.

So what actually occurred on the Bell plantation? Even allowing for distortion of some of the details with the passage of time, it seems that the principal events did take place. In 1849, the *Saturday Evening Post* investigated the case, and printed an article alleging that 12-year-old Betsy had engineered the whole thing. The Bell family lawyers obtained a substantial amount in damages, and the magazine printed a retraction. The hoax theory, then, seems patently absurd.

training seems to have been overcast by the superstition of rural 19th-century Tennessee. He threw the bottle into the fire, thereby disposing of the Witch's brew for good.

The following morning, John Bell was found dead in his bed; and the Witch marked his passing – whether or not this was by its hand – by singing ribald songs at his funeral.

DISSIPATED ENERGY

After the death of John Bell, the energy of the Witch seemed to dissipate until, at last, having achieved its ends, the Witch seemed content to go. The final phenomenon, which to Dr Fodor was 'highly symbolic of guilt release', took place some years later. Something like a cannonball rolled down the chimney and burst in a puff of smoke, and a clear voice called out: 'I'm going, and will be gone for seven years.'

This promise was fulfilled, for seven years later the Witch did indeed return. At the time, Mrs Bell and her sons, Richard and Joel, were the only occupants of the homestead, Betsy having married another man.

Scratching sounds were heard, and half-hearted pulling of bedclothes felt. The family agreed to ignore the manifestations; and after a fortnight, the

Brazil, a country much preoccupied by Spiritism, also suffers from frequent and sometimes severe outbreaks of paranormal vandalism. In one case, a pet parrot fell victim to a poltergeist's spite and had its tail feathers singed, as shown top; and in another, a group of people discovered that the settee on which they were sitting was being slashed by an invisible assailant, as above. But few people have suffered anything as extreme as the indignities and horrors of the Bell family.

As Dr Fodor pointed out, Betsy's fainting and dizzy spells – immediately followed by the voice of the Witch – seem very similar to the symptoms exhibited by a medium going into a trance. On the other hand, the Witch, although describing itself as 'a spirit from everywhere' on one occasion, denied all knowledge of life after death.

Dr Fodor concluded that Betsy Bell suffered from a split personality, and that in some mysterious way, part of her subconscious mind had taken on a life of its own, literally plaguing her father to death. The psychology of such splits is still a mystery, and similar cases are rare – but when they do occur, some powerful emotional shock is usually found to have been the triggering factor. Dr Fodor also made the purely speculative guess that John Bell had interfered with his daughter sexually during her early childhood, and that the onset of puberty and her awakening sexuality stirred the long suppressed memory of that interference – bringing into being the Bell Witch.

But Fodor admitted that no conventional psychologist would credit split personalities with manifestations and powers outside the range of the body. As he concluded: 'Obviously we are dealing with facts for which we have no adequate theories within normal or abnormal psychology.'

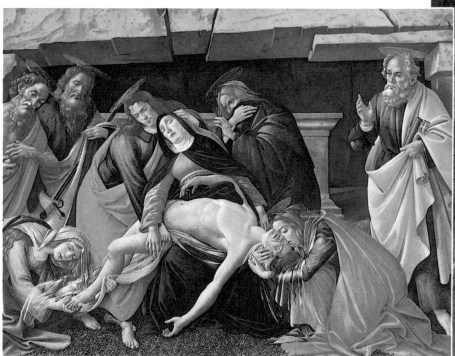

THE TEMPLAR INHERITANCE

IT HAS BEEN SUGGESTED THAT THERE EXISTS TODAY, IN FRANCE, A SECRET SOCIETY THAT GUARDS THE LINEAL DESCENDANTS OF CHRIST. FURTHERMORE, PAST LEADERS OF THIS SOCIETY ARE SAID TO INCLUDE SOME OF THE MOST ILLUSTRIOUS NAMES IN EUROPEAN HISTORY

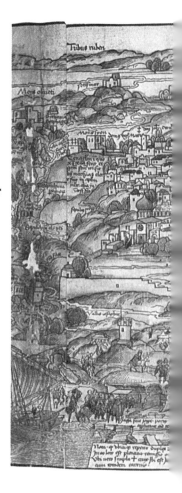

The French adore a conspiracy. So it is that hundreds of books have been published in France, setting out to prove that the Knights Templar were not wiped out in the 14th century; that secret societies claiming access to an 'esoteric tradition' derived from the Templars have played a significant part in political developments throughout Europe since then; and that they were even behind the French Revolution, on one side or the other, depending upon the individual author's predilections. In 1974, J.M. Roberts devoted a book of nearly 500 pages to *The Mythology of the Secret Societies*, setting out to demonstrate that there was no real evidence for this belief; but still the books proliferate.

There is, however, firm evidence that the Order of the Prieuré de Sion, guarding the descendants of Christ, actually existed at some time in the past. After Jerusalem fell to Godfroi de Bouillon in 1099, an abbey devoted to Notre Dame du Mont de Sion was built on the hill of Sion to the south of Jerusalem. It is mentioned in later documents, and figures in views of the city. A certain Father Vincent, for instance, writing in 1698, says: 'There

In **The Deposition,** *by Botticelli,* **far left,** *Christ's body, newly taken down from the cross, lies in the arms of his sorrowing mother, while Mary Magdalene passionately embraces his head. A theory has been put forward that Christ was married to Mary Magdalene, and that the interests of their descendants, who live in France, are guarded by a powerful and secret society called the Prieuré de Sion. Intriguingly, Botticelli,* **left,** *who chose to depict Mary Magdalene's grief so movingly, was allegedly himself a Grand Master of the Prieuré de Sion from 1483 to 1510.*

The 15th-century Dutch print of a perspective of Jerusalem, **below,** *shows the Temple and the Abbey of Notre Dame de Sion. The coincidence of names, as well as certain documentary evidence, suggest that the abbey may once have been the home of the Prieuré de Sion.*

were in Jerusalem during the Crusades... knights attached to the Abbey of Notre Dame de Sion who took the name of *Chevaliers de l'Ordre de Notre Dame de Sion.* And R. Rohricht, in his *Regesta Regni Hierosolymitani* (Roll of the Kings of Jerusalem) of 1893, cites two charters – one of 1116 by Arnaldus, prior of Notre Dame de Sion, and one of 1125, in which Arnaldus' name appears with that of Hugues Payen, the first Grand Master of the Temple. The existence of the Abbey of Sion until 1281 is also attested to by E.G. Rey in a paper in the proceedings of the French National Society of Antiquaries for 1887, which lists the abbots who administered the abbey's property in Palestine.

These are in fact the only historical documents referred to by Henry Lincoln, Michael Baigent and Richard Leigh in their book about the descendants of Christ, *The Holy Blood and the Holy Grail;* all other material appears to come from what they call 'the Prieuré documents', mysterious duplicated pamphlets that have been lodged with the Bibliothèque Nationale in Paris since 1965.

The *Dossiers Secrets,* allegedly by a certain Henri Lobineau, contain three lists of names. The first reproduces Rey's list, with two insignificant additions; and the second is taken by the authors as proof of the authenticity of the third. It is a list of the Grand Masters of the Knights Templar between 1118 and 1190, and it differs in certain respects from those given by most historians.

The authors of *The Holy Blood and the Holy Grail* write: 'We consulted all writers on the Order, in English, French and German, and then checked their sources as well. We examined the chronicles of the time... We consulted all the charters we

could find... As a result of this exhaustive inquiry, it became apparent that the list in the *Dossiers Secrets* was more accurate than any other...' They point out, too, that they spent over a year comparing material in this way.

INSIDE INFORMATION

The authors' conclusion is as follows: 'Granted, such a list might perhaps have been compiled by an extremely careful researcher, but the task would have been monumental. It seemed much more likely to us that a list of such accuracy attested to some repository of privileged or inside information – information hitherto inaccessible to historians.'

The third list claimed to be of the successive Grand Masters of the Prieuré de Sion, a succession that reached directly into the 20th century and included more than a few unexpected names, some of which are listed here.

Jean de Gisors	1188-1220
Marie de Saint-Clair	1220-1266
Guillaume de Gisors	1266-1307
Edouard de Bar	1307-1336
Jeanne de Bar	1336-1351
Jean de Saint-Clair	1351-1366
Blanche d'Evreux	1366-1398
Nicolas Flamel	1398-1418
René d'Anjou	1418-1480
Iolande de Bar	1480-1483
Sandro Filipepi (Botticelli)	1483-1510
Leonardo da Vinci	1510-1519
Connétable de Bourbon	1519-1527
Ferdinand de Gonzague	1527-1575
Louis de Nevers	1575-1595
Robert Fludd	1595-1637
J. Valentin Andrea	1637-1654
Robert Boyle	1654-1691
Isaac Newton	1691-1727
Charles Radclyffe	1727-1746
Charles de Lorraine	1746-1780
Maximilien de Lorraine	1780-1801
Charles Nodier	1801-1844
Victor Hugo	1844-1885
Claude Debussy	1885-1918
Jean Cocteau	1918-1963

As Lincoln, Leigh and Baigent write:
'The Prieuré de Sion would seem to be both modest and realistic. It does not claim to have functioned under the auspices of unqualified geniuses, superhuman "masters", illumined "initiates", saints, sages or immortals. On the contrary, it acknowledges its Grand Masters to have been fallible human beings, a representative cross-section of humanity – a few geniuses, a few notables, a few "average specimens", a few nonentities, even a few fools. Why, we could not but wonder, would a forged or fabricated list include such a spectrum?'

However, this seems to be more than a little naive on the authors' part. Few of the names are less than illustrious: even Charles Nodier, who is unlikely to be familiar to any English reader, was a prolific author, a Master Mason, and an active influence in the French Revolution; and Charles Radclyffe was the illegitimate grandson of Charles II.

As for the others, Nicolas Flamel is perhaps France's most famous alchemist, and Robert Fludd

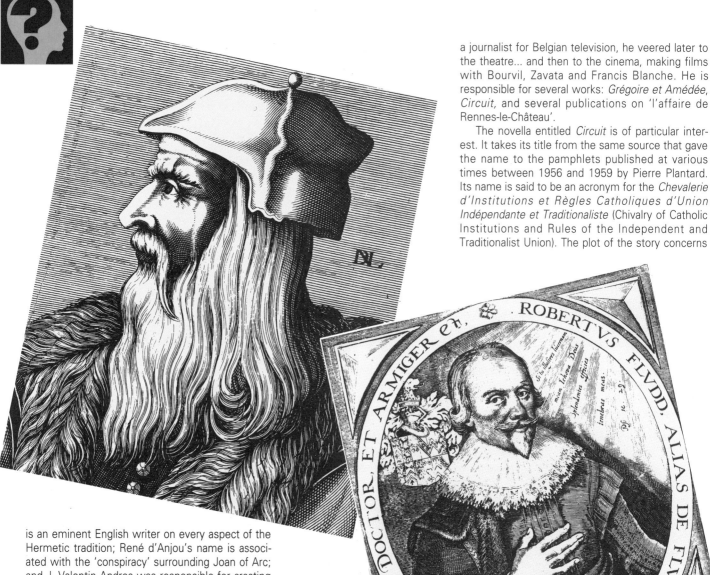
a journalist for Belgian television, he veered later to the theatre... and then to the cinema, making films with Bourvil, Zavata and Francis Blanche. He is responsible for several works: *Grégoire et Amédée*, *Circuit*, and several publications on 'l'affaire de Rennes-le-Château'.

The novella entitled *Circuit* is of particular interest. It takes its title from the same source that gave the name to the pamphlets published at various times between 1956 and 1959 by Pierre Plantard. Its name is said to be an acronym for the *Chevalerie d'Institutions et Règles Catholiques d'Union Indépendante et Traditionaliste* (Chivalry of Catholic Institutions and Rules of the Independent and Traditionalist Union). The plot of the story concerns

is an eminent English writer on every aspect of the Hermetic tradition; René d'Anjou's name is associated with the 'conspiracy' surrounding Joan of Arc; and J. Valentin Andrea was responsible for creating the myth of the Rosicrucians. Many of the remaining names on the list, meanwhile, belong to high-ranking – if obscure – European nobles. It seems clear, therefore, that any ingenious person who set out to fabricate such a list would, with a dictionary of dates to hand, find the task a simple one.

But who, following the death of Jean Cocteau in 1963, was to become the next Grand Master of the Prieuré de Sion? All the clues point to a modest Frenchman, Pierre Plantard, known as Pierre Plantard de Saint-Clair. This supposed Grand Master was described to author Franck Marie as:

'A very secret man who did not like one to inquire into his affairs. He lived in a little room on the sixth floor... in the 16th arrondissement of Paris. It was hardly comfortable: a table, a bed, some chairs, very little furniture... He left these lodgings in January 1973, forgetting to pay an important portion of his rent. His wife, Annie Hisler, died in 1971... It seems he was frequently visited by, and put up for the night, M. Philippe de Cherisey, who was *interdit de séjour* (forbidden to stay) in Paris...'

And so we meet Philippe de Cherisey, apparently Pierre Plantard's collaborator and spokesman. He was described by Jean-Luc Chaumeil in the following words:

'Born of a prominent family in the Ardennes... Philippe de Cherisey carries his 53 years well, with the lively eye and gentle regard of a poet. First of all

Leonardo da Vinci, top, was one of the most illustrious of the alleged Grand Masters of the Prieuré de Sion. He apparently ruled the society from 1510 to 1519.

Robert Fludd, above, the English physician and mystical philosopher, was allegedly Grand Master of the Prieuré de Sion from 1595 to 1637.

an extraordinary adventure underground in the vicinity of Rennes-le-Château, France, during which the hero discovers the tomb of an ancient Roman and an inaccessible treasure of solid gold.

MYSTIC TRIANGLE

According to Jean-Luc Chaumeil, in *Le Trésor du Triangle d'Or* (The Treasure of the Golden Triangle), Rennes forms one point of a 'mystic triangle' drawn upon the face of France, the other two points of which are situated at Gisors (an ancient castle of the Templars) and Stenay (where Dagobert II met his untimely end). There is, however, one great objection to the apparent significance of this statement: *all* triangles have three points – and there is nothing to distinguish this particular triangle from any other.

So what do we really know of Rennes-le-Château? Pierre Plantard claims it as the home of his otherwise undocumented female ancestor,

Gisèlle, daughter of the Count of Razès. Philippe de Cherisey, a friend of Plantard but apparently otherwise unconnected with the region, suggests that there is a buried treasure there. But the authors of *The Holy Blood and the Holy Grail* have pointed out that the first mention of this treasure in *Un Trésor Mérovingien à Rennes-le-Château (A Merovingian Treasure at Rennes-le-Château)* is 'a verbatim text, reset and reprinted, of a chapter in a popular paperback – a facile bestseller, available at newsstands for a few francs, on lost treasures throughout the world.' It is surely time to look once again at everything published since 1967 about Rennes, and to try to sift the known facts from the mass of allegation and supposition that surrounds them.

> **THE TRUE TREASURE, HE [M. PLANTARD] INSISTED, WAS SPIRITUAL. AND HE IMPLIED THAT THIS SPIRITUAL TREASURE CONSISTED, AT LEAST IN PART, OF A SECRET. IN SOME UNSPECIFIED WAY, THE SECRET IN QUESTION WOULD FACILITATE A MAJOR SOCIAL CHANGE.**
>
> **M. BAIGENT, R. LEIGH AND H. LINCOLN, THE HOLY BLOOD AND THE HOLY GRAIL**

NODIER.

The Irish-born scientist Robert Boyle, above left, was Grand Master of the Prieuré de Sion from 1654 to 1691. It is said that Boyle taught the secrets of alchemy to the great English scientist Isaac Newton, who was allegedly Grand Master from 1691 to 1727. Newton was followed by the Jacobite sympathiser and activist Charles Radclyffe, Earl of Derwentwater, above, who is said to have ruled the Prieuré from 1727 to 1746.

Charles Nodier, above, a prolific French writer who played an active part in the French Revolution, allegedly became Grand Master in 1801. He was succeeded in 1844 by his more illustrious colleague Victor Hugo, right. On Hugo's death in 1885, the title then passed to the composer Claude Debussy.

UFO WATCHING

THERE ARE SEVERAL EMINENT RESEARCHERS WHO HAVE DEVOTED MUCH TIME AND ENERGY TO LOOKING INTO THE NATURE OF UFO SIGHTINGS. WHEN, FOR INSTANCE, HARLEY RUTLEDGE SET OUT ON A ROUTINE UFO INVESTIGATION, HE DID NOT RECKON ON IT TAKING SEVEN YEARS. NOR WAS HE TO KNOW THAT HIS FINAL REPORT WOULD BE A MAJOR LANDMARK IN UFO RESEARCH

It was phenomena such as those in the sky at night over Piedmont, below, and Cape Girardeau, bottom, that started Harley Rutledge on his studies. Researchers had grown disenchanted with lights in the sky as evidence of UFO activity, since such sightings were open to many interpretations. But Rutledge's Project Investigation was to use monitoring techniques to prove that images, like the two shown here, were very definitely not the product of natural phenomena.

Practical ufology is, for many, a contradiction in terms. Indeed, faced with the elusive and often paradoxical nature of all the evidence that has been put forward by witnesses to date, a number of ufologists have reached the conclusion that there is no possible material explanation for the phenomenon.

But French-born ufologist Jacques Vallee is just one of a growing number of more advanced researchers who consider that the subject is, in fact, of a much more complex nature. As he declared in a paper delivered to the American Institute of Aeronautics and Astronautics: 'The UFO phenomenon is the product of a technology that integrates physical and psychic phenomena.' If this is so, then, since orthodox science is better equipped to cope with physical rather than with psychic material by way of evidence, it might well be best to concentrate primarily on investigating the material aspect of UFO sightings.

It was in just such a matter-of-fact frame of mind that Harley Rutledge embarked on what probably ranks as the most important piece of practical ufology yet carried out. It began in 1973 when, as professor of physics at South-East Missouri State University at Cape Girardeau, he was confronted with an intriguing challenge. Near the town of Piedmont, some 50 miles (80 kilometres) from

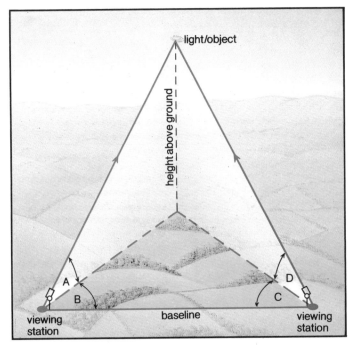

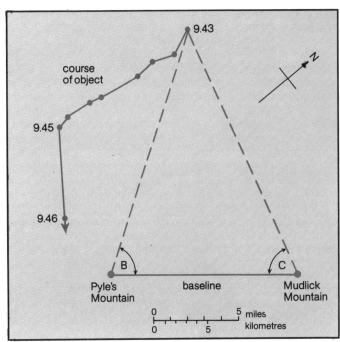

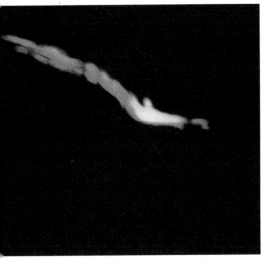

Cape Girardeau, curious lights had been seen on numerous occasions by many witnesses, in circumstances that seemed to defy any conventional explanation. As a scientist, Rutledge accepted the challenge to explain the phenomena, collecting together a team of specialists in various fields, gathering whatever monitoring and recording instruments he could find, and setting off for the site in the expectation that two or three weekends of expert observation should suffice.

But it was not until seven years later that his report on the investigation was published – the result of nearly 2,000 man-hours of observation by Rutledge and his team of colleagues. During that period, they observed 178 UFOs, 157 of which were recorded on their monitoring instruments, and combined visual observation and photographic records with radar and other forms of detection that were set up in separate locations for simultaneous monitoring.

The great majority of the phenomena observed by Rutledge's team took the form of lights in the sky, generally at night, with little or no discernible shape. This was unfortunate: there has been an

Principles of triangulation, as illustrated above left, can be used to plot an object's height and distance from the ground. To make the calculation, the vertical angles (A and D) and the horizontal angles (B and C) must be measured simultaneously from two points on the ground, a known distance apart (baseline).

The plan view, above right, is of the course of a UFO seen on 25 May 1973, as plotted by Project Investigation. *At 9.43 p.m., researchers at the observation posts at Pyle's Mountain and Mudlick Mountain, 11 miles (18 kilometres) apart, had the object in view. Using triangulation, they were able to measure the height and the distance of the UFO and thereby pinpoint its position. Between 9.43 and 9.46, nine such points were located at 15-second intervals.*

increasing tendency among ufologists to disregard this type of sighting unless there is very good circumstantial evidence surrounding it, because there is very little to be deduced from a blob of light. Besides, lights are the most easily misinterpreted of all visual phenomena: whereas a domed disc with portholes must be either a 'nuts and bolts' craft or an illusion of some kind, a light-blob can be anything from a car headlamp to a meteorite, a satellite or even light reflected off a flock of birds.

PRACTICAL APPROACH

However, Rutledge's highly practical approach, concerned only with the facts of the sightings, quickly eliminated any such obvious causes of misidentification. Using the surveyors' technique of triangulation, the precise location and course of the objects could be established and plotted, which meant that their size, altitude and speed could also be accurately established.

The following is a typical example of the observations made by Rutledge's team – a sighting recorded on 25 May 1973. That evening, two field units had been set up, one on Pyle's Mountain ('P') and the other on a fire tower on Mudlick Mountain ('M'), some 11 miles (18 kilometres) distant.

The two observation points were equipped with monitoring instruments, and were in radio contact with each other.

At 9.37 p.m., the four observers at P reported a light towards the west. The observers at M immediately confirmed this, and at once initiated the measuring of bearings and altitudes, which were transmitted every 15 seconds, and also recorded on video tape.

At 9.42, those at P reported the object as 'moving across the sky rather slowly; it is fairly bright, say a first-magnitude star. It is yellowish/orange in colour.' Those at M reported: 'We have it in full view now.'

By 9.43, with observers at both posts obtaining a clear view of the object, its precise location was calculated by triangulation. Between 9.43 and 9.46, nine such points were located at 15-second intervals: one point was missed because of radio interference, but those at *P* confirmed that the object was still on its apparent course. At 9.46, those at *M* lost sight of the object; then, at 9.48 and 9.50, those at *P* made two further observations; but in the absence of simultaneous observations from observers at *M*, these could be considered accurate only as far as direction was concerned.

The result of this series of matched observations was that the object was plotted precisely over an erratic course of more than 15 miles (25 kilometres) and less precisely over a considerably greater distance. Analysis of this data showed that the object was travelling initially at about 310 miles per hour (500 km/h), accelerating after changing its course to about 325 miles per hour (523 km/h). While this gives little positive information about the nature of the phenomenon, it eliminates many possible explanations. No car could be at such an altitude; no bird could fly that fast; no satellite could fly so low; no meteorite could change its course in such a way, for example.

MORE THAN COINCIDENCE

By such means, Rutledge's *Project Investigation* established beyond question the reality of the phenomenon and invalidated most, if not all, previous naturalistic explanations. Its instrumental record provided a solid basis for future research, too. What is more, Rutledge's observations also established that the objects seemed to respond specifically to the actions of observers. On at least 80 occasions, he registered an apparent synchronicity between something connected with the observers and the objects. But it was not a consistent pattern of behaviour that showed up – sometimes the objects would respond in one way, and sometimes in another. At the same time, however, such synchronicity occurred too often to be readily dismissed as no more than mere coincidence.

The events in themselves were trivial. For example, on 21 June 1973, Rutledge pointed his flashlight up at a stationary light – at once, it began to move, seemingly careful to avoid the observation post by veering away. On 20 June 1976, he was pointing at what seemed to be a new star and it immediately 'went out'. On several occasions, 'stars' halted, began to move, or changed course when observation began, a camera was aimed, or car headlights were switched on or off. There were even instances when the object seemed to respond to the voices of the observers – at a distance of 2 miles (3 kilometres) or more, to radio messages between observation posts – and even to the thoughts of the observers (although this, of course, cannot be established scientifically, and so could be dismissed). But such behaviour at least justifies the hypothesis that the objects probably possessed a certain degree of intelligence, or were controlled by intelligent beings. It also seems to indicate that they possessed very sophisticated means of registering the actions of observers who were, of course, at ground level – mostly in the darkness – and not easily detectable from the air.

Harley Rutledge is seen, below, with his portable battery-operated oscilloscope and spectrum analyser.

Workers on Project Investigation are seen bottom, setting up their equipment. Despite the preparations, UFOs – or those who control them – still seemed to play hard-to-get. Indeed, Harley Rutledge and his team noted that, on occasions, the objects appeared deliberately to move out of the line of vision whenever the monitoring devices were switched on by them.

No firm conclusions can be drawn from the results of Rutledge's project; but, certainly, no one has done more to establish the physical reality of the UFO phenomenon, and his investigations have provided much food for thought for ufologists.

Once hard facts have been established, they can be used as a basis for hypotheses that can be tested: this is the second form that practical ufology can usefully take. But because the 'facts' of ufology are themselves so much in dispute, opportunities for testing hypotheses are inevitably limited. Yet it is surprising how often ufologists fail even to take the most obvious practical steps. In Wales, for instance, investigator Peter Paget claimed that Stack Rock, in Dyfed, was being used as a secret UFO base. But even though he was researching in the area in 1979, he never took the step of visiting the island itself to establish the truth. If his claim had been correct, he would, of course, have made one of the most sensational discoveries in the history of the world. Instead, it was a BBC television reporter, Brynmor Williams, who chartered a boat to visit Stack Rock to see if he could find a UFO base there. He found none.

Researcher Alvin Lawson is seen below with Judy Kendall, who claimed to have been taken on board a UFO.

Is the object bottom, an alien spacecraft? Is it a UFO? The photograph was actually taken by the PROBE group from Bristol during an experiment to prove that a supposed UFO was in fact a balloon.

Those who put forward sensational claims should be able, of course, to back them with some kind of evidence. The PROBE group of Bristol, for instance, decided to test their theories about a UFO sighting at Warminster – this, they felt, sounded suspiciously as though it might have been a balloon. They did not doubt the sincerity of the witness, however, feeling that she had, indeed, seen an unidentified object; but the speed, direction and flight characteristics were such that a natural explanation seemed possible, and even quite likely.

So a balloon was obtained, and flown on a thread – along a course similar to that of the alleged UFO. The witness was invited to watch, and photographs were taken. Soon, she agreed that what she could now see was probably what she had originally seen. A further test in which the balloon was released – and duly lost – confirmed this opinion, and the conclusion was that 'the investigation and resultant tests showed that the UFO as reported

resembled, behaved like – and most probably was – a silver-red, plastic-aluminium laminate balloon, released some time before the sighting from a location west of Warminster.'

Such debunking operations may not be the most gratifying aspect of ufology, but they play an important part in eliminating false data, enabling genuine phenomena to be seen more clearly.

But one of the most dramatic experiments in practical ufology was almost certainly that conducted by Professor Alvin Lawson of California. His comparison of 'imaginary abductees' with individuals claiming to have been abducted on board UFOs relates only to a limited part of the UFO phenomenon, of course; but he and his colleagues have established that ordinary people, with little knowledge of the UFO phenomenon, are capable – in the hypnotic state – of fabricating an imaginary abduction event that matches, in extraordinary detail, the stories told by those who claim actually to have been abducted. Certainly, on first consideration, this tends to support the supposition that the 'real' abductees are simply fantasizing, but this is by no means an obvious conclusion.

Supporting the view that 'real' accounts may be what they claim to be is the fact that there are frequently marked differences in the ways the two classes of subject tell their stories. The descriptions of alleged abductions were very similar, but the 'real' witnesses seemed to have a greater emotional stake in their stories. Of course, this too may be accounted for in psychological terms: indeed, the way lies open for much further research, such as exploration of the possibility that abduction stories may reflect memories of birth traumas.

The evidence Lawson gathered for his hypothesis is very persuasive; but, as he himself was the first to insist, it remains nothing but a hypothesis. Nevertheless, the great achievement of researchers such as Lawson and Rutledge has been to demonstrate that some, at least, of the mass of ufological data can be tested. And it is this approach that will almost certainly solve the UFO riddle – one day.

MAGNETIC PHENOMENA

THE TURBULENT GEOLOGICAL HISTORY RECORDED IN THE EARTH'S CRUST SHOWS THAT THE PLANET'S MAGNETIC FIELD FREQUENTLY REVERSES. WHEN IT DOES, IT SEEMS THE RESULTS CAN BE DISASTROUS FOR LIVING THINGS

William Gilbert, above, *wrote* De Magnete, *one of the first works of modern natural science. He studied the magnetic fields of lodestones (natural magnets) and realised that the entire Earth is one huge magnet.*

For centuries, navigators have used a magnetic compass to find their way safely over the globe. The compass needle points roughly north-south, towards the Earth's magnetic poles, one of which lies in the Arctic, the other in the Antarctic. The Earth itself is in fact like a huge magnet, but a somewhat strange one, since the magnetic poles wander around the true North and South Poles (those points around which the Earth rotates). Recent research has also shown that the Earth can do something no ordinary magnet can: its magnetic field can spontaneously change direction. Indeed, if such a magnetic reversal occurred today, the end of a compass needle that had hitherto pointed north would suddenly begin to point south.

It was the ancient Chinese who discovered the natural magnetism of certain rocks in around the first century AD. About 1,200 years later, Western

The invisible 'lines of force' of the Earth's magnetic field, as depicted below, wreathe the planet. This field guides some of the cosmic rays from space into the atmosphere in the polar regions, giving rise to auroras. But some are trapped temporarily in radiation belts (orange) before reaching Earth.

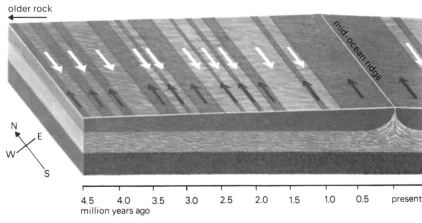

older rock ←

mid-ocean ridge

| 4.5 | 4.0 | 3.5 | 3.0 | 2.5 | 2.0 | 1.5 | 1.0 | 0.5 | present |

million years ago

Molten rock thrown out by volcanoes, left, solidifies with a weak magnetic field induced by the Earth's field. The ocean floors are formed by volcanic activity at the mid-ocean ridges and thus record the Earth's magnetic field throughout geological history, illustrated in the chart above. As the sea floor spreads from a mid-ocean ridge, the Earth's periodically reversing field magnetises the rock in 'stripes' of alternating direction. Man-made objects that are heated during manufacture or use also become magnetised as they cool: Gilbert made the point in the illustration of a blacksmith at work, below. A salt-drying hearth used in pre-Roman England, below centre, reveals recent changes in the Earth's field and hence the movements of the magnetic poles.

navigators began to use these 'lodestones' as compasses. But it was in the year 1600 that the Earth itself was first thought of as a giant magnet that aligns the compass needle, as proposed by Colchester-born William Gilbert, physician to Queen Elizabeth I. He showed that the Earth's magnetic field resembles that of a magnetised ball with one pole to the north of Siberia, so that a compass needle in London pointed about 11 degrees east of true north. Gilbert also disproved a few old superstitions about magnetism, such as the story that garlic can destroy the powers of a magnet.

SHIFTING FIELD

Although no one knew why the Earth should be a giant-lodestone, the idea seemed quite reasonable. Then, in 1634, the English astronomer Henry Gellibrand discovered that a compass in London no longer pointed 11 degrees east of north, but only 4 degrees east. Somehow, it seemed that the Earth's magnetic field was shifting within the body of the planet, so that by the 1650s, a magnetic compass in London conveniently pointed due north. Today, the magnetic pole is among the islands of northern Canada and gradually moving northwards.

Not only does the Earth's magnetic field shift its direction, however, it also changes in strength. Indeed, archaeologists can measure the strength of the Earth's field in the past by investigating ancient kilns and hearth stones. When these bricks or stones are heated and then cool down, they pick up a weak magnetism from the Earth's magnetic field that can be detected and measured, permitting scientists to calculate the strength and direction of the Earth's magnetism at the period when the kiln or hearth was last used.

Changes discovered by this technique are quite remarkable. Around 4000 BC, for instance, we now know that the Earth's magnetism was only about half its present strength; but it grew in intensity until, around AD 500, it was one-and-a-half times stronger than it is now. Since then, the field has been weakening.

Geologists can go back even further in time by looking at the magnetism of ancient rocks. When lava flows cool down, they pick up magnetism from the Earth's field, just as kilns and hearth stones do. As early 20th century geologists used new sensitive magnetometers to investigate old lava flows, they made an almost unbelievable discovery. In some

SEPTENTRIO.

AVSTER

hearth near Lake Monger in Western Australia , and lasted only 2,000 years – so each reversal of the field could have taken only a couple of centuries.

The origin of the Earth's shifting magnetic field is still something of a mystery. However, scientists now to tend to agree that it must arise in the Earth's outer core of liquid iron. Electric currents flow in the molten metal and generate a magnetic field – just as in an electromagnet such as the coil that pulls the hammer on an electric doorbell.

But what causes the electric currents? It is probably the motion of the liquid metal through the core's magnetic field. As long as there is just a little magnetism to begin with, the sloshing of molten metal in the core creates a degree of electric current; and this current then produces more magnetic field, which allows the production of further electric current. In fact, the core resembles a dynamo, in which electric currents are generated in wires as they move through a magnetic field that is itself generated by the current.

In this maelstrom of entangled magnetic fields, electric currents and super-hot streams of molten iron, it is not surprising that the Earth's magnetic field can change erratically in direction and in strength – or even flip over altogether.

places, the rocks were magnetised in directions quite different from that of the Earth's magnetism. Indeed, in some places, the rocks' magnetism was in the opposite direction to the Earth's field. As they investigated more lava outcrops, these geologists found rocks with such 'reversed' magnetism occurring just as commonly as 'normal' rocks, and soon a pattern began to emerge. Take samples of lava of any one age from anywhere in the world – Iceland, Hawaii, India or wherever – and you find they all have the same direction of magnetism, whether normal or reversed. In other words, this reversal cannot be a local phenomenon, and so the Earth's entire magnetic field must be able to reverse itself spontaneously.

EPISODIC FLIPS

Our planet thus has no preferred direction of magnetism; and over its long history, its magnetic field has as often been in the reversed direction as in its present orientation. Our present 'normal' period goes back only 700,000 years: before that, there was a 1,700,000-year period of reversed magnetic field; and, going back even further, a million years each of 'normal' and 'reversed' magnetism. But as geologists have looked in more detail, they have found that, within these main episodes, there have also been shorter periods of reversed magnetism. And if we add up the total, we find that the Earth's magnetism has flipped over at least 20 times in the last 4½ million years.

During a magnetic reversal, the Earth's magnetism drops dramatically in intensity and then regenerates itself with its direction reversed. The change can take few centuries – a mere moment, of course, in the thousands of millions of years of geological time. It is difficult to tell how long the older reversals took; but in 1971, Australian scientists made the astounding discovery that the Earth's magnetism flipped over to 'reversed' for a short while 30,000 years ago. This change is recorded in the stones of an ancient aboriginal

CONTINENTS IN MOTION

Although they cannot explain past flips of the Earth's magnetism, scientists have proved that one of the wildest theories ever proposed for our planet Earth is indeed correct. In the 1920s, a German meteorologist, Alfred Wegener, suggested that the continents wander over the surface of the Earth. Once, they were all joined as a single huge supercontinent, which he named *Pangaea* ('whole Earth'), but this broke up into fragments that are the continents we know now. Scientists thought Wegener was a crank, and for almost 40 years his ideas lay unheeded.

But, by 1960, geologists in Britain and Australia had evidence that forced them to reconsider continental drift. They had studied the magnetism of rocks in such detail that they could now calculate the position of the magnetic poles over the past 500 million years. Measurements showed that the

In the 1920s, Alfred Wegener, above, suggested that the continents drift over the Earth's surface. The idea was ridiculed for decades, but has now become the orthodoxy of geology.

As shown in the chart, right, ancient rock magnetism reveals the movement of the north magnetic pole. (The numbers show millions of years in the past.) But European and North American rocks yield different tracks. However, when the tracks are adjusted to compensate for the recent separation of the continents, the two tracks coincide.

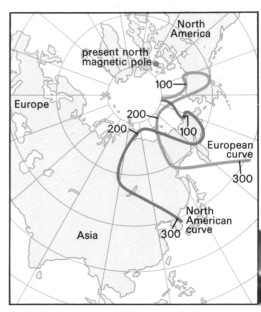

poles had apparently moved about. This was not surprising in itself; but the shock came when they compared data from different continents which seemed to show the magnetic poles to have been in different positions at the same time in the past.

There was only one way to make sense of the evidence: what had moved was not the magnetic poles – or not the poles alone – but the continents, and each continent had moved in a different way relative to the magnetic poles. Indeed, the continents are still drifting independently over the globe.

Not all scientists were yet convinced. But magnetism was to provide the final proof of continental drift in a different way. If the continents are separating from one another – say, South America from Africa – then new rocks must be coming up at the central crack between them – in this case, in the middle of the bed of the Atlantic Ocean. In 1960, American geologist Harry Hess pointed out that there is a volcanic ridge along the middle of the Atlantic floor, which could mark the split between America and Africa. As the Atlantic widens, new rock wells up here. So each half of the Atlantic sea bed should be a horizontal time chart: rocks at the centre are young, while the sea bed towards either side of the ocean is progressively older.

At the time, there was no evidence to support Hess's theory. But oceanographers had already discovered the vital key, without realising what they had found, for there are strange patterns of magnetism in the rocks of the ocean bed. The directions of the magnetism in the rocks form 'stripes': within

THE WHOLE PROBLEM IS SO COMPLICATED THAT SCIENTISTS CANNOT PREDICT HOW THE MAGNETIC FIELD WILL BEHAVE IN THE FUTURE, NOR DO THEY KNOW WHY IT HAS CHANGED AT PARTICULAR TIMES IN THE PAST.

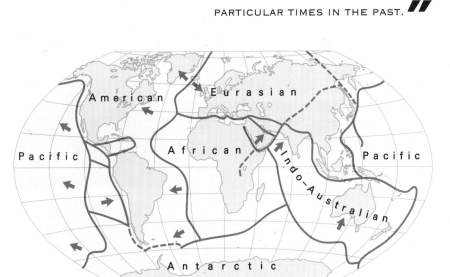

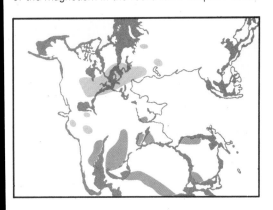

a given stripe, the rock is magnetised one way, roughly parallel to the mid-ocean ridge; and in neighbouring stripes, the rock is magnetised in the opposite direction.

In 1963, two Cambridge geologists, Fred Vine and Drummond Matthews, realised the simple truth. As Hess had suggested, new hot rock wells up at the mid-ocean ridges; and when it cools, it picks up magnetism from the Earth's field, just like any other lava. As the ocean bed gradually spreads, this rock is carried away on either side. If the Earth's magnetism flips over, new rock will show the new direction of magnetisation.

Knowing, from the evidence of continental rocks, when the Earth's magnetic field had reversed, Vine and Matthews could now work out what the magnetic pattern in the ocean floor should look like. And, indeed, the pattern matched up in every detail. The world's geologists were convinced, almost overnight, that continental drift does occur. And geologists who study the magnetic

The illustration, above, shows the system of plates that make up the Earth's surface and cause the ocean floor to spread and the continents to drift. New material is added to each plate at mid-ocean ridges. The plate as a whole rolls like a conveyor belt towards a 'subduction zone', where it plunges into the body of the Earth. The continents, consisting of lighter rock, ride on the plates.

The map, left, shows the modern explanation of the climatic variations that inspired the pole shift theorists. About 200 million years ago, the world's land formed a single supercontinent, Pangaea. Australia, India, southern Africa and southern South America lay, with Antarctica, near the South Pole and still show signs of glaciation (blue areas). Europe and North America were tropical (green areas). Here, the luxuriant forests of the Carboniferous era had given way to hot deserts, beneath which the world's great seams of coal were formed.

stripes in the ocean floor have confirmed the pattern of continental wanderings.

As the continents have drifted from equatorial regions to polar zones and back, so their climates have also changed. In the days of *Pangaea*, some 300 million years ago, the southern extremities of the land, including present-day India and Australia, were at the South Pole and lay under thick sheets of ice. At the same time, the far northern shores of *Pangaea* – modern Greenland and Europe – lay in a tropical climate astride the equator.

But while the Earth's magnetism has provided evidence that has solved many of the Earth's past mysteries, its future behaviour cannot be predicted. Study of old rocks shows that often, when a magnetic reversal has occurred, many living species have been completely wiped out. The reason is simple. The Earth's magnetic field acts as an invisible umbrella to protect us from cosmic rays from the Sun. When the field weakens drastically during a reversal, these rays can get through to Earth and damage the sensitive cells of living things. The extinction of the dinosaurs, among other plants and animals, for instance, has been blamed on the burst of cosmic rays that followed a magnetic reversal.

The Earth's magnetic field is dropping in intensity, and it is not known whether this is simply a short-term fluctuation, or if it heralds another magnetic reversal. Even if the trend does continues at the present rate, there is no need for panic, as the reversal would occur in only two or three thousand years time. But sooner or later, Man may have to live through another reversal of the Earth's wayward magnetic field, and face the ensuing threat of devastating radiation from space.

SURGEON FROM THE OTHER SIDE

IT WAS A PERSONAL TRAGEDY THAT TRIGGERED ISA NORTHAGE'S EXTRAORDINARY PSYCHIC ABILITIES. IT ALL STARTED WITH CLAIRVOYANCE AND WAS TO CLIMAX WITH MATERIALISATIONS OF A DECEASED SURGEON WHO PERFORMED OPERATIONS ON THE LIVING

I n 1916, a young woman named Isa Phillips was eagerly planning her wedding day when, in a vivid and horrifying vision, she saw her husband-to-be, Kit – at the time, away on active service – shot and fall from his horse: a few days later, she received news of his death.

A friend brought Kit's personal belongings home to Isa, and described to her how Kit had died: it confirmed Isa's psychic vision in every detail. Isa had also seen this man, Jack Northage, in her vision – he had gone to Kit's assistance – and, as things turned out, he also had a large part to play in Isa's

When a spirit guide advised medium Isa Northage, above, to concentrate on healing, she started a sanctuary at Pinewoods, in the beautiful grounds of Newstead Abbey, Nottinghamshire, below.

future. They became firm friends, and were eventually married in 1919.

Not long after this first demonstration of her psychic abilities, Isa began to hear a man's voice, which guided her whenever she was in danger. She also began to develop clairvoyant powers.

After the war, Isa formed a small orchestra, which flourished for a time. Then she began 'seeing' faces and people in front of her music stand while she was playing. These 'spirits' indicated that they wanted to speak to her and give her tunes that had a special meaning for their loved ones.

Eventually, the medium abandoned her musical career and devoted herself to passing on these communications from the dead to the living at Spiritualist churches and public meetings. During this early stage of her career, in the late 1930s, Isa was known as the 'concertina medium' because, during seances, she would often receive a psychic impression of a song or tune and would play it on her concertina, at the same time describing the spirit she could see clairvoyantly. She was often able to give the name and personal details of the spirit person, also conveying a message of comfort to the grieving relatives and friends.

Isa Northage was in great demand as a medium, particularly once it became known that her powers included the production of physical phenomena. The first public manifestation of this occurred in April 1937, at a meeting held in a well-lit hall in Matlock, Derbyshire. While Isa was speaking to the audience, some flowers on a table near her slowly lifted themselves out of their vase and floated above the heads of the assembled company. Then, almost as an encore, the table carrying the now empty vase itself rose off the ground. Isa later confessed herself astonished at this phenomenon.

In the early days of her physical mediumship, Isa used a light aluminium trumpet, with a broad luminous band painted around the end of the bell to make it visible in the dark. It served as a megaphone to amplify the voices of the spirits. She had three principal spirit assistants. The first was Chedioack, a West African, affectionately known to the sitters as Sambo. He had died after a bout of fever at the age of 19, and had appointed himself Isa's spiritual bodyguard while she was in trance. Ellen Dawes, an English girl who had also died aged

During a seance, Chedioack, one of Isa Northage's spirit helpers, manifested himself for 20 minutes in full light, giving one of the sitters, a Mr Ives, an opportunity to make a sketch of him, above.

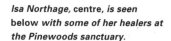

Isa Northage, centre, is seen below with some of her healers at the Pinewoods sanctuary.

19, acted as a helper and also communicated regularly with her mother. The third member of the spirit team was a Dr Reynolds, who had practised medicine 150 years earlier: it was his voice that had guided Isa at the start of her mediumship.

A KISS FROM BEYOND

In July 1939, the weekly Spiritualist newspaper *Two Worlds* carried an account of one of Mrs Northage's home sittings, during which a parrot materialised, flew around the darkened room and perched on someone's shoulder. Recognisable voices spoke through the trumpet, and there was also a full form materialisation – the wife of one of the sitters. She was clearly seen and heard; and her husband kissed her on the forehead before she returned to the curtained 'cabinet'.

Isa's powers increased dramatically during the next 18 months. At a seance in a private house in Doncaster, for instance, the 10 sitters saw 19 materialised forms and also spoke to other spirits through the three trumpets that were in use.

During the seances, each spirit form emerged from the medium's cabinet, then picked up a luminous plaque and held it close to its features so that it could be recognised. Occasionally, a spirit would pick up a red torch so that the sitters could see it more clearly.

At one particular seance, reported in *Two Worlds* on 15 December 1939, the spirit assistant Sambo asked a sitter to place her hands on the medium's knees. 'While she was still holding them,' the report continued, 'a spirit person materialised, left the cabinet, and walked across the circle to speak to and embrace her mother.' For some reason this seemed to the observer to be 'definite evidence that the medium was in her chair', although it was not made clear whether the medium was inside or outside the cabinet.

As Isa's mediumship grew stronger, more and more forms appeared at each sitting, and the materialisations appeared more convincing. One sitter at a seance in Ashington, Northumbria, said in an account published in February 1941:

'My wife and daughter materialised, and both of them talked to me, kissed me, and caressed me. They brought a flower from the cabinet and handed

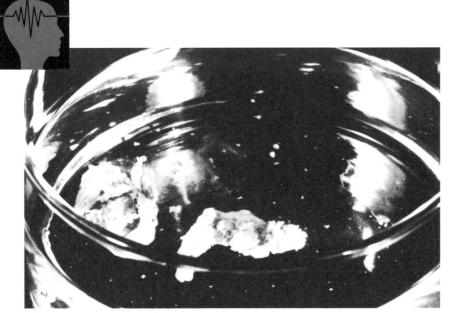

it to me. Then my brother came and spoke to us through the trumpet. I suggested that it was a pity we had not a violin with us, as he was a skilled violinist. He said: "Bring one tomorrow night and I will play it for you." We borrowed one, and on the following evening he picked up the violin from outside the cabinet and asked us to sing *Auld Lang Syne* while he played.'

Further details about the conditions under which Isa worked were given in August of the same year by G. W. Marshall, a journalist on the *Grimsby Advertiser*. A corner of a room in a private house was partitioned off by a thin curtain to make a cabinet. The sitters took their seats in a circle, and the lights were turned off. The medium entered the room and made her way to the cabinet, using a dim red light to find her way. When she had taken her seat, this light was also turned off. The reporter was allowed to examine the room both before and after the seance, which lasted two and three-quarter hours, and produced both direct voice and materialisation phenomena. 'I shall never forget that experience as long as I live,' wrote Marshall. Another sitter at this seance was A. F. Cutforth, vice-president of Louth Spiritualist Church, who testified that the materialised forms came from the cabinet and walked around among the sitters, after which 'most of them dematerialised through the floor in front of us, often talking until they were only an inch or two above the floor'. He also reported that two trumpets were levitated, and said of the phenomena that he witnessed:

'While one spirit was holding a conversation through the trumpet at one side of the room, a fully materialised form was conversing with friends and relations on the other side. Mothers, sons, husbands, wives, brothers, sisters, children and guides appeared as solid forms, and were able to shake hands with us and exchange kisses.'

At a seance in Skegness in April 1941, a dead sailor appeared to his mother from what was described as a 'bubbling mass of ectoplasm'. The spirit was said to be smiling and full of life, and held long, excited conversations with his brothers, sister, grandmother and parents. We are told: 'Then he stood in the middle of the circle and melted slowly away. He did not go to the cabinet, but dissolved before our eyes.'

Several witnesses saw the removal of tissue, top, by the materialised form of Dr Reynolds. Afterwards, some of the deceased tissue was analysed, and shown to be part of a duodenal ulcer. Had it remained in the sufferer's body, it would soon have proved fatal.

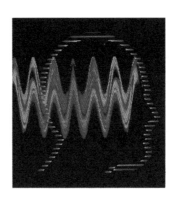

As depicted in the artist's impression above, mediums such as Isa Northage regularly receive psychic impressions from the 'other side', and are able to convey messages from the deceased to their loved ones.

After 1941, Isa's career entered a new phase when her guide, Dr Reynolds, told her to abandon public seances and concentrate on healing. As a result, she established a seance room, healing clinic and operating theatre in the grounds of her bungalow at Pinewoods, Nottinghamshire. The theatre was for spirit doctors, such as Dr Reynolds, to carry out 'psychic operations'.

Ernest Thompson, editor of *Two Worlds*, himself witnessed psychic surgery there on 21 May 1949. Eight people, including Isa Northage, gathered in the operating theatre in the wooden building in Isa's garden. The door was locked, the light turned out, and the meeting started with prayer. Isa was in her cabinet, in a trance; soon a trumpet rose into the air, and the sitters were addressed by the spirit helper, Ellen Dawes. Dr Reynolds's materialised form then appeared, discernible as a 'black silhouette against the red glow from the lamp on a trolley, on which were laid forceps, two red electric torches, one white electric torch and two luminous plaques'.

OPERATION SUCCESS

Dr Reynolds picked up a torch, switched it on, and turned towards the operating table on which lay a patient suffering from an acute duodenal ulcer. Two of the witnesses were not wearing masks, and the doctor asked them to remedy this before he began operating. He then placed cotton wool swabs on the patient's abdomen and assured him that there would be no pain. No anaesthetic was used. Dr Reynolds next explained how he would 'freeze' the portion of the body to be operated upon and then pass his hand, which would become dematerialised, into the side of the body and remove the ulcer. His hands moved to the side of the body and, as he did so, he asked the patient if he felt any pain. The patient apparently replied that he did not. Then a gurgling sound was heard, and Dr Reynolds reported that 'the ulcer was in a very bad condition, that it would not come away in a whole piece and that he was afraid of haemorrhage'. This difficulty was overcome, however, and portions of ulcer were brought through what Dr Reynolds described as a temporary opening in the abdomen, and placed on the swabs on the surface of the body.

When the seance ended, Thompson retrieved the human tissue from the swabs and put it in a bottle of surgical spirit. A few days later, he arranged to have it analysed, and the verdict was: 'It is an acute duodenal ulcer, contains Brunner's glands and shows from its condition that it was about to penetrate the intestine and would have proved fatal.'

Stories like this continued to appear in the psychic press throughout the 1950s. After Isa was involved in a car crash, however, her materialisations and psychic surgery ceased. But she continued to help the sick. In August 1967, the Scottish *Sunday Express* described how a bus driver, suffering from a stomach ulcer, visited Pinewoods. Before the astonished witnesses, Isa massaged his abdomen, which 'opened like a rose' and the ulcer was plucked out in two pieces. The patient told the newspaper: 'Before the operation, almost anything I ate gave me pain. An hour after, I was able to eat a five-course meal. I haven't had a twinge since.'

CURIOSITIES FROM CHINA

THE EXCEPTIONALLY TALL, THE HAIRY, THE TWO-HEADED AND THE HORNED: CHINA CERTAINLY SEEMS TO HAVE HAD MORE THAN ITS FAIR SHARE OF FREAK OR MALFORMED HUMAN BEINGS. BUT THERE ARE TALES, TOO, OF ELIXIRS MADE FROM ANTS THAT ARE SAID TO HAVE MIRACULOUSLY IMPROVED THE EYESIGHT AND HEARING OF THE VERY AGED

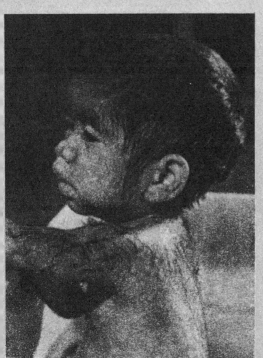

Zhu Xiulian, left, born in 1977 in Guangdong Province, was covered in black hair from birth, but in all other respects, she grew to be a perfectly normal, active and intelligent child.

One of the most famous of Chinese hairy children, Yu Zhenhuan, below, was born in 1977 to horrified parents who were tempted at first to let him die because of this.

With a population of 1.16 billion, it is perhaps hardly surprising that so many oddities of the human form occur in China. To take one example, the average Chinese is possibly the least hairy individual on the planet, so the phenomenon of the hairy child is all the more unusual in China. The Hong Kong newspaper *Ta Kung Pao* of 10 January 1980 reported that 32 such individuals had been found in China, spread over 10 provinces. Although isolated cases had been reported over the years, it was little Yu-Zhenhuan (whose name means 'shock the Universe') who made the condition famous. Unfortunately, Western journalists handled his story in their usual degrading fashion, calling him 'monkey-boy', 'wolf-boy', 'freak', 'mutant'... but, to the Chinese, he was simply *mao hai*, a hairy child.

Yu Zhenhuan was born on 30 September 1977, in the Shaotzugo People's Commune in Liaoning Province, north-east China. His parents, Yu Wenguang, 27, and Song Baoqin, 25, were horrified to find their baby covered in jet-black hair at birth: his eyebrows merged with the hair on his forehead, and his entire body – except for his lips, palms, soles and the tip of his nose – was hirsute. He even had hairy ears.

There was, it seems, some dispute as to whether Zhenhuan should be allowed to live, but he survived long enough to come to the attention of

Numerous stories of paranormal happenings have come out of the many regions of China, as plotted on the map above.

on her skin, 'but these hairs fall off as soon as the weather turns cold.' (Interestingly, one would expect that, if this were to happen, it would be when the weather turned warm.)

Then there were two brothers in Yunnan Province – Yang Tianzhao, 26, and Yang Tianshun, 21. Their hairlessness was accepted by their fellow villagers, simply because clean-shaven heads are a way of life in the region. Their peculiarity came to light only when a medical team carried out an investigation in the village. Though the brothers had no hair at all, not even in their nostrils, hair follicles could be seen under the skin in the pubic region and armpits, and on the scalp. The brothers seldom fell ill and they sweated normally, unlike certain other hairless people. Their youngest brother, who died at the age of 18 months, was also hairless. But their two surviving sisters had thick black hair on their heads.

Chen Li, 15, whose address was not reported, was congenitally unable to perspire, since he lacked sweat glands and hair. In summer, he bathed in rivers a dozen times a day to keep cool, and had to cover himself from head to toe with wet towels before he could fall asleep.

Another boy of 15, from Shiling Commune, Jiangsu Province, was known as 'fire body'. After falling ill in 1971, he refused to wear any clothing at all, even playing naked in the snow during winter. Throughout the previous 10 years, he had not caught cold or any other illness, and was growing up normally otherwise.

the Chinese Academy of Sciences, and after that his future was assured. His family was given a new house and a state subsidy to look after him; and at the age of eight months he starred in his first film, a documentary shot at Shenyang, the provincial capital. By the end of 1979, his hair had turned from black to brown. It varied in length in different parts of his body: 3 inches (7 centimetres) around the shoulders, 2 inches (4.5 centimetres) on his back, 1 inch (2.5 centimetres) on his abdomen. Apart from that, he was very much an ordinary child. All his senses were in good working order, and X-rays and intelligence tests showed nothing abnormal. He had a slightly enlarged heart, and at under six months was taller than an average child. His head and ears were large, and he cut his teeth late, at about one year. He laughed a lot and, apart from a little trouble with a boil and eczema, was perfectly healthy. The hair parted at the side of his body and thickened towards the mid-lines of the back and abdomen, forming whirls at various places.

Zhenhuan had a sister two years older than himself, who was perfectly normal. Apart from his maternal grandfather and uncle, who had slightly hairy calves and thick beards, none of his immediate relatives showed similar traits.

INHERITED HIRSUTISM

All human foetuses are covered with fine down after five to six months' development, but this hair is usually shed before birth. The cause of the *mao hai* atavism remains mysterious, but it has been determined that the trait is inheritable, and also that the hirsute individual generally keeps his pelt throughout his lifetime.

As if to balance these stories, reports of completely hairless folk soon began to emerge. In February 1981, the New China News Agency said that seven such people had been discovered in the eastern part of China. Zhang Juling, a 10-year-old girl, was one of these. Her father said that, with a magnifying glass, minute hairs could be detected

The two Siamese twins, Liu Sen-Ti and Liu Sen-Kai, right, were 64 years old when this picture was taken in the 1940s. In their prime, they had made a great deal of money touring Europe and America. Later, having fallen on hard times, they returned to vaudeville in Nanking. Their act was a simple one: it consisted of answering questions from the audience about the details of their everyday life.

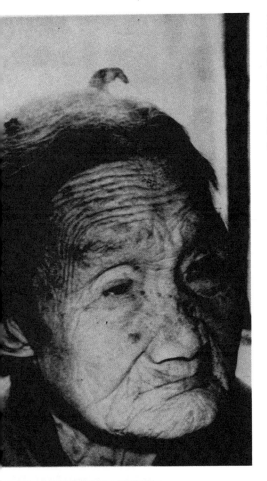

The 88-year-old woman, Zhao Lishi ('Madam Chow'), left, suddenly found herself growing small horns. It took about six months to reach the stage of development seen here. A similar condition, in which bony protrusions develop inside the skull, is not uncommon in elderly women.

Wu Xiaoli, a baby girl from Miangyang in Sichuan Province, and nicknamed 'fire baby', always felt hot and went naked because she was apparently allergic to clothes.

But perhaps the oddest freak story of all from China emerged at the beginning of 1980. Zhang Ziping, 35, a deaf-mute farmer from a remote mountain village in Huize County, Yunnan Province, had his second head surgically removed. The 'parasitic' head, in some sources reported as normal-sized but actually about 8 inches (20 centimetres) round, was growing on the right side of Zhang's face. It had hair and 12 teeth, but the eyes, eyelids, nose and mouth were not fully developed. The cranium was normally shaped and covered an egg-sized brain, which is said not to have functioned. Plastic surgery restored Zhang's face, and it was at this point that he decided to look for a wife.

Another two-headed baby was born on 16 August 1980 in an army hospital in Tianjin, to unidentified parents. Weighing 7 pounds (3.3 kilograms) at birth, the baby also had two oesophaguses, two respiratory systems and two stomachs, but one heart, liver and anus. When the left hip was injected, the left head cried; when the left head was fed, the right head cried.

Two other freak births – though not in China – were reported around this time in the *South China Morning Post*. A baby born at the Tsan Yuk hospital, Hong Kong, apparently had four legs and four arms. The infant died 13 hours after birth. And in Manila, in the Philippines, a boy with two heads, three feet and three hands was said to have died five hours after birth.

A surgical operation on a 3-month-old girl, carried out at Anshan in Liaoning Province on 4 December 1979, disclosed four parasitic foetuses that were growing in her abdomen. In total, they weighed 11½ ounces (325 grams). The largest was 6 inches (15 centimetres) long and had well-developed hands, feet and hair.

In 1980, Lin Eryi, a 17-year-old male of Gutian County, Fujian Province, complained of difficulty in breathing and vomited blood and human hair. Diagnosing a tumour, surgeons operated and discovered a foetus, carried since birth in the thoracic cavity. Weighing more than 21 pounds (1 kilogram), it had underdeveloped hair, teeth and eyes.

At the age of 68, Wang Yinge of Angua County, Hebei Province, had a calcified foetus removed. It had been embedded in her abdominal cavity for 31 years. All those years ago, it had burst out of the womb and entered the abdominal cavity, where it died at the age of about seven months and became calcified. It weighed 4 ounces (121 grams) and was 4½ inches (11.5 centimetres) long.

DEATH OF A MONKEY-MAN

According to the newspaper *Shanghai Wenhuibao*, in 1980, local scientists exhumed and examined the remains of Xu Yunbao, who had died in a fire in 1962, aged 23. Born in Sichuan Province, Xu had been entirely covered in hair and bent at the waist. His skull was only 3 inches (8 centimetres) in diameter at birth; and he grew to be only 3 feet 5 inches (105 centimetres) tall. Referred to as a 'monkey-man', Xu used all four limbs for walking, refused to wear clothing even during the winter, and preferred raw corn to eating cooked food. The paper denied he was either monkey or ape, but it admitted he had 'a strong wild nature and liked to catch people'. His mother, 72, his two brothers and his two sisters were still alive and apparently normal in every respect. There is a strange twist to this story, reported in the official *Guangming Daily*. The mother had apparently disappeared for 27 days in 1939, in a forest area said to be frequented by the 'wild men', or Chinese yeti, of Hubei Province. 'She admitted she had been seized by the ape-men but denied having any relations with them,' said the paper. The clear implication was that the hairy boy was a yeti-human halfbreed.

According to reports in May 1980, an old woman of 88 in Hebei Province grew two horns on the top of her head. The larger of the horns was said to be 1 inch (2.5 centimetres) long, yellowish-brown and without feeling. An American doctor, Martin Bruber, told the New York *Midnight Globe* that this was a case of *hyperosteosis frontalis*. 'This is a bony, tumour-like growth that normally occurs on the inside of the skull and is nearly always confined to elderly women, frequently suffering from diabetes or obesity.' But he had never heard of a case where the horns grew on the outside of the skull so that they were visible.

The less restrained *New Thrill* of Malaysia identified the woman as 'Madam Chow' of the Chiao Ho district in Hebei Province, and said she was in normal health, and neither obese nor diabetic. It also said that the horns grew to be 2 inches (5 centimetres) long. When both horns were that length, they started to turn downward, and allegedly came to resemble deer horns. The same newspaper mentioned an unidentified Japanese with 3-inch (7.5-centimetre) horns; and it referred to another report from China of a man with 10-inch (25-centimetre) horns, which later dropped off to leave stumps. These then started to form into an 'S' shape.

In February 1981, there were further tantalising reports in *New Thrill*. One concerned a five-year-old boy with a tail, who was said to be more advanced than other children of his age in many respects. A Peking newspaper, meanwhile, went to great lengths to debunk a reported mermaid and 'fish with legs', of which a picture (said to be a photomontage) had been circulating in Peking.

AN ELIXIR FROM ANTS

In the same month, the *Shanghai Wenhuibao* carried the story of 87-year-old Yan Zhongshan, who had discovered a wondrous tonic made from ants. It seems that, since 1964, he had been collecting ants, washing them in pure water, drying and grilling and then grinding them up into powder. He would then cook them up in an omelette, from which he made pills. A regime of one pill a day throughout the winter had given Yan exceptionally sharp eyes and ears, so the paper reported; and, having lost his teeth when he was 72, he had now grown a new set, strong enough to crack nuts... or so he claimed.

Luo Shijun of Jiangxi Province, in southern China, is said to have celebrated his hundredth birthday on 12 December 1981. According to the *Shanghai Wenhuibao* for 6 April 1982, he suddenly discovered one morning that 27 new teeth had grown from his previously toothless gums. An official in his village, who could not believe his eyes when shown the teeth, gave Luo a piece of dried meat which the peasant chewed readily. But there is no mention of ant pills here.

New teeth or not, some Chinese certainly do live on to a very ripe old age, and a candidate for the oldest Chinese emerged from the census of 1982. Lan Buping, of Guangxi Autonomous Region, was born on 13 April 1846, according to a report in a Canton newspaper. At 136, he still went occasionally into the mountains to cut firewood, said the paper, and could drink as much as 2 pints (1 litre) of rice wine at a sitting.

However, in September 1980, the journal *New Physical Culture* had reported that an ex-Buddhist monk, Wu Yunqing of Shaanxi Province, claimed he was born in 1838, making him 142 years old. He told interviewers he had prepared wood for his coffin three times. The first two lots rotted away, and the third now served as floorboards in his room. The old man gained national fame, but two journalists checked local records and established he had in fact been born on 13 December 1898, making him merely an 82-year-old fraud.

In April 1981, the Xinhua News Agency reported two giant children. Three-year-old Jin Rui already weighed 89 pounds (40.5 kilograms) and was polishing off 2 pounds (0.9 kilograms) of food a day. He weighed almost 15 pounds (6.8 kilograms) when he was born on 23 May 1978 in Hubei Province. One month later, he weighed 26 pounds (11.8 kilograms), and was eating four meals of porridge a

day. The report also mentioned Liu Debiao, aged 6, from Jiangsu Province, who was 4 feet 9 inches (1.45 metres) tall, weighed 91 pounds (41 kilograms) and could carry a man almost twice his weight on his back.

Rounding off this sombre cabinet of curiosities is the gruesome project of Dr (or Professor) Qi Yongxiang. In December 1980, the *Shanghai Wenhuibao* stated that, in 1967, a female chimpanzee had been inseminated with a man's sperm, and was three months pregnant when Red Guards smashed the laboratory and the chimpanzee died. Dr Qi, who was identified as a 'researcher in medicine' in the north-eastern city of Shenyang, was involved in the original project, and wanted to resume the experiments to create what he called a 'near-human ape'.

His aim was that, having an enlarged brain and tongue, it should be able to grasp simple concepts and learn to talk some kind of language. Organs from the monster could possibly be used as substitutes for human or artificial organs in transplants, it was thought. The creature might also have been able to drive a car, herd animals, guard forests and other natural resources, and be used for exploration of the seabed, outer space and the centre of the Earth, the researcher claimed.

Chimpanzees and humans are remarkably similar genetically. A chimp has 48 chromosomes, while a human has 46. It is assumed that the only major rearrangement has been the fusion, during human evolution, of two pairs of chromosomes to produce one pair. The differences between horses and donkeys, which can mate to produce the infertile mule, are considerably greater.

Professor Neil Moore, an associate professor in the department of animal husbandry at Sydney University, commented: 'You cannot say blandly the whole thing is stupid. All one can say is that it is possible to obtain fertilisation between many species, but the chance of survival of a man-ape embryo is remote.'

If such a hybrid could survive, though, it would have notable advantages as a worker, according to Dr Qi. And, he added, since it would be classed as an animal, there need be no qualms about killing it if necessary – an attitude many would oppose.

The two completely hairless brothers above – Yang Tianzhao, right, 26 when this picture was taken in 1980, and brother Yang Tianshun, five years younger – were from Yunnan Province.

Wu Yunqing, below, became a national celebrity in 1980 when he claimed to have been born in 1838. But journalists proved that he had in fact been born 60 years later.

The tallest woman in the world, Zeng Jin-Lian, left, stood 8 feet 1 inch (2.46 metres) high. She was only 17 years old when she died of diabetes in 1982.

Seen below at the age of 35 months, Jin Rui of Hubei Province already weighed a prodigious 89 pounds (40.5 kilograms) and was eating 2 pounds (1 kilogram) of food each day.

❚❚ ANOTHER TWO-HEADED BABY WAS BORN ON 16 AUGUST 1980 IN AN ARMY HOSPITAL IN TIANJIN TO UNIDENTIFIED PARENTS. WEIGHING 7 POUNDS (3.3 KILOGRAMS) AT BIRTH, THE BABY... HAD TWO OESOPHAGUSES, TWO RESPIRATORY SYSTEMS AND TWO STOMACHS, BUT ONE HEART, LIVER AND ANUS. WHEN THE LEFT HIP WAS INJECTED, THE LEFT HEAD CRIED; WHEN THE LEFT HEAD WAS FED, THE RIGHT HEAD CRIED. ❚❚

BIG CATS, TALL STORIES?

HAVE JUNGLE CATS FOUND HOMES IN THE WOODS AND FORESTS OF BRITAIN? INNUMERABLE REPORTS SUGGEST THAT, OFFICIAL ZOOLOGICAL DATA NOTWITHSTANDING, A FEW SUCH CREATURES MAY ACTUALLY BE THRIVING IN THE ENGLISH COUNTRYSIDE

The leafy lanes of Britain are an unlikely habitat for the puma and no less so, one would suppose, for the lion. Yet both these creatures have apparently been seen – the puma especially frequently. Neither beast is native to any part of the British Isles: the only native feral member of the cat family is the wild cat, which still survives in remote areas of Scotland. But the wild cat looks something like a domestic tabby and is not big enough to be mistaken for a puma or lion.

Yet puma sightings go right back to the 18th century, when the traveller and essayist William

On 18 July 1963, at Shooters Hill, south-east London, below, policemen, soldiers and citizens set off on a hunt for a 'cheetah' that had been reported by a lorry driver and by police in a patrol car. The threat was taken so seriously that the searchers even armed themselves – with pick-axe handles and hockey sticks.

Motor-cycle police joined in the Shooters Hill hunt, as shown top. Perhaps the authorities thought speed would be needed if their quarry should prove to be a cheetah, which can reach 60 miles per hour (95 km/h).

Most Britons would be hard pressed to identify a big cat such as the one above if they were to encounter it unexpectedly. Indeed, reports are almost never precise enough to permit the species of a mystery cat to be determined. This is in fact a North American puma (also known as a mountain lion or cougar).

ambulance crew and animal welfare officers combed 850 acres (340 hectares) of land. All they found was a set of large footprints in a muddy stream bed; and although the beast was apparently seen later in the week and the reports were followed up by the police, no cheetah was ever found.

MYSTERIOUS PRINTS

Pumas have also been seen in other parts of England, and the New Forest area of Hampshire seems to have been a favoured haunt. During September 1972, three young brothers saw a creature that certainly sounds suspiciously like a puma. Stuart Cron, aged 12, and his brothers Andrew, aged 10, and Donald, aged 6, were taking their dog for a walk when they saw a strange creature creeping through the grass on the forest edge. Andrew got closest to it, and later said: 'It was larger than an Alsatian dog but looked like a cat. It had a big head with stick-up ears, like cats' ears, and its eyes looked fierce.' It was tawny brown in colour. When Andrew slapped the dog's lead against his leg, the animal bounced off 'in big leaps'. The boys likewise ran off; and their Alsatian, which normally chased anything that moved, ran away with them. The boys' mother had earlier found mysterious large paw prints with claw marks in the area. This is not the first occasion on which such prints have been found around the time when unidentified big cats are reputed to have been seen. The puzzle is that members of the big cat family (except cheetahs) do not walk with their claws out. So what could these animals possibly be?

Early in 1979, a black 'puma' was reported from the Faversham area of Kent in south-east England. Students of American big cat sightings will know that black pumas (sometimes called panthers) are often seen in the United States, despite supposedly being extremely rare. In Britain, they should be nonexistent! However, farmer Chris Blood believed he saw one on this occasion. He said: 'At first people round here thought it was just a large domestic cat, but it was far too big for that.' Paw prints found on the farm and elsewhere were identified by experts as those of a dog; but despite an official pronouncement that local people could stop worrying, Chris Blood and others who had seen the beast were not so easily satisfied. This confusion as to whether a mysterious animal is a cat or a dog often recurs. Are we, perhaps, dealing with some sort of hybrid creature?

Further big black cats were reported in southern England during 1979. Colin Carter was walking on the South Downs near Eastbourne in Sussex at the end of June when a black, cat-like creature, the size of a pony, crossed his path and disappeared into the undergrowth. Early in September, John and Frances Clarke were walking in Tilgate Forest near Crawley in Sussex, 25 to 30 miles (40–48 kilometres) from the site of the previous sighting, when they spotted a large cat-like animal standing motionless about 75 to 100 yards (70–90 metres) away. It watched them for several seconds and then, when John whistled, it bounded into the undergrowth. The couple described it as 2 to 2½ feet (60–75 centimetres) tall, with a small head, pointed ears, and a long tail. It was dark in colour, and either brown or black.

Cobbett saw one in the grounds of the ruined Waverley Abbey near Farnham, Surrey, in southern England, when he was a boy. It was 'as big as a middle-sized spaniel dog' and was in a hollow elm tree. Cobbett was beaten for insisting that he had seen this strange creature

SCATTERED SIGHTINGS

Surrey is densely populated in parts but still retains a few quieter areas of wood and commonland. It is there that the creature, now known as the 'Surrey puma', has most widely been seen, with literally hundreds of sightings reported by apparently level-headed witnesses.

Since a puma has never been caught in England, the identification is really only a guess: indeed, sometimes the animal seen is called a cheetah or a lynx. What is more, the sightings are scattered over such a large area and such a long period that many separate animals must be responsible for them. There could in fact be a variety of explanations, with large dogs fleetingly seen at night being the cause of some reports by witnesses who have heard of the 'puma'. But that explanation cannot account for a number of daytime sightings, just as the well-worn explanations of pet pumas or escapes from a zoo cannot encompass all the reported sightings.

The elusive big cats are sometimes even seen by the people who are actively hunting them. One was the 'cheetah' that jumped over the bonnet of a police car in July 1963. This animal was first seen by a lorry driver, David Back, who stopped at Shooters Hill in south-east London to help what he thought was an injured dog lying by the roadside. The time was 1 a.m. Mr Back later reported: 'I walked over to it – and then it got up. I knew then it wasn't a dog. It had long legs and a long, pointed tail that curled up. It looked as if it had a mouthful of food. It ran off into the woods.' When a police patrol car went into the area, the 'cheetah' jumped over its bonnet – and the hunt was on. The policemen obviously thought that the animal was something more than a stray dog, because extra police were drafted into the area to search for it. In the end, 126 policemen with 21 dogs, plus 30 soldiers,

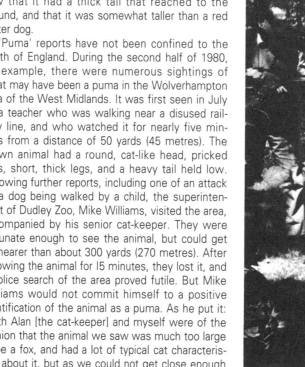

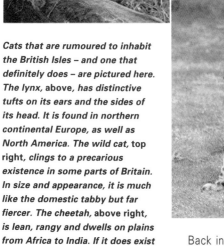

Cats that are rumoured to inhabit the British Isles – and one that definitely does – are pictured here. The lynx, above, has distinctive tufts on its ears and the sides of its head. It is found in northern continental Europe, as well as North America. The wild cat, top right, clings to a precarious existence in some parts of Britain. In size and appearance, it is much like the domestic tabby but far fiercer. The cheetah, above right, is lean, rangy and dwells on plains from Africa to India. If it does exist in Britain, however, it can scarcely be living in open spaces.

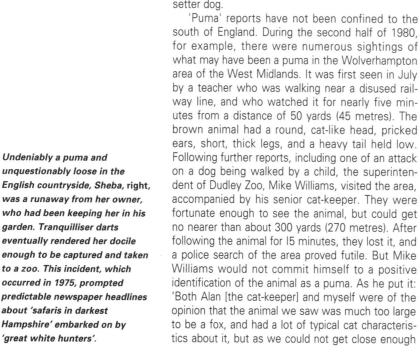

" IT WAS LARGER THAN AN ALSATIAN DOG BUT LOOKED LIKE A CAT. IT HAD A BIG HEAD WITH STICK-UP EARS... AND ITS EYES LOOKED FIERCE. "

Undeniably a puma and unquestionably loose in the English countryside, Sheba, right, was a runaway from her owner, who had been keeping her in his garden. Tranquilliser darts eventually rendered her docile enough to be captured and taken to a zoo. This incident, which occurred in 1975, prompted predictable newspaper headlines about 'safaris in darkest Hampshire' embarked on by 'great white hunters'.

Back in Surrey, puma-like creatures were still being seen as the 1980s dawned. On 27 June 1980, Mrs Vivien Wilkinson looked out of a window at her East Horsley home around 5 p.m. and saw a tawny cat at the bottom of her garden. As it loped across the lawn and through a gap in the fence, she saw that it had a thick tail that reached to the ground, and that it was somewhat taller than a red setter dog.

'Puma' reports have not been confined to the south of England. During the second half of 1980, for example, there were numerous sightings of what may have been a puma in the Wolverhampton area of the West Midlands. It was first seen in July by a teacher who was walking near a disused railway line, and who watched it for nearly five minutes from a distance of 50 yards (45 metres). The brown animal had a round, cat-like head, pricked ears, short, thick legs, and a heavy tail held low. Following further reports, including one of an attack on a dog being walked by a child, the superintendent of Dudley Zoo, Mike Williams, visited the area, accompanied by his senior cat-keeper. They were fortunate enough to see the animal, but could get no nearer than about 300 yards (270 metres). After following the animal for 15 minutes, they lost it, and a police search of the area proved futile. But Mike Williams would not commit himself to a positive identification of the animal as a puma. As he put it: 'Both Alan [the cat-keeper] and myself were of the opinion that the animal we saw was much too large to be a fox, and had a lot of typical cat characteristics about it, but as we could not get close enough

A tunnel in straw, allegedly made by an unknown animal in a barn at Llangurig, Wales, in October 1980, is shown right. Journalists and the police laid siege to the barn overnight, but they found no big cat inside it.

The unusual paw print below was found next to the barn, and was pronounced to be like that of a dog by experts. But big cat reports continued to come in from surrounding areas throughout the following months.

we could not give the police a positive identification. If it had been a large brown dog, it would surely have been found during the police search.'

He also said that he had no knowledge of an illegally kept puma having got loose, and presumably he would also have known of any puma that had escaped from a zoo.

A similar animal, possibly the same one, was seen again in the area in March 1981, walking along scaffolding and then jumping through an open window into a partly-built house. It was described as about 4 feet (1.2 metres) long and dark brown, with a cat-like head, and a long tail.

Despite being an area of remote, thinly populated land consisting of mountains, moorlands and forests, Wales is also the source of a number of big cat reports. Indeed, it may be that some of the many sheep-killings that occur there could be attributed to big cats, though they are usually blamed on dogs. However, in October 1980, the nation's attention was focused on Wales when a farmer at Llangurig, in Powys, reported that he thought he had a big cat holed up in his barn. Press, radio and television reporters soon gathered at the farm, together with armed police, but an all-night vigil ended without a sight of the supposed animal. Police tactics were not subtle, according to a farmer, Michael Nash: 'They hammered hell out of the asbestos [side of the barn] when they heard it snoring.' But if there was an animal there in the barn, it must have crept out entirely unnoticed to find a quieter nest. Later, however, a lair with wet straw and strange droppings was found.

The evidence for the animal's existence is enigmatic. Michael Nash had lost four sheep in 10 days, killed in a manner not typical of dogs. He had heard a snoring noise coming from the straw bales in the barn, and found large footprints in the muddy farmyard. But all this could be explained without needing the presence of a big cat. The sheep killings could have been the work of foxes; the snoring noise could have been owls; the droppings may have been owl pellets; and the paw prints could have been made by a large dog. Nash preserved one print: it measured 5 inches (12.7 centimetres) long by 3½ inches (7.6 centimetres) wide, and was later pronounced dog-like by zoologists.

But this negative assessment of the evidence does not dispose of big cats in Powys. Only three weeks before the events at Llangurig, a district nurse saw what, from her description, sounded like a lynx near Church Stoke on the border with England, 30 miles (50 kilometres) north-east of Llangurig. A month after the Llangurig events, and only 6 miles (10 kilometres) away, another farmer described a strange cat-like animal that had moved in leaps and bounds across his fields. There were other sightings throughout the autumn, too. Then, in June 1981, sheep and lambs were killed near Aberystwyth. One farmer saw a black animal, about 30 inches (75 centimetres) tall at the head; the police and RSPCA seemed almost certain it was a puma. They set traps baited with meat, but there were no reports of a capture, nor of any further sightings. As always, the cats – if cats they were – disappeared just as suddenly as they had appeared.

IS DEATH A DREAM?

IF, AS MATERIALIST PHILOSOPHERS BELIEVE, THE MIND IS MERELY A SHADOW OF THE BRAIN, THERE IS NO POSSIBILITY THAT CONSCIOUSNESS SURVIVES DEATH. BUT MANKIND STILL HAS A TENACIOUS BELIEF IN THE AFTERLIFE. IS THIS FAITH REALLY JUSTIFIED?

The overwhelming majority of Mankind has always taken it for granted that some aspect of the human personality survives bodily death. In many societies, ancestors are considered to live on in a rather shadowy form in a netherworld, where they can be contacted by shamans through dreams or trances. In the East, hundreds of millions of people are convinced that the core of the personality survives bodily death

A grotto of ancestor figures, below, overlooks growing crops at Toraja, inset, on the island of Sulawesi (formerly Celebes) in Indonesia. The inhabitants of the island believe that, in some sense, the spirits of their ancestors live on in the effigies, and that they can ensure a good harvest.

and comes back to this world in another physical body via the process of rebirth or reincarnation. And Muslims and Christians have generally believed in various kinds of afterlife that seem to depend for their nature on a person's faith and actions during his or her life.

By contrast, those who are followers of the philosophy of materialism fervently deny that any aspect of personal consciousness can survive the death of the physical body. They believe that the mind is nothing but an aspect, or a kind of shadow, of the activity of the brain. All mental activity must therefore cease completely when the brain stops functioning at the time of death. However, in spite of the fact that many highly educated people believe it, this theory of materialism has no truly persuasive logical or scientific basis.

But if, in contrast to the beliefs of the materialists, there *is* some sort of personal survival of bodily death, what is it like? The usual answer is to say it is a life of the soul. But what precisely is the soul? Is it, perhaps, what we normally think of as the mind? And if so, what kind of existence can the mind have without the physical body? We are so used to living in a physical form that it is almost impossible to imagine ourselves surviving without some kind of body. Certainly, our physical bodies disintegrate after our death.

One answer to these questions is suggested by the experience of dreaming. In dreams, we find ourselves in all sorts of places and situations. We see and hear things, talk to people and also move about. But meanwhile, the physical body is lying asleep in bed. So the body in which we find our-

selves in dreams cannot be our own body: it must be another body, which can conveniently be referred to as the 'dream body'. This dream body, like our physical body in waking life, is usually taken for granted within the dream and so seems real enough. Normally, it is only on waking up that we realise that we were dreaming, and that the dream world and dream body we experienced were not in fact what we would accept as being physically real.

In order to wake up, we need the living physical body. After death, of course, this is no longer possible. But perhaps we continue to exist in a kind of dream state from which we cannot awake. In this state, the dream body will seem real, and so will the world we experience, but it will not be physical – any more than our ordinary dreams are physical.

Fascinating insights into the nature of the dream world arise in lucid dreams, within which the dreamer becomes aware that he is dreaming. These are relatively rare, but many people have had occasional experiences of this type – for example, by realising during a nightmare that the events they are experiencing are only a dream after all. However, some people have lucid dreams quite regularly and even deliberately explore them. Indeed, they have found that the world they experience in lucid dreams is usually much more realistic

Many ancient societies believed that the dead should be buried with objects that they may need in the afterlife. In ancient Egyptian graves in the City of the Dead, above, just outside Cairo, for instance, extraordinary collections of household goods have been found. Many Viking burials often contain, in addition, a horn of plenty, top, holding belongings precious to the dead.

and consistent than in normal dreams, and sometimes almost indistinguishable from the ordinary world of waking experience. The main difference is that, within lucid dreams, they can do anything they like and go anywhere they like just by willing it.

Several people have described how, within lucid dreams, they have visited their own bedroom and seen themselves asleep in bed. Here, the centre of consciousness, within the dream body, seems to be directly and explicitly experienced as separate from the physical body.

CLOSE TO DEATH

The intriguing thing is that such states in lucid dreams seem to be almost the same as the out-of-the-body experiences that are relatively common in childhood, and that may occur in adult life under unusual conditions of stress – when someone is close to death, for instance. As in the case of lucid dreams, a number of people have cultivated the ability to travel out-of-the-body more or less at will. Indeed, those who are familiar with both lucid dreams and out-of-the-body experiences have observed that they are almost identical, except for the fact that the out-of-the-body state is entered via dreams in the one case, and directly from the waking state in the other. This seems to indicate that the centre of consciousness experienced in dreams – the dream body – and the centre of consciousness detached from the physical body in out-of-the-body experiences may be of the same nature.

Such experiences may indeed point to the kind of existence that continues after physical death. Numerous people who have nearly died have described how they found themselves outside their physical body – for example, looking down at it from somewhere near the ceiling of a hospital

room. In other words, these descriptions of near-death experiences involve an out-of-the-body state in which the centre of consciousness is detached from the physical body, just as it is in other out-of-the-body experiences and in lucid dreams. There is no logical reason why this centre of consciousness should not continue to exist, detached from the physical body, even after the physical body has decayed. And since science has not yet begun to be able to suggest what the nature of this centre of consciousness might be, there is at present, strictly speaking, no scientific objection either.

Assuming this happens, what sort of life might be possible after death? Again, individual experience of the non-physical dream world may give us some suggestions. The kinds of dream we have depend on our memories, hopes, fears, desires, beliefs – in short, on individual personality, including the unconscious mind. There is a certain amount of evidence to suggest that, in dreams, we may also be more open than usual to telepathic influences from others, and to precognitions of the future. Just as our normal dreams reflect our personalities and depend on our actions and beliefs while we are awake, so the world we enter after death seems likely to depend on what we have done and believed while alive in the physical body. Some people may experience a dream-like continuation of their life before death. Some may undergo the most fantastic adventures. Others may suffer from recurrent nightmares, trapped in some form of hell that has been created by their own minds. And others may experience a kind of paradise conjured up by their expectations: Muslims, for example, may tend to find themselves in green gardens with fountains, attended by dancing girls and serving boys, enjoying the pleasures described in Islamic literature. Roman Catholics may encounter St Peter at the Pearly Gates. Possibilities may be limited only by the capacity of the imagination.

FROM THE OTHER SIDE

If imagination governs the afterlife, it need not mean that we will be confined to a personal fantasy world, unable to communicate with others. Although in the absence of the physical body, normal kinds of communication through the physical senses can no longer take place, direct communication of a telepathic nature may be possible both among the departed, as well as between the departed and the living. Some of the communications 'from the other side' picked up by spirit mediums may be of this kind.

Another possibility is that the surviving personality re-enters a physical body and, as it were, wakes up again in the physical world. This taking over the body of a living person would correspond to what has traditionally been referred to as 'possession'. But if the surviving personality were to become associated with an embryo or a newly born baby, then this would amount to what many religious people regard as reincarnation.

The Dream of Ossian, by Jean-Dominique Ingres (1780-1867), left, shows warriors and languorous women summoned from the netherworld by the beauty of the poet's music.

A 16th-century Mogul Indian painting by Ram Das of the Emperor Babur receiving Uzbeck and Rajput envoys in his garden at Agra is shown right. It has been suggested that the nature of the world we enter after death depends upon our own expectations and experiences. For some, it may have all the luxury and comfort depicted in this painting; for others, it may be a dream-like or even nightmarish continuation of their life before death; or it may correspond to the expectations of the afterlife given by organised religion. The nature of the afterlife, in short, may be determined by the imagination of the individual.

An Attic kylix of around 430 BC, left, shows Pluto and Persephone, joint rulers of Hades. According to Greek mythology, it was Pluto's responsibility to supervise the trials and punishment of souls after death.

In addition to these possibilities, it is also conceivable that, in the kind of dreamlike existence after death, the personality may be open to spiritual influences coming from beyond the realm of the human mind and imagination. As in this world, such influences may lead to a progressive development of the personality, and a greater openness to the life of the spirit.

All this is inevitably a matter of speculation. We cannot find out from experience until we ourselves die. But even then, we are unlikely to obtain an objective view independent of our beliefs and expectations. For what happens to us seems very

In the Allegory of Purgatory by Giovanni Bellini (c.1430-1516), far left, the foreground represents a paradise garden with the tree of knowledge in the centre. Justice and punishment are suggested by the figure with the sword.

likely to depend on our own attitudes. In particular, the possibility of continued spiritual development may depend on our openness to this very possibility. Could it be that, if we close our minds to anything that lies beyond, we may condemn ourselves to remain trapped indefinitely within our present fears and limitations?

> THE CENTRE OF CONSCIOUSNESS WHICH WAS IN EXISTENCE BEFORE DEATH DOES NOT CEASE TO BE IN EXISTENCE AFTER DEATH AND... THE EXPERIENCE OF THIS CENTRE AFTER DEATH HAS THE SAME KIND OF CONTINUITY WITH ITS EXPERIENCE BEFORE DEATH AS THAT OF A MAN WHO SLEEPS FOR A WHILE AND WAKES AGAIN.

W. R. MATTHEWS, PSYCHICAL RESEARCH AND THEOLOGY

METAL THAT BENDS WHEN SIMPLY POINTED AT; COINS THAT BECOME AS SOFT AS PUTTY; AND BROKEN CUTLERY THAT CAN BE 'INVISIBLY' MENDED – THESE ARE JUST SOME OF THE PSYCHIC FEATS PERFORMED BY SILVIO MAIER

Silvio is seen, left, stroking a spoon in an effort to bend it psychically. Often he would wait until he felt that the metal 'wanted' to be bent before attempting to do so.

The photographs below, bottom, below right and right are part of a unique videotape showing the sequence of a coffee spoon being bent by Silvio. He merely pointed at the spot on the spoon handle that he intuitively felt was about to soften and eventually bend – which it did.

A NEW TWIST TO METAL-BENDING

In the early 1970s, the word 'paranormal' meant just one thing to most people – the metal-bending powers of Uri Geller. But then, gradually, other metal-benders, (or the 'Gellerini', as some Italians call the Geller imitators) started to appear, though many of them have never been heard of since. One was a psychic, usually known simply as 'Silvio', from Bern, Switzerland.

Silvio Maier first became aware of his power accidentally. In fact, he was just as startled as his friends when he suddenly found himself bending spoons in a restaurant one evening in 1974. To begin with, it was just something of a game, albeit an extraordinary one; but this quiet, sensible man had no idea quite how it was to influence his life.

Soon afterwards, a professional magician, Rolf Mayr (who had invented a considerable number of tricks to enable him to bend spoons and forks), approached Silvio after a local newspaper had carried a report on 'the Swiss Geller'. Mayr intended to disclose him as a fraud, but he ended up by telephoning Professor Hans Bender of the Freiburg Institute in Germany to tell him that Silvio's metal-bending performances deserved serious investigation, after all.

When Bender and his research team first met Silvio in December 1974, they encountered a tall man with a naive, childlike enthusiasm. He was always very co-operative, demonstrating his remarkable ability to bend cutlery whenever he was required to do so. Indeed, that first evening ended with seven pieces of bent or broken silverware. Still, the man who did it all had no idea how it had happened, nor even why he had suddenly found himself able to do it. His investigators were just as

puzzled – for other reasons. It seemed that Silvio's attitude to these objects was one of sympathy and friendliness: he would fondle a spoon, for instance, showing obvious pleasure when it 'agreed' to weaken and bend. He also not only bent coins, but actually caused them to soften so much that he was able to leave his nail prints on them.

In Silvio's words: 'I just hold the object and wait. I can't do anything other than wait. Of course, I want the spoon to bend, but it does not make any difference if I concentrate hard or if I just keep waiting.' And so he waited innumerable times in front of the research team's video cameras, and bent first one spoon, then another, and then another. 'It is as if something is coming towards me from very far away. I have to wait for it to come. Sometimes it comes; often it does not. But if it comes, I can feel it get closer; it feels very close behind me, and then it is in me.' Silvio's heart would start to beat faster whenever he felt this power approaching, and so he was able to predict when the spoon would bend. Indeed, one of the most extraordinary films on psychokinesis (PK) shows Silvio pointing his index finger towards the thinnest part of a coffee spoon, which is stuck into a piece of polystyrene, for a full 15 minutes. Then, the upper part of the spoon begins to bend and, within a few seconds, it has bent right through 180 degrees – without ever being touched by him or anyone else.

This amazed the Freiburg parapsychologists, who replayed the tape over and over again. Equally enigmatic are the filmed instances of objects moved by PK on a flat surface. One piece of film shows Nina Kulagina, the famous Soviet psychic,

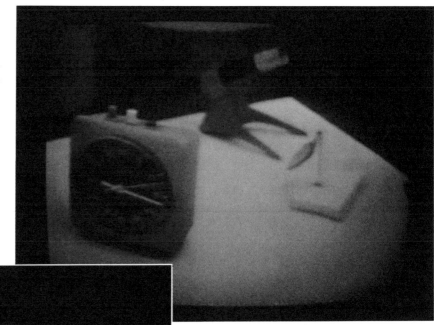

succeeding in moving small objects without touching them, but only with great physical and mental effort. Yet Silvio seems not to have exerted such strength. He simply waited, keeping his hands outstretched and motionless above an ordinary pencil, for example. Sometimes, the pencil made a sudden movement and then stopped abruptly.

Researchers and magicians have tried in vain to reproduce these strange movements using mechanical means, and physicists have tried to find the secret of Silvio's astonishing power by analysing single frames of the film of these experiments. But, unfortunately, these investigations, though thorough, have proved inconclusive.

At the start of the long-term research project with Silvio, Professor Bender and his colleagues thought about ways of obtaining evidence to prove it is possible to bend a metal object using PK. The easiest way would have been to seal an object in a glass container and then ask Silvio to move the

The magician Rolf Meyr, right, set out to expose Silvio as a fraud but finally recommended him to Hans Bender of the Freiburg Institute as a genuine psychic and worthy of an investigation.

object without touching the container. But, although they attempted this experiment, it was doomed to fail, partly for psychological reasons. It seems that Silvio, like many other PK psychics, needed to have physical contact with the experimental object or, at least, the option of this contact. This might be why Silvio never succeeded in moving a small piece of metal sealed in such a container. Eventually, a bottle was constructed that contained a spoon with a long handle that stuck out of the sealed closure. This bottle was secured in several ways against attempts at tampering. There were even devices to indicate whether thermal, magnetic or mechanical means might have been used to bend the part of the spoon inside the bottle. But every attempt to bend one of these spoons by PK was unsuccessful.

However, a spoon did break once, though in rather unusual circumstances. Silvio woke one day to find a strange woman, dressed in white, entering

On one occasion, Silvio broke a restaurant spoon and then 'psi-soldered' it back together, with the handle the wrong way round, as in the top spoon in the photograph, right.

The spoon in the sealed bottle, right, was set in motion by Silvio's psychic powers, the crack resulting from the force of the spoon's movement.

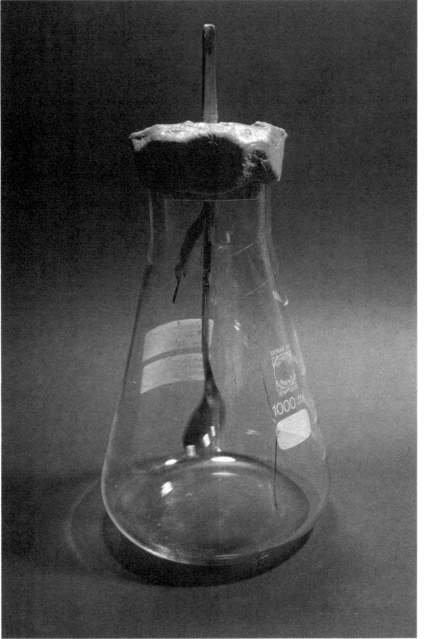

his bedroom. Who she was remains a mystery. He got up and went to his experimental room where he found the tablecloth, upon which objects for use during experiments had been lying, torn in pieces. Several items of silverware had also been deformed into bizarre sculptures or broken into bits, as was the spoon in the safety bottle. These broken objects, as well as the ones broken during experiments, were later examined at the Max Planck Institute for Metal Research in Stuttgart. The Institute reported that the breakages appeared to be no different from typical mechanical fractures. The broken spoon inside the safety bottle was particularly interesting: the bottle was cracked, and it was certainly arguable that it might have been thrown against something, so breaking the spoon inside. But Dr Sommer, a scientist at Freiburg's Frauenhofter Institute for Solid State Mechanics who examined the bottle, concluded from a structural analysis that the crack had been produced by a mechanical force coming from the inside. Obviously, when the spoon broke, it hit against the glass with great force.

AN ANGELIC VISITATION?

Another interesting point is that it seemed Silvio's powers were gradually becoming more varied – if, that is, it really was Silvio who stopped the church clock opposite his house from ringing after he had cursed its noise. Even stranger, and more interesting, is a slide that he showed to the Freiburg researchers in June 1975. Silvio had taken a walk through some woods shortly after his mother's death when he suddenly saw an intense ball of light in front of a row of trees. Startled, he raised his camera to photograph it. But there was to be a further surprise for Silvio. When the slide was developed, he saw the outline of a yellowish ball with a 'light figure' resembling an angel with wings in the centre. Photographic experts were unable to discover any evidence that the film had been tampered with in some way.

Many instances of Silvio's PK abilities involved things happening to him, rather than the psychic making them happen – as is most obvious in his metal-bending tests. In essence, it seems that the

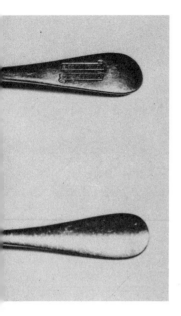

psychic had to be in the right mood, the right state of mind, and even then he did not know exactly what was going to happen. One incident in particular emphasizes the passive character of Silvio's powers. Bernhard Walti, a technician from Bern University and a researcher at the Freiburg Institute, was investigating Silvio's talents. Silvio had succeeded several times in moving a pencil on the table by PK, and the whole experiment was recorded on video. Some hours later, though, Silvio decided to end the session for some unknown reason. Bernhard Walti began to put away the equipment, but there was one spoon still left on the table, and the video camera had been left running.

Silvio left the room, then re-entered and looked with Walti at some photographs of a cave, standing about 6 feet (2 metres) away from the table. At that moment, the pencil rotated 20 degrees in a counterclockwise direction as Silvio had tried to make it do, in vain, just before the end of the session.

Interestingly, this event went unnoticed at the time, and was seen only later when the video tape was played back. Yet, perhaps, this is really not so strange. PK often occurs not when someone is trying to make it happen, but afterwards, as if somehow brought about by the sudden release of effort.

The most puzzling incident, though, occurred in the restaurant where Silvio first discovered his metal-bending faculties. He had deliberately broken some of the restaurant's silverware by PK when one of his friends warned that they might be thrown out if Silvio kept destroying the restaurant's precious property in this way. Why, instead, it was suggested, did he not try to 'psi-solder' the broken cutlery and repair the damage done? 'Silvio took the two parts of the spoon in his hands,' one of the friends explained, 'and held them between his fingers. He concentrated, and it did not take long until the spoon was in one piece. Again, he bent the spoon, broke it, and "psi-soldered" it together.'

Just some of the objects affected by Silvio's PK are shown right. Although most famous for his metal-bending, he also exhibited other paranormal talents, such as thoughtography. Shortly after his mother's death, Silvio was taking a walk through some woods when he saw a brilliant ball of light in front of some trees. He took a photograph of it and, much to his surprise, when the film was developed, the ball had transformed itself into the radiant, angel-like figure seen below.

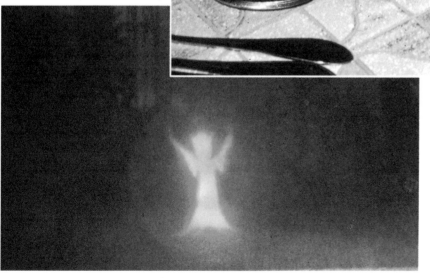

Certainly, no one believed this, including the Freiburg researchers who were shown such spoons (which in no way differed from normal spoons) until, finally, his friends asked him to break the spoon and 'psi-solder' it so that the side with the restaurant's name would be facing upwards, not downwards, as it had been when originally made. Silvio then did as they requested, and the spoon that he succeeded in rearranging now lies in the archives of the Freiburg Institute. It is indeed a strange artefact – a curious example of the unexplained or, perhaps, a key to a better understanding of psychokinetic metal-bending.

As UFOs continue to be reported all over the world, governments can no longer deny that such things exist, whatever their nature. Nevertheless, official attitudes tend to be alarmingly inconsistent

UFO enthusiasts, above, are seen some years ago at the United Nations. Among them were Dr Jacques Vallee, centre; the President of Grenada, Sir Eric Gairy, centre back; and Dr J. Allen Hynek, top left.

UFOs - CLOSELY GUARDED SECRETS

The governments of the world seem, despite protestations to the contrary, to take the subject of UFOs very seriously. The United States government, for example, certainly does, and even refuses to release key documents because, it claims, they would compromise national security. Britain, meanwhile, maintains a stiff upper lip on the subject, but all the evidence points to an active interest in UFOs at a high level. Several European nations admit openly to the reality of UFOs; and a leading scientist working with GEPAN, France's former government-funded UFO research project, went further and proclaimed that the phenomenon is produced by an intelligence that is actually the dominant form of life on this planet. Such widespread interest seems inconsistent with the commonly held opinion that ufology is, at best, a 'pseudoscience', and that it should stay that way.

Several of the smaller nations – such as those in South America – have issued bold statements concerning the reality and nature of UFOs. The media coverage of UFO reports in these countries is fairly extensive and rarely critical, so it is hardly surprising that they, too, should offer their view that UFOs are representatives of a higher intelligence.

In 1978, the President of Grenada, Sir Eric Gairy, tried to force a United Nations debate on UFOs. Eventually he succeeded; and several impressive depositions were made, including contributions from Dr J. Allen Hynek and Dr Jacques Vallee. But nothing beyond a resolution calling for further action emerged, and Sir Eric was unable to push for the resolution to be implemented.

For years, the situation in the former Soviet Union was characteristically complicated and obscured by officialdom. We know, for instance,

Hollywood's extra-terrestrial (E.T.) is seen proving that he loves Mankind, above. Despite his appearance, this creature has become a world-wide symbol of Man's longing to find – and understand – another race from another world. Some ufologists, however, feel that this sympathetic portrayal of aliens is merely a form of propaganda, preparing us to meet our planet's 'true rulers'.

The nature of UFOs, such as that shown right, is still essentially unknown. Nevertheless, the sincerity of witnesses cannot be doubted, whether what they have seen are 'nuts and bolts' craft or some form of hallucination.

that parapsychology was always treated with respect in the USSR, but very little was known about the official Soviet attitude to UFOs until 1967, when Dr Jacques Vallee paid a visit there. His trip coincided with the foundation of a scientific UFO research group, whose head was Dr Felix Zigel, professor of cosmology at Moscow's Institute of Aviation and the man responsible – under government direction – for the training of cosmonauts.

Working with him in UFO research was an air force major called Stolyarov. They claimed that the authorities promised them, when their group was properly established, that they would be given the 1,500 UFO reports in their possession. However, this promise was never kept, the group eventually being told: 'You are too small, and the UFO problem is too big.'

Stolyarov and Zigel were, however, given permission to appear on national television, which they did on 10 November 1967, telling the Soviet citizens: 'UFOs are a very serious subject, which we must study fully'. They also launched an appeal for UFO reports.

Shortly after this, however, Zigel suddenly adopted a low profile. Indeed, when US journalists Sheila Ostrander and Lynn Schroeder visited the USSR in the late 1960s to collect material for their book *Psychic Discoveries Behind The Iron Curtain*, the only scientist they were not allowed to meet was Felix Zigel.

On 14 June 1980 at 11.50 p.m., an orange, horseshoe-shaped UFO appeared in the sky to the north-west of Moscow, and was seen by thousands of people. The giant object cruised over the streets of the capital, causing great panic. Some people even fled into fall-out shelters, believing that the Third World War had started – but the object moved away without harming anyone. And next day, the Soviet media made no mention of this event. However, somewhat oddly, in view of his strange reticence on the subject of UFOs, Zigel suddenly spoke of craft detaching themselves from the horseshoe-shaped 'mother ship' and disgorging aliens on to the streets of Moscow. Yet Zigel must have known that the 'UFO' was very probably the satellite *Cosmos 1188*, shortly after its launch from

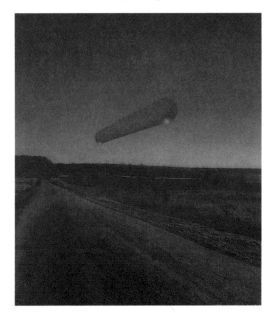

a site at Plesetsk, just north of Moscow. Western scientists were certainly well aware of this and – although ordinary Soviet citizens were generally kept in the dark about their own government's activities – Zigel, as a trainer of cosmonauts, must have known about it. His extraordinary claims may, in fact, be proof that, finally, he had been let into the secrets contained in the 1,500 official UFO reports – on condition, presumably, that he became a pawn of the Soviet government. And this, it has been suggested, may have involved using unlikely UFO stories to act as a cover for some kind of secret government activities.

Although Zigel published many articles about UFOs in the USSR, he seems to have been very reluctant to share his data with ufologists elsewhere. Perhaps it was simply too problematic to smuggle information out of the country, but others managed to do so, albeit with some difficulty. Nikita Schnee is one Soviet ufologist who regularly sent UFO reports to the West. Commenting on Zigel's cases, he said: 'We checked them out and not a single one was found to be true!'

Schnee worked at a scientific research establishment and, together with fellow scientist Vladimir Azhazha, attempted to set up a private UFO research institute between 1978 and 1979. But they were continually blocked by the Communist Party who, announcing that the study of UFOs was 'anti-state', set about breaking up their meetings. On one occasion, Zigel is alleged to have telephoned Schnee and to have said: 'Well, they dispersed you, eh! I fixed that for you!'

STATES OF CONCERN

Juri Lina is another Soviet ufologist who sent UFO reports to the West. These mirror the characteristics of typical cases elsewhere, including close encounters. However, Lina also suffered. Indeed, he claimed he was persecuted because of his activities and eventually managed to escape by entering into an arranged marriage with a Finnish ufologist. Although he went to live in Finland, Lina returned to the USSR to lecture about UFOs and, he said, the KGB continued to watch him closely. Thus the only realistic conclusion about ufology in the USSR is that it has been seen as dangerous, and therefore must be of great interest to the government.

The Australian authorities, on the other hand, seem only too eager to give researchers unlimited access to their UFO files. In late 1981, ufologist Bill Chalker was suddenly given the opportunity to see those UFO reports then in the possession of the Royal Australian Air Force (RAAF). During 1982, Chalker took up the offer with enthusiasm: he was even allowed to copy whatever he wanted – although, reasonably enough, he was required to sign a waiver to guarantee the confidentiality of the witnesses involved. No other restrictions were imposed.

The cases reported in the RAAF files apparently gave rise to the official pronouncement that 'nothing that has arisen from the three or four per cent of unexplained cases gives any firm support for the belief that interlopers from other places in the world, or outside it, have been visiting us'. However, according to Bill Chalker, many of the cases were extremely provocative.

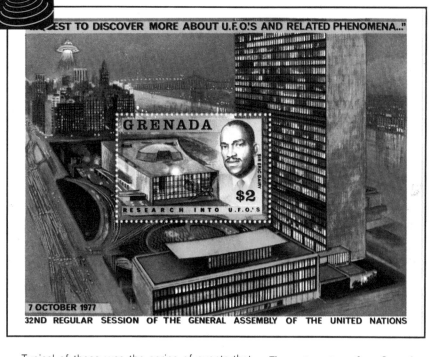

"...EST TO DISCOVER MORE ABOUT U.F.O.'S AND RELATED PHENOMENA..."

7 OCTOBER 1977

32ND REGULAR SESSION OF THE GENERAL ASSEMBLY OF THE UNITED NATIONS

Typical of these was the series of events that took place around Brisbane airport on 4 November 1976. Ground staff saw a pulsing light in the sky, and the crew of an *Elektra* transport aircraft observed the same object keeping pace with them before moving off southwards at one-and-a-half times their speed. A commercial jet was also 'paced', and a nearby light aircraft reported a close encounter. Both local weather radar and the airport radar tracked an unidentified object that seemed to match the sightings. The conclusion of the report in the RAAF files was that the light was most probably the planet Venus and that the radar returns were 'ships at sea', although the pilots all refuted the suggestion that they had been 'paced' by a planet, and the highly experienced radar operators said that they had never before picked up echoes from ships.

The RAAF had pursued the usual official line of enquiry, based entirely on concern over a possible threat to national defence. No scientific study was undertaken. Significantly, the files contain memoranda suggesting that some RAAF personnel were aware that a cover-up would be suspected. One of them says: 'We only foster the incorrect (but nevertheless widely held) belief that we have much vital information to hide.'

Chalker concluded that the openness of the assistance offered and the contents of the files themselves militate against the idea of an official cover-up. In fact, the files show that the RAAF was as puzzled as anyone else about the phenomenon; and there are many other cases, Chalker pointed out, that do not appear in the RAAF files – some of which 'are at the very least highly provocative'.

In 1981, Australia passed its own Freedom of Information Act; and, as a consequence, the official files were opened to Chalker. But perhaps such apparent openness may be merely an attempt to discourage ufologists to investigate further.

If one looks at the official changes of attitude to UFOs since the 1970s, a clear pattern seems to emerge. Spain released its files to interested parties in 1976; the so-called Blue Book documents

The postage stamp from Grenada, above, clearly shows its government's interest in UFOs.

Bill Chalker, below, was actually offered top secret UFO documents by his government – but why?

were made accessible to the American public in 1977; France set up an official UFO study group, which made some interesting statements, in the late 1970s; and in 1981, Australia opened up its files. Then, in 1982, Britain announced that its UFO files would be made public. In every case, the country concerned had maintained for years that UFOs did not exist, or that no such files had been kept.

PUBLIC REASSURANCE

All of this may, of course, simply be a coincidence. And perhaps such movies as *Close Encounters of the Third Kind* created such a sense of unease in the public mind that governments felt compelled to reassure people that there was, in fact, no sinister cover-up, releasing their files for public scrutiny. That may not be the whole story, however.

The fact that governments all over the world have kept records of UFO cases – and some of them spent vast sums of money on official studies – attests to the mystery surrounding the phenomenon. What is more, the fact that no government in the world has claimed to have solved the enigma must surely be significant.

One extraordinary explanation of the official attitude to UFOs was put forward by the Earl of Clancarty – otherwise known as the UFO writer Brinsley le Poer Trench – who believed that there has, indeed, been a world-wide UFO cover-up, but that it is gradually being replaced by a subtle 'UFO education' programme of which few people are aware. Lord Clancarty asserted that we are being conditioned to accept the truth. Indeed, perhaps enormously popular movies such as *E.T., The Extra-Terrestrial*, in which the alien is presented as extremely lovable, are part of such an education campaign. If it succeeds, then nobody will fear UFOs any more.

But if this is true, what are we being prepared for? Lord Clancarty – together with an increasing number of other ufologists – also voiced the suspicion that UFOs represent the real rulers of this planet. Such a revelation could not be sprung on the world without the most appalling panic – hence the need for the re-education programme.

If this is indeed the real reason for the curiously inconsistent behaviour of the world governments over the UFO issue, then they have an unenviable task ahead of them – that of ensuring that the millions of people on Earth, of widely different cultures, are prepared to receive the greatest news story ever. The world certainly has a right to know the truth about UFOs, be it disappointingly mundane or as astoundingly significant as Lord Clancarty's theory suggests. The evidence seems to point to a move towards discovering the truth. Perhaps the days of the cover-up are nearly over.

❚❚ WHAT IS MORE, THE FACT THAT NO GOVERNMENT IN THE WORLD HAS CLAIMED TO SOLVE THE ENIGMA MUST SURELY BE SIGNIFICANT. ❚❚

The illustration above shows
The Creation, from the
frontispiece of the Luther Bible
of 1534: 'In the beginning God
created the Heaven and the Earth.'
The modern scientific explanation
of the origin of the Universe
dispenses with the notion of a
Creator. Yet certain features of
the Universe suggest that it was
designed by an intelligent being
for intelligent beings to live in.

Natural theology – the attempt to prove the existence of God by argument from the observed features of nature, rather than from appeal to faith – is rather out of favour nowadays. The successes of science have encouraged the conviction that all facts about the world are to be explained as the outcome of forces operating blindly and automatically since the beginning of time, not as parts of a plan executed by a divine architect. Nevertheless, certain developments in modern cosmology actually make it look as if, when the mechanism of the Universe was set running, it was delicately adjusted with the interests of its future inhabitants in mind. Indeed, the physical world looks suspiciously as if it had been intended as a home for us, or at least for intelligent life of some kind. This idea, too loose to be called a scientific theory, now goes under the general name of the 'anthropic principle' (from the Greek *anthropos*, meaning 'human being'). And it could well lead to a revival of interest in natural theology.

LIFE IN THE BALANCE

Clearly, human life depends on many delicately balanced features of the environment. If the Earth were a little closer to the Sun, for instance, it would be too hot for life, and there would be no liquid water here. If it were a little farther away, it would be too cold, and any water that existed would be in the form of ice. In either case, it is almost impossible that any but the simplest organisms could appear on Earth. Again, without a protective layer of ozone in the upper atmosphere, the surface of the Earth would be subjected to bombardment by cosmic radiation, and in this situation it is inconceivable that life could ever have spread from the protection of the oceans on to the land.

But fortunate though such facts are for us, they do not constitute concrete evidence for any kind of design, for it can be argued that such circumstances are almost bound to occur somewhere among the 100,000 million stars that make up our Galaxy – let alone the billions of other galaxies. Doubtless, in this immensity, there are many planets suitable for life – but, so the argument goes, they are the ones that chance has favoured, far outnumbered by the ones that were not so fortunate.

But some of the remarkable facts that favour the existence of intelligent life are of a different kind. In the light of our present knowledge, it now looks like tremendous luck that galaxies, stars and planets were born at all – that the Universe did not remain a chaos of diffuse gas. And given that, at its birth, conditions were just right to permit the appearance of galaxies and the subsequent formation of stars, it seems like a further stroke of luck that the Universe was sufficiently long-lived to give intelligent life time to evolve. Still further coincidences – if that is what they are – are responsible for the existence of elements such as carbon, upon which life depends.

THE
SUCCESSFUL UNIVERSE

Such 'lucky' facts as these apply to the whole Universe, not just to some remote corner of it, such as planet Earth. And they raise the question of why the Universe should be the way it is, rather than taking another form that is less favourable to us. To appreciate our good fortune fully, however, we need to know a little about the history of the Universe.

Cosmologists now agree that the Universe was probably created in a single 'big bang' between 10 and 15 billion years ago. (One billion here means one thousand million.) Of what came before – if there was any 'before' – or what the first instants were like, we know nothing: but one hundredth of a second after the beginning, it has been calculated that the temperature was about 180 billion degrees F (100 billion degrees C). The density of matter was over 3 billion times that of water, while electromagnetic radiation was compressed into a 'soup' nearly a billion times as dense as water.

All the matter we can see today with our most powerful telescopes – that is, out to a distance of about 10 billion light years – was squeezed down into a volume less than one light-year across. This tightly packed matter was expanding as it blasted outwards, and the temperature and density fell. After 700,000 years, the Universe consisted of a thin gas, about 75 per cent hydrogen and 25 per cent helium, and was still expanding.

LUMPS IN THE UNIVERSE

At some point, the gas broke up into galaxy-sized lumps, each of which started to fall together under its own gravity. Luckily for us, the early Universe, though uniform, was not too 'smooth' – if it had been, the gas would never have broken up into galaxies. Fortunately, too, there was just enough 'lumpiness' – patches of matter of greater density – to trigger the formation of galaxies. Smaller lumps within each of these proto-galaxies shrank under gravity, releasing heat and becoming stars. These victories of gravity over the general expansion were purely local, however; and while numbers of galaxies grouped themselves into stable clusters, the clusters continued to recede from one other, as indeed they still do today.

The balance between the strength of gravity, the overall density of matter, and the rate of expansion of the early Universe was also fortunate for us. Had the expansion rate been a little too low (or to put it another way, had the density of matter and radiation been a little too high), the Universe would have stopped expanding and would have collapsed back on itself in a matter of some hundreds of millions of years – not long enough, as far as we can estimate, for intelligent life to evolve. And if the expansion rate had been too high (or the density too low), gravity could not have caused concentrations of matter to form into galaxies and stars. Such variations in the balance of forces, with their huge implications for the possibility of intelligent life in the Universe, depend on an infinitesimal adjustment of the density of matter during the first fractions of a second of the existence of the Universe. In other words, matter emerged from the big bang with just the right combination of density and speed of expansion to ensure that there would be the opportunity for intelligent beings to evolve.

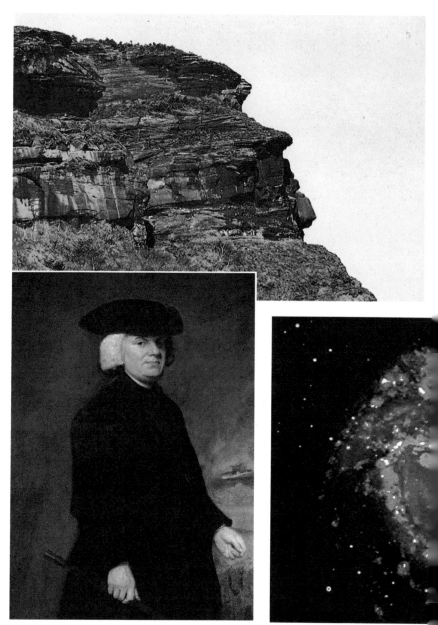

The profile of the rock formation at Helsby Hill, Cheshire, England, top, is so like a face that it is difficult to believe that it was formed by the natural forces of wind and weather. One of the popular 'proofs' of the existence of God in the 18th century was advanced with some force by Archbishop William Paley, above. Essentially, it stated that the very existence of the world implies it was designed by an intelligent force. But however miraculous the existence of the world may be, scientists argue, it is quite possible that, like Helsby Hill, it is here merely as a result of chance.

There is one more of these hair-fine 'adjustments' of the primordial Universe on which our existence depends. There seems to have been the minimum possible amount of turbulence, or swirling, in the expanding matter. If there had been any appreciable turbulence, it would have been evened out in the course of expansion; but as it did so, heat would have been generated – or alternatively, the cooling of the Universe would have been retarded. In either event, the result would be much the same today: the Universe would be a far hotter place, and intense 'background radiation' would fill intergalactic space. If the theories of the cosmologists are right, even a tiny amount of initial turbulence would lead to a colossally high temperature – far above, say, the boiling point of water – making life quite impossible anywhere.

When the first stars were born, conditions of the earlier Universe were duplicated within each one – but now heavier nuclei were built up. The most massive stars ran through their life cycles rapidly – in mere millions of years – and built up the whole range of stable nuclei. They then ended their lives

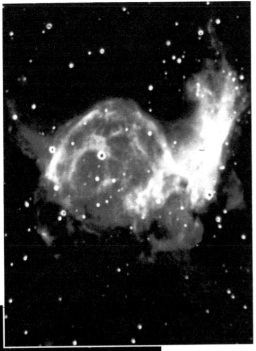

The nebula NGC 2359, left, is a cloud of gas surrounding a group of young stars. The gas contains elements essential to life, such as carbon, derived from the supernovae of other stars.

That galaxies, such as M83, below left, exist at all is the result of an extraordinarily fine adjustment in the events immediately after the 'big bang'. The expanding matter, below (1), developed 'lumps' that condensed into galaxies. If the rate of expansion had been too great, this condensation would not have taken place (2); while if it had been too small, the Universe would have stopped expanding and collapsed back on itself (3).

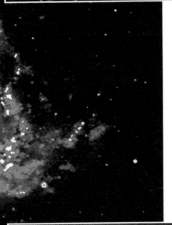

in supernovae explosions that scattered the newly created elements – notably those necessary for life, such as carbon, oxygen and nitrogen – through the galaxies to which they belonged. These elements were incorporated into planetary systems as they were formed from the swirling discs of gas surrounding the stars.

A further stroke of good fortune was pointed out by the astrophysicist Sir Fred Hoyle in a characteristically perceptive observation. Carbon is formed in the centres of stars in a two-step process: first, two helium nuclei collide to form a nucleus of beryllium; after a while, if this survives, another helium nucleus collides with this and forms the carbon nucleus. The success of that second step depends on the energy of the helium nuclei being just right: if they move too fast or too slowly, they are not likely to fuse with the beryllium nucleus and, since the latter is short-lived, the chances of carbon forming would be lost. As it happens – or perhaps as some intelligent agency intended – the temperatures in the centres of large stars are close to the optimum for the second step of the carbon-building process.

There is yet another piece of what appears to be luck here. Once formed, the carbon nucleus does not readily combine with helium nuclei to form heavier elements, so the stock of carbon nuclei is not depleted.

VITAL HYDROGEN

Neither of these happy coincidences would occur if the strength of the 'strong' force, which binds protons and neutrons together in nuclei, were only a few per cent different from what it is. Furthermore, if the strong nuclear force were only slightly stronger than it is, the matter that emerged from the first few minutes of the 'big bang' would not have consisted predominantly of hydrogen, with a small fraction of helium: all the protons and neutrons would have been built up into helium. With virtually no hydrogen in the Universe, there could be no water, which consists of hydrogen and oxygen; and, of course, as far as we know, water is essential to life. Stars that were 100 per cent helium when they began their lives would also have completed their life cycles so quickly that there might not have been time for life to evolve on their planets either.

Certain reactions among elementary particles take place through the action of the 'weak' nuclear force; and it is in connection with neutrino reactions that the weak force vitally affects the possibilities

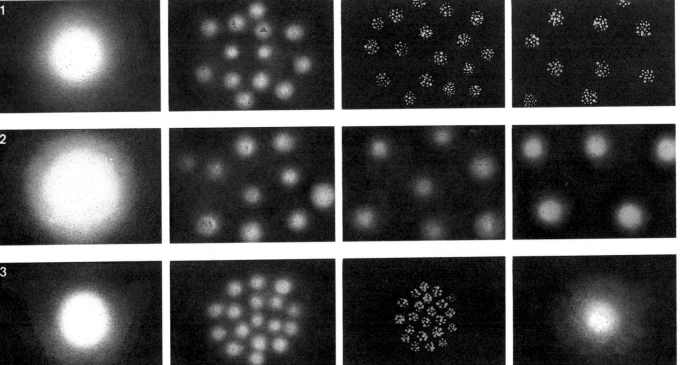

The powers by which carbon is formed in the nuclei of stars is shown below right. The entire phenomenon of life on Earth is based on carbon – but it is an extraordinary coincidence that carbon exists at all. It is formed when two helium nuclei collide to form a beryllium nucleus which then collides with another helium nucleus. The success of this operation depends on the temperature at the centre of the star being just right.

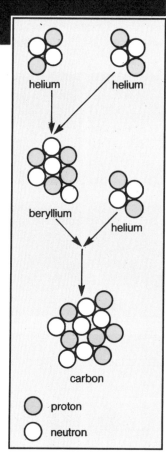

helium   helium

beryllium

helium

carbon

○ proton
○ neutron

for life. Neutrinos are the chargeless, probably massless, particles that pervade the Universe. At the end of its life, a large star begins to run out of nuclear fuel to support its own huge weight. It progressively shrinks, and then suddenly implodes catastrophically. The matter at the centre vanishes into a black hole, and a flood of neutrinos is released. These 'ghosts' of the nuclear world are produced in such enormous numbers, and the matter inside the star is so dense – denser than the matter of the Universe after its first hundredth of a second – that the neutrinos significantly interact with the matter. The outer layers of the star, rich in the heavy elements, are next torn off in a giant supernova.

If the weak force were slightly weaker than it is, the star would not be disrupted and the elements essential to life would not be scattered through interstellar space. And if the weak force were slightly stronger, the neutrinos would not succeed in escaping from the star's core in sufficient numbers to disrupt the outer layers, and again the heavier elements would remain trapped inside the star. In either case, the result would be a Universe in which the development of intelligent life was simply not possible.

But research might, of course, take a different direction: for it might be that the coincidences are exactly that – that they are as arbitrary as they seem to some, and that the whole of the Universe known to us is indeed the result of happy chance. That would imply that there could be other universes in which the dice did not fall so fortunately and in which life might never have emerged.

DEATH AND REBIRTH

One suggestion is that the Universe dies and is reborn repeatedly, for ever. The density of the Universe is unknown: if it is sufficiently great, the force of gravity will be sufficiently strong to bring the receding galaxies to a stop and then pull them back in towards each other until they vanish in a 'big crunch', like a reverse performance of the 'big bang'. This would presumably be followed by another explosion and the birth of another universe. But, this time, the fundamental forces of nature might not be as finely balanced – so that, for example, no stars might be formed from the interstellar gas, or else they might appear but carbon might fail to be formed in the nuclear furnaces. But this universe, too, would collapse, and a new one would be born. So the cycle would continue, universe following universe to eternity, the overwhelming majority of them never witnessing the birth of intelligent life. But in an infinitesimal number of them, conditions would be so finely balanced that observers could appear and wonder at their good fortune.

But an even more astonishing theory has been put forward to explain the fact that the Universe has been designed with the emergence of intelligent life in mind. According to this, the 'unsuccessful' universes – in which conditions are not right for life – are to be found, not in the past or future, but co-existing in parallel with the Universe we know, as proposed by American physicist Hugh Everett.

This many-worlds theory has been developed by a number of cosmologists as an alternative to the assumption that the world was designed by an intelligent being for other intelligent beings to live in. For although it may be true that the Universe was set in motion by a divine contriver, scientists agree that it would be abandoning the very idea of scientific explanation to admit, at the very foundation of our concept of the Universe, an assumption that is not itself understandable in terms of science.

ALTHOUGH ROMAN CATHOLICISM IS NOMINALLY THE PREVAILING RELIGION OF BRAZIL, LIFE THERE EVEN TODAY IS INTERWOVEN WITH THE PAGAN AND MAGICAL ELEMENTS OF ANCIENT SPIRIT CULTS THAT ARE AFRICAN IN ORIGIN

A massive statue of Christ, left, towers over Rio de Janeiro. Although Brazil's official religion is Roman Catholicism, many of the country's inhabitants also adhere to the beliefs of Macumba, the Brazilian form of voodoo. Rio's Copacabana beach, below, is both a pleasure resort and the scene of many Macumba rites, such as the one shown here in honour of the African sea goddess Yemanja.

Brazil has a population of around 145 million and is often described as the world's largest Catholic country. Nominally this is true: almost every child born in the country is baptised, and most Brazilians receive the last rites of the Church when they are mortally ill and, after death, a Catholic funeral. But while the Catholic churches are often crowded, the voodoo temples of *Candomblé*, *Umbanda* and other Afro-American spirit religions (in Brazil, collectively referred to as *Macumba*) are more crowded still.

The practice of *Macumba* rituals is widespread throughout the country and does not take place only inside temples. *Macumba* ceremonies are performed in isolated clearings in the the Amazonian jungle, at crossroads (traditionally, as in Europe, popular places for magic rites), and even on Rio de Janeiro's famous Copacabana beach, which is one of the world's most popular pleasure spots.

This dual role of Copacabana beach aptly illustrates the powerful hold that Afro-American religion and magic have on Brazilian life. By day, the beach is packed with sunbathing tourists; by night, it is thronged with *Macumbistas* worshipping a host of exotic gods and demons, and casting spells designed to obtain love, money or power, or even the death of an enemy.

On New Year's Eve, Copacabana is the site of a maior *Macumba* festival combining secular, religious and magical elements, at which the gods of pagan Africa are worshipped, together with the Catholic saints with whom they are identified. The principal object of adoration, however, is the African sea goddess Yemanja, who is often identified with the Virgin Mary.

DRUMMING UP THE SPIRITS

Yemanja was brought to Brazil by Yoruba slaves from the area of Africa that is now Nigeria. In Yoruba mythology, Yemanja was the daughter of heaven and earth. She married her brother, and then coupled with her son, who fathered on her a whole tribe of gods and goddesses, among them Shango, the god of storm and thunder (identified by *Macumbistas* with St John the Baptist); Ogun, the god of war and iron-working; and Orishako, a peasant god who rules over agriculture and female fertility. The name Yemanja is derived from the Yoruba words for 'mother' and 'fish': she is the 'mother of all fish' and therefore queen of the ocean and everything under and upon it. For this reason, her chief festival is held on the seashore, and the offerings dedicated to her are glven to the sea.

As sunset approaches on 31 December, *Macumbistas* make their way individually or in small groups to Copacabana beach. Some come on foot, some in cars (many of *Macumba*'s devotees belong to the prosperous middle classes). And since the New Year's Eve festival is of national significance, many more come in motor coaches from temples hundreds of miles away.

The worshippers are mostly dressed in white – Yemanja's favourite colour – and they carry candles and gifts to be offered to the goddess. Each devotee places lighted candles in a previously dug hole that is carefully walled with sand as a protection against the wind. The offerings – which can take many forms, including mirrors, bottles of scent, hair ribbons or, in the case of prosperous businessmen, expensive bottles of imported Bourbon – are placed nearby.

Each devotee then looks fixedly into the flames of the flickering candles and asks Yemanja for some favour. The more candles there are, the better: it seems that either Yemanja likes the smell of burning wax, or she wants her worshippers to spend as much money as possible to show their devotion.

On Copacabana beach at night, top, a priestess dedicates flowers, clothing and other items to Yemanja before consigning them to the waves.

David St Clair, above, was the victim of 'closing the paths', a particular technique of Quimbanda black magic.

At the Saida dos Santos ceremony, which celebrates the 'leaving of the saints', left, a dancer dressed in rich ceremonial robes represents the voodoo deity Oxum.

Whether the number of candles offered is odd or even is also important. If the devotee wants some material benefit, such as a wage increase or a new car, he must burn an even number of candles: for something to do with the emotions, such as a love affair or a better relationship with one's neighbours, the number must be odd. If the candles burn to extinction or are swept out to sea by the incoming tide, it is a sign the wish will be granted. If, however, they are blown out by the wind, the omen is unfavourable.

ORGIASTIC DANCE

As the myriads of candles are lit, the *Macumba* drums start to sound, and the dancing begins. At first, only a few people dance, rather mechanically, as if performing a necessary but boring duty. But as the evening wears on, the numbers increase, and a frenzied, almost orgiastic, quality becomes apparent. Eventually, as in the voodoo celebrations of Haiti, some of the dancers enter a trance state and become possessed: the gods descend and 'mount their horses'.

As in Haiti, those who are possessed seem to lose all consciousness of their own identity. When they return to normal consciousness, they cannot remember what happened during trance. Out of the great number of dancers on the beach, only a few will achieve this state: nevertheless, it is possible for the interested onlooker to move through the crowds and meet many members of the *Macumba* pantheon, such as the god of war, the god of thunder, 'the Old Black Slave' (a supernatural being, renowned for his powers of healing), or Exu, a sinister entity who is the nearest *Macumba* equivalent to Satan.

In due time, the tide sweeps away Yemanja's gifts, the entranced dancers return to normal consciousness, the worshippers make their way homewards, and the festival is over for another year.

But the New Year's Eve festival at Copacabana is no mere anachronistic survival from a past age of slavery and superstition. Belief in the existence of the spirit world is alive and well at every level of

Brazilian society. Peasants, factory hands, bankers and politicians – almost all believe in gods, demons and supernatural powers, even if they are not prepared to admit it to sceptical foreigners. This widespread acceptance of the supernatural would seem to extend even to such a prosaic institution as the Brazilian Post Office. In 1957 and 1964, it issued pictorial stamps in honour of *The Spirits' Book* and *The Gospel According to Spiritism*, both works by Allan Kardec, the founding father and first theoretician of Spiritism.

Kardec's Spiritism incorporates a belief in reincarnation, and its influence on *Macumba* varies from group to group. Some temples conduct ceremonies that are almost completely 'Kardecised'. When the devotees are in a state of trance, they follow a Europeanised pattern of behaviour and their actions are quite as restrained and unalarming as those of any French or English Spiritualist medium. In other temples that are less influenced by Kardec, however, those possessed by the gods will engage in remarkable and spectacular activities that are seen by the onlookers as evidence of genuine control by otherworldly beings. Such activities have been seen to include walking on broken bottles, inserting large needles into the cheeks, fire-eating, and drinking whole bottles of raw cane spirit within the space of a few minutes, all apparently without any untoward effect.

Yet manifestations of this kind are not as uncontrolled as they may appear. *Macumba* ceremonies follow a pattern that is quite as predictable, in terms of its own conventions, as any Christian service.

Brazilian **Macumba** *ceremonies are folk rituals in which all present participate to some degree. At the climax of a festival,* **above,** *dancers are seen prostrating themselves.*

The young girl, **below,** *dances vigorously in a trance to rhythmic hand-clapping and music played on simple instruments.*

Stylised drum rhythms, dancing, a charged atmosphere of religious expectation, and the practice of deliberate over-breathing (which produces changes in brain chemistry) induce a near-hypnotic state in all the participants. Finally, when the high priestess calls down the gods, the dancers stop moving one by one. Some of them bend down, and then straighten up, often with a scream, in a trance, supposedly possessed by a divinity.

CLOSING THE PATHS

But as in Haiti, so in Brazil there is a darker side to spirit religion. This is *Quimbanda*, an evil voodoo in which practitioners work black magic against their own and, for a fee, their clients' enemies. A favourite technique of *Quimbanda* is 'closing the paths'. This involves casting a spell that blocks the victim's progress to personal happiness. The person who has been subjected to this finds that love and financial matters cause nothing but trouble, that his physical and mental health deteriorate, and that problems arise for him in even the most ordinary everyday affairs.

The American writer David St Clair seems to have been the victim of just such a psychic attack during the time he lived in Brazil. First, his girlfriend left him, and money he was expecting did not arrive. Then, legal difficulties arose over an inheritance, and he contracted malaria. He attributed all this misfortune to nothing more sinister than bad luck – until, that is, a Brazilian friend, a *Macumbista* who claimed to have psychic powers, told him that 'his paths had been closed' by *Quimbanda*.

At first, St Clair thought this was superstitious nonsense. Soon afterwards, however, he received a message from a Spiritualist source: his maid, Edna, had employed black magic against him. Each week, it was alleged, she took an item of his clothing to a *Quimbanda* ceremony. There, it was buried while 'crossing spells' were chanted and ceremonial candles burned around it. In addition, said the Spiritualist, Edna was adding a magical 'closing powder' to his food. St Clair was still sceptical, but he had seen too many strange things in Brazil to discount completely the idea that black magic was being used against him. He decided to fight fire with fire, and to attend a *Macumba* ceremony himself, so that he could consult one of the possessed.

The votive offerings, right, have been dedicated to a deity to effect a cure. The images themselves (such as the feet and breast in the foreground), or a mark on an image, indicate the parts of the body that need to be healed.

The first part of the ceremony he attended followed the conventional pattern of drumming, dancing and possession. But then something extraordinary happened. The priestess, who was wearing the customary *Macumba* vestments and regalia – a spotlessly white blouse and skirt with a gold cross at her breast – suddenly left the temple. When she returned a few minutes later, her appearance was completely different. She was clad in filthy red satin tatters; and in place of the golden cross was the skull of a human infant, its jaws tied together with black tape, a dead snake wreathed between the staring eye sockets.

Rituals and dances often take place at night and can last for hours. Fatigue is evident on the faces of the followers, below, who urge on dancers with their rhythmic clapping.

Laughing insanely, the priestess seized a bottle of rum, gulped half of it down, and announced that she was Exu, the *Macumba* equivalent of Satan.

A long conversation ensued between St Clair, 'Exu' and two mediums, one of whom was possessed by 'Satan's dog'. Eventually 'Exu', who claimed he sometimes did good as well as evil, told St Clair: 'The curse has been lifted, and will come down doubly on the person who placed it on you.'

Within a few days 'the paths opened' for St Clair. His psychological attitude changed for the better and, perhaps because he no longer expected the worst, his health, finances and love-life all improved. Possession of a priestess by a voodoo deity had transformed his outlook on life.

This, perhaps, is the real power of voodoo, *Macumba* and other Afro-American spirit religions. Indeed, it is possible that possession by the gods offers the devotee something of greater therapeutic value to a diseased psyche than do orthodox Western remedies.

" Brazil has made a name for itself in recent years as a land of paranormal phenomena... It might be helpful for visitors to have signs put up outside São Paulo's Congonhas airport such as: Warning! You Are Entering a Poltergeist Zone, Materialisations Twice Nightly, or simply Welcome to the Capital of ESP. "

Guy Playfair, The Flying Cow

OF THE HUNDREDS OF MILLIONS OF CHINESE ALIVE TODAY, IT WOULD BE ODD IF SOME DID NOT DISPLAY UNUSUAL TALENTS. BUT IS IT TRUE, FOR INSTANCE, THAT STRANGELY GIFTED CHILDREN CAN READ USING THEIR EARS, OR EVEN OTHER PARTS OF THEIR BODIES?

A 12-year-old Chinese boy called Tang Yu was playing one day when he stumbled against a bystander. The boy said that, although only his ear touched the man's pocket, he was able to 'read' the brand name on a packet of *Flying Wild Goose* cigarettes in his breast pocket. To test the boy's claim, another man wrote a word on a sheet of paper and then crumpled it into a ball. The boy placed the wad of paper next to his ear and, after a while, was able to tell the man what he had written on it.

The local paper, the *Sichuan Daily*, published an article about Tang Yu's talent in March 1979. But it was severely criticised in Peking for publishing 'unscientific nonsense', and the mass media were advised to refrain from following up similar stories. One paper even accused little Tang Yu of sneaking a look when he performed these feats. It was recalled that a similar stir had been caused in the 1940s when the Chinese press carried a story about a girl, also in Sichuan, who was capable of surviving

THE SEEING EAR

without food for several months. The story proved to be a fake: the girl was eating in secret.

This time, however, once the first report had gained currency, many others began to surface in different parts of the country. The political climate in China was right for speculation about the world of the paranormal: there was widespread talk of seeking truth empirically and not blindly following the party line.

Most of the reports that emerged involved children who supposedly were able to 'read' not only with their ears but with the tops of their heads, their armspits, pigtails, buttocks, feet and so on. Many of the children were also said to have more than one such paranormal faculty. A 25-year-old woman, it was claimed, could read simultaneously and without confusion with five parts of her body; and a girl of nine was said to be able to read with any of 10 different parts of her body.

The front cover of the Chinese journal Nature *of April 1980, above, shows just some of the children said to be able to see with their ears, fingers and even their armpits. This trend in psychic abilities began in 1979 when 12-year-old Tang Yu (bottom right of picture) stumbled against a bystander and found he could read the name on a cigarette packet in the man's jacket pocket – with his ear. It seems that Chinese scientists are taking such claims seriously and are strenuously investigating them under strict laboratory conditions.*

Chinese historians found similar reports in classic works written over 2,000 years ago. The Shanghai scientific journal *Nature* argued the validity of such phenomena in a series of 10 articles; and for the rest of the year, ESP became a major topic of conversation, not only in tea house gossip, but also within the country's leading scientific and medical research establishments.

In an effort to determine the validity of these claims, scientists performed hundreds of tests on these children. The most elaborate were organised in Shanghai by *Nature* from 4 to 10 February 1980. There were 14 subjects, aged between 9 and 25, who were tested before 10 audiences, totalling more than 2,000 scientists, doctors, teachers and journalists, and the proceedings were filmed by the Shanghai Science and Education Studio. There was a holiday atmosphere at the tests, coinciding as they did with the Chinese spring festival.

113

The test subjects were seated in the centre of the hall. Behind each of them stood a monitor to minimize the possibility of trickery. Members of the audience left the hall, wrote words or pictures on sheets of paper, folded the papers, placed them in heavy paper bags or plastic boxes, and then returned to the hall where they presented them to the children, who examined them using their own particular methods. The expressions of the children differed widely: some closed their eyes, some bowed their heads, others smiled or looked shy.

Little Jiang Yan was the star of the test on 6 February. Her performance almost brought the house down, according to the report in the Hong Kong newspaper *Ta Kung Pao* for 31 July 1980. Her clear Peking accent rang from the loudspeakers: 'Mine is a cluster of yellow bananas painted on a green background!' She had 'read' this picture with the tip of her finger, with which she was allowed to feel about in a cloth sleeve. The six children tested on that day were given three papers each to 'read': the results were 17 correct out of 18.

TELEPATHIC ARMPITS?

Much attention was also focused on two young Peking sisters, Wang Qiang and Wang Bin. Not only could they read with their ears and armpits, but if one sister placed a message under her armpit, the other could read it telepathically.

In addition to being tested before large audiences, the 14 youngsters were also examined by a team of 30 experts and scholars in various fields. Some had been sceptics before the tests, but changed their minds afterwards. Among the converted was Wu Xueyu, director of the Eye, Ear, Nose and Throat Hospital of the Shanghai No 1 Medical College. 'I surrender,' said the 70-year-old doctor. 'There is no arguing with facts.'

The Chinese-American physicist Dr Chih Kung Jen was among a team of specialists who conducted tests on 12 psychic children in the autumn of

Could the ear, above, really be capable of vision? Or is it more likely that form of telepathy is involved?

1980. A 98 per cent accuracy in 'reading' concealed messages with parts of the bodies was achieved. When holding the wrapped paper, he said, 'the children told us they experienced both a warmth and a tingling sensation in their hands – like pin-pricks – and that the sensation travelled along the nerve lines of their bodies to their heads.'

A number of scientists involved in the tests had some singularly unenlightening ideas to offer by way of explanation, according to Meng Dongming, a reporter with the official *Worker's Daily*: 'Most researchers tend to the idea that the skin of people with these sorts of abilities gives off a certain kind of radiation which can pass through objects and relay information back to the body for interpretation by the brain.' He quoted a professor as saying that the basis of the strange powers was that 'thoughts have substance'.

Chen Shouliang, Dean of Natural Sciences at Peking University, studied a group comprising 40 children around the age of 10, who had been picked at random. He found that he was able to develop extra-sensory powers in 16 of them; and concluded that extra-sensory perception is in fact a latent human ability that can be brought to the fore.

Professor Wang Chu, deputy director of the Department of Radio Engineering at the same university, reported on the descriptions given by the children he had studied with Chen Shouliang. At first, the children said, the images appear in their minds as a disordered jumble of dots and lines, which gradually rearrange themselves until the pictures become clear to them. According to Chen and Wang's study, the faster this process takes place, the more likely the child is to get the correct answer. The process generally speeds up as the child becomes more experienced in the use of the special sense, and is also influenced to a degree by the state of the child's health.

When the sisters Wang Qiang and Wang Bin returned to Peking after the Shanghai tests, the Traditional Chinese Medicine Institute arranged for

Tu Ping and Tu An, a sister and brother who attended a primary school near Wuhan University, are shown, right, taking part in an eyeless-sight experiment. With their sight effectively blocked out, they were asked to read objects at a distance and showed marked telepathic abilities. Here, Tu Ping gleefully describes the target object – only five seconds after the beginning of the experiment.

an expert in *Qigong* to train them. *Qigong* is, literally, '*ch'i* work' – *ch'i* meaning 'breath', 'inner power', or non-muscular energy. It is this energy that flows along the acupuncture meridians, and is developed by practitioners of the 'internal schools' of martial arts, the most well-known of which is *t'ai chi chuan*. *Ch'i* masters are said to have extraordinary powers – 'rooting' themselves to the ground and thus resisting massive efforts to push them over; repulsing attacks by means of an invisible force; transmitting a surge of energy, resembling electricity, or a strong magnetic attraction; and so on. One master, out walking in the street with a friend, is said to have been hit in the back by a pedicab, which rebounded 10 feet (3 metres) and tipped over. The master, without a break in the conversation, walked on as if nothing at all had happened. There are also accounts of masters projecting *ch'i* beyond the body in order to ring bells and snuff out candles at a distance. Was this power perhaps used by two girls in Yunnan Province, discovered at the beginning of 1981, who allegedly could make tree branches break and flowers bloom?

> **"** IN FEBRUARY 1981... I ATTENDED A SCIENTIFIC CONFERENCE IN SHANGHAI... IN ONE DEMONSTRATION... A 12-YEAR-OLD BOY SHOWED US HE COULD USE HIS MIND POWER TO MAKE A WATCH OR CLOCK RUN FASTER OR SLOWER AT WILL. A 12-YEAR-OLD GIRL, NAMED CHEN YI, OPENED A LOCK WHICH HAD BEEN SEALED INSIDE A BOX ALONG WITH ITS KEY... **"**

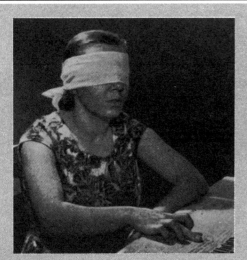

*In*Focus

THE FINGERTIP TEST

The ability to 'see' with parts of the body conventionally reserved for other functions is accepted as real by many scientists in the CIS (Commonwealth of Independent States, formerly the Soviet Union). Like Chinese researchers, they have put a great deal of effort into studying the faculty, and there have been public demonstrations by gifted people. One of the most famous is Rosa Kuleshova, who is allegedly able to recognise colours through her fingertips, as demonstrated *right*. She told this to her doctor in her home town of Takil, in the Urals, in 1962; and her demonstration so impressed him that he reported her abilities to colleagues, including Professor Abram Novomeysky, who began to study her intensively. At first, only two fingers of Rosa Kuleshova's right hand were sensitive; but with training, both hands and other parts of her body, including the elbow, became able to 'see'. She became so adept that she could 'read' print blindfolded, as *left*. Even more excitingly, Novomeysky found that many people can develop similar abilities. Some could even begin to distinguish colours within half-an-hour of making their first attempts.

Experiment has ruled out the possibility that skin vision is due to telepathy or clairvoyance. Nor could it be due simply to the different 'feel', in the normal sense, of differently coloured surfaces. Colours could be recognised through a sheet of glass, and some subjects could recognise them when they held their fingers some way above the material being 'viewed'.

Zhen Xiao-hui and her mother, left, pose at their Canton home. The little girl seemed able to read merely with her fingertips.

The group of psychically gifted children from Shanghai, below, demonstrated their bizarre talents to a group of visiting Americans.

States, witnessed many such demonstrations and described his experiences as follows:.

'In February of this year [1981], I attended a scientific conference in Shanghai in which 14 of the children demonstrated their really extraordinary abilities. In one demonstration, a young boy and girl sat holding stems with unopened flower buds in their hands. After about 20 minutes of concentration by these two subjects, these buds opened to reveal yellow blossoms... A 12-year-old boy showed us he could use his mind power to make a watch or clock run faster or slower at will. A 12-year-old girl, named Chen Yi, opened a lock which had been sealed inside a box along with its key. Chen Yi placed her hand upon the sealed box for about 20 minutes, then declared: "The key is now floating inside the box! Now the key is going into the keyhole and is turning the lock over." When the box was opened, the key was indeed in the lock and the lock had been opened...

In the autumn of 1981, the *Shanghai Wenhuibao* quoted Yu Guangyuan, vice-chairman of the National Science Commission, as saying that the

As a result of *Qigong* training, the armpit-reading sisters increased their already remarkable powers so that, during tests, they were able to indicate the location of scars on the body of a fully clothed person, and they successfully described the shape of a pendant hidden under the clothing of another.

Related observations have been reported involving an 11-year-old boy, Xie Zhaohui. Doctors said he had the ability to describe, without touching the mother, the position of a foetus in the later stages of gestation, whether the liver is grossly inflamed as compared with a picture of a normal liver, and whether a fracture is simple or compound.

X-RAY VISION

Another 11-year-old, Wei Ruoyang, appeared to have even more highly developed 'X-ray' vision. 'Researchers took him to a reservoir near Peking and asked him to indicate the location of underground water pipes,' according to Meng Dongming of the *Worker's Daily*.

The places he pointed to corresponded exactly with the locations as they were shown on official maps. Then they took him to the tombs of the Ming Dynasty emperors, situated to the north of Peking, and he correctly pointed to the location of two of the hidden entrances to one of the tombs. He also described the internal arrangements of another of the tombs; but, as the tomb had not been opened by archaeologists, it was not possible to check whether or not he was right.

The *Taiyuan City Daily* reported in March 1981 that over 100 children with unusual powers had been found in the city. The paper claimed that they were capable of the most amazing feats, stating that: 'Some children with supernatural powers develop from being able to read with their ears to having X-ray vision, telepathic powers, telescopic vision, and the ability to open locks, peel oranges, open and close flowers with the power of their thoughts alone.'

Zheng Rongliang, visiting professor of biophysics at Johns Hopkins University in the United

ear-reading (and related) stories were 'ridiculous propaganda' and that such things had long been a popular 'magic trick' in China. It is true that cautious commentators have pointed out that parapsychological researchers must be conversant with the tricks of the illusionist's trade: indeed, if a professional magician can duplicate a feat, then paranormal ability in achieving it cannot be regarded as proved.

On the other hand, is it likely that such a large number of young children from all over China would be skilled in the techniques of the stage magician?

To assess the truth of the bizarre stories that emerged from China until 1981, when the authorities clamped down on them, is even harder than it is in the case of similar reports in the West. In many respects, we must be grateful that we have been allowed even to glimpse this much of paranormal happenings in that country.

PHAETON – THE WORLD THAT NEVER WAS

DOES THE EVIDENCE FIT THE THEORY THAT ASTEROIDS ARE THE REMNANTS OF AN INHABITED PLANET, PHAETON? HERE, WE CRITICALLY EXAMINE THIS THEORY AND SUGGEST THAT THE FUTURE OF THE ASTEROIDS MAY BE AS INTRIGUING AS THEIR PAST

The artist's impression, top, is of a meteorite fall. It has been suggested that, when the planet Phaeton exploded a million years ago, some of the debris fell to Earth as meteorites. But studies have shown that the number of meteorites reaching the Earth has remained roughly constant over the last 3.5 billion years.

The Meteor Crater in Arizona, USA, above, is one of the largest in the world.

In the 19th century, it was believed that, a million years ago, a planet in our solar system, called Phaeton, blew up into the fragments we now call asteroids. It is no longer thought that this planet ever existed, however. So why was the Phaeton theory wrong? There are several reasons. First of all, the asteroids do not move as they would if they had come from a single explosion – and certainly not one that took place as recently, astronomically speaking, as a million years ago. Two pieces of an exploded planet would shoot off in different directions, and follow new orbits about the Sun. And if we draw these new orbits on a plan of the solar system, they will always intersect where the original planet would have been. The asteroid orbits do not intersect at a single point: so they cannot be debris from a single explosion.

The fragments from such an explosion would also have taken up orbits that – although they intersected – would be of different sizes and shapes. So the asteroid belt would, in theory, be a jumble of fragments of different types of rock and metal from different depths below Phaeton's surface. Astronomers roughly guage an asteroid's composition by analysing the way in which it reflects light.

117

Iron asteroids and 'peculiar' asteroids of unidentified composition each make up 10 per cent of asteroid numbers throughout the belt. But the rocky asteroids change systematically: near the inner edge of the belt, light-coloured 'silicaceous' asteroids outnumber the coal-black 'carbonaceous' asteroids by a ratio of three to one: further out, the proportions reverse. However, towards the outer edge, silicaceous asteroids are in the minority, outnumbered four to one by the carbonaceous variety. There is no known way that an explosion could possibly grade the asteroid types so systematically.

DAMNING EVIDENCE

Even more damning for the Phaeton theory, there simply is not enough matter in the asteroid belt to make up a planet anywhere near the size of the Earth. The largest asteroid, Ceres, is 620 miles (1,000 kilometres) across. All the other asteroids together contain no more matter than Ceres itself. Adding them all together would build up a globe 800 miles (1,300 kilometres) across – no larger than India. Such a world could not retain an atmosphere. It would be one third the size of our Moon, and just as barren.

We could, of course, suppose that the planet Phaeton – if it existed – was originally a lot bigger, roughly Earth-sized, and that the rest of it was blown clean away in the titanic explosion. But the asteroids together weigh less than one thousandth of the Earth. Any explosion would therefore have to have had tremendous power to eject 99.9 per cent of the planet's matter at a speed sufficient to throw it out of the solar system, against the Sun's immense gravitational pull.

Indeed, if it had done so, the entire solar system would now be full of chunks of rock, following orbits in as far as Mercury, and out to the distant planets. Even more relevant, if the explosion had indeed been of this magnitude, there would be no distinct asteroid belt.

If the solar system had been filled with such quantities of flying debris, then asteroid-sized chunks of rock and iron would have peppered other planets and gouged out huge craters. The Moon, Mars and Mercury are crater-pocked; but astronomers can date these craters, and all the major ones are more than 50 million years old – most of them dating back billions of years. The Earth certainly was not bombarded by asteroids a million years ago. Even one of the smaller asteroids would have blown a crater the size of Ireland! Detailed studies have also shown that the rate at which large meteorites have hit the inner planets has remained constant for the last 3.5 billion years, and that there was no upsurge a million years ago.

And that is not all. Fragments from an exploded planet would be broken shards, twisted irregular shapes much like shrapnel. But the largest asteroids are round, as spherical as the Moon. Their own

It is thought that many meteorites of the type shown right come from a particularly violent collision between an iron asteroid and a stony one, some 600 million years ago.

The cut surface of an iron meteorite is shown left. Only about 6 per cent of meteorites that reach the Earth are iron.

gravitation is not responsible for this: it does not have the strength to round them off, as Earth's gravity has done. The only reasonable explanation is that the largest asteroids are not fragments of a larger world, but that they built up gradually from smaller bits of rock, never part of a planet.

Two supporters of the Phaeton theory, however, have been Soviet science fiction writer Aleksandr Kazantsev and Professor Felix Zigel. Both believe that pumice and limestone meteorites found on Earth are from the sea-beds of Phaeton, which they claim broke up in a nuclear explosion.

But the evidence of meteorites does not support this claim. Most are small chips from asteroids, and they testify to the non-existence of Phaeton. No 'pumice' and 'limestone' meteorites are known, apart from those that Zigel claims to have studied. The meteorites called carbonaceous chondrites contain simple carbon compounds, but are almost certainly not the remains of living things. What is more, they cannot have originated in an "earth-like" Phaeton, because an oxygen-rich atmosphere like ours soon destroys such compounds.

The meteorites are even more damning in what they do *not* tell us: for instance, they contain no evidence of recent radio-activity. Yet Phaeton was supposed to have been destroyed in the most colossal nuclear explosion of all time – and we all know how much radio-activity a nuclear explosion creates.

Other arguments for Phaeton fare no better. The asteroids are so far from the Sun that any water on them would have been permanently frozen. In such conditions, life could not have arisen. Neither can a nuclear explosion trigger oceans to explode. Hydrogen bombs use heavy hydrogen as their explosive, not the ordinary type that makes up water. If water were a thermo-nuclear explosive, then the famous H-bomb test on Bikini Atoll in 1946 would have taken the entire Pacific with it!

The composition of the asteroids, as shown right, suggests that they could not have been formed from an exploding planet. Eighty per cent are stony (the rest are iron or of unknown composition), but the nature of the rock also varies according to its distance from the Sun. Silicaceous asteroids, light in colour, are predominant at the belt's inner edge. Dark carbonaceous asteroids are more numerous farther out. This regularity suggests an orderly formation: a violent explosion would certainly have jumbled the rock types.

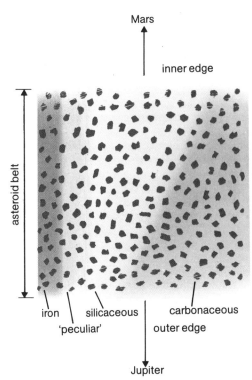

The turbulent cloud belts of Jupiter, right, are seen from the space probe Voyager I. *This giant planet probably attracted most of the material that could have formed a planet between it and Mars. The remainder formed the asteroids.*

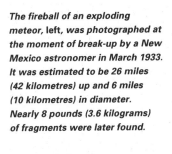

The fireball of an exploding meteor, left, was photographed at the moment of break-up by a New Mexico astronomer in March 1933. It was estimated to be 26 miles (42 kilometres) up and 6 miles (10 kilometres) in diameter. Nearly 8 pounds (3.6 kilograms) of fragments were later found.

Nevertheless, asteroids are interesting – and mysterious – in their own right. No one yet knows why the gap between Mars and Jupiter is filled with blocks of rock, but almost all astronomers agree that they are parts of a planet that never quite made it. In its early days, the solar system must have consisted entirely of such rubble circling the newly-born Sun. Most of the rocks amalgamated with their closest neighbours to build up the planets – from Mercury out to Pluto. In the asteroid region, for some reason, they did not.

The giant planet Jupiter is the likely culprit. It may have stolen for itself so much rocky material that there was not enough left to build a respectable-sized planet. And it could have been Jupiter's perturbing gravitational pull that prevented the asteroids from amalgamating into even a small planet. Jupiter's gravity affects the asteroids even today: its pull sweeps out the asteroids in certain orbits, where the orbital period is an exact fraction of Jupiter's. The result is to leave spaces, known as 'Kirkwood gaps' after 19th century asteroid astronomer Daniel Kirkwood, in the asteroid belt at certain distances from the Sun.

Although the asteroids' orbits do not all intersect, as they would if they had resulted from the explosion of a single world, there are some curious regularities. About one-third fall into ten orbital 'families', as first noticed by Japanese astronomer Hirayama. The asteroids in each family also have orbits which intersect precisely – indicating that these asteroids, at least, are fragments from ten original worlds.

These were not 'exploding planets', though, but only asteroids themselves – and asteroids smaller than Ceres. Each of the Hirayama families probably represents splinters broken off when two of the original worlds collided. Certainly the members of each family are made up of similar kinds of rock, as far as astronomers can tell from their reflected light.

And the meteorites that fall to Earth can tell us when these cosmic collisions happened. Most of the meteorites called H-group chondrites, for example, have been exposed to the cosmic rays of space for four million years: at that time, they must have been chipped off some unidentified asteroid by another. Iron meteorites known as medium octaedrites and many of the stony hypersthene chondrites are fragments from a single particularly violent collision between an iron asteroid and a stony one, some 600 million years ago.

These iron asteroids could be very important to our descendants. Judging by the iron meteorites that fall to Earth, they are a pure alloy of iron and nickel. Unlike iron ore on Earth, asteroidal iron needs no smelting, no refining. So, with the increasing difficulty and cost of mining iron on Earth, it may one day be cheaper to mine the asteroids. The potential is enormous. The meteorite that hit Earth 20,000 years ago and blasted out the famous Meteor Crater in Arizona, was only a small ingot by asteroid standards, less than 300 feet (100 metres) across. If it were still out in the asteroid belt, astronomers could not detect it even with the largest telescopes. Yet this object was a quarter-of-a-million tonnes of pure iron-nickel.

According to Dale P. Cruikshank, below, the puzzling asteroid Hektor may have a dumb-bell shape. A painting by his colleague William K. Hartman, bottom, shows how Hektor may look.

Asteroids can also approach one another without colliding. In 1978, astronomers were amazed to find an asteroid with a moon of its own – a smaller asteroid in orbit. Moons of the asteroids are too faint to be seen directly. But they can be observed by indirect means. In July 1978, the asteroid Herculina was due to pass in front of a distant star and block off its light. Sure enough, astronomers at the right spot on Earth saw the star disappear behind Herculina – but 1½ minutes before this, the star had also blinked off briefly. Something invisible, moving with Herculina but 600 miles (975 kilometres) away in space, had blocked off the star's light first. It must have been a moon, less than a quarter Herculina's diameter of 140 miles (220 kilometres). The story was repeated almost exactly six months later, when another asteroid, Melpomene, was due to eclipse a star. For all we know, it may be very much the rule for asteroids to have satellites of their own.

But the most unusual asteroid pair is called Hektor. It lies beyond the main asteroid belt, and at a point that forms the third corner of an equilateral triangle formed with the Sun and Jupiter. We cannot see its shape directly, but its brightness drops by two-thirds and recovers regularly as it spins round. This means that it must be spindle-shaped – three times as long as it is wide. Infra-red (heat) measurements indicate that it is a large, though very dark, asteroid – 200 miles (300 kilometres) in length. That is very odd indeed. The smallest asteroids are irregular in shape, because they are mere splinters. But Hektor is far too large to be merely a splinter from another asteroid.

CELESTIAL DUMB-BELL

American astronomers William K. Hartman and Dale P. Cruikshank propose that Hektor is, in fact, two spherical asteroids stuck together. They approached at such a slow speed that they did not strike splinters off one another and rebound. Instead, the two asteroids nudged gently together, and ended up held in permanent contact by each other's weak gravity, like a celestial dumb-bell.

When astronauts of the future reach the asteroid belt, what they will not find is evidence of an ancient civilisation. But what they will find may be equally exciting. Already we can predict that asteroids are often weirdly shaped, some – perhaps many – with moons of their own. The astronauts will be metallurgical prospectors, sounding out the iron asteroids for their commercial potential. They will also test the asteroids – their reflected light tells us they are 'peculiar' – to find just what odd kinds of rock they are made of, rocks left over from the birth of the solar system.

Another target for enquiry will be the carbonaceous asteroids. Although their carbon compounds are unlikely to be the products of life, they may well be the compounds from which life on Earth sprang, back in the early days of our own planet.

All we know of the asteroids comes indirectly at the moment. Astronomers study their motions, analyse their reflected light, and interpret meteorites as asteroid debris strayed from its home regions. When Man reaches the asteroids, these mysteriously diminutive worlds of the solar system will undoubtedly have more surprises in store.

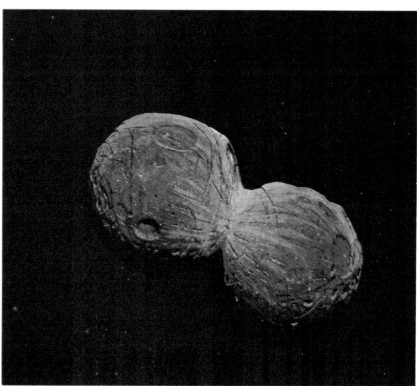

HOUDINI WAS THE GREATEST ESCAPOLOGIST OF ALL TIME – BUT HE IS ALSO FAMED FOR HIS EXPOSURE OF FRAUDULENT MEDIUMS

I n 1924, a contest took place in which Harry Houdini, established as the leading stage magician of his era, was for the first and only time defeated. But he did not admit defeat: on the contrary, he claimed to have exposed his opponent – the Spiritualist medium 'Margery' – as a fraud, just as he had exposed so many others. But in this Houdini lied, just as, unfortunately, by then – he had just entered his fifties – he was all too prone to do.

Houdini was born in Wisconsin in the United States in 1874, the son of Hungarian immigrants, Rabbi Samuel Weiss and his wife Cecilia, who had named him Erich. As a teenager, he read the memoirs of Robert-Houdin, the most famous magician of the previous era; and in response to these, resolving to take on his hero's mantle, he adopted the name 'Houdini' and took an act on tour.

However, it was not long before he realised that, in using Houdin's name, he had made something of a mistake – for he was destined to be even greater. It was too late to change his stage name, but by writing *The Unmasking of Robert-Houdin*, he effectively demolished the Frenchman's reputation. Indeed, this gives us a clue to Houdini's own character; for when Maurice Sardina went over the same ground, he realised that, although Houdini had indeed uncovered many of Houdin's weaknesses, he had also been unscrupulous in distorting the facts to fit his case.

HOUDINI'S SPIRIT EXPOSÉS

UNMASKED BY HOUDINI?

Mein Training   Meine Tricks

During his lifetime, Harry Houdini became a worldwide household name – principally for his skills in escapology. A German book cover, left, shows Houdini about to free himself from a fearsome array of manacles. He became known, too, for his replicating of Spiritualist phenomena, as illustrated above. Supporters of the Spiritualist movement, however, pointed out that reproducing phenomena by trickery did not necessarily detract from the authenticity of the mediums' manifestations.

Houdini made his name principally as an escapologist, and in that capacity he was supreme. By 1918, he had escaped from just about every form of confinement that ingenuity could devise, and was beginning to look for alternative sources of income – and fame. He had also starred in several films, and thought in terms of film-making as a career. But he had contracts to honour in Britain as an escapologist. He had signed these before the First World War; and in 1920, he arrived to fulfil them. It was then that he realised an old ambition – to meet the creator of Sherlock Holmes.

Sir Arthur Conan Doyle and Houdini took an immediate liking to one another. 'Apart from his amazing courage, he was remarkable for his cheery urbanity in everyday life,' Doyle was to recall after Houdini's death. 'One could not wish a better companion so long as one was with him.' When one was not with him, however, Houdini 'might do and say the most unexpected things' – unexpected, that is, by Doyle, who found it hard to believe that somebody with whom he got on so well could openly despise him behind his back. For, much as he liked Doyle, Houdini thought him hopelessly gullible in his dealings with Spiritualist mediums. At that time, they were flourishing as never before, thanks to the demand for their services created by the deaths of so many loved ones on the Western Front.

On the subject of Spiritualism, Houdini was, at this period in his life, ambivalent. He had been so passionately devoted to his mother that he was to say of her, in the introduction to his book *A Magician Among the Spirits*: 'If God in His infinite wisdom ever sent an angel upon Earth in human form, it was my mother.' After her death in 1913, he longed to communicate with her, and sat with several mediums in the hope that his mother would 'come through'. But she never did – not, at least, in a way that satisfied him, although Lady Doyle maintained that she had brought him a message from her. But there was something that aroused his suspicion – the fact that his mother's alleged spirit addressed him as 'Harry', a name by which she had never called him in life.

Houdini became increasingly interested in 'physical mediums' from a practical point of view: assuming they were fraudulent, how did they produce their materialisations? His magician's imagination was caught by this question: however, for a short time, Doyle seems to have persuaded him that physical mediums were worth investigating, not just to catch them cheating, but to see whether there might indeed be some psychic force involved.

As it happened, the celebrated Marthe Beraud, better known under her pseudonym 'Eva C', was in London being tested by the Society for Psychical Research. On 21 June 1920, Houdini went to a seance where he was able to watch two expert investigators, E.J. Dingwall and W. Baggally, put Eva C through a carefully controlled trial.

Born Erich Weiss, Houdini took on the name of Robert-Houdin, the French conjurer above, in modified form as a mark of esteem.

Sir Arthur Conan Doyle is seen below left with Lady Doyle and their family. The Doyles were committed Spiritualists who believed that Houdini was himself psychic.

Houdini shows, below, how easy it is to fake a spirit photograph, as he apparently communes with Abraham Lincoln.

Eva's speciality was materialising strange – apparently two-dimensional – human forms and faces. She had been doing this at seances for 15 years, carefully monitored and photographed by such experienced psychical researchers as Professor Charles Richet, Baron Schrenck-Nötzing and Dr Gustave Geley. Although her powers were gradually waning – and she had little success in her London trials – Houdini happened to be present on one of her better days, and he wrote an account of the sitting to Doyle the following morning.

Eva C, he said, had been made to drink a cup of coffee and eat some cake. He assumed they wanted 'to fill her up': in fact, it was a precaution against her having swallowed something before the seance – butter muslin, for example – and regurgitating it

as 'ectoplasm'). After she had been undressed, sewn into tights, and her face covered with a veil to make it impossible for her to disgorge objects from anywhere in her body, she manifested 'some froth-like substance, inside of net, 'twas long, about five inches [13 centimetres]'; then 'a white, plaster-looking affair over her right eye', and 'something that looked like a small face, say four inches [10 centimetres] in circumference'. Finally, she 'asked permission to remove something in her mouth, showed her hands empty, and took out what appeared to be a rubberish substance, which she disengaged, and showed us plainly. We held the electric torch, all saw it plainly; when, presto!, it vanished. It was a surprise effect indeed!'

'Doyle would doubtless receive a detailed report later', wrote Houdini, adding: 'I found it highly interesting.' He was certainly a sufficiently experienced magician to realise that there was no ready explanation for the ectoplasmic manifestation he had witnessed. He also hoped to visit W.J Crawford, the Belfast engineer who had thoroughly investigated the mediumistic Goligher family, and especially their most gifted member, the daughter Kathleen.

Houdini seemed impressed by what he had heard of Crawford's investigations. 'It is certainly a wonderful affair,' he wrote to him, 'and there is no telling how far all this may lead.' But as he had to return to the United States, he contented himself with asking Crawford for some of the photographs he had taken showing the ectoplasm that emerged from Kathleen Goligher, and also the effects of her psychokinetic powers.

Not long after he returned to the United States, however, Houdini began to exploit what he regarded as the 'tricks' of such mediums by giving public demonstrations of them. It was a profitable diversion from escapology. Soon, he even emerged as the great scourge of the Spiritualists, taking it upon himself to expose fraudulent mediums up and

Houdini was on friendly terms with many of those whose beliefs he professed to despise – the Conan Doyles and the flamboyant psychical researcher Harry Price, for instance, with whom he kept up a lively correspondence. Surprisingly, some of the mediums whom he exposed as frauds were willing to confess all. Anna Clark Benninghoffer, below, even posed for a satirical photograph with Houdini, the 'scourge of the Spiritualists'. This seems to argue that, whatever else he was, the magician was a man of considerable charisma.

down the country. And when, in 1923, he was invited to write articles on the subject for the *Scientific American*, although commitments prevented him writing them, his suggestion that the journal should sponsor an investigation into mediumship, in which he would assist, was accepted.

The *Scientific American* offered a reward of $2,500 for 'the first physical manifestations of a psychic nature produced under scientific control'. Mrs Mina Crandon, the wife of a Boston surgeon – who, as 'Margery', was to become the most celebrated of American mediums in the period – took up the challenge. Dr William McDougall, professor of psychology at Harvard; Dr Daniel Comstock, a physicist, formerly of the Massachusetts Institute of Technology; Walter Franklin Prince, research officer of the American Society for Psychical Research; and Hereward Carrington, the most experienced of American psychical researchers – all were appointed, along with Houdini, to carry out the investigation. Houdini, however, could not attend the early seances as he was on tour. Later, he was mortified to hear that the *Scientific American*'s nominee as secretary to the committee, J. Malcolm Bird, had decided that Margery's materialisations were genuine, and that she was likely to win the award.

Houdini had been promoting his forthcoming book *A Magician Among the Spirits* by boasting that he could expose any medium as fraudulent, and backing his claim with bets. Of Margery, he told the publisher of the *Scientific American*: 'I will forfeit a thousand dollars if I do not detect if she resorts to trickery.' By this time, Houdini had convinced himself that all materialisations must be fakes, and he now became utterly obsessed with proving that Margery was a fraud.

SABOTAGE

Margery's spirit 'control', or 'guide', was her dead brother Walter (who, apparently, behaved in the spirit world as he had in life – badly). Walter clearly relished the idea of a contest with Houdini, but Houdini's plan was to enclose Margery in a box, made to his specifications by his assistant, James Collins. It looked like an old-fashioned steam bath, with a hole at the top, out of which her head protruded, and holes at either side so that her hands could be held. Hardly had the seance begun when the whole contraption burst apart, as if exploded by a small bomb. And when Margery was re-installed, the voice of Walter accused Houdini of sabotaging the experiment. He had, claimed Walter, interfered with the box in which was the bell that Margery was to try to ring. Sure enough, a small rubber eraser had been inserted, presumably by Houdini, to prevent the bell sounding. Houdini, it seemed, was hardly playing ball.

For the next seance, Houdini and Collins reinforced the lid of the cabinet in which Margery was installed; but, again, Walter came through with his usual flow of words, which the note-taker deemed unprintable: 'Houdini! You – blackguard! You have put a rule in the cabinet.' Sure enough, in the cabinet, which Houdini was supposed to have searched and found empty, there was indeed a telescopic rule. (No doubt, had Margery caused objects to move, she would have been accused of doing so by working the rule with her mouth.)

But even if Margery could have conveyed the ruler to her mouth while her hands remained outside the cabinet, to have used it to move the objects at a distance, and to start the bell ringing in the box, would have been impracticable, as the ruler was only 2 feet (60 centimetres) long. The most plausible explanation was that Houdini had it put in the box as a last resort, in case he could not detect her in more obvious 'tricks'. Indeed, according to one of his biographers, Lindsay Gresham, Houdini's assistant, James Collins, later openly admitted that he had put it in the cabinet himself and had actually been asked to do so.

PHOTOGRAPHIC EVIDENCE

A later biographer of Houdini, the well-known magician (and sceptic) Milbourne Christopher, was to cast doubt on the story on the ground that it had been spread by a man with a grudge against Houdini. In Christopher's opinion, the story of Collins' confession was sheer fiction. Yet Christopher himself also disclosed how, at this time, Houdini had cheated his fellow investigators, and the public. During the seances, Houdini had asked and received permission to take photographs – to discover, he hoped, how Margery played her 'tricks'. He had asked a friend to have prints made from the negatives, saying 'she's the slickest ever.' The prints showed nothing suspicious, but one of them displayed what looked like a halo around Margery's head. As mediums often claimed to be able to impose such effects on negatives, Houdini suppressed the picture, telling his friend that Spiritualists might claim it proved her psychic capabilities, and adding: 'She's a fake – why should I help build up her following?'

Houdini's escapes from handcuffs, chains, ropes and locked containers of all kinds were so spectacular and considered to be so 'impossible' that his skills were widely thought to be paranormal, even diabolical, in origin. The cartoon, right, shows him as the Devil after his 'escape' from Liverpool jail in 1904. He issued a general invitation to the locksmiths, police and even other stage magicians of the world to confine him successfully, but he always escaped. He took up every challenge and took part in every form of entertainment, such as the circus, below, and always emerged the winner. But did he have paranormal powers, or was he simply a particularly well-rehearsed performer?

The *Scientific American* committee was divided: Bird and Carrington were sure that Margery had proved her psychic powers; Prince and McDougall thought she must be using trickery, but could not fathom how; Comstock accepted the reality of the phenomena, but refused to endorse them unless they could be explained in terms of electromagnetism. To the irritation of his colleagues on the committee, however, Houdini resumed his tour of the halls, claiming that he had exposed Margery. But his failure had clearly annoyed him; for when given another opportunity to try again a few months later, he accepted.

MAGICAL FEATS

The new chief investigator was Dr Henry McComas, a psychologist at Princeton University. Houdini, who by that time had learned caution, told him to attend a seance and report back what Margery did – 'the lady is subtle and changes her methods like any dextrous sleight-of-hand performer' – so that he would have time to work out how to duplicate her feats. McComas reported that Margery was now performing while enclosed in a glass case. Her feats had been spectacular, including the levitation of objects outside the case. Baffled, Houdini asked for time to decide how he could do what Margery was doing; but before he was ready, McComas had abandoned his investigation and returned to Princeton.

In 1926, an alleged spirit message came through at Conan Doyle's home circle: 'Houdini is doomed, doomed, doomed!' Other Spiritualists reported receiving similar communications. Then, on 24 October that year, one of Houdini's allies in the campaign against mediums was sitting in his room when a picture of Houdini, which the magician had given him, crashed to the floor. 'Maybe,' he wrote anxiously, 'there is something in these psychic phenomena, after all.' A week later, Houdini was dead. 'I knew him well,' said the author Walter Franklin Prince, 'and the world seemed poorer when his big heart and eager brain were stilled.'

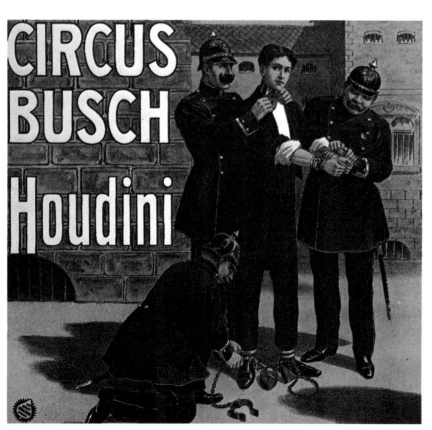

CIRCUS BUSCH
Houdini

The fall of Constantinople to the Turks in 1453 is depicted in a painting by Tintoretto, right. Halley's Comet, which made one of its periodic appearances at this time, was taken to be a portent of the event.

COMETS – PORTENTS OF CATASTROPHE?

THE IDEA THAT COMETS ARE PORTENTS OF DISASTER IS GENERALLY DERIDED BY ORTHODOX SCIENCE. BUT A NEW THEORY BY TWO BRITISH ASTRONOMERS SUGGESTS THAT THE OLD BELIEF MAY INDEED BE BASED ON FACT

One of Man's most ancient – and seemingly universal – beliefs is the idea that comets are makers of catastrophe. While the positions of the planets at the birth of an individual are thought, in mundane astrology, to govern the characteristics of that person and even to guide events in his or her life, the appearance of comets is associated with the likelihood of momentous and terrible happenings. The timely arrivals of Halley's Comet are well known: its coming in AD 66 was seen by the Romans to foretell the death of Nero and, by the Jews, the imminent destruction of Jerusalem. In 1066, it was thought to presage bad luck for the English at the Battle of Hastings; and in 1453, it appeared to mark the sack of Constantinople by the Turks. Roman literature is full of ominous references to comets – the one that was seen shortly after the Ides of March in 44BC, for instance, was thought to be a reflection of the killing of Julius Caesar. And right through the medieval period in Europe, comets were feared as signs of coming pestilence, floods or war – even the Apocalypse or Day of Judgement itself.

Comets are certainly the most wayward and surprising members of the solar system. But what in essence are these odd phenomena? Composed of a tiny 'head' of ice and dust, only a few miles across, they trail huge tails of incandescent dust

125

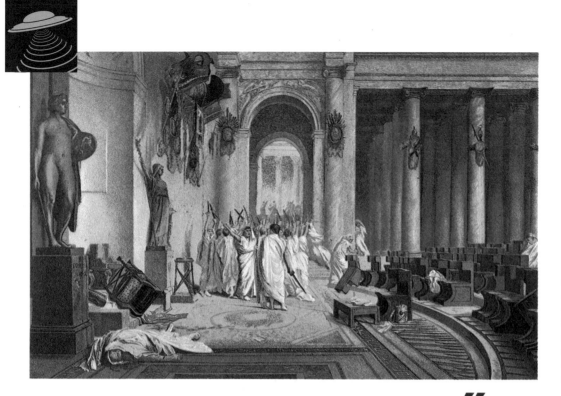

A comet was seen in the skies shortly after the assassination of Julius Caesar in 44 BC, depicted left. As Shakespeare wrote in his play Julius Caesar: 'When beggars die, there are no comets seen;/ The heavens themselves blaze forth the death of princes'.

and glowing gas when they are near the Sun. Some swoop into the centre of the solar system on vast orbits, crossing the sedate paths of the planets, and then swing around the Sun to travel outwards into the depths of interstellar space, never to return. Others – short-period comets such as Halley's and most of those we see from the Earth – are trapped in the gravitational field of the Sun and planets, reappearing to us at regular intervals.

DIRTY SNOWBALLS

The phenomenon we see as a comet is formed when a lump of ice and dust – 'dirty snowballs', as astronomers have whimsically nicknamed them – comes close enough to the Sun for the ice to begin to melt. A stream of dust particles is then driven away from the comet to form a glowing tail that may stretch for as far as tens of millions of miles. The mass of the material in the tail is usually a tiny fraction of that in the almost invisible nucleus; but a relatively small comet can provide a brilliant tail as long as one 'astronomical unit', which is defined as the distance between the Earth and the Sun, some 93 million miles (150 million kilometres). Playing in the solar wind, such a tail can take on all manner of fantastic patterns and forms: curving forks, twisted horns, sword-shapes, sickles and tridents, in colours that have been known to range from incandescent blue-white to deep bloody red.

A graphic description of a comet appears in an astronomer's record that dates back to an eyewitness account of 1882:

'As the Comet rose, the widened extremity of its tail passed the zenith and seemed to overhang the world. When the dawn came, the dark blue of the sky near the point of sunrise began to change into a rich yellow, then gradually came a stronger light, and over the mountain and among the yellow, an ill-defined mass of golden glory rose, in surroundings of indescribable beauty. This was the nucleus of the comet... with a tail about as long as the moon is broad.'

The computer-enhanced photograph, below, is of Comet Kohoutek, which passed close to the Earth in 1973. Although this particular comet was barely visible, it is easy to see how the spectacular appearance of many comets led to the belief that they were somehow connected with cataclysmic events.

" BRIGHT COMETS... ARE ALWAYS APT TO TAKE US BY SURPRISE: THE ONLY EXCEPTION IS HALLEY'S COMET WHICH... LAST RETURNED IN 1986. IT WILL BE BACK ONCE MORE IN THE YEAR 2061. "

**PATRICK MOORE,
MISSION TO THE PLANETS**

This kind of impressive and ornamental display has been seen very seldom during the 20th century. Shows such as that of 1882 can be witnessed only a few times a century. Most comets are rather disappointing, as was Comet Kohoutek, which was billed as the spectacle of the century – but in the event was hardly noticed by anyone when it came close to the Earth in 1973.

Comets can be breathtakingly beautiful, fascinating and perhaps awesome – but, viewed objectively, they are transient, hardly terrifying, phenomena. In historical time, there are no records of comets having caused direct damage on Earth. Why, then, have they evoked such unreasonable fear across the ages? The works of Shakespeare are replete with doom-laden images of 'comets, importing changes of time and states'. And as recently as

The scene from the Bayeux tapestry, above, shows the appearance of a portentous star – Halley's Comet. At the time, it was believed to presage bad luck for the English army.

1858, London eyewitnesses to the dazzling Donati's Comet spent the night in panic, fearing that the world was about to come to an end.

It is tempting to put this overblown fear of comets down to pure superstition, based on ignorance. But is this really the case? Is it not possible that Man has some kind of deep memory of a time when comets were perhaps not as harmless as they are today?

Two British astronomers, Dr Victor Clube and Dr Bill Napier, put forward a new theory that tackles a staggering range of apparently unrelated enigmas in the Earth's history – from the death of the dinosaurs and origins of the asteroid belt to the significance of Stonehenge and the true meaning of astrology. They claim to have demonstrated that at regular, and datable, periods in the past, the Earth has been assailed and devastated by swarms of comets. These periodic catastrophes have not only shaped the Earth's geological and biological evolution, they say, but have decisively influenced the religious and intellectual life of Man.

COSMIC SERPENT

The results of their research into cometary history have been published as a book, under the title *The Cosmic Serpent*. (The dragon, they argue, is simply early Man's way of describing the snake-like appearance of comets.) They make an impassioned plea for the recognition of the importance of comets – which are, they claim, both the heroes and villains of the world's prehistory. The authors are aware that they encroach on the ground of many scientific disciplines, and it is true that, as they mischievously announce in the introduction: 'There is something here to outrage everyone.' But while some of their endeavours – their attempt to revise the dates of Egyptian history, for instance – may be over-ambitious, the central core of their theory is a clearly argued and logical outcome from the problems posed by modern astronomical research. As they freely admit, not much of it is really new:

When Donati's Comet appeared in the skies above London on 4 October 1858, right, Londoners spent the night in panic, many of them convinced that the world was about to end.

127

wander off into deep space, while others are boiled away by the heat of the Sun into streams of dust. At the rate we lose them, calculations show that the Oort cloud should by now have been devastated, whittled down to a fraction of the size we now observe.

So where do all the comets in the Oort cloud come from? The obvious conclusion, as Clube and Napier show, is that rather than being 'born' together with the rest of the solar system, our cometary siblings come from outside it.

Our Galaxy is a gigantic spiral structure, a whirling spray of stars that rotates around a common centre. The Sun, one of the oldest stars in the Galaxy, moves slowly through successive arms of the spiral, crossing a new one roughly every 50 million years. Here, in these arms, as Clube and Napier discovered, is an ideal source for the periodic 'topping up' of the Oort cloud with cometary material. In between the stars, what were once thought to be empty gulfs or holes in the spiral arms have been revealed by radio-telescopes to be vast freezing dust clouds of inconceivable immensity.

These interstellar freezing clouds dwarf the stars and are easily the largest known objects in the Galaxy. Whereas astronomers had previously imagined that the Sun would glide peacefully through the void of interstellar space when traversing a spiral arm, a totally different picture emerges when the existence of these dust clouds – sometimes condensed into supercomets – is taken into account. Violent interactions would be inevitable, the scientists claim. Moreover, the gravitational pull of the interstellar cloud would not only tear away our previous comets, but at the same time provide us with a fresh influx of cometary material.

Clube and Napier used complex mathematics to construct a model of exactly what would happen in

the possibility of comet-caused catastrophes has been toyed with for at least 300 years. But only recently has enough information been gathered to form a plausible hypothesis.

As internationally recognized astronomers, Dr Clube and Dr Napier have, between them, published over 100 papers in scientific books and journals. And while the overall picture they paint seems somewhat unorthodox, the individual pieces of the puzzle are composed of the hard facts of 20th-century astronomical discovery.

Their study begins with the mystery of the extraordinary over-abundance of comets. There are presently estimated to be several thousand million comets associated with the solar system – but in terms of the currently accepted theory of the origins of comets, this is far too many.

THE OORT CLOUD

In 1950, a Dutch astronomer, Sigismund Oort, demonstrated from an examination of the orbits of comets that they originated from a ring or cloud of comets at the farthest edge of the solar system. This 'Oort cloud', as it is now known, is usually thought to have formed at the same time as the rest of the Sun's family – some 4.5 billion years ago. But as Clube and Napier point out, the solar system is constantly losing comets, some of which

The Whirlpool Galaxy, above, like our own, is clearly a spiral galaxy. For reasons that are not yet completely understood, stars move in and out of the arms of the spiral; and in our Galaxy, the Sun passes through a spiral arm roughly once every 50 million years. In The Cosmic Serpent, *Dr Victor Clube and Dr Bill Napier suggest that the passage of the Sun through the spiral arm causes a huge influx of comets into the solar system. These, in turn, are thought to cause catastrophic events on Earth.*

St George kills the dragon, right, in an anonymous medieval altar painting. Clube and Napier argue that dragons, as they appear in the religious imagery of many cultures, are in fact representations of comets.

this instance. It seems that roughly every 50 million years, when the Sun passes through another arm of the Galaxy, the solar system would become flooded with comets of a whole range of sizes. Gradually, the number of comets would dwindle until a new spiral arm is reached, and then the process would begin again. The subsequent effect on the solar system of these periodic saturations of comets would be devastating.

HUGE EXPLOSION

Comets are not, as *Hutchinson's Encyclopedia* would have it, 'completely harmless'. There is no reason why they should not strike the Earth. This may, indeed, have happened at Tunguska, Siberia, in 1908. Probably only a small fragment of a comet about 110 yards (100 metres) across fell, but its impact raised a column of fire 12 miles (20 kilometres) high, charring trees up to a radius of 45 miles (70 kilometres) and knocking people unconscious within a 60-mile (100-kilometre) radius, in an explosion around the order of 100 megatonnes.

A comet or asteroid about half-a-mile (around 1 kilometre) wide, at a typical speed of 80,000 miles per hour (130,000 km/h), would hit the Earth with the force of a 3 million megatonne bomb. (For comparison, the disastrous Hiroshima explosion was just one-fiftieth of a megatonne.) Such an impact could boil seas, raise global dust clouds and drastically alter our climate. Searing heat, the force of the blast, tidal waves and cyanide from the comet's tail would annihilate any life-forms within its range, and inevitably impose an entirely new environment on those who managed to escape the immediate catastrophic effects.

Clube and Napier's theory clearly fits neatly with the conclusions being reached by some geologists about the mysterious disappearance of the

An artist's impression below illustrates one possible way in which dinosaurs could have become extinct. Many writers have suggested that comet fragments were responsible for the catastrophe that wiped them out, and Clube and Napier's theory suggests a possible origin for the comet 63 million years ago. When dinosaurs became extinct, the Sun was entering a spiral arm of our Galaxy, and a number of comets may have entered the solar system at that time.

dinosaurs some 63 million years ago. In the rock stratum laid down in the period marking the boundary between the age of the dinosaurs and the following period of mammals, geologists have discovered, on a world-wide scale, anomalous amounts of the element iridium. While iridium is rare on the Earth, it is abundant in comets and meteorites. So perhaps the extinction of the dinosaurs was indeed caused by the impact of a massive comet or meteorite, as some palaeontologists believe.

It is the time-scale here that is all important. The last passage of the Sun through a spiral arm of the Galaxy took place about 10 million years ago. The previous one would have occurred around 60 million years ago, strikingly close to the time of the dinosaur extinction. Clube and Napier also pointed to a more general correlation with the 50-million-year encounters between the solar system and spiral arms. The interval between the major geological ages since life began is around 50 million years, and at the ends of these ages we find other biological extinctions, as well as changes in sea level and climatic upheavals. *The Cosmic Serpent* goes so far as to postulate a single cause for all these catastrophes.

If Clube and Napier are right, it is comets that shaped the early history of the Earth. And if their theory stopped there, we might feel tempted to say that the superstitions of the ancients were somehow vindicated – that our ancestors had intuitively sensed the devastating potential now shown by science to be stored in the comets. But the story of cometary origins and major geological changes is just one aspect of Clube and Napier's theory, for they also expressed a belief that, as recently as within the past 5,000 years, Man has himself witnessed – and survived – a whole remarkable series of cometary catastrophes.

THE POWER OF WITCHCRAFT

PEOPLE FEAR WITCHCRAFT BECAUSE THEY BELIEVE THAT IT HAS A SUPERNATURAL CAPACITY TO HARM THEM. BUT DOES IT REALLY HAVE SUCH MAGICAL POWERS? AND HOW DID THE PRACTICE OF WITCHCRAFT FIRST ARISE?

Under the laws of Hammurabi, right, king of ancient Babylonia from around 1792 BC to 1750 BC, anyone accused of witchcraft was to be thrown into 'the holy river'. Persecution of witches, both by ducking and by burning, was common in Europe, too, from the medieval period onwards. A witch is 'swum' in the 16th-century engraving, below right, and another is burnt in a German illustration of 1555, far right. In the reign of Aethelstan of England, below, however, the punishment for witchcraft laid down in AD 924 was no more than a mere 120 days of imprisonment.

On 9 March 1967, an odd advertisement appeared in the Personal columns of *The Times*: 'A witch of full powers is urgently sought to lift a 73-year-old curse and help restore the family fortunes of an afflicted nobleman. Employment genuinely offered.'

Some days later, it was revealed that the advertiser was the bankrupt 74-year-old Duke of Leinster, head of one of Britain's oldest families. Over 170 people offered assistance. Whether or not witchcraft helped, the destitute duke was able eventually to pay off his debts, and was welcomed back into society before his death in the 1970s.

Some of the 'witches' who came to the ageing aristocrat's aid were followers of Gerald Gardner who invented much of modern witchcraft; others were members of 'independent' covens, and some were lone operators: all of them believed – or apparently believed – that they were inheritors of a craft that had passed from master to apprentice through the ages. But can any of their claims to magical powers be historically substantiated?

To begin with, there appears to have been no time or place on Earth where witchcraft and magic have not been practised. Man's attempt to control and come to terms with exterior natural phenomena through ritual and ceremony is an essential part of his way of thinking and behaving. Indeed, the evidence of primitive sculpture and cave painting suggests the eternal preoccupation of Man with magic and its effect on fertility, rainmaking, success in hunting, warding off sickness and evil influences; and 'modern' witches, students of Gardner, would claim these are their concerns, too.

Events in his life took a decided turn for the better after the Duke of Leinster, right, placed an advertisement in the The Times, requesting the services of a witch to lift a 73-year-old curse on the family fortunes.

THINK OF THE POWER WIELDED BY SATAN'S CHOSEN BRIDE! SHE CAN HEAL, PROPHESY, PREDICT, CONJURE UP THE SPIRITS OF THE DEAD, CAN SPELL-BIND YOU, CAN TURN YOU INTO A HARE OR A WOLF... AND MOST FATAL OF ALL, CAST A LOVE CHARM OVER YOU.

JULES MICHELET, SATANISM AND WITCHCRAFT

By the time of the earliest written texts on magic, the Akkadean-Chaldean inscriptions of Nineveh dating from the second millennium BC, the practice of black and white magic had already developed into what E. M. Butler, in *Ritual Magic*, termed 'an extremely elaborate and well-developed demonology'. The practices described are almost identical to those associated with European witches in the Middle Ages. One inscription reads:

'He who has fashioned images corresponding to my whole appearance has bewitched my whole appearance; he has seized the magic draught prepared for me and has soiled my garments; he has torn my garments and has mingled his magic herb with the dust of my feet. May the fire-God, the hero, turn their magic to naught.'

The persecution of witches followed a familiar pattern, too. Hammurabi of Nineveh, in a legal code dating from the 17th century BC, laid down that:

'If a man has laid a charge of witchcraft on another man and has not justified it, he upon whom the witchcraft charge is laid shall go to the holy river, and if the holy river overcome him, he who accused him shall take to himself his house.'

The rules are rather different from 17th-century East Anglian witch-floating, but the instinct is very much the same.

The Bible even describes several encounters with witches, notably that between Saul and the witch of Endor. It also condemns them in texts that were used by medieval inquisitors to justify their own orgies of torture and burning. And wrongly, too, as it happens, since as early as 1584, Reginald Scot, in *Discovery of Witchcraft*, had pointed out that the most famous anti-witch text of all, 'Thou shalt not suffer a witch to live,' properly translates as 'Thou shalt not suffer poisoners to live.'

However, although *The Bible* speaks of individual practitioners of witchcraft, there is no evidence whatsoever to suggest that it was an organised religion of the kind claimed by Gerald Gardner and his followers.

MASS NECROMANCY

Many of the writers of ancient Greece also mention witchcraft as a practical reality, with necromancy – the raising of the dead – as one of its principal aims. Aeschylus, in his play *The Persians*, for example, describes the raising of Darius, while Homer in the ninth book of *The Odyssey* tells of a mass raising in gory detail.

The Romans Tacitus, Virgil, Horace, Tibullus, Livy and Pliny all describe witches as commonplace, and there is no doubt that witchcraft spread throughout the Roman Empire. After the break-up of the Empire in Britain, however, there are few literary mentions of witches, except as mild offenders against the law.

In the Saxon period, an edict was issued against those who 'practise any heathenship or in any way love witchcraft'. The penalty for such a crime was 10 half-marks: 'half to Christ, half to the King' Under Aethelstan in AD 924, even when witchcraft had apparently been responsible for death, the punishment was only 120 days of imprisonment. This was rather more lenient than the law issued by the pious King Edgar, in AD 959, who ordained death for anyone disobeying his edict that on Christian

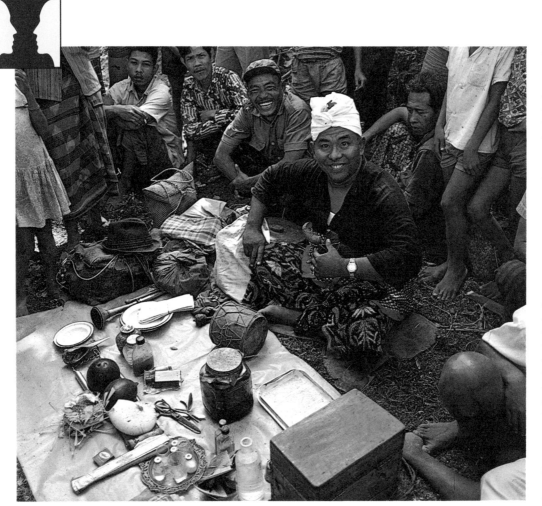

A witch-doctor, left, is seen offering cures at a market in Bali. Throughout Indonesia, witchcraft is accepted as a normal part of everyday life. In Europe, by contrast, witchcraft is generally regarded with suspicion, and the vogue that it enjoyed during the 1960s and 1970s was seen by many as threatening.

A detail from a 15th-century manuscript, below, shows members of the Manichee sect engaging in heretical practices. Primitive witchcraft was often confused with heresies such as Manicheism, and both were brutally dealt with by the Roman Catholic Church.

On the tablet, bottom, is inscribed 'May he who carried off Sylvia from me become as liquid as water. [May] he who obscenely devours her become dumb'.

feast days 'well worshippings, and necromancies and divinations and heathen songs and devil's games be abstained from.'

Undoubtedly, during this period there were still lingering traces of primitive 'heathenism' – the real 'Old Religion' of the pre-Christian era – throughout Britain. Many people clung determinedly to their old gods for several centuries after missionaries, such as Aidan and Columba, had begun preaching the Gospel. But those who continued to worship in the old ways were not by definition practitioners of witchcraft. In late Saxon and Norman times, there were indeed witches, but they tended to operate alone. William the Conqueror, for instance, called one in 'to disconcert by her magic all the warlike devices of the Saxons' at the siege of Ely in 1071. She was placed on a wooden siege tower that was promptly burned down by the defenders led by Hereward the Wake.

It was not until almost 100 years later, with the founding of the Inquisition in 1163 by the Council of Tours, that the Church began to confuse primitive witchcraft with the beliefs of such heretical sects as the Cathars and the Manichees. This misplaced notion gave rise to the ideas of Satanism and group Devil-worship by 'covynes' – Old French for 'coming together' or 'conspiracy' and from which the word 'coven' is derived. And so began the systematic persecution of people who were purported to be in cahoots with the Devil.

Why did the Church determine to stamp out the Cathars and the Manichees? The theology behind their reasoning is complex but was rooted in the idea of a 'dualism' with God on one side and the

powers of evil – Satan – on the other. While the Church held that Satan was the lesser power, operating within the 'permission' granted him by God, their opponents saw God and the Devil as equals, engaged in an eternal running fight, with Mankind as the battle-ground.

Once the great machinery of the Inquisition got rolling, there was to be no stopping it. With time, it was to crush the Manichees, the Waldensians, the

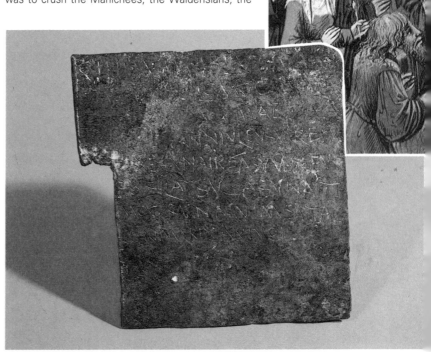

*In*Focus

A LORE UNTO THEMSELVES

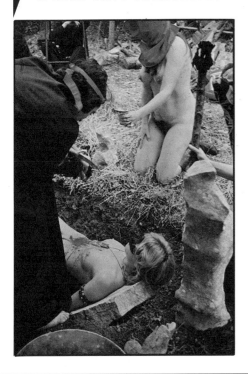

Throughout the year, modern witches meet on nights of the full Moon, and gather to celebrate certain high days known as 'sabbats'. There are eight of these: May Eve (30 April), Hallowe'en (31 October), Candlemas (2 February), Lammas (1 August), the equinoxes (21 March and 21 September) and the solstices (21 June and 21 December).

A typical sabbat will involve all members of the coven, ideally 13 in number but generally between 6 and 20. Usually, the ceremonies are conducted in the nude, which means they must be performed indoors or at some isolated site.

Traditionally, the coven is led by a High Priestess as

A modern coven conducts an initiation ceremony, left.

representative of the Great Goddess, but some groups have a male leader, most frequently referred to as High Priest or Magus. At the site of the sabbat, a magic circle is drawn, and a ring of witches is formed within it, hand to hand. The High Priestess, who should 'carry Phallic Wand, or Riding Pole, phallic or pine-cone tipped, if possible', enters the circle and is greeted by the senior male with the five-fold kiss on knees, genitals, breasts and lips. Then follows the ceremony of the 'drawing down of the Moon', and the initiation of new members.

The evening's ritual entertainment may conclude with the Great Rite, in which the High Priest and Priestess have sexual intercourse, either symbolically or in reality, possibly (although not usually) in front of the assembled company.

Cathars and the Knights Templar, before moving on to destroy individuals whose only crime may have been to foresee a neighbour's death in a dream. In such an environment, it was unlikely that the simple witchcraft of village 'wise' men and women could survive for long before becoming entangled with charges of heresy.

PACTS WITH THE DEVIL

Gradually, the process of trying and condemning witches became entirely divorced from ordinary law; and, in 1398, the University of Paris opened further floodgates by decreeing that any 'superstitious practice' that had results that could not 'reasonably' be accredited to God and nature had to be the result of a pact with the Devil. That, and subsequent judgements, spread terror throughout Europe: suddenly, it seemed witches and demons were everywhere, ready to strike down Christians, blight their crops, render them impotent and destroy their souls.

No doubt many of the accused actually believed themselves to be witches, and for every ten innocents tortured to extract a confession of guilt, there was probably an equal number who volunteered a confession, convinced that they were genuinely possessed by demons. Such a phenomenon is well known to modern police officers whenever a particularly sensational murder is committed: neither is it unknown for a spate of imitative crimes to follow shortly after a well-publicised killing. Likewise, 'group witchcraft' was originally the invention of the Inquisition; but it is probable that, in some isolated cases, a strong leader

could succeed in deluding a group of his or her neighbours into joining a coven for the thrill of it.

Undoubtedly there were, and still are, individuals who appear to have 'strange' powers. However, the traditional belief that they are the 'seventh child of a seventh child' is not so much a statement of fact as an indication of the comparative rarity of such people. The more down-to-earth lore associated with 'country witchcraft' today – wart curing, and knowledge of herbs and the habits of animals, for example – was widespread in a pre-industrial age, simply because people were closer to nature. They grew up knowing about the 'magic' properties of the plants that surrounded them. Today, when such skills are practised, however, they naturally smack of the truly 'occult' – in the sense of a hidden skill.

Curiously, it was a member of the Spanish Inquisition, Alonso de Salazar Frias, who in 1611 pronounced an opinion that may well have applied not only to his own time but to the myriad 'witch' cults that have spawned in Britain and the United States since the 1960s. Over a period of eight weeks, he is said to have talked to as many as 1,800 witches, many of whom had made voluntary confessions. His approach was astonishingly open-minded, and his conclusion salutary.

'Considering the above with all the Christian attention in my power, I have not found even indications from which to infer that a single act of witchcraft has really occurred... I deduce the importance of silence, and reserve from the experience that these were neither witches nor bewitched until they were talked and written about.'

CAN PRAYING TO THE VIRGIN MARY OR A SAINT ACTUALLY EFFECT A 'MIRACULOUS' CURE? OR ARE THERE MORE DOWN-TO-EARTH EXPLANATIONS FOR SUCH SUDDEN RELEASES FROM SERIOUS ILLNESS?

Christ's miracle cures – one of which is seen in The Raising of Jairus's Daughter *by G.P. Jacomb Hood,* **right** *– were usually accompanied by thought-provoking statements. In this case, 'the maid is not dead, but sleepeth' has been taken by many to mean that the girl was in a coma; but it could, of course, imply that Christ did not see physical death as irreversible.*

The 'miracle healer', five-year-old Linda Martel, is seen **below**, *being treated by Harry Edwards. She suffered from spina bifida herself; and although she died in 1961, she is still credited with healing powers – as are her clothes.*

When faced with an illness over which we have no immediate control, we tend to worry, perhaps even panic. This is a perfectly natural reaction; and the more critical the pain or the malady we know we have, or believe we have, the more fervently we wish it would pass. For many of us, that wishing is but a small step from praying – in the belief that, if we do so, some external agency (our guardian angel, God or one of the saints) will put an end to our suffering.

One of the possible outcomes of being ill is that we recover; another is that we die; a third, covering

MAKING MIRACLES HAPPEN

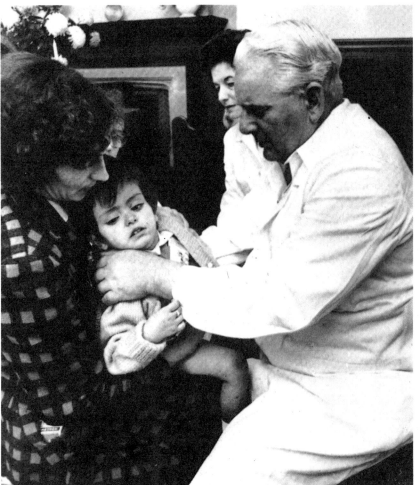

the majority of cases, is that we come to terms with the illness, mentally and physically, with the help of medical treatment and natural resistance, inherent in the human body. In the case of serious – even apparently terminal – illness, few doctors will deny that a small number of their patients experience temporary periods of remission. In some rare instances, they acknowledge, too, that the remission can be sudden, and lasting. Sometimes the body seems to mend in just a few days or perhaps hours, even where it has been broken down by some form of cancer, for example. Remission is not a fantasy, or a rumour, or even a matter of misinterpretation of the facts: it happens.

Bearing in mind our natural tendency to wish away our illnesses or to pray for release from them, it is hardly surprising that sometimes remission coincides with our most fervent prayers, or a more sophisticated form of attempting to secure divine intervention – the petitioning of a religious figure such as the Virgin Mary, or visiting a place of pilgrimage, such as Lourdes, for instance. But had the prayers remained unsaid, the Saint not called upon, and the pilgrimage not been undertaken, might the remission – be it temporary or permanent – have happened anyway?

The tradition of healing persists, and in the West it persists particularly as a belief in divine intervention, whether or not a human agent such as a priest or a healer is involved. In cases where healing is

apparently brought about by contact with religious objects, such as relics, or by visits to shrines or places of pilgrimage, the 'divine' influence is said to be 'direct'.

The Roman Catholic tradition of healing is undoubtedly the greatest repository of varied and vociferous claims for divine healing in the modern world, and healings that have apparently taken place within that tradition have given their title to those claimed in many others. Thus, the oddest and most unlikely healings are frequently given the general title of 'miracles'.

The evidence for alleged miracle cures outside the Roman Catholic Church is often skimpily investigated and therefore lacks real credibility. But reports of such cures continue to be filed throughout the world.

The *Shorter Oxford English Dictionary* defines a miracle as: 'A marvellous event exceeding the known powers of nature and therefore supposed to be due to the special intervention of the Deity or some supernatural agency; chiefly an act (e.g. of healing) exhibiting control over the laws of nature,

At High Mass on Ascension Day in Chartres Cathedral, France, above, the sick of the diocese gather to be blessed. Although the blessing is intended to be of a spiritual nature, there are few present who do not hope for a miracle cure of their physical ills.

Prayer, as right, is said to bring almost miraculous cures at times. But might this in fact be no more than coincidence?

and serving as evidence that the agent is either divine or is especially favoured by God.'

George Bernard Shaw, on the other hand, in his play *St Joan*, chose to describe a miracle as 'an event which creates faith'.

Both of these definitions apply to the healings of Sathya Sai Baba, the Indian mystic who is widely respected in both the West and the East. Many of his followers regard him as being a manifestation of God in this age. But even if we ignore such extreme claims, Sai Baba has certainly impressed those who have witnessed his 'miracles'.

His most spectacular healings have been two cases where he is said to have brought the dead back to life. Of the two, the most widely reported was his raising of V. Radhakrishna, aged 60, at an ashram (a religious community) at Puttaparti. There was no question in this case that the man was dead, for he had already begun to decompose when Sai Baba raised him to life, three days after he had been pronounced dead by doctors.

This is as direct an example of a miracle cure as one can expect to find; and it is either true or not. If it is false, then many people have been duped. But Sai Baba's record of producing other miraculous phenomena – such as 'apporting' hot food or 'sacred ash', apparently from nowhere – makes this raising from the dead more credible. Yet, as with many of Christ's miracles, there seems to be an obvious question left unanswered: if Sai Baba was able to revive the man from death, why did he permit him to die in the first place? What possible benefit could three days of widowhood have had for the man's wife? Does it become more of a self-promoting trick than a miracle in this context? The glib theological answers – that God's purpose is subtle but sure, and that miracles make us 'glorify the Lord' – do not seem to help that much.

YOUNG HEALER

Certainly much simpler and more straightforward in their motivation were the miraculous cures associated with Linda Martel, a hydrocephalic child who spent her short life in Guernsey, dying aged five in 1961. At the time of her death, the media were full of stories about her supposed cures, but gradually her name has faded into comparative obscurity, remembered only by her family and, presumably, by those whom she cured.

During her few years, Linda – who also suffered from spina bifida and whose legs were paralysed – showed herself to be very advanced intellectually, and often her most perceptive remarks were deeply religious. She would, for example, speak of 'my Jesus Christ' with a conviction that seemed to smack of experience, yet her family was not particularly religious, and are unlikely to have inculcated such an attitude in her. Like other leading healers, she seemed to have some power of diagnosis, as well as that of healing; but, again, such a small child is highly unlikely to have learned the skill of diagnosis in the conventional way, as an adult might have done. Her healing was occasionally direct, and she cured by touch in the presence of the sick; but most frequently it was brought about by the sufferer touching an item of clothing that Linda had worn. Such healings are reported to have

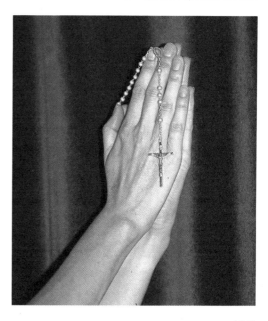

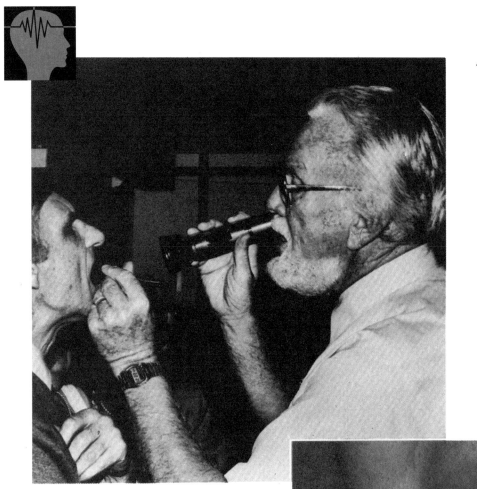

occurred both before and after her death, and the illnesses and problems cured are said to have included a spinal injury, haemorrhoids, eczema, warts, cartilage trouble, and cancer of the throat. A multitude of such cures were claimed in the years following her death.

In the case of Linda Martel, one must conclude either that those who claimed to have been cured with her direct or indirect help were deceived or deceiving – or that the cures were genuine. Healing by the power of the mind – by faith – no doubt accounted for a great many of the claims: cures were even attributed to her grave. But if the claims regarding the curing of spinal injuries or cancer are to be accepted as genuine, then we must start considering what the concept of 'miracle' means in this context. Could such a small and helpless child have the power to heal, and to impart that power in some way to the clothes she wore? Or was some external power working through her, so that those who associated themselves with her simple and naïve faith in Christ could benefit from his legendary healing powers? It is not an easy case to assess, but at least we do not have here any suggestion of self-promotion.

There is something compelling about some of the claims made for Linda Martel, despite the lack of a great deal of conclusive and verifiable evidence. Yet there is an American case, of some fame, in which there is both photographic evidence and abundant personal testimony that, though it fits the definition 'miracle', and undoubtedly concerns cures of a kind, many still find absurd and unacceptable. It concerns the healing ministry of Willard Fuller, a former Baptist minister with a marked evangelistic style.

American 'psychic dentist' Willard Fuller, a former Baptist minister who cured dental ailments by purely spiritual means, is seen top. After an initial inspection of the patient's mouth, Fuller would pray and, within minutes, fillings – and sometimes even new teeth – would appear, as above.

Initially, he healed all kinds of ailments, but one day a man, whose ulcer he had cured, came to him and said: 'Preacher, I have one cavity in a tooth back here. I believe that if God can heal an ulcer, He can fix this cavity for me. Will you lay hands on me and pray for me for the meeting of my dental needs?' Fuller did so, and the tooth was 'miraculously' filled. To quote Bryce Bond, writing in *Alpha* magazine:

'Those who have seen a filling gradually form describe it as a small bright spot which becomes larger until it fills the whole cavity, like the speeded-up picture of a rose blooming. Porcelain fillings are common occurrences and are of particular interest because they form fast enough for witnesses to watch the growth, but slowly enough to give many people a chance to witness at first-hand what is happening... Today, conservatively, there are some

25,000 people in America who have evidence of this 'miracle in the mouth'.

The minister of a church where Willard Fuller appeared and demonstrated his skills in 'miracle dentistry' in 1967 reported to an astounded congregation: 'Right before our eyes, teeth have been filled with gold, silver and porcelain – not just one night but every night. Over 200 people have experienced this miracle in two weeks. Last night, one man received seven silver and two gold fillings. This is done in such a way that there can be no doubt.'

Many apparent healings have a natural cause, and demonstrate no more than the exceptional potential of the body to heal itself in the right circumstances. Healers, such as Rose Gladden and Matthew Manning, recognise this, whatever they claim as the source of their healing powers. But there can be no argument about teeth that suddenly fill with gold, or silver, or even porcelain – it is a remarkable event that defies explanation. Yet its very banality – after all, there are plenty of dentists in the USA, and presumably they all know how to fill cavities with a variety of materials – seems to argue against any sort of direct divine intervention in Willard Fuller's 'miracles'. Many people wonder why the Almighty should fill the teeth of fortunate

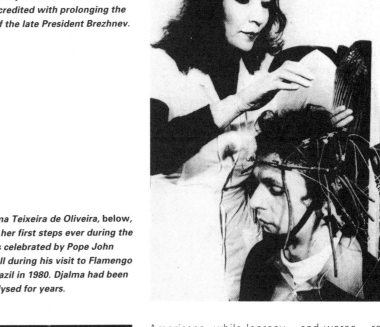

The Soviet faith healer Dzhuna Davitashvili wires up a patient, right, to determine the strength of his bio-field – a scientific version of the mystic's aura. The healer was credited with prolonging the life of the late President Brezhnev.

Djalma Teixeira de Oliveira, below, took her first steps ever during the mass celebrated by Pope John Paul II during his visit to Flamengo in Brazil in 1980. Djalma had been paralysed for years.

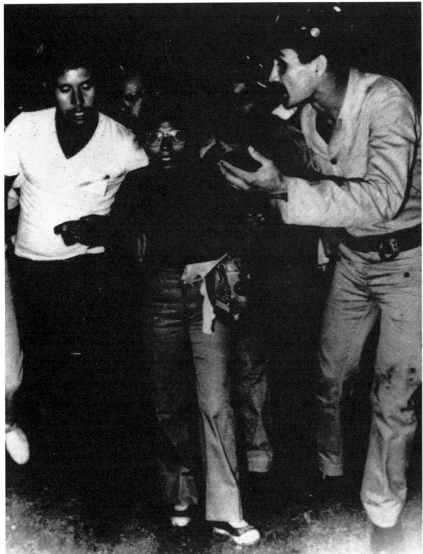

Americans, while leprosy – and worse – rage unabated in the Third World. If Fuller had this power, then it could be argued that it must be his, not God's. Or, if it is divine in origin, it seems to point to a somewhat whimsical deity.

But there are many examples to show that healers do not always concentrate their powers on the poorest or the most sick; and in this light, it is worth mentioning Dzhuna Davitashvili, the Soviet healer, who is said to have done much to sustain the late President Brezhnev during his prolonged last illness. The *Sunday Times* of 29 August 1982 reported that: 'The healer's credentials include testimonials from high Soviet officials, stage and literary celebrities and numerous distinguished foreigners who have written thanking her for curing stomach ulcers, hernias, double pneumonia, kidney ailments and malignancies.'

She is said to have healed by the laying on of hands, which apparently gave patients a sensation like a mild electric shock; and, although a Christian, she did not claim to work miracles on those she treated. But then, in the Soviet Union at that time, discretion may have been the better part of valour.

With so much research yet to be done on the nature and process of healing, it is surprising that those established churches that claim to demonstrate the power of God through healing by ordained priests have no clear idea of the nature of the gift, nor how it operates. In the early 1980s, there was a debate about faith healing in the *Church Times* – the Anglican newspaper – that one week gave an excited account of the spectacular healings said to have taken place in a Bristol church. Yet, only a short time later, it printed the warnings of another writer who said: 'Beware! For Satan himself masquerades as an angel of light. Not all healing is good and in Jesus' name; but happily there is the gift to distinguish between Spirits. Satan can "heal", and he does.'

HAUNTING OF A SCOTTISH CASTLE

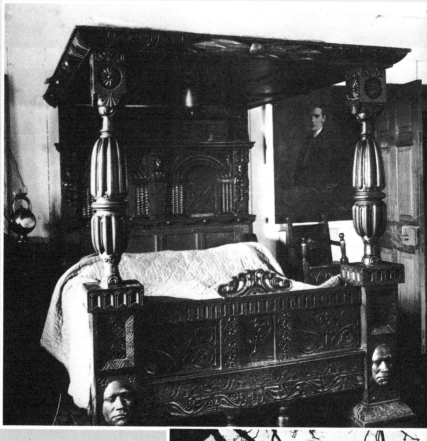

SHRIEKS, GROANS, HEAVY FOOTSTEPS AND THE UNCANNY SOUND OF SOMETHING BEING DRAGGED ALONG THE FLOOR MADE NIGHTS AT A LONELY CASTLE A TERRIFYING EXPERIENCE FOR THE OCCUPANTS. NO RATIONAL EXPLANATION HAS BEEN FOUND TO THIS DAY

The 17th-century painting of King Charles II, left, is now in the National Portrait Gallery, London. Because a massive carved bed had reputedly been slept in by Charles II, the room at Penkaet Castle containing it became known as the King Charles room. Many of the paranormal happenings at the castle, right, were connected with this room.

The four-poster bed in the main bedroom of Penkaet Castle, left, had been a present from students to Professor Holbourn, who bought the castle in 1923. The masks on either side of the bottom of the bed were said to be replicas of the death mask of Charles I, and the bed was believed to have been used by his son, Charles II. On several occasions, the bedclothes were found rumpled as if the bed had been slept in, even though no one had been in the room.

On a windy weekend in March 1946, a party of students gathered at Penkaet Castle in Scotland to rehearse a play they intended to perform at Edinburgh College of Art. After the first day of rehearsal, supper was served and the party retired to bed. Two of the girls, Susan Hart and Carol Johnstone, were put in the King Charles room, so called because it contained a massive carved four-poster bed, reputedly slept in by Charles II.

On either side of the bed a candle burned, throwing long shadows across the cavernous room. Although there was an oil heater, it was extremely cold, so cold that the girls found it impossible to get to sleep.

About midnight, both girls heard a sound, which they said was like 'something trundling across the floor above' or 'something going down a slope'. The strange sound was repeated from time to time, and they also heard footsteps.

At about 2 a.m., a new phenomenon presented itself. On the wall opposite the bed, they noticed a large, dark brown stain. It was on the right-hand side of the fireplace, giving the impression that part of the paper had come away from the wall and was now hanging down. The following night, to their surprise, the patch had disappeared. Although the girls experimented with the candles in an attempt to produce a shadow of the same shape and position, they were unsuccessful.

This was not the first time that Penkaet Castle had been the scene of inexplicable manifestations. Dating from the beginning of the 16th century, it stands near Haddington, Lothian. It is virtually unmodernised and retains many of its original historic furnishings. And there is a legend that a former owner, John Cockburn, killed his relative John Seton, and his troubled conscience is said to cause his ghost to haunt the place.

In the early 1920s, the castle was bought by Professor and Mrs Holbourn, who soon began to experience strange phenomena. 'When we first came here in 1923,' Mrs Holbourn was reported as saying in the *Journal of the American Society for Psychical Research*, 'we were often disturbed by the sounds of heavy footsteps going about the house, and the sound of something heavy and soft being dragged along. Various people who occupied the house [in our absence] complained of hearing shrieks and groans, and that doors which were shut and even locked at night were found open in the morning. One girl was so terrified that she refused to sleep alone.'

Sometimes, when Professor and Mrs Holbourn found the noises too persistent and annoying, the professor would admonish 'John', telling him he was behaving childishly and asking him to stop. The sounds would cease at once.

MUSIC AND MOVEMENT

While carols were being sung in the music room at Christmas 1923, a piece of wood carved with the family crest was seen to lean forward from the wall, 'hesitate' and then return to its former position. Two years later, a friend occupied the room containing the King Charles bed, and heard someone moving about on the ground floor during the night. She and the professor searched downstairs but could find no one. On their return to the first floor, they heard, from the room above, the sound of someone turning over in the bed that the friend had left.

Ten years later, when a Mrs Carstairs, recuperating from an illness, was sleeping in the King Charles bed, Mrs Holbourn's brother, who was in the room below, was wakened by urgent knocks apparently coming from overhead. Thinking that Mrs Carstairs had fallen out of bed and was knocking for help, he woke Mrs Holbourn, who found the lady sleeping soundly in her bed.

Other people (including Professor and Mrs Holbourn) spending the night in the bedroom below the King Charles room also heard sounds of movement from the room above when it was supposed to be empty. Sometimes, it sounded as if furniture was being moved around; and at other times, it sounded as if someone was 'stumbling and groping about the room'.

In 1924, a cousin was staying in the house while the Holbourns were away. One day, he took a visitor to see the King Charles bed and, when they entered the room, they found the bedclothes ruffled – as if the bed had not been made. The cousin mentioned this to the gardener's daughter, Mrs Anderson (whose job it was to make the beds), and

In March 1946, when a party of students spent the night at Penkaet, young Mr Holbourn and his wife slept in the dining room, *left*, and Mrs Holbourn Senior occupied the music room, *bottom*. All three were kept awake far into the night by loud, unexplained noises. Later in the year, in July, members of an East Lothian society visited the house. While they were in the library, *below*, a glass dome covering a model of Penkaet, *below left*, suddenly disintegrated.

she expressed surprise, maintaining that she had in fact made the King Charles bed that very morning. The incident was dismissed – until it happened again. The cousin took another visitor up to the room, this time someone who wanted to photograph the bed. Again the bedclothes were found to be disarranged, and again Mrs Anderson had to remake the bed. The visitor took his photograph and left, but returned a day or so later to say that the photograph had been under-exposed. When he and the Holbourns' cousin went up to the bedroom so that he could rephotograph the bed, they found that, once again, the bedclothes had been pulled about. This time, after Mrs Anderson had put the bedclothes straight, the cousin took the precaution of locking the two doors leading into the room and checking that the windows were secure. He also placed two bricks against the main door. The following day, the bricks had been moved and the bedclothes were again disarranged. At the time that these strange occurrences took place, the cousin was the only person living in the house.

Another incident that occurred in the very same room concerned a massive antique cabinet, which was very difficult to move. This was found 6 inches (15 centimetres) away from the wall. In addition, a brass jug and basin had been placed on top of the cabinet, and the jug was lying on its side.

In the summer of 1935, Professor Holbourn's son was working late one evening in the workshop on the ground floor. Although it was about 11 p.m., it was only just getting dark, and the son took the job he was working on outside in order to look at it in the fading light. While he was outside, the housekeeper, Betta Leadbetter, came to the window to tell him that someone was taking a bath. She had heard the taps running, someone splashing about in the bath, and later the water running out. As his wife had been in bed since 9 p.m., he decided to investigate.

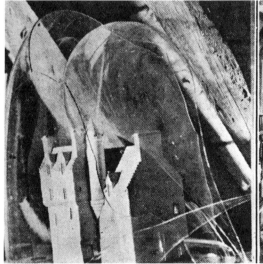

" ON THE NIGHT OF HER HUSBAND'S FUNERAL, MRS HOLBOURN SENIOR SAID THAT SHE HAD HEARD FOOTSTEPS COMING DOWN THE PATH OUTSIDE THE HOUSE; SHE ALSO HEARD THE FRONT DOOR OPEN AND SHUT. WHEN HER ELDEST SON INVESTIGATED, HE COULD FIND NOTHING TO ACCOUNT FOR THE SOUNDS. "

Legend has it that a former owner of Penkaet Castle, above, a certain John Cockcroft, killed a relative, and that his troubled spirit is responsible for the strange noises and other unaccountable happenings that have so often been reported there. At Christmas 1923, for instance, a piece of wood in the music room, carved with the family crest, was seen by several witnesses to lean forward from the wall, hesitate perceptibly, and then return to its proper place.

When he entered the bathroom, it was full of steam and the mirror and windows completely misted over, although the bath itself was quite dry. No one in the house admitted to having used the bath. The most bizarre feature of this incident concerned the soap. At the time, it was customary for large houses to order soap by the half-hundredweight (25 kilograms). The Penkaet Castle soap was all of one colour. What was found in the bathroom, however, was a square piece of white soap, totally unlike the other soap in the house.

It is well known that domestic animals are acutely sensitive to paranormal phenomena, and another incident at Penkaet Castle bears this out. On the night of her husband's funeral, Mrs Holbourn Senior said that she had heard footsteps coming down the path outside the house: she also heard the front door open and shut. When her eldest son investigated, he could find nothing to account for the sounds. But when he returned, the cat preceded him, showing every sign of being terrified. It took refuge under the table, lashing its tail from side to side.

On another occasion, Professor Holbourn's son heard a scratching sound at one of the two doors leading into the Middle Room. As the household possessed a Siamese cat at the time, he went to open the door for it. To his astonishment, when he was about 3 feet (1 metre) from the door, it suddenly swung wide open, the door at the opposite end of the room did likewise, and a curtain blew outwards, although there was no wind. As he stood there, footsteps were heard down the passage.

Among the students who had come to Penkaet Castle to rehearse their play that weekend in March 1946 was Professor Holbourn's son. Most members of the party arrived on the Saturday and, after a rehearsal and supper, they all retired to bed.

Because the house was so crowded, Mrs Holbourn Senior occupied the music room. During the night she heard, from somewhere above her, loud noises that continued until nearly 3 a.m. Her son and his wife spent the night in the dining room, and they too heard disturbing noises, so severe that they hardly slept at all. It sounded as if the other members of the group were rehearsing the play again – behaviour that seemed quite extraordinary at that time of night.

In the morning, the two girls who had occupied the room above were asked how they had slept. They had been much disturbed by peculiar noises, they complained, but had tried to ignore it all, thinking that perhaps someone was playing a trick.

When Carol and Susan, who had occupied the King Charles room, came down, they told the others about the noises they had heard, and the ghastly stain on the wall. They wondered if a certain William Brown (in the room above theirs) had been playing a trick on them; but when he came down, he said he had slept soundly.

Another member of the party, Margaret Stewart, had slept in the Long Room on the same floor as the King Charles room, sharing it with Carolyn Smith. She had also heard the trundling noise. She said that the room was very cold, and that she had the feeling that they were never quite alone.

STOPPED CLOCKS

Susan Hart had encountered another puzzling phenomenon. She had brought with her a clock, which had been in her possession ever since her schooldays and had never been known to go wrong. At Penkaet, she wound it up, but found that it would not go for more than five minutes continuously throughout her stay at the castle, even though she tried to get it working several times. Mr Holbourn said that he had discovered that any clock placed on the wall between the dining room and the next room would not go. He had also tried hanging a watch on that wall, and it stopped.

Two of the girls, Carol Johnstone and Margaret Stewart, said that they had felt ill throughout their visit. All in all, it seemed that the weekend produced a number of strange and inexplicable events.

On 6 October 1946, a trustee of the Edinburgh Psychic College took a statement from Mrs Holbourn. He also interviewed most of the members of the rehearsal party in Edinburgh on 4 December of that year. William Brown sent a statement from his army camp on 28 January 1947, in which he said that, on the Saturday night in question, all he did after the party retired to bed was to go to the library to look for something to read, go to his room, undress, and lie in bed reading. He said he was asleep long before midnight.

On 29 July 1946, public attention was drawn to the 'entity' that had disturbed the party of young people. It was the day that about 100 members of the East Lothian Antiquarian and Field Naturalists Society had an outing to the castle. In an upper gallery, used as a library, was a glass dome that covered and protected a model of the house. It was about 2 feet (60 centimetres) high, and stood on an oval base about 20 inches (50 centimetres) long. Suddenly, for no apparent reason, and with no one anywhere near it, the dome shattered. Could this perhaps have been a hint from 'John Cockburn' that he was tired of so many visitors?

THE EXPERIMENTER EFFECT

CAN THE SCIENTIST REMAIN DETACHED FROM THE PHENOMENA HE STUDIES? OR IS HE INEVITABLY SO BOUND UP WITH THEM THAT HE ACTUALLY CREATES MANY OF THE EFFECTS THAT HE OBSERVES?

A disturbing idea has gained currency in certain scientific circles in recent years, and is one that conflicts completely with the basis on which most scientists conduct their experiments – that of 'naïve realism'. Most scientists, most of the time, assume that the physical world is 'out there', quite independent of themselves (though the scientist's own body, with its sense organs, is clearly a part of that world). Science is considered to be, firstly, a process of describing that physical world, and then of devising hypotheses as to how things work. If the hypotheses are sound, they stand up under test, and assume the status of established theory. For example, the movements of the planets and other celestial bodies could be predicted with considerable accuracy by Newton's theory of gravitation; and, after two centuries of successes, the theory came to be regarded as unshakeable knowledge. However, when hypotheses do not stand up under test, they are changed, or scrapped and replaced by better ones. Thus, Newton's theory of gravitation was finally to be replaced by Einstein's fundamentally different general theory of relativity of 1915.

An experiment in psychokinesis (PK) is under way in the laboratory, below. J. B. Rhine, making notes, obtained results in dice-rolling experiments that convinced him subjects could mentally control the numbers that turned up on the dice. If this can happen in a deliberately contrived PK experiment, could it also happen unknown to experimenters involved in conventional research?

Most scientists would probably be willing to accept that, when constructing their theories, they are actually building mental 'models' representing experience. But they would probably react violently against the suggestion that the realist's view is never the whole truth. And if it were suggested that their mental activity could perhaps affect the results of an experiment, they would probably be completely incredulous. Indeed, they would no doubt point out that a most important step in the establishment of a scientific theory is that relevant experiments should be repeatable by other experimenters in other laboratories, in order to provide the assurance that the result obtained is not the product of chance, error or self-deception.

Admittedly, the attitude of modern nuclear physicists is perhaps a little different. In the models they have devised to explain the behaviour of elementary particles, very strange things do happen. Time runs backwards, and particles may disappear at one place and reappear in another without crossing the space between. Nuclear physicists on the whole do not worry too much about the physical interpretation of their equations. They believe that, provided these lead to correct predictions as to the outcome of experiments, their interpretation does not matter. Mental models cannot be visualised – they are abstract and mathematical. So it is that nuclear physicists are often far more

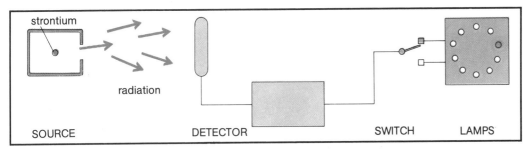

The chain of events that took place in Helmut Schmidt's PK experiments is illustrated left. Radioactivity from strontium 90 triggered a detector, which controlled a rapidly oscillating switch. Some subjects succeeded in influencing the lamps to light in a particular direction. But in doing this, were they influencing the strontium, the detector, or some other part of the intricate circuitry? In the experiment, below, light passes through a slit and forms a light patch on a screen. When a second slit is opened, an interference pattern occurs. Why are certain paths forbidden when the second slit is opened? Nature certainly seems to evade attempts to observe her closely.

open-minded than other scientists when it comes to matters of the paranormal.

Odd as it may seem, certain scientific theories also sometimes actually give room for paranormal happenings. It is an old idea that, just as everything we can learn about or become aware of in the Universe influences us, directly or indirectly – otherwise we could not gain knowledge about it – so we influence everything else in the Universe, to some degree at least. In quantum mechanics, this takes on a new twist. For instance, some of the most eminent physicists have claimed that, when a nuclear particle is observed by a scientist – or, perhaps, when a measurement is made of it by an automatic instrument – the observation directly affects the particle. If, for example, its position is measured, the particle acquires a definite position at that moment – having previously been in an indefinite, 'spread-out' state. According to this view, scientists intervene very directly in the phenomena that they study, both creating them as well as observing them.

GETTING SWITCHED ON

Many psychical researchers have been encouraged to look for the effects of the mind on physical processes at the micro-level. One of these, Helmut Schmidt, built a test machine using radioactive decay. The radioactive emissions from a sample of strontium 90 controlled a number of lamps arranged in a circle. When a Geiger counter recorded the arrival of radiation from the strontium, the equipment switched off the lamp that was illuminated at that moment, and then switched on a neighbouring lamp. A rapidly oscillating switch determined whether the neighbouring lamp in the clockwise or in the counterclockwise direction was lit. Schmidt's subjects were asked to try to influence the lamps to light up in a specific direction – say, clockwise – and his results indicated very strongly that they could.

Psychical researchers have long noticed apparent effects of mind on matter, and many fascinating experiments have been carried out to study the phenomenon. Dr Gertrude Schmeidler found, for example, in experiments that have been repeated many times, that subjects who had a belief in the possibility of psychic phenomena were more likely to be successful. Equally remarkably, subjects who strongly disbelieved in the very possibility of such phenomena were more likely to get results that were worse than would be expected by chance. This, too, involves an interaction of an unknown type between the subject and the system that the subject is trying to observe or influence. Schmeidler called the believing subjects 'sheep' and the disbelieving ones 'goats'.

Psychical researchers have also put each other under scrutiny. Some researchers frequently get good results with their subjects, and are referred to as 'catalysts'. (The term comes from chemistry, and refers to a substance that promotes some reaction between other substances.) Other experimenters regularly fail to demonstrate effects, and have been described, unflatteringly, as 'inhibitors'. Usually, such experimenters claim to be open-minded as to the possibility of psychic phenomena occurring in their experiments: if, therefore, they are causing their own lack of success, the reason may lie in their unconscious minds.

Sceptics might suggest that the results of the 'catalysts' are actually due to fraud or incompetence. But many of these experimenters have unblemished reputations.

So what consequences for science in general follow from this? Suppose a scientist, who has a

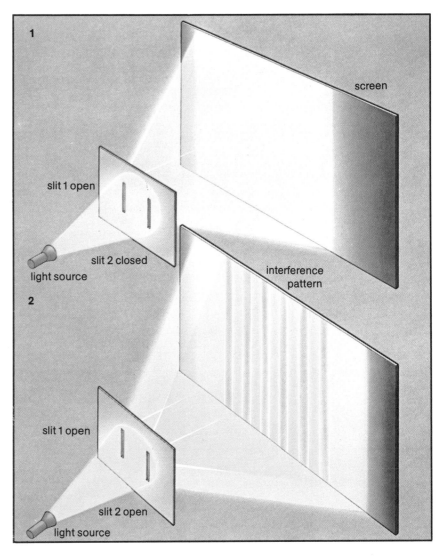

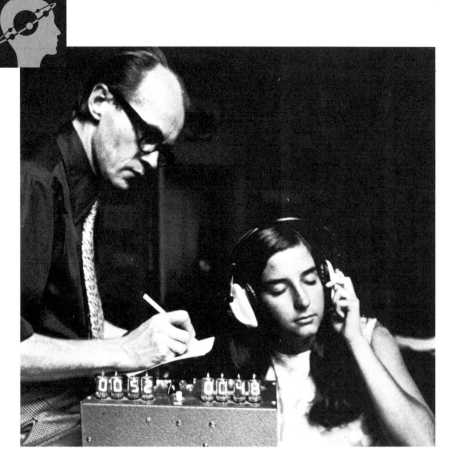

Helmut Schmidt is seen at work, above, with a random number generating device.

long-cherished belief in a particular physical theory, spends a great deal of time clarifying it in his mind, and conducts experiments that are suggested by the theory: it seems possible that physical effects confirming the theory could perhaps be created by his or her very thought processes.

There are in fact many cases of scientists who produced experimental results in accordance with some theory and were able to repeat them, while other workers were at first unable to do the same. This is usually attributed to the necessity for the other researchers to familiarise themselves with an experimental set-up and to learn the skills necessary to conduct the experiment. But might it not also be that scepticism somehow inhibited the effects that the original researcher achieved?

Every year new, short-lived elementary particles are discovered. Frequently their existence is predicted before their discovery, and it has been seriously suggested that they are produced, rather than discovered, by the sustained mental efforts of physicists around the world. It may seem impossible to those conditioned to accept 'naïve realism' as a result of a scientifically-based education, but such an idea cannot be dismissed out of hand.

'Naïve realism' is thus an inadequate basis for an experiment in psychical matters. If the experiment involves the mind of a subject or subjects (and what experiment does not?), then it is important to remember that the experimenter and any collaborators are essential parts of the experiment, too. In fact, the subject, the experimental team, their beliefs and their attitude towards the theory they are testing, the equipment, the laboratory and the world beyond – all form a *Gestalt*, or organised whole. Indeed, it seems to be impossible to draw hard and fast divisions between any of these and say that they cannot influence each other in any

way – even though, in certain circumstances, that influence may be very weak.

The idea that all human beings are part of a greater whole, and are therefore inextricably linked, is also a very old one. But it has only recently found its way into science, and many present-day scientists do not yet accept it. We are all – in the West, at any rate – conditioned from an early age to accept the very inadequate view that human beings are no more than a mass of complex tissues surmounted by a living micro-computer, and that we are all quite separate from each other and from the physical Universe in which we find ourselves. It is very difficult for us to accept any clear evidence that it is not so. 'We are members one of another,' wrote St Paul; and teachers from all the world's great religions have agreed with him. Scientific evidence that this is literally true is growing, too.

Western exponents of the idea that human beings and the rest of the Universe are one whole, the evidence for which keeps breaking through in so many ways, are not uncommon. The eminent South African statesman Jan Christiaan Smuts put forward the idea in his writings on 'holism' – the doctrine that 'wholes are greater than the sum of their parts', having new properties that are not reducible to the properties of the parts. (Interestingly, the word 'holy' has the same root as 'holism', denoting the idea of wholeness.)

The psychologist C.G. Jung, meanwhile, wrote about 'synchronicity' – the occurrence of meaningful patterns among things and events, inexplicable by cause and effect. Arthur Koestler, in *The Roots of Coincidence*, championed these ideas, as well as those of the biologist Paul Kammerer, on 'the law of series'. This is the alleged occurrence of meaningful coincidences in series of events that occur more frequently than expected by chance. Later, Koestler co-authored a work on various aspects of ESP and synchronicity, *The Challenge of Chance*, demonstrating that evidence produced by psychical researchers by no means stands alone.

GUIDED EVOLUTION

The most recent – and extremely controversial – evidence in this area is that presented by the biologist Rupert Sheldrake. He postulates the existence of 'morphogenetic fields' – non-physical structure-forming fields that carry biological 'information'. The development of an individual organism, and the evolution of a species, he says, are guided by these fields. The response of scientific orthodoxy to such a theory has been very like its response to Einstein's work. But the evidence in the case of relativity finally became so strong that it was irresistible, and the theories of Einstein are now 'establishment science'. Perhaps, in due course, Sheldrake's work will receive the same recognition.

The experimenter effect is, then, a phenomenon that does not accord with the basis of most modern scientific practice. However, there appears to be little doubt that it exists and cannot be ignored. What is more, its occurrence could have been foreseen from the teachings of various traditions, especially those of Eastern religion and philosophy. It even seems that the recognition of the experimenter effect may presage a most radical change in our way of looking at the world.

MEDIUMS ON TRIAL

WILLI AND RUDI SCHNEIDER BECAME CELEBRATED MEDIUMS DURING THE 1920S AND WERE STRINGENTLY INVESTIGATED BY LEADING PSYCHICAL RESEARCHERS. HOW AUTHENTIC WERE THE PHENOMENA THEY PRODUCED?

In the spring of 1919, rumours began flying around the small Austrian city of Braunau. It was said that spirits were being conjured up in the flat of Herr Josef Schneider. Twenty-five years later, the psychical investigator Harry Price was to write of Braunau as 'a charming frontier old-world village which is famous as the birthplace of three distinguished persons – Adolf Hitler, and Willi and Rudi Schneider, the Austrian physical mediums'.

Willi Schneider is seen below in a state of trance during a seance in Munich in 1922. Two German psychical researchers are acting as controllers.

Josef and Elise Schneider had 12 children altogether, nine boys and three girls, but only six boys survived: Karl, Hans, Fritz, Willi, Franz and Rudi.

Rudi, the youngest, was born on 27 July 1908. His parents, disappointed that he was a boy, put him in girls' clothing, curled his hair and even called him 'Rudolfine' for a time. He seems to have survived the ordeal, taking up the traditionally boyish pursuit of football and showing a special interest in

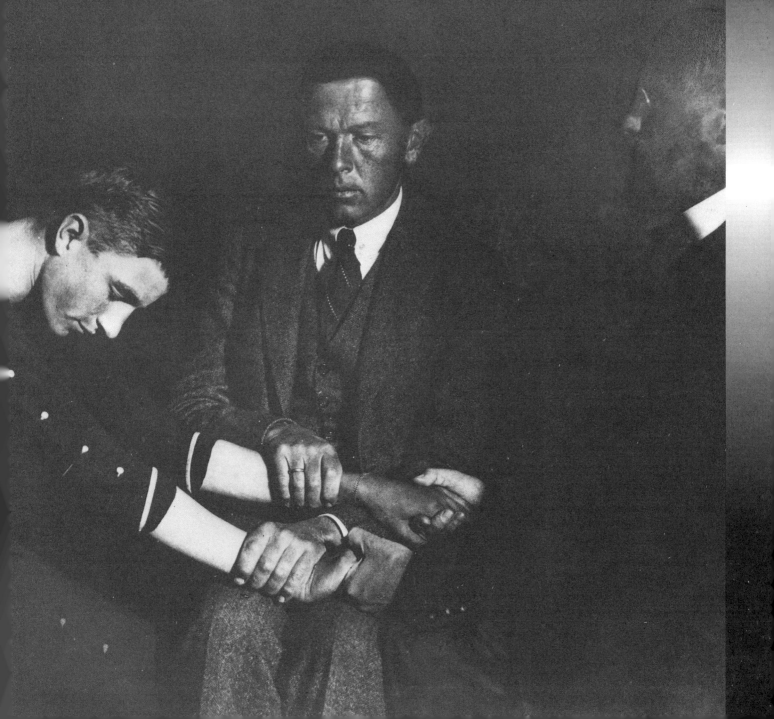

Josef Schneider, seen left with his wife and psychic sons, kept a detailed record of Rudi's seances in two thick exercise books. These became known as his 'ghost books'.

cars and aeroplanes – a preoccupation he shared with his brother Willi, five years his senior.

There are slight variations in the accounts of how their mediumistic activities began. The most widely told version is that in the early spring of 1919, officers stationed at Braunau began buying large quantities of paper from the print shop below the Schneiders' flat. The family discovered that the officers were holding spirit seances, and the paper was needed for recording spirit messages being spelt out by a *planchette* – a small board mounted on castors, and with a pencil attached.

Mrs Schneider and some friends decided to experiment with a *planchette* themselves, but without success. When some of the Schneider boys returned home one afternoon, they also tried but the *planchette* would not move. It was only when Willi arrived and took a turn that the *planchette* began to slide across the paper. Josef Schneider, who was affectionately known as *Vater* ('Father') Schneider, explained what happened:

'It began to write "Olga" in beautiful handwriting. Everyone was astonished and someone from the circle called out: "Well, what sort of an Olga are you then?" The reply was: "I was the mistress of the King of Bavaria, called Lola Montez." Now the questioning began and every day until midnight we did table turning and writing.'

Initially, the *planchette* appeared to move most fluently when Willi's hand was resting on it. Then, one day, it apparently moved when his hand was above it. As the questioning continued, Olga did not repeat or insist upon her claim that she was Lola Montez, a colourful and tempestuous Irish-Spanish dancer, created Countess von Landsfeld by King Ludwig I who had to abdicate his throne in 1848, some claim, because of his liaison with Lola.

Lola Montez, the dancer and famous beauty, right, had a notorious liaison with King Ludwig of Bavaria which may have cost him his throne. At first, Olga – Willi Schneider's spirit guide – claimed to be Lola; but Olga could not understand English even though Lola had been the daughter of a British army officer; nor could Olga give any details of Lola's life.

> **"** THE FACT REMAINS THAT RUDI HAS BEEN SUBJECTED TO THE MOST MERCILESS TRIPLE CONTROL EVER IMPRESSED UPON A MEDIUM IN THIS OR ANY OTHER COUNTRY AND HAS COME THROUGH THE ORDEAL WITH FLYING COLOURS. THE GENUINENESS OF THE PHENOMENA... HAS IMPRESSED... SCIENTISTS, DOCTORS, BUSINESSMEN, PROFESSIONAL MAGICIANS, JOURNALISTS, ETC. **"**
>
> **HARRY PRICE**

History tells how Lola could speak fluent English, whereas Olga could not even understand it. And, indeed, on later occasions, when Olga was asked to give details about Lola's life, she was unable to do so. It therefore seems likely that her identity was wished on her by the seance participants, but not by Willi.

Vater Schneider asked Olga if they could help her in any way. She wrote that they could indeed: would they have some masses said for the repose of her soul, please? The family were devout enough Catholics to comply with her request, though not sufficiently obedient members of their Church to desist from having seances. The masses were said, and seances continued. Olga was apparently grateful for their help and promised that, in return for their kindness, she would make their name famous throughout the world. It was a promise that she kept: the events that day signalled the beginning of a series of remarkable paranormal phenomena that were to startle the world.

Olga instructed the family to cover a kitchen stool with a large cloth and to place objects – including handkerchiefs and a basinful of water – near to it. Willi sat next to the stool and, within a short time, strange things started to happen. The water splashed out of the bowl, two tiny hands appeared to materialise from nowhere, the sound of clapping was heard, and objects placed near the

It was in the small Austrian city of Braunau, below, that Willi and Rudi Schneider were born and brought up.

Witnesses who saw the ectoplasm produced by Willi, below right, described it as a cobweb-like substance, or like an undulating, phosphorescent fog emanating from the boy's head.

stool were said to move. A handkerchief was also drawn beneath the cloth and then thrown out with knots tied in the four corners. Throughout the activities, Willi seemed unconcerned and to be enjoying the confusion that was being created around him.

KEEN OBSERVER

One of the witnesses was Captain Kogelnik, a man not naturally predisposed to believe in occult goings-on and rather inclined to dismiss them as antiquated, medieval rubbish. However, that first encounter with Willi Schneider's mediumship was to transform his outlook. According to Kogelnik, in those early days before Willi became an international celebrity, his ability to produce phenomena was at its height: 'Not even the slightest attempt was made by him to support the super-normal phenomena through normal means. He never fell into trance: he himself watched the manifestations with as much interest as any other person present.'

Kogelnik described how, on one occasion, the cloth over the stool lifted and a small hand emerged: 'I quickly and firmly grasped it and was just about to draw out from the table what I thought must be there – when I found my closed fist was empty and a heavy blow was dealt against it.'

As Kogelnik returned to the Schneider household and regularly witnessed Willi's skills, he became increasingly convinced that he was observing genuine physical phenomena. They were, he wrote, quite splendid:

'A zither was put on the floor, close to the tablecloth, and out from under the table there came a small hand with four fingers stroking the strings and trying to play. This hand was well visible, looked like that of a baby and was very well developed in every detail as far as the wrist, above which it passed off into a thin... glimmering ray which disappeared behind the tablecloth... A large brush was put before the tablecloth. The hand grasped it and began energetically to brush the floor in front of and behind the cloth... '

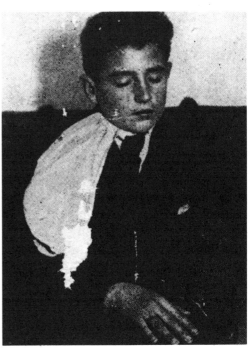

To begin with, Olga had written out her wishes and instructions while Willi was fully awake. After a time, however, she began to speak through him while he was in a trance. On these occasions, his voice came out as an unfamiliar hoarse whisper. Also at this stage, another odd phenomenon occurred: Willi began producing ectoplasm. Kogelnik described it as being a cobweb-like substance, first wrapped around the medium's face, but soon materialising on one shoulder, then the other. The substance seemed to disappear without a trace. One day, Olga invited Kogelnik to take a closer look. From a distance of about 10 inches (25 centimetres), he saw a faint, undulating phosphorescent fog being emitted from Willi's head. It eventually appeared to settle on Willi's hair and rested there like a cap, before being withdrawn into the body through his nose.

But this was not the most extraordinary occurrence. On one occasion, a phantom that stood 5 feet (1.5 metres) tall gracefully danced a tango for delighted onlookers before finally disappearing, perhaps in search of a partner, some of the witnesses ventured to suggest.

The flashlight picture, below, of one of Willi's sittings reveals a fake 'phantom' pinned to the curtain. But many people, including the novelist Thomas Mann, above, were convinced that Willi's powers were genuine.

*In*Focus

THE EYES HAD IT
Vater Schneider's ghost books, a complete record of Rudi's seances, were to help Rudi when an accusation of fraud was levelled against him. Two Viennese professors, Stefan Meyer and Karl Przibram, who had attended a seance with Rudi, later claimed that the controller had been influencing the sitting. Vater Schneider was able to defend his son's integrity by producing the very page, *right*, on which the two professors had endorsed the seance record, one of them adding for good measure the words '*Die Kontrolle war einwandfrei*' – 'the control was perfect'. They were therefore obliged to retract the claim that they had caught Rudi cheating, and instead had to content themselves with asserting that they had found a 'natural' way of producing such phenomena.

Not surprisingly, Willi's phenomena soon attracted local and then international attention. Various scientists went to Braunau in order to investigate. Among the most important figures in psychical research in Europe at that time was Baron von Schrenck-Nötzing. Kogelnik contacted him, aware that he would certainly be interested in Willi and the phenomena that he was producing.

SYSTEMATIC EXPERIMENTS
Schrenck-Nötzing began systematic experiments with the boy in December 1921. These were to continue for several years, and altogether he had 124 seances with Willi, publishing his findings in 1924. Twenty-seven university teachers and 29 other interested people, including doctors and writers, participated in these experiments, the results of which were claimed to be strongly positive. What is more, phenomena reported as happening in the Schneider household were said to have been repeated in the laboratory.

Among those who carried out investigations were Dr E.J. Dingwall and Harry Price who, together, visited Munich in May 1922. It was apparently with some amusement that Schrenck-Nötzing allowed the two Englishmen to search for trap doors and false walls. Having satisfied themselves that intruders could get in only through the front door, this was locked and sealed for the duration of the experiments. Unaffected by these conditions, Willi produced a number of extraordinary phenomena, including the levitation of a table, which rose with such force that Dingwall was unable to hold it down. After a series of tests, Dingwall thought the evidence strong enough to point to phenomena that were, indeed, the work of unexplained 'supernormal agencies'. At that point, he felt he could 'scarcely entertain with patience' the idea that all involved were engaged in a hoax. Unfortunately, however, Dingwall was not to maintain his conviction. Indeed, he suggested, some time later, that Schrenck-Nötzing must have somehow been

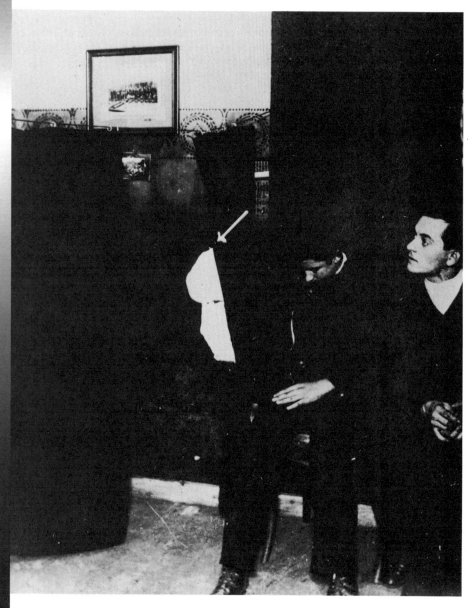

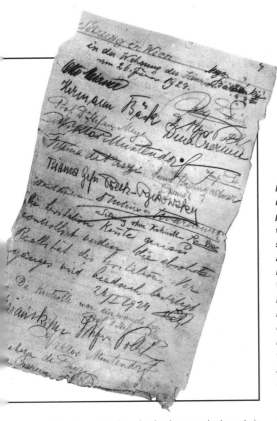

Rudi, below, was subjected to rigorous tests by the English psychical researcher Harry Price, who invited him to England for a series of investigations under the auspices of the National Laboratory of Psychical Research. While Rudi was staying in London, the laboratory paid his hotel expenses plus a stipend of £3 a week which, as Harry Price observed, was rather more than he would have earned in Austria at his apprenticed trade of motor mechanic.

learned what was needed by way of documentation and evidence. His long experience with Willi had helped to convince him of the need to keep a systematic account of every seance. In the case of Rudi, this was a substantial number.

Every time there was a sitting, he entered the names of those present, the date and the place in an exercise book. Then he – or someone appointed to do so — gave an account of what had happened at the sitting. And, finally, all those participating were asked to sign the record alongside any comments they cared to make.

The two thick exercise books that Vater Schneider managed to fill make fascinating reading. They were always described as Vater Schneider's *Geisterbücher* – or ghost books. He refused to be parted from them in his lifetime.

These books are fading now; the binding is extremely frail, but the accounts of the sittings can still be read quite easily. Altogether they contain details of 269 sittings, from 8 December 1923 to 1 January 1932, and the painstakingly collected reports provide good evidence for the genuineness of Rudi Schneider's psychic powers.

responsible for what they had witnessed, though it is difficult to see how the Baron could have achieved such a feat.

Willi's mediumship gradually began to wane and, by the time he came to be investigated in London in 1924, the only phenomena he now seemed capable of producing were, to say the least, very disappointing. However, in 1919, before the decline had become firmly established, Olga made one of her strangest announcements. In the hoarse, hurried whisper that was characteristic of Willi in trance, she stated that she wanted to contact Rudi, and that he was in fact a stronger medium than Willi. The Schneider parents objected: Rudi was only 11 years old, he could not stay up late, and he would be frightened. Olga was adamant. 'He will come!' she said. And he did; for even as the Schneiders were arguing with Olga, the door opened and Rudi entered the room. He looked as if he were sleepwalking: his eyes were tightly closed and his hands outstretched. The moment he sat down, phenomena started to occur.

RISING STAR

Rudi now went into a trance and spoke as Olga. Willi, meanwhile, appeared to take on a new personality who announced herself as being 'Mina' and who spoke in a voice that was quite distinct from the one previously used by Willi when in trance. Olga was never again to speak through Willi and, with the phenomena he could produce already in decline, his younger brother Rudi now became very much the focus of attention.

Schrenck-Nötzing took an interest from the earliest days of Rudi's mediumship, and experiments were begun at once. At first, they were held in Braunau but, later, the boy was investigated at the Baron's own laboratory in Munich. The powers that Rudi seemed to possess were equal to those that his brother once had.

From the outset, Vater Schneider decided to keep a record of Rudi's progress, and quickly

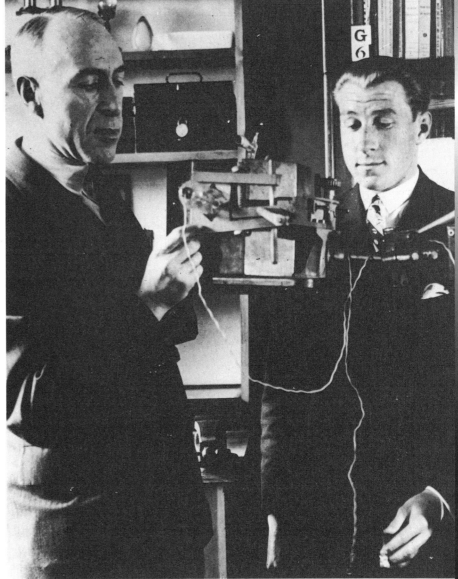

THE MAKING OF A SAINT

WHEN AN OBSCURE CARMELITE NUN DIED AT THE AGE OF 24 IN 1897, NO ONE COULD HAVE FORESEEN HER POPULARITY AS A SAINT. HERE, WE DESCRIBE THE LIFE OF ST THÉRÈSE OF LISIEUX, AND THE MIRACLES SAID TO BE ASSOCIATED WITH HER EVEN TODAY

It was in the main street of Alençon in northern France, below, that Zelie Guerin and Louis Martin were first drawn to each other, apparently by the hand of God. They married and had a large family. All the boys died in infancy and all the girls became nuns – among them the future saint.

Sister Thérèse is seen, right, in the convent garden, holding a lily – the traditional symbol of virginal purity.

As Zelie Guerin was crossing the bridge over the river Sarthe at Alençon in northern France one blustery day in October 1858, she saw a strange man walking towards her. At that moment, according to her own account, a voice within her told her: 'This is he for whom I have prepared you.'

His name was Louis Martin, a watchmaker in the town. The couple fell into conversation – an exceptional event, for both were modest and pious to an unusual degree – and found they had a great deal in common. Both were the children of army captains who had served under Napoleon. But even more remarkably, both had at one time felt religious

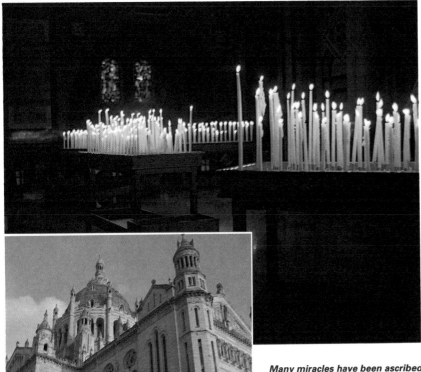

Many miracles have been ascribed to St Thérèse, whose popularity shows no sign of diminishing. Votive candles offered in the hope of her direct intercession burn brightly, above, in the great Basilica at Lisieux, left, which has gradually become a place of pilgrimage.

have been spoilt. This point did, indeed, later occur to the Promoter of the Faith who was appointed by the Pope to investigate the case for Thérèse's canonisation. But he found no evidence to suggest that she was anything other than a delightful child.

Not surprisingly, given the pious environment in which she grew up, Thérèse was a devout Catholic from her earliest years. She was later to write in her autobiography, *Histoire d'une Ame*, that: 'From the age of three, I denied God nothing.'

OBSTINACY OF SPIRIT

The Promoter of the Faith did, however, find one fault in her character – a marked obstinacy of spirit – which was said to be successfully curbed except when Thérèse believed she was prompted by the will of God. It was in this way that she was to justify the dramatic breach of etiquette that she committed during an audience with the Pope in 1887.

In that year, the Bishops of Normandy sponsored a public pilgrimage to Rome – a rare event. Thérèse, by now 14 years of age, had a particular reason for wishing to join it. Her three elder sisters had already become nuns and it was her fervent desire to follow them within the next year. Not unreasonably, the ecclesiastical authorities rejected her request to become a novice on the grounds of her extreme youth. For Thérèse, however, this was merely a bureaucratic obstacle in the path to which God had called her, and she determined to seize the chance to make a direct appeal to the Pope, Leo XIII. To the alarm of the clerics in charge of the pilgrims, she made no secret at all of her intentions. The priests told her firmly to hold her tongue, an order that was strongly reinforced in the ante-chamber of the Papal audience hall. Nevertheless, when her turn eventually came to kiss the Holy Father's extended hand, she grasped it and tried to present her case. Two of the Pope's helmeted Swiss Guards at once stepped forward to remove her. But, recovering from his astonishment, the Pontiff allowed her to continue, although his answer to her request was diplomatic: 'Well, you will enter the convent if it is God's will . . .'

So, astonishingly – and against all precedent – the authorities in France relented and Thérèse was received into the Carmelite Convent in Lisieux the following year. The régime of the order was harsh even by the standards of the day. The nuns ate no meat, and from September to Easter they took only one meal a day. From rising at 4 a.m. until rest at 10 p.m., most of their time was spent in complete silence. In addition, each nun was required to scourge her naked body several times a week with what is known as a *disciplina*, a sort of cat-o'-nine tails made of knotted leather thongs.

Thérèse accepted the daily suffering humbly and thankfully for the glory of God. Discussing the use of the scourge, her younger sister Céline confessed to her that she 'stiffened involuntarily in an effort to suffer less.' Thérèse expressed surprise: 'I whip myself in order to feel pain, as I want to suffer as much as possible. When the tears come into my eyes, I endeavour always to smile.' Later, however, she came to reject the use of instruments of mortification, emphasizing instead the importance of complete obedience to God in every aspect of life.

vocations, though frustrated in achieving them. Zelie had sought admission to the Sisters of St Vincent de Paul, and had been turned down without explanation. And Louis' earnest efforts to become a monk at the Grand St Bernard Abbey had come to nothing since he was unable to gain a sufficient mastery of Latin.

Within three months, the couple were married. By their own choice, it was a marriage of perfect monastic chastity. For 10 months, they lived happily as brother and sister, until Louis' father confessor, no doubt feeling that such a state was unnatural, advised them that it was God's will that they should have children. Louis and Zelie took him at his word, and over the next 14 years they produced five girls and four boys. The boys all died in infancy, but the five girls survived to succeed where their parents had failed in entering monastic life. And the youngest of them, Thérèse, was canonised a saint of the Roman Catholic Church in 1925, a mere 28 years after her death.

Zelie died from breast cancer when Thérèse was four years old, but the little girl's childhood in the old stone-built town of Alençon was nevertheless a happy one. Her father called her *ma petite reine* ('my little queen') and would deny her nothing – to the extent that a less exceptional child might

*In*Focus

CLAIMS TO HOLINESS

The process leading to the canonisation of Roman Catholic saints is a lengthy and rigorous one. The bishop of the diocese in which the candidate lived first holds an enquiry and then sends the results to Rome. Here, the case is put into the hands of a committee known as the Congregation for the Causes of Saints. The Congregation now appoints two men to examine the case further – the Postulator of the Cause, who argues for the case, and the Promoter of the Faith, commonly known as the Devil's Advocate, whose task it is to search out any reasons why the candidate should not be canonised and thereby made a saint.

The life and claims to holiness of the candidate are now examined: in the case of non-martyrs, two well-attested miracles are required for the initial step of beatification, which takes place before canonisation. A five-man committee is appointed by the Congregation to examine the case in greater detail. If it is successful, it goes back to the Congregation for discussion at three consecutive meetings. The Pope himself attends a final meeting; and if, after 'prayerful consideration', he supports the cause, yet another meeting is held. The Pope can now declare the candidate blessed.

The final step in the process takes place if a further two or more well-authenticated miracles are proved to have taken place through the intercession of the person declared blessed. These are discussed at three meetings of the Congregation. A final meeting is then held, and the Pope issues a document known as a Bull of Council, in which he states that the new saint is worthy of honour.

Thérèse is seen aged 15, below, with her widower father, just before she became the youngest nun in the Carmelite convent at Lisieux. M. Martin adored Thérèse, and her ardent sense of vocation convinced him that he should allow her to become a nun.

A statue of the dead saint, bottom, can be seen in the Basilica at Lisieux.

Thérèse lies dying, right, in 1897. The privations of her religious life took their toll, but she offered up her sufferings to God – and pledged to return from heaven to help the faithful. Her death, she said, would be only the beginning of her 'real work'.

Thérèse's devoutness and cheerfulness were exemplary, and were remarked upon by everyone who knew her. In recognition of these qualities, she was entrusted, at the age of 23, with the care and training of novices. Then, one morning, she suffered a severe haemorrhage. The privations of her life had taken their toll. Tuberculosis was diagnosed, and she was given a year to live.

Towards the end, she remarked to one of the nuns who tended her: 'I have never given God anything but love and it is with love that I will repay. After my death, I will let fall a shower of roses. Now I am in chains like Joan of Arc in prison, but free soon, then will be the time of my conquests.'

The infirmary sister, no doubt thinking to humour her, replied: 'You will look down from heaven.' 'No,' answered Thérèse vehemently, 'I will come down.'

On her deathbed, Thérèse was brought roses. Deliberately removing the petals one by one, she touched them to a crucifix beside her bed. A few fell to the ground; and seeing this, she cried earnestly: 'Gather them carefully! One day they will give pleasure to other people. Don't lose a single one of them.'

The final death agony was a long one. For hours, Thérèse fought for breath, her hands and face turning purple, her mattress becoming soaked with sweat. To add to her pain, the doctor's prescription of morphine was denied her by an eccentric and tyrannical Mother Superior.

Many Roman Catholics believe that Thérèse's sufferings were not in vain. After her death, there occurred a remarkable series of phenomena – perhaps miracles – many of them connected with the rose petals she had plucked when she was dying. Whether or not the rose is responsible, as some people think, these events defy rational explanation.

Take the case of Ferdinand Aubry. A man of 60, he was admitted in 1910 to the hospital of the Little Sisters of the Poor in Lisieux for treatment of ulcers of the tongue. His condition deteriorated rapidly,

and gangrene set in, causing the tongue to split and then fall apart. Medical opinion gave the man only a few days to live. In desperation, the Sisters begged one of Thérèse's rose petals from the nearby Carmelite convent, and Ferdinand was induced to swallow it. The following day, he was cured. His tongue, however, was so badly damaged that it took the nuns some minutes to interpret his first attempts at speech to mean: 'When will my tongue come back?' Sadly, they shook their heads. But three weeks later, as contemporary photographs attest, Ferdinand's tongue was restored. It was now whole and entire.

A year earlier, a Scotswoman, Mrs Dorans, had been admitted to a Glasgow hospital with an abdominal tumour. Having taken no food for 10 weeks, she was failing fast and her doctor gave her just days to live. Prayers were offered to Thérèse for her recovery by the local Catholic community.

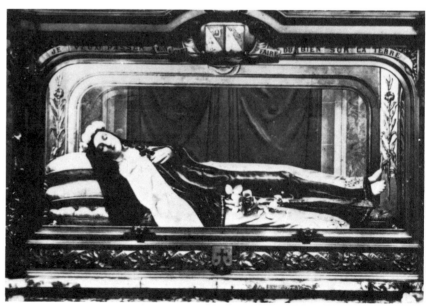

On the night when doctors expected her to die, Mrs Dorans felt what she later described as 'a light touch on her shoulder', although there was no one in the room apart from her sleeping daughter. Mrs Dorans then fell asleep and woke at 5.30 a.m., demanding tea and rolls. Later, doctors who examined her discovered that the tumour had regressed spontaneously, leaving a harmless lump the size of a marble.

A gardener's wife, Madame Jouanne, was rushed to a Paris hospital with peritonitis in 1912. She was operated on immediately, but so much pus was found when her stomach was opened that she was immediately sewn up and simply left to die. But the priest who came to give her the last rites slipped a little silk purse containing one of the miraculous rose petals under her pillow. It seemed to succeed where medicine had failed, for Madame Jouanne made an instant recovery. She left hospital a week later and lived for many years afterwards.

WORLDWIDE CONSPIRACY?

Comparable stories of the intercession of Thérèse have subsequently been gathered from Austria, Belgium, Spain, Switzerland, Italy, Africa, the United States, Canada and China. The authenticity of many of the cases is unquestionable – unless, as one writer put it, one is 'prepared to believe in a world-wide conspiracy of priests, nuns, doctors and men and women of every rank and condition'.

A mere 20 years after her death, the Church acceded to the tumultuous clamour that Thérèse be officially venerated as a saint, and the process of investigating her case began. Contrary to popular opinion, this process is, in modern times, a rigorous one. At least four miraculous cases must be proved to the satisfaction of a panel of medical specialists. We have space to put forward just two of the cases. Sister Louise de St Germain was considered to be dying of a stomach ulcer. On the night of 10 September 1915, she dreamt that Thérèse appeared to her and promised her recovery. When she woke next morning, her bed was surrounded by rose petals: no one could explain how they got there. Her condition, however, grew worse until the morning of 25 September, when she awoke to find herself completely recovered. Her cure is certified by a series of X-ray photographs.

Charles Anne was studying for the priesthood when, in 1906, he contracted tuberculosis. It had spread to both lungs, and he had suffered a number of severe haemorrhages. As the case was pronounced beyond the scope of earthly medicine, he was persuaded to wear around his neck a silk purse containing some of the saint's hair. He tells of his forthright prayer to Thérèse: 'I did not come to this seminary to die: I came to serve God. You must cure me.'

The next morning, his prayer was answered and he was cured from that day on. The doctor who was in attendance affirmed the cure to be 'absolutely extraordinary and inexplicable from a scientific point of view'.

What distinguishes the miracles associated with Thérèse from those of many other saints of the Roman Catholic Church is that they occurred in our time and have been submitted to scientific scrutiny. Indeed, Pope Pius XI and his cardinals needed little time to assess the evidence presented to them by their expert panel. In each of the cases examined, the evidence that was cited was incontrovertible. As we find in the Apostolic Decree proclaiming the sanctity of Thérèse of Lisieux: 'Each instance involved the healing of an organic malady, one produced by pathological and anatomical lesion rigorously determined... such that the forces of nature... could not heal.'

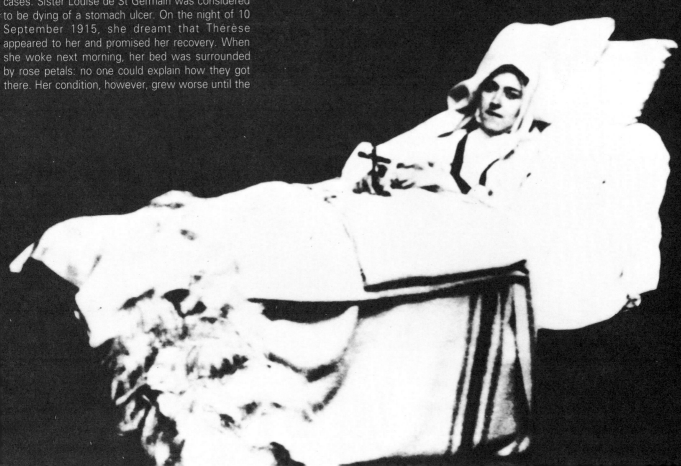

THE HUNTING OF THE QUARK

IN THE EARLY 20TH CENTURY, TWO LEADING THEOSOPHISTS CLAIMED TO HAVE PROBED THE ATOM BY CLAIRVOYANT VISION. ARE THERE IN FACT PARALLELS BETWEEN THEIR ACCOUNT AND MODERN SCIENTIFIC THEORIES?

hope of reconciling Besant and Leadbeater's work with orthodox science.

What, then, were Besant and Leadbeater 'seeing'? In the 1970s, a possible solution was presented, and a description from the two psychics of what they believed to be the hydrogen atom provided a vital clue.

In its normal state, hydrogen does not consist of single atoms. It consists of pairs of atoms, tightly bound together. This pair is the 'molecule' of hydrogen – the smallest quantity of hydrogen that exists under ordinary conditions. This much was well-known even when Besant and Leadbeater began

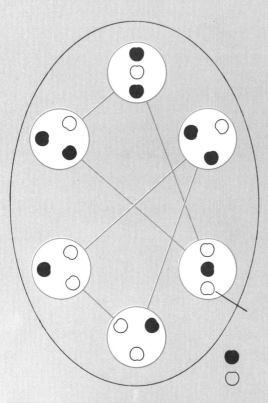

The structure, far left, believed by Annie Besant and C.W. Leadbeater to be the hydrogen atom, may have been derived from a pair of atoms, linked to form a molecule, left. The fundamental anu *would then correspond to hypothetical particles, known as subquarks. Three subquarks make up a quark, while the* anu *likewise occurred in triplets. Furthermore, subquarks come in two varieties, just as the* anu *did. Three quarks make up each atom's central proton, corresponding to each of the two triangular arrays seen by the psychics. It seems that the hydrogen atoms must have been disrupted and intermixed when observed psychically; and the two electrons did not appear.*

Today, when people ostensibly bend spoons without touching them and leather rings link themselves together of their own accord – even on film – the claims of Annie Besant and Charles W. Leadbeater that they observed fundamental particles by psychic means seem far less fantastic than they did in the early 1900s. But both prejudice and well-founded criticism have, until recently, made the two Theosophists' claims seem false and absurd to most scientists. Chemists as distinguished as E. Lester Smith, co-discoverer of Vitamin B_{12}, for instance, pointed out discrepancies between their descriptions of micro-psi 'atoms' and our current knowledge of chemical atoms. Even sympathetic scientists, therefore, soon lost any

interest in their work. Then it was discovered that each hydrogen atom consisted of a single proton – a positively charged particle around which an electron (a negatively charged particle, much lighter than a proton) revolves in an orbit.

In 1964, the 'quark theory' was proposed by two American physicists, Murray Gell-Mann and George Zweig, working independently. They both proposed that protons and neutrons – neutral particles of approximately the same mass as protons, occurring in all nuclei except the simplest, that of hydrogen – are made up of three fundamental particles that are called 'quarks'. So, too, are other relatively heavy particles studied by physicists. Several scientists have since gone further, suggesting the possible existence of 'subquarks' of which the quarks are supposedly composed.

Compare this picture with the micro-psi 'atom' of hydrogen, as described by Besant and Leadbeater. It consists of two intersecting triangular arrays, each comprising three bodies. Each of these bodies in turn consists of three particles that the psychics named 'ultimate physical atoms'. They also referred to them as *anu*, a Sanskrit word, meaning 'atoms'. But can we identify these with subquarks? If we can, then three of them form a quark, which we can identify with the body lying at each corner of one of the triangular arrays. And each triangular array is a proton. The micro-psi hydrogen 'atom' is actually a structure derived from the hydrogen molecule with its two protons.

This interpretation explains why micro-psi 'atoms' of hydrogen were never observed in pairs, as would be expected if they were chemical atoms. But as observed by the two Theosophists, the protons appeared to be much closer together than we now know them to be in the hydrogen molecule – 100,000 times closer, in fact. To explain this, it is necessary to suppose that the two atomic nuclei disintegrated and their constituent quarks then

Murray Gell-Mann, above, shared a Nobel prize for proposing the theory that certain types of fundamental particle are composed of yet smaller 'quarks'.

recombined, at least for the period during which they were being observed by micro-psi.

ELEMENTAL EQUATIONS

The atomic weight of an element is defined as the weight of one of its atoms relative to the weight of one atom of hydrogen. Thus carbon, for example, has an atomic weight of 12 because its atom is 12 times as heavy as hydrogen's. But since a hydrogen atom weighs almost the same as a proton, which in turn is very close in weight to a neutron, the atomic weight of an element is almost exactly equal to the number of protons and neutrons in its atomic nucleus. Different isotopes of an element have different numbers of neutrons in the atomic nucleus, and so their atomic weights will differ accordingly. Furthermore, on the theory we are here considering, the number of subquarks very nearly equals nine times the atomic weight (because there are three subquarks per quark, and three quarks per proton or neutron).

The number of subquarks in any pair of nuclei of a given element is therefore close to 18 times the atomic weight of that element. Besant and Leadbeater found that the number of *anu* in each

*In*FOCUS

THE TREE OF LIFE

Besant and Leadbeater related the structure of the *anu* to the ancient Jewish mystical doctrine of the Tree of Life. This is a kind of chart of reality, including the material Universe and its microcosm, the human body. The Tree is based on 10 *sephiroth* ('emanations') – the 10 stages in which God manifested himself in creation. Masculine qualities are placed on the right, feminine ones on the left. They are combined and reconciled in the central *sephiroth*. The highest is *Kether* (Crown, or godhead), giving rise to *Chokmah* (divine Wisdom) and *Binah* (divine Intelligence). A gulf separates this 'supernal triad' from the lower *sephiroth*. *Chesed* (Mercy) is a constructive, loving principle, contrasted with *Geburah* (Severity), which is associated with destruction and war. These two are united in *Tiphereth* (Beauty), representing the life force and symbolized by the Sun and by the heart. Next come *Netzagh* (Victory), representing instinct, the passions and forces of attraction, and *Hod* (Glory), standing for imagination, and also for reason, which is viewed as a negative quality. *Yesod* (Foundation) is linked with growth and decay, the Moon – which links the Sun and the Earth – and the genitals. *Malkuth* (Kingdom) is matter, the Earth, the body. To Besant and Leadbeater, the three major whorls of the *anu* corresponded to the supernal triad, and the remainder to the lower seven *sephiroth*.

micro-psi 'atom' was also about 18 times the atomic weight of that element. So it seems that the two researchers were observing pairs of nuclei that had disintegrated and recombined, and that they were succeeding in distinguishing the subquarks that comprised them.

Usually the number of *anu* in an atom was not exactly equal to 18 times the atomic weight of the element. So Besant and Leadbeater had to estimate the number of *anu* in the more complex micro-psi 'atoms' by counting them in individual 'spikes' or 'bars' and then multiplying by the number of such spikes or bars in the whole 'atom'. For example, the micro-psi 'atom' of one of the isotopes of neon is star-shaped. It consists of a central globe containing 120 *anu*, and six arms, each containing 46 *anu*. Besant and Leadbeater apparently counted 47 *anu* in one of these arms and thus overestimated the total number in the 'atom' by six. Almost all of the

Annie Besant and Charles Leadbeater, opposite, conducted their research into the constitution of matter over four decades, while also controlling the affairs of the Theosophical Society. Another of their shared concerns was a belief in reincarnation.

support this conjecture. One such anomalous object contained 2,646 *anu*, equivalent to an atomic weight of 147. This is the average of 102 and 192, the atomic weights of the most common isotopes of ruthenium and osmium, which had micro-psi 'atoms' of the same shape. Further 'impossible' structures could be formed by the combination of different isotopes of a single element.

STRING MODEL

Further confirmation of the objective character of the Theosophists' observations is provided by their descriptions of the forces binding the *anu* together. They support the 'string model', which accounts for the forces between quarks.

This theory was developed because free quarks have never been detected, despite extensive searches over the years. Physicists therefore concluded that these particles cannot escape from one another. The string model explains this in describing

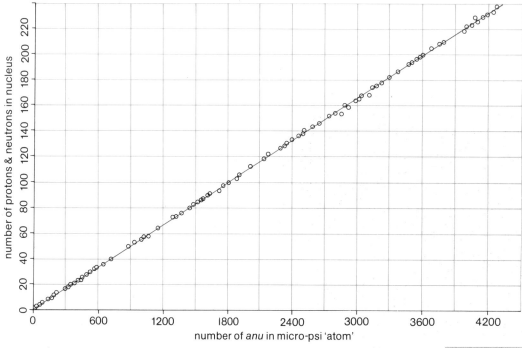

discrepancies in the numbers of *anu* reported by the psychics can be accounted for as the results of miscounting by just one or two in one part of the structure they were observing – a structure that was complex and shifting, and could contain thousands of *anu* so that such small errors are only to be expected .

Their observation by no means came easily. Indeed, Besant and Leadbeater commented on the difficulties they had in stopping the motion of the constituent particles by psychokinesis. Leadbeater once said: 'The molecule is spinning. You have to hold it still and then you have to he careful that you do not spoil its shape. I am always afraid of disturbing the things because I must stop their motion in order to give an idea of them.'

But what of the 'atoms' described by Besant and Leadbeater for which there are no places in the periodic table? These could have been formed from the nuclei of two different elements, with micro-psi 'atoms' of the same shape. The numbers of *anu*

The graph, above, shows the number of particles in each atomic nucleus – a number approximately equal to the atomic weight – against the number of anu seen in the atom by Besant and Leadbeater. If there were exactly 18 anu for each particle, all the points would lie on the red line. Small departures from the line could be due to small plausible errors in counting by the psychics. The graph is impressive evidence that they were observing something objectively real.

C. Jinarajadasa, below, was the collaborator and amanuensis of Besant and Leadbeater, taking down their descriptions as they made their psychic observations.

quarks as resembling the ends of a piece of string. If the model is correct, then we can no more hope to find a free quark than we can hope to find a piece of string with a single end. The quark is regarded as a magnetic 'monopole' – a single source of magnetic field.

The magnetic field can readily be visualised in terms of 'lines of force', or field lines like those traced out by iron filings that have been shaken on to a piece of paper held over a bar magnet. The field lines from a quark form a narrow tube or string – the physicist thinks of the lines as being squeezed together by surrounding space. A quark and its corresponding antiquark (which is its antimatter equivalent lying at the end of a single string) form one of a number of short-lived particles called 'mesons'. Three quarks lying at the ends of a Y-shaped string form other types of particles, including protons and neutrons. If a string breaks, new quarks appear at the severed ends.

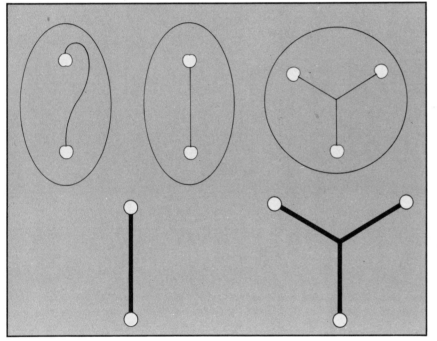

If quarks are regarded as composite particles, then they consist of triplets of subquarks, and it is these that lie at the ends of Y-shaped strings.

Compare this picture with the diagrams of pairs and triplets of the *anu* that were practically observed by Besant and Leadbeater. Some pairs were joined by single 'lines of force'. Sometimes three lines of force formed a Y-shaped configuration, each line ending on an *anu*. It is hard to credit at first, but such diagrams are, essentially, identical to depictions of subatomic particles appearing in the scientific journals of today.

Annie Besant took responsibility for observing how the *anu* were bound together, whereas Leadbeater was more concerned with the larger-scale structures, requiring less magnification. Besant depicted many string configurations, in addition to the single strings and Y-shaped strings. Together, these add up to further evidence that the *anu* were single magnetic poles bound by string-like lines of force. All in all, Besant's psychic observations give support from an unexpected direction –

The structures, above, described by Besant and Leadbeater, strikingly resemble modern 'string model' theories, shown below them, in which quarks (or subquarks) are the ends of 'strings' of magnetic lines of force.

that of extra-sensory perception – to a modern scientific theory of the strong forces acting between fundamental particles.

EXTRAORDINARY RESEARCH

The two Theosophists were assisted in their work by their friend C. Jinarajadasa, who wrote down their descriptions of the *anu* as they dictated them, following their psychic observations. At the end of the third edition of *Occult Chemistry*, he remarked in a summary of the Theosophists' work: 'With the information revealed in *Occult Chemistry*, a great expansion of our knowledge of Chemistry lies in front of us. It is just because this expansion is inevitable that our clairvoyant investigators have toiled patiently for thirty years. They have claimed no recognition from chemists and physicists, because truth accepted or rejected is truth still, and any fact of nature seen and stated clearly will sooner or later be woven into the whole fabric of truth. The fact that this generation of scientists hardly knows anything at all of an extraordinary work of research extending for 30 years matters little, when we contemplate the long vistas of scientific investigation which the imagination sees awaiting mankind.'

Today, the 'extraordinary piece of research' by Besant and Leadbeater has at last shown its intrinsic scientific merit by revealing a remarkably high degree of consistency with what are now well-established facts of nuclear and particle physics. Without knowing what they were observing, they described the subatomic world over 80 years ago in a way that agrees with important areas of modern research.

Scientists and lay people alike may find their claims difficult to believe. But no one can dismiss the Theosophists' claims as being fraudulent because their work was completed many years before pertinent scientific knowledge and theories became available. So a hoax was hardly possible, even in principle. Nor can we honestly reject these claims as unsupported by scientific thought, for the very opposite is true. How, therefore, can one account for Besant and Leadbeater's remarkable anticipations of the discovery of modern physics, except by admitting that they did indeed observe the microphysical world by means of extra-sensory perception?

THE BRITISH SCARESHIP INVASION

A POLICEMAN'S SIGHTING OF A HUGE AND MYSTERIOUS AIRSHIP EARLY IN 1909 STARTED A SPATE OF REPORTS OF SIMILAR TERRIFYING CRAFT. WERE THEY GERMAN ZEPPELINS – OR PERHAPS SOMETHING MUCH STRANGER?

In the early months of 1909, an aerial horror began to haunt the imaginations of the British people. The first sighting of a phantom airship to have a major impact on the public consciousness was made by a Cambridgeshire policeman, PC Kettle. He was patrolling Cromwell Road in Peterborough on the morning of 23 March when he heard the sound of a distant motor car. As he continued to hear what he thought was the steady buzz of a high-power engine, he suddenly realised that the noise was coming from above. On looking up, he saw a bright light attached to a long, oblong body outlined against the stars. This strange aerial object crossed the sky at a high speed, and was soon lost from sight.

News of this sighting met with a certain amount of scepticism. Nevertheless, it set the pattern for future 'airship' watchers, and reports from people

An early dirigible, the Zeppelin Mark 2, is seen above in flight over Lake Constance in April 1909. The same year, there was a spate of mystery airship sightings throughout Britain. Many people believed that the aircraft were German Zeppelins making reconnaissance flights in preparation for an invasion of Britain – but German airships were far too unreliable for it to be possible to employ them on such a dangerous mission.

It was at Cromwell Road, Peterborough, below, that the first 'scareship' sighting occurred.

who had seen bright, powerful lamps or searchlights attached to dark bodies making a noisy passage across the night sky soon became numerous. Another common feature of such stories was the happy habit of many self-proclaimed experts of submitting explanations for such visions. In the case of PC Kettle's sighting, a Peterborough police officer announced to the press that a 'very fine kite flying over the neighbourhood of Cobden Street' had been the cause. The bright light was easily explained as a Chinese lantern that had been attached to the kite.

'But how about the matter of the airship going at a tremendous pace?' asked a reporter.

'Oh, that was a little poetic touch on Kettle's part for the benefit of you interviewers. He did not officially report that, and the wind driving the kite would give the impression of movement,' replied the officer.

'But how do you get over the whirring and beating of engines?' asked the still puzzled reporter.

'Oh, that,' responded the officer, as he went to take his leave, 'was the motor which goes all night in the Co-operative Bakery in Cobden Street!'

This dismissal of PC Kettle's observation might have carried more weight if it had been released soon after the sighting. Instead, it took the police at least six weeks to arrive at this simple answer to the mystery of the airship. It seems they preferred to imply that PC Kettle was a simpleton who could not distinguish between a kite and an airship, rather than to see the Peterborough police force implicated in giving credence to such an unlikely story.

A clipping from the Cardiff Evening Express and Evening Mail of Wednesday, 19 May 1909, right, describes a sighting of the mystery airship made on 18 May on Caerphilly Mountain. The witness saw a huge 'long, tube-shaped object' lying on the grass at the side of the road. Newspaper cuttings relating to airship sightings and to German military matters were later found scattered over the area.

At first, PC Kettle's observation seemed to have been an isolated occurrence. But around the beginning of May, sightings began to be reported daily throughout south-east England. A typical report was made by a certain C. W. Allen. As he and some friends were driving through the village of Kelmarsh, Northamptonshire, they suddenly heard a loud bang. Then, above them, they heard the 'tock-tock-tock' of a motor engine. Although the sky was dark, they were able to see a 100-foot (30-metre) long, torpedo-shaped airship that carried lights fore and aft. It was moving swiftly, but this did not prevent the witnesses seeing a platform beneath the craft, which appeared to contain its crew. The airship then disappeared in the direction of Peterborough.

Prior to the First World War, Britain devoted very little research to airships, such as the Wellman, below, seen at the Aero Show of 1909. Government construction was begun in 1907; but by the outbreak of war in 1914, only five British ships had been built.

There were many more such reports. But what were these craft? The fact that the exploits of Count Zeppelin were well-known in Britain, combined with the antagonism between Germany and Britain at the time, soon led people to the conclusion that German airships were probably making a reconnaissance of southern England.

The major flaw in this hypothesis, however, was the sheer number of airship sighting reports, which soon came from all regions of Britain. At the time, Germany barely had the resources to make even one or two reconnaissance flights. For this reason, a few newspapers were prepared to discount the entire phenomenon as imaginary, and sent readers who had reported airship sightings to what they picturesquely called 'lunacy experts'. From one, they received this diagnosis:

'In every thousand men, there are always two every night who see strange matters – chromatic rats, luminous owls, moving lights, fiery comets and things like these. So you can always get plenty

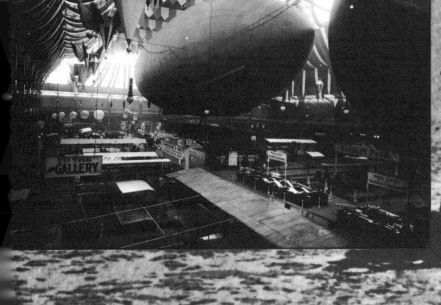

PERSPECTIVES

A PHANTOM FLEET?

Could the mysterious airships seen over Britain during 1909 have been German Zeppelins? It seems unlikely.

The pioneer of German airship research was Count Ferdinand von Zeppelin, *right*, who launched his first dirigible, the *Luftschiff Zeppelin 1* – or LZ1 – over Lake Constance in July 1900, shortly before his sixty-second birthday. LZ1, simply an enormous bag filled with gas and propelled by an engine, remained in the air for just over 17 minutes – but its short flight was impressive, and the future of airships seemed bright.

Count Zeppelin set in motion an ambitious airship-building programme; but by 1909, owing to a number of crashes and shortage of money, there were only three working Zeppelins in existence – the LZ3, rebuilt from an earlier airship that had crashed, the LZ5 and the LZ6. Of these, only two, the LZ3 and the LZ5, were in the hands of the German army. They were very much in their experimental stages, and certainly not capable of long and hazardous journeys, or of carrying out high-speed manoeuvres, such as those reported by the numerous witnesses of the British 'scareships'.

of evidence of this sort, particularly when you suggest it to the patient first.'

The most puzzling and sensational sighting was made by an elderly Punch and Judy showman, C. Lethbridge. With this report, made on 18 May, the focus for the airship's activities shifted from the east coast to mid-Glamorgan, Wales. By now, there were also well-attested reports of a 'long-shaped object' with red flashing lights seen over Belfast, now in Northern Ireland, on 17 May, and there seemed to be no area of Britain left unaffected by the scare. A few hours after his sighting which amounted to a close encounter, Lethbridge told reporters:

'Yesterday, I went to Senghenydd and proceeded to walk home over Caerphilly Mountain. You know that the top of the mountain is a very lonely spot. I reached it about 11 p.m. and, when turning the bend at the summit, I was surprised to see a

long, tube-shaped affair lying on the grass at the roadside, with two men busily engaged with something nearby. They attracted my close attention because of their peculiar get-up: they appeared to have big, heavy fur coats and fur caps fitting tightly over their heads. I was rather frightened, but I continued to go on until I was within twenty yards [18 metres] of them and then my idea as to their clothing was confirmed. The noise of my little spring-cart seemed to attract them and, when they saw me, they jumped up and jabbered furiously to each other in a strange lingo – Welsh or something else; it was certainly not English. They hurriedly collected something from the ground, and then I was really frightened. The long thing on the ground rose up slowly. I was standing still all the time, quite amazed; and when it was hanging a few feet off the ground, the men jumped into a kind of little carriage

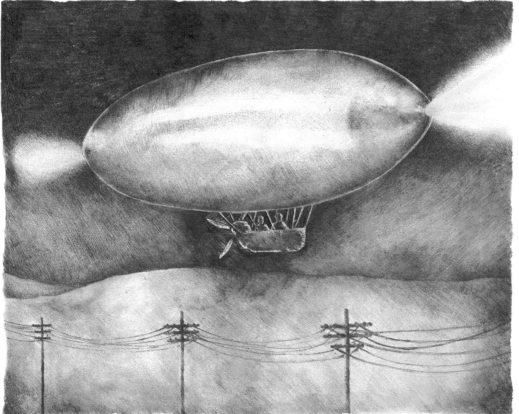

As depicted left, the 'scareship' seen on Caerphilly Mountain on 18 May 1909 'rose in the air in a zig-zag fashion' and sailed away towards Cardiff.

At Ham Common, on the outskirts of London, right, on the night of 13 May 1909, two witnesses saw remarkable airship. The pilots, described as a Yankee and a German, apparently steered their craft by pulling beer handles.

back

At the village of Kelmarsh, Northamptonshire, right, on 13 May 1909, another witness saw a 100-foot (30-metre) airship moving swiftly north-eastwards.

A cartoon published in Punch *for 26 May 1909, below, shows a sea serpent staring glumly at a headline in the* Daily Scare: *'Mysterious air-ship seen everywhere by night.' The caption reads: 'Well, if this sort of thing keeps on, it'll mean a dull August for me'.*

suspended from it, and gradually the whole affair and the men rose in the air in a zig-zag fashion. When they had cleared the telegraph wires that pass over the mountain, two lights like electric lamps shone out, and the thing went higher into the air and sailed away towards Cardiff.'

When Lethbridge, accompanied by reporters, returned to the site where he had his encounter, they found several traces of the airship's presence. The ground where the 45-foot (14-metre) long object had been seen was churned up as though by a plough-share. All over the area, they discovered a quantity of newspaper cuttings of accounts of airship sightings and references to the German emperor and army. Along with these items, they found a large quantity of papier-mâché packing material, a lid from a tin of metal polish, a few dozen pieces of blue paper bearing strange writing, and a metal pin with a red label attached to it. The label of the pin carried instructions in French and excited attention when some commentators thought that it was part of an explosive device, but further enquiry showed it probably to have been a valve plunger for a motor car tyre.

Several witnesses came forward to support Lethbridge's story. In Salisbury Road, Cathays, Cardiff, residents said that on the same evening, between 10.40 and 10.50 p.m., they had also seen an airship-like object in the air.

CIGAR-SHAPED

Additional testimony came from Cardiff dockers who, two hours after Lethbridge's encounter, saw a fast moving 'boat of cigar shape' flying from the direction of Newport, and going eastwards. The airship carried two lights, and its engines made a loud whirring noise. One witness said: 'We could not see those on board. The airship was too high up for that at night, but it was plain that it was a big airship.'

Two gentlemen made some even more extravagant claims, to the effect that they had seen a 200-230 foot (60-70 metre) long airship 'like a collection of big cigar boxes with the ends out' on Ham Common, London. The occupants of the craft, whom they met on the night of 13 May, were described as a clean-shaven Yankee and a German who smoked a calabash pipe. The German asked for some tobacco, which one of the witnesses supplied out of his own pouch. Although they were blinded by a searchlight that played on their faces, the witnesses were able to see that the 'Yankee' was positioned in a kind of wire cage: in front of him, he had a row of levers similar to draught beer pump handles. In front of the German was positioned a map with pins dotted all over it. The encounter apparently came to an abrupt end when the 'Yankee' pulled one of the levers down. Then he switched the light off, and the craft flew off, without either of the men saying good-bye.

With such a variety of bizarre reports, it is hardly surprising that the mystery of the phantom scareships that plagued Britain in 1909 has proved so difficult to solve.

" IN EVERY THOUSAND MEN, THERE ARE ALWAYS TWO EVERY NIGHT WHO SEE STRANGE MATTERS. "

The toad has, for centuries, been linked with magic and witchcraft. Used as an ingredient in witches' concoctions, it was supposed to give them powers of flight; and the stone, said to exist in certain toads' heads, was believed to have special curing properties. Until science was able to establish the biochemical features of this amphibian, many believed it also possessed certain evil characteristics and was closely linked with the Devil. Much of the evidence to support such beliefs has since been explained in more rational terms and has, at the same time, thrown light on why such beliefs originally existed.

Superstitions and strange practices involving toads seem to be linked in various ways with their evolution and bid for survival. Ancestral amphibians had been covered with fish scales that afforded protection. Toads, however, lost their scales and the whole body surface was converted into a single moist lung, so that toads breathed through their damp skin. The extra supply of oxygen allowed toads to adopt such habits as hopping and leaping and, somewhere in the course of evolution, they lost the tail.

With this soft skin, the toad became vulnerable to the bacteria, yeasts and fungi that thrived in its natural environment. So it developed a sophisticated battery of fungicides, and bacteriocides, which it emitted through its skin glands. This battery of poisons then grew to fulfil another function – that of attacking far larger enemies, such as snakes, mammals and birds that preyed on it.

SORCERY AND SCIENCE

The toad must have attracted the attention of Man at a very early stage. Since dogs would foam at the mouth and die in agony after just touching a toad, it was assumed the creature possessed magical properties. In a primitive world, magic was regarded as a weapon to control the environment. The Indians of the Amazon Basin, for example, dipped their arrows into toad poisons, and Chinese physicians used toad preparations in treating heart diseases.

Toads also possessed another hallucinatory ingredient called *bufotenin*. This hallucinogen works by mimicking the chemical molecule that carries messages from the nerve cells to the brain, flooding it with false, distorted messages and producing the hallucination of flight.

Witches are seen, above, flying to their unholy Sabbat on a strange assortment of mounts – lions, tigers, and other unlikely creatures besides the traditional broomstick. Secretions from toads were used in witches' 'flying ointment' in order to create such bizarre hallucinations.

THE DEVIL'S SCAPEGOAT

FOR CENTURIES, THE TOAD WAS BELIEVED TO BE EVIL INCARNATE – POISONOUS, REPULSIVE, AND A FAMILIAR OF WITCHES. WHAT IS THE TRUTH BEHIND LEGENDS CONCERNING THIS UNFORTUNATE AMPHIBIAN?

Toads are not the only source of hallucinatory poisons – angiosperms (high flowering plants) have poisons with similar effects as a defence against herbivorous insects. Mandrake, for example, contains *hyoscyamine*, which also gives an overwhelming illusion of flight. Many of the Solenaceae, such as henbane and deadly nightshade, also provide strong hallucinogens, with accompanying illusions of growing fur, feathers and warts, and of changing into animals or other objects.

There is evidence that witches often kept toads as pets or 'familiars'. In 1556, two Chelmsford women, Elizabeth Francis and Mother Waterhouse, admitted sharing a toad for which they had made a cosy nest of 'woll' (wool) in a pot, until, 'moued by pouertie', Mother Waterhouse used the wool. Alice Hunt of St Osyth confessed in 1582 to keeping two friendly toads named Tom and Robbyn. Instances have also been recorded where witches were said to have 'milked' their toads. And modern biochemical evidence suggests this is exactly what they did.

Hallucinations in the Middle Ages were not restricted to witchcraft: ordinary people could experience aerial flights and transformation into werewolves through such basic elements of their diet as

It is no doubt the ugliness of the toad, **left**, in addition to the poison it secretes, that had led to its close association with evil.

grain, for example. Clean grain was kept for the aristocracy and clergy, while contaminated, ergotised grain infected by the fungus *Claviceps purpurea*, which manufactures Lysergic Acid Diethylamide (LSD), was fed to the peasants.

Among the more lethal effects of this fungus is the feeling of being turned into an animal; so the innocent peasant, with no knowledge or experience of witchcraft, could find himself experiencing the hallucination of being turned into a toad or wolf just through eating the grain. There is a modern example of such an effect. In 1951, at Pont St Esprit in the Rhône Valley, nearly 300 people were affected by eating fungus-infected rye: five died and many were damaged for life. All suffered horrible hallucinations of being turned into beasts and attacked by tigers and red snakes.

As early as 1451, Alfonso de Torado, Bishop of Avila, suggested that the flights and 'shape-shifts' of witches were not supernatural, but were due merely to hallucinatory effects of the drugs in their concoctions – a remarkably accurate assessment for that

The illustration of a female mandrake, **above**, is taken from a medieval woodcut. Like the toad, the hominid-shaped root of the mandrake was considered magical. It contains hyoscyamine – a drug that gives an illusion of flight. Taken in excess, it can cause madness.

From the 12th century, a popular belief held that a lucky gem was embedded in toads' heads. The illustration, **right**, depicts its extraction.

time. Other explanations of the 'flying power' of witches using toad ointments have been rather less scientific. Reginald Scot, in his *Discovery of Witchcraft*, written in 1584, said: 'They [the witches] rub all parts of their bodies exceedingly, till they look red, and be very hot, so as the pores may be opened, and their flesh soluble and loose . . . by this means in a moonlight night, they seem to be carried by the air.'

FULL OF POISON

The diffuse antipathy towards the toad becomes rational enough when we examine its appearance and properties. It looks like a warty, dark-skinned homuncule, the kind of miniature devil figure which fits so exactly the concept of the witch's familiar. The toxic substances it exudes do not help improve its reputation, although the only way a European toad could be harmful to a human being is for that person actually to bite a living toad, in which case he or she would suffer nausea and mild but unpleasant hallucinations.

Nevertheless, the myth of the 'deadly' toad dates back at least as far as Pliny, who claimed the animal was 'full of poison'; while Aelian, writing in the third century AD, stated that a glass of wine to which a single drop of toad's blood had been added was instantly fatal. Even Milton, in *Paradise Lost*, relates how Satan transformed himself into a toad to infuse poison into Eve's ear.

It was popularly believed from the 12th century that the toad had power to charm as well as to poison. The belief was that certain toads carried a gem – the toadstone – in their skulls; the older the toad, the more precious the stone. 'There is to be found in the heads of the old and great toads,' wrote one commentator in 1569, 'a stone they call borax or stelon, which being used in a ring gives a forewarning against venom.' Ever one to make use of a popular myth, Shakespeare gives the Duke in *As You Like It* the lines:

'Sweet are the uses of adversity;
Which like the toad, ugly and venomous,
Wears yet a precious jewel in his head.'

Country mountebanks were also quick to spot an opportunity and took to selling toad-shaped stones – usually coloured pebbles – at fairs and markets. They argued that, if a toad leaped forward to snatch the stone, that one was genuine. Of course, to justify this claim, there was always a toad handy that would prove their point. Some even went further by using a boy to swallow, or pretend to swallow, the poisonous animal. The child would then go into writhing agonies, only to be promptly 'cured' with a touch from his master's magic pebble. These boys were usually ragged urchins reduced to 'toad-eating' for a living – hence the expression 'toadie', meaning 'yes-man'.

THE HERETICAL HOMUNCULE

But while the toad's toxic qualities, however exaggerated, gave it a sinister reputation, it was its humanoid shape that really caught the imagination of the superstitious. Pierre de Lancre, a French lawyer and fanatical witch-hunter, pandered to popular credence in 1609 when he wrote of 'some magicians who feed . . . little demons in the form of toads on a brew of milk and flour, giving them first morsel to taste. These magicians dare not leave their homes without asking permission. . .' He also wrote that one Gentien le Clerc reported that he had often seen 'Nevillon's puppet which looked like a big black toad covered with black fur. It was kept in a box beneath a tile in the floor, which lifted when the toad wished to be fed. Nevillon told him a dozen times that he would get one for him if he liked, and that there was more to be gained from the puppet than from God.'

Long before de Lancre, however, the Inquisition had upheld the toad as an adjunct of devil worship in their persecution of the Cathars, Waldensians, Bogomils, Templars and other heretical sects. In 1388, a member of the Waldensians of Turin confessed that the group worshipped the Great Dragon of Revelation, which was represented by a toad, and said initiates had to drink a potion made from the toad's excrement. Other heretical groups made a ritual of kissing a toad on the mouth and anus to gain magical insight, a practice which finds a distant but definite echo in the later fairy tales of a handsome prince turned into a toad, who had to be kissed by a maiden to regain his human form. During the so-called Age of Reason in the 18th century, a new underground vogue for Black Magic and Satanism sprang up among jaded intellectuals on the Continent, and the long-suffering toad was made to play a cruel part in their black masses and other sacrificial rites. Usually a toad was 'baptised' as Jesus Christ and then crucified upside down.

In his memoirs, Aleister Crowley, the British occultist, claimed that, as late as 1916, while living in Bristol, New Hampshire, he had performed a ceremony to raise himself to the status of Magus in the Order of Templars of the Orient, a quasi-mystical cult that had its origins in early 19th-century France. During the ritual, he had crucified a toad. In 1938, the American journalist William Seabrook had been shown what appeared to be a 'killing' spell cast by a witch in St Rémy in France. A doll had been stuck with pins and smeared with the blood of a toad, which had been crucified on a Bible.

In parts of South America, even today, the creature is roasted alive over a fire and its poison used

Few imaginary habits were deemed as disgusting as eating toads – and as dangerous, too, for toads were believed to be poisonous. Centuries ago, urchins were reduced to earning their keep by pretending to swallow toads, only to be cured by a master's magic stone. A 'yes-man' has thus become known as a 'toadie'. A wry cartoon by George Cruikshank, dated 1834, below, brings home the point.

to tip arrows. Here, however, the frog is usually preferred. Indeed, the poison arrow frog of the Amazon region gives off the deadliest natural poison in the world.

The toad's strange history and associations spread even further. In Togoland, West Africa, for example, the Hos tribe used the toad as a scapegoat for their collective sins, dragging it around the village on a palm leaf until finally it died. The Gilyaks of Northern Asia ritually sacrificed a bear, and then laid the guilt for the killing on a toad; while in Persia, the Zoroastrians simply believed the toad – an evil symbol – should be killed.

The toad remains for many an unattractive, loathsome and evil creature, and biochemical evidence offers an explanation for its use in superstitious and magical practices. There is, however, nothing intrinsically sinister about this unfortunate amphibian, whose characteristics developed with evolution – not as a result of evil practices.

The ritual 'magick' of Aleister Crowley, below, involved performing a ceremony in which he crucified a toad.

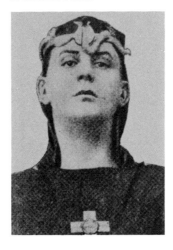

" KEEP THE TOADS SECURE SINCE ANY CRIMINAL WISHING TO ESCAPE DETECTION CAN DO SO BY CARRYING A DEAD TOAD WITH HIM. THEY ARE ALSO A FINE REMEDY AGAINST EPILEPSY. "

D. NORRIS AND

J. CHARROTT-LODWIDGE,

THE BOOK OF SPELLS

UFOs: THE CASE FOR A COVER-UP

THE US GOVERNMENT HAS LONG DENIED ANY INTEREST IN UFOs, YET IT KEEPS THOUSANDS OF UFO DOCUMENTS ON THE SECRET LIST. HERE WE REPORT ON A BIZARRE CIA PLOT, APPARENTLY TO MISLEAD THE PUBLIC

An unidentified flying object skims over the desert outside Phoenix, Arizona, on 12 September 1972. Checked by computerized enhancement techniques, the photograph has been declared genuine by Ground Saucer Watch. Despite such evidence, government agencies such as the CIA – whose official seal appears above – deny the existence of UFOs.

UFO researchers have long maintained that their governments know more about the UFO phenomenon than they officially admit. One reason for thinking this has been the unfailingly sceptical attitude taken by government officials when questioned about any particular sighting – even the best-documented reports are greeted with cries of 'weather balloons' or 'the planet Venus seen under unusual conditions'. Another cause for suspicion has been the peculiar interest that UFOs take in military establishments from time to time. Some, at least, of the infamous 'men in black' (MIBs) may have been genuine government agents, and the thought may linger in many ufologists' minds that the MIB's elusive nature is only the

smoke of folklore, behind which lurks the sinister fire of clandestine operations. In the United States, the idea of deliberate government attack on ufology was confirmed for many by the publication in 1969 of the Condon Report, widely regarded as, at best, complacent or, at worst, wilfully ignorant.

Documents obtained by Ground Saucer Watch (GSW) from the United States government under the Freedom of Information Act now confirm that there has indeed been a cover-up – right from the start of the modern UFO era in the late 1940s. But what is revealed by the documents is not that there is a world-wide plot to hide the true nature of UFOs – involving secret contact with extra-terrestrials or some gruesome conspiracy against humanity, or

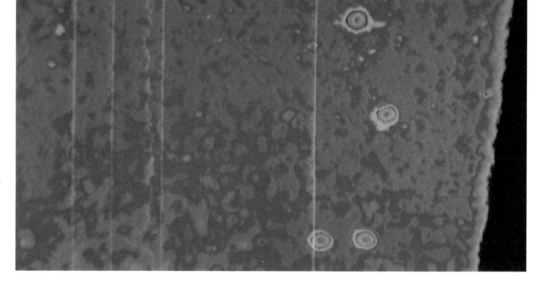

A still from the film shot by Delbert C. Newhouse on 2 July 1952, 7 miles (11 kilometres) north of Tremonton, Utah, USA, is reproduced above. Newhouse saw 'gunmetal coloured objects shaped like two saucers, one inverted on top of the other', near the eastern horizon. Mystified, he shot some 16-millimetre film of them. A few frames have been released to the public, but many more remain in CIA hands. Ground Saucer Watch (GSW) analysed the available frames with a range of techniques that included colour contrasting, right. This demonstrated that the objects were indeed solid. Sceptics have claimed the UFOs were birds or planes, but computerised images of these at comparable distances – centre right, a bird; far right, a plane – show quite different characteristics of shape, reflectivity and density. GSW concluded that the images in Newhouse's film represented craft about 50 feet (15 metres) in diameter and 5–7 miles (8–11 kilometres) distant.

be identified, were sufficient information on each sighting available. How can the man in the street argue with logic like that?

SCREEN OF DENIALS

The debunking campaign has been successful, too, because well-known military or government figures have weighed in against the UFO. Most people have an automatic respect for public figures, and so their statements are readily accepted. The few researchers who believed that they saw through the screen of official denials were therefore easily dismissed as mavericks or cranks. There was, according to the official line, nothing to research. The government knew about everything there was to be seen in the sky.

But perhaps the cover-up was itself so successful because no one could prove it was going on. There was also no hard evidence to back the claim that the government was not being completely honest with the public. Then again, if governments know so much, why have more ex-employees not come forward with their stories – revelations that are far more explosive, potentially, than any political scandal?

Despite all this, one's suspicions remain. Over the years, Ground Saucer Watch (GSW) has encountered numerous incidents that showed

some other outlandish suggestion. What is indicated, rather, is that the US government wishes to maintain a certain public attitude towards UFOs for its own reasons.

This atmosphere of doubt and derision has been created in a number of ways. Anyone can offer more or less plausible explanations for a UFO sighting: bright planets, unusual atmospheric conditions, meteorites, aircraft and so on. This approach cannot help but be successful, since as many as 95 per cent of alleged UFOs are indeed misinterpretations of known objects. Some sceptical investigators even maintain that if these statistics are valid, then all UFO reports must represent objects that could

every sign of direct or indirect government interference. Photographs went missing; ground markings were ploughed under; occasional witnesses talked about visits from military or intelligence officers who wanted to suppress the stories of their UFO encounters. Too many cases came to an abrupt halt because some of the evidence was missing, making it impossible to reach a firm conclusion.

Largely at the insistence of Todd Zechel of GSW, it was decided to attack the issue head on and approach the government directly. In the first instance, GSW questioned the US Air Force – with predictable results. Typical replies were that 'the phenomenon does not represent any advanced technology beyond our present capability and... poses no direct threat to the United States,' and that 'there is no evidence indicating that sightings categorized as "unidentified" are extraterrestrial vehicles.' This was no more than had been expected. The next step was to confront the CIA – most likely to be involved in suppressing UFO material. The CIA's reply to GSW dated 26 March 1976 is intriguing in the light of later events:

'In order that you may be aware of the true facts concerning the involvement of the CIA in the investigation of UFO phenomena, let me give you the following brief history. Late in 1952, the National Security Council levied upon the CIA the requirement to determine if the existence of UFOs would create a danger to the security of the United States. The Office of Scientific Intelligence established the Intelligence Advisory Committee to study the matter. That committee made the recommendations in the Robertson Panel Report. At no time prior to the formation of the Robertson Panel, and subsequent to this issuance of the panel's report [in January 1953], has the CIA engaged in the study of UFO phenomena. The Robinson Panel Report is the summation of the Agency's interest and involvement in this matter.'

The Panel's conclusions – after an intensive briefing by top airmen, astronomers and several CIA

Research director Todd Zechel, above left, and director William H. Spaulding, right, of Ground Saucer Watch, are seen discussing the UFO problem.

men – was that there was no cause for alarm, but the panel concluded that 'the continued emphasis on the reporting of these phenomena does, in these perilous times, result in a threat to the orderly functioning of the protective organs of the body politic.' Their recommendations were framed accordingly – debunk UFOs and educate people to recognise aerial phenomena.

In fact, the CIA did not let the matter drop there in 1953. Searches through the National Archives showed that many reports were missing from the files. When GSW made specific requests under the Freedom of Information Act, a few papers were released, but they were so highly 'sanitized' that only a mind-reader could have made sense of them. GSW then decided to attack in the courts. After 14 months of gruelling legal action, the government released, on 15 December 1978, close to 1,000 pages of documents. It was a major victory.

PSYCHOLOGICAL WARFARE

What do the papers show? Firstly, they indicate that CIA involvement in UFOs actually pre-dates the National Security Council directive to set up what became the Robertson Panel. Indeed, it seems it was the CIA that urged an investigation on the Council! Secondly, the implications for psychological warfare clearly attracted considerable attention. As one memo puts it: 'A fair proportion of our population is mentally conditioned to the acceptance of the incredible. In this fact lies the potential for the touching-off of mass hysteria and panic.' The third concern is with the vulnerability of US air defences: 'At any moment of attack... we cannot... distinguish hardware from phantom.:. ' The use of the word 'phantom' is interesting, for another memo, from the Deputy Director for Intelligence, CIA, dated November 1952, says bluntly: 'Sightings of unexplained objects at great altitudes and travelling at high speeds in the vicinity of major US defense installations are of such a nature that they are not attributable to natural phenomena or known types of aerial vehicles.'

In the light of that, it is not surprising that when Edward Tauss, then Acting Chief of the Weapons and Equipment Division of the Office of Scientific Intelligence, recommended that the CIA 'continue' (not 'begin') coverage of the subject in August 1952, he should add: 'It is strongly urged, however, that no indication of CIA interest or concern

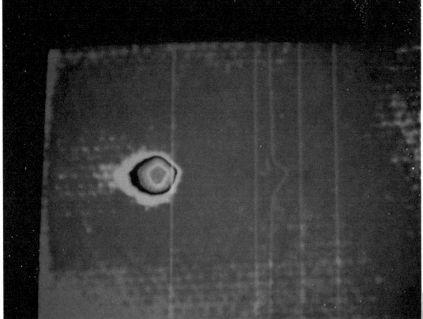

" IT IS CLEAR THAT THE CIA AT LEAST BELIEVED IN THE REALITY OF UFO PHENOMENA. IT WAS ALSO ALARMED BY IT. AND IT WAS DETERMINED TO KEEP WHAT IT DID KNOW TO ITSELF. "

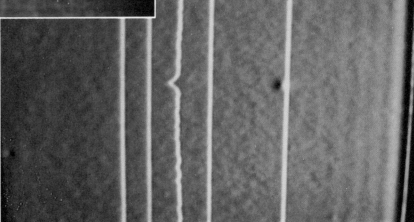

reach the press or public, in view of their probable alarmist tendencies to accept such interest as "confirmatory" of the soundness of "unpublished facts in the hands of the US government".'

It is clear then, that the government – or the CIA at least – believed in the reality of UFO phenomena. It was also alarmed by it. And it was determined to keep what it did know to itself.

Nor was the report of the Robertson Panel the last word, though the CIA pretended to accept its findings. The US Air Force, after all, maintained Project Blue Book until 1969, after the Condon Committee published its findings – though whether Blue Book was ever told the whole truth, either by the USAF itself or by other defence agencies, remains in some doubt. The probable fate of the film taken by US Navy Warrant Officer Delbert C. Newhouse in 1952 – the 'Tremonton movie' that

The last members of Project Blue Book, the US Air Force's full-time UFO investigation unit, who disbanded in 1969 while under the leadership of Major Hector Quintanilla (seated), are shown right. The project's tiny staff was unable to deal in any depth with the thousands of UFO reports that it received every year, suggesting that the USAF was dragging its feet over the UFO question. But another suggested explanation is that the real research was being done in secret by the CIA, leaving Blue Book as more of a public relations front.

*In*FOCUS THE MARINE, THE CIA AND THE UFO

One of the oddest UFO cases on record is the 1952 sighting by US Marine Ralph Mayher, *right*. It is odd not because of the sighting itself, which was as 'normal' as any UFO event, but because of what happened afterward to Mayher and the film he managed to take.

Ralph Mayher had heard that, on the night of 28 July 1952, a couple named Goldstein had seen a flying saucer near their home. He was an experienced movie photographer and was interested in UFOs,

so he arranged to meet the Goldsteins the next day and rented a camera – he had a theory that saucers sometimes appear on consecutive nights. At 9.30 p.m. on 29 July, Mayher heard a woman across the street shout that a UFO was in view. The Goldsteins and another neighbour, Herman Stern, also saw the object, which remained visible over the ocean for about three minutes. Mayher managed to shoot only some 40 frames of film because his view

was obscured by trees and buildings. The object was travelling horizontally toward the witnesses, then turned and shot away.

Mayher had his film processed at once and, as his unit commander had no objections, released frames – such as the one *below left* – to the press. He even recorded a radio interview. But within 48 hours, USAF investigators were on the scene and threw a security blanket over the case. Mayher was visited by a number of men with CIA credentials, who told him to keep quiet about the event. On enquiry, Mayher was also told that the USAF thought the 'pinpoints of light' (*sic*) too small to analyse properly. But the film was never returned.

The strangest part of the story is that while well-informed UFO investigators heard nothing of the film, ace debunker Dr Donald Menzel soon became familiar with it. With surreal inventiveness, he said it showed a cobweb. GSW's computer analysis, *below*, indicates the object is solid, 50 feet (15 metres) in diameter, and travelling at 2,500 miles per hour (4,000 km/h).

was shown to the Robertson Panel – is one indication of the CIA's true reaction to the evidence.

This film has been subject to several attempts at debunking. According to the witness, it shows a number of unusual craft travelling at enormous speed, some 10 miles (16 kilometres) from the camera. Newhouse's report of the incident (he was a trained Navy photographer) is confirmed by GSW's computerised tests on the film, as it was by the USAF photo laboratory at Wright-Patterson AFB, who first analysed it. The film was then handed to the Naval Photographic Interpretation Center (NAVPIC) at Anacostia, Maryland, and subjected to over 1,000 man-hours of study. The Navy had no explanation for the objects but said they appeared to be 'self-luminous' spheres travelling at up to 7,560 miles per hour (12,096 km/h). The Robertson Panel argued over the film for about two hours. They were also shown film of seagulls giving intense reflections of light in bright sunshine. The panel duly reported that 'the objects were considered strongly to represent birds.'

Who laid on that film of seagulls? Was it the CIA, experienced hands as they were at manipulation and suggestion? Whatever the case, what the CIA did not do was stop studying films of UFOs. As soon as the Robertson Panel had reported, NAVPIC was dissolved. Some of its members, however, were moved to the CIA to form the National Photographic Interpretation Center (NPIC). Material dating from at least 1950 is kept there. As GSW's Todd Zechel put it: 'There is a direct link between NAVPIC's work on the Tremonton analysis and the decision of the CIA to place the analysis programme under its direct authority. In other words, rather than thinking the Tremonton analysis was in error, as has been purported, the CIA was impressed enough immediately to transfer the project to its headquarters.'

A COVER FOR THE CIA

It is small wonder, then, that the USAF's Project Blue Book got such short shrift. According to Todd Zechel, Blue Book was 'in reality . . . no more than a PR front, primarily covering for the secret research being conducted by the CIA... to give Blue Book full support would have been a waste, since it would have been duplicating research already being conducted by the CIA. Therefore, and for the most part unwittingly, Blue Book's facade enabled the CIA to pull off the greatest propaganda fraud in history.'

The documents obtained by GSW support the view that the CIA has persisted in UFO research. Among them are numerous reports, dutifully filed by US embassies abroad, of UFO sightings. In 1976, for instance, there were multiple events in Tunisia, with many witnesses, radar tracking and police reports. A very concerned Chief of Military Security, General Balma, wanted to know if the US Sixth Fleet could shed any light on who or what they might be. Not only was this – and innumerable other cases – being reported in 1976, seven years after the US government had supposedly given up its interest in UFOs in the wake of the Condon Report, but all UFO reports from the embassies are thought to be sent to the CIA and the even more shadowy United States Defense Intelligence

The unexplained mass of light, above, seen over Ibiza in May 1974, remained stationary for a brief period before rapidly climbing to a high altitude and vanishing. Reports such as this have been collected by the CIA from all over the world. Despite official claims that the agency ceased to have an interest in UFOs in 1953, documents have been obtained from CIA archives detailing subsequent sightings.

Agency, the National Security Council, the Secretary of Defense and the Secretary of State.

Of course, it is in any government's interests to pretend that it can identify everything in the sky. But all the evidence indicates that the cover-up does not stop at a desire to prevent alarm and despondency from spreading among the people – just the opposite, in fact, if you happen to be a witness to a UFO. Agents from the CIA Directorate of Operations (Clandestine Services) and Domestic Operations Division (sometimes called the 'Contact Division') have been known to harass, intimidate and silence such people. And a more sinister game still is perhaps being played out. For while the intelligence services attempt to deflate the UFO controversy, they are in many ways also helping to feed it.

" ELEVEN PERCENT OF THE ADULT POPULATION, MORE THAN FIFTEEN MILLION AMERICANS, SAID THEY HAD PERSONALLY OBSERVED AN UNIDENTIFIED FLYING OBJECT. IN ADDITION, FIFTY-ONE PERCENT OF ALL PERSONS INTERVIEWED BELIEVED UFOS ARE REAL... "

JOHN WALLACE SPENCER,

NO EARTHLY EXPLANATION

FASHIONS IN PHENOMENA

GONE ARE APPORTS AND ECTOPLASM AS SUBJECTS OF PARANORMAL
INVESTIGATIONS. IN, INSTEAD, ARE SUCH AREAS AS TELEPATHY AND
POLTERGEISTS. WHY SHOULD THERE BE SUCH FADS IN THE UNEXPLAINED?

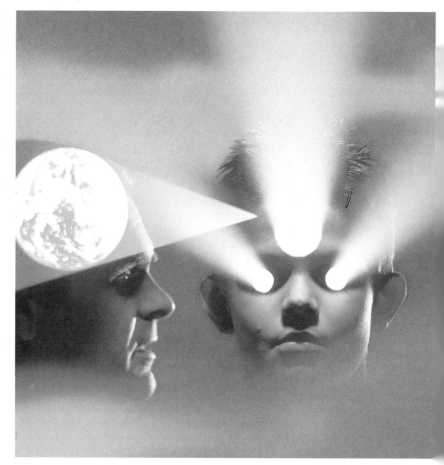

The early history of Spiritualism produced floods of ectoplasm, hosts of full-bodied materialisations, and enough apports to stock a department store. Yet, before and after a period bridging the late 19th and early 20th centuries, such phenomena of physical mediumship were almost unheard of. Fashions in phenomena have changed, and with them fashions in psychical research. Indeed, the investigators of today have all but deserted the seance for laboratory tests of metal-bending, ESP and the like.

Could it actually be that, as Charles Fort observed in the early 20th century: 'There are phenomena that exist relatively to one age, that do not, or do not so pronouncedly, exist in another age'?

One example of a phenomenon no longer in vogue is that of certain birds hibernating over the winter in dark, dry places, usually underground. Although this idea is not taken seriously by 20th-century naturalists, it was not dismissed by such eminent founders of the natural sciences as Linnaeus and Baron Cuvier. A number of cases were reported in 18th- and 19th-century scientific accounts and discussed in professional journals. Gradually, however, such reports ceased and the phenomenon was forgotten. This fact was noticed by Philip Gosse, the populariser of science, who included a not entirely sceptical review of the subject in the second volume of his celebrated *Romance of Natural History* (1861). Gosse wondered why the discoveries of hibernating birds 'instead of increasing in frequency with the increase of scientific research and communication, strangely become more rare'.

There are a number of possible reasons for this. Scientific literature has become more rigorous and academic, and the anecdotal and circumstantial nature of the evidence for bird hibernation is regarded as weak. In such a climate of scepticism, few scientists would risk their careers by opposing the almost universally accepted doctrine of bird migration. Then again, the adoption of explosives and heavy machines for demolition and earth removal could have destroyed evidence that might have been uncovered in the days of the spade and shovel. Finally, there may have been a change in the instinctive behaviour of the birds – something that is not unknown to happen in animals as the environment changes.

Of course, a distinction has to be made as to whether the appearance, or disappearance, of certain kinds of phenomenon are the result of increased knowledge or the product of social processes. The pioneering ufologist John Keel has shown, for example, that only a fraction of the UFOs seen ever get reported, and only a fraction of those reported ever get publicized. Consequently, he and other ufologists have warned of the shock to society if the true proportion of the phenomenon were ever disclosed. Similarly, it would seem that the once ubiquitous sea serpent has suffered virtual extinction – but not so, according to the world's greatest expert on these creatures, Dr Bernard Heuvelmans. After compiling a chronology of sightings between the years 1639 and 1964 for his book *In the Wake of the Sea Serpents*, Heuvelmans

Philip Gosse, the British naturalist, above left, discussed the discovery of frogs in stone – a widely reported phenomenon at one time – in his book Romance of Natural History, *in which the illustration, far left, appeared.*

A sea serpent was sighted by HMS Philomel *in 1879 in the Gulf of Suez, as depicted* above. *Once common in mariners' reports, such sightings have declined, especially since the second half of the 19th century.*

Parapsychologists are now widely investigating the powers of the mind – represented in the composite illustration, left – and do so in laboratory settings. A century ago, however, they were more likely to have been studying the nature of ectoplasm.

Telepathy is a principal area studied by parapsychologists today. Indeed, according to researchers within this currently 'fashionable' field of study, such communication, illustrated far left, may account for many other forms of hitherto unexplained phenomena.

remained convinced that they still averaged about two a year. The apparent decline, he said, was a product of the shyness of the creatures, the fact that modern shipping keeps largely to well-defined routes, and fear of ridicule. As he put it: 'The sound of laughter has driven away as many sea serpents as that of ships' engines.'

But nothing has driven away lake monsters, which have been regularly, if sporadically, sighted for centuries. Indeed, since the Loch Ness monster surfaced in 1933, sightings of huge serpent-like creatures have proliferated in lakes all over the world. Another long-lived phenomenon is that of stigmata, although the first instance did not occur until nearly 1,200 years after the crucifixion. Since St Francis of Assisi was stigmatised in 1224, however, there has hardly been a year without a report of a stigmata case.

STAGE-MANAGEMENT

To most of us, the things we perceive in our everyday lives are solid and real. They are the tangible proof of that state of existence we agree, by consensus, to call reality. It therefore seems preposterous that the furniture of reality could be subject to the whims of something as ephemeral as fashion. But there can be as many definitions of reality as there are people to perceive it. Research into the nature of coincidence has established strong links between the unconscious mind, of both individuals and the collective, and the phenomena of reality. The familiar story of how a lost or stolen item finds its way back to its owner, for example, often through a revealing dream, recurs consistently. The German psychologist Wilhelm von Scholz thought that the coincidences in such cases were so outrageous to the view of conventional physical causality that he was moved to believe they must be 'stage-managed... as if they were the dreams of a greater and more comprehensive consciousness... '

The theory towards which von Scholz was groping in 1924 is surely close to what many Forteans and others subscribe to today: that powerful

*A ring lost in a pool by Queen
Nest is found in a fish served up
to her husband, King Maelgwn
Gwynedd of North Wales, in the
presence of St Asaph, as
illustrated below right. This 6th-
century legend is one of many
throughout the ages in which lost
or stolen items find their way
back to their owner, seemingly
by coincidence.*

Dancing could be set off instantly by the sight of a
pointed shoe, a snatch of music, the colour red, the
rant of a preacher, the sight of someone already
dancing, or the imagined bite of a tarantula.

On the basis of the 'projections' theory, and by
extension of Le Bon's idea, one might reach the
conclusion that a 'crowd' need not be together
physically. Its constituents could be spread widely
apart – even over a whole country – and become
aligned through individual contact with the collective unconscious, so that an idea arising out of this
unconscious would occur to them all. An excellent
example of this curious form of collective hysteria
occurred in France in 1789, and is called the 'Great
Fear' by historians. It began immediately after the
fall of the Bastille in Paris. Entire villages were abandoned as rumours reached them of a huge army of
brigands killing and looting their way towards them.
Terrified people babbled of seeing the flames of
burning houses in the sky, of being captured and of
seeing friends killed by brutal bandits, and so on.
But the whole affair had been hallucinated. The
panic had not even spread out from Paris in the
ordinary way, as rumours carried by travellers.'
Instead, it seems to have sprung up independently
in several locations across France, and to have

projections from the unconscious of archetypal
forms or behaviour are able to manifest themselves
in what we call reality, or to alter that reality by
influencing related events. This semi-mystical view
is related to three converging streams of thought.
One explores the world of meaningful coincidence,
which C. G. Jung termed synchronicity. Another is
the hypothesis of 'formative causation' proposed by
Dr Rupert Sheldrake, which describes a mechanism
for the communication, beyond the normal restrictions of space and time, of form and behaviour in
nature. The third concerns 'tulpas' or thought forms
and the way a consensus can influence reality by
creating its own separate 'bubble' of reality.

MAGIC WAND

The crazes or obsessions that can grip a community, as well as an individual, exemplify this. In
Gustave Le Bon's neglected study, *The Crowd*
(1897), he showed how a community can be gal-
vanised in such a way that a particular set of ideas
or imagery – sublime or even trivial – may come to
dominate their perceptions, actions and rationalisa-
tions of their resulting unusual behaviour. The
'magic wand' that turns a group of individuals into a
crowd or mob is simply a shared state of height-
ened suggestibility. Le Bon thought that this was
brought about when any group of people in physical
proximity become suddenly aligned psychologically
by any unusual stimulus.

This type of phenomenon is characterized in the
title to Charles Mackay's pioneering historical study,
*Memoirs of Extraordinary Popular Delusions and the
Madness of Crowds*. In this book, he discusses the
medieval craze for relics, the South Sea Bubble
swindle, the frenzied witch-hunts, and the wild and
wasteful Crusades, among other topics. The
medieval dancing manias are another example of
some kind of unconscious collective behaviour.

*One theory of mass hysteria says
that the affected need not be a
group of people in close proximity,
as in the mob scene, below, at a
trial during the Reign of Terror in
France in 1793. It can affect groups
in different places as a result of
unconscious collective behaviour.*

spread out like a forest fire from each of these. Historians are at a loss to explain how such panic could grow faster than anyone could travel at the time, whereas the theory that people all over France formed a crowd goes far towards an explanation. The populace was in a state of suggestibility due to general anxiety about the political crisis, and became aligned by threatening images that can only be guessed at. The initial outbreaks needed only a simple stimulus, such as a flash of lightning – unusual natural phenomena were indeed recorded in association with the Great Fear – and rumour and panic did the rest.

Some phenomena have not varied much throughout history, however – among them pathological and mental illness, strange falls from the sky and ball lightning. But explanations for them have been subject to changing fashions in belief and, consequently, were attributed to a succession of gods, devils, elementals, ghosts, fairies, witches, psychic powers or even aliens.

Consider the huge flying machines, with powerful searchlights and 'foreign-looking crews', seen in the skies across North America in 1896 and 1897 by reliable witnesses – at a time when there were thought to be no such craft in existence. These

EN L'AN 2000

❝ ALTHOUGH OBJECTS IN

THE SKIES HAVE BEEN SEEN

SINCE ANCIENT TIMES AND...

RANDOMLY INTERPRETED

AS DIVINE LESSONS... AND

OMENS, UFO SIGHTING HAS

ONLY GRIPPED THE GENERAL

ATTENTION OF THE WORLD'S

NATIONS SINCE 1947. **❞**

CHARLES BERLITZ, WORLD OF

STRANGE PHENOMENA

Mass hysteria can take many forms, such as the medieval dancing craze, top, in which whole villages danced as if demented. During such 'fits', strange phenomena were reported, suggesting that mob behaviour of this sort can somehow transcend time and space. The spate of 'sightings' of airships over North America in 1896-1897, like the one illustrated above, may have spread in a similar way.

sightings cannot all have been misidentifications of natural phenomena; and, indeed, there is another possibility. The late 19th century was the heyday of the hero-inventor; and whereas today's mysteries of the skies are attributed to UFOs, that era attributed them to unidentified great inventors. It was only when Andrew Rothovius compared some of the 1897 incidents with the Great Fear (in *Pursuit* magazine, 1978) that the airship sightings were seen to have originated spontaneously, from apparently unconnected initial incidents in several different locations throughout the country, and then by rumour.

Jung thought that the UFO was a sign of changes in the constellation of archetypes in the human unconscious, and that such antigravity, dream-like discs of light were omens of the need for psychic unity at a time when the split between people's rational, scientific side and their instinctive, mystical side had never been greater. Jung could not have known of the later developments in UFO manifestations, bringing the frightening abductions and sinister behaviour of fantastic entities. But perhaps he would have agreed with ufologist John Rimmer that the UFO has become 'the antiscience symbol par excellence'.

Projections from the unconscious have the power of archetypes, and address themselves to our main personal and collective anxieties. They can possess us and direct our actions, sweeping through a community like a rumour. Indeed, Jung likened the UFO to a 'visual rumour'. The same might be said of today's frequent sightings of monsters. These appear in strikingly archaic forms, as though somehow attempting to remind us that we are eroding our psychic landscape as surely as we are spoiling the world's last wildernesses. Such weird phenomena, clearly 'fashionable' today, are in many ways like collective dreams, and there is surely much to be learned from them.

For years on end, a young American woman called Ruth, living in London, was afflicted by hostile hallucinations of her father, who lived on the other side of the Atlantic at the time. These hallucinations affected her senses of sight, hearing, smell and touch. Indeed, it was almost as if her father had been constantly physically present. Ruth thought she was going mad; but, through the treatment of a wise psychiatrist, she learned that her ability to fantasize was in its way a gift that she could – and did – develop for positive use. She was, unwittingly, what is known as a fantasy-prone personality, and the late developer of a talent that some fortunate people, perhaps 3 or 4 per cent of the population, possess all their lives.

There have been several studies into the nature of such personalities. Dr Sheryl C. Wilson and Dr Theodore X. Barber, both of Cushing Hospital, Framingham, Massachusetts, USA, for instance, tested 27 female fantasy-prone personalities together with a control group of 25 'normal' women. The fantasy-prone women were selected on the grounds of their extremely positive responses to certain standard psychological tests in guided imagining, hypnosis and suggestibility, and to other tests devised by the experimenters. With two exceptions, every member of the group was university educated. Their ages ranged from 19 to 63 years, with a mean of 28. All but four, in the experimenters' estimation, were either socially normal or exceptionally well-adjusted: the remainder, of whom one had been through a nervous breakdown, faced difficulties such as depression. Twenty-four had husbands or relationships with one or more boyfriends. It cannot be over-emphasized that, aside from their genius for fantasizing, the fantasy-prone women were perfectly normal people. They were, so to speak, at one extreme end of a curve representing a certain kind of ability. Otherwise, they were quite ordinary – just as a mathematician, artist or musician, exceptionally talented in his or her field, may be entirely ordinary in everything else.

The abilities of fantasy-prone people, Wilson and Barber found, generally begin in childhood. Many of them – like many sensitives – had childhood playmates as real as flesh-and-blood companions whom, as they sometimes learned through bitter experience, adults could not see. Not only this, they

THE FANTASY-PRONE

MOST OF US DREAM ONLY WHILE WE ARE ASLEEP.

BUT THERE ARE SOME WHO SEEM TO LIVE IN A CURIOUS

WORLD OF FANTASY MOST OF THE TIME

The genius for fantasizing is, in many ways, a gift that can be put to positive use. There is, for instance, a remarkable similarity between The Temptation of St Anthony, *from the Isenheim altarpiece by Mathias Grunewald (c.1460-1528), above, and a painting by a drug addict showing visions experienced as withdrawal symptoms, right. Dr Sheryl C. Wilson, top, and Dr Theodore X. Barber, above, of Cushing Hospital, Framingham, Massachusetts, USA, both investigated the experiences of fantasy-prone personalities.*

often 'became' characters from books they read, ceasing to be themselves in a way that is perhaps similar to that in which a great actor loses himself completely in the character he portrays. Fantasies are not without danger: a child who believed she was leading a lamb through a meadow, for instance, suddenly 'awoke' to find herself alone, surrounded by traffic in a city street.

A consciously developed ability to fantasize can also continue into adult life for a number of reasons. Adults significant to the child may provide encouragement through accepting the child's viewpoint supportively, and convincingly, as their own. A child may also use his fantasy world to escape from isolation, loneliness, a deprived or distressing environment or a particular activity that he dislikes, such as intensive piano practice.

SECRET TALENTS

Realisation that they are not like others in their fantasizing ability frequently makes the adult fantasy-prone individuals somewhat secretive about their talents. Consequently, they share their secrets with no one, not even their marital partners. Some, however, actually find relief in fantasizing during contact with strangers, pretending to be characters other than themselves.

Interestingly, fantasy-prone people often have psychic abilities above the average; and the 27 women in the Massachusetts experiment were found to be gifted in telepathy, precognition (waking and in dreams), premonitions (one subject forecast the Kentucky Derby winners for 10 years in succession but did not back them because she considered this a misuse of her faculty), psychometry, mediumistic trances, perception of the presence of spirits, encounters with apparitions (one apparition revealed to one of the subjects the existence of a missing will), 'seeing' people's thoughts in images above their heads, dowsing, automatic writing (felt

Fantasy-prone people often 'become' characters from books they read or films they see, ceasing to be themselves in a similar way to that in which great actors lose themselves in the characters they portray – just as Richard Burton did in the stage version of Camelot, *above, for example.*

175

to come from an entity outside the subject), and the capacity to affect the working of electrical appliances. Twenty-two subjects reported out-of-the-body experiences, while two claimed to carry out healing, and a third to minister to the dying during astral travel.

Like other psychics, fantasy-prone people have vivid imaginations. They do not merely recall events but relive them with the sights, smells, sounds, tactile impressions and emotions of the original experiences. Many of them also have a perfect auditory memory. Their recollections, like their fantasies, are in many ways similar to films – but films that they not only watch, but in which they play a part. Some fantasy-prone people are also able to eliminate unpleasant memories through amnesia. However, they have a tendency to confuse fantasy memories with memories of actual events.

TRANSPORTS OF DELIGHT

Fantasy-prone people live an outwardly normal life – but many of them admit to spending more than half their lives in a fantasy existence. In social contacts, they can fantasize about what is being discussed or described by their companions, or use fantasy to escape from boredom. They often react intensely to stimuli – a passing mention of Egypt, for example, can transport them to a pharaoh's court or to modern Alexandria. They can fly from routine or unpleasant experiences into a holiday world, a 'previous life', a trip into the future, travel to other galaxies or enjoy a sexual experience with a fantastic lover, who can give them greater orgasmic satisfaction than any live human being.

In idle moments, or while preparing for sleep, they can surrender to fantasy, set the stage, create the plot and characters and then sit back, as it were, to watch the play unfold. One third of subjects found it better to watch their 'home movies' with closed eyes; but to two-thirds, it did not matter whether

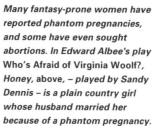

Many fantasy-prone women have reported phantom pregnancies, and some have even sought abortions. In Edward Albee's play Who's Afraid of Virginia Woolf?, *Honey, above, – played by Sandy Dennis – is a plain country girl whose husband married her because of a phantom pregnancy.*

The medium Mrs Ena Twigg, left, like many fantasy-prone people, had imaginary childhood playmates whom she was startled to realise others could not see.

their eyes were open or shut. All the subjects, however, reported that they experienced their fantasies with all their senses as real events. To all fantasy-prone people, 'real' life is a shadow of their fantasy existence. To be deprived of the latter would be, to them, a living death too terrible to contemplate.

DANGEROUS DAYDREAMS

But there are dangers and inconveniences associated with fantasies for adults, too. The fantasy of a child running on to a road from behind a parked car may make a driver brake suddenly and cause an accident, and fantasy-prone drivers have sometimes to try hard not to fantasize. Physical symptoms, even actual illnesses, may result from fantasies. Thirteen out of 22 women questioned in the Massachusetts project admitted having had at least one false pregnancy. Each had experienced several symptoms of the condition, and two had even sought abortions.

Another of the talents exhibited by many fantasy-prone people is the control of their autonomic bodily functions – heart rate, blood pressure, skin temperature and so on. They have the ability to feel hot or cold at will, a faculty that leads to the consideration that they may be practising some form of

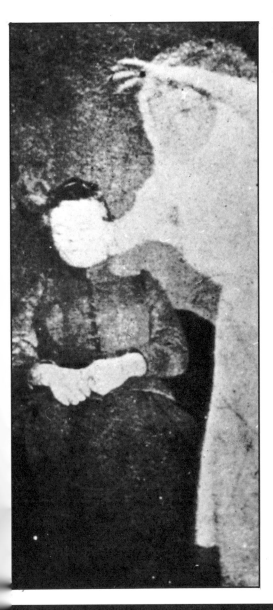

An early seance-room photograph, left, shows a medium and her spirit guide. Many fantasy-prone people have psychic gifts. It has even been suggested that spirits may be mass hallucinations of their fantasies.

self-hypnosis. Fantasy-prone people tend to make excellent hypnotic subjects. It has also been found that many of them respond well to suggestions of age regression and to visual and auditory hallucinations. They react well to negative hallucinations, too – that is, suggestions that something or someone who is actually present is not there. They can, however, if they wish, refuse to cooperate with a hypnotist and are able to ignore any therapeutic suggestions made by him or her.

Well over half the 27 women in the experiment frequently experienced hypnopompic and hypnagogic visions – that is, extremely realistic and vivid hallucinations seen in the states intermediate between sleeping and waking, and waking and sleeping. But they felt these to be different from their deliberately created fantasies and were relieved and grateful to know that they were not unusual in this.

The experiences of such fantasy-prone people are certainly significant for psychical research. Study of their characteristics may throw light on mediums, for example. Indeed, it is possible that some spirit guides and communications are actually created by subconscious fantasizing. Their experiences also challenge the nature of our very perception of reality, which we assume communicates itself, by stimulation of the senses, in approximately the same way to everyone experiencing it. Perhaps there is indeed another, inner or 'mirror' reality, that communicates in a different way. And just as the average person is ordinarily unaware of psychical phenomena, yet has perhaps one or two experiences of them during the course of his life, so perhaps he may have, very rarely, a momentary revelation of the fantasy-prone person's inner reality, in which he experiences an hallucination as real. The knowledge that there are personalities who constantly have such experiences may thus help the ordinary man or woman to come to terms with such a one-off event.

P E R S P E C T I V E S

COMING DOWN TO EARTH

Barber and Wilson's experiments revealed that most of their subjects could be labelled without exaggeration as 'fantasy addicts'. Of 17 subjects asked to estimate what proportion of the day they spent in fantasy, 11 estimated it to be over 90 per cent. In fact, they found it easier to estimate the amount of time during which they did not fantasize. One said that she tried consciously to refrain from it while she was driving, but that otherwise she fantasized all the time. But although she fantasized vividly with all her senses, this did not affect her ability to function normally in the real world.

The women studied in the experiment had some interesting stories to tell about their childhood. As a rule, they had spent all their time fantasizing and could not tell their fantasy worlds from the real world. One remembered her bewilderment when she was finally convinced that Santa Claus did not exist: she could not understand why adults should want to 'make him up', when all around there were real magical beings, such as elves, fairies and tree spirits.

Other subjects reported how they would pretend to be other people – orphans, princesses, animals or birds – and would become utterly engrossed in the role they were playing. One woman described how she had believed, not that she was pretending to be a princess, but that she was a princess pretending to be an ordinary little girl. She was brought back down to earth with a jolt when she took some of her school-friends home to see the magnificent castle she had described to them as her home. They, of course, seeing only the middle-class house that was actually there, accused her of lying. She could not believe that they could not see the castle: to her, it was more real than the world that her friends insisted was genuine.

THE FASCINATING TOAD

THROUGHOUT HISTORY, THE TOAD HAS BEEN LINKED WITH WITCHCRAFT AND SORCERY. IN THE COUNTRYSIDE, IT HAS LONG BEEN ASSOCIATED WITH CURSES AND BLIGHTS, TOO

Whatever beliefs about the toad have been explained in scientific or biochemical terms, there still remain certain strange and remarkable accounts. One, for instance, involved Charlie Walton, considered as a bit of a character by his neighbours in the English village of Lower Quinton, Warwickshire, where he lived with his unmarried niece. Although in his seventies and somewhat troubled by rheumatism, he could still turn his hand to most of the crafts so important to an agricultural community. He worked as a jobbing labourer and, since he was willing to put in a seven-hour day for one shilling and sixpence an hour, he was always in demand.

When he failed to return home for his tea on the evening of 14 February 1945, his niece Edith grew alarmed. Dusk had long since fallen on the slopes of Meon Hill, where the old man had been hedging and ditching for a farmer named Potter. Apart from the scattered lights of the village, the countryside lay pitch black under a moonless sky.

Summoning a neighbour, Miss Walton went to the farm. Mr Potter thought Walton had gone home long ago, but took a torch and went to the spot where Charlie had last been seen working that afternoon. He was found by a hedgerow, spread-eagled on his back. A rough, cross-shaped wound had been carved on his chest with a bill-hook, and his neck had been pinned to the ground with a pitchfork. Such force had been used that the head was all but severed.

STRANGE WAYS

The following day, a murder squad, led by the cele-brated Detective Superintendent Robert Fabian of Scotland Yard, arrived at Lower Quinton. But his team was met with what appeared to be a conspira-cy of silence. Those villagers who would talk merely muttered about the old man's 'strange ways'. He talked to birds, they said; and instead of cats or dogs, he kept natterjack toads. When Fabian visited Walton's cottage, he found numbers of these sinis-ter creatures wandering about the garden with their curiously loping gait.

As the days went by, the whole ambience of Lower Quinton – taciturn locals, the lonely secretive old man, the manner of his death, and the slimy

Toads were supposed to dance at witches' Sabbats, as illustrated in the engraving, **top.**

Detective Superintendent Robert Fabian ('Fabian of the Yard'), **above,** *investigated the bizarre murder in 1945 of Charlie Walton, who kept natterjack toads as pets.*

'familiars' breeding so profusely in the damp under-growth of his garden – began to smack of the influ-ence of witchcraft and the supernatural. This idea did not arouse contempt in Fabian, however. On the contrary, he began to examine it as a possible point-er to the motive for the old man's peculiar murder. He consulted Dr Margaret Murray, whose in-depth books on medieval witchcraft in Europe had attract-ed some controversy, and began to delve into aspects of local history.

During these investigations, he discovered a startling parallel to the Walton case. Seventy years previously, a man had been found guilty of murder-ing an old woman in the nearby village of Lower Compton. The man, believing the woman to be a witch, had killed her by pinning her to the ground and slashing her with a bill-hook. Fabian also discov-ered from one of the more talkative locals that Charlie Walton had used his amphibian pets for a strange purpose: he had harnessed them to a toy plough and sent them running across local fields with the plough in tow. This incident struck an immediate chord with Dr Murray, who was able to relate it to the case of Isobel Gowdie, a Scottish witch, who had been burned at the stake in 1662. Isobel had confessed to using a team of toads an

Toad of Toad Hall from Kenneth Grahame's Wind in the Willows, *is seen* right, *disguised as a washerwoman.*

Dr Margaret Murray, eminent witchcraft expert, above, was called in to advise on the Walton murder hunt.

Isobel Gowdie is seen below *consorting with the Devil. She confessed to using toads to blight crops by magic.*

a miniature plough in just the same way in order to blight crops by magic.

The spring of 1945 had come early and promised a good season for crops and animals; but both seedlings and livestock in the Lower Quinton area had failed to make good that promise. It seemed inconceivable in the middle of the 20th century, but to Fabian, the truth – however bizarre – seemed to be that old Walton had been cut down

because someone thought he was a witch and was convinced that he and his toads were to blame for blighting the crops. Fabian was certain he knew the culprit, but sporadic police enquiries over the next 20 years failed to turn up enough evidence. The killer was therefore never charged.

UNIVERSAL LOATHING

To folklorists, this episode fits a pattern that has remained constant for centuries all over the world – the deep-rooted, universal loathing of the toad. No other creature, not even the serpent that tempted Eve from Paradise, has inspired such hatred. Only Toad of Toad Hall, among all his literary kin, has had anything like a good notice – and even he is depicted in Kenneth Grahame's *Wind in the Willows* as a bombastic and stupid animal, an object of derision.

Ben Jonson, in his *Masque of Queens*, has one of his hags cry:

> 'I went to the toad that lies under the wall
> I charmed him out and he came to my call;
> I scratched out the eyes of the owl before
> I tore the bat's wings; what would you have
> more?'

And Jonson, in an annotation of his production for Elizabeth I, explained to the Queen that: 'These [toads] also, both by the confession of Witches and Testemonye of writers, are of principal use in theyr witch-craft.'

For centuries, toads have represented not just witchcraft but evil in general. Every French schoolchild knows the story of Clovis the Great and his banner or 'oriflamme' bearing the device of three toads. When he became King of France in AD 481, Clovis was a pagan and, as such, was certainly a believer in witchcraft and its powers. He launched a campaign against the Romans and defeated the

last Roman governor of Gaul at Soissons in AD 486 before going on to defeat the Alemanni, old allies of Rome. He now faced a major military challenge – the destruction of the Visigoth kingdom that was centred on Toulouse.

Marching towards his objective, he had the banner of the three toads fluttering at the head of the army. On the way, however, he saw a vision of his banner outlined in the clear blue sky. As he watched, the toads turned into three lilies, symbols of the Blessed Virgin. Clovis recognized this as a sign that he should embrace Christianity, a course he prudently took before going on to defeat his last great enemy. Since then, the oriflamme of France has carried the three lilies of the 'fleur-de-lis'.

VARIED REPUTATION

The toad's reputation varies to some extent from country to country. In Romania, for example, it was shunned and feared but never molested since, for some unknown reason, a man who killed it was considered capable of killing his own mother. In some areas, however, it was actually considered lucky. In England, for instance, a toad in a Cornish tin mine is a harbinger of a lucky strike. In parts of rural Cambridgeshire, it was also looked on with favour, since it ate spiders, which locally were believed to be the embodiment of Satan. It was also credited with foretelling thunderstorms and droughts by its periodic movements to and from breeding grounds.

In parts of East Anglia, particularly Norfolk, the toad was intrinsically linked with a sect of horsehandlers known variously as 'horse whisperers' or 'toadmen'. These skilled men are said still to exist in this area, where heavy horses are even today used in farming.

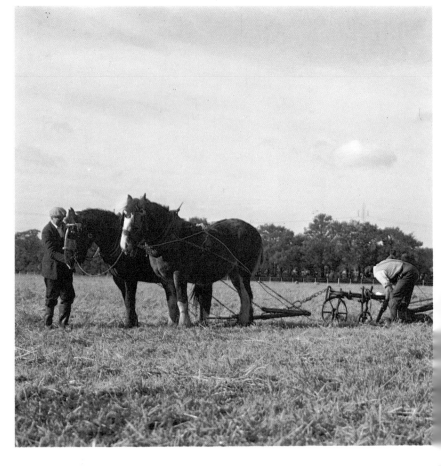

In East Anglia, the 'horse whisperers' or 'toadmen' gained total control over shire horses, such as those above, by the application of a lotion made from the powdered skeleton of a toad.

The pagan King Clovis of France is depicted, left, being baptised. His conversion in AD 489 was the result of a vision in which the three toads on his banner turned into three lilies, taken to be symbols of the Virgin.

One Norfolk horseman, Albert Love, who was born in 1886, described in detail how the connection existed. A natterjack toad was taken home, killed, and then put on a whitethorn bush for 24 hours until it was dry. It was next buried in an ant hill and left there until the appearance of a full moon. The skeleton of the toad was then taken to a stream and watched carefully in the moonlight to see whether the 'crotch bone' floated against the current. If it did, it was taken back home, baked, powdered and put in a box. This powder would be mixed with a special oil solution. If applied to a horse's tongue, nostrils, chin and chest, the horse would be your servant and do anything you wanted. In Suffolk, most horsemen used the bone whole, keeping it wrapped in linen: to 'jade', or stop, a horse they would touch it on the pit of the shoulder with the bone – and touch it on the rump in order to release it.

Many experts have suggested that the 'horse whisperers' in fact did just what their name implied – training their horses to respond to a whisper in the wind. Others are said to have used various scents and herbs to attract or repel their charges. Whatever the truth, they were a privileged breed in the days of horse power, and no doubt surrounded their real, yet secret, skills with such 'hex' stories as that involving the dead toad.

A further curious tradition, which has apparently been preserved in parts of the English Fens, is that of using a toad as a primitive form of compass. The Romans, for instance, used to place a dagger blade on a toad's back; and it is said that the creature would move around slowly until the dagger pointed due north and then stop.

How much of the legend of the toad is really true, we will probably never know for certain. But there is no denying its significance to people throughout the centuries as a creature surrounded by mystery. Certainly, its supposed sinister influence has never been lightly dismissed when no other acceptable explanation has been to hand.

The ingredients of the main dish in the macabre feast, above, include unbaptised babies and live toads. Eating the witches' brew supposedly confers the ability to fly on a broomstick or on a devilish beast.

The natterjack toad (Bufo calamita), left, was much-maligned for centuries.

> AT THE BEGINNING OF THE 18TH CENTURY, IT [TOAD VENOM] WAS ACTUALLY ADDED TO EXPLOSIVE SHELLS. PRESUMABLY THE COMMANDERS FELT THAT IF THE CANNON DID NOT KILL THEIR ENEMIES, THE TOAD TOXINS WOULD.

**WADE DAVIS,
THE SERPENT AND THE RAINBOW**

THE TERROR OF CROGLIN GRANGE

THE MACABRE STORY OF A SHRIVELLED, BONY CREATURE THAT ATTACKED A YOUNG WOMAN BY NIGHT SUGGESTED THAT A FIEND WITH A LUST FOR BLOOD WAS LOOSE IN VICTORIAN ENGLAND

Apart from medieval legends of the vampire, the British Isles have been curiously free of that particular plague – free, that is, until 1900 when Augustus Hare's tale of vampirism in Cumberland (now Cumbria) was first published. Many writers have quoted it, but few have attempted to trace the creature to its lair. Indeed, the trail left by Hare has proved difficult to follow.

The vampire of Croglin Grange makes its appearance in the fourth volume of Hare's autobiography, *The Story of My Life*. The book is a rambling series of anecdotes, tall stories and excerpts from his journals. The vampire story had apparently originated with a certain Captain Fisher, who said his ancestors had once owned property in Cumberland – Croglin Grange. When, long ago, they had moved south to Guildford, in Surrey, they had rented the property to two brothers and their sister.

The lease was to run for seven years. The trio proved popular among their neighbours, spending a happy first winter at Croglin. However, throughout

Croglin Low Hall in Cumbria, below, was supposedly the original of the Croglin Grange in Captain Fisher's vampire story. But his description of the house, with its veranda lawns and elegant trees, does not seem to match the forbidding granite construction of Croglin Low Hall, nor the barren landscape that surrounds it.

the hot and stifling summer that was to follow, the young woman found it difficult to sleep and would lie in bed gazing out for hours at the moonlit lawn beyond her window. One night, she saw a creature dart from the shadows. In a moment, it was at her window scratching at the glass. The window was shut fast, but the figure began picking away at the lead. A pane of glass was loosened and fell into the room. A long, bony finger released the catch, and suddenly the creature was in the room. Twisting it

shrivelled fingers through her hair, it dragged her towards it, and then bit her on the throat.

The woman's screams alerted her brothers, who chased the vampire out of the house, across the lawn and over the neighbouring churchyard wall. Although the woman's wound was to heal in time, her doctor urged a change of scene; so the siblings decided to holiday in Switzerland. Once the young woman had fully recovered, the threesome returned to Croglin, and the following winter passed without event. Then, one night in March, the young woman was woken by a scratching at her window. The creature was there again: this time, her screams brought her brothers running to the rescue armed with pistols. In the ensuing mêlée, the creature was hit in the leg but, despite this, it managed to evade capture. However, the men saw where it went to ground – in an old family vault in the churchyard . The following day, local villagers opened the vault and found a horrible scene of broken coffins and mangled corpses. Only one coffin stood intact. When the lid was prised open, 'there – brown, shrivelled, mummified but quite entire – was the same hideous figure which had looked in at the windows of Croglin Grange, with the marks of a recent pistol shot in the leg. And they did the only thing that can lay a vampire: they burnt it.' This is how Augustus Hare concluded his account of Captain Fisher's narrative. England had acquired its first authenticated vampire, and the story was soon being included in anthologies of British hauntings.

PARTY PIECES

Augustus Hare and Captain Edward Fisher had first met in June 1874 on the eve of Fisher's marriage to Hare's cousin, Lady Victoria Liddel. At dinner, Hare – a renowned raconteur – told alarming ghost stories that he had collected during his wide travels in Europe, leaving Fisher compelled to relate a story of his own. He began by telling the assembled company that his family had not always lived at Thorncombe near Guildford. Then followed the vampire tale, which he recounted much as Hare related it in his autobiography. It was an exceptionally graphic account. Hare was proud of his memory and the mass of detail he invariably included in his writings – indeed, to his publishers' despair, he always refused to cut any of his material.

Only a little is known of Fisher's later life. Following his marriage in July that year, he made his home at Thorncombe, an elegant estate 5 miles (8 kilometres) from Guildford, where he continued to charm Hare as 'one of the kindest, cheeriest, pleasantest fellows who ever entered a family'. Fisher, whose full name and title were 'Edward Rowe Fisher-Rowe, Late Captain of the 4th Dragoon Guards', was to die at Thorncombe on his 77th birthday, on 8 November 1909. His wife, who died in 1935, lies by his side in Holy Trinity Church at Bramley.

But what of Fisher's ancestors? Did they really own a Croglin Grange? Twelve miles (19 kilometres) south-east of Carlisle is Croglin Water, a lonely Cumberland stream. A poem by Wordsworth establishes its setting:

Down from the Pennine Alps, how fiercely sweeps
Croglin, the stately Eden's tributary!

The mangled corpses in broken coffins, above, present a similar scene to the one said to have greeted the eyes of the Cumberland villagers when they opened the vault in which the vampire had gone to ground.

Augustus Hare, below, first published the story of the Croglin vampire in the fourth volume of his autobiography.

However, investigations into whether there is a Croglin Grange reveal that there is no house by that actual name, only a scattering of lonely farm houses of which one, Croglin Low Hall, is the main contender for the title. Parish records and gravestones reveal that the Fishers were the local landowners and farmers certainly as far back as the 1730s. And it is possible that Captain Fisher could have been the grandson of Edward Fisher (1762-1833) and his wife Deborah, whose memorials stand in Ainstable graveyard.

Bramley parish records, however, suggest that there were no Fishers at Thorncombe before the Captain moved there, so his assertion that his family went south many generations earlier is misleading. Equally misleading is his description of Croglin Grange's veranda, lawns and elegant trees. The heavy granite walls of Croglin Low Hall and the barren landscape that surrounds the building certainly do not spell elegance, and there are neither lawns nor verandas. The cobbled yards even suggest the Hall was a working farm.

There are other discrepancies, too. Either Fisher or Hare was wrong about the churchyard. There is, indeed, a church at Croglin, a Victorian building on the site of a Norman church. It is, however, almost 2 miles (3 kilometres) from Croglin Low Hall, high on a hill above Croglin Water – a prodigious run for the healthiest vampire. At this point, we have to face the facts: the Croglin Grange of the story retold by Hare is possibly not the Croglin that exists in Cumberland. It may be that Hare invented details to enhance a sketchy description given by Fisher, or that the Captain, not wishing his aristocratic friends to know he came from humble farming stock, deliberately misled the assembled company to gain his family a more stately origin. Oddly, though, Hare's description of the Grange matches the Thorncombe estate – Fisher's home in Surrey – in many respects.

small diamond pane in the window to gain entry.

Both vampires, we find, slip in bony fingers to release the catches and open their windows. Fisher's vampire twisted its long bony hands into the girl's hair, dragging her forcefully to the side of the bed so that it could attack and bite at her throat. What of Varney's technique? How similar is it? This is Rymer's version:

'...the figure seized the long tresses of her hair, and twining them round his bony hands he... drags her head to the bed's edge. He forces it back by the long hair still entwined in his grasp. With a plunge, he seizes her neck in his fang-like teeth: a gush of blood and a hideous sucking noise follows.' The similarities are striking.

As long ago as 1929, Montague Summers quoted both texts in his book, *The Vampire in Europe*, but he failed to comment on the curious similarities. He may well have noted them, but perhaps preferred to let Fisher's story stand and not to 'lay' Croglin's ghost at that point.

Subsequent owners of Croglin Low Hall said they had a ghost of a pig on their estate, but they rejected the vampire story absolutely. It may appear heartless to deny England her only resident vampire, but it seems its origin may well not have been in Cumberland, but within the pages of James Rymer's fascinating book.

Allowing, then, that Hare got both his geography and his dates wrong, the existence of the three tenants and their uninvited summer visitor has still to be substantiated in some way. The letting of the Grange to the anonymous tenants would certainly appear to be no more than a fiction. So where did Fisher find his vampire?

A ROMANTIC FICTION

It may be necessary to look no further than the work of James Malcolm Rymer (1804-1882), a writer of extremely successful 'penny dreadfuls'. In 1847, *Varney the Vampire, or the Feast of Blood*, a romance in 220 chapters, made its first appearance; and in 1853, its 868 pages were reprinted in 'penny parts'. They were to capture the public's imagination, inspiring not only ballads but also numerous theatrical melodramas.

Varney was not quite the first of the genre. In 1816, the story-telling sessions that inspired Mary Shelley's *Frankenstein* had also given birth to John Polidori's *The Vampyre*, a short story published three years later. There were no vampire tales in Britain prior to this date, despite the European vampire 'epidemic' of the 1700s. Although the story of *Varney the Vampire* is well-known, the text virtually disappeared for over a hundred years until it was republished in America in 1974, and it must be supposed that earlier writers overlooked the strange, intriguing similarities between Varney and the Croglin Grange vampire.

A comparison between the two vampires' first appearance is fascinating. Fisher sets his action in a ground-floor bedroom of a country house on a hot summer's night. Rymer's location is a medieval chamber in a city during a hailstorm. Both rooms have large fastened windows. Fisher's heroine is awake, watching a shadowy figure on the lawn; Rymer's girl sleeps through the storm but then wakes to the sound of fingernails drumming on the glass. She thinks it is the sound of hailstones until she sees a figure standing on her window ledge. Fisher's girl is horrified by the sound of scratching and picking at her window. Varney breaks a small pane of glass to enter, and the Croglin vampire picks the lead from around a

Tombstones in Ainstable graveyard near Croglin Low Hall, above, reveal that the Fisher family had been living in the area since the 1730s.

The illustration below is from James Rymer's Varney the Vampire, published in 1847.

TALES TO WONDER AT

EVERYONE HAS HEARD —
IN PUBS, CLUBS OR
LOCKER ROOMS — THE KIND OF STORY
THAT BEGINS 'YOU'LL NEVER
BELIEVE IT . . . BUT IT HAPPENED
TO MY COUSIN'S BOYFRIEND'S
LITTLE SISTER.' HERE, WE
EXAMINE THE AUTHENTICITY OF
SUCH TALES, AS WELL AS
THEIR ORIGINS AND HOW THEY
USUALLY SPREAD

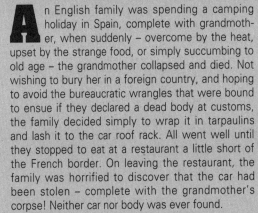

An English family was spending a camping holiday in Spain, complete with grandmother, when suddenly – overcome by the heat, upset by the strange food, or simply succumbing to old age – the grandmother collapsed and died. Not wishing to bury her in a foreign country, and hoping to avoid the bureaucratic wrangles that were bound to ensue if they declared a dead body at customs, the family decided simply to wrap it in tarpaulins and lash it to the car roof rack. All went well until they stopped to eat at a restaurant a little short of the French border. On leaving the restaurant, the family was horrified to discover that the car had been stolen – complete with the grandmother's corpse! Neither car nor body was ever found.

This tale may sound familiar and, not surprisingly, similar stories are constantly related in pubs, clubs, at parties and in locker rooms. Generally, they happen to 'a friend of a friend' or 'my friend's cousin's girlfriend'. Rarely is the individual who is telling the story the person involved in the incident; and here lies a clue, for many of the events described in such stories never actually happened.

For instance, have you heard about the girl, back in the 1960s, who had a magnificent beehive hairdo?

185

On the previous page, the finishing touches are applied to the appearance of a model, complete with bouffant hairstyle, top. A story often told in pubs and clubs concerns a girl who kept her beehive hairstyle perfect by never washing it, but simply applying lacquer. One day, she fell down dead, apparently because bees that had made their nest in her hair had gnawed through her skull to her brain. This tale appears to originate in the era of beehive hairstyles of the 1950s and 1960s – but was also extant in the 18th century, when bouffant hairstyles were fashionable, as illustrated on the previous page, too.

An illustration of the 13th-century Welsh legend of Gellert, by the 19th-century artist John Byam Liston Shaw, is shown above right. One day Llewellyn, Prince of North Wales, went hunting leaving his faithful hound Gellert at home to guard his infant son. On his return, he was greeted by a gory Gellert standing by a bloodstained cot. Thinking that Gellert had killed his son, he plunged his sword into the dog's side. Only then did he notice his son, safe and sound – and a huge wolf lying dead by the cot. This legend now circulates in the form of a story of a woman who comes home to find her dog choking on two fingers bitten from the hand of an intruder who is later found hiding in a cupboard.

She was very proud of it, and kept it perfect by never washing her hair, but simply lacquering it to make it keep its shape. One day, sitting in a milk bar, she suddenly keeled over, dead. It turned out from the post-mortem examination that bees had made their nest in her hair and had finally gnawed through her skull to the brain.

This is a chilling story, certainly, but it is doubtful whether it ever happened. Bees live on pollen, not on human flesh; and if they had made their hive inside the girl's hair, one would have expected to see them flying in and out as they foraged for food. In any event, surely she would have heard them buzzing? One suspects that the reference to bees was simply suggested by the name of the bouffant hairstyle – 'beehive'; and the discovery that the same story has been reported, with minor variations, over hundreds of years in different locations lends substance to the suspicion that it never actually occurred. The insects in the hair are most often bees – but sometimes they are cockroaches or, more convincingly, black widow spiders. The story was reported – without supporting evidence – in *Esquire* magazine in March 1976, as an example of teenage 'Folklore from the Fifties':

'A girl managed to wrap her hair into a perfect beehive. Proud of her accomplishment, she kept spraying it and spraying it, never bothering to wash it again. Bugs began to live in her hair. After about six months, they ate through to her brain and killed her. Moral: Wash your hair or die.'

What is perhaps even more extraordinary is that virtually the same story appears in a 13th-century *exemplum* – a moral tale; and, like the *Esquire* example, it is a stern warning against vanity in women. It appears in the *Speculum Laicorum* ('Mirror for the Laity'), a book of improving texts for churchgoers.

There is also a sermon story of a certain lady of Eynesham, in Oxfordshire, who took so long over the adornment of her hair that she used to arrive at church barely before the end of Mass. One day, the devil descended upon her head in the form of a spider, gripping with its legs, until she well-nigh died of fright. Nothing would remove the offending insect, neither prayer, nor exorcism, nor holy water until the local abbot displayed the holy sacrament before it. The story of the vanishing hitch-hiker, too, is an ancient one with roots reaching back into the traditional folklores of cultures as geographically widespread as the United States, Britain, Sweden, Malaysia, Sicily, Pakistan and South Africa. It seems, too, that perhaps we should include the reports of visits by men in black in this category for, whether or not they are true, the stories appear in startlingly similar forms all over the world.

FACT OR FICTION?

So what is it that makes such stories so persistent? They are always told as true – but in the absence of any substantiating evidence, it is extraordinary that many of them have persisted for hundreds of years. They may once have had a basis in fact – but have now become what folklorists refer to as legends.

Legends can be described as traditional narratives that, in the society in which they are told, are considered to be truthful accounts of what happened in the historic past. As such, they contrast sharply with myths – narratives that are considered to be truthful accounts of what happened in some distant and heroic past – and with folktales, which are regarded as fiction and told primarily for entertainment. Legends generally focus on local people and places, events and situations. As such, they constitute a form of traditional narrative that is still very much alive in the 20th century. Folklorists call legends that deal with the immediate past contemporary legends, and study of these in Great Britain and the United States

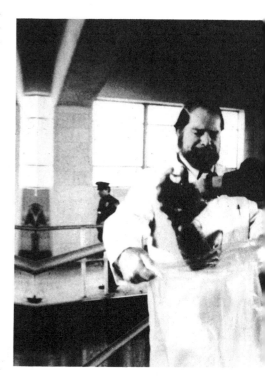

The still, right, is from the 1980 movie Motel Hell. The plot is centred on a story that occurs repeatedly in contemporary legend: guests in a motel or hotel are killed, sawn up and then served as meat at dinner.

A persistent rumour alleges that visitors to the Everglades, Florida, bring home baby alligators – such as those below – as pets. Then, growing tired of them, they flush them down the lavatory. As a consequence, the New York sewers are said to be full of huge alligators. The 1980 movie Alligator made use of this story. In the still, bottom, Detective Madison, played by Robert Forster, realises something is afoot when human limbs – in this case, an arm – are recovered from the sewers.

reveals how astonishingly widespread occurrences of the same tale may be.

One of the best-known such stories, instances of which have been collected all over the United States and in Britain, is known as the 'hook' story. It concerns a teenage couple who have driven to the local 'lovers' lane' to listen to music on the radio and indulge in pubescent sex. Suddenly, the music is interrupted by an announcement: that there is an escaped convict in the area. He is described as having a hook instead of a right hand. The girl is frightened, and wants to go home; but her partner interprets this as rejection of his advances. He turns on the ignition, puts his foot down hard on the accelerator, and off they roar. When they arrive back in town and the girl gets out of the car, she finds on the door handle a bloody hook.

This is among the best-known and most widespread tales to have been studied by folklorists. Generally, the 'lovers' lane' in which it is situated is a real place in the locality; and inevitably, it happened to 'my friend's cousin's boyfriend'. The earliest examples of the story date from the 1950s; and it seems to be one of those legends that surface, die away, and surface again in exactly the same form years later.

So why is it told? It is, of course, a good story, with the classic ingredients of suspense, sex, fear and mutilation. It also has a kind of ghastly plausibility and, perhaps most important, it is, like the beehive hairdo story, a moral tale with a warning. On 8 November, 1960, the story appeared in a letter included in a popular newspaper column written by Abigail Van Buren. The letter began: 'Dear Abby, If you are interested in teenagers, you will print this story. I don't know whether it's true or not, but it doesn't matter because it served its purpose for me.' A graphic account of the 'hook' story followed, and the letter ended: 'I don't think I will ever park to make out as long as I live. I hope this does the same for other kids.'

MICROWAVE HORROR

Other warning tales concern new technological inventions with which people are still less than familiar. A widespread story of this kind is that of the young man who is staying at his aunt's house to look after her beloved cat while she is on holiday. During a dreadful storm, the cat stays out all night, and arrives home shivering, bedraggled and miserable. The young man takes pity on the cat and decides to warm it up – by putting it in his aunt's microwave oven. Most versions of this story end with the cat 'exploding'.

Many contemporary legends also relate to the world of business. Rumours that cheap Chinese restaurants serve rats or Alsatian dogs as meat are so common that they are hardly taken seriously. News of extraordinarily good deals – the teller claims that his cousin's brother-in-law was able to take advantage of such an offer, or invites his audience to do so – circulates constantly in pubs and bars, too. One of the best-known of these is the story of the sports car that is going for an incredibly cheap price. There seems to be nothing wrong with

> *GHOSTS STORIES ARE, ONE WAY OR ANOTHER, STRANGE FRAGMENTS OF HUMAN EXPERIENCE, ATTESTED TO BY OUR FELLOW MEN AND WOMEN. THEY REVEAL TO US SOMETHING ABOUT THE WAY IN WHICH WE FUNCTION; THEY INVITE US TO THEORIZE, TO PROBE OUR LIMITED UNDERSTANDING.*
>
> **MICHAEL GOSS, THE EVIDENCE FOR PHANTOM HITCH-HIKERS**

*In*Focus

LET THEM EAT CAKE

A story from the United States tells how a woman boarded a bus and started handing out cards bearing the recipe for a 'red velvet cake'. She was eager to press the recipes on to people. When asked why, she explained that she had recently dined at the Waldorf Astoria Hotel in New York, and had tasted this delicious cake. She had enjoyed it so much that she had sent her compliments to the chef and, when she returned home, wrote to the hotel asking for the recipe. It duly arrived – together with an invoice for something like $350 from the chef.

Her lawyer advised her that she would have to pay the sum he demanded – and the woman apparently thought that the best way to get even with the chef would be to hand out copies of the recipe for nothing.

Variations on this story are to be found all over the United States. Generally, the location of the woman's home town is specific, as is the sum she has allegedly had to pay. The hotel is always the Waldorf Astoria, and the story always includes the recipe for the cake. But is there any truth in the

it – but everyone who gets into the car notices a strange, lingering smell. It turns out that the previous owner died at the wheel – and that the body stayed undiscovered in the car for some weeks.

A group of stories that deserve to be considered on their own are those that allege conspiracy on the part of big business. Indeed, the McDonald hamburger corporation has come in for harsh treatment at the hands of such a legend. Early in 1977, the rumour spread that McDonald's was donating a hefty part of its profits to a satanic cult. Hardly had this died down when, in late 1977, another one replaced it, alleging that worms were being added to Big Mac hamburgers to supplement the protein. It was, of course, ridiculous. But it was in vain for McDonald's to protest that, pound for

Diners enjoy a meal at a Chinese restaurant in Britain, left, while the carcass of a dog hangs in a butcher's stall in a market in Canton, mainland China, below left. Rumours that Chinese restaurants in Britain serve Alsatian dog meat are so common that they are hardly taken seriously any more – or are they?

pound, worms were actually more expensive than beef – all that could be done was to wait until the story died down of its own accord. Marlboro cigarettes suffered in a similar way when a rumour circulated linking the manufacturers, Philip Morris, with the Ku Klux Klan through the design of the Marlboro pack. There was, naturally, no truth at all in the rumour.

Another story concerns parts of mice found floating in soft drinks containers. According to one version, collected in Minnesota in 1976, two old ladies stepped into a restaurant to have a little lunch and ordered two Seven-Ups. It came in old green bottles. The ladies finished their first glass and one of them noticed something towards the bottom of the bottle, but could not make out what it was. Finally, they tried to pour it out and what emerged was a decomposed mouse. The two ladies promptly fainted. After they got home, they consulted their lawyers, sued the Seven-Up company and made thousands of dollars on the lawsuit.

tale? Was there indeed a woman who was landed with a bill of $350 for a recipe?

Professor Jan Harold Brunvald, of the Department of English in the University of Utah, USA, wrote to the Waldorf Astoria in 1965. The reply claimed: 'We have letters and clippings in our files going back more than ten years which give numerous versions of this story... A thorough check was made here at the hotel when the story first cropped up and it is completely false.'

False or not, life has begun to imitate folklore; the Waldorf Astoria now distributes the recipe to anyone who asks for it.

The curious thing about this particular story relating to a soft drinks company is that it is actually based on fact – but on fact that was some 30 years old, and also rather inaccurately reported. Professor Gary Alan Fine, a scholar of contemporary legend who has made a special study of legends as they relate to subsequent court actions, managed to locate a report of the actual lawsuit on which the story was based:

'On the night of July 24, 1943, the plaintiff and her sister went to the Spa Sweet Shop, sat at the counter and each ordered a bottle of Coca-Cola... Plaintiff placed a straw in each bottle... According to

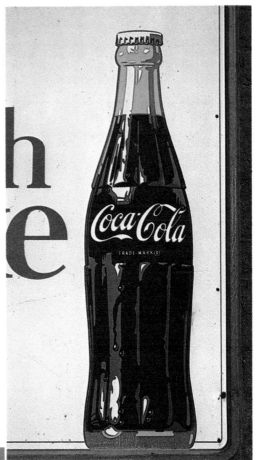

An advertisement for Coca-Cola is shown left. A rumour that surfaces again and again in the United States concerns parts of mice found in Coca-Cola bottles – an embroidered and amalgamated version of several such cases in which the Coca-Cola corporation has been taken to court.

During the late 1970s, McDonald's, below left, had to face the (unfounded) rumour that the meat in its 'Big Mac' hamburgers was being supplemented by worms. It was, of course, in vain for McDonald's to protest that, pound for pound, worms were actually more expensive than beef.

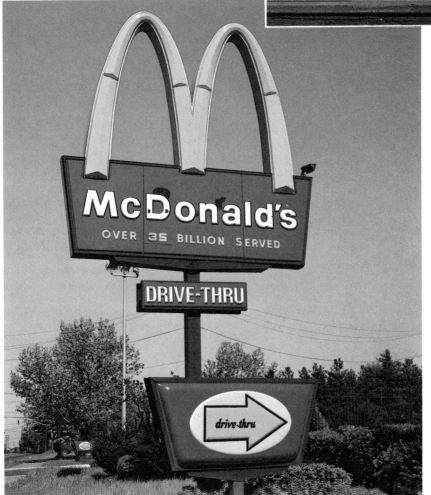

plaintiff, the following exchange then occurred: "When I got half way down, I remarked to my sister that it had an awful taste to it. She said hers was all right. I kept on drinking, and when I came to the bottom of the bottle, the straw hit something. I picked up the bottle and looked at it, and there was a mouse in it." '

Clearly, the process of folklore has here taken over from legal and newspaper reports to make a more vivid – if less accurate – story. But the story impugns the wrong product – and, as for the claim that the plaintiffs made 'thousands of dollars on the lawsuit', Professor Fine's researches show that the average amount of money to be made was far below what rumour placed it as and really quite modest. Such exaggerations are part of the stuff of contemporary myth.

So are tales of the paranormal to be classed with contemporary legends? Certainly, they share many of the same characteristics. Often, they spread by word of mouth, and lack convincing corroborative evidence. Frequently, too, the details are vague – the events, as we have see, usually happened to a friend of a friend, and at an indeterminate time and place.

But to ask such a question is not to say that reports of paranormal events are always mere fiction – any more, or any less, than contemporary legends are always entirely fiction. But it has been suggested that an analysis of contemporary legend may perhaps one day give us some new insights into certain aspects of the paranormal.

A PERILOUS MEDIUM

THE BRAZILIAN PSYCHIC CARMINE MIRABELLI HAD AN EXTRAORDINARY RANGE OF PARANORMAL SKILLS THAT WERE OFTEN AN EMBARRASSMENT TO HIS FAMILY AND COLLEAGUES

One day in 1911, a young man who was working as an assistant in a shoe shop in São Paulo, Brazil, was dismissed from his job. Apparently, his employer objected to the fact that shoe boxes kept flying off the shelves when the young man was near by. The dismissed employee, whose name was Carmine Mirabelli, afterwards spent 19 days in an asylum under the observation of two unusually sympathetic doctors. One of these, Dr Felipe Ache, declared that, while the young man was not normal, he was not sick, either. He concluded that his psychic abilities were 'the result of the radiation of nervous forces that we all have, but that [he] has in extraordinary excess'.

Dr Ache's colleague, Dr Franco da Rocha, described how Mirabelli was able to make a skull rotate on top of a glass without the need for touch – just by looking at it. 'Nor was that all,' the doctor added. 'When I picked up the skull, I felt something strange in my hands, something fluid, as if a globular liquid were touching my palm. When I concentrated my attention further, I saw something similar to an irradiation pass over the skull, as when you rapidly expose a mirror to luminous rays.'

This was the beginning of the remarkable career of the Brazilian medium Carmine Mirabelli, who was born in 1889, the son of a Protestant pastor of Italian origin. Credited with the ability to produce every known phenomenon of a medium's repertoire, he was possibly the greatest medium of all time. In addition to regular demonstrations of telepathy, clairvoyance and precognition, his reported feats included automatic writing in more than 30 languages, and producing paintings and drawings in various styles. Although he was musically untrained, he could, while in a state of trance, sing and play the piano with skill. He was also able to paint or write at the same time that he was singing, and write a message in one language while conversing in another.

In addition to all this, he was a focus for poltergeist activity for a period of some 40 years. In his presence, both in and out of doors, objects would move around, appear out of thin air, catch fire or vanish with such regularity that members of his family came to regard such happenings as routine. He was also said to have the skill of levitation, and to be able to produce visible materialisations of the dead.

Not only did Mirabelli have extraordinary mediumistic gifts, he also had a tremendous zest for normal life. Someone who knew him well for 20 years – his biographer Eurico de Goes – describes him as a man of great energy and charisma, who was excitable, impulsive and impatient, yet tolerant and good natured. He was quite capable of buying as many as 10 suits at a time and giving most of them away. Nevertheless, he showed a considerable

*Carmine Mirabelli, **right**, had psychic powers that were first discovered in 1911. In addition to clairvoyance, psychokinesis and automatic writing, he was said to be able to levitate, and to produce materialisations of the dead. His most celebrated demonstration of levitation took place during a seance in São Paulo, at which his son Luiz was present. The medium rose slowly into the air and remained there long enough for the photograph, **left**.*

business acumen, and was always able to earn a good living by 'normal' means. Mirabelli embraced the Spiritist cause, and founded and directed centres in several towns in Brazil. But he was unpopular with orthodox Spiritists because of his tendency towards exhibitionism, his fondness for physical demonstrations, and the fact that he sometimes charged money for his services. But even one of his most severe critics, the Spiritist historian Carlos Imbassahy, had to admit that there was no doubt that his mediumship was genuine.

In his book *O Espiritismo a Luz Dos Fatos* ('Spiritism in the Light of the Facts'), which was published in 1952, Imbassahy relates an incident when Mirabelli was brought, uninvited, to his house. 'There was nobody I less wanted to see,' Imbassahy wrote; for he feared 'this perilous mediumship' would start smashing his crockery.

Instead, the 'perilous medium' embarked on a detailed account of the life of one of Imbassahy's friends (whom Mirabelli had never met). Then a servant brought in some bottles of water and put them on a table some 16 feet (5 metres) from where Mirabelli was sitting. 'Immediately,' said Imbassahy, 'in full view of us all, one of the bottles rose halfway up the height of the others and hit them with full force for five or ten seconds, before returning to its place... This was seen and heard clearly, with no shadow of hesitation.'

Meanwhile, both the medium's hands were being held. Imbassahy would have been only too happy to denounce Mirabelli as a fraud, but he was honest enough to state that he was left 'with the unshakeable certainty' of his abilities.

Eurico de Goes' biography of Mirabelli is crammed from start to finish with detailed accounts of an enormous variety of phenomena, some of them quite extraordinary. At one seance, for instance, the handcuffed medium rose into the air and dematerialised. The handcuffs fell to the floor.

> *"The phenomena of materialisation were astounding. The figures were not only complete, they were not only photographed, but medical men made minute examinations which lasted sometimes as long as for fifteen minutes and stated that the newly constituted human beings had perfect anatomical structure."*
>
> **Nandor Fodor, Encyclopedia of Psychic Science**

*The seance room where the levitation took place is shown **right**. The room was recognised as being the one in the levitation photograph when a team of psychical researchers visited the house in 1973. The essential clues were the mouldings round the light fitting in the ceiling, the two doors (partly hidden here by the dividing screen) and the fact that light coming through the window would have cast a shadow similar to the one in the levitation picture. Since the room is about 16 feet (5 metres) high, it is estimated that Mirabelli rose to about 8 feet (2.5 metres) from the ground.*

Mirabelli was eventually found, lying down and chanting in Latin, in a nearby locked room.

On another occasion, when Eurico de Goes was on his way to visit Mirabelli, he remembered he had left his umbrella at home. As he entered Mirabelli's house, his umbrella promptly fell from the ceiling. Apparent teleportation was also witnessed by the British poet-diplomat Sir Douglas Ainslie, who arrived at a private house in São Paulo and found his travelling clock on the hall table. He had last seen it inside a suitcase in his hotel room.

EXPRESS JOURNEY

In another incident related by Eurico de Goes, Mirabelli was waiting for a train with a group of friends when they suddenly noticed he was nowhere to be seen. His worried friends telephoned to the house they were heading for, in a town 50 miles (80 kilometres) away. They were told the medium was already there.

In 1973, the Brazilian Institute for Psychobiophysical Research (IBPP) appointed a team of investigators to compile a file on Mirabelli. The team was headed by the leading Brazilian parapsychologist Hernani G. Andrade. In a few weeks, the file was bulging with firsthand testimony. They managed to locate and interview three of the medium's sons, none of whom claimed to have inherited any of his father's paranormal skills. Cesar Augusto Mirabelli was a police investigator with São Paulo's flying squad. He was highly critical of the Spiritist movement, 99 per cent of which, in his opinion, was 'deceit, mystification or bad faith'. He added: 'If my father were a fraud, I would certainly say so.' However, Cesar insisted, fraud was out of the question; and phenomena were often produced just for the family. Among several examples he described was the following: 'We had an ornamental porcelain vase, about 60 centimetres [2 feet] high, weighing, I suppose, three to four kilos [about 7 pounds], standing on a kind of tripod... Suddenly, Father started to look at the corner where the vase was, and I started to look as well. The vase just rose into the air about 40 centimetres [16 inches]. Then, all at once, it turned, picked up speed and smashed itself to pieces against a wall, 2 metres [6 feet] away.' This kind of thing, Cesar said, would happen 'almost every day, any time and at any place'.

BURIED ALIVE

Regene Mirabelli, a businessman and amateur hypnotist, also had plenty of memories of an unusual home life. Once, on hearing an extraordinary noise, he rushed into the living room to find his mother buried beneath a pile of all the furniture. His mother was, he said, resigned to this sort of thing. Indeed, it was not unusual for her to spend half an hour laying the table, only to find, the moment her back was turned, the whole setting swept to the floor.

Mirabelli's eldest son, Luiz, had become a successful hardware salesman. He remembered a car journey in the open country during which the driver was suddenly slapped violently in the face by an invisible assailant. Mirabelli then told him to engage first gear, 'because "they" are trying to push us backwards'. Whereupon, said Luiz, the car – in first gear – did indeed start to move in reverse.

This remarkable series of pictures shows Mirabelli apparently controlling the gradual materialisation of a complete human form. The entity's robe and hair suggest an African or Indian origin for the materialisation.

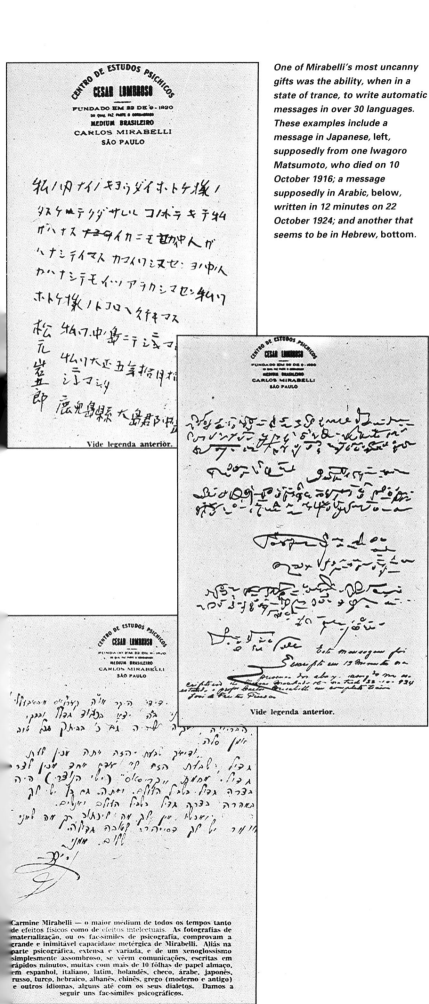

One of Mirabelli's most uncanny gifts was the ability, when in a state of trance, to write automatic messages in over 30 languages. These examples include a message in Japanese, left, supposedly from one Iwagoro Matsumoto, who died on 10 October 1916; a message supposedly in Arabic, below, written in 12 minutes on 22 October 1924; and another that seems to be in Hebrew, bottom.

Luiz was also present at one of the most celebrated incidents in his father's life. It happened during a seance in a well-lit room. Mirabelli rose slowly into the air, stayed there long enough for a photograph to be taken, and then descended to the ground slowly. But Luiz described the incident as if it were nothing especially remarkable .

During the IBPP investigation, the team met a São Paulo estate agent named Fenelon Alves Feitosa, who had known the medium well, and still held weekly Spiritist meetings in his memory. As it happened, Senhor Feitosa had just been asked to sell a house that he recognised as being one of Mirabelli's former centres.

The team went to visit the house, at 6 Rua Natal, in the Tucuruvi district. As they were going through the rooms, they recognised one of them as the scene of the levitation photograph. It seemed that the light coming through the window would have cast a shadow similar to the one seen in the photograph. The room was about 16 feet (5 metres) high and, in the photograph, Mirabelli's feet appear to be at least half that distance from the floor.

MOVING EXPLANATION

In December 1935, the Journal of the Society for Psychical Research (SPR) in London carried a long report on Mirabelli by Theodore Besterman that added to the controversy surrounding the medium. Besterman had witnessed a number of incidents involving the movement of objects, but remained sceptical. He asserted that 'hidden threads' were the explanation, although he admitted that he had never found any. He had watched a piece of board revolving on top of a bottle – which puzzled him – and had also witnessed Mirabelli writing more than 1,700 words in 53 minutes in French, a language that he is thought not to have learned.

'Mirabelli left me in no doubt that he was purely and simply fraudulent,' Besterman said in 1973. 'Once I had expressed this opinion, none of his followers would talk to me.'

Fortunately, other investigators were not so tactless. The eminent embryologist Hans Driesch, who was also a president of the SPR, witnessed at least one 'most impressive' demonstration of psychokinesis in 1928. And in 1934, May C. Walker of the American SPR described 'the most impressive telekinesis I have ever seen' after a session in which, among other things, a fan began to 'wriggle about, as if alive' in her hand.

One of the few Brazilians to make a systematic test of Mirabelli's skills was a well-known doctor and public health official, Dr Thadeu de Medeiros. The medium worked for a time in the doctor's clinic as a paranormal diagnostician. But bottles of medicine kept flying around the room, so this phase of his career also came to an abrupt end.

In 1960, Dr E. J. Dingwall of the SPR lamented that the Mirabelli case 'remains another of those unsolved mysteries with which the history of parapsychology abounds'. He put much of the blame on Besterman, for not keeping proper records.

Mirabelli died in 1951. His son Cesar has movingly described how, while they were on the way to the local cinema, the medium dashed across the road to buy his son an ice cream. He was hit by a car, and died without regaining consciousness.

DOLPHIN INTELLIGENCE

SCIENTISTS AGREE THAT DOLPHINS ARE HIGHLY INTELLIGENT. CERTAIN RESEARCH EVEN SUGGESTS THAT THEY ARE BRIGHTER THAN HUMAN BEINGS IN SOME WAYS

Dolphins have figured in literature and art since ancient times. The fine dolphin fresco, far right, for example, is from the royal palace at Knossos, Crete, and dates from 1500 BC. The friendship of men and dolphins was often celebrated. On a coin, below right, from the Greek city of Tarentum, in southern Italy, the city's founder, Phalanthus, is shown riding on a dolphin. But a killer whale, right, closely related to the dolphin and nearly as intelligent, here shows itself less willing to be used as a mount.

A bottle-nosed dolphin – one of those lovable extroverts that delight the crowds at large aqua-zoos by playing with beach balls, leaping for fish, and even removing the top halves of bikinis worn by female attendants – learned to speak an English sentence with, admittedly, a strong Hungarian accent.

So said Dr John Lilly, a neurophysiologist who studied dolphins over many years.

The dolphin that allegedly spoke, and whose words were recorded on tape after being picked up on one of Dr Lilly's array of underwater microphones, made a simple enough demand. 'Throw me a ball,' it said, in a pronunciation suggesting it might have spent its calfhood in Budapest.

Not all those researching dolphin behaviour and intelligence are prepared to accept Dr Lilly's remarkable claim. He was trying, some say, to turn dolphins into 'floating Hobbits'. His theories concerning their intelligence were 'speculative to the point of irresponsibility', they say, stating that the vocal equipment of cetaceans – dolphins and whales – is quite incapable of ever producing human language. As for the English sentence recorded by Dr Lilly, it is clear, so it is asserted, that some electronic fault in a microphone caused it to pick up words spoken by Dr Kert, the Hungarian-born physicist who was leading a research team in the vicinity.

Dr Lilly remained unabashed. He was convinced that the words came either from Joe or Rosie, a dolphin pair that had frequently heard the voice of Dr Kert and that had picked up their English pronunciation from him.

Whatever the truth of the matter, there is no doubt that dolphins have a highly developed brain structure, more complex even than that of apes, and that they have a considerable native intelligence. They are also extraordinarily friendly to Mankind, noticeably lacking the responses of fear and hostility to human beings that characterise most wild animals.

This endearing friendliness was commented upon by Greek and Latin writers. The Greek historian Plutarch, for example, remarked in the first century AD that wild animals avoid men because they are afraid of them, that tame animals are friendly to men out of self-interest, because they are fed by them, and that: 'To only the dolphin, Nature has given that which the philosopher seeks, friendship for no advantage; though it has no need of any man's help, yet it is a genial friend to all, and has helped Man.'

A century after Plutarch, the poet Oppian told a story illustrating the friendship between Man and dolphin. On the island of Poroselene, he said, lived a youth who, from childhood, had been loved by a dolphin. The boy would swim with the dolphin, play with it, and even ride on its back. The dolphin formed a strong emotional attachment to its human companion 'being fain to kiss and embrace the youth', and when the boy died, 'like one sorrowing, the dolphin visited the shores in quest of the companion of its youth: you would have said that you truly heard the voice of a mourner, such helpless grief was in it. And although the islanders called it often, it would no more listen to them nor accept food they offered it, and very soon it vanished from that sea and none saw it any more.'

For almost 2,000 years, this and many similar tales dating from classical times were taken to be no more than pleasant fantasies. Modern research and observation, however, have shown that there is

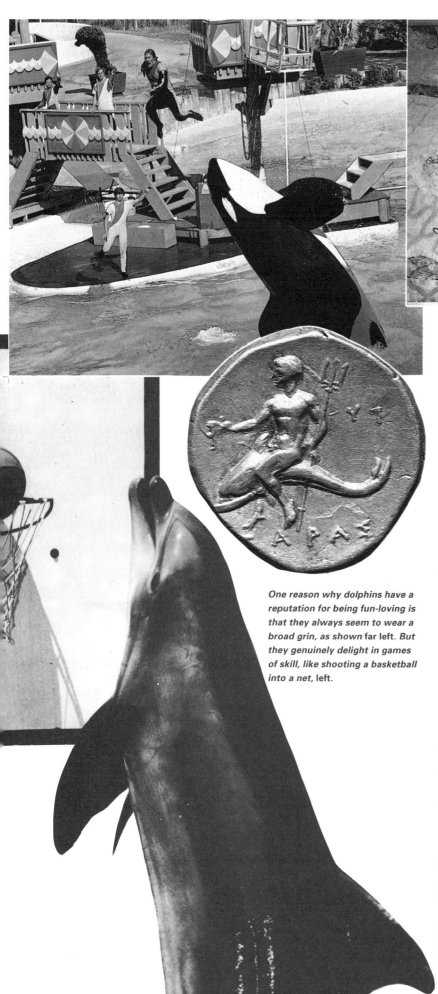

One reason why dolphins have a reputation for being fun-loving is that they always seem to wear a broad grin, as shown **far left**. But they genuinely delight in games of skill, like shooting a basketball into a net, **left**.

no reason to disbelieve the existence of a factual basis for such stories. Several present-day observers of dolphins, among them the writer Ronald Lockley, have experienced a relationship with dolphins similar in essence to that described by Oppian. Even the dolphin's supposed attempts to 'kiss and embrace the youth', which might be thought to be a flight of poetic fancy, are in complete conformity with modern observations of dolphin behaviour. Dolphins, like most advanced mammals, even seem to enjoy masturbating; and those in captivity have been seen to attempt to do so by rubbing themselves against humans swimming in their tanks.

SEEKING COMPANIONSHIP

Nevertheless, it would be wrong to think that human-dolphin friendship is only, or even usually, a product of the animal's sexual drive. Thus, Opo, a young female dolphin who, during 1955 and 1956, made friends with some of the inhabitants of the New Zealand village of Opononi, seems to have had no other motive than a desire for companionship .

Possibly she was an orphan – certainly, she first came to human attention when she began to nudge dinghies and other small boats in a manner that suggested she was looking for some lost parent or friend. By the autumn of 1955, she was allowing the crews of such craft to touch and even tickle her. Her liking for human beings steadily increased, and she soon began to swim into shallow waters and introduce herself to bathers, making it clear that she desired physical contact with them.

By the summer holiday – which in New Zealand falls at Christmas and New Year – a newspaper had reported her activities. Hundreds of sightseers made their way to the beach to watch bathers tickling and playing with Opo. She showed no signs of fear and even allowed some favoured swimmers to hold her. When introduced to a beach ball, she quickly learned to play with it, using her tail or head to throw it high in the air.

Opo did not like her human friends to be too boisterous in their play; if they became too rough she made no attempt to retaliate but simply swam away, indicating her displeasure by smacking the

*In*Focus

SENSE AND SENSIBILITY

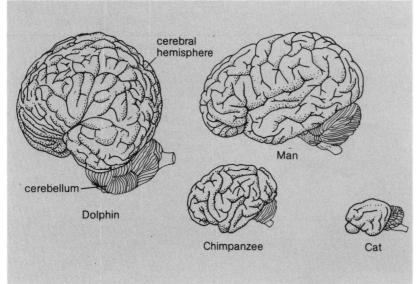

Brains of four mammals are seen drawn to scale, above. The dolphin's brain is slightly larger and heavier than Man's, but the human brain has a greater proportion of neocortex, responsible for higher intellectual functions.

cerebral hemisphere

cerebellum

Dolphin

Man

Chimpanzee

Cat

The degree of development of the different parts of an animal's brain can often be related to a creature's way of life. The part of the brain called the cerebellum, for example, is responsible for balance and posture, and so is more highly developed in birds than in fish, for whom these functions are less important. In mammals' brains, the cerebellum has highly developed side lobes, which govern the movement of the limbs. In the primates, they regulate the delicate movements of the hands or paws, and of the fingers; but they are almost as important to the dolphin.

The distinctive abilities of the higher mammals are largely due to the neocortex, the outermost part of the cortex – the layer of nerve cells that covers the cerebellum and the cerebral hemispheres. The surface of the small brain of the cat is smooth, whereas the surfaces of the large brains of chimpanzees, men and whales are deeply folded. This folding results in a large surface area, and hence a high proportion of neocortex. Eighty per cent of the human brain is neocortex – more even than in the dolphin brain. Certain areas of the neocortex are concerned with specific senses; and the remaining 'association areas' are crucially important to intelligence, for they are concerned with learning. They form over three-quarters of the neocortex in the cleverer mammals – chimpanzees, humans and dolphins.

water with her tail. Children were her special delight, presumably because they were more gentle than adult swimmers, and she became a particular friend of Jill Baker, a 13-year-old whom she allowed to take brief rides on her back.

DEATH OF A DOLPHIN

One day, in April 1956, Opo was missing from her favourite playground. The next day, she was found dead, trapped by the shore in a rock inlet from which the tide had receded. It is possible that her liking for human companionship had killed her, that she had gone so near the shore in the hope of making new friends. One thing is certain: in the 10 months or so of her contact with human beings, she provided hard evidence that the classic 'fairy stories' of dolphins' friendliness and intelligence, and of dolphins with human riders, almost certainly had a factual basis. Even the tales told by ancient Greeks of sailors being saved from drowning by dolphins who held them above the waves until rescue arrived may well have been true. Certainly, modern observers have witnessed dolphin mothers spending many hours holding aloft sick calves, when their young have lacked the strength to reach the surface in order to breathe.

There are indications that the friendliness dolphins show to living beings of other species is related to their brain structure. The central nervous system of dolphins, like that of the other cetaceans, is very highly developed. It is difficult to compare the dolphin brain directly with that of land mammals, however. In the 30 million years or so since the mammalian ancestors of the cetaceans took to the sea, the dolphin nervous system has evolved in specialised ways that help it to survive in its marine environment. Much of this mechanism is not fully

understood. Nevertheless, the complexity of its brain is such that the dolphin is now generally regarded as more intelligent than other advanced mammals – the dog, seal or chimpanzee, for example. It is even possible that dolphins are more intelligent than human beings. The human brain has more neocortex, but the ratio of the dolphin's neocortex – its 'thinking brain' – to its limbic area – the oldest and most primitive part of the brain – is larger than in most human beings. This provides a clue to dolphin psychology. Evidence from human beings seems to indicate that damage to the neocortical 'association neurons' (nerve cells) correlates with impairment of the sense of humour, the capacity for emotional self-control, and the power of abstract thought – including philosophical speculation and problem-solving by insight. The high degree of development of the neocortex in dolphins suggests that corresponding faculties may be well-developed in these creatures.

So, while we cannot know whether dolphins engage in philosophic or religious speculation, there seems no reason to disbelieve that they are capable of doing so. It has even been suggested that they quite naturally go in the directions we call spiritual, and get into meditative states quite easily.

Whether dolphins actually meditate is likely to remain an unanswered question until someone develops a language that a dolphin can learn and use as a means of communicating with human beings. Such a step forward in the relationship between human beings and cetaceans is not impossible. At the University of Hawaii, for instance, Dr. Louis Herman, a psychologist who for some years worked with a pair of bottle-nosed dolphins, taught his subjects to understand a vocabulary of about 30 English words. The dolphins responded to these

words not only individually – which might indicate the type of learning by rote that is displayed by performing circus animals – but also in hundreds of combinations. Dr Herman also reported a curious fact concerning his dolphins' understanding of the word 'in'. This seemingly simple English word has several different uses: it can be a preposition, an adverb, an adjective – even a verb. When Dr Herman used it in a different way from any he had used before in his 'conversations' with dolphins, they showed an immediate understanding. This would seem to indicate that Dr Herman's pupils had acquired a rudimentary awareness of English grammar and wanted to use this knowledge in order to communicate with human beings.

DOLPHIN TONGUE

It has been suggested that dolphins have a language of their own – 'Delphinese' – in which they hold long conversations with each other. There is no doubt that they do communicate with one another. Experiments have even shown that, when two previously unacquainted dolphins are put in adjoining tanks, they use sounds as a means of communication. Clicks seem to be dolphins' usual mode of communication, but they also make a sound somewhat similar to human whistling. The behaviour of dolphins in this experimental situation always seems to follow a similar pattern: one listens politely while the other clicks away, then the talker falls silent in order to listen to the reply.

Various types of whistle seem to express distress of one sort or another – anything from a mild unease to the dolphin equivalent of a scream for help. Nearby dolphins, hearing a whistle of the 'scream' type, immediately hurry to the rescue and, even if their distressed fellow is not obviously in need of air, they push it to the surface in order that it may breathe easily. After the distressed creature has taken his first deep breath, there is often a prolonged exchange of clicks and whistles among the entire group. This was considered by Dr Lilly and others to be 'evidence of meaningful exchanges in the vocal sphere' – in other words, conversation.

It is difficult to devise experiments to test whether dolphins have the capacity for 'insight' – the ability to solve problems by thinking about them and then acting, rather than by blind trial and error. But observation of captive dolphins suggests that they do possess this quality.

Yet, in spite of the possibility that the communication barrier between Man and dolphin may be broken down, there seems little likelihood of our ever fully understanding cetacean consciousness. For dolphins have a sonic sense: they can 'illuminate' objects with sound pulses and, from the echoes, can judge the objects' positions. No human can understand what it is like to 'see' such a sound picture, any more than the sightless can understand what it is like to look at a sunset. We may one day come to comprehend dolphin intelligence, but may never share their perceptions of the world.

A trained dolphin 'stands' in the water, above, keeping itself up by thrashing its tail rapidly, as it takes food from its handler.

A US Navy trainer, left, holds out an acoustic homing device to a porpoise, Tuffy, being trained as a messenger for a Sealab underwater laboratory. Dolphins and porpoises have also been trained for more sinister purposes – as 'frogmen', to carry explosive charges and detonate them against the sides of enemy ships, for instance.

" IT HAS EVEN BEEN SUGGESTED THAT THE ACOUSTIC MEMORY OF WHALES IS SO ELABORATE THAT THEY COULD PERHAPS LISTEN TO AN ENTIRE SYMPHONY JUST ONCE AND THEN HAVE A MENTAL PLAYBACK LATER, REMEMBERING NOT ONLY EVERY PHRASE BUT ALSO THE WAY THEY FELT WHEN HEARING IT FOR THE FIRST TIME. "

LYALL WATSON, LIFETIDE

197

APOCALYPSE NOW?

CERTAIN GROUPS OF UFO CONTACTEES OFTEN GIVE DETAILED WARNINGS OF IMPENDING DISASTERS. WHAT IS MORE, THESE CULTS INVARIABLY INSIST THAT ONLY THEIR OWN CHOSEN FEW WILL BE SAVED – A PROMISE THAT, NOT SURPRISINGLY, ATTRACTS MANY HOPEFUL DEVOTEES

Most UFO cults have appeared in the United States, long the home of countless eccentric religious groups. The story of one of these cults is told in full by a trio of sociologists, Leon Festinger, Henry Riecken and Stanley Schachter. They planted observers in a developing group centred on a UFO 'communicator' in 'Lake City', Utah. (The sociologists used fictitious names throughout in order to protect their subjects.) The communicator was 'Marian Keech', who believed she had received the initial message from her late father. She sat quietly and regularly thereafter, waiting to produce automatic writing, and was soon contacted by 'higher forces' – firstly, by 'the Elder Brother', and then by entities from the planets Clarion and Cerus (neither of which is known to conventional astronomy). She received communications especially from a certain Sananda of Clarion, who claimed to have been Jesus in an earlier time. Marian did not publicise her messages enthusiastically, but others from existing UFO groups and mystical or occult groups soon showed an interest. In August 1954, a press release was issued. This summarised not only the more philosophical part of the communications, in which the media took little interest, but also predictions regarding a coming disaster of vast proportions. The nature of the event, as reported by Marian, varied at times; but as interest in the group grew, its details became more firmly fixed. At the end of September, the *Lake City Herald* published this typical report:

'Lake City will be destroyed by a flood from Great Lake just before dawn, December 21st, according to a suburban housewife. Mrs Marian Keech of 847 West School Street says the prophecy is not her own. It is the purport of many messages she has received by automatic writing... The messages, according to Mrs Keech, are sent to her by superior beings from a planet called "Clarion".

In a still from a television science fiction play, **left**, a throng of young people, controlled by armed police, gather at an ancient stone circle in the expectation that UFOs are about to take them to a new existence beyond the Earth. At gatherings such as this, badges like those, **inset**, find a ready market. Many older and rather more staid people, however, have also expected to be contacted by UFOs and delivered from imminent cataclysm.

These beings have been visiting the Earth, she says, in what we call "flying saucers". During their visits, she says, they have observed fault lines in the Earth's crust that foretoken the deluge. Mrs Keech reports she was told the flood will spread to form an inland sea stretching from the Arctic Circle to the Gulf of Mexico.'

By now, Marian Keech was referring to a group of communicators whom she called the 'Guardians', though Sananda remained the most important. Once the media had started to publicise the group, Mrs Keech and her associates began to be afflicted by the problems that always beset UFO contactees. Increasing numbers of visitors called at her house, often when group members were present. She had explained to the group that, if they did the right thing and were gathered together, ready, at the appointed time, they would not be drowned in the forthcoming flood but would be carried away in one or more flying saucers. The extra-terrestrials could come to make contact at any time and in any way: so Mrs Keech and her group had to decide whether or not the visitors they had were extra-terrestrials, and also whether they in fact were good or evil extra-terrestrials.

THE LAST DAYS

The cult had now fallen into the classical pattern: it had a communicator, an explanation for the UFO mystery, a message of great importance, and a 'task' for its members – not so much to publicise the disaster as to prepare themselves to survive it. As the chosen date approached, the group became more outlandish. Members gave up jobs, possessions and relationships, and some took up unusual diets. All came together to await the fulfilment of their expectations. One condition of escape required by the 'Guardians' was that all metal should be removed from the participants' persons. This led to some interesting arrangements for clothing, and a lively discussion about dental fillings.

Salvation from ageing and death was promised by George van Tassel, the Sage of Giant Rock. Supposedly on instructions from extra-terrestrials, he built the structure above, the 'Integatron', at Giant Rock Airport in California, USA. It was intended for research into the unseen truths of life and for development of techniques of preventing and even reversing the processes of ageing in the human body. The structure, four storeys high, was made mostly of timber and contained no metal.

The last few days before 21 December were traumatic for the group members, as their hopes were first raised and then dashed by increasingly strange messages and predictions, all proving to be inaccurate. The greatest shock came on the day itself, when no flood arrived, nor any spacecraft to save them from it. The group now fell prey to disillusion and, in due course, dispersed.

Another group that purveyed warnings of catastrophe transmitted from space beings called itself the 'Light Affiliates'. They were active in the late 1960s in Burnaby, British Columbia, Canada. Their launching statement read: 'We wish to notify all those interested that a phenomenon has occurred here in Vancouver. A young girl, age 22, suddenly began channelling on 23.10.69. Her source is a being identifying himself as Ox-Ho, who is relaying transmissions from a galaxy close to our own... Her material is phenomenal in that she has been informed of the coming disasters, when to expect them, and what to do pertaining to the necessary evacuation of the danger areas and food supplies that will be needed.' The real name of the 'channel' was Robin McPherson, but she was renamed 'Estelle' by the 'being'. Her mother Aileen became 'Magdalene', her friend Sally became 'Celeste', and a young man involved in the early communications was given the evocative name 'Truman Merit'.

Ox-Ho explained that the day of judgement would begin during 22 November 1969. In these final hours, Man would be 'given a last opportunity to repair his decadent house before the terminal series of disasters'. If he did not take the opportunity to change, 'the Space Brothers would remove the Chosen and return them to Earth after the planet had once again "crystallised", and been spiritually, as well as physically, restructured.' This 'restructuring' would involve the tilting of the Earth on its axis and the disappearance beneath the sea of large land areas. Members of the 'Light Affiliates' were also exhorted to evangelise wherever possible.

Nothing seems to have happened on the predicted date to fulfil the expectations of the 'Light Affiliates'. Robin McPherson then ceased to communicate, but her mother continued the task. In an interview with the writer Brad Steiger, in the mid 1970s, she explained where the predictions had gone wrong:

'We misinterpreted them, Brad, because it all happened so suddenly. The first visions I was given of destruction were very upsetting. I can see things now in a much broader perspective... The thing is that it is the first ascension, and it is a mental ascension. The Brothers are trying to get as many people as possible into the Kingdom... You know, I've been told by the Brotherhood that Earth is like an encounter therapy centre for the psychotics of the Universe... I have been shown that the Earth is also wobbling very drastically on its axis.'

It is sometimes less painful to find ways of showing that your beliefs are fundamentally correct by means of some elaborate reinterpretation than to concede that they are simply mistaken.

Claims that intelligent beings can visit us from the planets of the solar system have been made implausible by space exploration. Alien entities must come from distant star systems, even from other galaxies, of which science presently knows little. Some UFO cults – though by no means all – have adapted to the growth of knowledge by placing the source of their communications in suitably remote places.

The group that made the greatest impact during the 1970s was called 'HIM' – Human Individual Metamorphosis. This group appeared in California in 1975 and appealed to some of those who had dabbled in the drug culture, personal spiritual development and New Age mysticism. The movement was run by a middle-aged man and woman. They adopted names that were modest enough – Bo and Peep – and their teaching offered the advantages of life after death without the inconvenience of dying. Instead, the adherents were to ascend physically.

*Joan Culpepper, seen **above**, with two members of the cult, told reporters about her life with Human Individual Metamorphosis (HIM), run by a couple calling themselves Bo and Peep, **below right**. HIM offered its followers the prospect of being transported physically to a realm beyond the Earth's atmosphere. Joan Culpepper subsequently left the cult and set up a half-way house to assist other disillusioned former adherents.*

One of the cult's publicity posters read:

'UFOs: why they are here. Who they have come for. When they will land. Two individuals say they were sent from the level above human and will return to that level in a spaceship within the next three months. This man and woman will discuss how the transition from the human level to the next level is accomplished, and when this may be done... If you have ever entertained the idea that there might be a real physical level in space beyond the Earth's confines, you will want to attend this meeting.'

MORE THAN HUMAN

Bo and Peep – formerly known as M.H. Applewhite and Bonnie Nettles – had convinced themselves that they were more than human, and had the strength of will and personality to maintain that impression. Converts were clearly quite overwhelmed by them. At first, they claimed that they would one day be assassinated and then would be resurrected after three days. Later, these claims were set aside. As in other such groups, members were expected to make sacrifices – to give up their names and possessions, abandon the use of drugs, alcohol, radio and television, and not to indulge in sex, or even read books. The members generally lived in semi-permanent camps. The words of Bo and Peep, in an interview recounted by Brad Steiger, make their attitude to the family and other personal relationships clear:

'Husband and wife can take the trip at the same time – but not together. It would be impossible to become an individual if you went together on the trip... In order to leave this Earth's atmosphere, you

must go alone and overcome whatever needs you have for any other individual or thing of this Earth. Anything for which you depend on another human being or any thing on this Earth must be overcome'.

Being a member of 'HIM' was more like being a Moonie than participating in a traditional religion or even a traditional UFO cult. But the structure of the group was like that of other groups already described: there was a communicator, a message, and a task.

No one has yet ascended to another physical realm above the atmosphere. Not many people seem to have got their money back, either. It turned out that Bo and Peep had met each other in a psychiatric hospital, where she was a nurse and he was a patient. Yet plenty of people remained willing to believe them and to accept their discipline. Like so many fringe religions, it seems to have met spiritual needs that were shared by many people at that time.

Let us look, finally, at one further vision of salvation by UFOs – one that has been experienced in dreams by Sue and John Day, an English couple. They claim to have been taken on board an alien spacecraft near the village of Aveley in Essex. In their dreams, they saw a deep red Sun and a dark sphere hanging in a blood-coloured sky. Columns of weary men, women and children made their way through a devastated landscape towards the summit of a high hill. There, they waited for perhaps days, until their eyes caught the first glinting reflections from a formation of shining UFO-like craft appearing over the murky horizon, heading slowly in their direction. As they drew nearer, a number of these craft broke away and descended over the

hilltop. Then they began to lower ramps. The people seemed to know that, at last, 'they' had come to take them away from the devastated planet Earth.

This series of dreams seemed to the Days to be a presentiment of a possible, but avoidable, future – a future holding disaster, but also salvation for a fortunate few through the intervention of UFOs. Quite when this event is due, however, still remains unknown.

Dragon Hill, near Uffington in Oxfordshire, below, is one of England's most mysterious ancient sites. It was recognised by two contactees, John and Sue Day, as the scene of dreams foreshadowing some future disaster for the world. UFOs figured in the dreams, and saved a disease-ravaged remnant of the human race.

> " CERTAIN CULTS HAVE ADOPTED THE BELIEF THAT THE MISSION OF UFOS IS SPIRITUAL AND THAT ALL PHYSICAL EFFORTS TO DETERMINE THE NATURE OF UFOS MUST NECESSARILY FAIL. WHILE SUCH MAY BE THE CASE, EVIDENCE TO SUPPORT IT IS CLEARLY LACKING. "
>
> **ROBERT EMENEGGER: UFOS – PAST, PRESENT AND FUTURE**

ODD TRICKS OF FATE

SOME PEOPLE SEEM TO BE ABLE TO SENSE IN ADVANCE THE CLUSTERINGS OF RANDOM EVENTS THAT WE CALL COINCIDENCES, AND USE THEM TO ADVANTAGE

In 1891, an unknown Englishman named Charles Wells became an overnight sensation as 'The Man that Broke the Bank at Monte Carlo'. Using no apparent system, he three times 'broke' the 100,000 franc 'bank' allocated to his roulette table at the famous Monte Carlo casino, seen above left, and in a contemporary drawing from the Illustrated London News, above right. After winning for the third time, Wells disappeared, taking his secret with him. He was never seen again.

It was only when his train steamed into Louisville station that George D. Bryson decided to break his trip to New York and visit the historic Kentucky town. He had never been there before and had to ask where to find the best hotel. Nobody knew he was in Louisville and, purely as a joke, he asked the desk clerk at the Brown Hotel: 'Any mail for me?' He was astonished when the clerk handed over a letter addressed to him and bearing his room number. The previous occupant of Room 307 had been another, and entirely different, George D. Bryson.

This was a remarkable coincidence, by any standards, but was made particularly piquant by the fact that the man who has told it most frequently is Dr Warren Weaver, the American mathematician and expert on probabilities. Weaver believes in the theory that coincidences are governed by the laws of chance, and rejects any suggestion of the uncanny or paranormal in coincidences.

On the opposite side of the fence are those who follow the 'seriality' or 'synchronicity' theories of Paul Kammerer, Wolfgang Pauli and Carl Jung.

Although these three men approached the theory of coincidences from different directions, their conclusions all hinted at a mysterious and barely understood force at work in the Universe, a force that tries to impose its own kind of order on the chaos of our world. Modern scientific research, particularly in the fields of biology and physics, also seems to suggest a basic tendency of nature to create order out of chaos.

The sceptics, however, stand firm. When events are happening at random, they argue, you are bound to encounter the clusterings we call coincidence. It is even possible to predict such clusterings or, at least, to predict the frequency with which they are likely to happen, so it is claimed.

If you toss a coin many times, the laws of probability dictate that you will end up with an almost equal number of heads and tails. However, the heads and tails will not alternate. There will be runs of one and runs of the other. Dr Weaver calculates that, if you toss a coin 1,024 times, for instance, it is likely that there will be one run of eight tails in a row, two of seven in a row, four of six in a row and eight runs of five in a row.

The same is true of roulette. Remarkably, 'evens' once came up 28 times in succession at a Monte Carlo casino. The odds against this happening are around 268 million to one. Yet the randomness experts claim that, as it *could* possibly happen, it did happen – and will indeed happen again somewhere in the world, if enough roulette wheels keep spinning for long enough.

Mathematicians use this law to explain the fantastic series of winning numbers that earned

Dr Warren Weaver, above, the American mathematician and probability expert, made a study of coincidence that led him to oppose any suggestion that a paranormal force is involved.

When a commuter train plunged from an open drawbridge into Newark Bay in New York, below, over 30 people lost their lives. By an ironic coincidence, this tragic incident won many New Yorkers large sums of money. A newspaper picture of the accident, left, showed the number 932 on the rear coach of the train and many people, sensing some meaning in the number, put their money on it in the Manhattan numbers game, and won.

Charles Wells the title – in song – of *The Man that Broke the Bank at Monte Carlo.*

Wells – a fat and slightly sinister Englishman – became the subject of the popular music-hall ditty in 1891, when he broke the bank at the Monte Carlo casino three times. He used no apparent system, but put even money bets on red and black, winning nearly every time until he finally exceeded the 100,000 francs 'bank' allocated to each table. On each occasion, attendants lugubriously covered the table with a black 'mourning' cloth and closed it for the rest of the day. The third and last time Wells appeared at the casino, he placed his opening bet on number five, at odds of 35 to 1. He won. He left his original bet and added his winnings to it. Five came up again. This happened five times in succession. Out came the black cloth; and out went Wells with his winnings, never to be seen there again.

GETTING LUCKY

The seriality and synchronicity theorists – and those who have extended the work of Kammerer, Pauli and Jung – accept the idea of 'clusters' of numbers. But they see 'luck' and 'coincidence' as two sides of the same coin. Indeed, telepathy and precognition – recurring elements in coincidences – might offer an alternative explanation of why some people are 'luckier' than others.

Modern research breaks coincidences down into two distinct types: trivial (like spinning coins, runs of numbers and amazing hands of cards) and significant. Significant coincidences are those that shuffle together people, events, space and time – past, present and future – in a manner that seems to cross a delicate borderline into the doubtful region of the paranormal.

Sometimes, a coincidence occurs that seems to link, almost capriciously, the rival theories. After a New York commuter train plunged into Newark Bay – killing many passengers – work started on recovering the coaches from the water. One front-page newspaper picture showed the rear coach being

winched up, with the number 932 clearly visible on its side. That day, the number 932 came up in the Manhattan numbers game, winning hundreds of thousands of dollars for the hordes of people who – sensing an occult significance in the number – had put their money on it.

Modern researchers now divide significant coincidences into several categories. One of these is the warning coincidence, with its presentiment of danger or disaster.

COINCIDENCE AND PREMONITION

Warning coincidences often have an extraordinarily long reach both geographically and in time, which is why many are ignored or go unrecognised. That was certainly the case with three ships, the *Titan*, the *Titanic* and the *Titanian*. In 1898, the American writer Morgan Robertson published a novel about a giant liner, the *Titan*, which sank one freezing April night in the Atlantic, after hitting an iceberg on what was her maiden voyage.

Fourteen years later – in one of the world's worst sea disasters – the *Titanic* sank on a freezing April night in the Atlantic after hitting an iceberg on her maiden voyage.

But the coincidences did not end there. The ships, both fact and fiction, were around the same tonnage, and both disasters occurred in the same stretch of the ocean. Both liners were also regarded as 'unsinkable', and neither carried sufficient lifeboats.

With the extraordinary story of the *Titanian*, the *Titan-Titanic* coincidences begin to defy human belief. On watch one night in April 1935 – during the *Titanian*'s coal-run from the Tyne to Canada – crewman William Reeves began to feel a strong sense of foreboding. By the time the *Titanian* reached the spot where the two other ships had gone down, the feeling was overpowering. Could Reeves stop the ship merely because of a premonition? One thing – a further coincidence – made the decision for him. He had been born on the day of the *Titanic* disaster. 'Danger ahead!' he bellowed to the bridge. The words were barely out of his mouth when an iceberg loomed out of the darkness. The ship avoided it just in time.

Coincidence links the fates of the **Titanian**, *above, and the famous* **Titanic**. *Both hit icebergs in the same waters; but the* **Titanian** *survived.*

The dead body of Charles Coghlan, below, made an immense sea journey before being cast up on the shore of his home town.

Another category is the 'it's-a-small-world coincidence', which brings together people and places when least expected – a phenomenon that was vouched for by Arthur Butterworth, of Skipton, Yorkshire, England.

During the Second World War, while serving in the army, he ordered a secondhand book on music from a London bookseller. The book eventually reached him at his camp, disguised by the usual military postcode, in the grounds of Taverham Hall, near Norwich. Standing at the window of his army hut, he opened the parcel and, as he did so, a picture postcard – presumably used as a bookmark – fell out. The writing on one side showed the postcard had been written on 4 August 1913. To his astonishment, when he turned it over, the picture showed 'the exact view I had from my hut window at that very moment... Taverham Hall.'

If coincidence can reach so easily across time and space in its quest for 'order out of chaos', it is not surprising that it can stretch beyond the grave.

While on a tour of Texas in 1899, the Canadian actor Charles Francis Coghlan was taken ill in Galveston and died. It was too far to return his remains to his home on Prince Edward Island, in the Gulf of St Lawrence more than 3,500 miles (5,600 kilometres) away by the sea-route, so he was buried in a lead coffin inside a granite vault. His bones had rested less than a year when the great hurricane of September 1900 hit Galveston Island, flooding the cemetery. The vault was shattered and Coghlan's coffin floated out into the Gulf of Mexico. Slowly, it drifted along the Florida coastline and into the Atlantic, where the Gulf Stream picked it up and carried it northwards.

Eight years passed. Then, one day in October 1908, some fishermen on Prince Edward Island spotted a long, weather-scarred box floating near the shore. Coghlan's body had come home. With respect and a sense of awe, his fellow islanders buried the actor in the nearby church where he had been christened as a baby.

Was this chance, destiny, a mere trick of 'randomness', or that strange and powerful force, striving to make sense of the Universe, that some call coincidence?

A STROLL INTO THE PAST

THE EXPERIENCE OF TWO ENGLISHWOMEN AT VERSAILLES IN 1901 WAS TO BE A MATTER OF CONTROVERSY FOR YEARS AFTERWARDS – FOR THE LADIES CLAIMED TO HAVE WALKED BACK INTO THE 18TH CENTURY, TO THE TIME OF MARIE-ANTOINETTE

When Miss Moberley and Miss Jourdain visited the palace of Versailles on 10 August 1901, everything appeared to be perfectly normal. After leaving the Galeries des Glaces, right, they ventured out into the grounds to find the Petit Trianon, below, the small secluded mansion that had once belonged to Marie-Antoinette. It was then that they found themselves in what seemed to be another age.

On a warm afternoon in August 1901, two middle-aged British schoolteachers, Miss Anne Moberley and Miss Eleanor Jourdain, decided to enliven their Parisian holiday by visiting the Palace of Versailles, which neither of them had seen. Both women were interested in history, and both had some claim to academic standing: Miss Moberley was the Principal of St. Hugh's College, Oxford, while Miss Jourdain was head of a girls' school in Watford, near London. Neither woman was inclined to be gullible or over-emotional in her reactions to her surroundings.

Having toured the Palace, they came to rest temporarily in the Galerie des Glaces. Soon, however, the open windows allowed the scent of the

The route taken by Miss Moberley and Miss Jourdain during their walk on 10 August 1901 is shown on an enlarged section of a map, right, drawn by Richard Mique, Marie-Antoinette's architect and landscape gardener.

flowers in the gardens to tempt them out again in the direction of the Petit Trianon, the château built in the grounds of Versailles by Louis XV and given by his successor, Louis XVI, to Queen Marie-Antoinette. Eventually, they came to a long lake with a woodland glade away to its right, and thence to another stretch of water, beside which rose the Grand Trianon, a château constructed for Louis XVI. They next arrived at a broad, green drive.

By now, the women were not at all sure of their direction, and instead of walking down the drive, which led to the Petit Trianon, they crossed it and took a side lane. Miss Moberley remembered noticing a woman shaking a white cloth out of the window of a building at the corner of the lane and was surprised that her friend did not stop to ask the way. Miss Jourdain, she learned later, had not done so because she had seen neither the woman nor the building.

At this point, the two ladies were unaware of anything odd in their surroundings and were absorbed in talk about England and friends there. They turned right, past some buildings, and glimpsed the end of a carved staircase through an open doorway. They did not pause but took the centre path of three that lay ahead of them. The only reason for this choice was that two men appeared to be at work on it with a kind of wheelbarrow and a pointed spade. This suggested that they were gardeners, though the women thought their dress unusual – they were wearing long, greyish green coats and small, three-cornered hats. The two men directed them straight ahead, and the friends continued as before, still deep in conversation.

About this time, however, both began to feel somewhat depressed, but independently, not mentioning the fact to each other until later. They also noticed a curious flatness about their surroundings, and each had the impression that the landscape had somehow become two-dimensional. These sensations soon became overpowering as they approached 'a light garden kiosk, circular, and like a small bandstand, by which a man was sitting'. Neither lady liked the look of the man, for his face was dark and repulsive. He wore, they noticed, a

Miss Anne Moberley, above left, and Miss Eleanor Jourdain, above right, were determined to discover what lay behind their experience. The two women therefore made further trips to the Petit Trianon but found that the layout of the gardens had altered considerably since their first visit.

cloak and sombrero-style hat. Although they were still unsure about which way to go, nothing would have induced them to pass the man at the kiosk.

The sound of running footsteps behind them came as a relief; yet, when they turned, the path was empty. However, Miss Moberley noticed another person standing nearby, who seemed to have appeared with some suddenness. He seemed to be 'distinctly a gentleman... tall, with large dark eyes and... crisp, curling black hair'. He, too, wore a sombrero and dark cloak, and he seemed excited as he directed them to the house. He smiled in what they regarded as a peculiar fashion; but as soon as they had passed him and turned round to call out their thanks, he had disappeared. They now heard running footsteps again, which seemed close beside them, though they could see no one.

The two ladies next crossed a bridge over a miniature ravine, noticing a small cascade that tumbled down beside it, and finally reached 'a square, solidly built, small country house' with a terrace on the north and west sides. Miss Moberley saw, seated on the grass with her back to the terrace, a lady

Miss Moberley believed she saw seated the ghost of Marie-Antoinette (1775-1793), Queen of France, right, on the grass near the terrace of the Petit Trianon. It was the discovery that Miss Jourdain had not seen the figure at all that led the ladies to write down independent accounts of their expedition.

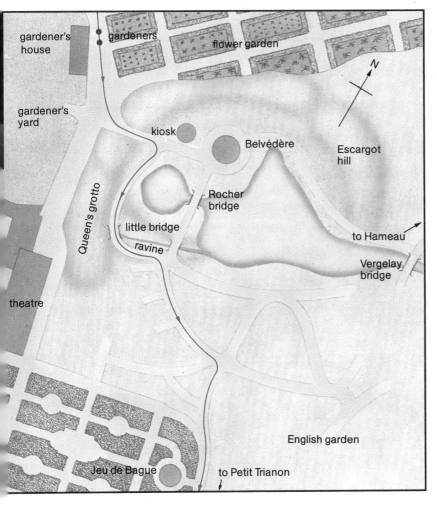

Full accounts were written by both women, separately, three months after their visit. This lapse of time was one of the factors that gave rise to scepticism on the part of later commentators. Memories of an event recorded three months afterwards, they pointed out, were likely to be far less accurate than those recorded within hours. In other words, the Misses Moberley and Jourdain were suspected of 'imaginative reconstruction' rather than accurate recollection.

Supportive legends relating to the Trianon were found to exist, however. A Parisian friend of Miss Jourdain's, for instance, told her that people from the village of Versailles had seen Marie-Antoinette one August day, seated in the gardens of the Petit Trianon, wearing a pink dress and a floppy hat. The whole place – the people who were present and the amusements that were provided – had appeared, the friend said, to be an exact representation of Trianon on the fateful 10 August 1792, the day of the sacking of the Tuileries, the royal family's flight to Paris, and the King's and Queen's imprisonment in the Temple. Miss Moberley and Miss Jourdain wondered if they might perhaps have entered some memory of the Queen, either projected by her upon the Trianon or retained by the place itself. Mystified by what they had encountered, they determined to check the details of their experience with the facts by returning to Versailles.

A CIRCLE OF INFLUENCE

Miss Jourdain revisited the Trianon alone the following January and again she sensed a strange quality about the place. Yet there were differences. The kiosk, for example, did not seem to be the same building, and at first there was no sense of eeriness. It was not until she walked over a bridge to reach the Hameau, where Queen Marie-Antoinette and her friends used to retire to play at being peasants, that she felt as though a line had been crossed, and a circle of influence entered. She noticed a cart being filled with sticks by two labourers wearing tunics and hooded capes. She turned her head fractionally to look at the Hameau; and when she looked back, both the men and the cart had vanished.

whom she thought to be busy sketching. The lady looked the women full in the face as they walked by. Miss Moberley commented that, though rather pretty, the lady's was not a young face, and she did not find herself attracted to its owner. This did not prevent her from noticing the lady's dress, which was of light material, with a low-cut neckline, and her plentiful fair hair, which was topped by a white, shady hat.

The two Englishwomen passed her without speaking and stepped up on to the terrace, Miss Moberley feeling as though she were walking in a dream. She then caught sight of the lady again, this time from behind, and felt a wave of relief that Miss Jourdain had not paused to ask if they might enter the house. Miss Jourdain, as it happened, had not seen the figure at all.

They had now reached the south-west corner of the terrace. As they turned, they noticed a second house, from which emerged a young man (with 'the air of a footman'), who offered to show them round. They were presently joined by a lively wedding party, and their spirits revived.

During the following week, the events of that afternoon were not discussed between them. It was not until Miss Moberley came to write her description of the events that she again experienced a sense of depression, and she asked Miss Jourdain: 'Do you think the Petit Trianon is haunted?' Miss Jourdain did. It was only then that they compared notes and learned how their perceptions of certain events differed.

A plan of the proposed gardens at the Petit Trianon, drawn in 1774 by the head gardener Antoine Richard, is reproduced below. The ringed area shows a kiosk of the kind seen by Moberley and Jourdain, but there is no firm evidence that it was ever erected.

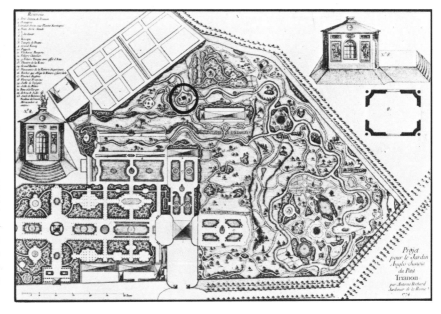

There were other incidents, too – the sight of a cloaked man moving through trees, the rustle of silk dresses, a feeling of being hemmed in by throngs of invisible people, the sound of a distant band playing light music – but nothing to match the events of August 1901.

The two friends returned to Versailles several times afterwards but never relived their earlier experiences. On the contrary, they discovered that the plan of the garden had changed considerably since their first visit. Woods had disappeared; paths had been removed; buildings had been altered; the kiosk had vanished; walls had been destroyed; and the ravine, little bridge and cascade had gone. The 20th-century Trianon bore little resemblance to the one they had originally seen. Mystified and intrigued, the two women now undertook their own investigation into the history of Marie-Antoinette's Petit Trianon.

It should be remembered that little was known about large-scale retrocognitive experiences at this date. Since the Moberley-Jourdain adventure was both intricate and complex, the simplest explanations seemed to be that the women had been hallucinating, that their memories had been inaccurate, or that they were romanticizing their experience. Much was made, too, of the fact that neither woman realised at the time that she was seeing things that did not exist.

But Miss Moberley and Miss Jourdain apparently felt sufficiently convinced of the strangeness of their experience to wish to check its facts; and over the next few years, they took considerable trouble to research the details of the Trianon's original structure, the way the gardens were landscaped and by whom, the workmen who may have been employed there by the Queen, and the uniforms that were thought to have been worn in her time. In the light of the results, the jibe of one reviewer – that the women had seen actual 1901 people in actual 1901 settings and clothes – does not appear to stand up to scrutiny. The gardeners' grey-green

The Jeu de Bague, above, with its semicircular screen, once stood in the Trianon grounds. Léon Rey, one of the critics of the Moberley-Jourdain account, identified this as the kiosk in their story, but the ladies disagreed.

During their research, Miss Moberley and Miss Jourdain found much evidence that confirmed their belief that they had slipped back into the world of Marie-Antoinette. Illustrations of costume of that period, left, showed a style of dress very similar to that worn by the people they had encountered. And, on reading descriptions of the Comte de Vaudreuil, a member of the Queen's close circle of friends, above, they concluded that he was the 'repulsive' man seated by the kiosk.

uniforms and tricorn hats were certainly not worn by officials at the Trianon in 1901, for 'green was a Royal livery, and no one now wore it at the Trianon', according to the records of Moberley and Jourdain's research, published in later editions of their book, *An Adventure*. Could the apparitions, therefore, have been masqueraders, and the ghostly music that of a real orchestra playing out of sight? But why should masqueraders have been running through non-existent woods? As for the music heard by Miss Jourdain in 1902, she discovered immediately afterwards that no band had been playing out of doors that afternoon.

IMAGINATIVE AFTERTHOUGHT?

The kiosk they had seen bore some resemblance to one that had figured in the original plans of the Trianon as a *ruine* – that is, a decorative folly – but there is some doubt about whether it was ever built. In fact, the kiosk proved a source of difficulty, for Moberley and Jourdain, in their struggles to identify it with an original Trianon feature, tended to waver and to modify their opinions. It had 'a slightly Chinese effect', they thought. A French critic, Léon Rey, writing in the *Revue de Paris*, identified it with a building called the Jeu de Bague, which was vaguely Chinese in style. The two Englishwomen, however, disagreed with this and pointed out the discrepancies between the kiosk of 10 August 1901 – which, after all, they had seen and Rey had not – and the Jeu de Bague. Their reference to a 'Chinese effect' was not made until 1909, which does suggest the possibility of imaginative afterthought. Nevertheless, there are grounds for thinking that, in 1774, Marie-Antoinette's head gardener, Antoine Richard, had sketched plans that included a light garden kiosk of the kind the two women thought they saw in 1901.

As one examines the 'facts' recounted by Moberley and Jourdain and the charges and counter-charges levelled against them over the years, their account and its interpretation grows increasingly confused. The swarthy man to whom the women felt such aversion was 'identified' as the Comte de Vaudreuil, who had played a sinister part in Marie-Antoinette's last few months as Queen. But another critic has suggested that the figure could have been that of the old Louis XV, who built the Petit Trianon. Indeed, there was hardly a point in the narrative of the two women that was not later challenged, and often contradicted, by some even wilder explanation.

The Hameau, above, is the miniature village built for Marie-Antoinette in the grounds of the Trianon. When Miss Jourdain went to Versailles alone in January 1902, she sensed nothing strange until she reached the village. Then, the feeling of depression of the previous year became particularly noticeable.

Some critics believed the Temple de l'Amour, below, could have been the kiosk, but Moberley and Jourdain declared it was definitely not the building they had seen in 1901.

Critics not only contradicted Moberley and Jourdain, they also contradicted each other, and leaned over backwards to show that the women had imagined what they had seen or had misinterpreted, distorted and romanticized it. Their researches had not been thoroughly or reliably carried out, said the critics: they had allowed later research to influence the evidence and had embroidered their experiences to accord with what they had discovered. The critics claimed, in other words, that Moberley and Jourdain had systematically 'cooked the books' to produce proof of their story. The two ladies, whose intelligence seems to have been every bit the equal of that of their critics, were damned by implication as a couple of gullible elderly spinsters, whose heads were filled with romantic nonsense about the tragic Queen of France.

Yet this is not the impression gained from reading the Moberley-Jourdain papers. The women appear to have been balanced, sensible and genuinely puzzled by what they had encountered that August day in 1901. Their later enquiries are also as thorough as opportunity and the availability of material could make them; and although the two women were accused of altering their original story to suit later revealed facts, it may well be that they did not understand what they had seen until the discovery of certain facts made it clear to them. However, Moberley and Jourdain did fail to keep meticulous records of what had happened, perhaps because it never occurred to them that these would be necessary to prove their veracity.

It is not possible to judge what actually happened on 10 August 1901. But it seems likely that the women encountered a large-scale hallucination consistent with the conditions of a retrocognitive timeslip. And by far the most interesting aspect is the sustained interchange that apparently took place between figures from the past and those in the present. Two other English women underwent a similar experience at Dieppe some 50 years later. Is it the air of France, or her history, that somehow promotes such curious encounters?

THE DAY THE NORFOLKS DISAPPEARED

ONE OF THE MOST FREQUENTLY REPEATED STORIES OF MYSTERIOUS DISAPPEARANCES CONCERNS 267 SOLDIERS FROM THE ROYAL NORFOLK REGIMENT – WHO WERE ALLEGEDLY ABDUCTED BY A UFO IN 1915

There are many strange accounts of people having been abducted by UFOs. In most cases, the unfortunate victim is returned to Earth and is able to tell his or her story, often to an incredulous audience who, not unnaturally, express considerable disbelief. But sometimes the victim disappears forever, his fate to remain unknown. These cases are rare because a number of witnesses are required if more prosaic explanations for the disappearance are to be dismissed.

Troops are seen below, landing at Anzac Cove, Gallipoli, in 1915. Conditions were appalling; dysentery decimated the ranks and corpses lay everywhere, adding to the nightmare.

In this latter category can be counted the case of the vanishing First-Fifth Norfolks, a battalion of the Royal Norfolk Regiment, one of the most bizarre of all disappearances, and one which has been subsequently featured in numerous books about UFOs, the Bermuda Triangle, and other 'paranormal' mysteries. But can it possibly be true?

The incident allegedly took place in August 1915, during the ill-fated Gallipoli campaign. According to a statement made by three of the original witnesses, 22 members of a New Zealand field company saw a large number of British soldiers, later identified as the 'First-Fourth Norfolk Regiment', march into a strange loaf-of-bread shaped cloud that was straddling a dry creek bed. After the last man had entered, the cloud lifted and moved off against the wind. Not one of the soldiers was ever seen again.

The New Zealanders' story contained obvious errors, however. The First-Fourth Norfolk was not a regiment, but a battalion of the Royal Norfolk Regiment, for example. Yet none of the errors has ever been corrected in any of the books that feature the story, which suggests that it has never been substantiated, authors simply having copied the myth from one another.

THEATRE OF WAR

This opinion is supported by one further and very important fact: the First-Fourth Norfolk did not disappear from Gallipoli in August 1915, nor at any time or place thereafter. Indeed, there is ample evidence to show that they were in active service until the end of the year, when they were withdrawn from Gallipoli and sent to another theatre of war.

This fact would be sufficient to dispose of the New Zealanders' story of cosmic abduction as a figment of someone's imagination; but, perhaps coincidentally, it is a matter of undisputed historical fact that another battalion of the Royal Norfolk Regiment, the First-Fifth, *did* disappear at Gallipoli in August 1915, their fate never having been satisfactorily ascertained. So, if the New Zealanders did see any Norfolks abducted, it could only have been the First-Fifth. Is it possible that, bizarre though their story most certainly is, the members of this New Zealand field company did witness the fate of

Digging in, as shown below, was a necessary evil in a slow-moving war, and provided both shelter and cover. But the overcrowding and less than perfect sanitation, as well as the heat and flies, meant a squalid death for many before they had fired a shot. It was in such chaotic conditions that the Norfolks 'disappeared'.

Turkish artillery fire, bottom, during the advance on the hills of Tekke and Kavak Tepe.

the First-Fifth Norfolk? If they did not, where did their story come from, and what was the fate of the First-Fifth battalion?

The twisting trail in search of a solution to the mystery begins in Dereham, a small market town not far from Norwich, England. It was here, as part of the predominantly East Anglian 163rd Brigade, that the First-Fourth and First-Fifth Norfolks prepared to go to war.

The Norfolks were members of the reserve force known as the Territorials – and called 'Saturday night soldiers' by men of the regular army – but they belonged to a regiment with a long and distinguished history, which could be traced back to 1685, when it was raised by King James II at the time of Monmouth's Rebellion. At that time, it was known as Colonel Henry Cornwall's 9th Regiment of Foot.

The Norfolks embarked for Gallipoli on 29 July 1915. The Gallipoli campaign was fought for control of the Dardanelles – the ancient Hellespont – a long, narrow channel extending some 40 miles (65 kilometres) along the Gallipoli Peninsula in Turkey and connecting the Mediterranean with the Black Sea, for which reason it had acquired strategic importance following the alliance between Turkey and Germany.

The Gallipoli Peninsula is exquisitely beautiful in spring and early summer; but from May onwards, it bakes under a relentless sun and, by August, it is one of the most inhospitable places on Earth. It was on 10 August, at the height of the terrible summer, that the Norfolks landed at Suvla Bay and surveyed what had already become a graveyard for so many unfortunate soldiers.

Not far from the beach was a large salt lake. Dry in summer, it reflected the harsh glare of the sun. Beyond the beach lay the battlefield, Suvla Plain, and in the distance a semicircle of bleak hills stretched from north to south, giving the plain the appearance of a giant arena. The northernmost hill was named Kiretch Tepe, in the middle were the twin heights of Kavak Tepe and Tekke Tepe, and to the south was Sari Bair.

The Gallipoli campaign has gone down as one of the worst theatres of war in recent military history; and to those Norfolks who had deluded themselves that they were off on a great adventure, the sights that met their eyes must have seemed like a nightmare vision of hell.

TRENCH WARFARE

Conditions were appalling. The trenches were like ovens: a hot wind, pungent with the stench of death, stirred a fine dust across the plain; the food, the trenches, the latrines and the corpses were infested with a vile, bloated green fly – called the 'corpse fly' by the men because it feasted on the bodies of the dead and wounded. It spread a particularly virulent form of dysentery from which no soldier escaped and that reduced many to walking skeletons.

The troops, riddled with disease, were exhausted. Corpses lay about in great numbers and it was by no means unusual to see the face or hands of a hastily buried comrade protruding from the ground. Morale was low and an atmosphere of defeat hung heavily in the air.

The Norfolks had no experience of combat, and in normal circumstances, they would have been given time to acclimatize in a quiet sector. But Sir Ian Hamilton, Commander-in-Chief of the Mediterranean Expeditionary Force, believed that the only chance of wresting victory from the jaws of dreadful defeat lay in the use of fresh forces in a major offensive.

Hamilton envisaged a bold, sweeping attack on Tekke and Kavak Tepe; and it was arranged that, under cover of darkness on the night of 12 August, the 54th Division (of which the Norfolks' brigade was a part) should advance to the foothills and prepare to attack at dawn the next day. However, it was believed that a cultivated area called Kuchuk Anafarta Ova, over which the night advance would take place, was held by enemy snipers.

The effects of delay in burial and the burning heat made identification of corpses often impossible, as demonstrated, top.

Under the command of Major-General Sir Ian Hamilton, Commander-in-Chief of the Mediterranean Expeditionary Force, above, some 46,000 men lost their lives – including the 267 men of the Norfolks.

Accordingly, it was decided that the Norfolks' 163rd Brigade should move forward and clear the area during the afternoon of 12 August.

The advance that afternoon was a complete and utter fiasco, a prime example of the muddle and incompetence that marked the whole Gallipoli campaign. It was to begin at 4 p.m. with artillery support, but there was a delay of 45 minutes. However, faulty communications prevented the artillery from being informed and they opened fire as scheduled, thereby wasting their support. The area had been totally unreconnoitred, commanding officers were unfamiliar with the terrain and uncertain about their objective, and most of the maps hurriedly issued at the last moment only depicted another part of the Peninsula. The strength of the enemy was completely unknown.

The 163rd Brigade, with the First-Fourth Norfolk bringing up the rear, had advanced no more than about 1,000 yards (900 metres) when it became obvious that a serious mistake had been made in trying to cross the open plain in daylight. The strength of the enemy was greater than had been supposed, and the main body of the brigade – encountering heavy machine-gun fire – was forced to ground. However, on the right flank, the First-Fifth Norfolk encountered less stiff opposition and pressed forward into battle.

Sir Ian Hamilton described the following events in a dispatch to Lord Kitchener, the Secretary of State for War:

'In the course of the fight, creditable in all respects to the 163rd Brigade, there happened a very mysterious thing... Against the yielding forces of the enemy, Colonel Sir H. Beauchamp, a bold, self-confident officer, eagerly pressed forward, followed by the best part of the battalion. The fighting grew hotter, and the ground became more wooded and broken. At this stage, many men were wounded or grew exhausted with thirst. These found their way back to camp during the night. But the Colonel, with 16 officers and 250 men, still kept pushing forward, driving the enemy before him... Nothing more was seen or heard of any of them. They charged into the forest and were lost to sight or sound. Not one of them ever came back.'

Two hundred and sixty-seven men had vanished without trace!

The failure of the advance that afternoon delivered a crushing blow to Sir Ian Hamilton's hope of turning the tide of the campaign, and evacuating Allied forces at the end of 1915 was a major defeat. The Gallipoli campaign had lasted eight-and-a-half months and cost the lives of about 46,000 soldiers, a horrific number by any previous standards of modern warfare.

In 1916, the Government appointed a Royal Commission to investigate the causes of the defeat. The heavily censored report was released in

The poster, above, celebrates the Turkish victory over the invading forces, in Gallipoli, 1915.
The Turkish troops, below, knew the terrain, were used to the climate and were far better organized. Their victory rapidly became inevitable.

1917 with another one following in 1919. It was not until 1965, however, that a declassified edition was made available – a significant date as we shall see.

The fate of the First-Fifth Norfolk remained a mystery for four years until, in 1919, there was a further development in the story.

At the end of 1918, the British returned to Gallipoli as the ultimate victors. A soldier of the Occupation Forces was touring the battlefield when he found a cap badge of the Royal Norfolk Regiment, and on making enquiries he learned that a Turkish farmer had removed a large number of bodies from his property and dumped them in a nearby ravine. On 23 September 1919, following the unpleasant task of recovering the bodies, an officer commanding a Graves Registration Unit triumphantly announced:

'We have found the Fifth Norfolk – there were 180 in all: 122 Norfolk and a few Hants and Suffolks with 2/4th Cheshires. We could only identify two – Privates Barnaby and Carter. They were scattered over an area of about one square mile [2.5 square kilometres], at a distance of at least 800 yards [730 metres] behind the Turkish front line. Many of them had evidently been killed in a farm, as a local Turk, who owns the land, told us that, when he came back, he found the farm covered with the decomposing bodies of British soldiers which he threw into a small ravine. The whole thing quite bears out the original theory that they did not go very far on, but got mopped up one by one, all except the ones who got into the farmhouse.'

'We have found the Fifth Norfolk... ' Although this is generally considered the last word on the fate of the First-Fifth Norfolk, it is evident that this statement was somewhat premature. Only 122 Norfolks were found, which leaves more than half the men unaccounted for. Their fate remains a mystery – unless, of course, the New Zealanders' story of the strange cloud is true.

TWILIGHT OF THE GODS

TODAY, WE SEE NO SIGN AT ALL OF THE GODS AND GODDESSES WHO CROWDED THE ANCIENT WORLD. HOW COULD THEY HAVE BEEN SO REAL TO OUR ANCESTORS AND YET SO REMOTE TO US?

In the minds of most of our pre-Christian ancestors, the whole of nature seemed to be suffused with divine spirit – crowded with gods who controlled every aspect of the world, from the Sun, Moon and stars to the mountains, winds and rivers. In the ancient Near East, the enormous family of gods was also thought to control Man's life intimately, from day to day.

In ancient Sumer (the southern part of which is now Iraq), one of the earliest urban cultures, with origins dating back to 5000 BC, if not earlier, the gods were believed to be the owners of cities.

Achilles, the greatest warrior among the Greek besiegers of Troy, is seen below, slaying Hector, son of King Priam and foremost of the city's defenders. Achilles is guided to his foe by the goddess Athena who hovers overhead. The guidance and advice of the gods was an ever-present reality for the characters of Homeric poetry.

Man, it was said, had been created solely to relieve the gods from the tedium of work, and to provide a slave force to carry out chores such as irrigation, agriculture and building.

The temples built by the Sumerians were also believed to be the homes of their gods. They housed the images of local gods or goddesses and were focal points of the city's economy. A considerable proportion of the country's produce – grain, dates, meat and beer – would be brought to the temple for the deity's consumption. The priests were like valets to a divine aristocrat, responsible for clothing, washing, repairing and 'feeding' the idols. In turn, the gods issued commands for the running of state business, appointed kings as their deputies, and were ceremonially transported, when necessary, to meet the gods of other cities for high-level discussions.

The rule of the gods in the Near East has also been explained as a way of maintaining authority by the priests, who exploited the gullibility of the people. The promise of eternal life has often been used as a device to justify poverty and servitude in this life. But whilst this explanation might work, to some extent, for the Sumerians, it does not explain the behaviour of the Babylonians. In their minds, the afterlife consisted of a shadowy existence in a bleak underworld, regardless of one's record in life. Bearing this in mind, it does not seem very likely that the priests were guilty of a deliberate confidence trick.

The ancient Egyptians, Phoenicians and Greeks also seem to have had comparable arrangements with the divine. Large proportions of the gross national product of these ancient civilizations were spent on the housing and daily needs of their gods. Witness the pyramids, each of which was destined to be the tomb of the king who built it – the king being regarded as a living god. Witness, too, magnificent buildings such as the Parthenon and the other costly temples of the Acropolis at Athens. The ancient peoples who created these structures –

Many, today, would insist that religious belief has never been anything but a more or less conscious deception that serves to maintain the power of a priestly class. The prophet Daniel, who exposed two false Babylonian deities, would probably have agreed. The Babylonians brought 12 bushels of fine flour, 40 sheep and 50 gallons of wine to the idol of the god Bel each day. These vanished overnight. When King Cyrus cited this as proof of Bel's divinity, Daniel laid a trap by scattering ashes secretly on the temple floor. In the morning, the footprints of the priests were visible, showing that they were the ones who had been enjoying the food and wine. A dragon was also worshipped by the Babylonians, as illustrated left. Daniel exposed its non-divinity, too, by feeding it with pitch, fat and hair, whereupon it died.

provided the focal point for the economic and social structure of the state, just as in the Old World. And human sacrifice, regularly performed on the Aztec pyramids of Mexico, expressed a concern to appease the gods even more compulsive than that of ancient Sumer.

The ancient Meso-American cults, like those of the Near East and Greece, seemed to have been dominated by the worship of planetary gods. The major Aztec deity, Quetzalcóatl, in many respects resembles Dionysus and Shiva as a heroic god whose own death and resurrection gave the promise of renewed life to his followers. But the closest parallels to Quetzalcóatl are to be found in Ishtar, the Babylonian equivalent of Aphrodite. Ishtar and Quetzalcóatl were both warrior deities and were worshipped in the forms of a dragon and the planet Venus.

Babylonian and Mexican myths tell similar stories about their 'deaths', how they spent a period in the underworld and how they were subsequently resurrected to return to the sky as the morning star. The simplest explanation of these parallels is that they were independently originated, and were based on observations of the planet Venus. For long periods, Venus is invisible, as if it has 'gone to the underworld'.

A more sinister aspect of the planets was emphasized by the rebel scholar and writer Immanuel Velikovsky. Velikovsky's case for the occurrence of global catastrophes within the last

many of which, though ruined, still inspire awe after thousands of years – believed firmly in the reality of their gods and backed their beliefs with lavish gifts.

Several of these ancient civilizations even worshipped almost identical pantheons of deities under different names. Most were sky gods, conquerors of earlier, primeval deities, and masters of natural forces, such as lightning.

TWIN ORACLES

There seems to have been a general awareness throughout the ancient Mediterranean of the common heritage of their religions. The oracle of Zeus at Dodona in northern Greece and the oracle of the Egyptian god Amun in the Libyan desert, for instance, performed identical functions as the mouthpieces of closely similar deities. And we can glean from the writings of Herodotus, the Greek traveller and historian of the fifth century BC, that the two oracle centres kept in touch by pigeon post (though the 'pigeons' were actually doves). Their priests even agreed that the oracles had a common origin, although they differed in their stories of how this had come about.

Some such similarities can be explained simply by cultural diffusion. But such arguments leave several unanswered questions. They might explain similarities in form (common symbols, oracle cults, temple procedures), but they leave the basic driving force behind the evolution of the ancient polytheistic religions a mystery.

So how can we account for the many similarities between the pantheons of the ancient Mediterranean world and those of pre-Columbian America? The hierarchy of the New World gods

The tablet, above, is from the Sumerian city of Lagash. It records the building of a temple about 2550 BC. The prince is shown carrying a basket of stones, symbolizing the earnestness with which the Sumerians, both high and low, served their gods.

few thousand years is based on the world-wide concordance of ancient myth. Legends around the globe do, indeed, seem to tell the same story of portents in the sky and the appearance of a monstrous comet-like body, followed by destructive rains of stones and fire, with cataclysmic earthquakes and tidal waves. As Velikovsky stresses: 'The stories are told very differently in different parts of the world, but the theme is always the same.' Indeed,

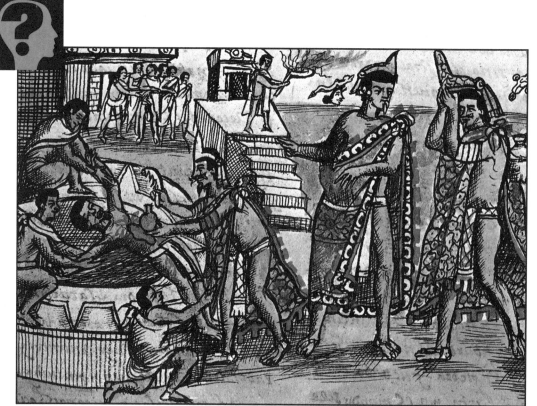

The picture of human sacrifice among the Aztecs, left, comes from a 16th-century account of the American Indians. The still-beating heart is newly torn from a victim. The sacrifice may have been made to Huitzilopochtli who, by the time that the Spanish arrived in America, had become a terrible god of war, demanding huge numbers of human victims. In the New World, tribute to the gods took a particularly bloody form.

the core of the world's mythologies, as he pointed out, is 'theomachy', the war of the gods.

The gods in question, Velikovsky argued, were actually the planets, which had been in turmoil in historical times. Jupiter, for instance, had been disrupted by a gigantic explosion and had ejected a huge 'comet'. Wandering too close to the Earth, this body had caused the parting of the Red Sea, the plagues of Egypt and later the collapse of Jericho. The comet, he claims, later settled down to become the planet Venus.

This could explain why the gods Jupiter and Venus, and their Greek equivalents Zeus and Aphrodite, held far more prominent positions in ancient pantheons than the Sun and Moon gods, even though their corresponding celestial bodies are mere pinpricks of light in the sky.

The British astronomers Victor Clube and Bill Napier have argued that Velikovsky's theories of planetary misbehaviour are dynamically impossible. But they do accept the validity of his case for the occurrence of certain major catastrophes, and claim that comets were indeed responsible for them. Whatever the truth, it seems we should accept that very real dangers from the sky were responsible for the awe in which the planetary gods were held by all the ancient peoples.

We are thus left with several theories, all purporting to explain the origins and resemblances of the world's ancient pantheons: cultural diffusion of some original religion, dating from the very earliest times; the worship of the planets and fears of cosmic catastrophes, caused by the heavenly bodies; and the worship of natural forces.

Other factors to consider are the various 'spectral' phenomena, such as UFOs and encounters with fairy folk. It may be possible to view the Greek gods as intelligent forces that operated in the ancient world like a race of poltergeists, functioning in a region somewhere between material existence and the purely psychological realm.

It is not, however, very satisfying to explain the origins of religions in terms of paranormal factors which are themselves mysterious. So, is there any possible unifying explanation in terms of something that is at least partly understood? Do we perhaps know of a mechanism that could convert different kinds of 'input' – memories of outstanding human leaders, or natural forces, for instance – and turn them into 'gods'?

A GOD-MAKING MECHANISM

Such a mechanism was suggested by the American psychologist Julian Jaynes. He provided a neat explanation of the ancient mind in terms of modern knowledge of the structure of the brain. It is well-known that the right and left hemispheres of the brain control different aspects of human behaviour. One – usually the left – deals with language, mathematics and analytical functions. The right is responsible for spatial abilities and is somewhat more involved in emotional responses than the other hemisphere. It has been claimed that intuitive and artistic activities are also handled by this hemisphere (usually the right). Indeed, in the schizophrenic, and in some epileptics, there is a discernible lack of cooperation between the two sides of the brain. In the schizophrenic, the left side of the brain can be a source of 'messages' that, after processing by the right side of the brain, are interpreted as the voices of other people or that take the form of vivid visual hallucinations.

Examining the religious and epic literature of the ancients, Jaynes was struck by the similarity between the thought processes of our ancestors and those of modern schizophrenics.

In the *Iliad*, for example, Homer's famous epic poem about the Trojan War, the heroes are never seen to make a decision for themselves. They never sit down and ponder a problem: rather, the answer is always described as coming directly from a god. Even in the heat of battle, Achilles might be

Zeus, above, brandishes a thunderbolt. According to a traditional view of the origins of the gods, they are personifications of the natural phenomena most significant to human beings – wind, rain, streams, the sea, thunder and lightning. But this theory offers no explanation of why human characteristics should be attributed to such things, nor why people once believed themselves able to hold 'conversations' with the gods.

> **THE PEOPLES OF THE PAST WERE PREPARED TO SEE MIRACLES IN UNUSUAL OCCURRENCES; FOR THIS REASON MODERN MAN, WHO DOES NOT BELIEVE IN MIRACLES, REJECTS THE EVENT TOGETHER WITH THE INTERPRETATION. BUT AS WE FIND THE SAME EVENT IN THE TRADITION OF MANY PEOPLES... ITS HISTORICITY CAN BE CHECKED...**
>
> **IMMANUEL VELIKOVSKY, WORLDS IN COLLISION**

Religious people, today, generally seek divine inspiration in a still, small voice within. The ancients, however, regularly heard the gods as strong clear voices from without – from such oracles as the one at Dodona in Greece, below. In the Old Testament, communication with God is also often highly direct. A rather different form of divine communication, however, is that of speaking in tongues, as the disciples did at Pentecost, right.

The serpent, bottom, is thought to have been part of the treasure sent to Hernando Cortés (1485-1547), the Spanish conqueror of Mexico. Montezuma, the last ruler of the Aztec empire in Mexico, believed Cortés was the returning god Quetzalcóatl.

devotees' minds. If this was the case, it is easy to understand why the ancients made and then pampered their idols, and there is no need to assume they were gullible or stupid.

Jaynes' theory also explains why the ancient gods seem to have been so 'human' in their behaviour. We can also begin to see why the 'gods' maintained their hold on the minds of the Sumerians, Babylonians, Egyptians, Aztecs and Greeks for so many thousands of years – for as long, in fact, as our somewhat schizophrenic ancestors continued to hear their 'voices'. Today's bicameral phenomena – religious ecstasy, speaking in tongues, prophecy, spirit possession – can even be seen in this light as the swansong of the gods, flickers of 'divine' activity in a human psyche that is now far more evolved than that of our polytheistic ancestors of three millennia ago.

interrupted by an appearance of the war goddess Athena, telling him to make for a particular foe. Could this be a straightforward description of the behaviour of the people of that age – behaviour that we, today, would regard variously as schizophrenic or inspired?

Jaynes' theory can be applied to a wide range of phenomena that seem commonplace in the ancient world: to the voices heard by ancient prophets, the 'muses' that inspired the poets, or the commands that issued from graven images. All these can be seen as the products of minds that operated in a schizophrenic manner – or, as Jaynes calls it, a 'bicameral' (two-chambered) manner, a term that alludes to the two halves, or chambers, of the brain. Jaynes expressed a belief that this bicameral aspect of the human mind began to fade at some time between 1500 and 700 BC, perhaps as the result of natural catastrophes. Only after that time did consciousness, as we know it, evolve.

Idols may thus have been constructed as 'focal points' to enhance the bicameral activity of the

THE UNKNOWN PROPHET

IN 1914, AN UNIDENTIFIED FRENCHMAN WAS CAPTURED BY GERMAN FORCES. DURING QUESTIONING, THE MAN MADE A NUMBER OF QUITE EXTRAORDINARY PROPHECIES

A ndreas Rill, a carpenter from Untermühlhausen on active service in Alsace, wrote two letters to his family in Bavaria, Germany, in August 1914. In these letters he told how he and another soldier had captured a Frenchman who proved to be a somewhat unusual prisoner. After the man had been taken prisoner, he was questioned all through the night; and during the questioning, he began to speak about the future of the war. In his first letter, Rill wrote that the Frenchman was a 'strange holy man who said incredible things. If we knew what would happen during the years to come, we would throw away

Andreas Rill, a Bavarian carpenter above left, sent home some letters while on active service in Alsace that were more than a little out of the ordinary. In one of them, left, he told of a French prisoner who had been able to tell him the course that the war was to take.

Andreas Rill's second letter contains details of the predictions of the end of this war. 'The man and his sign will disappear,' he was told, and hatred and envy would be rife. 'When there is a 4 and 5 in the year [1945], Germany will be pressed from all sides and totally plundered and destroyed.' Foreign powers would then occupy Germany. But, by virtue of its resourcefulness, Germany would recover. In the first letter, Andreas Rill noted further that: 'Italy will be against us in this war within a year and will be on our side in the second war'.

It was also said that many German soldiers would die in Italy. The letters tell, too, of a third war beginning with an invasion by Russia of south-east Germany. This was to happen during 1947 or 1948. During the war that was to follow, the 'mountains will spit fire'. Between the Danube and the Inn, it was said, 'everything will be totally erased'. The prophecy then continued: 'the streams are so shallow that no bridges will be needed to pass'. In Russia, the Frenchman said, the rulers would be killed; and there would be so many dead people that there would be no one to bury them.

SUSPICION OF AUTHENTICITY

At first sight, the letters are astonishing. The details in them are extraordinarily accurate, even down to dates. It is not surprising, therefore, that when they were presented for examination to the Freiburg Institute for Border Areas of Psychology and Mental Hygiene, the first reaction was suspicion as to the authenticity of the letters. But experts in criminology testified that there are no signs that the letters are forged, nor that parts of them were altered after they were written.

After the first predictions had proved to be accurate, Andreas Rill told the story of the strange Frenchman to several of his friends in local pubs. Reportedly, Rill became almost blasé, and somewhat fatalistic, after he saw one prediction after another fulfilled: the German defeat in the First World War, inflation and, finally, the upsurge of Nazism under Hitler. Soon, the prophecies of the unidentified French prisoner became widely known

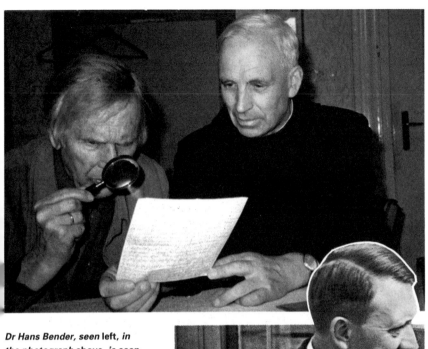

Dr Hans Bender, seen left, in the photograph above, is seen examining the Rill letters with Father Frumentius Renner. Father Renner came across these letters in the 1950s, and published them in a mission journal. Unaccountably, they passed almost unnoticed.

According to Rill, the unknown Frenchman not only predicted the course of the First World War, but also forecast the rise to power of Hitler, right.

our weapons today.' Then the carpenter reported what their unusual prisoner told them: that the war was going to last for five years and Germany was going to lose it; after which there would be a revolution. Everyone would become a millionaire; and there would be so much money that it would be thrown out of windows; but no one would bother to pick it up. (Here, the author of the letter remarked: 'Ridiculous!')

At this time, the prisoner continued, the Antichrist would be born: he would be a tyrant, passing new laws every day; and the people would soon become poorer without realising it. This time would begin around 1932 and would last for nine years. In 1938, preparations for war would begin – a war that would last three years, ending badly for the dictator and his followers. The people would rise against him in anger; things would become known 'that are simply inhuman'; everyone would be very poor; and Germany would be torn apart.

> **"** THEN THE CARPENTER REPORTED WHAT THEIR UNUSUAL PRISONER TOLD THEM: THAT THE WAR WAS GOING TO LAST FOR FIVE YEARS AND GERMANY WAS GOING TO LOSE IT; AFTER WHICH THERE WOULD BE A REVOLUTION. EVERYONE WOULD BECOME A MILLIONAIRE; AND THERE WOULD BE SO MUCH MONEY THAT IT WOULD BE THROWN OUT OF WINDOWS; BUT NO ONE WOULD BOTHER TO PICK IT UP. **"**

in Bavaria, and one day a police crime squad showed up at the Rill's home to question him about his conviction that the future would bring tyranny. According to his son, Siegmund, it was only by chance that his father escaped imprisonment in a concentration camp.

During the 1950s, the letters came into the possession of Father Frumentius Renner, who published them in a mission journal, where they passed almost unnoticed. No efforts were made to examine their authenticity, nor to establish the true identity of the mysterious prophet. It was a comparatively easy matter, at the Freiburg Institute, to have the letters checked by criminologists, but it was the work of some years to uncover the visionary.

Through careful tracing of members of the Rill family and a minute analysis of the war journal of the company with which Andreas Rill had served, Professor Hans Bender and Elmar Gruber tried to find the exact spot at which the Frenchman had been captured. Andreas Rill's sons revealed that the visionary was apparently a rich man who gave away all his earthly wealth to join a monastery in Alsace. Before that, he was said to have belonged

It was to the monastery at Sigolsheim, Alsace, above, that the search for the identity of the mysterious French prophet eventually led. Research revealed that a Frater Laicus Tertiarius – a person who lives in a monastery as a guest of the religious community – had died at Sigolsheim in 1917. Rill had captured the French prophet in 1914. Later, in 1918, when his company was stationed at Turckheim – indicated on the map, left – Rill apparently walked to a monastery to look for the visionary, but was told he had died. Turckheim is within walking distance of Sigolsheim. Could the French prophet therefore have been the unknown Frater Laicus Tertiarius?

to a Freemasons' Lodge in Colmar. Researches revealed that Rill's company must have been around Colmar in Alsace when the prophet was interviewed, and Siegmund Rill was indeed certain that his father met the visionary in a Capuchin monastery at Sigolsheim, six miles (10 kilometres) from Colmar, at the time. Some years later, in 1918, Rill and his company were stationed at Turckheim, near Colmar. Rill took the opportunity to go, on foot, to the monastery to look again for the visionary, but was told that he had died.

Checked lists of inhabitants of all the Capuchin monasteries in the area have provided one slight clue that might point towards the unknown prophet. In the Sigolsheim monastery, there had lived a certain Frater Laicus Tertiarius who had died at some time after 1917 but before Rill's second visit to the place. A Frater Laicus Tertiarius is a person who is not a member of a monastery, but who is permitted to live there as a guest. It could well have been that the prophet would not have been immediately accepted as a member of the monastery, particularly if he had been a rich man and a Freemason in his earlier life.

There are also several passages in the war journal that might have a bearing on the prophecies. One prediction the Frenchman made – noted in one of the Rill letters – was that a certain Corporal G. who ridiculed the visionary, would not come home from the war and that his body would not be buried but would be eaten by ravens.

True enough, on 23 September 1914, Corporal G. did go missing while on a patrol, and the war journal notes that his remains were found and identified in February 1915. There is also a note concerning Corporal G. and dated the day of his disappearance, from the private journal of Colonel Schleicher, putting it on record that Corporal G. was 'seeing spirits again.'

But why did such detailed and important prophecies not become better known? Why should the Frenchman tell his visions only to his German captors? Were these the only prophecies he ever uttered? And how reliable is Rill's evidence?

Andreas Rill's first letter is an account of what the Frenchman said, while the second represents

Rill's reflections on his experience with the visionary. The second letter, written some days after the first, also gives details about a third world war, and it seems that Rill selected from the prophet's words only those aspects of this prophecy that related to his home, Bavaria. In considering the predictions of the three wars, we should bear in mind that the prophet was French; and although the prophet is said to have spoken several languages (it is most probable that he spoke German with the soldiers), misunderstandings may have arisen through the prisoner's imperfect command of the German language. In any event, considering the Frenchman was interviewed for many hours at night, it is hard to believe that Rill could have remembered all he said.

> " IT SEEMS SAFE TO CONCLUDE
>
> THAT THE FUTURE CAN BE
>
> AVAILABLE TO OUR UNDERSTANDING
>
> IN THE PRESENT. YET IF WE ACCEPT
>
> THIS STATEMENT WE COULD BY
>
> IMPLICATION, ACCEPT THAT PAST,
>
> PRESENT AND FUTURE (THE MAN-
>
> MADE CONVENIENCE-DIVISIONS OF
>
> TIME) EXIST SIMULTANEOUSLY. "
>
> **JOAN FORMAN, THE MASK OF TIME**

Shown on this page are Warsaw Pact manoeuvres in Poland in 1981, above, and an anti-nuclear demonstration that also took place in 1981, in Bonn, then the capital of West Germany, right. The unknown French prophet had forecast a third world war that was to take place between 1946 and 1948. This did not, of course, happen. But could he perhaps have been 'tuning in' not to actual events in the future, but to the general climate of anxiety about the nuclear arms race following the atomic explosions that ended the Second World War?

Indeed, psychological studies have shown how poorly, in general, people are able to recollect events they have experienced. One should not forget, too, that the prisoner's prophecies were of the highest interest among the soldiers and that discussion may have prompted embroidery of the truth.

But the prophecies do, with astounding accuracy, forecast political developments in Europe for many years to come. They include the duration of the First World War from 1 August 1914 to the armistice of 11 November 1918; revolution and the establishment of the Weimar Republic on 9 November 1918; the leftist revolution and its failure to retain power; inflation until 1923; the election of the Nazi party in January 1933; the occupation of Czechoslovakia in March 1939; the attack on Poland in August 1939; the occupation of Norway and Holland in May 1940; the attack on Russia in June 1941; the landing of Allied forces in Sicily in July 1943; Hitler's suicide; the surrender of Germany in May 1945, and its occupation by American, English, French and Soviet troops; the loss of German territory and the division into two states; and the rapid recovery of the Federal Republic of Germany under Chancellor Adenauer.

And what of the predictions concerning a third world war? A psychic who gives an accurate prediction in one case may, of course, be totally wrong in another. The time when it was supposed to take place, 1946 to 1948, has passed. This may mean that the prediction is erroneous. But the dates may also

have been noted wrongly, or the French prophet, speaking German, may have given them incorrectly.

There is no question that a third world war, with its horrifying potential for destruction, has been felt as a constant imminent danger. The psychic may therefore have 'picked up' this general anxiety and mistaken it for the events actually happening.

Whatever the truth, the case of the anonymous French prophet remains a puzzling footnote in the extensive files of parapsychology.

**DID THE SUN CATCH
A CHILL A FEW
MILLION YEARS AGO?
AND WILL IT THREATEN
HUMAN LIFE BY WARMING
UP AGAIN IN THE FUTURE?**

During the 1930s, nuclear physics and astro-physics came into head-on collision in a debate that made headlines, even in the popular press. Physicists knew that the only pro-cesses that could keep the Sun hot were nuclear reactions. Since hydrogen is the most abundant ele-ment in the Sun, and helium the second most abun-dant, it was clear that hydrogen nuclei must be fus-ing together to make helium nuclei – a reaction that would release energy.

But, according to astronomers, the centre of the Sun must be at a temperature of about 27 million degrees Fahrenheit (15 million degrees Centigrade). The nuclear physicists said that, according to their most reliable theories, this temperature was too low to permit a sustained hydrogen fusion reaction.

Confident that, whatever the nuclear physicists might say, the Sun continues to shine steadily as it has done for many millions of years, the pioneering astrophysicist Arthur Eddington is reported to have

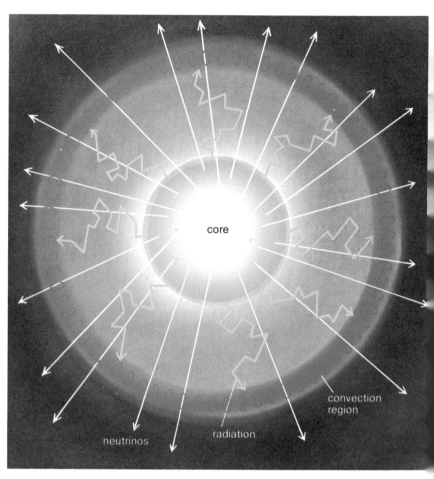

core

convection region

neutrinos

radiation

THREATS FROM THE SUN

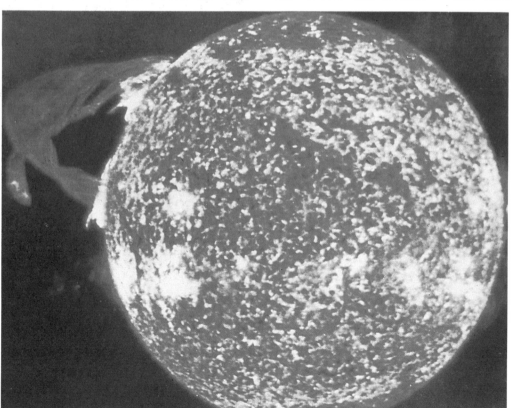

The solar powerhouse, illustrated above, is a relatively small region at the centre of the Sun. Heat, light and other radiation take a million years to struggle out through the Sun's middle layers. In the outer layers, heat is transferred by convection: hot gas moves outwards, radiates heat and light into space, cools and then moves inwards again.

Hotter and cooler areas on the Sun appear as brighter and darker patches when viewed through an ultraviolet light filter, left.

told his colleagues to 'go and find a hotter place' – a polite way of telling them to forget their theories.

In due course, the nuclear physicists did indeed find that their theories were incomplete. Improved theories showed how fusion reactions could go on inside the Sun at this temperature. These improved theories led eventually to the hydrogen bomb, and now point the way towards taming the power of the Sun in a fusion reactor on Earth.

Today, however, a new mystery surrounds the nuclear physics that describes conditions inside the Sun and the reactions that go on there. For those same equations that successfully explain how the Sun's heat is maintained predict that a flood of particles called neutrinos should be streaming out of the Sun and across space towards the Earth and beyond. But the neutrinos, or most of them, are missing. Once again, there is a head-on clash between observation and theory.

The Sun began its life as a large, cool cloud of gas. It was made chiefly of hydrogen and helium, which have the simplest of all atoms. But it contained a smattering of elements with heavier atoms, debris from earlier generations of stars. The

At the high temperatures and pressures in the Sun, atoms are stripped of their outer electrons. The atoms' nuclei, made of positively charged protons and uncharged neutrons, collide continually. Hydrogen nuclei (single protons) are built up in a series of steps to form more complex nuclei. This can happen in a variety of ways. In the sequence shown below left, deuterium ('heavy hydrogen') is formed while a positron (a positively charged electron) and a neutrino are emitted. Then, helium 3 ('light' helium) is formed, and a photon – a 'packet' of electromagnetic energy – is given out. Nuclei of helium 3 collide to form ordinary helium 4, releasing two protons.

The Helix Nebula, below, an enormous globe of gas, shows us the fate of the Sun in the far future as its nuclear fires die. First, the Sun will become a 'red giant'. Then its outer layers will swell, engulfing the Earth and ultimately the entire solar system.

cloud collapsed and, as it did so, its centre warmed up. It was warmed first by the release of gravitational energy (just as water at the foot of Niagara Falls is warmed by its fall), and then by the nuclear 'burning' of hydrogen.

Originally, the Sun was approximately 25 per cent helium and 75 per cent hydrogen. A small proportion of heavier elements was also present. The Sun has been converting hydrogen into helium for nearly 5,000 million years since then. And today, in the centre of the Sun, the proportions are nearly reversed – 65 per cent helium and 35 per cent hydrogen.

How can we be so sure of this? The basis for these statements is the success of our 'models', or theories, of stellar evolution. From a given original mass of a star, the proportions of the original hydrogen-helium mix, and the laws of physics, the model predicts how the star will 'evolve' as it burns its fuel. The calculations require powerful computers: all the calculations successfully 'predict' the sizes and temperatures that stars – and especially the Sun – are observed to have.

The picture of the Sun's interior that is provided by our present knowledge is a dramatic one. Half of the total mass lies close to the centre – inside a sphere with a quarter of the Sun's radius, or just 1.5 per cent of the total volume. In this tiny volume, 99 per cent of the Sun's energy is released, and conditions are extreme indeed: the temperature is close to 27 million degrees Fahrenheit (15 million degrees Centigrade) and the density is 12 times that of lead. Yet the material of the Sun's centre is still a fluid, not a solid.

The temperature and pressure prevailing here support the vast weight of the overlying matter. The Sun's mass is one third of a million times that of the Earth. But occupying a volume that could

hydrogen   hydrogen

deuterium

helium 3   helium 3

helium 4

○ proton   ○ positron

○ neutrino

○ neutron   ∿∿∿→ photon

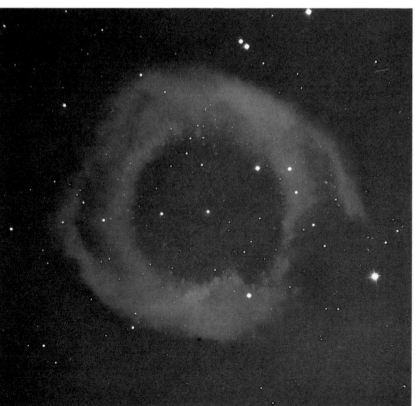

could comfortably accommodate 1,300,000 Earths. This gives rise to an average density which is just 1.4 times that of water.

It is surprising that any particle can escape from the depths of the Sun. Yet the neutrino is such an elusive particle that it does just that. The neutrino has no electrical charge. Indeed, it is not known whether it has zero mass, as long believed, or a very small mass. The chance of a neutrino interacting with any other particle it meets is incredibly small: the result is that it behaves like a ghost, able to slip through immense quantities of matter without any effect whatever. Neutrinos created by nuclear reactions at the Sun's core fly outwards at the speed of light, scarcely noticing the surrounding matter, which has a maximum density of 4.5 tonnes per cubic foot (160 tonnes per cubic metre) – and some of them reach the Earth just eight minutes later. In fact, 26,000 million neutrinos pass through

The first solar neutrino detector at the bottom of a gold mine in South Dakota, USA, is shown below. Since it has come into use, it has registered fewer neutrinos from the depths of the Sun than theorists originally had expected.

each square inch (4,000 million per square centimetre) of the Earth, or of our bodies; and every second, the minutest fraction of them react with particles in the atoms they meet.

Astrophysicists have measured the intensity of this flood of neutrinos with special detectors. Paradoxically, these 'neutrino telescopes', designed to study the heart of the Sun, are built deep underground. The purpose of this is to screen out other forms of radiation, such as cosmic rays and background radioactivity. To be sensitive enough to interact with the neutrinos, the detectors have to be very large.

The world's first solar neutrino detector, about as big as a swimming pool, was built at the bottom of a gold mine in South Dakota, USA. The tank was filled with perchloroethylene – dry cleaning fluid. It contained a high proportion of chlorine, with which one of the billions of passing neutrinos would occasionally interact. This interaction would lead to the emission of an electron which can easily be detected. In the 100,000 gallons (400,000 litres) of the fluid, experimenters calculated that they would catch some 25 neutrinos each month. In fact, they

observed an average of only eight solar neutrinos each month.

The earliest experiments failed to detect any neutrinos and some theorists therefore suggested that the Sun might have 'gone out' – that the reactions in its centre had ceased but the surface had not yet cooled off.

If this were true, it would take about one million years for the surface to go cold. That is the time it takes electromagnetic energy light – ultraviolet radiation and X-rays – to work its way outwards from the centre. The radiation bounces from electron to electron in the densely packed matter at the Sun's core, like a ball bouncing in a pinball machine.

Now that neutrinos have been detected, we know that the Sun has not gone out at all. But since they are fewer than expected, it may be that the Sun has, in effect, 'gone off the boil' and cooled off a little at the centre.

If the temperature were 10 per cent lower than the astrophysicists expected, the low neutrino intensity would be accounted for. But this temperature is too low to keep up the observed output of heat and light from the surface. So might this only be a temporary departure from the Sun's normal long-term state? This raises intriguing possibilities. Has the Sun been 'off colour' for the past few million years? If so, could that possibly tie in with the spate of ice ages that has afflicted the Earth during roughly that time?

In the 1930s, physicists had to change their ideas to account for what the astronomers knew of the conditions inside the Sun. The boot may now be on the other foot. Astronomers may have to revise their notions of how stars work to take account of the physicists' knowledge of nuclear reactions. For standard theories do not admit the possibility of stars varying – temporarily, we hope – in this way.

But should we even hope for a return to 'normal'? After all, human beings only evolved during the last million years or so. The conditions on Earth that we regard as normal – ice ages included – may be due to a temporary 'misbehaviour' of the Sun. If so, a return to the Sun's 'normal' state might mean a return to tropical conditions that are far too extreme for the human race to tolerate.

// THE SUN RISES... IT MEANS, JUST FOR A START, THAT THE SUN SHINES. THAT FOUR MILLION TONS OF MATTER ARE DESTROYED ON ITS SURFACE EVERY SECOND IN A RAGING NUCLEAR STORM... AND ALL THE TIME, THE MASS OF OUR STAR IS BEING REDUCED AND ITS VOLUME AND DENSITY ARE CHANGING. //

LYALL WATSON, LIFETIDE

SATANIST OR SAINT?

SOME HAVE SUGGESTED THAT SORCERY WAS THE SECRET OF JOAN OF ARC'S UNCANNY SUCCESS IN BATTLE. WHAT EVIDENCE IS THERE FOR SUCH CLAIMS CONCERNING HER SUPPOSED PARANORMAL POWERS AND CLOSE INVOLVEMENT WITH THE BLACK ARTS?

A·M·D·G

St JOAN of ARC

TO COMMEMORATE THE VISIT OF
H.H. PRINCESS MARIE LOUISE
21ST JUNE 1951

J oan of Arc's enemies, the English, believed that she was a sorceress and a harlot, in league with the powers of darkness. There could, in their eyes, be no other reason to explain the ignominious defeats they had suffered at her hands. This English view of Joan – known both as the Maid of Orléans and *La Pucelle* (the Virgin) – was described 150 years after her death in Shakespeare's play *Henry VI, Part I*. In this, she is dragged away to the stake, begging for mercy. To escape the flames, she claims she is with child, naming first the Duke of Alençon and then the King of Naples as the father. When this ruse fails, her last act is to curse the Duke of York, who retorts:

'Break thou in pieces and consume to ashes
Thou foul accursed minister of hell!'

The suggestion that Joan had, in her last moments, claimed that she was pregnant in order to escape being burnt was a calumny of particular significance. Indeed, an important element in Joan's sexual mystique was her claim throughout her life that she was a virgin since, in the 15th century, it was a recognised fact that the Devil could have no dealings with a virgin.

Earlier in the same scene in Shakespeare's play, Joan speaks up for herself, maintaining that she is not only immaculate and chosen by God, but also of royal birth:

A quarter of a century after her death, Joan was formally exonerated; and almost 500 years later, in 1920, she was canonised. The stained glass window of St Joan, left, is in the chapel of Croft House School, Dorset, England.

Joan's birthplace, above, was near the church at Domrémy in Lorraine where, as a young girl, she began to hear 'voices'. One of these, Joan claimed, belonged to the archangel Michael, right. At Joan's trial, her voices were taken as evidence that she was a 'disciple of the fiend', as was her admission that, as a child, she had danced round the Fairies' Tree, said to be frequented by evil spirits and those who practised spells. Further evidence of her paranormal powers was the fact that she was able to tell Robert de Baudricourt in Vaucouleurs the outcome of the Battle of Herrings, below right, on 12 February 1429, on the very day it was fought 200 miles (320 kilometres) away near Orléans.

'First let me tell you whom you have condemn'd:
Not me begotten of a shepherd swain,
But issued from the progeny of kings:
Virtuous and holy, chosen from above
By inspiration of celestial grace,
To work exceeding miracles on earth.'

The play thus draws together two opposing views of Joan – one view that she was a witch and a whore, and her own view that she was the Virgin of God; and it gives a powerful impression of the confusion that surrounded her trial.

The result of her trial was a foregone conclusion. The English wanted her dead at all costs; and on 2 September 1430, they paid the colossal sum of 10,000 francs to her Burgundian captors for 'the purchase of Joan the Maid, who is said to be a sorcerer, a warlike person, leading the armies of the Dauphin.' Joan was a thorn in their side and one best removed as soon as possible. The justice that disposed of her was a 15th-century justice – vastly different from modern justice. As Edward Lucie-Smith points out in his *Joan of Arc:* 'The trial was merely to legitimise the burning.' Nevertheless, the case against Joan had to look good.

She was initially indicted on 70 counts, many of them charges of witchcraft and sorcery. But by the time the crucial stage of her trial was reached, the number of counts had been reduced to 12 and all references to witchcraft had been eliminated, save one. She was eventually condemned chiefly for her resistance to 'the Church on earth' – in essence, a theological crime.

The one remaining reference to witchcraft in the trial records concerned the 'Fairies' Tree', under which Joan had often played as a child. An account of her supposed involvement in strange ceremonies there appeared in the Acts of Accusation:

'Near the village of Domrémy stands a certain large and ancient tree, commonly called *l'arbre charmine faée de Bourlemont,* and near the tree is a fountain. It is said that round about live evil spirits, called fairies, with whom those who practise spells are wont to dance at night, wandering about the tree and the fountain. The said Joan was wont to

may genuinely have believed that Joan was a witch; the rank-and-file soldiers who had retreated before her in battle certainly thought she was one. Without the help of the Devil, so they reasoned, it would have been impossible for her to prevail against them. After Joan's relief of Orléans, the Duke of Bedford wrote to the English King Henry VI that the retreat from Orléans had been due to:

'A disciple and lyme of the fiend, called the Pucelle that used fals enchauntments and sorcerie, the which... nought oonly lessed... the nombre of your peuple there, but as well withdrowe the courage of the remenant, in marveilous wyse, and couraged your advers partie and enemy's.'

But apart from the Maid's uncanny success in battle, what other reasons were there to connect her with the black arts?

First and foremost, she did appear to be something of a seer. Indeed, her most controversial prophecy was foretelling the English victory at the so-called Battle of Herrings on 12 February 1429 at Rouvray, near Orléans. On that very day, Joan (hundreds of miles away at Vaucouleurs) told Robert de Baudricourt that the French had been heavily defeated; and when the news was confirmed two days later, Baudricourt took it as a sign that Joan was divinely inspired, sending her on her way to the Dauphin. In his book *Jeanne d'Arc*, W. S. Scott suggests that this knowledge might have been the result of precognitive vision.

There was also the matter of her psychic knowledge of the Dauphin's secret prayer. When Joan first met him at Chinon, he naturally enough needed to be convinced that this girl had indeed been sent by God to lead his armies. Joan is said to have been able to tell him about a secret prayer he had made – that if he were indeed the rightful ruler of France, God would defend him, or allow him to escape to Spain or Scotland in safety.

PSYCHIC DISCOVERY

Yet another strange event concerned the sword of Fierbois. While she was being equipped to join the Dauphin's armies, Joan said that her battle sword would be found buried behind the altar at St Catherine's Church at Fierbois. The sword was searched for and found, even though no one had known of the existence of any such sword. Joan thus seemed to have some inexplicable sixth sense, if not actual psychic powers.

Joan's refusal to repeat the Lord's Prayer at her trial was also taken as an indication that she was a witch. At that time, it was a common belief that no witch could say the Lord's Prayer without faltering: if Joan had inadvertently stumbled over the words, she might have seemed condemned out of her own mouth.

A dangerous ally for the Maid was the Franciscan friar, Brother Richard, whom she had first met at Troyes in July 1429. At her trial, she described how she countered his first overtures with some wit: 'When he came to me... he made the sign of the cross, and threw holy water, and I said to him: "Approach boldly – I will not fly away".'

Brother Richard was already a controversial figure for a series of sermons he had been preaching in Paris on the subject of the imminent coming of the Antichrist. Joan and he quickly established a

frequent the fountain and the tree, mostly at night, sometimes during the day; particularly, so as to be alone, at hours when in church the divine office was being celebrated. When dancing, she would turn around the tree and the fountain, then would hang on the boughs garlands of different herbs and flowers, made by her own hand, dancing and singing the while, before and after, certain songs and verses and invocations, spells, and evil arts. And the next morning, the chaplets of flowers would no longer be found there.'

But perhaps Joan herself, as she claimed in her defence, had taken the flowers away – or perhaps they just blew away. In any case, to hang a charge of witchcraft on a child's participation in what sounds like a country custom was ridiculous, even by 15th-century standards of justice.

Belief in, and the persecution of, witches was at its height in Europe at the time, and the English

Joan's triumphal entry into Orléans, above, was painted by the French artist Jean Jacques Scherrer (1855-1916).

religious rapport, and he became one of her confessors, as well as her standard-bearer at Charles' exhausting coronation. But he encouraged Joan in her deviations from religious orthodoxy, and made extravagant claims for her that did not help her image:

'[She] had as much power to know God's secrets as any saint in paradise... and... she could, if she wanted, make the King's army enter over the walls in any way she wanted.'

Eventually, there was a rift in their relationship, but the damage had been done: the sensational sermons and sorcerer's image tainted Joan's reputation to a marked degree.

Joan's trial from the 16th-century Armagnac manuscript is shown below. The trial lasted five months and was presided over by Pierre Cauchon, bishop of Beauvais (an English sympathiser) and Jean Le Maître, deputy inquisitor. After Joan had recanted of her supposed crimes, she was condemned to perpetual imprisonment; and when she relapsed, she was burnt at the stake.

" JOAN'S REFUSAL TO REPEAT THE LORD'S PRAYER AT HER TRIAL WAS ALSO TAKEN AS AN INDICATION THAT SHE WAS A WITCH... IT WAS A COMMON BELIEF THAT NO WITCH COULD SAY THE LORD'S PRAYER WITHOUT FALTERING: SO... SHE MIGHT HAVE SEEMED CONDEMNED OUT OF HER OWN MOUTH. **"**

In a scene from the film Saint Joan, right, *Joan (played by Jean Seberg) hears the sentence of the court. A friar (played by Kenneth Haigh) kneels beside her as she prays for strength.*

The Maid's apparent lack of sexual identity also led to speculation as to whether she was in fact a girl. During her lifetime, Joan was examined three times to verify both her sex and her virginity: the evidence was that she was both female and *virgo intacta*. But, psychologically at least, she seemed to suffer from some confusion as to her sexual role. Her choice of male clothing was, she said, guided by her voices; but she certainly seemed to feel more comfortable in male dress. However, it also has to be said that dressing like a man encouraged her soldiers to think of her as a comrade in arms; and, certainly, it would have been uncomfortable for her to ride astride a horse in skirts.

FALSE MAIDS

Witch or not, Joan of Arc was condemned and, supposedly, burnt at the stake on 30 May 1431. But there is a theory that she escaped execution, and that a *bona fide* witch was burnt in her place. Several 'Joans' appeared in the years following her execution, the most convincing of whom was one who turned up in Orléans on 28 July 1439 and lodged there for a few days under the name of the Dame des Armoises. She received a payment for her past deeds on behalf of the city, and was apparently acknowledged by both Joan's brother and the king as the real Maid.

However, most contemporary chroniclers took the Dame des Armoises' claim with a pinch of salt; and in 1457, it was reported that she was released from prison 'having long called herself Jeanne la Pucelle, and deceived many persons who had seen Jeanne at the siege of Orléans.' She was never heard of again.

The false Joan fuelled speculation that the Maid might have been saved from the stake by order of the English regent, the Duke of Bedford, because she was of royal descent. Rumour had it that she was the illegitimate daughter of the promiscuous Queen Isabella (the Dauphin's mother) and Louis, Duke of Orléans. But unfortunately for this myth, the Duke had died years before Joan was born.

That a simple country girl should so seize the imagination of a monarch, an army and a people and lead them to triumph is scarcely credible; but the knowledge of what really inspired Joan of Arc almost certainly perished with her in the fire.

CREATIONS OF THE SUBCONSCIOUS?

UNDER HYPNOSIS, A PERSON CAN ASSUME AN ENTIRELY DIFFERENT PERSONALITY. BUT IS THIS AN ECHO OF A PAST LIFE OR A CREATION OF THE SUBCONSCIOUS MIND? HERE WE SUM UP THE EVIDENCE THAT HYPNOSIS OFFERS FOR – AND AGAINST – REINCARNATION

F ew accounts of 'previous lives' recalled by people under hypnosis are free of inconsistencies or historical inaccuracies. But these in themselves are not sufficient to destroy the possibility that some cases of hypnotic regression are true reports of events that happened in a previous life. Psychologists have developed their own theories to account for hypnotic regression. And some, while denying that reincarnation is involved, accept that something outside the range of normal scientific explanation is at work. Broadly, then, there are two views taken of hypnotic regression: the 'normal' and the 'paranormal'.

According to the 'normal' view, suggestibility plays a large part in the relationship between the hypnotist and his subject. Indeed, the knowledge that the hypnotist is conducting an experiment in regression may be enough for the subject to respond by providing details of an imagined past life that are manufactured for the purpose. There is certainly evidence that the subconscious creative capacity of human beings is extraordinarily powerful. Under hypnosis, the subject may display a talent for acting, drawing, painting, writing or musical performance or composition far exceeding not only his own conscious ability but also the ability of most other people. The manufacture of a past life simply to gratify the hypnotist's expectations may therefore be carried out and enacted at short notice and with startling conviction.

The material for such 'lives' may come from many sources. A dream that is felt to be significant because of its vividness or recurrence, for instance, can sometimes provide the foundation. Alternatively, there may have been subconscious imprinting by parents or others in the subject's childhood – or even earlier, for there is evidence that the foetus can hear and register impressions in the

womb during the months immediately prior to birth.

There are other possibilities, too. An individual who is widely read in historical material could use such knowledge to create a number of different lives, each focused on a different period of history. Ideas that are communicated, either consciously or subconsciously, by the hypnotist can also be picked up and elaborated upon by the hypnotic subject, while even someone unversed in hypnosis can elicit a response from the subject by innocently asking leading questions.

Hypermnesia, arousal of acutely detailed memories, and cryptomnesia, the tapping of hidden memories, may also provide reincarnation material; and events recalled in this way may be stage-managed by the subconscious to create a fantasy past life based on experiences in this incarnation. There are instances of hypermnesia, for example, in which a

The automatic painting, above, was created by London housewife Madge Gill, who died in 1961. She ascribed such drawing to the intervention of a spirit called 'Myrninerest' – but could it have been the work of her subconscious mind?

The 17th-century so-called little Prophets of Cévennes, right, are said to have been able to preach even before they could converse. Was genetic memory perhaps at work?

reader in a library glances at a printed page of, say, some archaic language for a few minutes and, decades later, is able to reproduce the same text in the minutest detail.

Such stage-management by the subconscious mind may provide an explanation for the case of Virginia Tighe, an American, who was regressed under hypnosis to become 'Bridey Murphy', who had apparently lived around 100 years previously. The *Chicago American,* in its exposé of the case, argued that certain facts disproved the theory of reincarnation.

As a child, Mrs Tighe had lived in Chicago, opposite an Irish family by the name of Corkell, and one of her childhood friends had been Kevin Corkell. 'Bridey Murphy' said she had lived in Cork and had a friend called Kevin. Even more revealing, the newspaper claimed, was the fact that Mrs Corkell's maiden name was Bridey Murphy; and Mrs Tighe's sister had fallen down a flight of stairs in circumstances strangely similar to the fall that caused Bridey's death, as revealed under hypnosis.

But this evidence does not succeed in either disproving or establishing the argument that 'Bridey Murphy' was just the childhood memory of Mrs Tighe or that Virginia Tighe was the reincarnation of 'Bridey Murphy'. Thus, the case remains open.

*In*Focus

CAYCE'S COSMIC KNOWLEDGE

The famous American clairvoyant Edgar Cayce was an active churchgoer all his life, and was inclined to dismiss reincarnation as un-Christian. One day, however, in 1923, a small boy climbed upon his lap and said: 'We were hungry together at the river.' This shook Cayce. He once had a dream, known only to his immediate family, of fleeing from Indians on the Ohio River and being killed. An old friend and religious thinker, Arthur Lammers, then persuaded Cayce to use the trance state to investigate a possible past life.

At first, Cayce was wary of such an unorthodox idea. But after examining the results – he appeared to have been a high priest in ancient Egypt, an apothecary in the Trojan War and a British soldier during the colonisation of America – he began to believe.

Cayce said that the readings of past lives that he went on to provide were culled from a universal or 'Akashic record' (from the Sanskrit *akasha,* meaning the fundamental etheric substance of the Universe). These are complete records of everything done and said since the beginning of time.

The recall of genetic, racial and folk memories provides another possible explanation for regression phenomena. We undoubtedly inherit some traits from our ancestors, but whether we inherit their memories is another matter. The claim that genetic memory can account for such cases as the Little Prophets of Cévennes – French Huguenot children who, in times of persecution in the 17th century, preached Protestant sermons with ecstatic fervour before they could hardly talk – is usually countered by the argument that, even if you accept the considerable contemporary evidence, there are still too few cases to justify the theory.

It is also said that some former lives described by subjects under hypnosis are too close to the present for such memory to have taken effect.

FOLK FEARS

According to this way of thinking, the last of Jane Evans' six recorded lives, that of Sister Grace, for instance, was not only too close to her in time, but she was also a celibate nun, so there could be no physical bridge across which her memories could have been passed to Jane. But there may be, in all of us, archetypal 'folk fears' – of being burnt as a witch or heretic, for example, or of suffering from chronic poverty – which, under hypnosis, are expressed as events in a 'previous life'. A Jewish girl, too young to have known of concentration camps except as a fact of history, nevertheless dreamed vividly and recurrently as a child that she was immured in one.

Dissociated personality – in which the human body may be inhabited by up to a dozen or more 'individuals' – is a rare form of mental illness. But sometimes, when apparently normal people are hypnotised for therapeutic purposes, such a personality, or personalities, may emerge whose existence would otherwise never have been suspected.

HIDDEN PERSONALITIES

It may be that some people harbour compensatory personalities in their subconscious, either as a means of expressing a personality whose fulfilment has been denied them by circumstances or as a way of making up for some quality missing in their conscious lives. An argument often presented against this possibility, however, is that the majority of regressed lives are dull or unhappy, and most end in violent death.

Indeed, the same argument may be raised against the psychological explanation of subconscious role-playing. When we daydream consciously, we see ourselves as happier, more fulfilled people than we really are. Why should so much subliminal role-playing, then, emphasize the dull, the sordid and the wretched?

Students of psychodynamics – the examination of personality in terms of past and present experiences with regard to motivation – believe that regressed lives are based on unconscious memory, revealing a connection between the subject's conscious personality and the one that emerges in the course of hypnosis.

In one particular case, for example, it was found that the subject's relationship with his grandfather lay at the heart of his regressive 'imaginings'. The grandfather disliked his grandson – the subject – because he had once borrowed his grandfather's mare without permission. This had aroused the old man's fury, and he told the parents that their son had bad blood in him – something which the grandson overheard. Under hypnosis, the subject became 'Brian O'Malley', claiming to be a British

officer in the Irish Guards, born in 1850, who had a number of French mistresses and was killed in 1892 by a fall fom his horse. This character seems closely modelled on a certain Timothy O'Malley who, in real life, ran the subject's grandfather out of Ireland and was later killed in an accident with his horse.

Acknowledging the historical inaccuracy – the Irish Guards were not formed until 1900 – E.S. Zolic, who investigated the case, ascribes the former 'life' to the subject's identification with his grandfather's enemy, the real O'Malley.

Another subject became 'Dick Wonchalk' (1850-1876), who seems to have led a solitary life after his family was massacred by Indians when he was a child. But this 'life' could be taken as a reflection of the subject's real feelings of isolation in childhood, his concern about loneliness, fear of not being accepted by people, and self-blame for his inadequacies.

There may indeed be a definite purpose behind the incubation of such lives. The physical body, when attacked by disease, produces antibodies that counterattack the invaders and, in a strong body, eventually gain supremacy. It is conceivable that,

Images of a Nazi concentration camp, such as the one shown left, recurred in the vivid dreams of a Jewish girl who was too young to have known about them.

The illustration below depicts a witch being burnt at the stake in France in 1680. Deaths like this are frequently described under regression hypnosis, but may be a reflection of a commonly held fear of a violent end.

Alexander Cannon, bottom, was a Spiritualist whose hypnotic subjects also used Spiritualist vocabulary to describe intermission periods between their former lives. Were they perhaps influenced telepathically by his own beliefs?

From the very beginning, Vassy and I both believed we had known each oher in at least one previous lifetime. For that reason as well as many others, we were spiritually compatible.

**SHIRLEY MACLAINE,
DANCING IN THE LIGHT**

The actor Fredric March is seen, below *and* below right, *in two very different guises in the 1931 film version of* Dr Jekyll and Mr Hyde. *The characters of Jekyll, and his alter ego Mr Hyde, symbolise conscious and subconscious forces inside all people that can come to the surface under hypnosis.*

One hypnotised subject told how, in another life, he had become an orphan after his family had died at the hands of Indians attacking their wagon train – a scene depicted above. *Psychologists think this 'life' dramatised his deep sense of loneliness and social inadequacy.*

in similar fashion, the mind produces mental antibodies, which by 'explaining' present weakness in terms of a past life, heal the patient psychologically and psychically. Thus, the American high-board diver, who was unaccountably panic-stricken by a shadow in the water as she was about to dive and could not jump, may have neutralized her irrational fear under hypnosis by 'explaining' it as the result of an event in a former life, in which – just as she was about to jump in the water – she saw the shadow of an alligator that then killed her. This 'explanation' in turn removed the fear, which no longer appeared irrational.

Paranormal explanations for past life accounts include telepathic tapping of the hypnotist's mind and also clairvoyance – the obtaining of information from, for example, closed books in libraries that the subject has never visited. There is even a theory of General-ESP or Super-ESP, which suggests that the mind of the hypnotised subject can have access to

information in books or in other people's minds. By selecting and arranging this from many sources, the subject may present an accurate account of an actual life once lived.

Spiritualists, meanwhile, who reject reincarnation, ascribe the accuracies reported in regressed lives to efficient spirit communication, and inaccuracies to communication difficulties. It is just as hard, they say, for spirits to communicate with us as for us to break through to them. Some people, however, claim that it is from the Akashic records of everything said and done since the world began that the details in regressed lives are obtained, although why particular lives should be selected and why the subject usually fails to show any other psychic ability are not explained.

So it is that the nature of past life regression remains elusive. In time, perhaps, we may come to understand whether it is indeed a matter of memory or merely invention.

LOST, BELIEVED KIDNAPPED

FIFTY YEARS AFTER THE GALLIPOLI CAMPAIGN, THREE OLD SOLDIERS CAME FORWARD WITH A BIZARRE TALE OF A CLOUD THAT SEEMED TO HAVE KIDNAPPED A WHOLE REGIMENT

On 12 August 1915, the best part of the First-Fifth Battalion of the Royal Norfolk Regiment disappeared. The decomposing corpses of slightly less than half the battalion were later found, but the precise fate of the remaining troops remains a mystery. However, a solution may lie in a story which has featured in several books about UFOs and other phenomena. According to a statement made by three of the original witnesses, members of a New Zealand field company saw a large number of British troops abducted by what was described as a strange cloud, perhaps a UFO. The troops were identified as the First-Fourth Norfolk and the event allegedly happened on 21 August. However, as there is ample proof that the First-Fourth Norfolk did not disappear, it seems that the New Zealanders' story is either a complete fabrication or describes the fate of another body of men

The British troops, below, were part of the hastily formed Naval division and lacked proper training in land fighting. Other divisions deployed at Gallipoli were equally inadequately prepared. The Norfolks, for example, consisted mainly of raw recruits and Territorials (so-called Saturday soldiers) whose exposure to the conditions at Gallipoli came as a brutal, and in many cases, fatal shock.

altogether, perhaps the disappearance of the First-Fifth Norfolk on 12 August.

What the New Zealanders allegedly saw is described in a statement signed by three of the original witnesses:

'August 21, 1915. The following is an account of the strange incident that happened on the above date, which occurred in the morning during the severest and final period of fighting which took place on Hill 60, Suvla Bay, ANZAC.

'The day broke clear, without a cloud in sight, as any beautiful Mediterranean day could be expected to be. The exception, however, was a number of perhaps six or eight 'loaf of bread' shaped clouds – all shaped exactly alike – which were hovering over Hill 60. It was noticed that, in spite of a four- or five-mile-an-hour [6-8 km/h] breeze from the south, these clouds did not alter their position in any shape or form, nor did they drift away under the influence of the breeze. They were hovering at an elevation of about 60 degrees as seen from our observation point 500 feet [150 metres] up. Also stationary and resting on the ground right underneath this group of clouds was a similar cloud in shape, measuring about 800 feet [245 metres] in length, 220 feet [65 metres] in height, and 200 feet [60 metres] in width. This cloud was absolutely dense, solid looking in structure, and positioned about 14 to 18 chains [280-360 metres] from the fighting in British-held territory. All this was observed by twenty-two men of No 3 Section, No 1 Field Company, N.Z.E., including myself, from our trenches on Rhododendron Spur, approximately 2,500 yards [1,350 metres] south-west of the cloud on the ground. Our vantage point was overlooking Hill 60 by about 300 feet [90 metres]. As it turned out later, this singular cloud was straddling a dry creek bed or sunken road [Kaiajik Dere] and we had a perfect view of the cloud's sides and ends as it

rested on the ground. Its colour was a light grey, as was the colour of the other clouds.

'A British regiment, the First-Fourth Norfolk, of several hundred men, was then noticed marching up this sunken road or creek towards Hill 60. However, when they arrived at this cloud, they marched straight into it, with no hesitation, but no one ever came out to deploy and fight at Hill 60. About an hour later, after the last of the file had disappeared into it, this cloud very unobtrusively lifted off the ground and, like any cloud or fog would, rose slowly until it joined the other similar clouds which were mentioned at the beginning of this account. On viewing them again, they all looked alike "as peas in a pod". All this time, the group of clouds had been hovering in the same place, but as soon as the singular cloud had risen to their level, they all moved away northwards, i.e. towards Thrace [Bulgaria]. In a matter of about three-quarters of an hour, they had all disappeared from view.

'The regiment mentioned was posted as missing or "wiped out" and on Turkey surrendering in 1918, the first thing Britain demanded of Turkey was the return of this regiment. Turkey replied that she had neither captured this regiment, nor made contact with it, and did not know it existed. A British Regiment in 1914-18 consisted of any number between 800 and 4,000 men. Those who observed this incident vouch for the fact that Turkey never captured that regiment, nor made contact with it.

'We, the undersigned, although late in time, this is the 50th Jubilee of the ANZAC landing, declare that the above described incident is true in every word. Signed by witnesses: 4/165 Sapper F. Reichardt, Matata, Bay of Plenty; 13/416 Sapper R. Newnes, 157 King Street, Cambridge; J. L. Newman, 75 Freyberg Street, Octumoctai, Tauranga.'

UNSEASONABLE FOG

This statement is sometimes accompanied by an extract referring to the event from an unspecified 'official history' of the Gallipoli campaign: 'They were swallowed up by an unseasonable fog. This fog reflected the sun's rays in such a way that artillery observers were dazzled by its brilliance and unable to fire in support. The two hundred and fifty men were never seen or heard from again.'

The New Zealanders' statement contains several obvious errors: ANZAC was not a place at the time (although there is a faint likelihood that they could have been referring to an area that was invested with that name), but an acronym for Australia and New Zealand Army Corps. The First-Fourth Norfolk was also a battalion of the Royal Norfolk Regiment and not itself a regiment. It is difficult to believe that anyone familiar with the British Army or the Gallipoli campaign would have made such mistakes, which suggests that the statement may not have been written by those who signed it and that signatures were provided without the statement having first been checked for accuracy. Most important, of course, is the fact that the First-Fourth Norfolk did not disappear but were in active service throughout the Gallipoli campaign. The Norfolks who disappeared were the First-Fifth Battalion, and they disappeared on 12 August, not 21 August.

It is perhaps possible, but highly unlikely, that the First-Fifth, disorientated after the fighting, wandered around Suvla Plain for nine days, but a more likely explanation for the difference in the dates – assuming that the New Zealanders' story relates to the First-Fifth – is that Sapper Reichardt, who seems responsible for telling the story, confused them. After all, 21 is the reverse of 12.

As for the substance of Reichardt's story, research has failed to locate any account of the 'kidnapping cloud' predating the signed statement (except the alleged entry in an 'official history'). But the statement is not contemporary with the events it describes, having been signed at an old comrades' reunion to celebrate the 50th anniversary, in 1965, of the ANZAC landing.

One can only wonder why Reichardt and his companions did not report such an unusual occurrence at the time, but perhaps they feared ridicule. Whatever the reason, the story rests with the testimony of those who signed the statement.

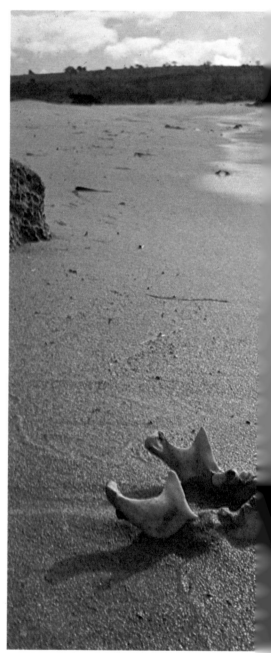

A grim relic of the Gallipoli campaign – a human jawbone washed up by the Aegean Sea 50 years after the Dardanelles invasion by the Allies – is seen below. Such was the carnage that tides are still washing up fragments of the fallen and their equipment.

The rough trench, below, is congested with walking wounded and stretcher cases. Rudimentary medical attention patched up the wounded until they could be carried out to the hospital ships moored offshore. However, the heat and dust – and the ever-present corpse fly – combined to produce fever and infection, which wiped out thousands of the wounded.

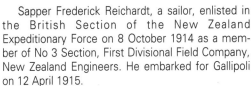

Attendants, **left,** *look after graves in one of the 31 cemeteries maintained on the Gallipoli Peninsula by the Commonwealth War Graves Commission. Thousands of the dead, however, were never identified and many soldiers simply disappeared.*

Sapper Frederick Reichardt, a sailor, enlisted in the British Section of the New Zealand Expeditionary Force on 8 October 1914 as a member of No 3 Section, First Divisional Field Company, New Zealand Engineers. He embarked for Gallipoli on 12 April 1915.

Suvla Plain is dominated by a semicircle of hills stretching from north to south, the southernmost being Sari Bair, which has three summits: Koja Cheman Tepe, Besim Tepe, and Chunuk Bair. The most practical route to the summit of Chunuk Bair is along the Rhododendron Spur, named by the Allies because of the red flowers (not actually rhododendrons, and therefore wrongly identified) that had blazed along its length during the early days of the campaign. It was from Rhododendron Spur that Reichardt claims to have seen the First-Fourth abducted.

One-and-a-half miles (2.5 kilometres) to the north of Chunuk Bair is a small hillock called Hill 60, towards which Reichardt claims the troops were marching when abducted by the cloud. A further three miles (5 kilometres) to the north is Kuchuk Anafarta Ova, the scene of the Norfolks' advance on 12 August.

According to the *War Diary* of the First Divisional Field Company, No 3 Section was away from the Rhododendron Spur until 13 August, and was transferred there on that date. This being the case, Reichardt and his companions were in no position to observe the Norfolks' advance on the afternoon of 12 August. However, it is possible that No 3 Section was moved to the Spur during 12 August in order to begin work there at dawn the following day. Reichardt could have had an unimpeded view of the Norfolks' advance, but he was at least four-and-a-half miles (7 kilometres) away and must have had acute powers of observation if he could accurately see what was happening at such a distance – in the midst of a battle.

There are also many errors in Reichardt's story: he names the wrong battalion; he calls it a regiment; he gives the date of 21 August, nine days after the First-Fifth disappeared; he calls ANZAC a place; and then he waits 50 years before telling his story. All this weighs against believing the main substance of his story.

A STRANGE MIST

However, in the final report of the Dardanelles Commission, on the page facing the account of the First-Fifth's advance on 12 August, is the following:

'By some freak of nature, Suvla Bay and Plain were wrapped in a strange mist on the afternoon of 21 August. This was sheer bad luck as we had reckoned on the enemy's gunners being blinded by the declining sun and upon the Turks' trenches being shown up by the evening sun with singular clearness. Actually, we could hardly see the enemy lines this afternoon, whereas to the westward targets stood out in strong relief against the luminous light.'

There can be no doubt that this is the extract used to support Reichardt's story. And it refers to events that took place on 21 August 1915.

'Freak of nature', 'strange mist' and 'luminous light', are words to conjure with, but the report in fact describes an unseasonable but otherwise perfectly normal mist that descended shortly after noon on 21 August and caused havoc with what was, in terms of numbers, the greatest offensive ever launched at Gallipoli.

During that afternoon, a composite ANZAC force of 3,000 men attacked Hill 60. The battle raged for a week before the Allies withdrew, leaving a corpse-strewn hillock behind them. It was in the late afternoon when, as the final report says, the mist reflected the sun. The Sherwood Rangers, led by Sir John Milbanke VC, could not see the enemy, but the enemy could see the Rangers only too well and wiped them out. It is this incident that Reichardt seems to have confused with the disappearance of the First-Fifth Norfolk to produce the story of the 'kidnapping cloud'.

The Norfolks' fate is still a mystery and in all probability will remain one. People do disappear in time of war. Of the 34,000 British and Empire troops who died at Gallipoli, as many as 27,000 have no known grave. In the light of such widespread carnage, how many more 'strange disappearances' do such statistics hide?

> "THE FOG REFLECTED THE SUN'S RAYS IN SUCH A WAY THAT ARTILLERY OBSERVERS WERE DAZZLED BY ITS BRILLIANCE... THE TWO HUNDRED AND FIFTY MEN WERE NEVER SEEN OR HEARD FROM AGAIN."

BORLEY: A HAUNTING TALE

WAS BORLEY RECTORY REALLY 'THE MOST HAUNTED HOUSE IN ENGLAND' — OR WAS ITS FAME BASED ON A PUBLICITY STUNT BY GHOST-HUNTER HARRY PRICE? INDEED, WAS PRICE NO MORE THAN A HEADLINE-SEEKING FRAUD?

Borley parish church stands on a hillside overlooking the valley of the river Stour, which marks the boundary between the counties of Essex and Suffolk in England. Borley is hardly large enough to merit being called a village. The hundred or so inhabitants of this country parish, mainly agricultural workers and weekend cottagers, do their shopping and socialising in Long Melford or Sudbury, the two nearest small towns on the Suffolk side. For more important business, they must make the journey from Borley Green to Bury St Edmunds, a town that lies about 25 miles (40 kilometres) away.

Harry Price, the well-known ghost-hunter, psychical researcher and author, put the parish of Borley on the map when he wrote a book about the haunting of the rectory of the parish church, seen below.

But, in 1940, the publication of a book entitle[d] *The Most Haunted House in England* sudden[ly] made the community world-famous. Then, in 1946 a further volume, *The End of Borley Rectory*, se[t] the seal on its fame. Both were written by the flam[-]boyant ghost-hunter Harry Price, who put psychica[l] research into the headlines in his day. The tw[o] books claimed that Borley Rectory, a gloom[y] Victorian house that had burned down in 1939, ha[d] been the focal point of some remarkably varie[d] paranormal phenomena. These included a phantom coach, a headless monk, a ghostly nun (who may o[r] may not have been the monk's lover), the spirit of a former vicar, eerie lights, water that turned into ink[,] mysterious bells, and a variety of 'things that wen[t] bump in the night'.

'One of the events of the year 1940' was how the first book was described by *Time and Tide* in its glowing review, while the *Church Times* said that i[t] would 'remain among the most remarkable contri[-]butions ever made to the study of the paranormal'[.] Price, who professed to have devoted 10 years t[o] his study of Borley's ghosts, continued to lecture

broadcast and write on the subject until his death on 29 March 1948. An obituary in *The Times* the following day summed him up as a psychical researcher with 'a singularly honest and clear mind on a subject that by its very nature lends itself to all manner of trickery and chicanery'.

Not everyone who knew or worked with Price agreed with this glowing testimonial, however. Some months after his death, and with the danger of libel safely out of the way, an article by Charles Sutton of the *Daily Mail* appeared in the *Inky Way Annual,* a World's Press News publication. Writing of a visit he had paid to Borley with another colleague, in 1929, in the middle of Price's first investigation, Sutton said that he had discovered what might be fraud on Price's part. After a large pebble had hit Sutton on the head, he found that Price had bricks and pebbles in his pockets.

GRAVE SUSPICIONS

On a more careful investigation, two members of the Society for Psychical Research (SPR) – Lord Charles Hope and Major The Hon. Henry Douglas-Home – confessed that they had serious doubts about certain phenomena that they, too, had witnessed at the rectory in the late 1920s. Both of them filed testimony with the SPR, stating that they had grave suspicions. Douglas-Home went so far as to accuse Price of having a 'complete disregard for the truth in this matter'. He told how, on one occasion, he was accompanying Price around the rectory in the darkness when he heard a rustling that reminded him of cellophane being crumpled. Later, he sneaked a look into Price's suitcase and found a roll of cellophane with a torn edge.

It was as a result of this testimony that the Council of the SPR invited three of their members, Dr Eric J. Dingwall, Mrs K. M. Goldney and Mr Trevor H. Hall, to undertake a new survey of the evidence. They were given access to Price's private papers and correspondence by his literary executor, Dr Paul Tabori. They also had access to documents in the Harry Price Collection, which Price had placed on permanent loan with the University of London in 1938 and which was bequeathed to that institution on his death. This survey took five years to prepare

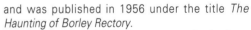

In the picture above, ghost-hunter *Harry Price speaks on the radio direct from a haunted house in Meopham, Kent, in 1936. On a much publicised trip to Germany with C.E.M. Joad,* below, *Price is seen helping to recreate a magical scene on the Brocken in the Harz Mountains in 1932.*

and was published in 1956 under the title *The Haunting of Borley Rectory.*

The reviews of this book were as enthusiastic as those of Price's two volumes in the 1940s, although for diametrically different reasons. The *Sunday Times* said that the Borley legend had been demolished 'with clinical thoroughness and aseptic objectivity'; while Professor A.G.N. Flew in the *Spectator* commented that the 'shattering and fascinating document' proved that Borley had been 'a house of cards built by the late Harry Price out of little more than a pack of lies'.

There, perhaps, the matter should have rested, but due to a combination of factors it did not. The principal reason may have been that Borley had made sensational copy for the world's popular newspapers for over a quarter of a century, and even the most objective of reporters dislikes seeing a good source of news dry up.

The media glossed over the painstaking evidence of Dingwall, Goldney and Hall. One account referred to them as 'the scoffers who accused Harry Price, the greatest of ghost-seekers, of rigging the whole legend'. And once more, the events described by Price were said to be 'puzzling, frightening, and inexplicable'. Peter Underwood, president of the Ghost Club, and the late Dr Tabori, returned to Price's defence in 1973 with a book entitled *The Ghosts of Borley: Annals of the Haunted Rectory,* dedicating it to 'the memory of Harry Price, the man who put Borley on the map'.

237

In his book *The Occult*, Colin Wilson made a fair and scrupulously unbiased summing up of the evidence for and against the Borley case. His conclusion was that 'a hundred other similar cases could be extracted [from SPR records]... Unless someone can produce a book proving that Price was a pathological liar with a craving for publicity, it is necessary to suspend judgement.'

Then, in 1978, SPR investigator Trevor H. Hall set out to prove Price 'a pathological liar with a craving for publicity'. The title of his book, *Search for Harry Price*, was a pun based on Price's own autobiography, *Search for Truth*.

Had it been less carefully documented, Hall's book could have been fairly described as a piece of muckraking. He revealed, for instance, that Price's father was a London grocer who had seduced and married Price's mother when she was 14 and he was over 40. Price himself, in his autobiography, had claimed to be the son of a wealthy paper manufacturer who came from 'an old Shropshire family'.

Price also stated that his childhood had been spent between the London stockbroker suburb of Brockley and the family's country home in Shropshire. He said that he usually 'broke his journey' there on the way to and from school, implying that he was educated at a boarding school. But Hall's researches clearly show the family home to have been in New Cross, far less salubrious than Brockley. Price, said Hall, attended a local secondary school, Haberdasher's Aske's Hatcham Boys' School, a perfectly respectable lower middle class establishment, not a boarding school. And the only connection with Shropshire was that Price's grandfather was landlord of the Bull's Head at Rodington.

Peter Underwood, above, was the president of the Ghost Club who came down on the side of Price in the controversy over his integrity.

The ruins of Borley Rectory, below, are as they appeared four years after the building was completely destroyed by a mysterious fire. This did not end the speculation over its haunting, however.

According to Price, he had held a directorship in his father's paper manufacturing company after leaving school, spending the 10 years between the end of his schooldays and his marriage in 1908 as an amateur coin collector and archaeologist. In fact, according to Hall, Price earned his living in New Cross in a variety of odd ways. He took photographs of local shopfronts for advertising purposes; hired out his portable gramophone and records for dances, parties and other functions; performed conjuring tricks at concerts – a skill that he was later accused of using during his Borley investigation; and peddled glue, paste and a cure for foot-rot in sheep from door to door in the Kent countryside. But Harry Price certainly had a flair for writing, as the impressive sales of his books – he wrote 17 in all – testify.

EXTRAVAGANT CLAIMS

In 1902, Price wrote an article for his old school magazine, *The Askean*, about the excavation of a Roman villa in Greenwich Park, quoting as his source a book written by the director of the project. But by 1942, in *Search for Truth*, he was claiming that he had actually helped to excavate the site. Price also contributed a series of articles to the *Kentish Chronicle* on coins and tokens of the county, following this up with another series for Shropshire's *Wellington Journal* on 'Shropshire tokens and mints'.

Hall asked the Reverend Charles Ellison, Archdeacon of Leeds and a leading authority on numismatics, to examine Price's writings on coins. The archdeacon found them to be straight plagiarisms from two obscure works on the subject. 'It is unsafe to rely on any statement made by Harry

The school where Price was educated is today Haberdasher's Aske's Hatcham College Boys' School, left.

Price bequeathed to London University his outstanding collection of thousands of books on magic and the occult, as shown below. *He tried to get the university to establish a psychical research department but failed. Some say that the institution was scared off by his flamboyant approach to psychical research.*

she was a French woman called Marie Lairre. On the subject of this and subsequent seances he held, Sydney Glanville was almost apologetic to SPR researchers Dingwall, Goldney and Hall, admitting that suggestion had played a part: all three Glanvilles had studied the history of the Borley hauntings.

After the story of the nun's ghost had appeared in *The Most Haunted House in England,* Price received an elaborate theory from Dr W. J. Phythian-Adams, Canon of Carlisle, to the effect that Marie Lairre had been induced to leave her convent and marry one of the local landowners. She had been strangled by her husband and buried in a well on the site of the rectory. The canon also suggested that the ghost of the former nun stole a French dictionary from the residents of Borley Rectory in the 19th century so that she could brush up on her English in order to communicate with them.

Despite other preposterous twists in the canon's theory, Price seized on it eagerly; and Hall even accuses him of manufacturing and planting evidence to back it up. Part of this evidence was two French medals that Price claimed had appeared as 'apports' during his first visit to the rectory in 1929. One was a Roman Catholic confirmation medal and the other, a badge or pass issued to

Price which lacks independent confirmation,' he abruptly concluded.

Hall reported that Price's financial independence came from marriage to Constance Knight, who inherited a fortune from her father. It was her means – and not family wealth as Price claimed – that gave him the leisure to put his days of peddling behind him and embark on his career as psychical researcher and book collector. The assembling of a library of occult and magical books running into several thousand volumes was, said Hall, 'Price's most useful achievement during his life'.

Even the library seemed to offer opportunities for chicanery, however. In the collection, Hall found several valuable books clearly marked with the imprint of the SPR. Price had catalogued them as his own, even attaching his own book-plates.

Price's book-plates were a source of interest and amusement for Hall, as well as another example of Price's deviousness. Price used two crested plates. One featured a lion rampant, which proved on investigation to be the family crest of Sir Charles Rugge-Price of Richmond, with whom Harry Price had no connection. The other, bearing a crest and coat of arms, carried the name 'Robert Ditcher-Price' and the address 'Norton Manor, Radnor'. Hall's investigations revealed that the crest and arms were those of Parr, Lancashire, and that Norton Manor belonged to Sir Robert Green-Price, Baronet, whose family had lived there since the 17th century. A letter from Lady Jean Green-Price unequivocally stated that she had never heard of Robert Ditcher-Price and that she was 'quite certain that he never resided at Norton Manor'.

In his first book on Borley Rectory, Price used a version of a 'nun's tale' supplied by the Glanville family – father Sydney, son Roger and daughter Helen. While holding a seance with a planchette at their home, Helen Glanville elicited the information that a nun had been murdered at Borley and that

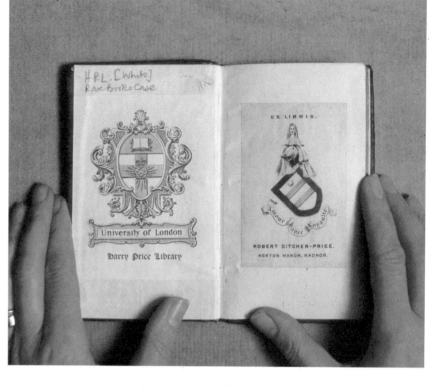

members of the National Assembly after the French Revolution. Yet, previously, Price had said that there was only one apported medal, as Price's faithful secretary confirmed.

PUZZLING FINDS

Hall also recounts how Price had excavated what he called a 'well' in the ruined cellars of Borley Rectory in 1943, discovering a human jawbone in the soft earth. The well turned out to be a modern concrete basin; and during the demolition of the ruins, a switch and lengths of wire were found in the cellar, though the house had never been supplied with electricity. In this account, there is an implicit suggestion that Price used this equipment to light the cellars as he secretly buried the jawbone for later discovery.

Price's accounts of psychical research projects are shown time and again to be inaccurate, almost entirely invented, or presented over the years in different versions with contradictory details. *Search for Harry Price* certainly fulfils Colin Wilson's criterion: it even shows Price as a confirmed liar and publicity-seeker. An absurd experiment in which Price and Professor C. E. M. Joad conducted a magical ceremony in the Harz Mountains in Germany for a regiment of press photographers certainly seems to prove the latter.

But does the tarnishing of Price's character necessarily mean that the haunting of Borley Rectory was fraudulent? From the year the rectory was built in 1863 until 1929, when Price first became interested in it, stories circulating in the area had seemed to suggest a succession of paranormal happenings at the site. Furthermore, from 1930 to 1937, Price visited Borley only once, and yet at least 2,000 allegedly paranormal incidents were recorded during that time. In a year straddling 1937 and 1938, when Price rented the empty rectory and recruited a team of independent witnesses through

Three of Harry Price's book-plates are shown above. The one on the far right, bearing the name of 'Robert Ditcher-Price' and the address 'Norton Manor, Radnor', was investigated by Hall.

an advertisement in *The Times* to live there with him, several incidents were reported even in Price's absence. And between Price's residency and 27 February 1939, when the rectory was 'mysteriously' destroyed by fire at midnight, several other extremely odd events occurred, as we shall see in the next part of this series.

> MORE DAMAGINGLY, PERHAPS, EYEWITNESSES CAME FORWARD TO TESTIFY THAT PRICE HAD DONE MORE THAN BIAS THE RESULTS... AND WHEN LIFE MAGAZINE PUBLISHED A PICTURE OF A BRICK APPARENTLY TELEPORTED INTO THE AIR AT BORLEY, WHY DID PRICE 'FORGET' THAT DEMOLITION WORK WAS IN PROGRESS AND THAT THE BRICK HAD ACTUALLY BEEN THROWN BY A LABOURER WHO WAS HIDDEN FROM THE CAMERA LENS?
>
> **JOHN FARLEY AND SIMON WELFARE,**
> **ARTHUR C. CLARKE'S WORLD OF**
> **STRANGE POWERS**

THE ART OF MASS MIND CONTROL

ACCORDING TO ONE OF THE MOST DISTURBING RUMOURS TO ARISE IN THE LATE 20TH CENTURY, THE SOVIETS NOT ONLY MASTERED THE ART OF MASS MIND CONTROL, BUT ACTUALLY SET ABOUT USING IT

American psychic Shawn Robbins, right, revealed that the US Navy once invited her to take part in a project similar to Stanford Research Institute's remote viewing experiments. There is some evidence that many other psychics have also been approached by their governments as potential subjects in large-scale ESP experiments.

Astral espionage; subliminal propaganda by telepathy; thought-moulding of Western leaders; bioenergy as an anti-personnel weapon; knocking out military equipment and space vehicles with psychokinesis – these are not jottings from a science-fiction writer's notebook but some of the techniques solemnly discussed in two reports compiled in 1972 and 1975 for the US

The early warning station, below, is designed to detect incoming missiles. But what warning would we have if an enemy state chose to direct weapons of mind control against us?

Defense Intelligence Agency (DIA) under the titles *Controlled Offensive Behavior – USSR* and *Soviet and Czechoslovak Parapsychology Research*. The former was scheduled for declassification only in 1990, but was released under the Freedom of Information Act. While parts of the documents may strain the credulity of even the most avid of science fiction fans, a study of them in conjunction with other published information points to the very real possibility that the Third World War was well under way by the mid 1970s – and that the West was slowly losing it.

According to the DIA reports, the Soviets had a start of several decades over the West in officially funded research into psychic phenomena, especially telepathy, and their top priority was always its practical application. In other words, while the West was holding psychical research at arm's length, or even arguing it out of existence, the Soviets were looking for – and finding – ways of making telepathy and psychokinesis (PK) work for them.

PSYCHIC WARFARE

However, a 1976 report (allegedly funded by one of the US intelligence agencies) was more cautious. Surveying the published literature on what its authors term 'novel biophysical information transfer' (NBIT) – comprising both telepathy and PK – it concluded that, although most published material was 'confusing, inaccurate and of little value from a scientific point of view', there was good reason to suppose that secret *psi* research was indeed going on in the Soviet Union, and that the results were intended to be used by the military and secret police. One of the authors of the report was later quoted as saying: 'I believe the Soviets are actually building prototype equipment for psychic warfare.'

It became known in 1980, thanks to successful use of the Freedom of Information Act by US journalist Randy Fitzgerald, that the Central Intelligence Agency's involvement in psychic matters could be traced back at least to 1952.

In a CIA document dated 7 January of that year, the remarkable claim was made that: 'It looks as if... the problem of getting and maintaining control over the ESP function has been solved.' It was also recommended that 'suitable subjects' should be trained and put to work as psychic spies. A well-known American psychic, Shawn Robbins, later revealed that she had been invited to take part in a US Navy project along the lines of the remote

Jack Anderson, left, a US columnist and investigative reporter, announced in early 1981 that the Pentagon had been training a 'psychic' task force (which he dubbed 'the voodoo warriors') since 1976. Although he treated the subject lightheartedly, other writers, including senior officers of the US Army, viewed it with grave concern.

A secret Soviet installation, observed at Sary-Shagan in Kazakhstan, far right, was believed to house a laser or particle beam weapon. Thomas E. Bearden, however, believed it was based on a Tesla invention and used to form a 'bubble' of energy – a force field that could be employed as a defensive shield. Alternatively, it could be used as an offensive weapon against enemy aircraft.

Could there indeed be weapon systems that operate on the power of the mind alone, as illustrated symbolically, below?

viewing experiments carried out at Stanford Research Institute (SRI) with researchers Ingo Swann and Pat Price.

Then, early in 1981, psychic warfare made headlines in the USA when columnist Jack Anderson announced that the Pentagon had been maintaining its own secret 'psychic task force' since 1976. 'The brass hats,' he said, 'are indeed dabbling in the dark arts.' Anderson does not seem to have taken the activities of what he calls 'the voodoo warriors' very seriously; yet by a curious coincidence, the first of his two columns appeared just after a much more thoroughly researched piece on psychotronic warfare in *Military Review,* the professional journal of the US Army.

The article, entitled *The New Mental Battlefield,* was humorously subtitled 'Beam me up, Spock', a reference to the TV series, *Star Trek.* But there was nothing funny in the eight-page text, written by Lieutenant-Colonel J.B. Alexander, a holder of three university degrees who had clearly done his homework. Psychotronic research had been under way for years, he wrote, and its potential use in weaponry had been explored. 'To be more specific,' he went on, 'there are weapons systems that operate on the power of the mind and whose lethal capacity has already been demonstrated.' After a candid and open-minded survey of his subject, he admitted that some would find it ridiculous 'since it does not conform to their view of reality'. However, he added, 'some people still believe the world is flat', and he called for more co-ordinated research into the paranormal, recommending that leaders at all levels should be provided with 'a basic understanding of weapons systems they may encounter in the not-too-distant future'.

Some indication of just what these weapons might be was given by Thomas E. Bearden, a retired US Army officer with long experience in nuclear engineering, war games analysis and air defence systems. He described a terrifying arsenal of some 26 devices, ranging from machines that modify the weather and broadcast 'disease patterns' to the 'hyperspace nuclear howitzer' and even an earthquake generator. Bearden uses quantum mechanics and Jungian psychology to build a model of psychotronic reality that is unlikely to conform to the views of many, although Lyall Watson, who discusses Bearden's theories in his book *Lifetide,* finds some of his ideas 'horribly plausible' and senses 'a rightness in his approach'.

But before the psychotronic scenario gets even more bizarre, two questions must be asked: who is winning the *psi* arms race, and is there any real evidence that any *psi* weaponry has ever been used?

According to Richard Deacon, author of several studies of international espionage, the first country to take the lead in *psi* warfare techniques could achieve 'something like total superiority'. And, he pointed out, the country with the most active interest in and best information on the subject is neither

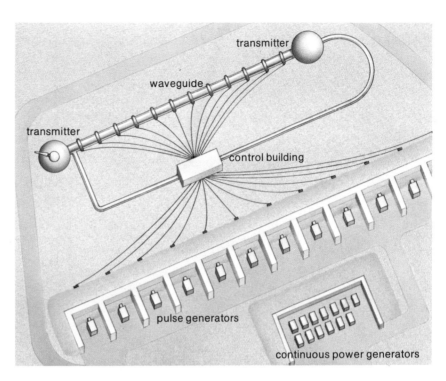

P E R S P E C T I V E S

A PAWN IN THEIR GAME

Anatoli Karpov, Soviet grand master, and Viktor Korchnoi, the Soviet defector, are seen below during their intense battle of wits at the 1978 World Chess Championship at Baguio City in the Philippines.

Who really won the 1978 World Chess Championship – Soviet grand master Anatoli Karpov, Soviet defector Viktor Korchnoi, or a mysterious man named Dr Vladimir Zukhar? According to the record books, it was the seemingly unflappable Karpov who retained his title after winning five games out of the first six, losing the next four, and finally returning to form and sweeping the board.

Korchnoi thought otherwise. Dr Zukhar, he alleged, was a psychic saboteur sent to the Philippines to make sure that Karpov avoided losing to a defector.

Korchnoi obviously believed that psychic powers could affect his game, for he took countermeasures of his own, in the form of training in yoga and meditation from two American members of the Anand Marg sect who happened to be in town. They also taught him a Sanskrit mantra to ward off evil, which he claimed to have used against Zukhar with devastating effect.

This was not the first time psychic matters had been raised at a world chess tournament. Interestingly, it was the Soviets who cried foul play at the 1972 confrontation between Bobby Fischer and Boris Spassky, suggesting not only that Fischer's chair was wired to receive messages from accomplices, but that Fischer, or at any rate somebody, was actually trying to cast an evil spell over Spassky. And at the world title elimination bout in 1977, Spassky had part of the stage screened off, so that he could hide from both Korchnoi and the audience. The former was paralysing his mind, he said, while the latter were beaming rays at him.

Could Dr Zukhar have helped Karpov win in 1978? By then, the Soviets had more than 50 years of state-backed research in telepathy to draw on; and if scientists in the 1920s could broadcast suggestions that subjects should scratch their noses, it seems possible that Zukhar could make Korchnoi move the wrong pawn at the wrong time.

'Chess is almost the perfect game for PK effects to make a real difference,' commented Dr Carl Sargent, a parapsychologist and chess enthusiast. 'One lapse of concentration may mean the blunder which costs the game or even the match.' A feature of the Korchnoi-Karpov games was indeed the number lost by apparent mistakes rather than won by skill.

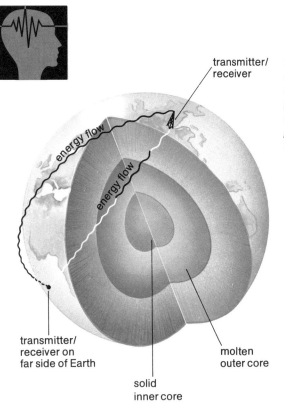

transmitter/
receiver

energy flow

energy flow

transmitter/
receiver on
far side of Earth

molten
outer core

solid
inner core

The diagram, left, *shows the theoretical application of one of Nikola Tesla's ideas – that of beaming radio waves through the Earth's core in order to carry psychotronic signals designed to destroy human brain waves.*

of the so-called 'superpowers', but Israel. Quoting intelligence sources, Deacon stated that the Israelis have first-hand knowledge of military *psi* research in seven Russian cities and at least four Eastern European countries. One of Israel's most alarming claims, according to Deacon, is that the Soviets were working in the mid 1970s on 'subliminal conditioning' by telepathy, through 'transference of behaviour impulses'. So has telepathic mind control already been put into practice?

In 1976, one possible means by which this could have been done became public knowledge. In that year, a number of new Soviet radio stations went on the air, mystifying listeners around the world by confining their programme content to a loud and steady rattle. One of these stations, at Gomel (near Minsk), was believed to have 20 times the peak output of any previously known transmitter. The Soviet 'woodpecker' (which is what it sounded like) was splashing across several frequencies on the short-wave band and was even interfering with telephones.

RADIO DISRUPTION

Telecommunications companies, amateur radio societies and several governments complained to the Soviet Union. The Soviets apologised, saying they were carrying out 'experiments' and promised to minimise disruption. But they never explained what they were doing, and early guesses were that they were working on a new form of over-the-horizon radar. Then, in 1977, the American psychical investigator Andrija Puharich startled a London audience with a detailed account of what he believed was really going on.

The Soviets, Puharich said, had put into practice an idea originally thought up by the scientific genius Nikola Tesla (1857-1943) around the turn of the century, and were using their transmitters to set up a colossal stationary wave passing through the core of the Earth and carrying a signal tuned to resonate with the Earth-atmosphere system. This signal was

being pulsed in the extremely low frequency (ELF) band, at 4 to 15 pulses per second, a range of special importance to the human brain, and comprising the theta and alpha bands.

In laboratory experiments, Puharich found that brain rhythms fell into step with whatever frequency in these bands was being beamed at them, even when the subject was in a shielded metal Faraday cage. Fine tuning of the pulse rate could also produce a wide range of symptoms, from tension headaches and nausea to drowsiness. This sinister process of 'bioentrainment' was, he claimed, being tried out on a country especially selected for the Soviet 'experiment' – Canada.

This was not all. Puharich claimed that ways had been found to get the psychotronic effect, in the form of a telepathic signal, on to the woodpecker signal. Something like this had been specifically predicted in detail by the authors of the 1976 report. So, fantastic as it may seem, it is an idea that has occurred to others besides Puharich. Indeed, it has often been noted that the physicist Dr Ippolit M. Kogan put forward a hypothesis in the 1960s on the use of ELF waves as carriers of telepathy and that, after 1969, Kogan's name completely disappeared from the published literature. Western observers also noticed that any accounts of psychical research published by the Soviets after 1970 described old, well-known experiments, as if their real work in this field had suddenly been deemed top secret.

In a scene from the 1977 MGM film Telefon, below, *Soviet 'sleepers' in America – activated by a hypnotic code – have just blown up a US military base.*

> **FIGHTING IS THE MOST PRIMITIVE WAY OF MAKING WAR ON YOUR ENEMIES. THE SUPREME EXCELLENCE IS TO SUBDUE THE ARMIES OF YOUR ENEMIES WITHOUT HAVING TO FIGHT THEM.**
>
> **SUN TZU, EARLY 4TH CENTURY BC**

A NIGHT TO REMEMBER

AFTER BETTY AND BARNEY HILL HAD SEEN A UFO AT CLOSE QUARTERS, BETTY DREAMED SHE HAD BEEN ABDUCTED AND INTIMATELY EXAMINED BY MEMBERS OF AN ALIEN SPECIES

In September 1961, Betty Hill and her husband Barney were taken on board a spacecraft from another world, subjected to examination and given information by the alien crew members. That, at least, was what the Hills believed. Their case is one of many; and more of the same kind are constantly being reported. But the Hills' account is

Betty and Barney Hill, below, were returning from a short vacation when they claimed to have seen a UFO during a night drive along a lonely highway in New Hampshire, USA. Two years after the incident, they both began to suffer from chronic ill health and nervous disorders. Betty was also experiencing disturbing dreams and Barney complained of stress, exhaustion and other anxiety symptoms.

particularly interesting and one of the most fully documented and thoroughly investigated abductions.

Whether their experience was just what it seemed or some kind of fantasy, it is important that we should know exactly what happened to Betty and Barney Hill that night, for it is part of a widespread pattern. The Hills lived at Portsmouth, New Hampshire, in the eastern United States. Barney, who was black, was aged 39 at the time. He worked as a mail sorter in Boston, a job he was glad to have, even though it was somewhat below his capacity and involved not only night work but also a daily car journey of 60 miles (100 kilometres) each way. Outside his work, Barney was known to be active in the campaign for civil rights for blacks. Betty, aged 41, was white and a child welfare worker. Both had been married before and had children by their earlier marriages, though the children were all living with their other parents. To all appearances, it was a happy and successful marriage: the couple were popular and had many friends.

Late on 19 September 1961, the Hills were on their way home after a short holiday trip to Niagara and Montreal. They were driving through the night because they had run low on money, the trip having been undertaken on the spur of the moment. They stopped for a snack at a roadside restaurant, which they left a little after 10 p.m. to drive on down Highway US3. During their journey that night, the Hills passed no other cars and saw only one other person. What happened to the couple on the journey home was described by Betty in a letter to a UFO investigator five days later:

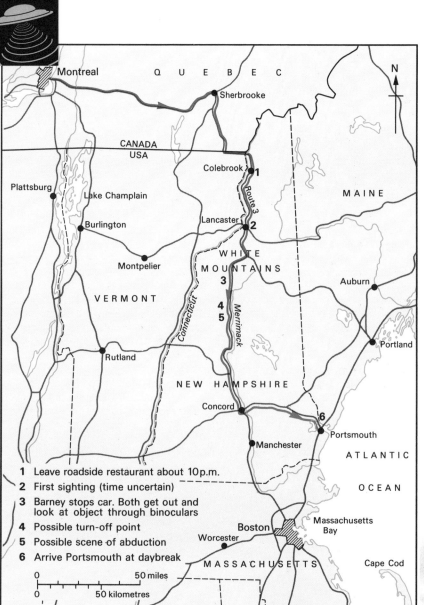

1 Leave roadside restaurant about 10p.m.
2 First sighting (time uncertain)
3 Barney stops car. Both get out and look at object through binoculars
4 Possible turn-off point
5 Possible scene of abduction
6 Arrive Portsmouth at daybreak

0   50 miles
0   50 kilometres

'My husband and I have become immensely interested in this topic [UFOs] as we recently had quite a frightening experience, which does seem to differ from others of which we are aware.

'About midnight on September 20th, we were driving in a National Forest Area in the White Mountains, in N.H. [New Hampshire]. This is a desolate, uninhabited area. At first we noticed a bright object in the sky, which seemed to be moving rapidly. We stopped our car and got out to observe it more closely with our binoculars. Suddenly, it reversed its flight path from the north to the southwest and appeared to be flying in a very erratic pattern. As we continued driving and then stopping to watch it, we observed the following flight pattern: the object was spinning and appeared to be lighted only on one side, which gave it a twinkling effect.

'As it approached our car, we stopped again. As it hovered in the air in front of us, it appeared to be pancake in shape, ringed with windows in the front through which we could see bright blue-white lights. Suddenly, two red lights appeared on each side. By this time, my husband was standing in the road, watching closely. He saw wings protrude on each side and the red lights were on the wing tips.

'As it glided closer, he was able to see inside this object, but not too closely. He did see several figures scurrying about as though they were making some hurried type of preparation. One figure was observing us from the windows. From the distance this was seen, the figures appeared to be about the size of a pencil and seemed to be dressed in some type of shiny black uniform.

> **ALTHOUGH THEIR OCCUPATIONS DO NOT ESPECIALLY QUALIFY THE WITNESSES AS TRAINED SCIENTIFIC OBSERVERS, I WAS IMPRESSED BY THEIR INTELLIGENCE, APPARENT HONESTY, AND OBVIOUS DESIRE TO GET AT THE FACTS AND TO UNDERPLAY THE MORE SENSATIONAL ASPECTS OF THE SIGHTING. HILL HAD BEEN A COMPLETE UFO SCEPTIC BEFORE THE SIGHTING.**
>
> **JOHN G. FULLER,**
> **THE INTERRUPTED JOURNEY**

The route taken by Barney and Betty Hill on the night they saw the UFO is shown left.

It was on Highway US3, below, that the Hills stopped their car and got out to look at the flying object. Betty described it as pancake-shaped with windows in the front through which could be seen bright blue-white lights, as illustrated right. The object also appeared to have fins tipped with red lights.

'At this point my husband became shocked and got back in the car, in a hysterical condition, laughing and repeating that they were going to capture us. He started driving the car – the motor had been left running. As we started to move, we heard several buzzing or beeping sounds, which seemed to be striking the trunk of our car.'

This letter, written to Donald Keyhoe of the National Investigations Committee for Aerial Phenomena (NICAP), effectively summarises what the Hills remembered of their experience. But what it lacks is the emotional response of the couple, more vividly described by John G. Fuller in his definitive account of the Hills' experience, entitled *The Interrupted Journey.*

MISSING TIME PUZZLE

It was not until 25 November, two months later, in the course of questioning by UFO investigators, that a 'missing time' puzzle emerged. Here are Barney's own words: 'They were mentally reconstructing the whole trip. One of them said: "What took you so long to get home?" They said: "You went this distance and it took you these hours. Where were you?" Well, when they said this, I thought I was really going to crack up... I became suddenly flabbergasted to think that I realised for the first time that at the rate of speed I always travel, we should have arrived home at least two hours earlier than we did.'

The Hills had taken seven hours to travel 190 miles (305 kilometres), on empty roads, often at 65-70 miles per hour (105-112 km/h).

Ten days after their return, Betty started to experience a series of disturbing dreams. By this time, she had already written her letter to Major Keyhoe, quoted earlier, but had not yet been visited by any investigator. She had told friends and relatives about the experience and was not just puzzled but very disturbed by it. Not surprisingly, her dreams reflected her anxiety.

But they did more than that. While taking the UFO sighting as a starting point, her dreams seemed to continue the incident. In fact, they present a highly detailed account of happenings that, though extremely bizarre, follow on logically from the sighting itself.

Betty's own account of her dreams is included as an appendix to Fuller's book. But unfortunately, he does not indicate when the notes were made; nor does he make it clear how many dreams there were, and whether they repeated the same material, or whether some of the story was contained in each, as fragments that Betty later combined to form a coherent narrative. In other words, we cannot be sure that the smooth, continuous flow of her narrative was also a characteristic of the dreams themselves, or whether it was the result of her own re-telling of the dreams. In the light of subsequent events, the coherence and detail of Betty's account of her dreams are of crucial significance.

The dream experience begins at a point immediately following the UFO sighting. Betty sees a very sharp left-hand turn in the road, which then turns back to the right. A group of eight or eleven men are standing in the middle of the road. Barney

247

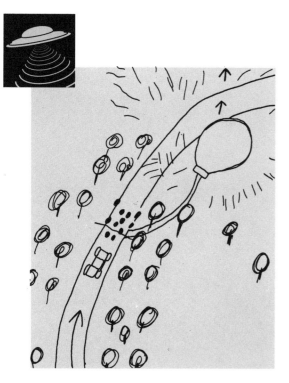

ONE WRITER HAS INTIMATED THAT THE HILLS ARE OBVIOUSLY EMOTIONALLY ILL... IT SEEMS CLEAR THAT IT WAS THE EXPERIENCE THAT CAUSED THE EMOTIONAL IMBALANCE, AND NOT THE EMOTIONAL IMBALANCE THAT CAUSED THE EXPERIENCE. "

T. M. WRIGHT,
AN INTELLIGENT MAN'S GUIDE
TO FLYING SAUCERS

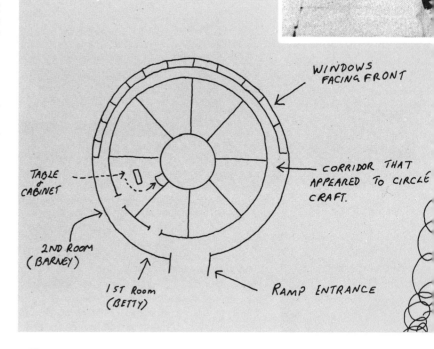

slows down, and the motor dies. As he tries to start the motor, the men surround the car. The couple sit motionless and speechless. Betty is terrified. The men open the car doors, reach in and take Barney and Betty by the arm.

Next, Betty seems to be walking along a path in the woods, with men ahead of, beside and behind her. Barney is similarly accompanied. She speaks to him but he does not seem to hear her: it is as though he is sleepwalking. The man on Betty's left, hearing her say Barney's name, asks if that is his name. She does not answer. He tries to assure her that there is nothing to be frightened of, and that no harm will come to them.

Soon they reach a small clearing, where a disc-shaped craft is parked. Betty described it as 'almost as wide as my house is long'. There are no lights or windows to be seen. They climb a ramp towards a door in the craft and, reluctantly, Betty goes in. They then emerge into a corridor, curving with the shape of the disc. Betty is taken into the first room opening off the corridor, but Barney is led further along. When Betty objects, the leader explains that only one person at a time can be tested in each room, and that it will be quicker to examine them separately .

The men leave Betty in the room and a pleasant, reassuring man, who speaks English, enters: he is the examiner. He asks several questions about her age, her diet and so on. Then he makes her sit on a stool while he carries out a superficial inspection, taking samples of hair and ear wax, fingernail clippings and scrapings from her skin.

Next, he asks Betty to lie down on a table. He examines her with a machine that has needles on the end of wires. This, he explains, is to check her nervous system. During this test, her dress is removed. With a needle 4 to 6 inches (10 – 15 centimetres) long, the examiner carries out what he calls a pregnancy test, which consists of jabbing the needle into her navel. The test is extremely painful, but the leader, who has returned to the room to watch the examination, clears the pain by waving his hand before Betty's eyes. She senses his concern, and from this point loses all fear of him.

That concludes the testing, and the examiner leaves to help with Barney, whose testing is taking longer. Alone with the leader, Betty examines the room and begins to chat with him. He apologises for frightening her and offers to answer her questions.

They are interrupted when some of the men enter. After a brief conversation, the leader turns to Betty, opens her mouth, and touches her teeth as though trying to move them. He is puzzled by the fact that Barney's teeth are movable while Betty's are not; so Betty explains about Barney's dentures. This leads to a discussion of old age, which the man seems not to comprehend, for he asks Betty about time and how it is measured.

Betty asks for some proof of the incident. The leader agrees; and when she looks round the room and sees a book, he says she may take it. Discussion of the book leads to questions about the Universe; and the leader pulls out a kind of map

Barney, top, shows his drawing of the spacecraft as he remembered seeing it – with fins either side, tipped with red lights, and members of the alien crew looking out of the windows. Although he had no conscious memory of being abducted, he was able – after hypnosis – to draw the plan, above, of the arrangement of rooms inside the craft, and sketched the area, top left, where the craft landed. His diagram shows the Hills' car on the highway and the group of spacemen (shown as dots) who abducted the couple.

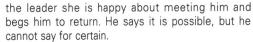

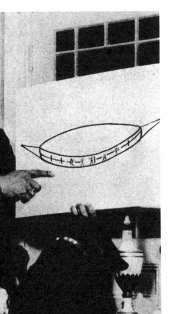

from a case, on which are marked a number of stars. Betty tells him that she knows little about such matters, but that there are others on Earth who do, and a meeting should be arranged with them. As she speaks, Betty is wondering whether she herself might be able to bring about such a meeting.

At this point, some men return with Barney, who is still in a daze. When Betty speaks to him, he does not answer. The leader assures her that he will be back to normal when they return to their car. They start to walk towards the door, and then one of the men says something that provokes an excited discussion. The leader takes the book away from Betty, saying that the rest of the crew feel that no one should know of this experience and that even Betty herself will not remember it. When she insists that she will remember somehow, he agrees that perhaps she will, but he says nobody will believe her.

They leave the disc and walk back through the woods. All the men accompany them. Betty tells

The artist's impressions of the alien crew of the spacecraft, left, are based on the Hills' verbal descriptions. In Betty's dreams, the aliens put the couple into separate rooms aboard their craft and carried out physical examinations.

the leader she is happy about meeting him and begs him to return. He says it is possible, but he cannot say for certain.

Barney seems to become more alert once they approach the car, but shows no emotion and behaves as though this were an everyday occurrence. They get into the car. The disc becomes a bright glowing object, seems to roll like a ball, turns over three or four times, and then sails into the sky. Betty turns back to Barney and says it is the most marvellous, most unbelievable experience of her entire life. Barney starts driving. So far he has not uttered a word. She turns to him and asks: 'Do you believe in flying saucers now?' He replies: 'Don't be ridiculous!'

Intriguing though they were, Betty's dreams figured in the case only because they confirmed the impact made on her by the sighting. The investigators who visited the couple were concerned only with the waking experiences reported by the Hills. Walter Webb, an astronomer who served as one of NICAP's scientific advisers, was impressed by the Hills' testimony.

In his report, Webb wrote: 'It is the opinion of this investigator, after questioning these people for over six hours and studying their reactions and personalities during that time, that they were telling the truth, and the incident occurred exactly as reported except for some minor uncertainties and technicalities... I was impressed by their intelligence, apparent honesty, and obvious desire to get at the facts and to underplay the more sensational aspects of the sighting.'

FEARS, REAL AND IMAGINED

Significantly, Webb went on to observe: 'Mr Hill believes he saw something he doesn't want to remember. He claimed he was not close enough to see any facial characteristics on the figures, although at another time he referred to one of them looking over his shoulder and grinning, and to the leader's expressionless face. However, it is my view that the observer's blackout is not of any great significance. I think the whole experience was so improbable and fantastic to witness – along with the very real fear of being captured adding to imagined fears – that his mind finally refused to believe what his eyes were perceiving and a mental block resulted.'

In the course of the ensuing year, it was Barney's 'mental block' that gradually assumed overwhelming importance. His health deteriorated, and with it his mental state: his ulcer became more pronounced, and he became exhausted and depressed. Seeking a cause, it was not surprising that the Hills should wonder whether their UFO experience had played any part in it. They suggested this to their doctor, who proposed hypnosis as a means of discovering more about the sighting and its effect on them. Already, during the investigation of their story, hypnosis had been proposed as a means of acquiring further data, so the Hills welcomed the suggestion.

But Betty had an additional reason for seeking what hypnosis might reveal: 'The moment they suggested hypnosis, I thought of my dreams, and this was the first time I began to wonder if they were more than just dreams... '

ENIGMAS

ONE OF THE STRANGEST STORIES TO HAVE EMERGED FROM THE CLOUD OF MYSTERY THAT SURROUNDS THE ANCIENT SCIENCE OF ALCHEMY IS THAT OF THE ELUSIVE MODERN MASTER KNOWN AS FULCANELLI. WHAT DID HE ACHIEVE? AND IF HE INDEED DISCOVERED THE ELIXIR OF LIFE, COULD HE STILL BE ALIVE TODAY?

THE HIDDEN FACE O

T he name Fulcanelli has flickered tantalisingly in and out of modern occult literature and speculation for more than half a century. Yet the true identity of the 20th-century alchemist working behind this pseudonym remains to this day a complete mystery.

It was in the early 1920s that the Fulcanelli legend started, as Parisian occultists and alchemists began overhearing oblique and intriguing references to an actual master, alive and working secretly in their midst. These references came mainly from a certain Eugène Canseliet – an intense, slightly-built man in his early twenties who was known to be an enthusiastic researcher into alchemy. They were also bandied about by his constant companion and friend, the impoverished artist and illustrator, Jean-Julien Champagne, who was 22 years Canseliet's senior. The pair, who rented adjacent quarters on the sixth storey of a dilapidated tenement at 59 *bis*, rue de Rochechouart, in the Montmartre district of Paris, had become the focal point of a small, select circle of occultists, and were frequently seen in the city's great libraries – the Arsenal, the Sainte Geneviève, the Mazarin and the Bibliothèque Nationale – poring over rare books and manuscripts.

Those on the periphery of this informal study-group heard hints that the Master Fulcanelli was elderly, distinguished, rich, immensely learned and possibly of aristocratic or noble lineage. He was said to be a genuine, practising alchemist who, if he had not done so already, was on the brink of perfecting 'the Great Work' – the manufacture of the Philosopher's Stone and the Elixir, which could prolong life indefinitely.

But who the Master really was remained unknown. Few had apparently met him – except, so they claimed, Champagne and Canseliet. Certain sceptics even began to question the very fact of his existence.

Then, in the autumn of 1926, evidence of the Master's reality – or at least the reality of someone – appeared. It came in the form of a remarkable

*In*FOCUS

THE MYSTERY OF THE CATHEDRALS

In his book *Le Mystère des Cathédrales,* Fulcanelli takes the reader on a guided and interpretative tour of many of France's finest examples of Gothic architecture, including the Cathedral of Notre Dame in Paris. Like many mystical commentators before him, he sees architecture as a means of passing on esoteric knowledge, encoded in the form and proportion of a building.

FULCANELLI

ULCANELLI

The name of Fulcanelli – whose signature is shown far left – is a phonetic approximation of 'Vulcan', the Roman fire-god, below, and 'Helios', the Greek Sun-charioteer, right. This may be an allusion, perhaps, to the flames used to heat the mysterious substances that combine to form the Elixir of Life.

The bracket in the mansion of Lallemant in Bourges, top, far left, shows a medieval adept holding the Vessel of the 'Great Work', in which the Elixir of Life is prepared.

Eugène Canseliet and Jean-Julien Champagne, reputedly pupils of the mysterious Fulcanelli, both lived at the house above left.

Marguerite de France (1553-1615), below, is believed by some to have known the secret of the 'Great Work'. Rumour suggested that Fulcanelli might have been descended from her.

His enthusiasm for Gothic architecture is reached via a circuitous route that involved a kind of punning logic. Thus, he interprets Gothic Art, *Art Gothique,* as *argot-hique* – reminding us that *argot* (cant or slang) is defined in dictionaries as 'a language peculiar to all individuals who wish to communicate their thoughts without being understood by outsiders.' Fulcanelli claims that those who use this secret language are descendants of the sailors who accompanied Jason on his search for the Golden Fleece – aboard the ship *Argo.* They, he claims, spoke the *langue argotique* [language of the *Argo*]... while they were sailing towards the felicitous shores of Colchos... '

But how does Fulcanelli's method work in practice? In the Portal of the Virgin of Notre Dame Cathedral, *left,* for instance, he sees the medallions of the sarcophagus as symbols of the seven planetary metals. According to standard alchemical interpretation, the Sun stands for gold, Mercury for quicksilver, Saturn for lead, Venus for copper, the Moon for silver, Jupiter for tin and Mars for iron. Taken as a whole, Fulcanelli claims, the portal gives clues as to how to transmute these metals. But Fulcanelli has not made matters too easy, and the final step in interpretation is left to the alchemist. Nevertheless, as Fulcanelli's pupil Canseliet reveals in his introduction to the book: 'The key to the major arcanum is given quite openly in one of the figures.'

book, *Le Mystère des Cathédrales* (The Mystery of the Cathedrals), published in a limited luxury edition of only 300 copies and subtitled *An Esoteric Interpretation of the Hermetic Symbols of the Great Work.* Its preface was by Eugène Canseliet, then aged only 26, and it contained 36 illustrations, two in colour, by the artist Champagne. The text itself was ascribed simply to Fulcanelli. The book purported to interpret the symbolism of various Gothic cathedrals and other buildings in Europe as encoded instructions of alchemical secrets, a concept only darkly hinted at by previous writers on the esoteric in art and architecture. Among occultists, it caused a minor sensation.

In his preface, the young Canseliet intimated that his Master, Fulcanelli – the name is a phonetic approximation of Vulcan, the blacksmith god, and Helios, the Sun-charioteer – had attained the Philosopher's Stone, thereby becoming mystically transfigured and illuminated, and then disappeared. As Canseliet put it: 'He disappeared when the fatal hour struck, when the Sign was accomplished... Fulcanelli is no more. But we have at least this consolation that his thought remains, warm and vital, enshrined for ever in these pages.'

SECRET OF LONGEVITY

Perhaps understandably – especially in view of the immense scholarship and unique haunting qualities of the book – speculation about Fulcanelli's true identity ran wild within the occult fraternity. There were even suggestions that he was a surviving member of the former French royal family, the Valois. Although they were supposed to have died out in 1589 on the demise of Henri III, it was known that members of the family had dabbled in magic and mysticism and that Marguerite de France, daughter of Henri II and wife of Henri IV of Navarre, had survived until 1615. What is more, one of her many lovers was the esoterically inclined Francis Bacon (whom many still claim as an adept to this day). She was divorced in 1599 and her personal crest bore the magical pentagram, each of the five points carrying one letter of the Latin word *salus* – meaning 'health'. So could the reputedly aristocratic Fulcanelli be a descendant of the Valois, and did the Latin motto hint that some important alchemical secret of longevity had been passed on to him by the family? These were, at least, possibilities.

But there were other, more or less plausible identifications. Some claimed Fulcanelli was the bookseller-occultist, Pierre Dujols; and that, together with his wife, he ran a shop in the rue de Rennes in the Luxembourg district of Paris. But Dujols was already known to have been only a speculative alchemist, writing under the *nom de plume* of Magophon. It seemed unlikely he would hide behind two aliases. Another suggestion was that Fulcanelli was the writer J.H. Rosny, the Elder. Yet this author's life was too well-known to the public for the theory to find general acceptance.

There were in fact three practising alchemists in Paris at around this period, operating under the respective pseudonyms of Auriger, Faugerons and Dr Jaubert. But the argument against any of them being Fulcanelli was much the same as that against Dujols-Magophon: why use more than one alias?

Finally, there were Eugène Canseliet and Jean-Julien Champagne themselves, both of whom were directly connected with Fulcanelli's book, and both of whom claimed to have known the Master Fulcanelli personally.

But the argument against Canseliet's identification as the Master was fairly straightforward: he was far too young to have acquired the erudition and knowledge so obviously and remarkably demonstrated by the text of *Le Mystère des Cathédrales*. And a study of his preface showed a distinct difference in style from that of the text, a difference that remains notable in Canseliet's later writings.

Champagne seemed, at least to some, the more likely contender. He was older and more experienced, and his work as an artist could have taken him around the various cathedrals, châteaux and other curious monuments imbued with symbolism that Fulcanelli had obviously studied and interpreted in great detail as keys to the 'Great Work'.

On the other hand, Champagne was a noted braggart, practical joker, punster and drunkard, who

Eugène Canseliet, above, claimed to be a pupil of Fulcanelli but did not reveal his identity.

Many suspected that the writer J. H. Rosny the Elder (1856-1940), above, was the figure behind the pseudonym 'Fulcanelli'.

Jean-Julien Champagne, left – artist and illustrator, and constant companion of Fulcanelli's supposed pupil Eugène Canseliet – was a braggart and practical joker. His habit of trying to pass himself off as Fulcanelli added to the confusion about the true identity of the master alchemist.

frequently liked to pass himself off as Fulcanelli – although his behaviour was entirely out of keeping with the traditional solemn oath of the adept that promises he will remain anonymous and let his written work speak for itself.

Two examples of Champagne's wicked sense of humour suffice to show the great gap between his own way of thinking and that of the noble-minded author of *Le Mystère des Cathédrales*. Champagne once persuaded a gullible young follower that he should stock up with a massive supply of coal to ensure that his alchemical furnace was constantly burning at the required temperature. The naïve youth lugged sack after sack of the fuel up to his garret until there was barely room in which to lie down and sleep. Champagne then announced to the would-be alchemist that the quest was an utterly vain and dangerous one – leaving him almost banished from his apartment by coal and, presumably, considerably out of pocket into the bargain.

FAKE LETTER

Another carefully contrived prank of Champagne involved the forging of a letter, purportedly from Paul le Cour, who edited and published a periodical called *Atlantis*, to the publisher of the *Mercure de France*. In it, the fake le Cour urged the setting up of a fund by the *Mercure's* subscribers to build a monument for the victims of the fabled lost continent – a cenotaph that, since he suggested it be placed in the middle of the Sargasso Sea, would have to be unsinkable. Champagne sat back and laughed while the unsuspecting 'real' le Cour received an indignant volley from the publisher of the *Mercure*.

To crown all of this, Jean-Julien Champagne's huge and almost insatiable appetite for absinthe and Pernod finally killed him. The poor artist died in 1932, of gangrene, in his sixth-floor garret, his friend Eugène Canseliet having nursed him through his long, painful and particularly unpleasant illness. (Champagne's toes actually fell off before his death at the age of only 55.)

Only three years earlier, a second work by the mysterious Fulcanelli had been published. This appeared under the title *Les Demeures Philosophales* (The Dwellings of the Philosophers). It was issued in two volumes and was double the length of the first book. Like its predecessor, it interpreted particular architectural embellishments, such as ornate ceiling panels – this time, in 12th- to 15th-century mansions and châteaux – as encoded alchemical secret knowledge.

The appearance of this book inspired yet another theory about Fulcanelli's possible identity. Inside the rear cover of the second volume were the armorial bearings of Dom Robert Jollivet, a 13th-century abbot of Mont St-Michel, known to have dabbled in alchemy. This, according to one theory, implied that the name of Jollivet was intended to indicate that his modern near-namesake, F. Jolivet Castelot, was in fact Fulcanelli. Jolivet Castelot was President of the Alchemists' Society of France from around 1914 and also a prominent member of the *Ordre Kabbalistique de la Rose-Croix*. Between 1896 and 1935, he had published many studies in hermeticism, alchemy and spagyrics – the art of

Some believed that F. Jolivet Castelot, below, was in fact Fulcanelli. But he said he was a practising 'archimist' – someone who tries to use ordinary chemical methods to transmute base metals into gold – rather than an alchemist.

> **THE LEADING ALCHEMISTS IN CHINA DECIDED THAT THE PHILOSOPHER'S STONE WAS RED CINNABAR (MERCURIAL SULFIDE). ONE SAID THAT THIS, COMBINED WITH HONEY, AND TAKEN FOR A YEAR, WOULD RESTORE YOUTH AND ENABLE THE INDIVIDUAL TO FLY. TAKEN FOR MORE THAN A YEAR, IT WOULD CONFER IMMORTALITY.**
>
> **STAN GOOCH,**
> **CITIES OF DREAMS**

Could the inscription on Jean-Julien Champagne's gravestone, below, have been a last attempt to convince people that he was the mysterious alchemist?

making special concoctions using alchemical principles. But he made no secret of the fact that he was an 'archimist' rather than an alchemist – that is, a researcher who tries to effect transmutation by orthodox chemistry, rather than a more mystically inclined alchemist.

There was, however, an even stranger heraldic shield on the final page of the original edition of *Le Mystère des Cathedrales*. The occult scholar Robert Ambelain – who, in the 1930s, made one of the most thorough investigations into the Fulcanelli mystery – was the first to draw attention to this shield. Among many other alleged clues, Ambelain pointed out that the dog-Latin motto beneath the shield was *uber campa agna,* a phonetic approximation of Hubert Champagne. And, he claimed, Hubert was the middle name of the artist, Jean-Julien Champagne. He also noted that the pseudonym Fulcanelli is an anagram of *l'écu finale* (the final shield), indirectly indicating the heraldic device and its motto.

Eugène Canseliet, however, flatly and consistently denied the identification of Champagne as Fulcanelli – or of anyone else, for that matter. Furthermore, Hubert was not the artist's middle name, he claimed – although it is, by sheer coincidence, that of his own maternal grandfather. In any case, he further asserted, the damning shield was inserted into the first edition of the book by Champagne without the permission or knowledge of the Master Fulcanelli, or of himself – as another of his practical jokes.

DECEPTIONS AND FORGERIES

Canseliet, who claimed to be Fulcanelli's sole surviving pupil, similarly claimed that an inscription on Champagne's gravestone, along with a deliberate forgery of Fulcanelli's signature by the artist, were further attempts to deceive or mislead. The epitaph, at the cemetery of Arnouvilles-les-Gonesses, reads:

'Here rests Jean-Julien Champagne
Apostolicus Hermeticae Scientiae
1877-1932.'

Another alleged Fulcanelli signature, meanwhile, also appeared in a handwritten dedication of the original edition of *Le Mystère des Cathedrales*, which was given by Champagne to an occultist named Jules Boucher. It was signed A.H.S. Fulcanelli – the same initials as those of the Latin motto on the gravestone of Champagne at Arnouvilles-les-Gonesses. And, interestingly, in Jules Boucher's *Manual of Magic,* the author's dedication is to 'My Master Fulcanelli'.

Curiously enough, despite all his alleged evidence to the contrary, Ambelain reaches the conclusion that Champagne actually did achieve the Philosopher's Stone – the stone that transmutes base metals into gold and allows the manufacture of the Elixir of Life – some three years before his dreadful death.

But if Ambelain is correct, how could this explain Champagne's untimely death through over-indulgence in drink at the age of just 55?

And yet, more than one person has attested to Fulcanelli's success in transmutation, in his perfection of the 'Great Work', and his continued existence even into the 1990s – which would make him more than 140 years old!

IT WAS AN ELDERLY
'WITCH' AND HER
SECRET USE OF THE
MAGICAL PENTAGRAM THAT
FIRST INTRODUCED
PSYCHICAL RESEARCHER
TOM LETHBRIDGE TO THE
WORLD OF THE PARANORMAL

N o one who is interested in the paranormal can afford to ignore Tom Lethbridge. When he died in a nursing home in 1971, his name was hardly known to the general public. But today, many of his admirers believe that he is the single most important name in the history of psychical research. Indeed, his ideas on such subjects as dowsing, life after death, ghosts, poltergeists, magic, second-sight, precognition and the nature of time cover a wider field than those of any other psychical researcher. Moreover, they fit together into the most exciting and comprehensive theory of the 'occult' so far advanced.

Tom and Mina Lethbridge, below, were keen and accomplished dowsers.

It was at Ladram Bay, Devon, below, that Lethbridge first experienced the 'blanket of fear'.

These ideas were expressed in a series of small books published towards the end of his life. The odd thing is that Lethbridge took no interest in psychic matters until he retired to Devon, in southern Britain, in his mid-fifties. He had originally trained as an archaeologist and a historian, and spent most of his adult life in Cambridge as the Keeper of Anglo-Saxon Antiquities at the University Museum. But, even in that respectable setting, he was a maverick; and in 1957, he left Cambridge in disgust at the hostile reception given to one of his books on archaeology. Together with his wife, Mina, he then moved into Hole House, a Tudor mansion on the south coast of Devon. He meant to spend his retirement reading and digging for bits of broken pottery. But, in fact, the most amazing period of his eventful life was about to begin.

The person most responsible for this change of direction was an old 'witch' who lived next door. This white-haired little old lady had assured Lethbridge that she could put mild spells on people who annoyed her, and that she was able to leave her body at night and wander around the district – an ability known as 'astral projection'. Lethbridge was naturally sceptical – until something happened that finally convinced him.

The witch explained to him one day how she managed to put off unwanted visitors. What she did was to draw a five pointed star (known as a

POWER OF THE PENTAGRAM

pentagram) in her head, and then visualise it across the path of the unwanted visitor – for example, on the front gate.

Shortly afterwards, in the middle of the night, Lethbridge was lying in bed, idly drawing pentagrams in his head, and imagining them around his wife's bed, and his own, when Mina woke up with a creepy feeling that there was someone else in the room. At the foot of the bed, she could see a faint glow of light, which slowly faded as she watched it. The next day, the witch came to see them. When she told them that she had 'visited' their bedroom on the previous night, and found the beds surrounded by triangles of fire, Tom's scepticism began to evaporate; and Mina politely requested the old witch to stay out of their bedroom at night.

Three years later, the old lady died in peculiar circumstances. She had been quarrelling with a neighbouring farmer, and told Lethbridge that she intended to put a spell on the man's cattle. By this time, Lethbridge knew enough about the 'occult' to take her seriously. He warned her about the dangers of black magic, and that it could rebound on her. But the old lady ignored his advice. One morning, she was found dead in her bed – in circumstances that made the police suspect murder. The cattle of two nearby farms also suddenly developed foot and mouth disease. However, the farmer she had wanted to 'ill wish' remained unaffected. Lethbridge was convinced that the spell had gone wrong, and that it had somehow 'bounced back'.

THE INVISIBLE WORLD

The old lady's death also resulted – indirectly – in one of Lethbridge's most important insights. Passing the witch's cottage one day, he experienced a 'nasty feeling', a suffocating sense of depression. With a scientist's curiosity, he walked around the cottage, and noticed an interesting thing. He found he could step right into the depression and then out of it again, just as if it was some kind of invisible wall.

The depression reminded Lethbridge of something that had happened when he was a teenager. He and his mother had gone for a walk in the Great Wood near Wokingham. It was a lovely morning; yet, quite suddenly, both of them experienced 'a horrible feeling of gloom and depression, which crept upon us like a blanket of fog over the surface of the sea'. They hurried away, agreeing that it was something terrible and inexplicable. A few days later, the corpse of a suicide was found, hidden by some bushes, a few yards from the spot where they had been standing.

About a year after the death of the witch, another strange experience gave Lethbridge the clue he was looking for. On a damp January afternoon, he and Mina drove down to Ladram Bay. As Lethbridge stepped on to the beach, he once again experienced that feeling of gloom and fear, descending like a blanket of fog upon him. Mina wandered off along the beach, while Tom filled the sacks with seaweed. Suddenly, Mina came hurrying back, saying: 'Let's go! I can't stand this place a minute longer. There's something frightful here!'

The next day, they mentioned what had happened to Mina's brother. He said he also had experienced the same kind of thing in a field near

Hole Mill, above, was the home of Lethbridge's neighbour, a 'witch' or 'wise woman', whose strange powers convinced Lethbridge that the world of the paranormal was worth investigating. Hole House, a Tudor mansion next door, became the Lethbridges' home after Tom left Cambridge in disgust at the reception of one of his books.

Avebury, in Wiltshire. Mention of the word 'field' made something connect in Tom's brain. He remembered that field telephones often short-circuit in warm, muggy weather. 'What was the weather like?' he asked. 'Warm and damp,' said his brother-in-law.

Suddenly, an idea began to take shape. Water... could that be the key? It had been warm and damp in the Great Wood, and it had been warm and damp on Ladram beach.

The following weekend, they set out for Ladram Bay a second time. Again, as they stepped on to the beach, both walked into the same bank of depression – or 'ghoul', as Lethbridge called it. Mina led Tom to the far end of the beach, to the place where she had been sitting when overwhelmed by the strange feeling. It was now so strong that it made them both feel giddy. Lethbridge described it as the feeling you get when you have a high temperature and are full of drugs. On either side of them were two small streams.

Mina wandered off to look at the scenery from the top of the cliff. Suddenly, she walked into the depression again. Moreover, she had an odd feeling, as if someone – or something – was urging her to jump over. She went to fetch Tom, who agreed that the spot was just as sinister as the place down on the seashore below.

BALEFUL SHADOW

Nine years after Lethbridge's initial experience of depression on those cliffs, a man committed suicide there. Lethbridge now wondered whether the 'ghoul' was a feeling so intense that it had become timeless, imprinting itself on the area and casting its baleful shadow on anyone who stood there. Whether from the past or from the future, feelings of despair seemed to have been 'recorded' on the surroundings – but how?

The key, Lethbridge was now convinced, lay in water. As an archaeologist, he had always been mildly interested in dowsing and water-divining. The dowser walks along with a forked hazel twig held in his hands; and when he stands above running water, the muscles in his hands and arms convulse and the twig bends either up or down. As for the

Simply by visualising a pentagram, such as the one below, Lethbridge's neighbour believed she could ward off unwelcome visitors.

mechanism involved, Professor Y. Rocard of the Sorbonne, Paris, discovered that underground water produces changes in the earth's magnetic field, and that this is what the dowser's muscles respond to.

Significantly, magnetic fields are the means by which sound is recorded on tape covered with iron oxide. Suppose the magnetic field of running water can also record strong emotions – which, after all, are basically electrical activities in the human brain and body. Such fields could well be strongest in damp and muggy weather.

MAGNETIC EMOTIONS

This would also explain why the banks of depression experienced by Lethbridge seemed to form a kind of invisible wall. Anyone who has ever tried bringing a magnet closer and closer to an iron nail will know that the nail is suddenly 'seized' by the magnet as it enters the force field. Presumably, the magnetic field of water has the same property. And if it can 'tape record' powerful emotions, then you would feel them quite suddenly, as you stepped into the field. Both Tom and Mina had noticed that the 'ghoul' they experienced on Ladram beach came to an end quite abruptly

Lethbridge was also convinced that his electrical theory applied to ghosts. In 1922, when an undergraduate at Cambridge, he had seen a ghost in the rooms of a friend. He had been just about to leave, late at night, when the door opened and a man wearing a top hat came in. Assuming he was a college porter who had come to give his friend a message, Lethbridge said goodnight, and went out. The man did not reply.

The next morning, Lethbridge saw his friend, and asked casually about the identity of the man in the top hat. His friend flatly denied that anyone had come in. When Lethbridge brooded on it, he realised that the man had not in fact worn a porter's uniform, but hunting kit. So why had he not recognised the red coat at the time? Lethbridge then recalled that it had been grey – a dull grey, like a monochrome photograph. So it was that Lethbridge realised he had seen a ghost. Moreover, his friend's rooms overlooked the river, so there was a damp atmosphere.

Tom had also seen a ghost in the witch's garden, the year before she died. He had been sitting on the hillside, looking down at the witch's house, when he suddenly noticed two women who were

> **" ALTHOUGH HE [LETHBRIDGE] WAS INCLINED TO BELIEVE THAT GHOSTS ARE TAPE RECORDINGS, HE ALSO BELIEVED THAT THERE IS A REALM BEYOND DEATH THAT IS, TO SOME EXTENT, ACCESSIBLE TO LIVING CREATURES. "**
>
> **COLIN WILSON, MYSTERIES**

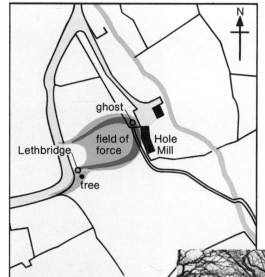

The map, left, shows the position of the ghost seen at Hole Mill in relation to the underground stream and its field of force. Lethbridge plotted the area 'blind' with his hazel twig. Later excavation showed him to be correct in every detail.

Lethbridge saw the ghost of an old lady and experienced a curious tingling sensation when he stood over an underground stream, at the spot shown right. He later discovered that the two experiences were connected.

The Reverend Bishop Leonidas Polk, below, intrigued Professor Joseph Buchanan in the 1840s by being able to detect brass in the dark, simply by touching it with his fingers.

in the yard. One was the witch; the other was a tall old lady dressed in rather old-fashioned grey clothes. Later, he saw the witch and asked her about her visitor. The witch looked puzzled. Then, when Lethbridge described the figure, she said: 'Ah, you've seen my ghost.'

This happened in 1959, before Lethbridge had his important insight on Ladram beach. So it never even entered his head that the ghost was a form of 'tape recording'. His first thought was that the old lady in grey might be some kind of thought-projection – in other words, a kind of 'television picture', caused by someone else thinking about the ghost, and somehow transferring the thought into his own mind. Then it struck him that ghosts are supposed to reappear on anniversaries. So he and Mina decided that they would go to the same spot, at the same time, the following year, to see if anything would happen.

They stood quietly at the same spot, on a fine, warm morning, but the old lady failed to reappear.

However, Lethbridge and his wife sensed a kind of electrical tingling in the atmosphere. There was a tiny underground stream running down the lane – under a drain cover – and they felt the tingling most strongly when standing on top of it. Lethbridge was only to realise the significance of that tingling feeling after his experience on Ladram beach. He then decided to explore the stream and see where it led. The result confirmed his suspicions. The stream turned at right angles quite close to the witch's house; and it was directly above this stream that he had seen the ghost of the old lady in grey. He had been connected to the spot, it seemed, by the magnetic field of the flowing water. But the witch, standing a few yards away from the underground stream, had seen nothing.

So Lethbridge had been quite mistaken to believe that his 'old lady' was some kind of 'television picture' projected by someone else's mind, or a ghost that would return exactly a year later. It was almost certainly just another 'recording', but in black and white, just like the huntsman he had seen in his friend's rooms at Cambridge.

It would be very satisfying to be able to add that Lethbridge decided to investigate the apparitions, and found that a huntsman had died of apoplexy in the room in Cambridge, or that the old lady had drowned in the underground stream. But no such neat, satisfactory solutions can be provided – and neither are they necessary. The huntsman had probably been a previous inhabitant of the rooms; and the old lady had probably lived most of her life in Hole Mill – the witch's house. (From her clothes, Lethbridge thought she dated back to before the First World War.) But there is no earthly reason why the 'force field' of water should record only unpleasant emotions. The old lady might have been unusually happy or excited when she was 'photographed'. Or perhaps she passed over the spot so often that her image finally became indelibly imprinted there.

How much evidence is there for the Lethbridge theory of ghosts? To begin with, it is worth noting that his 'tape recording' theory was by no means new. In America, in the 1840s, a professor named Joseph Rhodes Buchanan was intrigued when a

American professor Joseph Rhodes Buchanan believed that all substances – even a tree, such as that illustrated above – have a force field around them, on which human feelings can be recorded, to be 'played back' later.

In the mid-19th century, William Denton gave a piece of volcanic rock to a sensitive who immediately saw a volcano erupt, such as the one below. This was one of the first serious experiments into psychometry (or object-reading).

certain Bishop Polk told him that he could detect brass in the dark by touching it with his fingers, since it produced an unpleasant taste in his mouth. Buchanan tested him and found it was true. He discovered that certain of his students also had the same curious ability. In fact, some of them could even detect different substances when these were wrapped up in brown paper. Buchanan decided that the nerves produce some kind of force field – he called it the 'nerve aura' – which streams out of the finger ends, and which operates like an extra sense.

A STRANGE TALENT

What really puzzled him was that some of his sensitives could hold a sealed letter and describe the person who had written it, remarking upon whether the writer was sad or happy at the time. Buchanan explained this by suggesting that all substances give off emanations (or force fields) on which human emotions can be recorded.

Buchanan's friend, William Denton, a professor of geology, took the theory even further. He tried wrapping a piece of Hawaiian volcanic rock in paper and handing it to a sensitive, who immediately saw in his mind an island in the midst of blue seas, and an exploding volcano. When handed a pebble of glacial limestone, the sensitive saw it frozen in deep ice; and the fragment of a meteor produced a picture of the depths of space, with glittering stars. Denton was so excited by all this that he believed he had discovered a new – or forgotten – human faculty, and that one day we shall be able to look back into the past just as easily as we can now look at stars (which may have died millions of years ago) through a telescope.

Buchanan and Denton called this strange faculty *psychometry,* and for a few years it caused considerable excitement in the scientific world. Then, with the influence of Darwin, a more sceptical climate began to prevail, and it was forgotten. Even so, Sir Oliver Lodge, the notable scientist who dared to be interested in psychical research, wrote in 1908:

'Take, for example, a haunted house. . . wherein some one room is the scene of a ghostly representation of some long past tragedy. On a psychometric hypothesis, the original tragedy has been literally photographed on its material surroundings, nay, even on the ether itself, by reason of the intensity of emotion felt by those who enacted it.'

It may seem that Lethbridge's discovery was not so remarkable after all: but to believe this would be a mistake, for it was to prove only part of a far more comprehensive and important general theory of the paranormal.

> *I MUST STICK TO MY ORIGINAL*
> *THESIS THAT THE SUPERNATURAL*
> *WILL CONFORM TO NATURAL LAWS,*
> *EVEN IF WE DO NOT KNOW THE*
> *LAWS AS YET.*
> **T.C. LETHBRIDGE,**
> **GHOST AND GHOUL**

Large, dark and ugly, Borley Rectory seemed to invite haunting. And with the arrival of ghost-hunter Harry Price, it became a veritable hive of paranormal activity. But was someone perhaps helping things along?

Presented to The Rev. Henry Foyster Bull on his Marriage by the Choir and Organist of Borley Church. September 12. 1911.

Although it served as rectory to the 12th-century Borley Church, which stood amid ancient gravestones on the opposite side of the Sudbury road, the 'most haunted house in England' was only 76 years old when it burned to the ground in the winter of 1939. It was an ugly, two-storey building of red brick, its grounds dotted with tall trees that cast gloom on many of its 23 rooms. The rectory had been built in 1863 by the Reverend Henry D. E. Bull, who was both a local landowner and rector of Borley Church, to house his wife and 14 children.

The Reverend Harry Bull – seen posing with the choir of Borley Church, above – like his father before him, perpetuated the story of the haunting of the rectory by a nun.

The gloomy 23-room rectory is seen, below, in a photograph taken from the tower of the church.

Immediately behind and to one side of the house lay a farmyard bounded by a cottage, stabling and farm buildings. When an extra wing was added to the house in 1875, a small central courtyard resulted. The dining-room fireplace was carved with figures of monks, a decoration suggesting that the Reverend Bull may have believed a local legend that a 13th-century monastery had once occupied the spot. It was one of the monks from this monastery who gave rise to the first ghost story about the site. This monk was said to have eloped with a nun from

BORLEY: THE TENSION MOUNTS

a convent at Bures, some 8 miles (13 kilometres) away. But the couple were caught and executed, he being beheaded, while she was walled up in the convent. Their ghosts were said to haunt the area. But the roots of this tale were cut away in 1938 by a letter from the Essex Archaeological Society to Sidney Glanville, one of the most diligent and honest volunteer investigators for ghost-hunter and author Harry Price. It stated that neither the monastery nor the nunnery had ever existed.

However, there is evidence that both the Reverend Henry Bull and his son and successor as rector, the Reverend Harry Bull, enjoyed telling the story. Indeed, it gained currency particularly among Sunday school children, many of whom presumably grew up believing it – in view of its source – to be 'gospel' in every respect.

Before this first 'nun's tale' was replaced by a later version, reports grew that various members of the Bull family – notably two of the sisters, Millie and Ethel – had seen a shadowy figure in the long rectory garden moving across what then became known as the 'nun's walk'. This route followed the path of an underground stream, along which clouds of gnats were inclined to drift on warm summer evenings. The two sisters told Price that they had seen the nun in July 1900, adding only that it was 'evening' and 'sunlit' – so no one can be sure it was not in fact a formation of gnats. A later rector, the Reverend G. Eric Smith, told of being startled by a 'white figure' that turned out to be the smoke from a bonfire; while V. C. Wall, a *Daily Mirror* reporter, saw a similar apparition that proved to be the maid.

The Bull family lived at Borley Rectory in basic discomfort – without gas, electricity or mains water – for almost 65 years. When his father died in 1892, Harry took over as rector and continued to live in

Harry Bull dozed away his last years in the summer-house, above. He claimed that he saw the ghostly nun and other apparitions while he rested here.

At the spot below, the ghost of the nun was said to disappear after her walk around the rectory garden.

the house with his numerous siblings. At least three of the family remained in occupation until Harry's death in June 1927, but he moved across the road to Borley Place when he married in 1911, returning to the rectory in 1920, presumably after his wife's death.

CURIOUS ACOUSTICS

Despite the architectural gloom of their surroundings, the younger Bulls seem to have been a lively crowd, according to the testimony of friends and acquaintances who contacted researchers in the late 1940s and early 1950s. The house had curious acoustics that lent themselves to practical jokes. According to Major the Hon. Henry Douglas-Home of the Society for Psychical Research, footsteps in the courtyard at the rear of the house and voices in the adjoining cottage could clearly be heard in the rectory, along with noise made by the hand pump in the stable yard. These provided plenty of thumps and groans, he said. Another source told researchers that the young Bull sisters took a delight in telling maids that the house was 'haunted'; and one old servant mentioned that, after being primed in this way by Edith Bull, she had heard 'shuffling' noises outside her room.

As he grew older, Harry Bull added his own contributions to the village gossip. He appears to have had narcolepsy, a condition in which the sufferer is always drowsy, and took to sleeping for most of the day in a summer-house. After his snoozes, he claimed he had seen the nun, had heard the phantom coach in which she had eloped with the monk, and had spoken to an old family retainer named Amos, who had been dead for years. By 1927, when Bull died and the family finally left the rectory, it had become a 'haunted house' in local imagination, and this reputation was probably enhanced as the house lay empty and dilapidated for over a year.

In October 1928, the new rector of Borley arrived. The Reverend G. Eric Smith had spent his early married life in India; but when his wife fell seriously ill there, he decided to return home, take holy orders, and seek a living. Desperation may have been setting in when he accepted Borley, for he took it on trust. He and his wife were dismayed when they discovered the rectory's condition.

259

To add to their troubles, during the first winter, the Smiths soon heard that the house was 'haunted'. The 'ghosts' themselves did not trouble them, however. As Mrs Smith was to write in a letter to the *Church Times*, neither of them thought the house haunted by anything but 'rats and local superstition'.

Smith's main worry was that the more nervous of his parishioners were unwilling to come to the rectory for evening meetings. So when he failed to talk them out of their fears, he took what was perhaps the fatal step of writing to the editor of the *Daily Mirror* to ask for the address of a psychical research society. He hoped that trained investigators could solve the mystery in a rational way and allay the fears of the locals.

Instead, the editor sent reporter, V. C. Wall; and on Monday, 10 June 1929, he filed the first sensational newspaper account about Borley Rectory. His story talked of 'ghostly figures of headless coachmen and a nun, an old-time coach, drawn by two bay horses, which appears and vanishes mysteriously, and dragging footsteps in empty rooms...'

The spectral nun and the phantom coach, believed to haunt the site of Borley Rectory, are illustrated below. In some versions of the story, the drivers of the coach were beheaded, which accounts for the headless figures in this picture.

The figure, bottom, points out the place where the apparitional coach would vanish.

The *Mirror* editor also telephoned Price, who made his first visit two days later. With Price's arrival, 'objective phenomena' began for the first time. Almost as soon as he set foot on the premises, a flying stone smashed a window, an ornament shattered in the hallway, and showers of apports – pebbles, coins, a medal and a slate – rattled down the main stairs. The servants' bells jangled of their own accord, and keys flew out of their locks. During a seance held in the Blue Room – a bedroom overlooking the garden with its 'nun's walk' – rappings on a wall mirror, supposedly made by the late Harry Bull, were heard by Price and his secretary, Wall, the Smiths, and two of the Bull sisters who were visiting the house.

Price made several trips to the house during the weeks that followed, and during each visit experienced strange phenomena that were duly reported in the *Daily Mirror* by Wall.

The results were predictable: far from quelling his parishioners' fears, the Reverend Smith had not only unwittingly increased them but added another dimension to his catalogue of woes, for the district

> *AT BORLEY RECTORY, REPORTED PHENOMENA OVER A LONG PERIOD INCLUDED MATERIALIZATIONS OF THE NUN... BELL-RINGING, FOOTSTEPS, RAPS... DOOR-LOCKING AND UNLOCKING... FIRES AND SMOKE... A GLUEY SUBSTANCE, FACE-SLAPPING... THESE AND OTHER ACTIVITIES WERE REPORTED BY UPWARDS OF EIGHTY WITNESSES.*

PETER UNDERWOOD, EXORCISM!

became invaded by sightseers night and day. Coach parties were even organized by commercial companies and the Smiths soon found themselves virtually under siege. On 14 July, distressed by the ramshackle house and its unwelcome visitors, they moved to Long Melford; and Smith ran the parish from there before taking another living in Norfolk in April 1930.

Price must have been made uneasy on at least two occasions at Borley. One of these was when some coins and a Roman Catholic medallion, featuring St Ignatius Loyola, 'materialised' and fell to the ground at about the same time as some sugar lumps flew through the air. When they were picked up, they were, recalled Mrs Smith, strangely warm to the touch, as if from a human hand. Her maid, Mary Pearson, a known prankster, gave her the solution: 'That man threw that coin,' she explained, 'so I threw some sugar.' An even more farcical incident marked the second near-miss for Price during a further seance in the Blue Room. Heavy footsteps were heard outside, accompanied by the slow rumble of shutters being drawn back. In the doubtless stunned hush that followed, Price asked aloud if it were the spirit of the Reverend Harry Bull. A guttural voice, clearly recognizable as that of a local handyman, replied: 'He's dead, and you're daft.'

Rats, Mrs Smith later averred, lay behind the bell ringing – the bell wires ran along rafters under the roof. As for a mysterious light that 'appeared' in an upstairs window, it was well-known locally as a trick reflection of light from the railway carriages that passed along the valley.

For six months after the Smiths left Borley parish, the rectory was unoccupied once more. Then, on 16 October 1930, the Reverend Harry Bull's cousin, Lionel A. Foyster, moved in as the new rector. The Reverend Foyster, a man in his early fifties, had moved back home from his previous post as rector of Sackville, Nova Scotia, which he had held between 1928 and 1930. He suffered

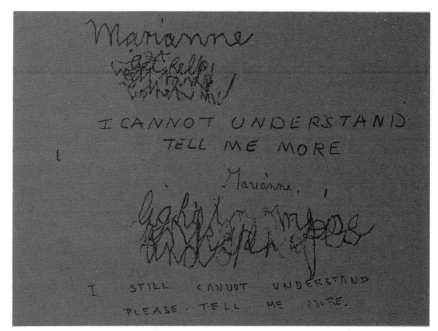

Paranormal phenomena increased when the Foysters came to live at Borley Rectory, and included the spirit writing, top.

Investigation of the Borley haunting is one of the most controversial aspects of the career of Harry Price, seen above in his laboratory.

All manner of apports – including coins and pebbles – arrived at the foot of the main stairs of the rectory, left, soon after Harry Price's arrival.

from rheumatism but, despite this painful illness, he was a kindly and well-liked man. He was also deeply devoted to his attractive wife Marianne, some 20 years his junior, and their adopted daughter Adelaide, a child of about two-and-a-half.

During the five years that the Foysters lived at Borley, an estimated 2,000 'incidents' occurred, most of them within a period of about 14 months. These included voices, footsteps, objects being thrown, apparitions and messages scribbled in pencil on walls. It is probably true to say that, with one possible exception, none of these could be attributed to Harry Price, who visited the rectory only once while the Foysters were there. The day after his visit, on 15 October 1931, he wrote one of the few straightforward statements he was ever to make on the Borley mystery in a letter to a colleague: 'Although psychologically, the case is of great value, psychically speaking there is nothing in it.'

Six months had elapsed since the Smiths' departure and the Foysters' arrival, and in that time Borley Rectory had become more dilapidated than ever. According to her husband's cousins, the Bulls, Mrs Foyster hated the place from the moment she saw it. She made no friends locally, and her only companion, apart from Lionel, was a family friend, François D'Arles, a French-Canadian who was much nearer her own age. He rented the cottage at the rear of the house, and investigators from the Society for Psychical Research got the impression that he dominated the household. By 1932, Marianne Foyster and D'Arles had opened a flower shop together in London and returned to Borley only at weekends, the implication being that they had become lovers. Mrs Foyster often behaved oddly, if not hysterically, fainting when frustrated. Once she flung herself on her knees before assembled investigators to pray to St Anthony for 'vindication' when no manifestations were forthcoming – as though she expected to be able to produce them. And when the 'hauntings' of Borley Rectory began again shortly after the Foysters' arrival, villagers went so far as to accuse Marianne Foyster – to her face – of being behind them.

THE MIRACLE MACHINE

A HUNGARIAN-BORN PHYSIOTHERAPIST LIVING IN BRITAIN INVENTED A SONIC HEALING MACHINE THAT HAS PRODUCED MIRACULOUS RESULTS ON PEOPLE, ANIMALS AND PLANTS

Stephen von Mehesz is a larger-than-life character with an insouciant air that seems to suggest surprise at his own achievements. Indeed, there is something almost puckish about him, although von Mehesz is far too earthy and practical a person to be called a mystic. Yet he undoubtedly has talents that can be classed as paranormal, and has invented a healing machine that baffles scientists.

Born in Hungary in 1912, Stephen von Mehesz witnessed quite early in life the healing gifts of his mother and may have inherited them. He once watched her heal a sick bird. Later, when his own pet bantam broke a wing, he dealt with it in similar fashion. He cosseted the bird in his bedroom, and the damaged wing healed quite quickly. This talent for healing remained with him into adult life. Once, for instance, some children brought an inert hamster to him, saying it was dead. 'Instinctively,' he said, 'I picked up the animal and touched its ear.' Immediately, the animal came to life and promptly ran away. 'How could I explain the situation to small children?' he asked. 'The centre of balance is in the ear, and I think the animal's reaction had something to do with this.' The hamster had completely recovered from whatever had ailed it.

In 1944, with the Soviet invasion of Hungary imminent, von Mehesz fled from Budapest and eventually managed to reach Britain. After staying for a short time with the famous film-maker Sir Alexander Korda, a family friend, he tried to join the British Army. Despite the fact that he was a highly skilled and experienced intelligence officer, he was turned down. Instead, the British Ministry of Labour directed him to work as a stoker at the Dorchester Gas Works.

After a spell there, he changed his job and became a bus conductor; but a lengthy chat one day with one of his passengers – she was a hospital matron – encouraged him to embark on the study of physiotherapy and osteopathy. He subsequently qualified as a physiotherapist, and went on to practise as such from his home in Dorchester in the south of England.

Stephen von Mehesz, above, invented a sonic healing box that has apparently treated cases of migraine, broken limbs, muscle injury and arthritis with amazing success.

The portable model of von Mehesz's machine, left, is small enough to fit into a briefcase. It runs off batteries, making it easy to use at the farms and stables where von Mehesz treated numerous animal patients.

Throughout his professional career, von Mehesz – now retired – tried to apply to this work his own distilled wisdom, which includes elements of Hungarian gypsy folklore, a smattering of acupuncture learned from a Chinese and, perhaps most important, a feeling that he had a mission to heal people. As von Mehesz himself put it: 'I also wanted to prove to the Home Office, that when they gave me British citizenship, I could do something for my new countrymen in return.'

What he did was to develop the von Mehesz sonic bleep machine, the result of many years of experiment. The original prototype measured about 2 feet (60 centimetres) square by 1 foot (30 centimetres) high, and looks rather like a piece of hi-fi equipment at first glance. It incorporates a cathode-ray oscilloscope, and runs from the electricity supply. The later, commercial model is smaller and portable: it fits into a briefcase and is battery powered. Von Mehesz says of his invention:

'My machine is based on the theory of using sonic energy to cure. It took me 12 years to perfect the theory and the machine, which exemplifies a completely new law of physics based on sound. Electricity is used to power sonic beams of varying strengths, and these are directed to vital parts of the body by carefully placed pads. The basic

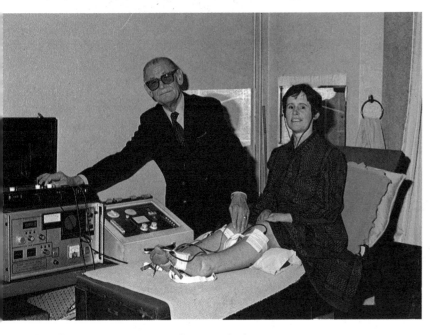

Von Mehesz used his prototype machine, below, to treat a client for migraine. In directing the sonic energy to the legs and feet, he used, he said, a form of reflex therapy.

principles of the machine can be easily grasped... It has succeeded beyond even my wildest dreams.'

Although the astonishing performance of the machine is something that even its inventor cannot easily explain, it is thought that the special frequency used produces sound waves that agitate living cells to such an extent that they shed any toxic substances they contain. However, there may also be some human element involved. As von Mehesz himself has suggested: 'Sometimes I wonder whether it is a question of the machine plus myself doing the trick... whether some healing talent of my own comes into it.'

During treatment for an arthritic hip condition, for instance, two wet pads are strapped across the hip. Clips are attached to the pads and linked up to the machine, which is then switched on. There is nothing dangerous about the treatment, nor is it unpleasant. The sensation experienced is rather like a mechanical crab moving its claws over the body.

After about 20 minutes of such treatment, a patient reported that all pain had gone, and that he felt very fit and able to walk with ease. The feeling of well-being lasted two to three days.

The machine has also been successful in treating rheumatism, rheumatoid and osteo-arthritis, fibrositis, sciatica, fractures, dermatitis, lumbago

and migraine. One sufferer from multiple sclerosis, who contracted the illness when he was 25, writes: 'Doctors have pointed out that there is nothing constructive they can do, as there is no known method of alleviating the symptoms. After four visits [to von Mehesz], I noticed that the coldness in the legs gradually disappeared, and for the first time in three years I was able to run on the spot, denoting a definite increase in mobility.'

ENERGETIC PLANTS

The 'miracle box' has also achieved wonders for crops. Indeed, subjecting seeds to the treatment has a remarkable energizing effect. The seeds are placed in a muslin bag and immersed in water; and metal plates in the water connected to the machine transmit sound waves through the water and 'irradiate' the seeds. A Batcombe farmer, Edward Vardy, had his barley seed treated by the machine before planting; and the resulting bumper crop showed a 150 per cent increase compared with untreated seed. It was also completely free from disease.

Outsize tomato plants have also been grown from seeds treated, soaring to the roof in von Mehesz's greenhouse. And an experimental plot of sugar beet, grown from treated seed, was sensationally successful.

Some of von Mehesz's most amazing results have been achieved with animals. His machine is even said to have saved the life of a severely injured fox-hound and a broken-down racehorse.

Richard Mitchell, who runs a training stables in Dorset, was sent a four-year-old named *Northern Eclipse* from Yorkshire in December 1981. The horse was in such a bad state that it could not even trot. One of its hind legs would not bend at all.

For four months, Stephen von Mehesz took his machine out to the stables once a week to treat the sick animal. At the end of this time, the horse had not only recovered but was able to race again.

Examples of outsize sugar beet, grown from seed treated by sonic energy, are held up for inspection by von Mehesz and a farmer client, right.

Later, he raced at Salisbury and in Belgium, where he actually won.

The machine also cured Mitchell's wife of the persistent migraine from which she had suffered for several years.

But von Mehesz's most impressive success story must be the case of Bowman, a 10 month-old fox-hound that had been seriously injured when it was kicked and battered by a cow. X-rays showed a fracture of the spine and dislocation of the last lumbar vertebra. The veterinary surgeon found the injuries so appalling that he suggested the animal should be put down.

As a last resort, it was decided that the animal should be taken to the Mitchell stables for treatment on the von Mehesz machine. 'When I first saw the animal,' von Mehesz said, 'it had lost all control of bowel and bladder, it was emaciated, and the two paralysed legs were just skin and bone... If the hound had been a human specimen, his ailment would have been called paraplegia and only a neurosurgeon could have done anything for him. Even so, in only two cases out of 100 is the operation partially successful.'

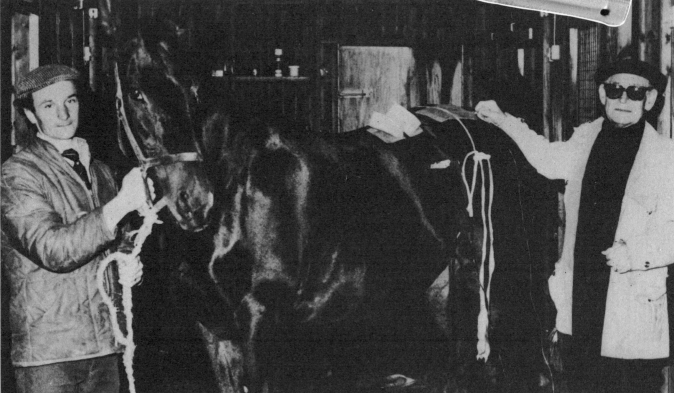

Amazingly, after five weeks' treatment, Bowman was almost back to normal. He started to put on weight, began chasing other dogs, and his bowel and bladder control returned. 'Soon', said von Mehesz, 'he was exercising with the horses, and running around the farm.'

Tests with the machine were carried out at Cardiff University and at the Royal Infirmary and University at Hull in connection with the treatment of fractures and neurological ailments. Experiments were also conducted at a stud farm in Yorkshire, where yearlings responded with an all-round improvement in growth and physique after being

The photograph, top, shows heads of barley grown together in the same field. The topmost head, from seed treated by von Mehesz, was healthy, while the rest succumbed to a fungus infection.

The broken-down racehorse Northern Eclipse, above, was treated by von Mehesz in the stables of Richard Mitchell, seen on the left.

'wired up'. The Irish Sugar Beet Corporation, meanwhile, expressed interest in the machine's effect on plant growth and health. Many scientists have been impressed by the performance of the machine; but since they cannot account for it in scientific terms, reserve judgement. It may be that von Mehesz's talent for healing worked along with his invention; but others have also operated the machine with apparent success. Von Mehesz is a forceful personality who admits to having a gift for hypnotism; so possibly the effects of his machine are helped by auto-suggestion. But whatever the explanation, his 'miracle box' has helped many friends and clients.

THE SCIENCE OF SOLECTRICS

EARLY THIS CENTURY, A BRITISH SEA CAPTAIN INVENTED A METHOD OF PREDICTING DISASTERS, SUCH AS EARTHQUAKES AND STORMS. HOW SUCCESSFUL WAS HIS SO-CALLED THEORY OF 'SOLECTRICS'?

In the Chilean city of Valparaiso on the evening of 16 August 1906, there was a dreadful tension in the air. The naval garrison was on alert. Its commander, Captain Gomez Carreño, had made preparations for a state of emergency. He now waited impatiently as dusk fell. Would what was widely expected come to pass?

The cause of his agitation was a warning published by the Meteorological Office – a warning not of bad weather but of an earthquake. The source of this prophecy was an English seaman, Captain Cooper of the Pacific Steam Navigation Company (PSNC). He had made his prediction of this natural disaster as the result of a complicated calculation involving the positions of the Sun, Moon and planets relative to the Earth.

One of the city's British residents telephoned friends at 8 o'clock that night, jokingly reminding them that an earthquake was due. He had only just made the call when the first tremor struck the city.

Elsewhere in the city, another British family fled from their dinner table. The last person to take his place had remarked in jocular vein that, in a few minutes, it would be time for 'Cooper's earthquake'.

It was a calm night, with light rain, when the city began to shake. In the harbour, Captain T. M. Taylor of the PSNC rushed on to the deck of the *Orissa*, remembering the prediction. As he recalled:

Scenes of desolation and looting in the Chilean city of Valparaiso after the earthquake of 16 August 1906 are shown below and inset right. The disaster had been predicted by Captain Alfred Cooper of the Pacific Steam Navigation Company, using a theory of his own invention – solectrics, involving analysis of what was believed to be a 'solar electric' force.

'The 100-ton crane at the end of the mole [jetty] came tumbling down, and all the chains of the other cranes were rattling, and we could hear the people on shore wailing, and the noise of the buildings tumbling down. I said to Mr Gowans, who had come to see me about getting steam: "We are the only people left alive in the world." Five minutes afterwards, the city was in darkness. I could see electric flashes, all along the face of the hill just like serpents, and directly the place was in a blaze, and lit the bay up just as if it were daylight.'

Captain Carreño took prompt action. Looters were rounded up and executed in the public square. 'Before order was assured, 680 persons paid the death penalty,' reported *The Times* of London.

It was later estimated that 10,000 people died and £20 million worth of damage was caused by that cataclysm. The main shock of the earthquake, which was unprecedented in the city's memory, lasted 4 minutes and 50 seconds. The people of Valparaiso were to pay special attention to the opinions of Captain Cooper thereafter.

Alfred J. Cooper, son of a Sunderland solicitor, had taken up his first command, the PSNC's steamer *Valdivia,* in 1877, at the age of 30. He was a fine navigator and a man of intellect. He patented a sounding device, and wrote an unorthodox book on the stability of ships. The former was widely adopted; but the precepts of the latter were not. He was a stern autocrat, an abstainer from drink and tobacco, a polemicist and a moralist.

One subject was the object of his burning passion. He somewhat understated this when he wrote:

'Having suffered shipwreck, occasioned by storms, three times on three consecutive voyages, I naturally acquired an interest in the questions as to why storms happen on the Earth, and where they come from...'

He hit on an explanation that promised to solve the mystery:

'On the west coast of South America, I was frequently disappointed by the non-arrival of a calculated storm, until it became apparent that, on these occasions, an earthquake took the place of an absent storm.'

The full theory was expounded in the book he wrote in his retirement, entitled *Solectrics,* with an ambitious subtitle: *A theory explaining the causes of tempests, seismic and volcanic disturbances and other natural phenomena.* It was a wide-ranging compendium of meteorological and seismological reports, astronomical charts and polemics against adversaries. The theory was guaranteed to provoke the scorn of every scientist who encountered it – and yet it earned the approbation of numerous practical seamen.

ILL-OMENED PATTERNS

Captain Cooper believed in the existence of a 'solectric' (solar electric) force, streaming between the Sun, Moon, Earth and all the other planets and satellites of the solar system. This force, he believed, was constantly entering the Earth and accumulating in various regions precisely determined by the positions of the heavenly bodies. When these positions were unfavourable, a solectric force would accumulate in great strength at certain places, and would strive to break loose, especially from the peaks of hills and mountains. If it did so, some form of natural disaster was likely to occur. If the moment passed without such a catastrophe, however, that region was safe until the heavenly bodies should again group themselves into some ill-omened pattern. The times at which a particular place was threatened could be precisely calculated, Cooper held, though it was a laborious task.

On 2 August 1906, Captain Cooper, in charge of the *Oriana,* anchored in Valparaiso Bay. He was greeted by two Chilean officers who were interested in his theory. They told him that, with its aid,

they had predicted a severe storm two weeks hence; but Cooper calculated that the situation would become worse than that – indeed, he predicted that there would be a storm and an earthquake to boot. Accordingly, he urged them to inform the press and shipping, and that was how Valparaiso received its warning.

That year, Captain Cooper retired, and began to work more energetically on his theories. Six years later, he discovered that misfortune was again on its way to Valparaiso. He wrote to the British Consul in the city with predictions of unseasonable bad weather on three days during September, and of an earthquake on 29 September:

'I am sorry not to feel justified in predicting definitely, because I can but spell out the messages of the heavenly bodies, and am unable yet to read them at sight. In this case, we have various powerful combinations and I am anxious to know their effects, if any.

'Personally, if I were in Valparaiso during the night of September 29th, I should be on the alert for signs of Earth unrest and displays of natural forces... '

In his comments on the accompanying astronomical charts, he was more emphatic. For 29 September, he wrote:

'Volcanic action is indicated. Earthquakes and storm are probable. Between the hours of 2 a.m. and 5 a.m. on September 30th, caution is necessary and a study of the weather. If animals are uneasy and rain sets in, walk outside between 2 and 5 a.m., after that there is safety.'

The Consul thought it his duty to publish this letter, and speculation and alarm mounted in Valparaiso as a result. The Director of the Seismological Office was moved to write a crushing rejoinder to the presumptuous seaman. But he could not attack the theory directly for, as he himself admitted, he did not understand the calculations involved. He therefore made do with describing the inglorious history of seismic prophecies, named some followers of Captain Cooper who had abandoned his theories, and then dwelt on his own refutation of a completely different theory linking earthquakes directly to the phases of the Moon. He ended his rejoinder:

'As for me, I shall be very calm on the 18th and 30th of September, thinking that only God knows whether an earthquake threatens or not, and I declare myself to be totally ignorant in this regard. Even should Captain Cooper's prophecy come to pass, I would not believe his theory. I am in good company – the company of all seismologists.'

Captain Cooper, however, would have regarded that as singularly poor company to be keeping. And such reproofs from the learned only deepened his lifelong scorn for official experts and 'pretentious professors'.

As each date for which Captain Cooper had made predictions came and went, his meteorological predictions were confirmed. Indeed, the weather was the worst in living memory for the southern springtime, and the inhabitants of towns in the area at which he had pointed his warning finger became increasingly agitated. As Cooper wrote:

Captain Alfred Jopling Cooper, above, was the inventor of the theory of solectrics, which – according to the inscription on his gravestone, left – enables us to understand the forces that cause many natural disasters. A practical seaman, Cooper also turned his capable mind to many inventions, such as the depth sounder, far left.

The false colour satellite image of Hurricane Alicia, right, was taken with an infra-red scanner on 17 August 1983. It was meteorological phenomena such as this that Cooper believed he could foretell by means of solectrics.

'At the instance, no doubt, of the non-intelligent section of authority, the President of Chile cabled to the Foreign Office in London, and I was twice hunted up by police – so that I might use means to turn off the predicted earthquake!'

Many citizens remained calm, however. These included traders, who published advertisements advising their customers to stock up in preparation for the coming disaster. In Valparaiso, the Hotel Monte Mar announced in an English-language advertisement that it would remain open all night to allow guests to watch the destruction of the city to the accompaniment of a hot supper and the sounds of an orchestra. But British residents dissociated themselves from such tasteless levity.

APPROACHING PANIC

During September, Captain Cooper became 'the best abused man in the world, and certainly the most grossly misunderstood man in Chile'. By the night of 29 September, the town-dwellers of central Chile had been 'reduced to a state approaching panic', according to *The Times*. Many left the towns, while others spent the night in tents: one such was the President himself. Military bands played to soothe the anxious citizens.

At 2 a.m., rain began to fall in Valparaiso, and a low moan escaped from the crowd. The downpour lasted all through the night. But there was no earthquake. Almost on the stroke of 5 a.m., the crowds, as if reprieved, hurried for their homes.

But during that night, there were more than a dozen tremors in the surrounding areas; and a strong earthquake took place beneath the ocean, throwing up three new islands.

Some Chileans were incensed at Captain Cooper; but many more were inclined to give him credit for his predictions of the unprecedented bad weather. Cooper, meanwhile, regarded himself as fully vindicated and pressed on with his work.

The outbreak of the First World War afforded Cooper fresh subject matter. In its early days, he wrote to the Admiralty with the advice that special precautions should be taken against a storm

Alfred Cooper Rollinson, Captain Cooper's great-nephew, right, continued to test the theory of solectrics by analyzing planetary positions at the time of earthquakes.

threatening in the North Sea towards the end of September. For some reason this prompted the attentions of the Special Branch, and Captain Cooper found a pair of plain-clothes detectives looking around his garden one day, searching for a secret radio transmitter and expressing great interest in his solectric theory. On 30 September 1914, what was described as 'the heaviest gale in living memory' swept over the North Sea.

The Captain soon discovered that his theory could explain more and more phenomena – exploding warships, for instance; and the pages of *Solectrics* are replete with cases of ill-fated ships that he showed – after the fact, unfortunately – to have been at the focus of malign solectric activity at the moment they blew up.

But among these cases there is one remarkable piece of detective work not attributable to

The illustration, below, shows our Sun and its planets (from left to right: Mercury, Venus, Earth, Mars, Jupiter, Saturn, Uranus, Neptune and Pluto). Cooper believed that a solar electric force streamed within the solar system and accumulated in various regions on Earth according to the positions of the heavenly bodies.

The letter was delayed, only reaching *El Mercurio* of Valparaiso on the evening of 3 December. The tremors were slightly late, too – striking at 3.15 and 7.40 the following morning. The shocks were not severe in Valparaiso, but the city of Copiapó was completely destroyed by a shock at 7.50 a.m. So, too, was the town of Vallenar. *El Mercurio* was impressed by the nearly simultaneous arrivals of the prophecy and its fulfilment, and Captain Cooper's reputation was confirmed.

In England, Captain Cooper's young great-nephew, Alfred Cooper Rollinson, waited expectantly for newspaper reports of events in Chile on 3 and 4 December. When they finally came, he turned to his father and told him triumphantly: 'There is uncle's earthquake!'

Young Alfred was among the mourners at his great-uncle's grave five years later. All his life, he was to be fascinated by the intricate calculations and grandiose sweep of Captain Cooper's theory; and when major earthquakes occurred, he would try his hand at drawing diagrams for them in the manner expounded by Captain Cooper in his book. After

hindsight. On 30 December 1915, the armoured cruiser *Natal* blew up and sank in harbour. Captain Cooper resolved to determine the cause 'because the idea of treachery in our midst begets nervous anxiety and a desire for cruel reprisal'.

It was a difficult problem, for the position and exact time of the disaster were kept secret. A British warship could have been in any one of countless harbours around the world at that time. After two days' work, Captain Cooper decided that the ship must have been in a Scottish port, Cromarty Bay, and he calculated two times at which astronomical combinations gave rise to solectric forces sufficient to cause gases from defective ammunition to explode.

IMPRESSIVE FEAT

In 1917, when he published these conclusions in the second edition of his book *Solectrics*, the facts of the *Natal*'s loss were still secret. It was only later that he heard from eye-witnesses that the explosion had indeed occurred in Cromarty Bay. The time of the explosion, however, was between the times that he had predicted. Nevertheless, to cite its location was an impressive feat.

Explosions in mines, explosions in ammunition dumps – Captain Cooper scrutinised all these, and time and again found a solectric cause for them. He also analyzed heat waves and cold spells, and found the interactions of the celestial bodies responsible. A number of riots, or 'brain storms', in lunatic asylums were analyzed solectrically, with the usual success, too.

On 10 October 1918, Captain Cooper sent another of his doleful predictions to Chile. He stated that on 3 December, from about midday until about an hour past midnight, there would be signs of natural disturbances – bad weather and perhaps volcanic tremors. The centre of the astronomical 'combination' would be near Valparaiso. He asked that a 'slight warning' be published.

The armoured cruiser Natal, top, *blew up on 30 December 1915. Captain Cooper determined to find out the cause. Within two days, his solectric theory had revealed the site of the explosion, which had been kept secret by the government – remote Cromarty Bay on the Moray Firth in the north of Scotland,* above. *He was less accurate about the time of the explosion, however: his theory yielded a choice of two possible times – and the actual hour of the disaster, as later revealed, was between them.*

his retirement from a lifetime's career in banking, he was able to give more time to the theory, and tried to attract the attention of the scientific world.

But the time required for a definitive test of the theory was not available to Cooper Rollinson. Labouring over the large charts, and covering them with the same tidy copperplate script with which he had once filled bank ledgers, he was painfully aware that it would take him years to do what a modern computer could do in days.

One day, he wrote to *The Unexplained*, which had announced that it was interested in prophecies and premonitions of all kinds. One of the publication's advisers, Professor Archie Roy of the University of Glasgow, was contacted; and through his good offices, one of his colleagues in the Department of Astronomy, Dr Ian Walker, agreed to put a computer to work in order to settle once and for all the question of the value of solectrics. Once again, the scientific world was paying attention to the ideas of Captain Cooper, as we shall see in a forthcoming feature.

Joanna Southcott, left, made the amazing claim – in late middle age – that she was pregnant with 'the Lamb' (or Messiah). Presumably, she had astonishing charisma in order to persuade several thousands of followers that she was, indeed, a channel for divine revelation.

KNOWN FOR A WHOLE RANGE OF BIZARRE BELIEFS, THE 19TH-CENTURY DEVON PROPHET JOANNA SOUTHCOTT STILL HAS A SMALL, BUT FERVENT, FOLLOWING

JOANNA SOUTHCOTT – NOTORIOUS PROPHET

While Joanna Southcott's milder critics called her an 'enthusiast', her enemies referred to her as a 'fanatic'. Her family, however, simply thought her mad. It is hardly surprising: neither she nor her principal disciples ever achieved anything they promised to do. Yet such was the personality of the former Devon milkmaid that, when she claimed to be pregnant with the 'new Messiah' in 1814, the cream of London society showered her with expensive gifts. And nearly 50 years after her death, with her prophecy of the coming of the 'second Jesus Christ' unfulfilled, one of her more extreme disciples was still able to build a mansion costing £10,000 from the offerings of 'Southcottians' in Melbourne, Australia, alone – subscriptions that would have been worth about £1 million today. Even nowadays, around the world, small but active groups of followers continue to await the opening of her enigmatic sealed box. This, they believe, contains the secret of world peace, happiness, and the millennium, as foretold in the *Book of Revelation*.

Joanna Southcott, the unlikely centre of all this spiritual speculation, was born in the hamlet of Gittisham, Devon, and baptised in the parish church of Ottery St Mary on 6 June 1750. Her father,

The cartoon, below, dating from 1814, is entitled Joanna Southcott, the prophetess, excommunicating the bishops. *Southcott is depicted as the archetypal man-hater, uttering the line: 'I put no more trust in bishops than men.' She believed all normal, sexual, or even romantic associations beneath her; only God was good enough to make her pregnant.*

I will Dust their Woolsacks and make in drunk in my fury. I will bring down i Strength to the earth.

Lay it on hip and thigh Brave Tonzar while the unbelievers. I put no more trust in Bishops as men. than I do in their Chariots and Horses but my trust is the Lord of Hosts

ETESS EXCOMMUNICATING THE BISHOPS. having already cutt off Four Bishops for refusing to hear her Visitation.

William, was a small tenant farmer of moderate religious beliefs; and her mother, who died when Joanna was a small girl, was a devout Wesleyan. Both mother and daughter were, according to William Southcott, 'too religious by far'.

Despite Joanna's fanatical church-going, her early years were normal enough. While tending her father's cattle, she even had a passionate love affair with Noah Bishop, a neighbouring farmer's son and friend of her brother Joseph, who helped the couple to keep their liaison secret.

GROWING MAD

At the age of 20, she moved to Honiton, Devon, to work as a shop girl, rejecting several suitors as beneath her – although some, at least, were property owners. By now, she was already developing the obsession that her body was too good for mortal men, referring to herself as the 'temple of Shiloh', the legendary sanctuary of the Ark of the Covenant. She also caused a minor domestic scandal when employed as a maid in a country house, claiming that a footman had molested her. But the footman denied the charge, telling his employer – who believed him – that Joanna was 'growing mad'.

Whatever the truth of the matter, the footman's claim seemed to have some foundation, for Joanna wrote later that 'divine command' had brought about her dismissal so that she could move to the county town of Exeter, where she was to work as a shop girl in an upholstering establishment for the next 20 years. Her employer later testified that, during this time, her 'character was blameless and her service faithful'. For, all these years, she shunned the society of men and spent most of her spare time at church and chapel.

Every Sunday, she went to communion twice, attending an early service in her parish church and a later morning service at the cathedral, while spending the afternoons and evenings at the local Wesleyan chapel.

At Christmas 1791, she became a full member of the Wesleyan congregation. It was to be a short and unhappy association. On Easter Monday 1792, the 42-year-old convert interrupted the Bible class. She had, she announced, been 'sent by God to Exeter' 20 years before to reveal to the world that she was 'the Lamb's wife' and would henceforth be his earthly representative.

'The announcement was not well received,' according to a contemporary account. 'There was uproar and cries of "shame" and "blasphemy" in the room, while Joanna fell into a fever and fits.'

Sympathetic members of the congregation carried the writhing figure across country to the home of her sister, Mrs Carter, at Plympton. For 10 days, Joanna lay in delirium – or, as she later described it, 'struggling with the powers of darkness'. Then she awoke and began writing 'prophecies' in rambling prose and doggerel rhyme.

There was never anything profound about the prophecies of Joanna Southcott – except perhaps her final foretelling of the impending 'birth of the second Christ'. Her 'prophecies' were either vague generalities concerning famine, war and pestilence at some time in the future, or particular omens and warnings that might or might not have meaning for an individual.

ENIGMAS

Joanna Southcott spent much of her free time in devotional studies at Exeter Cathedral, right. Indeed, she was to announce to the local Wesleyan congregation that she had been 'sent by God to Exeter' to reveal to the world that she was to be 'the Lamb's wife'. When the cries of 'shame' and 'blasphemy' became unbearable, she promptly had convulsions.

Certainly, the majority of her specific prophecies failed to materialise. One of the first examples was that the quality of the harvest for 1792 would be 'so bad that the best wheat would not fetch four shillings and sixpence a bushel'.

When her sister, Mrs Carter, read this in her farmhouse, surrounded by the nicely ripening corn, she wrote to their father echoing the opinion of the footman all those years previously: 'Joanna,' she said, 'is growing out of her senses.'

SEALED PROPHECIES

In fact, Joanna was only just getting into her stride. In her days as a shop girl, she had been sweeping up one day when she found a small oval seal bearing the initials 'I.C.' with two small stars. She decided that this was divinely sent – 'I.C.' meaning 'Iesus Christus' – and, with it, she began to seal up bundles of her prophecies to be opened at a future time as a test of her abilities. She wrote to every clergyman in Devon, from bishops to curates, demanding recognition. Then, in 1798, she moved to Bristol where, two years later, she published a booklet, *The Strange Effects of Faith*, inviting 'any twelve ministers' to try her claims. It was an unimpressive document at first sight – the printer's bill included the item: 'For correcting the spelling and grammar of the prophecies, 2/6d.'

By a strange chance, the Southcott publication coincided with the incarceration in the lunatic asylum at Islington, North London, of another 'prophet', Richard Brothers, a former naval lieutenant whose own lurid claims had attracted the attentions of King George III himself. Discharged on half pay after completing 13 years' meritorious service, Brothers had decided that the loyal oath required for him to continue collecting his pay was blasphemous, and wrote to the King, Speaker, and Members of the House of Commons in 1791, demanding that he be proclaimed by the House 'the nephew of the Almighty'. In his letter, he forecast – accurately – the forthcoming violent deaths of the King of Sweden, Gustavus III, and Louis XVI of France, as a result of which his book, *A Revealed*

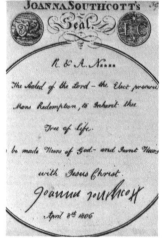

The design of Joanna's 'seal', copied from one she had found in the shop where she had worked as a young girl, is shown above. She took the initials 'I.C.' to stand for 'Iesus Christus'.

Richard Brothers, above right, was the self-appointed 'Prince of Hebrews and Ruler of the World'. King George III was so annoyed by Brothers' ravings that he had him put away in an asylum. Yet such was the general willingness to believe in anything prophetic that Brothers' cause actually helped further that of Joanna Southcott.

RICHARD BROTHERS
PRINCE OF THE HEBREWS

Knowledge of Prophecies and Times, published in 1794, enjoyed brisk sales. But one of its 'prophecies' claimed that, on 19 November 1795, he would be 'revealed as Prince of Hebrews and Ruler of the World'. This so upset King George – himself the victim of bouts of insanity – that, on 4 March 1795 Brothers was arrested by two King's Messengers on a royal warrant issued by the Duke of Portland. After being examined by the Privy Council, he was thrown into Islington asylum.

Despite such manifest eccentricities, Brothers had attracted a considerable number of converts one of them William Sharp, a well-to-do engraver who had made sufficient money to build a house in Chiswick from the proceeds of such best-selling pictures as *Hector, The Old Tower Lion*, a portrait of John Hunter the pioneering surgeon, and copper plate versions of paintings by Reynolds and Gainsborough. Just before Brothers' arrest, Sharp had published a portrait of him as the 'Prince of

William Sharp, left, a wealthy engraver, did much to publicise the prophecies of Richard Brothers. After Brothers had been incarcerated in an asylum in North London, Sharp became one of Joanna Southcott's most devoted disciples – one of the inner circle, referred to as her 'Seven Stars'.

Hebrews', with rays of heavenly light radiating from his head. The portrait was dedicated to Brothers from 'a true and devout believer'.

All his life, Sharp seemed to need to believe in philosophical and religious novelties. He had been a friend and admirer of Tom Paine, author of *The Rights of Man,* before being converted to the ideas of Mesmer and Swedenborg, and finally to those of Lieutenant Brothers. Now, with Brothers safely locked away, Sharp read Joanna Southcott's booklet and became interested in the new 'prophetess'.

In January 1802, Sharp – accompanied by three respectable Church of England rectors (Stanhope Bruce of Inglesham, Wiltshire, Thomas Foley of Old Swinford, Worcestershire, and Thomas Webster of Oakington, Cambridgeshire) and three other gentlemen – visited Joanna and held what was to become known as the 'First Trial' of her sealed writings at the Guildhall, Exeter. When the seals were broken,

each man found something in the writings that seemed to have a profound bearing on himself; and at the end of the session, all acclaimed Southcott as a 'true prophet'. For her part, she welcomed them as her 'Seven Stars'.

Public recognition by seven such respectable figures helped the Southcott cause immensely; and at Sharp's suggestion, she moved to London. In May 1802, she settled into High House, Paddington, and received growing audiences, many of whom came to mock but remained to pray. Perhaps her popularity lay in the scarcity of female prophets, plus her own undoubted personal magnetism. But apart from an emphasis on universal brotherly love, there was nothing revolutionary about her general teachings. In the spring of 1805, an Exeter-born 'dissenting' minister named William Tozer, who opened the first 'Southcottian Chapel' at Duke Street, Southwark, London, even used an orthodox Anglican prayer book.

But after a short while at Paddington, Joanna became increasingly convinced that she personally was the one vehicle of salvation. At Exeter, she had caused trouble by describing herself as 'the Lamb's wife'. In October 1802, she was more specific: 'I am bringing forth to the world a spiritual man,' she declared, 'the second Jesus Christ.'

> **//** EVEN NOWADAYS, AROUND THE WORLD, SMALL BUT ACTIVE GROUPS OF FOLLOWERS CONTINUE TO AWAIT THE OPENING OF HER ENIGMATIC SEALED BOX. THIS, THEY BELIEVE, CONTAINS THE SECRET OF WORLD PEACE... **//**

PERSPECTIVES

THE NEW MOSES

The Southcottians are considered by those who know of them to be frankly odd. The Church of Jesus Christ of Latter Day Saints (Mormons) also believes its leader to be a prophet, but is increasingly considered to be part of the Establishment.

It was not always so. After the martyrdom of the first 'prophet', Joseph Smith, in 1844, his successor, Brigham Young – 'the new Moses' – led the faithful away from persecution to 'the promised land'. They had no idea where they were going but still they followed this tough and charismatic man thousands of miles across America, until he suddenly pointed at an expanse of inhospitable salt flats. 'This is the place,' he declared. 'The desert shall blossom as a rose.' Against all the odds, it did; and the Mormon centre of Salt Lake City was founded there.

By 1873, when the print of Salt Lake City, *right,* was made, the community of Mormons had grown considerably, spreading out across the landscape. Today, Salt Lake City is the state capital of the American state of Utah.

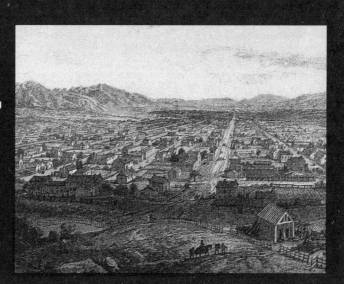

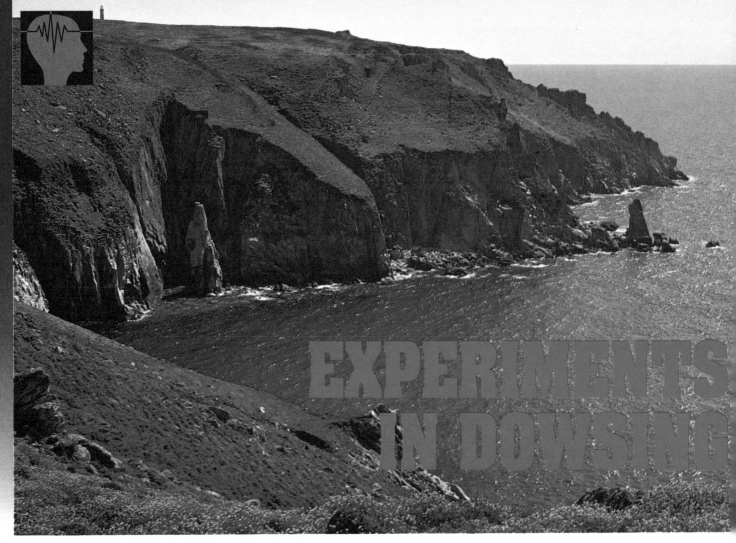

EXPERIMENTS IN DOWSING

DURING HIS CAREER AS AN ARCHAEOLOGIST, TOM LETHBRIDGE DISCOVERED HOW TO DOWSE NOT ONLY FOR WATER BUT ALSO FOR OBJECTS BY PICKING UP THEIR ELECTRICAL FIELDS. THIS WAS TO BE ONLY THE BEGINNING OF AN IMPORTANT SERIES OF EXPERIMENTS

Tom Lethbridge, above, as a result of experiments in dowsing, gradually came to believe in worlds beyond death.

It was on the island of Lundy in the Bristol Channel, top, that Lethbridge conducted his first experiment in dowsing. Using a forked hazel twig, he and a colleague dowsed for volcanic seams. The hazel twig located the seams by twisting violently when held over them.

Although Tom Lethbridge had no interest in ghosts or 'ghouls' before he retired to Devon, in southern England, he had always been deeply fascinated by dowsing.

It all started in the early 1930s, when he and another archaeologist were looking for Viking graves on the island of Lundy in the Bristol Channel. They located the graves; then, having time on their hands while they waited for the boat back to the mainland, they decided to try some experiments

with dowsing. Hidden under the soil of Lundy Island are seams of volcanic rock that pass up through the slate. Lethbridge decided to see if he could locate these. So he cut himself a hazel twig, allowed his friend to blindfold him, and was led along the cliff path, the forked hazel twig held tightly in his hands. (The twig has to be held with the forks bent slightly apart, so it has a certain amount of 'spring'.) Every time he passed over a volcanic seam, the hazel fork twisted violently in his hands. His friend had an extra-sensitive magnetometer, so he was able to verify that Lethbridge had accurately located every single one of the volcanic seams.

This may seem remarkable; but to Lethbridge it was all logical enough. Like running water, a volcanic seam has a faint magnetic field. Presumably he was somehow able to pick up these fields through the hazel twig, which reacted like a sensitive instrument. In one of his earlier books, he wrote: 'Most people can dowse, if they know how to do it. If they cannot do it, there is probably some fault in the electrical system of their bodies.'

The garden of Lethbridge's house in Devon was full of interesting archaeological remains, some of them dating back to Roman times; and, soon after moving in, Lethbridge remembered an experiment he had seen performed in the University Museum of Archaeology and Ethnology in Cambridge. Someone had asserted that a pendulum can tell whether a skull is male or female, and demonstrated this by dangling one over an ancient skull. The pendulum swung back and forth, which meant, apparently, that it was a man's skull. (If it ha swung round in a circle, the skull would have been female.) A similar method – dangling a wedding ring tied to a piece of thread over the stomach of a pregnant woman – is sometimes used in an attempt to determine the sex of an unborn baby.

But how can such a method possibly work? It sounds completely absurd. Male and female skulls do not have electrical fields; and even if they did, there seems to be no reason why one of them should make a pendulum swing back and forth, and the other make it swing in a circle.

Lethbridge now set out to test the method for himself. His first question was: if a pendulum can somehow respond to different substances, then how does it do it? A pendulum is, after all, just a weight fixed to the end of a piece of string. It must be the unconscious mind – or possibly the muscles – of the dowser that respond. But to what do they respond? The answer seemed to be that they respond to some kind of vibration – in which case, it seemed a fair assumption that different lengths of the pendulum respond to different vibrations.

The characteristic movement of a forked hazel twig when actively dowsing is shown in the diagram below. Its usual – though not invariable – reaction when held over a subterranean stream is to turn in a circle from right to left.

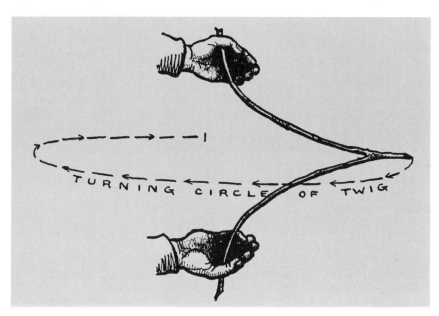

The twig must be held with the forks bent slightly apart, as shown left, when dowsing, in order to allow for a certain amount of natural 'spring'.

It was the most fruitful assumption Lethbridge ever made; and he set out to test it by putting a wooden bob on the end of a long piece of string, and then winding the string round a pencil, so he could lengthen or shorten the pendulum at will. Next, he put a piece of silver on the ground, held the pendulum over it, and carefully began to lengthen the string. When he had unwound about 2 feet (60 centimetres), the pendulum suddenly began to go into a circular swing. Lethbridge measured his string: it was precisely 22 inches. (Lethbridge believed one could only dowse successfully using imperial measurements. Feet and inches, he said, were 'natural' measurements based on the human body, whereas metric measurements were 'unnatural'. So pendulum 'rates' are given in inches only.)

THE PENDULUM REACTS

Next, he went out into the courtyard of Hole House, which dates back to Tudor times, and walked around with his pendulum. At one place, it went into a circular swing. Lethbridge dug down carefully, and eventually located a small piece of Rhineland stoneware pottery. He tried his pendulum over it, and once more it went into a powerful circular swing. That puzzled him greatly, until he tried his 22-inch pendulum over a piece of lead, and found it also went into a circular swing. Apparently, 22 inches is the 'rate' for both silver and lead. (Rhineland pottery in the 17th century was glazed with lead.)

Now very excited, Lethbridge kept the pendulum at the same length and walked around the courtyard until it again went into a circular swing. He dug down at that point, and found a bit of lead from an Elizabethan window. It seemed the pendulum was accurate. He now tried holding the pendulum over a copper pot, and found that it reacted at 30½ inches. He again walked around the courtyard until the pendulum responded, and this time, dug up a tiny copper tube. It was very small, so evidently the pendulum was extremely sensitive.

Convinced that he had made a major discovery, Lethbridge spent days testing all sorts of different substances with his pendulum and discovered, to his delight, that every one of them had its own 'rate': glass, sulphur, iron, slate, amber – even alcohol, garlic and apples. When he held it over a bottle of Australian Burgundy, the pendulum responded at 14, 20, 25½ and 32 inches, which Lethbridge proved to be the 'rates' for glass, vegetable matter (presumably, the label), alcohol and iron.

He even tested a truffle – that delicious fungus used in foie gras. The pendulum responded at 17 inches. Trying to locate buried truffles, Lethbridge stood with his pendulum in one hand, while pointing his other hand around in a slow semi-circle. When the 17-inch pendulum began to swing, he drew a straight line in the direction he was pointing. Then he went and stood several yards away, and repeated the experiment. Where the two lines crossed, he dug down with a trowel. There, he located a tiny, dark object and sent it to the Science Museum in London for identification. Incredibly, it turned out to be a rare variety of truffle.

There were still a number of minor mysteries – such as how to distinguish between lead and silver, when both react at 22 inches, or between truffles and beech wood, both of which respond to a

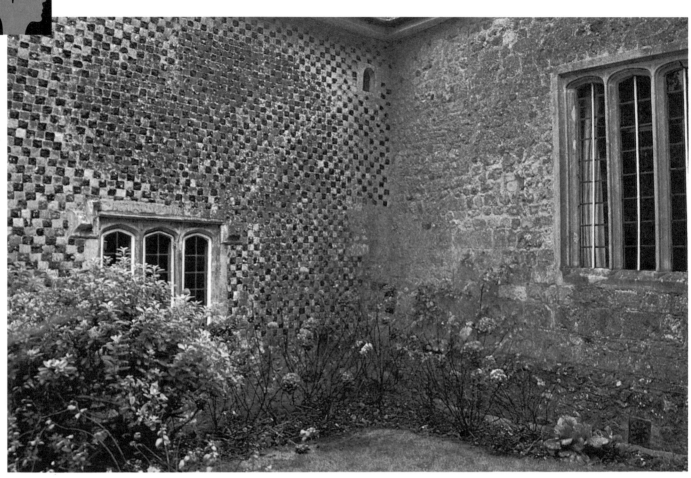

Dowsing revealed a number of buried objects in the corner of the courtyard at the Lethbridge home, Hole House in Devon, above.

The illustration below shows how dowsing with a pendulum works.
A. The dowser's psyche-field.
B. The static field of an object.
C. The pendulum – where A meets
  B, it begins to move in a circle.
D. The pendulum length,
  as controlled by dowser.

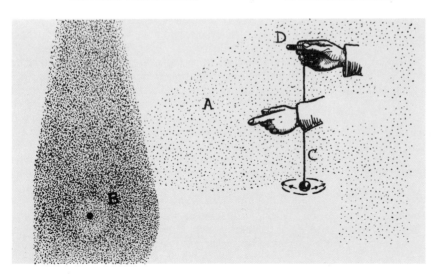

17-inch pendulum. Further experimentation solved that one, and the number of times the pendulum gyrated was found to be equally important. For lead, it gyrates 16 times, then goes back to its normal back-and-forth motion; for silver, it gyrates 22 times. It now looked as if nature had devised a simple and foolproof code for identifying any substance. And not just substances. The pendulum also responded to colours – the natural colours of flowers, for example: 22 inches for grey, 29 for yellow, 30 for green. Lethbridge next found himself wondering whether the pendulum would respond to thoughts and emotions as well as substances.

During his last excavations near Cambridge, Lethbridge had collected a number of sling-stones from an Iron Age fort. He tried his pendulum over them, and found that they reacted at 24 inches and also at 40. He fetched a bucketful of stones from the beach and tried the pendulum over these. They failed to react at either 'rate'. Now he divided the stones into two piles, and told his wife, Mina, to throw half of them at a wall, while he threw the rest. He tried the pendulum again. All Mina's stones now reacted at 29 inches (the 'rate' for females) while those he had thrown reacted at 24. So it looked as if the Iron Age stones had been thrown by males. But what about their reaction to a 40-inch pendulum? Could it, he wondered, be the rate for anger or death? Lethbridge set the pendulum at 40 inches and thought about something that made him angry; immediately, the pendulum began to gyrate. So it looked as if 40 was indeed the rate for anger. He later ascertained that it was also the rate for death, cold and blackness.

Now all this, as we have said, seems absurd. Yet Lethbridge repeated the experiments dozens of times, and each time he got the same result. The pendulum responded to ideas like evolution, pride, life, danger and deceit just as readily as to substances. Moreover, Mina got the same results. Through his experience of psychometry, Lethbridge realised that there is nothing very odd in a pendulum responding to ideas. If a 'sensitive' can hold an unopened letter, and somehow feel the emotions of the person who wrote it, then it seems reasonable to assume that human beings possess some 'sense' that registers these things, just as our eyes register colours and shapes – a sixth sense perhaps? In fact, you could say that a pendulum is merely an aid to psychometry. A psychometrist – or sensitive – can pick up vibrations directly; non-sensitive people, like Lethbridge, can only feel them indirectly through the pendulum.

After months of experiment with the pendulum, Lethbridge constructed tables of the various 'rates'; and it became clear that 40 inches was some kind of limit. Every single substance that he tested fell between zero and 40 inches. And at this point, he discovered something rather odd. Sulphur reacted to a 7-inch pendulum. If he then extended the pendulum to 47 inches – 40 plus 7 – it would still react to a heap of sulphur, but not when directly over the heap. It only reacted a little to one side. The same was true of everything else he tried beyond 40 – the pendulum reacted, but a little to one side.

Forty inches is also the 'rate' for death. Was it possible, Lethbridge wondered, that when the

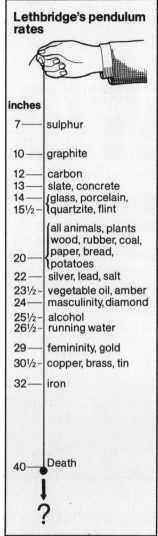

Lethbridge's pendulum rates

inches	
7	sulphur
10	graphite
12	carbon
13	slate, concrete
14	glass, porcelain,
15½	quartzite, flint
20	all animals, plants wood, rubber, coal, paper, bread, potatoes
22	silver, lead, salt
23½	vegetable oil, amber
24	masculinity, diamond
25½	alcohol
26½	running water
29	femininity, gold
30½	copper, brass, tin
32	iron
40	Death
	?

The table, above, shows the pendulum 'rates' as discovered by Tom Lethbridge in the course of his experiments. Through trial and error, he came to realise that the pendulum reacted consistently at certain lengths to specific substances, qualities and even abstract ideas.

Moreover, Lethbridge found that, if he lengthened the pendulum beyond 80 inches, he got the same result all over again, as if there is yet another world – or dimension – beyond that one. And this 'third world' also has a reaction for time. But when Lethbridge lengthened the pendulum beyond 120 inches, he discovered that the 'world' beyond that again had no reaction for time.

Tom Lethbridge's own explanation of this strange 'power of the pendulum' is that there is a part of the human mind that knows the answers to all questions. Unfortunately, it can only convey these answers to the 'everyday you', the busy, conscious self that spends its time coping with practical problems. But this 'other you' can convey its messages via the dowsing rod or pendulum, by the simple expedient of controlling the muscles.

Lethbridge had started as a cheerfully sceptical investigator, trying to understand nature's hidden codes for conveying information; but his researches led him into strange, bewildering realms where all traditional ideas seemed to be turned upside down. He compared himself to a man walking on ice, when it suddenly collapses and he finds himself floundering in freezing water. Of this sudden immersion in new ideas, he said: 'From living a normal life in a three-dimensional world, I seem to have suddenly fallen through into one where there are more dimensions. The three-dimensional life goes on as usual; but one has to adjust one's thinking to the other.' He did more than adjust his thinking: he set out boldly to explore the fourth dimension – and came to highly significant conclusions.

pendulum registers beyond 40 inches, it registers a world beyond death – another dimension? He remembered an experience of being at the dentist, under anaesthetic, and finding himself outside his body, hovering up in the air, and slightly to the left – just like the 'displacement' reaction of the pendulum to the heap of sulphur.

He also noticed another odd thing. Below 40 inches, there is no 'rate' for the concept of time; the pendulum simply would not respond. But when he lengthened the pendulum to 60 inches, he got a strong reaction for time. He reasoned that because 'our world' – that is, the world that registers below 40 – is in time, there is no reaction to the idea of time itself, just as you could not appreciate the speed of a river if you were drifting down it at the same speed as the current. But there is a reaction to the idea of time in the 'world beyond death'.

The mended pots, left and right, were originally found in fragments in the courtyard and orchard of Hole House solely through dowsing. Lethbridge later dowsed them to find their ages, finally coming up with the dates he scratched on the bottoms. Lethbridge achieved a high degree of accuracy: his dates for certain standing stones, for example, were later proved by carbon dating to be correct. As he himself said: 'It may seem absurd, but it delivers the goods'.

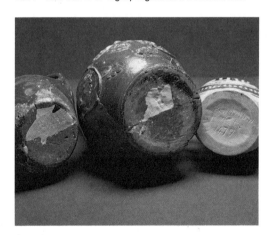

> **" MOST PEOPLE CAN DOWSE, IF THEY KNOW HOW TO DO IT. IF THEY CANNOT DO IT, THERE IS PROBABLY SOME FAULT IN THE ELECTRICAL SYSTEM "**
> **OF THEIR BODIES.**
> **TOM LETHBRIDGE**

ALIEN REVELATIONS

SENSATIONAL INFORMATION ABOUT ALIEN VISITORS EMERGED WHEN BETTY AND BARNEY HILL'S MEMORIES OF THEIR CLOSE ENCOUNTER WERE PROBED BY HYPNOSIS

Barney and Betty Hill presented themselves at the office of Dr Benjamin Simon on 14 December 1963 to begin a series of hypnosis sessions that was eventually to last seven months. Dr Simon was a practitioner of experience and repute, ideally suited for the task in hand; and his open-minded attitude enabled the troubled couple to present their stories in an atmosphere of sympathetic understanding, free from any risk of bias or prejudice.

It is important to remember why hypnosis was tried. In Betty's words:

Betty and Barney Hill are seen above, under hypnosis during their seven-month course of treatment. Their hypnotherapist – Dr Benjamin Simon, right – was concerned with 'the cumulative impact of past experiences and fantasies on their present experiences and responses', not with the existence of UFOs. In an introduction to the published account of the case, he was careful to say that hypnosis is a pathway to the truth 'as it is felt and understood by the patient'.

The artist's impression, left, shows Betty and Barney being led to the mysterious craft by members of its crew. Betty felt great fear at this point, but Barney later insisted he had felt none.

'We went to Dr Simon to get relief from the emotional trouble, and to determine what its cause was. In other words, we'd gone for medical help, not to find out about a UFO experience.'

The sessions were not part of a wider course of psychoanalysis, but were designed to see what relevance the alleged UFO sighting might have had to Barney's physical and psychological state. They therefore do not give us a general picture of the couple's psychological background. Indeed, there are many questions we would like answered about them – about their attitudes to such matters as their interracial marriage, their previous marriages, their separation from their children, their involvement with social work and civil rights, for instance, all of which could have some bearing on how we evaluate their story. But no such information is forthcoming: Dr Simon's probing, and his subsequent comments, were limited to the task in hand.

Each subject was hypnotised separately, with the other out of the room, one after the other. They

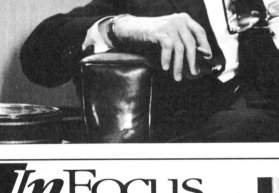

did not hear each other's sessions at the time, nor the tapes of their own sessions. Only when Dr Simon judged that he had accomplished all he could and had brought the sessions to an end did he invite the couple to hear the tapes for the first time. They chose to listen to them together.

All this was done at the Hills' own instigation. Apart from the emotional ordeal, seven months of sessions with a consultant of the highest qualifications must have cost a great sum of money. So there must have been an exceedingly strong motivation for such a financial burden.

TWO VIEWPOINTS

Under hypnosis, the Hills independently told a story that closely matched the dreams that had so troubled Betty in the weeks following their supposed sighting. But there was a difference: the histories were now recounted as the experiences of two people, each describing the events as seen from his or her individual viewpoint. During the phases of the story when the couple were together, each account confirmed the other; but when they were separated, they had their own stories to tell, and told them with an immediacy and intensity that give a vivid impression of re-living an actual experience. According to Barney:

'I started to get out of my car, and put one foot on the ground. And two men were standing beside me, helping me out. I felt very relaxed, yet very frightened. They didn't say anything. I knew I was walking, or moving down the road from the position of where my car was parked. And I could see the ramp that I went up... I could hear a humming sound that they seemed to be making. I was afraid to open my eyes. I had been told not to open my eyes, and it would be over with quickly. And I could feel them examining me with their hands. They looked at my neck, and I could feel them touching my skin right down my back. As if they were counting my spinal column. And I felt something touch right at the base of my spine, like a finger pushing, a single finger.'

Betty's account was equally detailed: 'They led Barney right past the door where I'm standing. So I said: "What are you doing with Barney? Bring him

---

*In*FOCUS

MERELY STAR-STRUCK?

The American UFO sceptic Robert Sheaffer, *right,* declared that the Hills' experience began when they misidentified the planet Jupiter as a UFO. Betty, he explained, first saw a bright 'star' near the Moon; later, a second one appeared and seemed to be moving. Jupiter and Saturn were visible near the Moon that night: and had there been a UFO, Sheaffer said, Betty would have seen three 'stars'. Sheaffer also dismissed Betty's other claims – that the UFO acted 'much like a yo-yo', had passed in front of the Moon in silhouette and flashed 'thin

pencils of different-coloured lights, rotating around an object which at that time appeared cigar-shaped'. He cited other cases, too, in which witnesses have produced fantastic misinterpretations of bright stars.

At various times, the Hills put the UFO encounter at around 11 p.m., between midnight and 1 a.m., and at around 3 a.m. Furthermore, Barney recalled that, as the UFO approached them, he drove extremely slowly; and on the homeward journey, he stopped at least once, for reasons he could not remember. Sheaffer insisted that there is so much uncertainty as to the times and their speed of travel that there is no reason to believe in the supposed 'loss' of the two hours – a loss that in any event was discovered only weeks later.

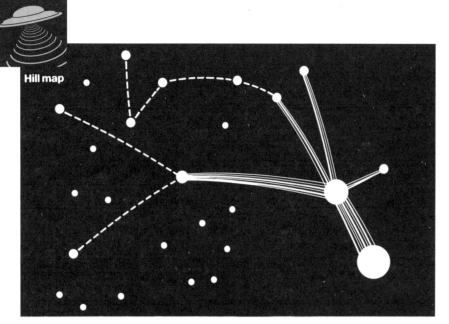

Hill map

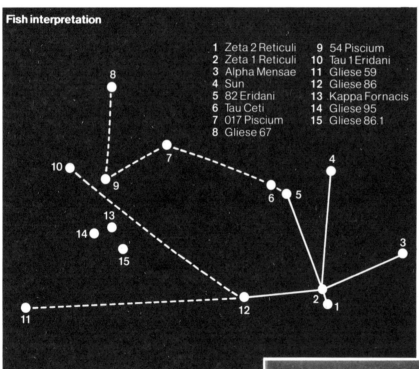

Fish interpretation

1 Zeta 2 Reticuli	9 54 Piscium
2 Zeta 1 Reticuli	10 Tau 1 Eridani
3 Alpha Mensae	11 Gliese 59
4 Sun	12 Gliese 86
5 82 Eridani	13 Kappa Fornacis
6 Tau Ceti	14 Gliese 95
7 017 Piscium	15 Gliese 86.1
8 Gliese 67	

in here where I am." And the man said: "No, we only have equipment enough in one room to do one person at a time. And if we took you both in the same room, it would take too long. So Barney will be all right, they're going to take him into the next room. And then as soon as we get through testing the both of you, then you will go back to your car. You don't have to be afraid."...And they rub – they have a machine, I don't know what it is. They bring the machine over and they put it – it's something like a microscope, only with a big lens. I had an idea they were taking a picture of my skin. And they both looked through this machine... Then they took something like a letter opener and they scraped my arm here, and there was like little – you know how your skin gets dry and flaky sometimes, like little particles of skin? And they put something like a piece of cellophane or plastic, they scraped, and they put this that came off on this plastic.'

ALIEN STAR MAP

One of the practical applications of hypnosis is to bring into the conscious mind information that is stored in the subconscious – things experienced but not consciously noted by the witness. This was used to good effect by Dr Simon in connection with the star map that Betty Hill said she had been shown by the 'leader' of the aliens. Dr Simon suggested that, after the session, when she got home, she might care to try to draw what she remembered of the map. To judge from her account, given here, it could have provided a valuable clue as to the origin of her abductors.

'I asked him where he was from. Because I said that I knew he wasn't from the Earth... and he asked if I knew anything about the Universe. And I told him no. I knew practically nothing... And he went across the room... there was an opening. And he pulled out a map... It was an oblong map... And there were all these dots on it... Some were little, just pinpoints. And others were as big as a nickel ... there were curved lines going from one dot to another. And there was one big circle, and it had a lot of lines coming out from it. A lot of lines going to another circle quite close but not as big... And I

" PSYCHOLOGISTS GENERALLY AGREE THAT WHAT A PERSON SAYS WHILE UNDER HYPNOSIS NEED NOT NECESSARILY BE ACTUAL FACT BUT RATHER REPRESENTS WHAT THE PERSON BELIEVES TO HAVE HAPPENED. HYPNOSIS IS OF LITTLE VALUE IN SEPARATING FACT FROM FANTASY. **"**

ROBERT SHEAFFER, THE UFO VERDICT

Betty Hill recalled being shown a star map, rather like the one reproduced top left. The stars, seen from an unknown viewpoint, form unfamiliar patterns. After several years work, Marjorie Fish arrived at the interpretation, shown centre left. The aliens' home system, zeta 1 Reticuli, she believed, is about 37 light-years from us. Marjorie Fish arrived at her result by making a model of stars near the Sun, and using beads mounted on threads, as shown bottom left.

asked him what they meant. And he said that the heavy lines were trade routes... the solid lines were places they went occasionally. And he said the broken lines were expeditions... So I asked him where was his home port, and he said: "Where were you on the map?" I looked and laughed, and said: 'I don't know.' So he said: "If you don't know where you are, then there isn't any point of my telling where I am from." And he put the map... back in the space in the wall...'

Betty drew the map to the best of her recollection; but with no names and no points of reference, it was totally meaningless. However, in 1968, a schoolteacher and amateur astronomer, Marjorie Fish, realised that there must be a limited number of actual configurations of stars that would match up to the points on the map. She started by making a three-dimensional model of Betty's map out of beads and string, and then set about seeking a match for it among the not-too-distant stars. After five years, she felt satisfied that she had found such a match.

random among the numerous stars in the neighbourhood of the Sun. By way of testing this, Charles W. Atterberg offered an alternative conjecture as to the region shown in the map. It is a measure of how debatable the findings are that the UFO sceptic Robert Sheaffer should find the Atterberg model superior to the Fish version, whereas Dickinson claims that it is more arbitrary in its selection of stars and contains several inconsistencies.

PREDICTIONS CONFIRMED

Additional support for the Fish model appeared in 1969, when a revised star catalogue, containing information that was simply not available in 1961, was published for the first time and confirmed predictions made by Fish on the basis of the Hill map. Though this is still not definite proof, it is strongly supportive of the Hill-Fish suggestion. But the question remains as to how much reliance can be placed on the recollections, by someone totally unversed in astronomy, of a map seen – under distinctly bizarre conditions – more than two years earlier.

The star map is the most tangible aspect of the Hill case, and lends itself to testing. For the rest, it is a matter of evaluating the Hills' personal testimony, but in the complete absence of any physical evidence – how valuable the book that Betty was offered would have been, if she had only been allowed to bring it away! – evaluation is limited to assessing the credibility of the Hills themselves. No critic has questioned their honesty and sincerity; rather, it is their interpretation of their experience that has to be questioned. It is in this respect that the lack of information about the Hills' personal background becomes important. For it is clear that there are factors in the Hills' personal circumstances that could be very relevant to the way we judge their story. We have already noted such external factors as their previous marriages, and Barney's state of health; and there is also considerable evidence to show that Betty was a much more unusual person than she is generally presented as being.

Barney Hill died in February 1969, five years after the sessions with Dr Simon, of a cerebral haemorrhage, like his father before him. Thereafter, Betty enjoyed the mixed blessings of fame. Her case has been featured in books and magazines, and was even presented as a full-length movie. She made countless public appearances at lectures and conferences, and was a guest on many radio and television shows. Some time after the hypnotic sessions, she gave up her work and devoted herself full-time to UFO research. As something of a celebrity, she was even recognized on the most unlikely occasions. As she herself recounted:

'At a recent lobster festival, the man on the mike looked up, saw me and said: "Welcome, Betty Hill! You've put us on the map with the greatest landing area for UFOs in the world!"'

Cynically, one could say that she developed a vested interest in having people believe that her experience was genuine, but there seems little question that she was completely sincere in her belief that the abduction really took place.

She also became no less convinced that a great number of strange events happened to her following the alleged abduction.

The illustration above shows the Hills' first close-up view of the aliens as they approached the couple's stalled car. This careful reconstruction of Betty and Barney's descriptions appeared in the UFO magazine Flying Saucer, after the case had caught the public's imagination.

The Fish map started a controversy almost as lively as that engendered by the Hills' original sighting. An astronomer, Terence Dickinson, was favourably impressed and presented the case for the Fish model in an authoritative article:

'Basically, the Fish interpretation is a view from a few light-years beyond the stars zeta 1 and zeta 2 Reticuli, looking back towards the Sun and the star 82 Eridani, which is about midway between us and the Reticuli pair. The 15 stars shown on the map are all basically like the Sun and could theoretically have planets like Earth. These are the types of stars some astronomers are currently examining in search of signals from alien intelligences. It is therefore a reasonable assumption that this type of star may be the only type on the map... No other interpretation of the Hill map includes all of the solar-type stars within a specific area of space containing the Sun... and makes sense in terms of logical travel between the stars.'

The Fish model provoked much debate, largely related to the chances of finding such a pattern at

WRITING ON THE WALLS, BELLS THAT RANG OF THEIR OWN ACCORD, APPARITIONS AND MYSTERIOUS FIRES – SUCH WERE THE NON-STOP PARANORMAL PHENOMENA THAT OCCURRED AFTER THE FOYSTER FAMILY MOVED INTO BORLEY RECTORY

In 1878, a young woman named Esther Cox suddenly became the centre of 'mysterious manifestations' at her sister's home in Amherst, Nova Scotia. Esther saw apparitions visible to no one else. Objects were thrown, furniture was upset, small fires broke out in the house, and messages addressed to the girl were found scribbled on the walls. The 'hauntings' subsequently became the subject of a book, *The Haunted House: A True Ghost Story . . . The Great Amherst Mystery* by Walter Hubbell. It was a huge success, running through 10 editions and selling over 55,000 copies. But, in 1919, the American Society for Psychical Research printed a critical study by Dr Walter F. Prince, suggesting that the Amherst case was not in fact a poltergeist manifestation. It was, he said,

Hauntings at Borley Rectory, above, seemed to reach a peak when Marianne Foyster lived there. But it is still an open question as to whether she created the events herself.

The cottage, below, was once part of the Borley Rectory property and the home of François D'Arles.

trickery on the part of Esther Cox while in a state of dissociation, or conversion hysteria.

The township of Amherst is about 5 miles (8 kilometres) from the equally small community of Sackville, where another of Esther Cox's married sisters resided and where, 50 years afterwards, the Reverend Lionel Foyster and his wife Marianne lived. The Foysters would certainly have heard of the Amherst case; and the fact that Foyster used the pseudonym 'Teed' – the married name of Esther Cox's sister – when writing of the happenings at Borley Rectory during his stay there offers what is tantamount to proof that he not only knew

BORLEY REVISITED

of the Amherst case but was familiar with its details. It seems likely, therefore, that his wife also knew of the case, though whether she made deliberate – if unconscious – use of it for her own behaviour is a matter for conjecture.

The resemblance between both cases is indeed striking; and Dingwall, Goldney and Hall, in *The Haunting of Borley Rectory*, offer no less than 19 points of general concurrence, including the ringing of bells, throwing of objects, setting of small fires, and mysterious messages written on walls.

Shortly after Marianne Foyster arrived at Borley and took such an instant dislike to the place, she began to see 'apparitions'; but no one else did. Then the manifestations, so similar to the Amherst case, began. Her husband, loyal and devoted, answered villagers, who accused her of faking, that *he* could not see the visions because 'he wasn't psychic'; and, in her 'defence', he began to keep a rough record of events. This was not perhaps as helpful as he hoped it might be because, as he admitted, much of it was written later.

Ghost-hunter Harry Price, left, and Mrs K. M Goldney of the Society for Psychical Research, right, pose below with the Foyster family at Borley Rectory. The Foysters' adopted child Adelaide and an unidentified playmate complete the group portrait.

One of several messages that appeared on the walls of the rectory is reproduced, bottom. All of them were scribbled in pencil in a childish hand, and most were addressed to Marianne Foyster.

In October 1931, in answer to a plea from the Bull sisters, Harry Price returned to Borley once more. It is interesting to speculate on the motives behind the Bulls' concern: perhaps because they knew the source of the pranks and hoaxes during their own tenancy, they suspected the genuineness of the new 'haunting'. The same might be said of Harry Price, for he returned from his visit convinced that Mrs Foyster was directly responsible for fraud.

In their examination of the alleged phenomena, Dingwall, Goldney and Hall analyzed the incidents described in Foyster's first record, which he later elaborated upon. Treating the constant bell ringing as a single phenomenon, they isolated 103 different instances. Of these, 99 depended totally on Mrs Foyster's sincerity, three were readily attributable to natural causes, and only one was in any way 'inexplicable'.

Among the most suspicious incidents was the appearance of pencilled writings on the walls. Some seven messages appeared during the Foysters' tenancy, most of them addressed to Marianne and

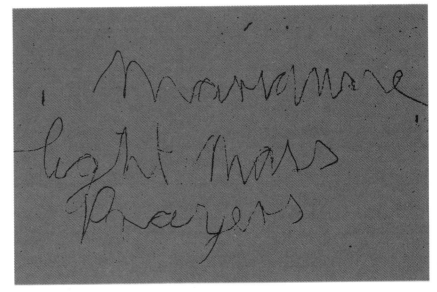

"

> WHAT SEEMS CLEAR FROM ALL ACCOUNTS OF THE PLACE IS THAT THE GROUND ITSELF IS HAUNTED, AND CONTINUES TO BE SO... BORLEY IS A PLACE OF POWER, THE KIND OF PLACE THAT WOULD BE CHOSEN FOR A MONASTERY, AND THAT PROBABLY HELD SOME PAGAN SITE OF WORSHIP LONG BEFORE THAT. "

COLIN WILSON, POLTERGEIST!

appealing for 'light, mass, prayers'. Another, not noted by Price in his Borley books, spelled 'Adelaide', the name of the Foysters' adopted daughter. All the messages were in a childish scribble. It has been speculated that little Adelaide may even have been responsible for one or both of the mysterious small fires that broke out in the rectory, for she was caught on at least one occasion trying to set fire to bedclothes.

In 1933, when the Foysters went on leave for six months, they left Canon H. Lawton as locum. Nothing untoward happened, though the canon – like Major Douglas-Home of the Society for Psychical Research – noted the curious acoustics of the house and surroundings. In any case, by then, Mrs Foyster was spending most of her time in London with François D'Arles at their flower shop. An exorcism by a group of Spiritualists the previous year, when Marianne and François first left to open their shop, seemed to have got rid of what the Foysters cosily called 'the goblins'. Or was it that Marianne Foyster was no longer on the premises?

In October 1935, the Foysters left Borley. When the Reverend A.C. Henning was appointed five months later, he chose to live elsewhere; and since this time, the rectors of Borley have lived at Liston or Foxearth rectories, parishes amalgamated with Borley since the 1930s.

But the battered, drama-ridden old house had still another four years of life to run. On 19 May 1937, Harry Price rented the rectory, and a week later inserted an advertisement in *The Times* asking for 'responsible persons of leisure and intelligence, intrepid, critical and unbiased' to form a rota of observers at the house. If, he later stated, they

One of Price's 48 volunteer investigators takes a break from his duties at the rectory, above. Price rented Borley for a year and gathered a team of observers through an advertisement in **The Times** *to work with him there. He did not ask for experience in psychical research but required his volunteers to have 'leisure and intelligence' and to be critical and unbiased.*

'knew nothing about psychical research, so much the better'.

Whether or not Harry Price and Marianne Foyster had used fraud for their own personal ends, a trickster who came on the scene in November 1938 was working for purely financial gain. He was Captain William Hart Gregson, who bought Borley Rectory six months after Price's tenancy expired. He immediately asked Price's advice about organizing coach trips to see his new property and broadcast on the radio, recounting several minor 'phenomena'. But his coach tour plans were brought to an abrupt end at midnight on 27 February 1939 when fire gutted the building, leaving only a few walls, charred beams and chimney stacks.

Sidney Glanville, one of Price's volunteer researchers and of impeccable reputation, said that, at a seance held at the Glanville home, an entity named 'Sunex Amures' had threatened to burn down Borley Rectory. But the real cause of the destruction of Borley Rectory was flatly stated by Sir William Crocker in his autobiography *Far from Humdrum: a Lawyer's Life*. Crocker, a distinguished barrister, and Colonel Cuthbert Buckle, an insurance adjuster, were both set the task of investigating the claim made by Gregson on behalf of the insurers. Crocker states: 'We repudiated his impudent claim for "accidental loss by fire"... pleading that he had fired the place himself.'

HOCUS POCUS

The ruins of Borley Rectory were finally demolished in the spring of 1944 and the site levelled. An orchard and three modern bungalows now occupy the spot. During the demolition, Price took a *Life* magazine photographer and researcher, Cynthia Ledsham, to Borley; and by sheer fluke, the photographer captured on film a brick that was apparently 'levitated' by unseen forces but was in fact thrown by a worker. *Life* published the photograph over a jokey caption; but Price, in his book *The End of Borley Rectory*, claimed it as a final 'phenomenon'. Cynthia Ledsham was astounded, calling it 'the most bare-faced hocus pocus on the part of... Harry Price.'

The truth is that the haunting of Borley Rectory was the most bare-faced hocus pocus from start to finish, with Price feeding his craving for personal publicity from it in the most short-sighted way. For, as was shown after his death, his shallow frauds could not hope to withstand investigation.

In a letter to C.G. Glover in 1938, Price wrote: 'As regards your various criticisms, the alleged haunting of the rectory stands or falls not by the reports of our recent observers, but by the extraordinary happenings there of the last 50 years.'

But Harry Price was to write to Dr Dingwall in 1946 in reference to the occasion when a glass of water was 'changed' into ink: 'I agree that Mrs Foyster's wine [*sic*] trick was rather crude, but if you cut out the Foysters, the Bulls, the Smiths, etc., something still remains.'

One great irony certainly remains. Despite the demolition of Price's pack of lies, ghost-hunters of the 1960s and 1970s doggedly persisted in investigating the area. And they may finally just have stumbled on something truly paranormal – not at the rectory site, but in Borley Church itself.

STARTING A COSMIC DIALOGUE

ARE WE ALONE IN THE UNIVERSE? IF NOT, HOW CAN WE SET ABOUT GETTING IN TOUCH WITH INTELLIGENT ALIEN RACES?

For thousands of years, human beings have looked at the heavens and wondered whether there were worlds out there with life on them. Authors have written innumerable stories in which Earthmen have gone to the Moon or to the planets and found all manner of strange creatures there. Lucian's *Vrea Historia*, published in the second century AD, was one of the first: the hero is carried beyond the Pillars of Hercules (the Strait of Gibraltar) in his ship and is swept up in a whirlwind to the Moon. He finds it inhabited and has all kinds of adventures there. Rather more recently, H.G. Wells wrote his famous science fiction thriller *The War of the Worlds*. Wells was doubtless inspired by the claims of the astronomer Percival Lowell that the planet Mars might well be inhabited by an intelligent race. In *The War of the Worlds*, they reveal their presence by a system of giant canals carrying water from the polar-caps.

We know now from the Moon landings and from a study of the lunar samples brought back that not only does the Moon not have any life, but it is extremely unlikely ever to have had any. We also know from the *Mariner* spacecraft sent to Mars, and especially from the *Viking* soft-landers, that there is no Martian civilization and no canal system. If there is any form of life on that planet, it is probably of the most primitive sort. Venus and Mercury,

Communication with intelligent aliens was first foreseen centuries ago. In The Strange Voyage and Adventures of Domingo Gonsales to the World in the Moon, *right, published in 1638, the hero was carried into space by bird power. But we now know that we shall have to look much farther than the Moon for intelligent life. And delays in conversation will probably be huge. If we sent a radio message to the Horsehead Nebula, below, for instance, we should have to wait over 2,000 years for a reply to reach us.*

and indeed all of the planets and moons so far explored, bear witness that, at least within our solar system, the Earth is probably unique in carrying an intelligent species.

Nevertheless, Man's fascination with the problem of extra-terrestrial life is undiminished; for, when all is said and done, the solar system is only a tiny part of the Universe. Surely, among the billions of stars scattered throughout the Universe, there must be some possessing planets with life – in some cases, intelligent life? And if so, surely some of these species would be interested in exploring the Universe, or at least in getting in touch with other intelligent races?

For generations, science fiction writers have speculated in magazines, novels, films and television on the theme of extra-terrestrial life. Some treatments have been thoughtful and sober, exploring the problems of a first encounter with an alien race, and demonstrating that, more often than not, even with the best will in the world, the most tragic consequences could ensue. But many such stories have, unfortunately, been mere rubbish – even dangerously misleading – with the authors paying no attention to scientific fact. In the 1950s, for example, a series of science fiction films was churned out, inspired by purely commercial motives. One even had the title *I Married a Teenage Werewolf*

The idea that Man might encounter alien races in space took firm hold in the science fiction boom of the 1950s. Usually, they were viewed as terrifying enemies rather than potential friends. The Thing of Venus, above, for example, is clearly a threat to Earthly womanhood.

The tightly packed ball of stars, above right, is called a globular cluster and lies in the constellation Pegasus. This computerized picture accentuates the reddish hue of the comparatively old stars making up the cluster. The orbits of planets would be so highly disturbed by neighbouring stars in the cluster that life would be unlikely to develop on them. But in the immensity of an entire galaxy, right, there may be an enormous number of planets suitable for life.

" OCTOBER 1992 SAW THE BIGGEST ATTEMPT YET TO DISCOVER EXTRA-TERRESTRIAL LIFE, WITH THE US SPACE AGENCY INVESTING £65 MILLION IN CONNECTING COMPUTERS TO TWO HIGH-POWERED RADIO TELESCOPES WHICH WILL SCAN THE COSMOS. "

Astronomy's 'first fact of life' is the scale of the Universe, illustrated right. Light takes over eight hours to cross the solar system (1) and 100,000 years to cross our Galaxy, in which there are about 100,000 million stars (2). Galaxies are grouped into clusters, typically 10 million light-years across, held together by mutual gravitational attraction (3). The observable Universe is about 20,000 million light-years across (4).

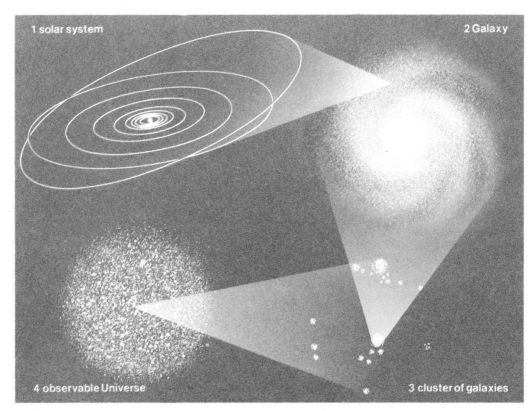

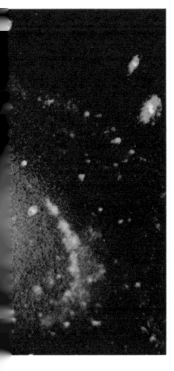

from Outer Space. It had all the most lurid themes in one package – sex, horror, teenage neuroses, and the menace of space. These films used a small number of stock plots. There was usually an old scientist with a pretty daughter or female assistant with whom his young colleague could fall in love. There would be an uncle, aunt or old friend whose job it was to intone: 'Man was not meant to meddle in such realms' or 'You realise... this means the end of civilization as we know it!' just before he or she was eaten by the monster from 20,000 fathoms, outer space or the centre of the Earth. The human race is just about to be defeated in its gigantic struggle against the menace when the young scientist, no doubt inspired by the pretty daughter/assistant's acceptance of his love, suddenly gasps: 'But is it possible they cannot withstand popcorn, salt water or the sound of Elvis Presley?' At the end, the young lovers were usually seen in a clinch, after which the camera would glance over their shoulders at the heavenly backdrop and we would receive the warning, spoken or implied: 'You know, the Universe is a big place. What other horrors may be waiting for us out there?'

ASTRONOMICAL FACTS OF LIFE

But what do astronomy and space research actually teach us about the Universe that is relevant to the question of extra-terrestrial life? We learn that there are three main astronomical facts of life; and it is only by considering these that we can, in any way, discuss life in the Universe sensibly.

The first fact is the size of the Universe. If a scale is taken such that the known Universe is as large as St Paul's Cathedral, then the 100,000 million galaxies it contains will be the size of specks of dust, and the average distance between neighbouring specks will be about half-an-inch (1 centimetre). If we choose one – our Galaxy, say – and imagine it

expanded to the size of the continent of Asia, then we find that it, too, is made of specks of dust – neighbouring specks being about 300 feet (100 metres) apart. These specks are the stars, about 100,000 million of them. Choose the one that is the Sun and place a penny on it: that penny is the size of the solar system. Now, finally, expand the penny to the size of Asia, and the Earth will be about the size of a small house.

The second relevant astronomical fact of life is the uniformity of the Universe. Throughout the known Universe, the same chemical elements appear in much the same proportions – about 70 per cent hydrogen, about 27 per cent helium, some two per cent made up of carbon, nitrogen, oxygen and neon, and the remaining one per cent consisting mostly of sodium, magnesium, aluminium, silicon, calcium and iron. The other 80 naturally occurring elements comprise no more than, so to speak, a pinch of seasoning in the cosmic brew. And wherever we go in the Universe, the same chemical and physical processes operate: gravitational and electromagnetic fields manipulate objects with their spectral fingers, while nuclear reactions act at the hearts of stars, transmuting element to element in ways that the ancient alchemists would envy. Whatever physical processes have happened in our corner of the Galaxy have been happening everywhere and are still happening.

The third astronomical fact that is important in this context is the age of the Universe. Astronomers now believe that the Universe has been a going concern for anything between 20,000 million and 30,000 million years, ever since it was created in the 'big bang'. Such immense durations, stated baldly, are impossible for the human brain to appreciate. Nevertheless, if we accept the upper figure and take a scale on which a second represents 1,000 years, then the Universe is one year

287

old. By the end of 1 January of that year, the process leading to our present-day Universe had essentially been completed. By June, our Galaxy had been created, and by the beginning of November the solar system, including the Earth, was in existence. The first signs of life were appearing on the Earth about 14 December, and Man, in much his present form, was beginning to use his primitive intelligence to master his environment about half-an-hour before midnight on 31 December. Mankind, as a species, is put into perspective when we realise that the earliest civilizations of which we have any record came into being about 8 seconds before midnight, while the last three-and-a-half centuries of our much vaunted scientific and technological age have occupied the last one-third of a second in the year-long history of the Universe.

SUITABLE ENVIRONMENTS

So how many places are there in such a vast Universe where life could survive? Since the only living things of which we have any knowledge are those found on the planet Earth, we must provisionally confine our enquiry to forms of life akin to those. Our forms of life consists of complex organisms composed of carbon, nitrogen, oxygen and hydrogen, with only one per cent of anything else. For most of these forms to survive, they must be supplied with water, food and air and be exposed to the correct ranges of temperature and pressure, and the right kind of radiation.

We do know, of course, that living creatures have demonstrated extraordinary powers of adaptation to widely different environments. Some blue-green algae are found in water at a temperature of 185°F (85°C), for example, while some plant seeds

The artist's impression, below, is of the Pleiades (M45) as seen from an imaginary nearby planet. The Pleiades are a cluster of stars some 400 light-years away in the constellation of Taurus. Could it be that intelligent life exists at such a distance? And might 'they' already be trying to contact us?

can be taken to temperatures as low as –310°F (–190°'C) without dying. The astronauts of *Apollo 12* were sent to find out how the instruments of the unmanned spacecraft *Surveyor 3* had withstood two years on the Moon's surface. There is no atmosphere there and the temperature in daytime is above the boiling point of water, falling to about –330°F (–200°C) during the night. The explorers found *Streptococcus mitis* bacteria still alive on the television camera. Living things have also been found at the bottom of the deepest oceans on Earth, where no sunlight penetrates and the pressure is many tonnes to the square inch.

If, therefore, we confine ourselves to Earth-like planets orbiting Sun-like stars – at distances at which the temperature range allows water to exist in liquid form and does not compel it to take the form of steam or ice – we will presumably be selecting suitable places for life, as we know it, to survive.

Proceeding in this way, we can estimate that, in the visible Universe, the number of Earth-sized planets orbiting Sun-type stars at about the right distance is about 6 million million million. And the question of vital importance is: would life originate on any of these hospitable planets?

STEPS TOWARDS LIFE

The experiments of Dr Stanley Miller, first carried out in 1953 and subsequently modified and confirmed by many other researchers, demonstrate that, in the atmosphere and surface conditions that existed on Earth before life began, ultraviolet radiation and electrical discharges would have formed many of the amino acids, complex molecules that are the building bricks of life. Miller did not prove that life would necessarily arise in such conditions, but he and other investigators showed that the first steps would be taken. In fact, in recent years, it has been discovered that, in interstellar space, all kinds of complicated molecules exist, such as formaldehyde and alcohol. Such discoveries strengthen the belief that what has happened in our part of the Universe has happened everywhere else. Nevertheless, it is important to realise that we do not know if life exists elsewhere, let alone whether it is intelligent.

The only civilization we know of, namely our own, has already reached the stage where it has sent products of its technology out of the solar system. *Project Daedalus*, the star-probe study made by the British Interplanetary Society, has also shown that, using technology that is now available or might reasonably be expected to be achieved by the end of the century, we could design and build an interstellar probe capable of voyaging to Barnard's star, six light-years away, and examine its planets. It has also been pointed out that the energy already stored in nuclear weapons would suffice to power a ship capable of taking 1,000 passengers to the nearest stars. The rapid technological rise of our civilization began but three centuries ago; and in that short time, we have come to a point where potentially, we can venture out into the Galaxy.

One of the most astounding deductions that can be made is that, once interstellar travel has been achieved, it would take only 10 million years or so to colonize the entire Galaxy! It does not seem to matter very much which values one takes for the

And so the question becomes pressing: 'Where is everybody?' The exciting thing is that, today, we may well be in a position to find out. October 1992 saw the launch of the biggest attempt yet to discover extra-terrestrial life, with the US Space Agency investing £65 million in connecting computers to two high-powered radio telescopes which will scan the cosmos. One is in Puerto Rico, at Arecibo; the other, in California's Mojave Desert. As astronomer Jill Tarter, working at Arecibo, put it: 'I'm certain there's something out there to find, even though it's a bit like looking for a needle in a cosmic haystack.'

There are indeed encouraging signs. Scientists have, at times, heard mysterious signals – from the constellations of Virgo and Sagittarius, for instance – but none has ever been repeated for long enough to be studied in detail. There are those, however, who feel that our galactic neighbours – if they exist – are best left alone, and that starting a cosmic dialogue may cause problems if other civilizations are far more advanced than our own.

various factors in the problem, such as the time of travel of starships or the time it takes a colony to develop to the stage where it can itself send out starships: all calculations end up with much the same figure. Now, the Galaxy is at least 10,000 million years old, so colonization time is only one thousandth of that figure (as eight hours compared to one year). We also have reason to believe that, billions of years ago, millions of Earth-like planets should have got to the stage our planet reached just before life appeared on it. If life appeared on those planets, so the argument goes, the whole Galaxy should have been colonized long ago.

IS ANYBODY THERE?

But perhaps, for some reason, life has not yet got started elsewhere, and we are the first intelligent race to evolve in the Galaxy. As a consolation, however, there would be an entire Galaxy waiting to be populated by us.

Some astronomers, such as Frank Drake, have argued that there is an alternative to those extreme views that suggest the number of intelligent races in the Galaxy is either enormous or vanishingly small. It is possible that a civilization would not think the enormous expenditure of resources and energy required to launch colonizing ships worthwhile. Or perhaps a civilization would prefer to stabilize its population and use its resources to maximize its standard of life? Or it may have evolved to some spiritual level at which colonization of other planets is irrelevant. Or else it may have destroyed itself, as we, periodically, seem in danger of doing.

And yet, if life has appeared in our Galaxy over the past few thousand million years, surely, it is argued, some forms of life, arriving at a high scientific and technological level, would have decided to explore and colonize the Galaxy? And if even just one of these alien civilizations decided so to do, in a dramatically short time they should have spread throughout the Galaxy.

In 1953, Dr Stanley Miller, top, simulated the conditions in the primeval Earth's atmosphere. Passing artificial 'lightning strokes' through inorganic chemicals, he created complex 'precursor' molecules, rather like those from which the earliest life developed.

The photograph above shows one of a system of hundreds of channels on the planet Mars, apparently carved by flowing water in the distant past. Liquid water is now absent on Mars; and though simple life may exist on the planet, there are certainly no beings advanced enough to hold a conversation with us.

" YET ACROSS THE GULF OF SPACE, MINDS THAT ARE TO OUR MINDS AS OURS ARE TO THOSE OF THE BEASTS THAT PERISH, INTELLECTS VAST AND COOL AND UNSYMPATHETIC, REGARDED THIS EARTH WITH ENVIOUS EYES AND SLOWLY AND SURELY DREW THEIR PLANS AGAINST US. "

H. G. WELLS,

THE WAR OF THE WORLDS

289

WHEN JOANNA SOUTHCOTT ANNOUNCED SHE WAS PREGNANT WITH THE MESSIAH, SHE WAS 64. BUT THE ECCENTRIC CLAIMS SHE MADE AT THE END OF HER LIFE WERE AS NOTHING COMPARED WITH THOSE MADE BY LATER 'PROPHETS'

A s Joanna Southcott's idiosyncratic ministry gained momentum, her pronouncements became increasingly bizarre. Eternal salvation would be the lot of only 144,000 souls; moreover, to gain admittance to heaven, her followers would have to be 'sealed' by her. She therefore began issuing what amounted to share certificates for a stake in paradise.

These certificates were half-page printed sheets reading: 'The sealed of the Lord – the elect precious man's redemption – to inherit the tree of life – to be made heirs of God and joint-heirs with Jesus Christ – Joanna Southcott.' The impression of her oval seal with its stars and the initials I.C. (Iesus Christus) was appended in red wax at the bottom of each certificate.

By 1805, when 10,000 of these certificates had been issued, Joanna was accused, probably falsely, of selling them; but even if the accusations were true, the bottom fell dramatically out of the market in 1809, when a particularly brutal murderess, named Mary Bateman, was hanged publicly at York and – embarrassingly for Joanna's movement – was found to be a certificate-holder.

In any case, money was plentifully forthcoming from other sources. In 1803, a second 'trial' – or public debate – of Joanna's prophecies was held before a wealthy invited audience at High House, Joanna's home in Paddington, London. Nearly 60 people received 'personal messages' when the sealed documents were opened and read out, and all of those attending the debate made handsome offerings. Another source of income was the second Southcottian chapel opened at Bermondsey, east London, the same year. Here, an apprentice, Henry

The contemporary cartoon, above, entitled The impostor or obstetric dispute, *shows the ridicule afforded by 64-year-old Joanna Southcott's announcement that she was carrying 'Shiloh' – the new Messiah, who would be born on Christmas Day. Oddly, eminent doctors agreed that she showed all the symptoms of pregnancy which, had it run its natural course, would have ended with the birth of a child on 25 December, 1814. Sympathizers showered her and the unborn child with gifts such as these, left, including – somewhat incongruously – a Bible, with which a Messiah would surely be familiar*

PROPHECIES OF A NEW MESSIAH

The Southcott 'seal', above, was appended to certificates issued by the prophetess to the 144,000 souls lucky enough to be approved by her to gain admittance to paradise. There was a rumour that a place in paradise could be bought, but the bottom fell out of the market when a notorious murderess was found to be a certificate-holder.

The elegant crystal goblets, right, were used by the Southcottians for their communion services and were a gift from a wealthy believer. Yet more funds helped establish chapels, such as that in Bermondsey, London, below.

'Joseph the Dreamer' Prescott, and his spiritual manager, Elias Carpenter, 'dreamed' for the benefit of the poorer classes of London. And the working classes of northern England were catered for in the autumn when Joanna went to Salford, Leeds and Stockton-on-Tees, setting up chapels in each town. A third and final 'trial' of her writings took place before a packed crowd in December 1804. Thereafter, to all intents and purposes 'Southcottism' finally became an established, if eccentric, part of English religious life.

At the height of Joanna Southcott's popularity, the 'prophet' Richard Brothers was released, a broken man, from the lunatic asylum at Islington, north London, and went to live quietly in St John's Wood. As both prophets had attracted the attention of the wealthy engraver William Sharp, Joanna's name had been linked with that of Brothers, although they had never met. Joanna's personal ambitions knew

no bounds, however. Now she spent two days carefully defacing as many as 1,000 copies of Sharp's engraving of Brothers as the 'Prince of Hebrews', only to order Sharp to make a similarly dramatic engraving of herself in January 1812, for distribution among the faithful.

Her next public move, too, echoed that of Brothers 18 years before – but was, if anything, more extreme. In the late summer of 1813, she wrote personal letters to every bishop, peer, and Member of Parliament, as well as messages to *The Times* and *Morning Herald*, announcing that she would shortly become 'the mother of Shiloh'.

'In ten years from the fourth of the century,' she said, 'the Messiah will come.' On 13 October 1813,

Engraved from an Original Painting by R.Bull.

she retired permanently from public life to her house at 38 Manchester Street, Manchester Square, in London's West End, with two female disciples, Jane Townley and Ann Underwood.

In late March 1814 – 'ten years from the fourth of the century' – news leaked out that the prophetess was ill, but it was not until 1 August that Jane Townley called for the assistance of nine prominent medical men. They included Dr Joseph Adams, editor of the *Medical and Physical Journal*, Richard Reece, a leading fellow of the Royal College of Physicians, and Dr John Sims, a fellow of the Royal Society and a noted scientific polymath.

It was Dr Adams who issued a cautious statement about Joanna's health to the press on behalf of himself and his colleagues. Joanna Southcott was now 64 years old; but, he confessed, in a

Dr Richard Reece, top, was one of the medical men who confessed themselves bewildered by Joanna Southcott's 'pregnancy' at the age of 64. It was to Dr Reece that Joanna finally announced that, instead of giving birth to the Messiah, she was 'gradually dying', although he could find nothing wrong with her. Yet, only a few days later, she was dead.

The Rev. George Turner of Leeds, above, took over the Southcottian movement after Joanna's death.

younger woman, her symptoms would indicate a pregnancy of four months. If such a pregnancy were to run its course, the child would be born on Christmas Day.

Not unnaturally, the news caused a sensation at every level of society. Medical aspects of the case were discussed avidly in the better newspapers and journals, while gifts of money, jewellery and clothing poured in to Manchester Street. In September, a crib costing £200 was made to order by Seddons of Aldersgate, a leading furniture company, and £100 was spent on a set of silver 'pap-spoons'; while–somewhat superfluously, perhaps, if the child were to be the Messiah – a richly bound vellum Bible, hand tooled and blocked in gold leaf, was sent to await the birth.

On 19 November, however, when Dr Reece called to examine her, Joanna announced that she was 'gradually dying'. As far as Reece could see, she was in good health, but nevertheless she insisted on giving him written instructions to 'open her body' four days after her death, and over the next few weeks all the gifts for 'Shiloh' were returned.

On Christmas Day, growing weak, she gave her last instructions to her female companions: her body was to be 'kept warm' until the post-mortem. And on 27 December, Joanna Southcott died. On New Year's Eve, Dr Reece performed the autopsy, watched by Dr Adams and Dr Sims, and later published a pamphlet of his findings. As far as he had been able to tell, there had been no physical 'pregnancy' and there was no functional disorder or organic disease in the body. Probably all the mischief lay in the brain, which was not examined owing to the high degree of putrefaction – hastened, of course, by the blazing fires kept going in the house on Joanna's final instructions. It was, apparently, a classic case of hysterical pregnancy, but one that, had it run its course, would – in view of Joanna's claims – have been timed with uncanny accuracy.

GREATER THINGS IN STORE

On New Year's Day 1815, Joanna was buried privately at St John's Wood cemetery, not far from the spot where Richard Brothers, her old rival, was to be interred 10 years later. On her tombstone were engraved the words: 'Thou wilt appear in greater power.'

After Joanna's death, her 'movement' was taken over by George Turner, minister of the Southcottian chapel at Leeds, who was assisted by Jane Townley. Their belief was quite unshaken by the non-appearance of Joanna's promised messianic offspring 'Shiloh'. She had, after all, promised that he would be a 'spiritual man' and, reasoned Turner, this 'spirit' could have entered into any one of Joanna's followers. According to the Bible, a 'prophet is without honour in his own country'; but it would be unforgivable of the Southcottians not to recognize him when he did arrive. In effect, therefore, the title was open to all comers.

One of the first to claim it was Mary Boon, an illiterate who, like Joanna, came from Devon. Her prophecies were written out for her by John Ward, a Baptist lay preacher who had joined Boon when she began to prophesy in 1818, four years after Joanna's death. It was Ward, in fact, who was next to be acclaimed as Joanna's 'Shiloh', though George Turner and Jane Townley were suspicious of him. Ward had been born – significantly, some might think – on Christmas Day 1781 in Cork.

At 12, he was an apprentice shipwright in Bristol with a drink problem, but his alcoholism did not prevent him distinguishing himself on *HMS Blanche* at the battle of Copenhagen in 1801. When he was paid off two years later, he gave up drink, married, and became a shoemaker – and turned to religion. Brought up as a Calvinist, he was next attracted to the Methodists and then to the Baptists, finally taking up with Mary Boon. In 1826, he pronounced himself 'illuminated by the Lord', and declared himself to be Joanna's promised 'Shiloh', though he was popularly known as 'Zion' Ward. His wife, neglected and without income, pronounced him mad and brought him before a magistrate who committed Ward to the workhouse.

When Ward was released, he and a companion, Charles William Twort, evolved a new method of prophecy, divining meanings not only from the words of the King James Bible but also from the actual shape of the print. Their enthusiasm gained them not only followers but 18 months in Derby jail for blasphemy, a punishment that was so unpopular that Parliament debated it and finally cut the sentences short. Ward, described as 'gentle, modest, with a high moral tone' and the preacher of 'spiritual pantheism', died on 12 March 1837, already eclipsed by his more vigorous rival, John Wroe.

RAVING HUNCHBACK

Wroe, a year younger than Ward, was the sickly son of a farmer from Bowling, near Bradford, Yorkshire. As a boy, he had carried a window stone up to the second floor of his father's house, damaged his back and 'was never straight again'. In later years, his hunchback lent his ranting sermons an extra aura of wildness.

Two years after Joanna Southcott's death, in 1816, the first signs of mania appeared in Wroe, who was by this time established as a farmer and woolcomber, although he was very much in debt. He took to reading the Bible as he tramped through his fields, saw visions, fell into spontaneous trances and suffered temporary phases of – presumably hysterical – blindness.

In about 1820, he paid a visit to George Turner's chapel at Leeds; but strangely, although Turner looked suspiciously on gentle John Ward, he was impressed by the wild-eyed Wroe. When Turner died in September 1821, Wroe took over his duties as 'Southcottian' leader, and the movement almost instantly fell foul of the law.

Wroe's peculiarities grew more noticeable as time passed. First, he ordered the Southcottians to discard the names of the months, numbering them instead. Then, he began to grow his beard, demanding that all his male disciples do likewise. He also made two highly publicized attempts to walk on water. When his attempts failed hilariously, he hastily announced that he had been undergoing 'public baptism'.

Certainly, Wroe had the courage of his strange convictions. On 17 April, 1823, he was publicly circumcised at a meeting of believers. But the incident had tragic repercussions. One of his disciples,

Henry Lees of Ashton, circumcised an infant called Daniel Grimshaw, who bled to death.

Wroe's trial came about as a result of his sexual tendencies, although the charge of 'swindler' was also levelled at him. In 1827, a 12-year-old girl, Martha Whitley, accused him of having had intercourse with her. At first, Wroe denied the charge; but when, three years later, three more young girls accused him of sexual interference during 'cleansing' ceremonies, he was called to answer.

However, after the trial – an unruly proceeding by all accounts – 'a very considerable number of [the Southcottians] left him and shaved off their beards', including Henry Lees, the over-enthusiastic circumciser. Wroe was never welcome in Ashton again – although, for 40 years afterwards, many of his followers were to be found in the town.

The charge of swindling was almost certainly true. In 1856, Wroe ordered his followers to wear gold rings; but although they paid for the gold, the rings were actually brass. And in 1842, when his printing shop at Wrenthorpe, Wakefield, was broken into by burglars, Wroe's perjury convicted three innocent people, a fact that came to light only when the real culprits were caught, five years later.

Wroe's final prophecy had the same germ of truth as that of Joanna Southcott. In the 1840s, he had forecast that the Millennium would begin in 1863 – but on 5 February of that year, he died suddenly after breaking his collarbone, at Collingwood, Melbourne, Australia, and is buried there.

No portrait exists of Wroe for, unlike Southcott, he thought such things sinful. Possibly his appearance had something to do with the omission, for he was described as having a 'savage, haggard look', with a 'hump back and very prominent nose'.

'There must have been a strange fascination about the man', wrote a late-Victorian commentator, 'for his utterances are but fatuous insipidities with a Biblical twang, having neither the pathetic earnestness of Joanna Southcott, nor the crude originality of her other improver, John Ward.'

*In*Focus

JOANNA SOUTHCOTT'S BOX

The whereabouts of Joanna Southcott's mysterious box remains a secret, but it is said to contain important writings that would guide the Church on to new and wiser paths. Moreover, it should be opened by a convocation of bishops. In 1927, psychical researcher Harry Price claimed to have been given a key to the box. It contained, he said, only an old nightcap, a flintlock pistol and various other oddments. He therefore believed the box to be a hoax. Her supporters maintain, however, that whatever Price opened, it was not Joanna's box.

Crime and banditry, the distress of nations and perplexity are still said by Joanna Southcott's followers to continue until her box of sealed writings is opened by the bishops or their representatives. Indeed, they quote, somewhat enigmatically, from *Revelations* in this connection, as follows: 'And the temple of God was opened... and there was seen the Ark [Chart or Box] of his Testament [or Will]... And round about the Throne were four-and-twenty... Elders [Bishops] sitting... and they fall down and cast their crowns [their Wisdom] before the throne... '

GATEWAY TO OTHER WORLDS

TOM LETHBRIDGE PROGRESSED FROM FINDING HIDDEN OBJECTS THROUGH DOWSING TO EXPLORING THE TIMELESS WORLDS BEYOND DEATH. WHAT DID THIS 'EINSTEIN OF THE PARANORMAL' DISCOVER ABOUT SUCH OTHER REALMS?

I n 1962, five years after his move to Devon, Tom Lethbridge's ideas on ghosts, 'ghouls', pendulums and dowsing rods began to crystallize into a coherent theory, which he outlined in a book called *Ghost and Divining Rod*. This appeared in 1963, and it aroused more interest than anything he had published so far. It deserved to be so popular, for its central theory was original, exciting and well-argued.

He suggested that nature generates fields of static electricity in certain places, particularly near running water. These 'fields' are capable of picking

Saddell Abbey, below, in Strathclyde, Scotland, is a place of curiously strong and varied atmospheres: menacing in the castle, melancholy in the abbey ruins and peaceful at the wishing well. Tom Lethbridge, above, believed that 'atmospheres' are powerful 'emotions recorded in the electrical field of water'.

up and recording the thoughts and feelings of human beings and other living creatures. But human beings are also surrounded by a mild electrical field, as the researches of Harold Burr of Yale University in the United States revealed in the 1930s. So, if someone goes into a room where a murder has taken place and experiences a distinctly unpleasant feeling, all that is happening is that the emotions associated with the crime (such as fear, pain and horror) are being transferred to the visitor's electrical field, in accordance with the laws of electricity. Similarly, if we are feeling full of energy, excitement, misery or anger, the emotional transference may flow the other way, and our feelings will be recorded on the field.

But if human emotions can be imprinted in some way on the 'field' of running water, and picked up by a dowser, then this world we are living in is a far more strange and complex place than most people give it credit for. To begin with, we must be surrounded by hidden information – in the form of these 'tape recordings' – that might become accessible to all of us if we could master the art of using the dowser's pendulum.

It looks – said Lethbridge – as if human beings possess 'psyche-fields' as well as bodies. The body is simply a piece of apparatus for collecting impressions, which are then stored in the psyche-field. But in that case, there would seem to be a part of us that seeks the information. Presumably, this is what religious people call the 'spirit'. And since the information it can acquire through the pendulum may come from the remote past, or from some place on the other side of the world, then this spirit must be outside the limits of space and time.

It was this last idea that excited Lethbridge so much. His experiments with the pendulum seemed to indicate that there are other worlds beyond this

one, perhaps worlds in other dimensions. Presumably, we cannot see them – although they co-exist with our world – because our bodies are rather crude machines for picking up the required low-level vibrations. But the 'psyche-field' – or perhaps the 'spirit' – seems to have access to these other invisible worlds.

DREAMS OF THE PAST

It also seems to have access to other times and other places. In May 1964, a BBC camera team went to Hole House to record an interview with Lethbridge about dowsing. A young cameraman looked so dazed and startled as he got out of the car that Lethbridge asked him: 'Have you been here before?' The cameraman shook his head. 'No. But I've dreamed about it.' He asked if he could look behind the house. Pointing to a wall that Lethbridge had knocked down and rebuilt, he said: 'It wasn't like that years ago. There used to be buildings against it.' That was true – but not in Lethbridge's time. In the herb garden, the cameraman said: 'There used to be buildings there, but they were pulled down.' In his dream, a voice had said: 'Now we shall be able to see the sea.' Again, it was true – but many years before, at the turn of the century. Now a row of trees blotted out the view of the sea.

The cameraman had never been in the area before, and he had no friends or relatives there who might have told him about it. Yet, on five occasions, he had dreamed about Hole House – as it was before he was born.

Lethbridge had always been interested in dreams, ever since he read J.W. Dunne's *An Experiment with Time* in the 1930s. Dunne was an

The diagram, above, illustrates Lethbridge's theory about the creation of the worldwide belief in nymphs 1. An aroused youth pauses within the static field of a stream (A), and vividly creates the image of a girl bathing (C) in his own static field (B). The image leaks into the weaker field (A) where it is 'recorded'. 2. Perhaps years later, a passing youth with a weak psyche-field (D) comes into contact with (A), from which the image of the girl (C) leaks into his field (D). He thinks he has witnessed a supernatural being, when he has really only seen the recording of a thoughtform.

J. W. Dunne, author of An Experiment with Time, *dreamed accurately of the eruption of the volcanic Mount Pelée, Martinique, right, some time before it happened. This and other dreams convinced him that we dream regularly of future events but do not always remember these dreams.*

aeronautics engineer, and around the turn of the century he had a number of impressive dreams of the future – for example, he dreamed accurately about the forthcoming eruption of the volcano, Mount Pelée, on Martinique. Dunne had suggested that time is like a tape or a film, which may get twisted or tangled, so that we can catch glimpses of other times. He used to keep a notebook and pencil by his bed, and jot down his dreams the moment he woke up. He was convinced that we all dream about the future – probably every night of our lives – but that we forget it almost as soon as we wake up.

Lethbridge decided that, if he wanted to study such dream mysteries, he should keep a dream notebook. It was soon filled with his own vivid and idiosyncratic observations.

He became convinced that Dunne was correct in believing that we all dream of future events, but that most of these dreams are so trivial – or so brief – that we fail to remember them. One night, he woke up dreaming about the face of a man that seemed to be looking at him out of a mirror. He was doing something with his hands, which seemed to be moving in the area of his chin. Lethbridge thought he might be shaving.

PREMONITION FULFILLED

The next day, Lethbridge was driving slowly along a narrow lane; a car came round the corner, and at the wheel was the man he had seen in his dream. His face was framed by the windscreen – which Lethbridge had mistaken for a mirror – and his hands were moving in the area of his chin, on top of the steering wheel. Lethbridge was certain that he had never seen the man before.

He also noted that some of his dreams seemed to go backwards. He once dreamed of a furry, snake-like object coming into his bedroom; but all the furniture in the room was reversed, as in a mirror. The snake-like object was recognized as the tail of their Siamese cat, walking backwards. A friend also told him about two 'backward dreams' she had

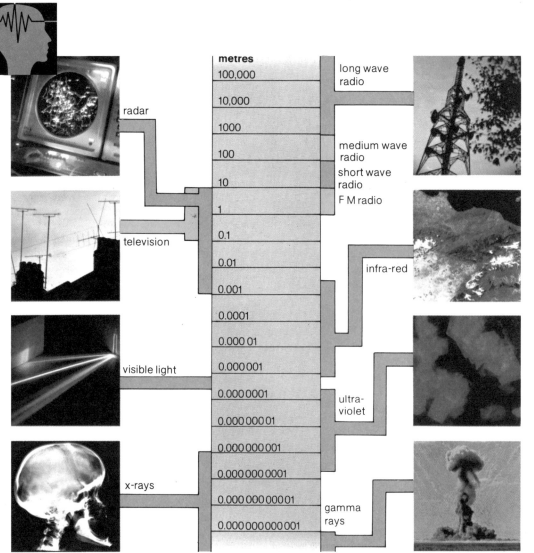

metres	
100,000	long wave radio
10,000	
1000	
100	medium wave radio
10	short wave radio
1	F M radio
0.1	
0.01	
0.001	infra-red
0.0001	
0.000 01	
0.000001	
0.0000001	ultra-violet
0.00000001	
0.000 000 001	
0.0000000001	
0.000 000 00001	gamma rays
0.000000000001	

radar

television

visible light

x-rays

The chart, left, shows the spectrum of electromagnetic (EM) vibrations. EM waves consist of electric and magnetic fields, vibrating with a definite frequency corresponding to a particular wavelength. In order of increasing frequency and decreasing wavelength, the EM spectrum consists of: very long wave radio, used for communication with submarines; long, medium and short wave radio (used for AM broadcasting); FM radio, television and radar; infra-red (heat) radiation which is recorded in the Earth photographs taken by survey satellites; visible light; ultraviolet light which while invisible, stimulates fluorescence in some materials; X-rays; and high-energy gamma rays which occur in fallout and in cosmic rays. The progressive discovery of these waves has inspired speculations concerning unknown 'vibrations' making up our own and higher worlds.

experienced: in one, she saw a couple she knew walk backwards out of their door and drive their car backwards down a lane. In another, she saw some men walking backwards carrying a coffin. One of them uttered the baffling sentence: 'Burnt be enough good woods any.' On waking up, she wrote down the sentence, then read it backwards, and realized that it actually said: 'Any wood's good enough to be burnt.'

But why, Lethbridge asked, should time sometimes go backwards in dreams? The clue was provided by his pendulum, which informed him that the energy vibrations of the next level – the world beyond ours – are four times as fast as those of our world. Lethbridge speculated that during sleep, a part of us passes through this world to a higher world still. Coming back from sleep, we pass through it once again to enter our own much slower world of vibrations. The effect is rather like that experienced when a fast train passes a slower one; although the slow train is moving forward, it appears to be going backwards.

More impressive examples of precognitive dreams came from his correspondents. One woman dreamed of the collapse of a building as the side was blown out and heard a voice say: 'Collapsed like a pack of cards.' A month later, a gas explosion blew out the side of a block of flats called Ronan Point in east London, and a newspaper report actually used the phrase 'Collapsed like a pack of cards'. Another correspondent described a

A gas explosion ripped through the London tower block, Ronan Point, right, causing death and devastation. One woman had dreamed precognitively of the disaster, hearing the very words of the subsequent newspaper headline – 'Collapsed like a pack of cards' – spoken clearly.

dream in which he saw a square-looking Edwardian house with many chimneys being burnt down: a few days later, Tom saw a house of this description being burnt down on a television newsreel.

The more he studied these puzzles, the more convinced Tom Lethbridge became that the key to all of them lies in the concept of vibrations. Our bodies seem to be machines that are tuned to pick up certain vibrations. Our eyes will only register energy with a wavelength that is between that of red and violet light. Shorter or longer wavelengths are invisible to us. Modern physics also tells us that, at the sub-atomic level, matter is in a state of constant vibration.

WORLDS BEYOND WORLDS

According to Lethbridge's pendulum, the 'world' beyond our world – the world that can be detected by a pendulum of more than 40 inches – consists of vibrations that are four times as fast as ours. It is all around us, yet we are unable to see it, because it is beyond the range of our senses. All the objects in our world extend into this other world. Our personalities also extend into it, but we are not aware of this, because our 'everyday self' has no communication with that 'other self'. But the other self can answer questions by means of the pendulum. When Tom and Mina Lethbridge visited a circle of stones called the Merry Maidens, near Penzance in Cornwall, Lethbridge held a pendulum over one of the uprights and asked how old it was. As he did so, he placed one hand on the stone, and experienced something like a mild electric shock. The pendulum then began to gyrate like an aeroplane propeller, and went on swinging in a wide circle for several minutes – Lethbridge counted 451 turns in all. Arbitrarily allowing 10 years for each turn, Lethbridge calculated that the circle dated back to 2540 BC – a result that sounds highly consistent with carbon 14 dating of other megalithic monuments, like Stonehenge. His 'higher self' – outside time – had answered his question, so it seemed.

In 1971, Lethbridge was engaged in writing his book on dreams – *The Power of the Pendulum* – when he became ill and had to be taken to hospital. He was a huge man, and his enormous weight placed a strain on his heart. He died on 30 September, leaving his last book unrevised. He was 70 years old, and his life's work was by no means

The ancient circle of standing stones known as the Merry Maidens near Penzance, Cornwall, is shown below. While dowsing over the stones, Lethbridge experienced a mild electric shock, as if the stones were some kind of battery. But, persisting with his pendulum, he was able to dowse for the age of the stones. Later, more sophisticated techniques – such as carbon 14 dating – were used to date the Merry Maidens, and Lethbridge's dating was confirmed.

complete. Yet, even in its unfinished state, it is one of the most important and exciting contributions to parapsychology in this century.

Lethbridge's insistence on rediscovering the ancient art of dowsing also underlined his emphasis on understanding the differences between primitive and modern Man. Ancient peoples – going back to our cavemen ancestors – believed that the Universe is magical and that Earth is a living creature. They were probably natural dowsers – as, indeed, the aborigines of Australia still are – and responded naturally to the forces of the Earth. Their standing stones were, according to Lethbridge, intended to mark places where the Earth force was most powerful, and perhaps to harness it in some way that is now forgotten.

Modern Man has suppressed – or lost – that instinctive, intuitive contact with the forces of the Universe. He is too busy keeping together his precious civilization. Yet he still potentially possesses that ancient power of dowsing, and could easily develop it if he really wanted to. Lethbridge set out to develop his own powers, and to explore them scientifically, and soon came to the conclusion that the dowsing rod and the pendulum are incredibly accurate. By making use of some unknown part of the mind – the unconscious or 'superconscious' – the dowsing rod and the pendulum can provide information that is inaccessible to our ordinary senses, and can tell us about realms of reality beyond the 'everyday' world of physical matter.

Lethbridge was not a spiritualist. He never paid much attention to the question of life after death or the existence of a 'spirit world'. But by pursuing his researches into these subjects with a tough-minded logic, he concluded that there are other realms of reality beyond our world, and that there are forms of energy that we do not even begin to understand. Magic, spiritualism and occultism are merely our somewhat crude attempts to understand this vast realm of hidden energies, just as alchemy was Man's earliest attempt to understand the mysteries of atomic physics.

As to the meaning of all this, Lethbridge preserved the caution of an academic. Yet, in his last years, he became increasingly convinced that there is indeed a meaning in human existence, and that it is tied up with the concept of our personal evolution. For some as yet not understood reason, he believed, we are being driven to evolve.

THE HAUNTING OF BORLEY CHURCH

WERE HARRY PRICE, HIS DETRACTORS AND HIS DEFENDERS CHASING GHOSTS IN THE WRONG PLACE BY CONCENTRATING ON BORLEY RECTORY? THERE IS, IT SEEMS, A CASE FOR A GENUINE HAUNTING ACROSS THE ROAD AT BORLEY CHURCH, STILL UNDER INVESTIGATION

The major part of Borley church, below, was constructed in the 15th century. Should the many who investigated the Borley rectory hauntings have looked here instead?

In all his Borley investigations and writings, Harry Price paid scant attention to the 12th-century church itself. He was aware of a story, told to him by Ethel Bull in 1929, that coffins in the Waldegrave family vault under the church had been mysteriously moved at some time during the 19th century, but he made little attempt to follow up the matter. Thus, Price may have missed his real chance to confront the paranormal: for, since the early

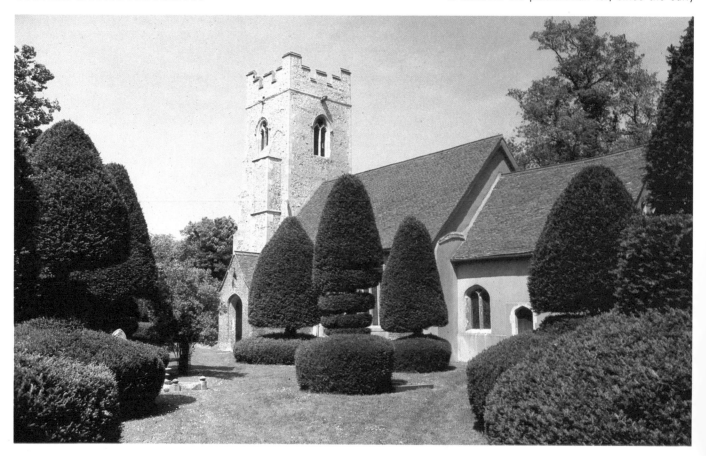

1970s, unexplained events in and around the church – many of them recorded on tape – have proved to be far more baffling than anything that happened in the old rectory.

The manor of 'Barlea' – the Anglo-Saxon for 'boar's pasture' – was mentioned in the Domesday Book, at which time a wooden church served the locality; and the south wall of the present church contains remnants of the flint and rubble building erected in the 12th century. The chancel, the north wall of the nave, and the west tower were added in the 15th century, followed a hundred years later by the red brick south porch.

In the little churchyard itself, planted around with clipped yews and horse chestnut trees, lie the graves of the Bull family. Vandals have broken the stone cross on that of the Rev. Harry Bull, the Victorian rector who drowsed away his last days in the summer-house and who reported seeing a ghostly nun and phantom coach. Geoffrey Croom-Hollingsworth, leader of a small psychical research group at Harlow, Essex, believed, as a result of his investigations, that the cause of the rector's death in 1927 was syphilis. Advanced syphilis is accompanied by a constant drowsiness, during which the sufferer hallucinates – a fact that would explain the rector's 'visions' neatly. But for Croom-Hollingsworth, this was not the whole answer, for he and an assistant, Roy Potter, claimed to have observed the phantom nun themselves.

Croom-Hollingsworth came upon the Borley controversy in the 1960s and decided to examine the facts. He and his group therefore began a series of vigils at Borley. Like subsequent investigators, they chose to keep watch at night to avoid interruption. Over a period of years, in very differing weather

The Enfield Parapsychical Research Group are seen at Borley church, above left. Ronald R. Russell, far right, a founding member, tended towards Price's side in the controversy over Borley's hauntings. But the group found the church itself of most interest and carried out many tests with cameras and sound equipment, as in the photograph, right.

The Reverend Harry Bull's grave in Borley churchyard was subject to vandalism, as shown above right.

conditions and at different times of year, they heard an assortment of noises – raps, heavy panting and furniture being moved. On one occasion, while in the orchard, something huge and dark, 'like an animal', approached them from between the fruit trees and banged loudly on the fence.

On another night, at about 3 a.m., the group heard 'laughter and merriment... which seemed to be coming up the road towards Borley church'. The night was misty, but there was sufficient light to see that nobody was in the roadway. Assuming that the voices were those of late-night revellers, but puzzled by the direction of the sound, Roy Potter got into his car and coasted down the road towards nearby Long Melford with his engine off. He met nobody. Using his walkie-talkie link with Croom-Hollingsworth, he had arranged the experiment of shouting at various points along the Long Melford road to see if the sound carried. The listeners in the churchyard heard nothing. In an attempt to record similar noises, a tape recorder was set up in the porch of the church, while the group kept watch from a distance. Nobody was seen to enter the porch, but the group heard a loud crash and found the tape recorder 'pretty well battered'. The tape had been torn from its reels and lay in a tangle.

But it was the sighting of the nun that convinced the Harlow group that something was indeed strange about Borley. One clear night, Croom-Hollingsworth was standing in the orchard, looking towards the 'nun's walk':

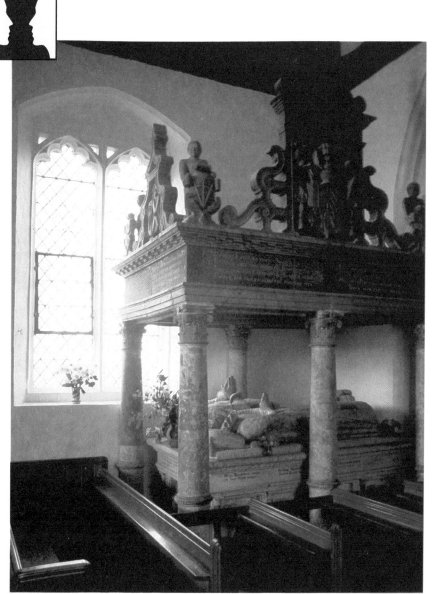

'Suddenly, I saw her quite clearly, in a grey habit and cowl as she moved across the garden and through a hedge. I thought: "Is somebody pulling my leg?" Roy was out in the roadway, and I shouted to him. The figure had disappeared into a modern garage, and I thought that was that; but as Roy joined me, we both saw her come out of the other side. She approached to about 12 feet [3 metres] from us, and we both saw her face, that of an elderly woman in her sixties, perhaps. We followed her as she seemed to glide over a dry ditch as if it wasn't there, before she disappeared into a pile of building bricks. Neither of us was frightened. It was an odd sensation, but peaceful and tranquil.'

Not surprisingly, in view of his experiences, Croom-Hollingsworth had little time for the critics who point to discrepancies in Price's account of the haunting. On the other hand, he said:

'I don't give a damn if Price invented things or not. The basic question is – is the place haunted? And, you can take it from me, it is. I have invented nothing. Roy and I saw the nun quite clearly for a period of about 12 minutes...'

Croom-Hollingsworth's determination impressed Denny Densham, a film director and cameraman. In 1974, he got permission to experiment with tape recorders in the church. The results – which were used by the BBC as a basis for a television programme – are, Densham said, 'quite baffling'.

The first taping began at midnight during the winter months. After the church had been carefully examined and searched, a cassette player was placed by the altar and the investigators sat at the other end of the church. The tape picked up a series of bumps and raps. Next, two tape recorders were locked up in the church, one by the altar and the other halfway down the aisle. Both picked up the unmistakable sound of a heavy door being opened and slammed shut, complete with the squeaking of a bolt. Neither the porch door nor the

" WE ALL FELT WATCHED AND A CURIOUS TINGLING SENSATION WAS FELT; ODDLY ENOUGH, THE MACHINES SEEMED TO PICK UP A LOT OF STATIC AT THIS POINT. WE RECORDED STEALTHY SOUNDS NEAR THE ALTAR, THE SOUND OF A DOOR SHUTTING AGAIN, A CRASH AS OF SOMETHING BEING KNOCKED OVER, AND THEN THE SOUND OF HOLLOW, HEAVY FOOTSTEPS... "

The Waldegrave tomb, above, is a memorial to an old and influential Borley family. Local gossip had it that the Waldegrave coffins in the vault under the church were mysteriously moved in the 19th century.

One of the stained glass windows of Borley church, right, is dedicated to the Reverend Henry Bull. His retelling of the story of the ghostly nun seen at Borley rectory gave a boost to the reputation of his family home as a haunted house.

smaller chancel door had been opened – the researchers had kept watch on the church from outside – and examination showed that the chancel door bolt did not squeak.

CHURCH VIGIL

The following week, Densham and his team started their vigil at 12.30 a.m. They set up a sophisticated stereo tape with two high quality microphones, again placing one near the altar and the other halfway down the aisle. An additional cassette machine was also positioned in front of the altar. Then half the team were locked into the church and the other half kept watch in the churchyard.

'Suddenly there was a curious change in the atmosphere,' said Densham. 'One of the team felt as if he was being watched, and we all felt very cold.' During the next few minutes, the tapes picked up a clatter, as if something had been thrown down the aisle. There were also knockings, rappings, the sound of the door opening again – although both doors remained locked and bolted – and, chillingly, the sound of a human sigh. Afterwards, the team found that the small cassette recorder had jammed, and the tape had been extracted and tangled up.

In July, the party visited Borley again. At 1.45 a.m., they felt a change in the atmosphere .

'We all felt watched, and a curious tingling sensation was felt; oddly enough, the machines seemed to pick up a lot of static at this point. We recorded stealthy sounds near the altar, the sound of the door shutting again, a crash as of something being knocked over, and then the sound of hollow, heavy footsteps, like those of a very large man walking by the altar rail. We could not reproduce them normally: the floor there is of stone, heavily carpeted.'

The observers then saw a glow of light near the chancel door, followed by a terrifying grunt. On this, their final visit, the team saw pinpoints of light in the curtains by one door, and heard the sound of a heavy crash. Densham said:

'Frankly, I am at a loss to explain what goes on at Borley. We made every effort to ensure that our legs weren't being pulled, and the tapes were new and untampered with. No theory I have tried to put forward seems to pan out. We tried leaving pencil and paper in the church, asked the thing to rap and so on, but it doesn't seem to be trying to communicate, unless the damage to the tapes and the throwing of invisible objects in our direction meant that it resented our presence. One's left with the feeling that whatever causes the phenomena is indifferent to or perhaps unaware of observers.'

After that summer of 1974, one of the most regular researchers at Borley was Ronald R. Russell, a member of the Enfield Parapsychical Research Group and professional photographer. Frank Parry, an electrical engineer, and John Fay, a mechanical engineer, usually worked with him. Russell achieved odd results while taking photographs of the area with an Agfa CC21 camera, in which the film is contained in a cassette and processed in the Agfa laboratory.

'Sandwiched between perfectly normal frames we got "ectoplasmic" stuff in the churchyard, shadows where no shadows should be, and a thin light near the north door. As a photographer, I'm at a loss to explain this as camera or film malfunction.'

The altar in Borley church. is shown, above. In 1974, some strange sounds – including raps, crashes and mysterious footsteps – were picked up here on a cassette recorder.

Frank Parry used a graphic analyser, an eight-channel recording machine with slider controls that adjust pitch and level, cut out interference, and enable its operator to 'pinpoint' sounds. As Ronald R. Russell said:

'We have recorded hundreds of extraordinary noises, footsteps, crashes and so on. On one occasion we located a centre of disturbance near the Waldegrave tomb; it was tangible, like a swirling column of energy. When you passed your hand through it, you felt a sort of crackle, like static electricity. On another occasion, we heard a deep, grunting voice, which reminded me irresistibly of Lee Marvin singing *Wandering Star*.'

The church authorities are non-committal, however, preferring to avoid discussion of the topic. But in the parish guidebook, under the heading 'ghosts', is a footnote:

'There are, of course, those who suggest the church itself is haunted. Many old churches and buildings have noises and chill areas which some would classify as ghostly, but those who have lived long in the village, and we who worship in the church, have not experienced anything which would support such thoughts... Visitors should please remember that this is God's house and treat it with reverence.'

"... THERE SEEMS TO BE SOME SORT OF POWER CONCENTRATED IN THE CHURCH ITSELF... WHEN YOU TRY DOWSING IN THE CHURCH, THE ROD PRACTICALLY TWISTS FROM YOUR HANDS... I WOULD SUGGEST THAT THE POWER IS BOOSTED BY THE PRESENCE OF OBSERVERS... "

RONALD R. RUSSELL

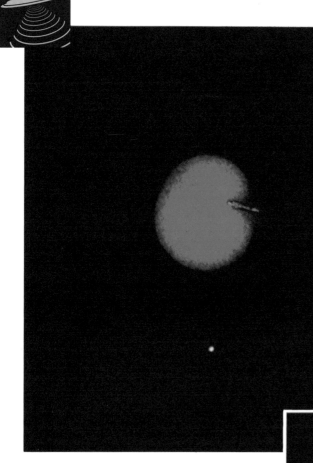

THE UNENDED JOURNEY

THE MOST FAMOUS OF UFO CLOSE ENCOUNTERS, THE ALLEGED ABDUCTION OF BETTY AND BARNEY HILL, CONTINUED FOR LONG AFTERWARDS. HERE, WE DESCRIBE THE SUBSEQUENT EXTRAORDINARY EXPERIENCES IN WHICH BETTY WAS INVOLVED

Not long after her UFO encounter, Betty Hill came home to find leaves piled inexplicably on her kitchen table. Among them were the ear-rings she had been wearing at the time of the sighting. Stranger and stranger incidents then occurred over the years. There were unaccountable noises around the house, and remarkable things happened to appliances: wires were pulled out of a central heating pump; a burglar alarm tripped off inexplicably; and faults developed in electrical equipment such as the refrigerator, toaster, iron, radio set and television, which just as strangely managed to right themselves. Betty finally claimed that her telephone had been tapped both by the Air Force and by some organization calling itself the 'Federal Agency'. Her mail disappeared; she saw and heard prowlers; and she was visited by all kinds of strangers.

While, for some of this, there is external confirmation – neighbours did indeed see prowlers round

PERSPECTIVES

NAZI ALIENS

At many points in the transcript of his hypnotic sessions, the latent fears of Barney Hill, *right*, come to the surface. While recalling watching the light in the sky, he says: 'Betty! This is not a flying saucer. What are you doing this for? You want to believe in this thing, and I don't.' When the object is close enough to appear like 'a big pancake, with rows of windows', he says: 'Can't somebody come and tell me this is not there?' One of the men on board apparently looked friendly, but another figure had an evil face: 'He looks like a German Nazi. He's a Nazi... '

Not surprisingly, considering he was black, Barney was terrified: 'His eyes! His eyes! I've never seen eyes like that before.' But after the experience, when he drove homeward, his former attitude returned. Betty asked him if he believed in flying saucers now, and he replied: 'Oh, Betty, don't be ridiculous.'

A huge red ball, filmed coming straight down from the sky, above left, and a double cylinder travelling along a beam, left – these are Betty Hill's descriptions of the objects that she filmed with a Super 8 movie camera in New Hampshire, not far from her home.

Betty Hill, left, reported frequent paranormal experiences and several sightings of UFOs each week. Sometimes investigators accompanied her, and reported that she misidentified aircraft and street lights. She believed, however, that she had found an actual UFO landing site in New Hampshire and that this accounted for the fact that she saw so many strange aerial objects.

Betty's home – most of it depends on Betty's own personal affirmation. However, in connection with another of her claims, she welcomed other witnesses: this was her UFO-hunting, which she went on to do several nights a week, whether with visitors or alone. She told the ufologist Allan Hendry that she often saw as many as 50 to 100 UFOs a night in a 'special area' in New Hampshire. In an interview, she told of one such incident:

'One particular UFO comes in almost every night. During the winter of 1976-1977, when I saw it often, it was quite spectacular – a sort of flattened disc with brightly coloured lights. One night in January 1977, it landed and turned on twelve big white lights around the rim. Under them, there were two white headlights. I was out there one night with a retired military officer and his wife. When he saw the UFO, he got out of the car and started walking towards it. Suddenly, a large swirling mass shot out from the object. I don't know what it was, but it looked like a red ball rolling over and over and heading directly toward him. I jumped out and tried to film this with my movie camera. But then – I know this sounds incredible – a green light hit my camera and burned out the switch and the circuitry so my camera wouldn't work. When the officer saw this red ball coming at him, he turned and ran back to the car. The red ball stopped, rolled back to the craft, and disappeared.'

But Hendry noted that 'a number of UFO field investigators have accompanied Mrs Hill to her special site, only to confirm that the lights in the night sky that Mrs Hill calls UFOs are only planes and street lights'; and he pointed out that 'she also related other tales involving robots, her neighbour's cat levitating, and a "militant" UFO that burned the paint on her car when she didn't leave the area soon enough to suit them.'

While it is fair to say that these bizarre incidents may be a consequence of her original experience,

and do not therefore invalidate that experience, they cannot be dismissed as irrelevant. In a case that depends entirely on personal testimony, we must know just what kind of person is making the testimony. Psychology, not astronomy, may therefore best help us to understand the Hill case.

We should note that the Hills' story contains many incongruous or inconsistent features. It is not clear, for example, whether Betty is communicating with the aliens in speech or by telepathy: sometimes one is suggested, sometimes the other. In either case, the way the 'leader' used colloquial English is surprising in view of the ignorance the aliens displayed in some areas.

An example of seeming inconsistency is also afforded by the Hills' statement that, in being abducted, they walked – apparently, for some distance – through the woods with their abductors before reaching the clearing where the UFO was parked, whereas after the examination they were soon back at their car, from which they were able to watch the UFO's departure. Such details are not particularly important in themselves, but they serve to remind us that the Hills' story is by no means a precisely detailed and watertight narrative.

SOURCES OF STRESS

In the search for an explanation, the Hills' psychological history should be considered. Barney's health deteriorated during the year following the sighting, but it was by no means perfect before it. Barney did not develop an ulcer in 1962 – rather, the ulcer he already had grew worse. And an ulcer is notoriously the physical expression of psychological disturbance, usually stress. We have noted that both the Hills had been married previously and were separated from the children of those marriages; and, although their present marriage was, to all appearances, a happy one, it was none the less an inter-racial marriage in a society in which this was, at the time, exceptional, and it remained a potential source of stress.

Betty was employed in child welfare work, while Barney worked at nights, commuting 120 miles (200 kilometres) each day, and was involved in the civil rights movement: both these occupations were liable to produce anxiety.

Furthermore, Betty had a history of psychic experiences: she believed that psychic abilities were common in her family and said that she herself had traumatic precognitive dreams as a teenager. Curiously, this ability was also shared by her adopted daughter. 'Actually,' Betty told Dr Berthold Schwarz, a psychologist with an interest in UFOs, 'all my close family members have witnessed UFO sightings: my parents, my sisters and brothers, my nieces and nephews.' Poltergeist

incidents of the type that occurred in the Hill household after the sighting had also been commonplace in her childhood home, where they were attributed to a 'ghost' named Hannah.

How does all this relate to their UFO sighting? Schwarz offers one possibility:

'In Betty's abduction case, as in some UFO contactee examples, there is the overall impression that the involved individual is a unique type of person, whose talents (such as the ability rapidly to enter a deep hypnotic trance, dissociative traits, and high-quality *psi* potentialities), latent or otherwise, are necessary for the UFOs, or the forces behind them...'

But Schwarz's view begs the question of whether any external agency was necessarily involved in Betty and Barney Hill's encounter. An alternative possibility is that there were no UFOs, nor any other external agency manifesting itself in that form, but that the whole experience was a 'projection' from an internal source, Betty's own mind. Many people have taken it for granted that Betty's dreams and the couple's hypnosis narratives are consistent with each other because both were derived from the same source – that is, an actual UFO encounter. But this, in many respects, is a naïve and unwarranted assumption – for it is no less possible that the stories recounted under hypnosis derive from Betty's dreams.

Two more of Betty's UFOs, filmed near the coast, show a disc on edge with a small remote-controlled object under it, top, and three mushroom-shaped objects travelling together, above.

In fact, the moment we focus on Betty's dreams as a record of fact, the insubstantiality of the case becomes apparent. So what is the likelihood that Betty's dreams offer a reliable account of a factual experience? This is not what most dreams do; they are generally either total fantasy, or reworkings of material drawn from a whole variety of sources – the dreamer's daily life, books and television, wishes and fears. We must therefore be wary of supposing that Betty's dreams are any exception to this rule.

Dr Simon, the Hills' hypnotist, never committed himself to a definite statement, but put forward the possibility that Betty's recounting of her dreams had in turn influenced Barney, who then relived them as his own recollections of reality. It is noteworthy that, though Barney's UFO examination supposedly took longer than Betty's, his account of what was done to him during his experience is far less detailed than hers.

But why would Barney fantasize? He may, of course, have been looking for an external cause on which to blame his internal trouble, just as all of us are apt to do at times. The UFO sighting offered a convenient scapegoat. So Barney took Betty's fantasy and used it, albeit unconsciously, for his own purposes. But Dr Simon ruled out any question of conscious collusion, let alone deceit: whatever process was operating, it was completely on an unconscious level.

Dr Simon further warned that hypnosis is not a royal road to the discovery of truth, and further evidence has emerged in later years to confirm this. Hypnotic regressions, in particular, have been shown in numerous cases to produce narratives that are nothing more than fantasy. There is some evidence, on the other hand, for repressed experiences emerging as coherent, detailed and accurate narratives in dreams.

Inevitably, such an interpretation of the Hills' 'memories' of their abduction is bound to be pure conjecture. But it is not more conjectural than the hypothesis that the dreams and hypnosis stories recounted by Betty and Barney Hill are based on a real-life experience of a medical examination by beings from another world.

CELESTIAL HARMONIES

THE SYMBOLISM USED IN THE CONSTRUCTION OF RELIGIOUS BUILDINGS IS BASED, IN GENERAL, ON VARIOUS SYSTEMS OF SACRED GEOMETRY. WHAT SORT OF SECRET LANGUAGE IS INVOLVED?

Among the Hopi Indian tribe of North America, the timing of many religious ceremonies is determined by the alignment of the stars. At particular seasons of the year, the priests and chosen members of the tribe descend into underground chambers, known as *kivas*, and watch the passage of the stars through the entrance slit. Rituals are performed during the time that it takes the relevant constellation to pass overhead. The duration of the entire ceremony, as well as its timing, is thus determined by astronomical – and astrological – conditions.

This megalithic tomb at Maes Howe, Orkney, was carefully aligned so that the setting Sun would shine down the long entrance passage only at the winter solstice. Christianity also aligned its buildings by the Sun, and assimilated other pagan practices. The painting, by an unknown 16th-century artist, of St. Géneviève sitting in a megalithic stone circle, below, dramatically illustrates the blending of Christian and pagan elements.

The 17th-century icon, below, from Bulgaria, depicts St George and the dragon. Christian churches built on the site of pagan temples were often dedicated to St George or St Michael, both dragon-slayers, in a bid to eradicate the old pagan religion centred on dragons.

The precise motives of the megalith-builders in Europe have been the subject of much conjecture, but it seems reasonable to suppose that the megalithic monuments were constructed for a similar purpose. The stars were certainly studied for practical reasons in ancient societies, and not merely for the timing of religious ceremonies. In ancient Babylonia, for example, the time for sowing crops was the 40 days during which the Pleiades were invisible. And research in Britain by, among others, Sir Norman Lockyer and Professor Alexander Thom suggests strongly that megalithic monuments are subtly aligned to form observatories from which the movement of the stars could be accurately charted.

The Christian missionaries who evangelised Britain during the seventh and eighth centuries found a country of heathens who worshipped a confused pantheon – a mixture of Celtic and Roman gods and deities of more ancient origin. The missionaries, therefore, feared that their Christian God would be adopted as just one more divinity on a level with all the others. Indeed, many Christian feasts and rituals were taken from, and celebrated as thinly disguised versions of, pagan counterparts. Moreover, well into the medieval period, pre-Christian festivals at the equinoxes or solstices were celebrated with dancing in churches or churchyards. These were often led – despite repeated injunctions by higher Church authorities – by the priests themselves.

The custom of dancing at ancient sacred sites marked by megalithic monuments also persisted,

much to the dismay of the Church, which regarded the continuance of pagan religious practices as a direct threat. It was in order to stamp them out that churches were often built on the very sites of ancient pagan monuments. Indeed, they were frequently dedicated to St George or St Michael, both of whom were dragon-slayers – the dragon being the symbol of the 'old religion'.

But even though churches were built on ancient sacred sites to eradicate pagan influences, church architecture, curiously enough, preserved at least one pagan element – the practice of precise astronomical alignment. Following the ancient tradition of the sacred geometry of the temples of Greece and Egypt, churches were built on an axis that pointed in the precise direction of sunrise on the morning of the feast-day of the saint to whom the church was dedicated. When this axis had been determined, the master mason and his assistants would lay out the foundations of the church using a knotted cord, just as their ancient Egyptian counterparts had done.

Medieval churches were also designed to harmonise with the world as medieval Man perceived it. As Nigel Pennick remarks in *Sacred Geometry*:

Two members of the warlike order of Knights Templar are dressed for battle in the 18th-century engraving, left. The Templars built churches with a circular plan, intended to represent the physical universe of material forces, but this was eventually condemned as heretical.

The 13th-century Templar chapel, below, at Vera Cruz, Segovia, Spain, is also round.

*In*Focus

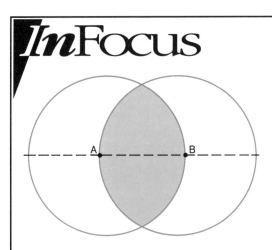

MEDIEVAL MOTIF

The sacred symbol of the *vesica piscis* (literally 'fish's bladder') is a crucial motif in medieval churches throughout Europe (as in the 12th-century decoration of a reliquary at Limoges, France, *above right*). The shape is formed by the intersection of two circles of equal radius, the centre of each lying on the circumference of the other, as *above*. Using the *vesica piscis*, it is possible to construct – with only a ruler and compasses – all the regular figures of plane geometry, and so the figure was extensively used in the laying out of sacred buildings.

Perhaps because of this, the *vesica piscis* is seen as the symbol of creation and regeneration – and has even in certain cultures represented the genitals of the Mother Goddess, from whom all physical life is believed by some to spring.

The Christian Church, meanwhile, has regarded the *vesica piscis* as a symbol of Christ, because of its fish shape, which was used by early Christians as a secret sign for Christ. The symbolism is reinforced by the overlapping circles that compose the figure: Christ is seen as the meeting point of heaven and earth, spiritual and material, creator and created.

'Physical manifestations of the *summa theologiae*, the microcosmic embodiment of the created universe, cathedrals in their perfect completed form, united in their position, orientation, geometry, proportion and symbolism, attempt to create the Great Work – the unification of man with God.'

True enough, the physical fabric of the church was, to the educated medieval mind, a rich metaphor of the world as organised religion taught Man to see it. The traditional nave-and-transepts of most churches reflected the fundamental symbol of Christianity – the Latin cross. It also represented the human form. The French theologian Durandus of St Pourcain (c. 1270-1334) wrote in *Rationale Divinorum Officiorum* ('Explanation of the Divine Office'):

'The arrangement of a material church resembles that of the human body; the chancel... represents the head, the transepts, the hands and arms, and the remainder – towards the west – the rest of the body. The sacrifice of the altar denotes the vows of the heart.'

By the Renaissance, architectural theorists were using similar arguments to insist that the only correct form for church design was the nave-and-transepts plan. Among them was Pietro Cataneo who argued, in *I Quattro Libri dell' Architettura* ('The Four Books of Architecture'), published in 1554, that the temple was symbolic of the body of God, and that churches should also celebrate the crucified Christ and therefore take the shape of the cross. Thus, the church would represent both the body of Man (made in the image of God) and the crucifixion of Christ.

A separate, but parallel, tradition of building round churches came to be regarded, in consequence, as heretical. These churches represent the *imago mundi* (image of the world), and they hold a special place in Christian architecture. It was, in fact, the round form that was chosen for the Church of the Holy Sepulchre in Jerusalem, which marked the tomb of Christ and (so it was believed) the centre of the world.

In the late medieval period, round churches also became associated with the fabulously wealthy military order of the Knights Templar. When the order was brutally suppressed in 1312, its members were accused of numerous heresies – such as blasphemy – and their form of church-building, too, was branded as heretical.

Unlike the nave-and-transepts design, the round form did not represent the body of a man, the body of God, or the cross on which Christ was crucified. It represented, instead, the physical universe – the domain of material and ungodly forces. The Templars believed that the place of God in the Universe had been usurped by his evil counterpart, the *rex mundi* ('king of the world'), and that these two waged an incessant battle over men's souls, in which it was by no means certain that good would win. At the centre of Templar churches stood an altar in the form of a perfect cube, symbol of the Earth within the heavens.

With the suppression of the Templars, the building of round churches virtually ceased until Renaissance architects reintroduced the form, following their study of certain classical temples.

The cruciform plan of Chartres cathedral, in France, left, symbolises both the crucifixion of Christ and the body of Man, made in the image of God.

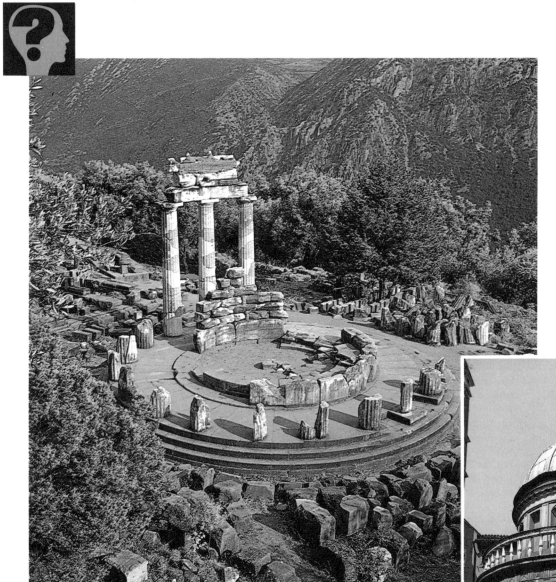

But it was soon suppressed again by Church authorities, on the grounds that pagan designs should not be used for Christian buildings.

That sacred symbolism of this kind was taken very seriously is clear. Indeed, medieval churches abounded with paintings and statuary in which more geometrical symbolism was to be found. The circle, for example, was the symbol of the infinite Universe – the cosmos; the square represented the microcosm, the finite Earth; the triangle stood for the Holy Trinity – Father, Son and Holy Ghost. In medieval art, the shape of the *vesica piscis* (literally, 'fish's bladder') also had a complex symbolism.

In addition to these, there were several systems of proportions that, although commonly used in classical and medieval times, did not become fully articulated until the Renaissance. Chief among these were the proportions defined by a triangle with sides measuring three, four and five units. This derived from the surveying instrument used by the ancient Egyptians, and the so-called Golden Section, known since the time of the ancient Greek mathemetician, Euclid. To see just how far such use of proportion can be taken, it is interesting to consider a document describing the design of the church of San Francesco della Vigna in Venice, Italy. The church was begun in 1534, under the direction

Little remains of the fourth-century BC marble rotunda in the sanctuary of Athena Pronaia at Delphi, above; but of its original 20 Doric columns, three have been re-erected. It was classical Greek buildings such as this that inspired the Renaissance architects to revive the round form in church architecture. Bramante's little Tempietto church in Rome (completed in 1502), above right, exhibits many such classical features.

of the architect Jacopo Sansovino. But arguments had arisen over the proportional system suitable for such a building, and a Franciscan monk, named Francesco di Giorgi, was called in to advise.

Giorgi suggested a system of proportion based on the number three – symbolic of the Trinity. His overall system was also related to the proportions of Vitruvian Man – the ideally shaped human devised by the ancient Roman engineer and architect, Vitruvius. Heavily symbolic and rigorously proportional, this design system was approved by the painter Titian, the architect Serlio, and the humanist philosopher Fortunio Spira. The facade of the church was completed 30 years later by Palladio, who used the very same system of proportion.

The ancient tradition of sacred geometry can be read as an attempt to make the buildings of Man harmonise with the world in which he finds himself and to be physical expressions of fundamental truths, both temporal and eternal. Sacred geometry has an explicit foundation in the natural world. As the preamble to Nigel Pennick's *Sacred Geometry* puts it: 'Geometry underlies the structure of all things – from galaxies to molecules. Each time a geometrical form is created, an expression of this universal oneness is made... Sacred geometry is responsible for the feeling of awe generated by a Gothic cathedral as well as for the "rightness" of a Georgian drawing-room.'

Examples cited to support this include the beautiful double-helix of the DNA (deoxyribonucleic acid) molecule; the manifestation of the logarithmic spiral (based ultimately upon the golden ratio) in the shell of the nautilus mollusc; and the harmonic intervals (similar to those in music) in atomic energy levels. All these seem to be manifestations of a transcendent geometrical order. This belief has yet to be proved by science; but what is beyond doubt is the beauty of the material language it has generated.

The Venetian church of San Francesco della Vigna, seen above in a painting by Canaletto (1697-1768), was based on the classical proportions of Vitruvian Man.

An 18th-century church mural of the Trinity, from Bulgaria, left, shows the Father, Son and Holy Ghost (represented by a dove) within a circle – the symbol of the cosmos. The square represents the finite Earth within the cosmos.

> WHEN FIFTEENTH-CENTURY WRITERS SPOKE OF DERIVING ARCHITECTURAL FORMS FROM THE HUMAN BODY, THEY DID NOT THINK OF THE BODY AS A LIVING ORGANISM, BUT AS A MICROCOSM OF THE UNIVERSE...
>
> **JAMES S. ACKERMAN, THE ARCHITECTURE OF MICHELANGELO**

PERSPECTIVES

THE CANDLESTICK OF FAITH

While religious symbolism permeates much of Christian art and architecture, the far older religion of Judaism has its own objects of symbolic importance. One of the central motifs of Judaism is the menorah – the seven-branched candlestick that was originally made for the Tabernacle (holy sanctuary) of the desert-dwelling Hebrews. This menorah was eventually placed in Solomon's Temple at Jerusalem, and its successor vanished with the destruction of the Second Temple in AD 70.

Since then, the menorah – in both its seven- and eight-branched forms – has come to embody for Jews not only the memory of the Temples' destruction, but Messianic hope, as well as personal and national redemption. The very shape of the menorah also has meaning: it is thought to represent the sacred Tree of Life – a common metaphor in Jewish tradition. According to rabbinical literature, the seven lights also represent the seven days of Creation.

After the loss of the Temple menorah, rabbinic law prevented Jews from making copies of the original for ritual use. It was only in the 12th century that Jews began to use menorahs in the synagogue and the home, especially over Chanukah, the Festival of Lights. (It was for this festival that the eight-branched version was developed, with the central, or ninth, light used to kindle the others, as pictured here.) Today, the menorah is one of the most popular images of Jewish art and religion – a symbol of everlasting light, hope and faith.

GELLER'S GURU

PSYCHICAL RESEARCHER ANDRIJA PUHARICH HAS BEEN DESCRIBED AS ONE OF THE MOST BRILLIANT MINDS IN PARAPSYCHOLOGY. HE EVEN BECAME URI GELLER'S MENTOR AT ONE TIME

At about 11 a.m. on 11 January 1971, the scientist and psychical researcher Andrija Puharich was sitting in his New York office when the telephone rang. A woman asked him if he had any comment to make about the death of the Brazilian healer, Arigo. Puharich had been planning to carry out detailed investigations into this famous 'psychic surgeon', and he asked the caller if she was quite sure that Arigo had died: she replied that she was. She gave Puharich her name and telephone number, and he spent the rest of the day trying to confirm the news. Eventually, friends in Brazil told him that it was true and that Arigo – whose real name was José Pedro de Freitas – had

Andrija Puharich, above, has a wide-ranging interest in the paranormal and is apparently able to trigger psychic powers in others. In 1952, for example, the Hindu scholar Dr D. G. Vinod, right, went into a trance soon after entering Puharich's laboratory. In this state, Vinod acted as a channel for 'M', one of the extra-terrestrials that claimed to take an interest in Puharich's work and the future of the Earth.

died in a car crash at 12.15 p.m. near his home in Congonhas do Campo, Brazil. Since there is an hour's time difference between Congonhas and New York, the accident happened at 11.15 a.m. New York time, a quarter-of-an-hour *after* Puharich had received the telephone call. But when Puharich looked on his notepad for the caller's name and telephone number, these details had vanished without trace.

The sensible and logical explanation for this bizarre sequence of events is that Puharich had simply mistaken the time at which he received the telephone call, and that he had mislaid the woman's name and number. But what really puzzled Puharich was that, ever since he had started researching into the paranormal in the 1950s, he had undergone similar experiences. Indeed, he

believed that he had been selected as the 'target' for a series of seemingly preposterous events in order to force him to the conclusion that our scientific view of the Universe is too narrow and rigid.

This sequence of events began at the end of December 1952, when Puharich was conducting a series of laboratory experiments into telepathy. One day, a Hindu scholar, Dr D.G. Vinod, visited Puharich and soon afterwards went into a trance. He began to speak in a deep, sonorous voice, quite unlike his own high-pitched voice, and with a perfect English accent. The voice identified itself as 'M', one of the 'Nine Principles and Forces' superhuman intelligences who apparently intended to help the human race.

'M' spoke impressively and lucidly for 90 minutes and referred to a version of Einstein's famous equation relating mass and energy, and to the number seven which was, apparently, the key to understanding the mind and its paranormal powers. 'This is one of the most secret insights,' said 'M'. However, when Dr Vinod came out of his trance, he could not remember anything of what he had said.

During the next occasion when Dr Vinod went into a trance, a large ball of cotton-like material, consisting of strange threads, suddenly appeared on the floor beside him. Everyone present agreed that it seemed to have emerged from out of the floor. Then the same voice expounded the philosophy of the 'Nine'. Puharich was very impressed because its utterances were more intelligent and contained much more detailed information than is usually given by an entranced medium.

Three years later, Puharich was travelling in Mexico with the psychic Peter Hurkos when he met an American doctor, Charles Laughead. Once Laughead learned that Hurkos was a psychic, he told him that both he and his wife had attended sessions in which a young man went into a trance and delivered messages from 'space beings'. Puharich thought the Laugheads a little mad and forgot all about them until, one day, he received a letter from Laughead explaining that the 'space beings' had asked him to pass on certain information to Puharich. He was amazed to find out that

José Arigo, the world-famous Brazilian healer, is pictured left with friends. In late 1970, he confided to a former president of Brazil, Dr Juscelino Kubitschek, above, that he, Arigo, was about to die a violent death. In January 1971, Puharich, who had been planning to research the psychic surgeon's work, received a mystery telephone call telling him of Arigo's death in a car crash 15 minutes before it actually took place. Instead of going to Brazil, Puharich went to Israel and met, for the first time, a young entertainer called Uri Geller, whose powers impressed him greatly.

the messages began 'M calling', and that they contained messages from the 'Nine'. Puharich argued that it would have been impossible for Laughead to have found out about Dr Vinod's seances and the 'Nine'. Suddenly, it began to look as if the 'Nine' might be more than a mere invention of Dr Vinod's unconscious mind.

It was in 1963, when Puharich was on an archaeological expedition to Brazil, that he had heard about Arigo and the way in which he would go into a trance and perform the most unlikely operations with an old penknife. According to Puharich's informant, Arigo had started performing

these operations in 1950 when he had been staying in a hotel with the politician Lucio Bittencourt, who was suffering from lung cancer.

Early one morning, Arigo wandered into Bittencourt's room in a trance, holding an open razor, whereupon Bittencourt blacked out. When he woke up, he had a large wound in his back and felt weak and faint: a medical examination showed that the cancer had vanished. As for Arigo, he could remember nothing whatsoever of what had happened. Later, he became convinced that, during these 'operations', his body was taken over by the spirit of a German surgeon, Dr Fritz, who had died in 1918.

Puharich was somewhat sceptical, but nonetheless drove to Congonhas to meet Arigo. The following day, he watched him perform a further 'operation' and was shocked to see Arigo thrust a penknife into a man's eye, scrape around vigorously while the eyeball rested on the patient's cheek, and haul out a large lump of pus. And, the very next day, Arigo hacked a lipoma – a benign tumour – off Puharich's own arm with the same penknife. Puharich deliberately refrained from applying disinfectant to the wound; yet, three days later, it had almost healed.

> **PUHARICH CAME TO BELIEVE THAT GELLER WAS AN EXCEPTIONALLY GIFTED PSYCHIC WHO POSSESED ASTONISHINGLY UNUSUAL POWERS.**

*In*Focus

VOICES FROM SPACE

There seems little doubt that it was Andrija Puharich's total commitment to the space beings – known as the 'Nine' – that led to the parting of the ways between Uri Geller and himself.

At one point, the 'space beings', speaking on tape with metallic voices, told Puharich

that they intended to land on Earth in their starship *Spectra*. Unfortunately for his credibility, they did not. Even so, the aliens continued to haunt those around Puharich, such as medium Phyllis Schlemmer, *left,* who became the 'voice' for the 'Nine' after a previous psychic channel, Bobby Horne, left Puharich's home in confusion and disgust. He had apparently been the dupe of cosmic hoaxers who, in the words of author Colin Wilson, appeared 'to be led by the spirit of W.C. Fields'! Yet, even after splitting up with Puharich, Horne's psychic collaborators continued to receive messages from 'space beings' who talked of universal peace.

Puharich's most famous protégé was Uri Geller, above, whose telepathic powers and paranormal metal-bending are still controversial, even among parapsychologists. Puharich also associated openly with such people as Dr Charles A. Laughead, above left, who lost his post at Michigan State College after he declared he knew when the world would end. The world continued to turn, however, as usual, after the given date.

Puharich carried out a careful study of Arigo, and tried out his German on Dr Fritz, only to discover that the doctor's German was as poor as his own. However, Puharich decided that Arigo's extraordinary surgical abilities were genuine, and that he must have been taken over by an intelligence; moreover, this intelligence possessed 'second sight' because Arigo had no medical training, yet could diagnose a patient's illness simply by looking at him.

In late December 1970, Arigo was visited by the former president of Brazil, Dr Juscelino Kubitschek, and calmly told him: 'This is the last time we shall meet. Soon I shall die a violent death.' He also told the editor of a local newspaper that 'my mission on earth is over.' Two weeks later, in a heavy rainstorm, the vehicle in which Arigo was travelling had a collision with a pick-up truck. Arigo died immediately.

At the very time that Puharich heard the news of Arigo's death, he had been preparing to make another trip to Brazil to carry out further investigations into Arigo's extraordinary powers. Now, instead, he went to Israel to see Uri Geller, who was demonstrating his psychic powers in a nightclub in Haifa. Puharich watched Geller mind-reading

successfully, and saw him break a ring held by a woman, merely by placing his hand above hers. The following day, in Puharich's hotel room, he also saw Geller deflect a compass needle and then raise the temperature of a thermometer simply by concentrating on each object in turn.

But the feat that really convinced Puharich that Geller must be a genuine psychic was comparatively simple. Geller wrote something on a notepad, then placed the pad face down on a table and asked Puharich to think of three numbers. Puharich chose four, three and two. Geller then told him to turn the notepad over: the very same numbers were written on it – in other words, Geller had anticipated Puharich's thoughts before he even gave shape to them.

WHO PROGRAMMED GELLER?

Puharich came to believe that Geller was an exceptionally gifted psychic who possessed unusual powers; and in 1971, his investigations took a new turn. During a hypnosis session, which Puharich recorded on a cassette, Geller went into a trance in which he described how, at the age of three, he had fallen asleep in a garden in Tel Aviv. Suddenly, he had been awakened by a shining, bowl-like object above his head – apparently a spacecraft – and had been struck to the ground by a beam of light. As Geller recalled these events, a strange metallic voice began to speak from above his head. It identified itself as one of the 'space beings' who had 'programmed' Geller at the age of three, and it then announced that world peace was about to be endangered by an immensely destructive war that Geller could avert. However, when Geller woke up, he could remember nothing about what had transpired. Then, as Puharich began to play back the recording of this voice, Geller snatched the cassette – and it promptly vanished from his hand.

At a later hypnosis session, the voice of the 'space man' was heard again. This time, it identified itself as one of the 'Nine'. From then on, hardly a day passed without some extraordinary event occurring. On one occasion, for example, Geller dematerialised the cartridge of Puharich's pen that was locked in a wooden box. Later, he took Puharich for a drive at night and, to Puharich's amazement, they both saw a great disc-like craft in a field, with a flashing blue light above it. With considerable alarm, Puharich watched as Geller walked

The photograph, right, of an alleged UFO in mid-flight – identified by the jagged line on the left – and a space being', right, was taken by Puharich at Mill Hill, North London, on 24 May 1974. UFOs often seem to appear to those who are psychic; and although Puharich apparently discovered such abilities in others, he never made claims to be particularly psychic himself, but spent time researching the chemical origins of life in his laboratory in North Carolina, below.

towards it and climbed in. Ten minutes later, he emerged from the craft and handed Puharich the cartridge from his pen. Meanwhile, Puharich took many photographs of the craft; but when he went to remove the film from the camera, he found that it had vanished.

Two years later, Puharich retold this story, and many others, in his book *Uri: a Journal of the Mystery of Uri Geller.* Given Puharich's reputation as an investigator, it should have caused a world-wide sensation. But Puharich's statement that Geller's powers came from 'space beings' was received with incredulity.

As Colin Wilson puts it in his book *Mysteries:*

'There was something comic in the assertion that Geller was the ambassador of superhuman intelligences, and that the proof lay in his ability to bend spoons... The opposition could be divided into two factions: those who believed Puharich had been hoodwinked by Geller, and those who believed that Geller and Puharich were trying to hoodwink the rest of the world. Not long after the book's publication, Geller and Puharich divided to go their separate ways.'

It was an unfortunate outcome for a man who had attained a considerable reputation for himself

THE CURSE OF FYVIE CASTLE

AN ANCIENT CURSE LAID ON FYVIE CASTLE IN SCOTLAND IS SAID STILL TO BE EFFECTIVE TODAY. IS THERE TRUTH BEHIND THIS MACABRE LEGEND OF A MELANCHOLY GHOST?

Alexander Forbes-Leith bought Fyvie Castle in 1889. With it, he acquired both a curse and, perhaps, the only ghost that has ever signed its name in stone for later generations to see.

The castle, which stands some 30 miles (50 kilometres) north-west of Aberdeen, has been described as the 'crowning glory of Scottish baronial architecture'. Its foundations were laid before the Norman Conquest in 1066 and, since the 14th century, it has been held by only five great families.

Like many a blight on old Scottish families, the 'Fyvie curse' was the work of the ubiquitous Thomas the Rhymer. Although he was shrouded in legend and superstition, it seems certain that Thomas of Erceldoune was a real person. He was born in 1220 and is mentioned as witness to a deed at the Abbey of Melrose around 1240. In Peter of Langtoft's early 14th-century *Chronicle*, it is also stated that he was a poet.

In his own day, Thomas the Rhymer was widely credited as being the lover of the 'Queen of Elfland'. It was she who had given him the power of prophecy; and when he vanished, it was presumed that she had carried him off. It is more likely, however, that he entered a monastery or, as Sir Walter Scott believed, was murdered by robbers.

While he was alive, his travels were well-recorded both in local lore and in contemporary

The magnificent south front of Scotland's Fyvie Castle, above, was extensively rebuilt in the early 16th century by Alexander Seton, Lord Fyvie, right. According to legend, three 'weeping stones' of ill omen had been built into the earlier fabric of Fyvie Castle: as long as they remained there, no heir would be born within the castle's walls.

documents. But he cannot have been a welcome guest, since his prophecies invariably foretold disaster; bloodshed and general mayhem were his stock-in-trade. Nevertheless, few of the lairds visited by Thomas the Rhymer cared to turn him away in case even worse befell them. According to James Murray, the 19th-century editor of the five ancient manuscripts that tell Thomas' story, the gates of

Fyvie Castle had stood 'wall-wide' – that is, open for seven years and a day, awaiting his inevitable arrival. When he finally turned up, it was in a typically ostentatious style. 'He suddenly appeared before the fair building, accompanied by a violent storm of wind and rain, which stripped the surrounding trees of their leaves and shut the Castle gates with a loud crash. But while the tempest was raging on all sides, it was observed that, close to the spot where the Tammas [Thomas] stood, there was not wind enough to shake a pile of grass or a hair of his beard.' Not surprisingly, Thomas was far from pleased that the Castle gates should have slammed shut in his face. Angrily, he uttered the following blood-curdling prophecy:

> 'Fyvie, Fyvie, thou's never thrive
> As lang's there's in thee stanis [stones] three.
> There's ane intill [one in] the oldest tower,
> There's ane intill the ladye's bower,
> There's ane intill the water-yett [water gate]
> And thir three stanes ye's never get.'

This somewhat obscure pronouncement was taken to mean that three stones, known collectively as the 'weeping stones', which had originally been taken from a nearby church property, would act as evil omens to Fyvie Castle as long as they remained part of the building. Only one of the stones, the one originally in 'the ladye's bower', has been found as yet, and so the curse remains.

Today, this stone stands in a wooden bowl in the charter room. At times, it is bone dry, and at

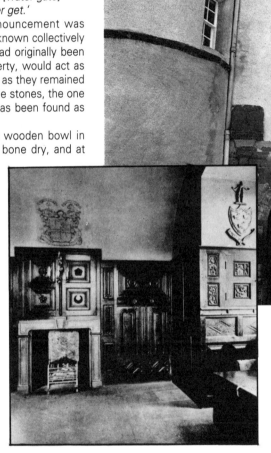

The Seton Tower, above right, over the main gate, was being rebuilt by Lord Fyvie when he married his second wife in 1601. Because the new apartments in it were not ready for occupation, the couple spent their wedding night in a room in the older part of Fyvie Castle.

others is seen to be 'exuding sufficient water to fill the bowl'. The stone said to be beneath the 'water-yett' has never been located; and the third one may have been built into what is now the Preston Tower since once, records an ancient document at the castle, 'when the rightful but dispossessed heir to the property approached, the water gushed forth in mournful salutation.'

Although Thomas the Rhymer was far from specific, the actual nature of the curse was interpreted as meaning that no heir would ever be born in the castle, and this is said to have been true since 1433. Furthermore, the castle would never pass from a father to his eldest son. This claim has held good. Indeed, among the Forbes-Leith family,

The panelled charter room, above, decorated with crescents, cinquefoils and the arms of the Seton family, was another of Lord Fyvie's improvements to the castle. The only one of the three 'weeping stones' that has been located is reputedly kept in a wooden bowl in this room.

the last private owners of the castle, no first-born survived to inherit it. Perhaps none ever will; since 1984, Fyvie Castle has been in the hands of the National Trust for Scotland.

But there is another mystery surrounding Fyvie Castle. It, too, concerns a stone, and one that is situated immediately above the charter room. It forms a window-sill three storeys up the sheer face of the castle wall. The puzzle, which dates from the night of 27 October 1601, has so far defied any rational explanation. At that time, the laird was Alexander Seton, Lord Fyvie, afterwards first Earl of Dunfermline, and Lord President of the Scottish sessions.

In 1592, Seton married Dame Lilias (or Lilies) Drummond, daughter of Lord Patrick Drummond, another peer connected with the ruling house of Stuart. Dame Lilias was a handsome, happy woman, and for nine years she and her husband were contented together. In that time, she bore five daughters, four of whom survived to marry influential noblemen. However, Lilias was not as strong as her appearance suggested; and on 8 May 1601, she died at her husband's house in Fife, where she was buried.

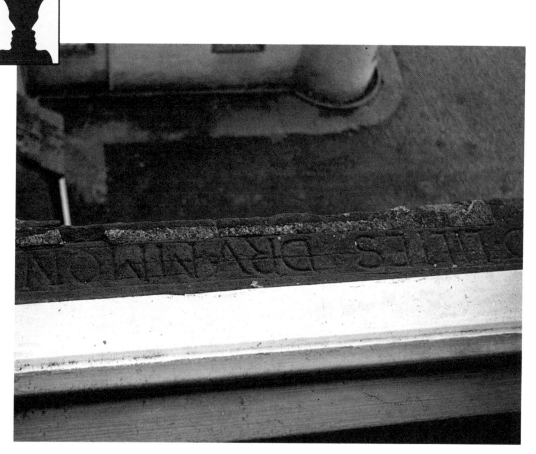

On the stone window-sill, left, the name of Lord Fyvie's first wife, D. LILIES DRUMMOND, has been carved upside down in characters nearly 3 inches (7 centimetres) high. The room, called the Drummond Room, is said to be the one occupied by Lord Fyvie and his second wife on their wedding night in 1601. During the night, they heard deep sighs; and in the morning, they discovered Dame Lilias' name incised outside the window.

Dame Lilias was not quite 30 when she died. According to the historical record, Seton seems to have mourned her death, and the fact that he remained on good terms with his brother-in-law bears this out. Tradition, on the other hand, asserts something different: tired of waiting for the son and heir who never came, Seton had begun an affair with the beautiful Lady Grizel Leslie, daughter of the Master of Rothes, whose home was 20 miles (32 kilometres) from Fyvie. Because of this, legend has it, Dame Lilias had died of a broken heart.

Although history and hearsay would appear to part company in their accounts of Seton's behaviour immediately after his wife's death, there can be no doubt that he lost little time in wooing the said Lady Grizel Leslie. Within six months, they were married.

On the night of 27 October, they retired to their temporary bedchamber, a small room at the top of the spiral staircase in the older part of the castle, as their new quarters – in what is now Seton Tower – were not yet finished.

That night, they both heard heavy sighs coming from outside their room; but even though Seton went out to investigate and roused a servant, no intruder was found. With the dawn, however, they discovered a startling indication of the intruder's identity. Carved upside down on the window sill, in neat 3-inch (7-centimetre) high letters, was the name D. LILIES DRUMMOND.

The carving, still clear and quite unworn, is over 50 feet (15 metres) from the ground in the old defensive wall of the castle, which had deliberately been built without any footholds.

Various suggestions have been put forward ever since as to an origin for the carving; but none seems tenable. The precision of the work and the perfection of the lettering show that, however it was done, it took great skill, so that any 'hoax' on the part of Seton or one of his ordinary household can probably be ruled out. Besides, why should the laird do something so calculated to terrify the young wife with whom he was obviously in love? And if he

PERSPECTIVES

SYMPTOMS OF A HEX

Hexes or spells have been placed on humans from time immemorial. Although modern urbanites may dismiss them as nothing but superstitious nonsense, their power to instil fear – and even, ultimately, to kill – is still reported from places as far apart as Haiti, London, Oklahoma City and West Africa.

The threat of death must be the most potent of the hexes. In so-called 'voodoo deaths', the victim suffers extreme anxiety

attacks, which appear to influence the sympathetic nervous system (affecting involuntary muscles, such as the heart). The heart beats too fast and collapses into a state of constant contraction. Some victims become frozen with fear, and their lungs cannot function, failing to provide the body with sufficient oxygen. These are the physical results of a hex; what provokes them is the victim's deep belief that death is unavoidable.

or someone else in the castle did it, why write it upside down?

Seton was the great architect of Fyvie as it stands today, and work is known to have been underway at the time of his second marriage. It has been suggested that one of his masons inscribed the name out of respect for the dead mistress. But, again, why do it upside down on a window-sill and

Another of Lord Fyvie's additions to the castle was the great stone wheel staircase, below. It is on this staircase that the Green Lady, the ghost of the unhappy Dame Lilias, is sometimes seen. She is dressed in a shimmering green gown and her appearance often heralds a death in the family. A portrait, right, that hangs in the castle is said to be of the Green Lady ghost rather than of Dame Lilias: it is dated 1676, 75 years after Dame Lilias died.

where it could be seen only from the interior of the room? Commemorative plaques, consisting of initials and coat of arms, were normally carved on stone and let into the surface of the wall where they could be seen. But the room was not in general use; in fact, it was far from the sumptuous new apartments Seton was then building, and was chosen at the very last moment. To reach the window-sill, it would have been necessary to erect scaffolding – a lengthy process. The mason would then have had to climb the scaffolding and noisily hammer out the deeply incised lettering. Yet, all the newlywed couple heard were 'deep sighs'.

LUMINOUS LADY

Whether natural or supernatural, the mysterious topsy-turvy writing marked the beginning of the haunting of the staircase, and the corridors leading from it, by a luminous 'Green Ladye', as 17th-century documents call her. Naturally, it was presumed that she was Dame Lilias, although a portrait dated 1676 that hangs in the castle, and reputedly that of the ghost, bears only a slight resemblance to the portrait of Seton's first wife. It is clad in a blue-green dress, and a faint iridescence seems to radiate from the enigmatic features.

The 'Green Lady' and her nocturnal rambles up and down the great wheel staircase were periodically documented over the years; and each account tells of the greenish-glow that surrounded her. Sometimes, however, she was seen simply as a flicker of light at the end of a dark corridor. Colonel Cosmo Gordon, fifth Laird of Gordon of Fyvie, who had the castle from 1847 to 1879, recorded that, on one occasion, he was shaken out of bed by unseen hands; while on another night, a wind arose inside the castle – when all outside was quiet – and blew the bedclothes off him and his various guests.

Presumably, Dame Lilias was in a boisterous mood on that occasion.

The Gordons came to Fyvie in 1733, and the apparition was seen so many times that they came to adopt the 'Green Lady' as their own, believing that her existence was personal to them. One story told by Colonel Cosmo Gordon seems to bear this out. A lady and her maid, named Thompson, happened to be staying for a weekend. At breakfast one morning, the visitor remarked that her maid had seen a lady she did not know in a green dress going up the principal staircase.

'It must have been the Green Lady,' said the Colonel, adding rather possessively, 'though she only appears to a Gordon.'

'Oh,' exclaimed the visitor, 'I always call my maids "Thompson" as a matter of course. Her real name *is* Gordon!'

Just before he died, Cosmo Gordon saw a figure beckoning him from the shadows of a room, and took the apparition to be an omen of his own impending death. A few days later, his younger brother saw the 'Green Lady' walking towards him in the gloomy December light that shone through the inscribed window. As she reached him, she curtseyed. The following morning Cosmo died.

ILLUMINATED PICTURES

During the First World War, a Canadian army officer left an account of his brush with supernatural forces at Fyvie, the most impressive in the castle's annals. A mining engineer by profession, he was formerly a complete sceptic: 'If anyone had told me before I came here that there were such things as ghosts or anything supernatural, I should have looked upon that man as an arrant fool,' he said.

On the first night of his stay, the officer retired to bed and fell asleep. Some time later, he woke up to find the light on, or so he thought, and got up to switch it off: 'But so doing, to my amazement, I found that I had switched it on. I extinguished it once more, but the light remained. The room was illuminated from some other cause, and as I watched, the light got gradually brighter. It was like little flames playing around the pictures, and I could see the colours of the pictures quite distinctly.'

The same phenomenon occurred every night until the end of his stay; and although no apparition apart from the strange light appeared, there was, said the Canadian, a feeling of 'someone or something in the room – something I wanted to hit.'

Lord Leith of Fyvie, who bought the castle in 1889 and died in 1925, had not only seen the same phenomenon, but had it investigated scientifically. At the same time, he had the only known 'weeping stone' examined. The latter proved to be a form of porous sandstone, which absorbed and exuded moisture by a natural process; but no 'scientific explanation' for the carving on the window-sill, or the wanderings of the 'Green Lady' and her luminescence, was forthcoming. Since Lord Leith's death, the 'Green Lady' has been glimpsed only periodically by visitors, but the enigmatic carving remains for all to see. Whatever the truth behind the stories of Fyvie Castle, Lord Leith's motto on the subject seems to have been a sound one: 'Never combat the supernatural,' he told a guest. 'Meet it without fear, and it will not trouble you.'

EARTHQUAKES AND VIOLENT STORMS ARE, ACCORDING TO THE THEORY OF SOLECTRICS, CAUSED BY UNFAVOURABLE POSITIONS OF THE CELESTIAL BODIES. WHAT EVIDENCE IS THERE FOR THE ACCURACY OF SUCH PREDICTIONS?

I n his theory of solectrics, Captain Alfred Cooper attempted to show that, when the Sun, Moon and planets take up certain positions relative to each other, an earthquake or some other terrestrial disaster is likely to happen soon afterwards. Cooper even gave detailed accounts of how his theory could be used to give warning of the approaching event. In three instances, he seems actually to have predicted earthquakes: on 16 August 1906, on 29/30 September 1912 and on 4 December 1918. But how remarkable are these alleged proofs of his method?

In order to investigate Captain Cooper's theory, we must first master some elementary geometry. The positions of celestial bodies can be described in terms of angles, just as we can describe the positions of places on the Earth in such terms. We speak, for example, of London as having a latitude of 51° north – that is, it is sited 51° north of the equator. This means that, if a line is drawn from the centre of the Earth to London, and then to a point on the equator, there will be an angle of 51° between them. In the same way, we can speak of, say, the Sun and Mars being 30° apart on the celestial sphere (an abstract sphere surrounding the Earth with poles and equator that are projections of corresponding features on Earth). The 30° is the angle between imaginary lines drawn from Mars and the Sun to the centre of the celestial sphere (which is also the centre of the Earth).

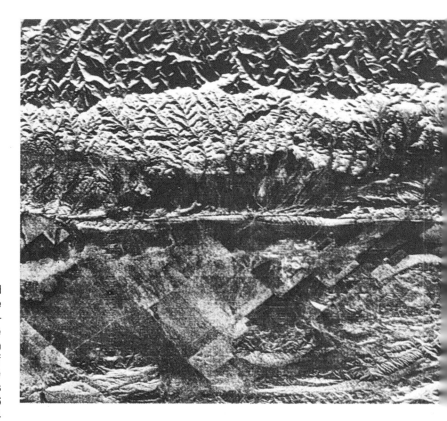

INVESTIGATING SOLECTRICS

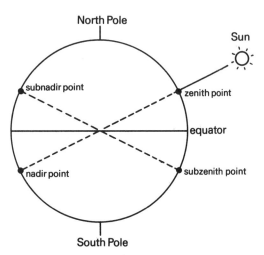

The San Andreas fault, above, running across California on the American west coast, shows up clearly in a picture built up by radar scanning from a high-flying aircraft. Many people fear that a major earthquake will hit this seismically disturbed area – but can the theory of solectrics predict the precise date when it will occur?

The solectric theory is based on the positions of the Sun, the Moon and the eight planets. For each of these, there are four key 'z-points' on the Earth, shown left. The 'zenith point' is directly beneath one of these bodies (in this case, the Sun). The 'nadir point' is on the other side of the world, opposite the zenith point. The 'subzenith point' is due north or south of the zenith point on the opposite side of the equator and equally distant from it; while the 'subnadir point' is opposite the subzenith point.

According to the theory of solectrics, there are four important places on the Earth's surface associated with each celestial body. Take, as an example, the four points related to Jupiter at a particular moment. Cooper called the point directly beneath Jupiter on the Earth the 'zenith point', because Jupiter is in the zenith – that is, directly overhead – at that place. The 'subzenith' is the point that has

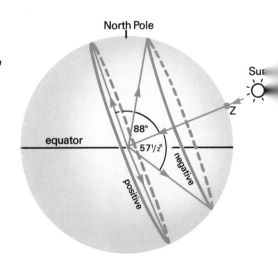

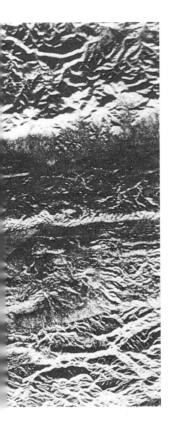

'Solectric force', illustrated below left, allegedly flows from each celestial body to the Earth's centre, splits into 'positive' and 'negative' parts and flows back to the surface, affecting two huge circular areas centred on the 'zenith (z) point'. Further flows of 'force' cause similar effects centred on each of the other 'z-points', according to Cooper.

The simplest of the many complicated interactions among the circular belts of solectric force are illustrated right. The belts are said to be centred on the 'zenith' (z) and 'subzenith' (sz) points of one celestial body, the places at which they intersect receiving 'warnings' of earthquakes. A complete diagram would show no fewer than 80 such circles, with many hundreds of places receiving warnings. As the Earth turns, the pattern sweeps across the surface. Any place that finds itself at the intersection of several circles on two occasions within a few days was regarded by Cooper as being at risk.

the same longitude as the zenith point, but is on the opposite side of the equator and at an equal distance from it. Thus, if the zenith point of Jupiter is 20° N, 50° E, the subzenith is the point 20° S, 50° E.

Another of the four important positions is the 'nadir point'. This is the place on Earth from which the heavenly body is in the nadir – that is, directly beneath the observer. In our example, the nadir point is at 20° S, 130° W – the point on Earth directly opposite to the zenith point. And corresponding to the nadir is the 'subnadir', on the opposite side of the equator, at 20° N, 130° W. At any moment, there are no less than 40 of these 'z-points', scattered over the Earth's surface – four for each of the 10 heavenly bodies in Cooper's solectric theory.

According to Cooper, warnings of cataclysmic events occur under the conditions when the Moon is at its maximum distance north or south of the celestial equator; when the Moon is precisely 57½° away from the Sun; or when the Sun crosses the celestial equator (which it does at the spring and autumn equinoxes).

But such warnings apply only to certain areas on the Earth – the two types of circular belts that surround each z-point: the belt of 'negative' solectric force, and the belt of 'positive' force.

There are 80 such belts altogether. So, at any moment, the Earth's surface, according to Cooper, is covered by an intricate network of belts of solectric force. Each place that lies on one of the belts of force associated with the Sun receives one warning. But warnings may also be given by proxy, so to speak. The Sun can act through the Moon or any of the planets in the correct circumstances – when one of the Sun's four z-points is about 57½° or 88° from the z-points of another celestial body. To put it another way, this occurs when any of the second body's z-points is to be found lying on one of the Sun's belts of force.

The Sun can also act through more than one body, in a chain. Thus, the second body might be at about 57½° or 88° from a third body, which means that places lying at the appropriate distances from this third body receive warnings. In his book, Captain Cooper illustrates many such chains.

The times of particular risk from earthquakes are those that, within a short period (generally five days or less), receive two distinct types of warning. For example, if the Moon comes to its maximum

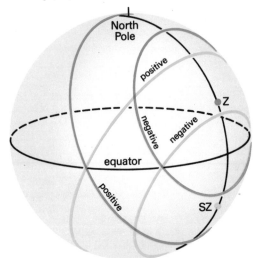

distance north or south of the celestial equator and then, a few days or perhaps even hours later, reaches an angular distance of 57½° from the Sun, that constitutes such a double warning. The violent event is now imminent .

But, as we have seen, this warning applies only to certain areas. So how many places on Earth could receive this double warning?

Places at risk are those that lie on the Sun's belts of force at the time of the first warning and, again, at the time of the second warning. We need to look at the areas where the eight belts of force at the first warning date intersect the eight belts of force at the second. There can be as many as 128 such regions of intersection, and no fewer than 64.

But, in general, there will be other places that receive warnings indirectly, through the Moon or through the planets. And in the unlikely case that the Sun is solectrically connected to the Moon and all eight planets, a maximum of 12,800 places could be put on alert for a forthcoming earthquake.

AN EXCESS OF WARNINGS

This is admittedly an extreme case. *The Unexplained* arranged to have hundreds of calculations made on a computer, and found that at any date and time whatsoever, on average the Sun will be 'solectrically connected' directly to two other celestial bodies. This means that, on average, a double warning is given to as many as 1,536 places.

Furthermore, the double warnings are not rare occurrences. On the contrary, they happen four times every month; for there are two occasions each month when the Moon is 57½° away from the Sun, and two when it is at its maximum distance from the celestial equator. It is therefore not surprising that many disasters should be found to occur within five days of a warning.

But the theory is somewhat looser in its predictions than this. Captain Cooper stated that he regarded it as acceptable to use the position of the Moon – not when it was precisely at its extreme position north or south, but when it was anywhere within 1/3,600 of a degree of that position. But this introduces an imprecision of one hour in the timing of this event. During that hour, the Earth turns through 15°, and the areas of intersection of the solectric belts sweep across 15° of longitude. That is equal to the distance from Berlin to London.

Worse still, Captain Cooper allowed even more laxity in calculating the moment when the Moon was 57½° from the Sun. He allowed a range of 3° either way, as a repetition of his calculations reveals. But this allows a total uncertainty of 12 hours in the timing of these events – in which time, the Earth performs half a revolution.

It is no wonder that Captain Cooper found the configurations of the heavenly bodies fitted his theories so well. For the theory predicts far too much. At any moment, virtually any area on the Earth is at risk, if the limits of error adopted by Cooper are used. And the chances are that there will have been a 'first warning' in the previous few days.

Study any disaster after the event, and a solectric alignment can be found. It follows, too, that you cannot use the theory in the way that Cooper used it to make predictions. But it might be argued that he did in fact successfully predict three Chilean

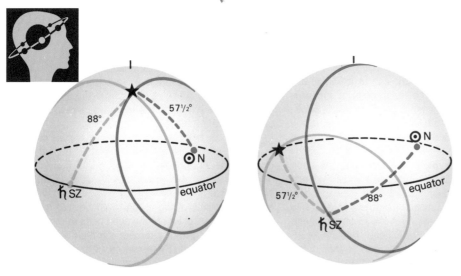

earthquakes. So how did he accomplish this? Part of the answer can be found by considering which regions of the world Captain Cooper thought to be most at risk from earthquakes.

In his book, we read: 'A sudden escape of pent-up forces is only possible near districts in which there are mountainous peaks. These peaks, being thrust far through the insulating atmosphere, constitute excellent solectric conductors.'

This makes the western coast of South America especially vulnerable because of the presence of the Andes mountains.

This area is, of course, a zone of frequent earthquakes, but not for the reasons given by Captain Cooper. The coastline marks the boundary between two of the tectonic plates that make up the Earth's crust. One, the plate that underlies part of the Pacific, is sliding underneath the plate on which South America rides. This process has thrown up the Andes mountains over millions of years, and continues to inflict earth tremors on the region. Captain Cooper's theory therefore 'predicts', but for the wrong reasons, the general locality of the earthquakes. But how did he get the correct timing on a number of occasions?

Unfortunately, Captain Cooper does not tell us how frequently earthquakes occurred in Chile. But on 29 November 1912, he wrote to the South American supplement of *The Times*, outlining the predictions he had made for the period 18 to 30 September, and the events that had actually occurred. In reply, *The Times* says: 'There was... no

There are two ways in which solectric warnings were said by Cooper to be intensified. In the first case, above left, a place on Earth (marked by a star) lies on two belts of force, 88° from the subzenith point of Saturn, and 57½° from the nadir point of the Sun. In the second case, above right, the place is 57½° from one z-point (the subzenith point of Saturn), which in turn lies 88° from another (the nadir point of the Sun).

The diagram, right, shows how a given warning affects a large area of the Earth. As the planet turns from west to east, the solectric pattern sweeps 15° westward every hour. Captain Cooper permitted a variation of many hours in some of his calculations – with a corresponding uncertainty in predictions of areas at risk.

real earthquake on the 29th, as is testified by a newspaper cutting which Captain Cooper forwards to us. There occurred merely a slight shake... the same newspaper says, "hardly a week goes by without one or two shakes being recorded". ' Now, if there were one or two tremors each week and the warnings used by Captain Cooper occurred four times every month, it is not particularly surprising that at least one tremor should match up with his prediction.

On a closer examination of the facts, we find that only for the earthquake of 16 August 1906 at Valparaiso did Captain Cooper give exactly the place and time. His prediction of an earthquake for 29/30 September 1912 at Valparaiso was actually wrong:

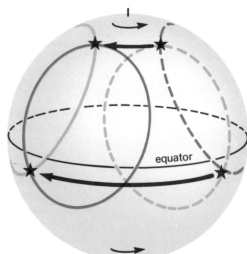

the tremors occurred in neighbouring areas. He also predicted volcanic activity.

This indeed occurred, but 450 miles (720 kilometres) off the Chilean coast and therefore well outside the solectric belt of force that supposedly caused these phenomena.

The earthquake of 4 December 1918 occurred at 7.50 a.m., but Captain Cooper had predicted that by 1 a.m. the danger would be past. Furthermore, the centre of the earthquake area was about 300 miles (480 kilometres) north of Valparaiso – again, outside the belt of solectric force that Captain Cooper claimed was responsible.

PERSPECTIVES

FEELING THE WEATHER

Our moods are often deeply affected by the weather. Before storms, for example, the drop in the barometric pressure often makes us feel sluggish. As soon as it starts raining, however, alertness increases and we feel more invigorated. Such sensitivity is particularly marked among sufferers of rheumatism and arthritis, who tend to experience increased pain as the storm approaches, but improve afterwards.

According to the 19th-century American neurologist, Weir Mitchell, around the 'rain area' of a storm lies a belt which may be called the neuralgic margin of the storm and which precedes the rain by about 150 miles. It is this belt, he believed, with its electric or magnetic force, that provokes the

pains of sufferers. In their own way, they are as much sentinels of approaching storms as meteorologists.

One researcher into climatic effects on humans, Ellsworth Huntingdon, has stated that: 'The rates of pulse and breathing, the blood-pressure... and other bodily functions all vary systematically with the coming and going of tropical and polar air masses.' Even intelligence may be affected. Students at a Massachusetts college in 1938 were taking psychological tests at the same moment that a hurricane struck their town. When the so-called 'hurricane papers' were marked, examiners – who expected average results – discovered that the students had attained the highest grades ever achieved by the college.

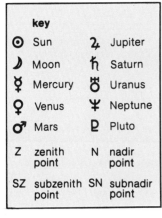

key

☉	Sun	♃	Jupiter
☽	Moon	♄	Saturn
☿	Mercury	♅	Uranus
♀	Venus	♆	Neptune
♂	Mars	♇	Pluto
Z	zenith point	N	nadir point
SZ	subzenith point	SN	subnadir point

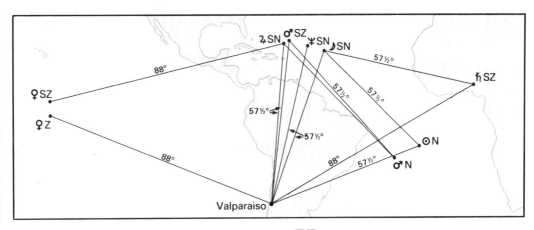

The solectric pattern, above right, is for Valparaiso in Chile, on 16 August 1906 at 8.17 a.m. local time – the moment of a devastating earthquake. Symbols can be identified from the key, above. Direct influences on the city seem to come from eight 'z-points' and are reinforced by several indirect ones. Captain Cooper was impressed by such a wealth of apparently significant relationships – but equally striking diagrams can be drawn for many times and places at which no disasters take place.

From all this, it is clear that the theory of solectrics will 'predict' a disaster at any place and time if the margins of error used by Captain Cooper are permitted. However, such margins are too generous. We need to limit the number of predictions by demanding that the positions of the celestial bodies be very precisely specified.

When, some years ago, a large number of predictions based on solectrics were made with the aid of a computer, especially for *The Unexplained*, double warnings occurred for Pakistan, Arizona, Alaska, Yugoslavia, Turkey and Chile on certain dates – but nothing transpired.

The science of solectrics must therefore join the long list of unsuccessful attempts to predict earthquakes. Unfortunately, Captain Cooper himself never realised this because, by the time he made his predictions, he had become utterly convinced of the accuracy of his theory and thought that any shortcomings were due to slight errors in calculating the positions of the Sun, Moon and planets. It simply never occurred to him to cast doubt on a theory that seemed to fit so well – too well, perhaps – with so many past earthquakes, volcanic eruptions and other violent events.

"AMONG THE INFORMATION... INCREASED SO AS TO OVERWHELM CONSCIOUSNESS IN AN EARTHQUAKE ARE THE SUBSONIC VIBRATIONS, CHANGES OF ELECTRICAL CHARGE IN THE AIR, MAGNETIC STORMS AND VERY HIGH BAROMETRIC PRESSURE... VISIONS OF FLYING SAUCERS HAVE BEEN ATTRIBUTED TO CHARGED AEROSOLS RISING FROM THE GROUND... AND PRODUCING A FORM OF TRANCE."

PETER REDGROVE, THE BLACK GODDESS AND THE SIXTH SENSE

*In*FOCUS

EARTHQUAKE ALARMS

Among the various attempts to predict earthquakes is the use of the seismograph – a highly sensitive instrument that measures vibrations in the ground before, during and after disturbances. The low-frequency vibrations in the ground that are known to precede earthquakes can, however, be picked up by what are virtually living forms of the seismograph – animals. In the Far East, a region prone to serious earthquakes, the Japanese have traditionally kept goldfish to warn them of impending disaster. As soon as pre-earthquake vibrations begin – falling into a range between seven and 14 cycles per second – the goldfish begin to swim frantically around in their ponds, alerting

their owners to danger. Other animals, too, are said to be sensitive to earthquakes; and deer and rabbits have been recorded running from the epicentre. One suggestion is that they can detect both the vibrations and the magnetic changes built up by pressure in subterranean rocks. As yet, however, there is no telling how far in advance of the earthquake these animals are responding: it may be they are picking up the tremors only minutes beforehand.

But vibrations are not the only known forewarnings of earthquakes. In 1965, a year before the great earthquake of Tashkent in Kirghizia, Central Asia, a build-up of the inert gas argon was found in the city's water supply. This quadrupled the day before the earthquake. Unfortunately, gas build-ups are not common to earthquake activity, and so this cannot be taken as a universal warning. Thus far, the art of accurate earthquake prediction remains as elusive as ever.

THE LONG SHADOW OF FEAR

MEN IN BLACK EXCITED A GREAT DEAL OF ATTENTION WHEN THEY BEGAN TO THREATEN UFO WITNESSES IN THE 1950S. BUT THE POWERFUL SYMBOL OF THE SINISTER BLACK-CLAD FIGURE IS CENTURIES OLD

UFO percipients and investigators are by no means the only people to receive visits from Men in Black (MIBs). Researchers Kevin and Sue McClure, investigating the North Wales religious revival of 1905, found accounts that bear at least a *prima facie* similarity to the more recent MIB phenomenon:

'In the neighbourhood dwells an exceptionally intelligent young woman of the peasant class, whose bedroom has been visited three nights in succession at midnight by a man dressed in black. This figure has delivered a message to the girl which, however, she is forbidden to relate.'

The young woman in question (a farmer's wife-

Montague Summers (1880-1948), above, was a writer who traced a number of historical MIB cases – years before the first modern, UFO-related MIB encounter in 1953.

In The Last Judgement, below, *by Fra Angelico (c.1400-1455), the damned, seen on the right, are being dragged off to Hell by black demons. Some modern writers have gone as far as to suggest an identification between these sinister figures and MIBs.*

turned-preacher), Mary Jones, one of the leading figures of the religious revival, was well known for the mysterious lights that appeared as she pursued her mission. On one occasion, when she encountered her sinister visitor at night, Mary was 'rescued' by one of her lights, which darted a white ray at the apparition. The MIB promptly vanished.

It all sounds like the wildest fantasy – except that there is substantial evidence for some of the phenomena reported, many of which were seen by independent witnesses, some of them avowedly sceptical. But does this mean that the MIBs really existed, and actually appeared in the bedroom of that 'intelligent young woman of the peasant class'? What we are learning about the modern wave of MIBs may help us to understand similar cases reported in earlier periods.

Men in Black turn up, in one form or another, in the folklore of almost every country of the world, and periodically emerge from legend into everyday life. On 2 June 1603, a young country lad confessed, before a court in south-west France, to several acts of werewolfery, culminating in the kidnapping and eating of a child. He stated that he was acting under the orders of the Lord of the Forest, to whom he was bond-slave. He described the Lord of the Forest as a tall, dark man, dressed in black, and riding a black horse.

UNDER COVER OF DARKNESS

Montague Summers, who reports the case in his book *The Werewolf,* has no hesitation in identifying this, and all other MIBs, with the Devil of Christian teaching, and it continues to be a widespread interpretation. Even today, there are theorists who claim that UFOs are diabolical in origin, and that consequently the MIBs must be Satan's agents. In those parts of the world where the prevailing religious doctrine presupposes two warring factions of good and evil, good is equated with light and evil with darkness. The agents of good tend to be blond and dressed in white, while the agents of evil have dark hair and are dressed in black. Other connotations inevitably follow. Under cover of darkness, all kinds of tricks can be carried out and crimes committed. Darkness is also associated with winter, and so with death: in almost all parts of the world, death rites and customs are also associated with the colour black.

So, whatever his specific role, the MIB is a distinctly sinister figure. He is a trickster, and he stands for lies rather than truth, death rather than life.

But because of the obviously symbolic elements involved, many theorists speculate that MIBs are not flesh-and-blood creatures at all, but mental constructs projected from the imagination of the percipient, and taking on a form that blends traditional legend with contemporary imagery. But it cannot be quite that simple: too many of the accounts show

Among many cultures, the colour black represents dark and sinister elements. The representation of the demon god Kal Bahairab from the Hanuman Doka temple in Nepal, below, shows him with a hideous face, four arms and black skin. Human beings were, in former times, sacrificed to this god to satisfy its lust for blood.

intelligence officers, are a big part of the complex UFO phenomena which is in turn part of another big and complex phenomena (*sic*). It is known that projects by them are now under way for the complete control of... political, financial, religious and scientific institutions. They – the MIBs – have a very long background and history that stretches back for centuries, indicating a massive build-up of concentration to where it is today.'

MYSTERIOUS ORIGINS

MIBs are often reported as being dark skinned, and having either a defective command of English, or conversely an over-precise way of talking that suggests that they are not speaking their own tongue. Mary Hyre, a West Virginia journalist, noted that a strange visitor picked up a ball-point pen from her desk and examined it with amazement, as if he had never seen anything like it before. And UFO percipient Mrs Ralph Butler, who received a visit from a man who claimed to be an Air Force major, was astonished to find that he was so unfamiliar with American food that he had to be shown how to eat it. The implication is that they are foreigners, an attitude encouraged by American xenophobia. Curiously, though, no witness appears to have suggested that the MIBs are of Russian origin.

Where specific details are mentioned, it is always implied that they are vaguely 'oriental'. Slanting eyes are frequently reported; and the deadpan faces suggest the supposedly inscrutable Asian. Sometimes, heads are totally bald. (By linking 'the yellow peril' with the 'man in black', of course, it is possible to frighten oneself with two bogeymen for the price of one!)

Although witnesses rarely state openly that they believe their visitors to come from beyond Earth, this is often clearly implied. The three men reported by Albert Bender of Bridgeport, Connecticut, USA, in 1953 – at the start of the modern MIB wave – were clearly of alien origin. Other MIBs have displayed behaviour traits that seem to suggest that they are able to function for only a limited timespan. After a while, they insist that they have to leave, or take pills, or drink water, and sometimes show signs of losing strength. A further possibility remains – that the MIBs are neither flesh-and-blood (even extra-terrestrial flesh-and-blood), nor some form of hallucination/illusion, but something in between. The entities encountered in a recent French case even seem to have existed, if 'existed' is the word, on some alternative plane of being.

The alleged abduction, in December 1979, of Franck Fontaine for seven days on board a UFO was one of the rare French cases to have attracted worldwide attention. The abduction itself was, of course, the central event of the case, but it was only the start of a series of incidents. One of these, involving MIBs, concerned another member of the trio, Jean-Pierre Prévost, who told this story:

'The night of Friday the seventh to Saturday the eighth of December 1979, Franck, Salomon and I had sat up talking for a long time, and went to bed sometime around 5 to 5.30 in the morning. At 7 a.m., there was a ring at the door. Salomon and Franck didn't hear it, so I went to open the door. I found myself in the presence of three fellows. One was of average height, very well dressed in dark

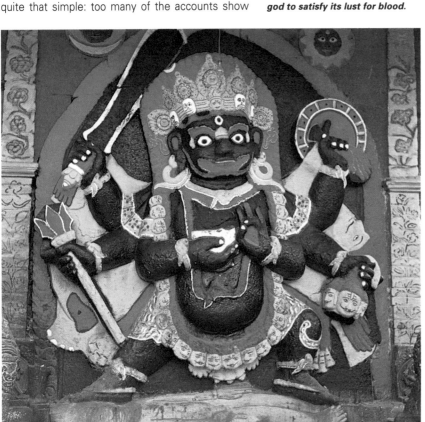

evidence of relating to physical creatures moving in the real, physical world.

There are several possible explanations. At their most concrete, the MIBs who visit today are supposed to be the representatives of an official department – sometimes as straightforward and above board as the Air Force, sometimes a more covert organisation, such as the CIA or FBI. The average American, in particular, seems far from convinced that investigative bodies, such as the CIA, are necessarily working in the public interest. The same attitude of mind that has evolved the conspiracy theories about UFOs – that a gigantic cover-up is being mounted by the government – suggests that the MIBs are part of this operation, their sole object being to conceal the facts by silencing witnesses and purloining photographs and other evidence of encounters with extra-terrestrials.

The fact that the identities of a great many MIBs have been checked, and that they have invariably been found not to be the persons they purport to be, lends strength to such suspicions, which can amount to virtual paranoia. In 1970, an American theorist, Tony Kimery, wrote in all seriousness:

'The mysterious MIBs and the entire collection of their thugs, henchmen, and highly trained

Richard Baxter, below, was a 17th-century writer who recounted the tale of a London woman of the time – a 'pious, credible woman' – who was encouraged to hang herself by the Devil in the shape of a big black man. The archetype of a black figure as a symbol of evil appears repeatedly in legend.

green, almost black, black tie, white shirt, and waistcoat to match his suit;
he had a fringe of beard, black like his hair, and a moustache. His general appearance was pretty good. The others were bigger than him, taller and more heavily built.

'What follows, I haven't told the police – I reported the visit itself to them – because we've already had enough of being taken for crackpots! But these two types, with the bearded man, didn't really exist, that I'm certain of! In the first place, they had no sight. That's hard to explain: they fixed me with their eyes, but those eyes were nothing but a white mass, all over. They were terrifying!

'The bearded fellow asked me: "Are you one of the three?" He obviously meant, was I one of the three people concerned in the Ciergy-Pontoise case? I said yes, and he went on: "Good, in that case, you can pass the word to your companions: you've already said too much. An accident will happen to you. And if you say any more, it will be more serious than that...

'And, with that, they vanished; but how, that's something I can't begin to explain. They didn't take the lift, I'd have heard it if they did; and even more so if they'd used the stairs – the door makes a deafening row! I went to the window that overlooks the parking lot. I can tell you definitely that, all night, at least until 5 a.m. or later, we'd noticed a Ford Capri in metallic green standing beneath our window, a Ford that we didn't recognise. Well, when I looked down, there was this Ford, just starting up. How had they managed to get to it without using the stairs or the lift? Complete mystery.

'I woke up Franck and Salomon and we went to the police, without giving them the unbelievable details about the two toughs. The police said: "So long as they didn't actually attack or wound you, there's nothing we can do, so get back home." And that was that.'

FORCES OF EVIL

Jean-Pierre told investigators that he saw the three men on several subsequent occasions – either from across the street or at a market. On one occasion, he received another warning while he was in a tobacco store buying cigarettes. He was told to keep quiet about their experiences and was also threatened. Subsequently, under hypnosis, Jean-Pierre indicated that the entities were not extra-terrestrials but *intra-terrestrials*, forces of evil originating from inside the Earth. He also added – intriguingly – that the bearded man had been real, but that his two henchmen had been 'unreal'.

Cases such as this are made baffling by their inconsequentiality. But one thing seems certain: just as the MIB visits seem to originate from some psychic or mental link between the MIBs and the witness, so the consequences of the visit depend less on the MIBs than on the attitude adopted by the witness. If the percipient takes the MIBs at their face value, and believes their threats, he or she is liable to find himself heading for a breakdown. Paranoia may develop, and he may believe himself followed everywhere, harassed by paranormal happenings, such as strange telephone calls and poltergeist phenomena. It is possible that these second-stage phenomena are genuine as far as the

The three men, top – from left to right, Salomon N'Diaye, Jean-Pierre Prévost and Franck Fontaine – were involved in a famous case of alleged abduction by the UFO shown in the sketch, above. Prévost was later the victim of a threatening visit from MIBs.

victim himself is concerned. Although they are manifestations of fears, they are none the less real for that and will not disappear until he capitulates and gives up his UFO studies, if he is an investigator, or keeps quiet about what happened during his experiences, if he is a witness.

If, on the other hand, he braves the matter out – if he refuses to abandon his investigation, and continues to tell the world of his experiences – it seems the MIBs are powerless against him. Carlos de los Santos, stopped on his way to a television interview by a gang of tough, threatening characters, was momentarily scared; he turned his car round, went home and cancelled the interview. But a friend reassured him and persuaded him not to let himself be intimidated. A fortnight later, he gave the interview – and he heard nothing subsequently from the MIBs!

The MIB phenomenon is clearly worth studying carefully. Whatever the nature of the MIBs – whether they are wholly illusory, or whether there is a measure of reality in them – they exert a great deal of power over the minds of their victims. The better we understand them, the more we may learn about how such power may be deployed. If for no other reason, the MIB phenomenon is important because it gives the sociologist a chance to study a legend in the making. Indeed, the sinister MIB masquerade provides us with contemporary phenomena that rank with the witch, the vampire and the werewolf of times past.

> **"**
> I HAVE IN MY FILES HUNDREDS
> OF CASES... IN WHICH YOUNG
> MEN AND WOMEN OBSESSED WITH
> THE UFO PHENOMENON HAVE
> SUFFERED FRIGHTENING VISITS
> FROM THESE APPARITIONS...
> **"**
> JOHN A. KEEL,
> UFOs – OPERATION TROJAN HORSE

MASTER OF THE SACRED DANCE

George Ivanovich Gurdjieff, left, earned his living as a stage hypnotist, and travelled in search of 'a certain knowledge, of certain powers and possibilities exceeding the ordinary possibilities of Man'. Having apparently found them – although, even to his closest disciples, he would never say where – he put this secret knowledge to use by inventing a philosophical system 'for the harmonious development of Man'. Gurdjieff founded his first institute for tuition in this system in Tiflis, Georgia, below, in 1919.

IN THE 1920S, THERE APPEARED AN OBSCURE ARMENIAN WHO CLAIMED TO BE ABLE TO TEACH A METHOD OF REALISING MANKIND'S HIGHEST POTENTIAL

On 9 January 1923, the New Zealand writer Katherine Mansfield died at the Institute for the Harmonious Development of Man at Fontainebleau, near Paris. She had been fighting a losing battle with tuberculosis for several years. Disillusioned with conventional treatments, she had entered the Institute some weeks before, convinced

The New Zealand writer Katherine Mansfield (1888-1923), right, became a devotee of Gurdjieff's system through her friend A.R. Orage, below right, editor of the English literary journal New Age. Katherine Mansfield died peacefully of tuberculosis at Gurdjieff's Institute for the Harmonious Development of Man at Fontainebleau near Paris. 'One has,' she wrote some weeks before her death, 'the feeling of having been in a wreck and by the mercy of Providence got ashore... It's a real new life'.

Gurdjieff's philosophical system, upon which his Institute was based, proposed that, ordinarily in Mankind, the physical, emotional and intellectual faculties (which Gurdjieff called 'centres') were unintegrated and out of balance, and Man therefore functioned inefficiently and mechanically. By following a programme of rigorous physical and psychological exercises, Gurdjieff's pupils hoped to develop their centres harmoniously, and eventually to make contact with a source of higher energy that would put them in possession of psychic powers not normally available to Man. As Gurdjieff said in a talk reported by his pupil C.S. Nott, 'directed' attention, in which all three centres – physical, emotional and intellectual – take part, is real concentration: then, 'a man can move a mountain.'

Although Katherine Mansfield died before she had an opportunity to advance in the Gurdjieff system, there is no doubt from her letters that she found peace and happiness in the last weeks of her life at the Institute: 'I believe Mr Gurdjieff is the only person who can help me,' she wrote on 24 October 1922. 'It is a great happiness to be here...

that, by achieving spiritual regeneration, she would also achieve a physical cure for her illness. She wrote to her estranged husband, John Middleton Murry, that she hoped to get 'really cured – not half cured, not cured in my body only and all the rest as ill as ever'. The Institute had only recently opened; and the physical conditions of life there for a tuberculosis patient were hard – it was extremely cold, and all the residents had to engage in strenuous physical work. Nevertheless, Katherine obviously found a great deal of solace in the few weeks she spent there. 'One has,' she wrote in a letter on 20 October 1922 – 10 weeks before her death – 'the feeling of having been in a wreck and by the mercy of Providence got ashore... It's a real new life.'

ARCANE KNOWLEDGE

Katherine's husband and friends were horrified that she had put herself in the hands of the dubious character who ran the Institute. George Ivanovich Gurdjieff was an Armenian Russian, who claimed to have acquired arcane knowledge during prolonged travels in the Middle and Far East. He had run study groups for 'the harmonious development of Man' in the early years of the century in St Petersburg and Moscow, and was trying to establish his first formal Institute in Tiflis when the Russian Revolution forced him to flee and take refuge in France. It was rumoured that a wealthy English Theosophist admirer had provided the funds to purchase the lovely house and grounds of the Prieuré at Fontainebleau, a former Carmelite monastery, where he set up his second Institute. Gurdjieff, at this time, was aged about 50. He was a man of great vitality, who enjoyed good food and company – and was extremely attractive to women. One observer described him as 'altogether Eastern in appearance', with long black moustaches and piercing eyes; Katherine Mansfield said he looked 'exactly like a carpet-dealer from the Tottenham Court Road'.

Such beautiful understanding and sympathy I have never known in the outside world .'

Katherine had heard about Gurdjieff and his Institute through her friend A.R. Orage, editor of the literary journal *New Age*. Orage became Gurdjieff's chief English disciple, and later ran a group of his own in New York.

Other well-known people became Gurdjieff followers during the 1920s and 1930s, including the American architect Frank Lloyd Wright, and Dorothy Caruso, wife of the operatic singer Enrico Caruso.

So how had Gurdjieff arrived at the remarkable philosophical 'system' that had such an influence during this period? It is not easy to determine the facts of his youth and formative years, partly because he himself was apt to give conflicting accounts of his early days to different disciples. It seems probable, however, that he was born in 1872 in Armenia. His father was Greek, his mother Armenian, and he himself had Russian nationality. From an early age, he was fascinated by the occult and magic. He told Peter Ouspensky, his chief Russian disciple, how – as a child – he had come into contact with a group of 'Devil-worshippers', the Yezidis. He had observed, for instance, how a Yezidi boy would find it impossible to step out of a circle that had been traced around him on the ground by another Devil-worshipper.

According to Ouspensky's account in his book *In Search of the Miraculous*, Gurdjieff gradually became convinced 'of the existence of a certain knowledge, of certain powers and possibilities exceeding the ordinary possibilities of Man, and of people possessing clairvoyance and other miraculous powers'. While still in his teens, he started to travel with the definite intention of finding this knowledge. Ouspensky and his other disciples were convinced that he did find it; but where he found it, Gurdjieff would never say. Even to Ouspensky, he was vague: he mentioned 'Tibetan monasteries, the

Disciples of Gurdjieff, left, perform one of his sacred dances. At the left of the front row is Madame Ogilvanna Lloyd Wright, wife of the renowned American architect, Frank Lloyd Wright. Learning the movements which were understood to be derived from ancient Dervish dances, below, constituted a physical discipline that was designed to give the participants a superhuman control over their faculties.

Chitral, Mount Athos; Sufi schools in Persia, in Bokhara, and eastern Turkestan; and he mentioned Dervishes of various orders, but all of them in a very indefinite way.'

According to John Bennett's account in *Gurdjieff: a Very Great Enigma*, Gurdjieff became convinced that the Caucasus, where he was born, was still the repository of some ancient secret wisdom, possibly going back 4,000 years. Accordingly, he embarked on a 20-year quest for this esoteric knowledge, during the course of which he allegedly discovered 'practical and powerful methods for Man to produce and control the fine substances' needed to produce psychic and spiritual changes in himself.

How Gurdjieff supported himself during these prolonged travels is not clear. He may have traded in oriental carpets, as he did later in life. Suggestions have also been made that he worked as a Russian spy. In any event, towards the end of his travels, he had acquired sufficient proficiency in hypnosis and auto-suggestion to be able to earn a living as 'miracle-worker' or healer.

POWERFUL CHARISMA

Eventually, Gurdjieff returned to Russia. There, he set up practical groups to work at his 'system' in St Petersburg and Moscow. It was in Moscow, in 1915, that Peter Ouspensky first met him, in a back-street cafe:

'I saw a man of an oriental type, no longer young, with a black mustache and piercing eyes, who astonished me first of all because he seemed to be disguised and completely out of keeping with the place and its atmosphere.'

He wore a black overcoat with a velvet collar, and a black bowler hat; and he spoke Russian incorrectly with a strong Caucasian accent – which was also, apparently, the way he spoke English. Ouspensky visited Gurdjieff's apartment on the Bolshaia Dmitrovka, which was furnished in Eastern style with the floors and walls covered in carpets, and the ceilings hung with silk shawls; it had a special atmosphere, and pupils who visited Gurdjieff there would often sit down and simply remain silent for hours. But chance visitors would react strangely to this atmosphere by starting to talk non-stop 'as if they were afraid of... feeling something'. Ouspensky said that another special quality of the apartment was that it 'was not possible to tell lies there'.

The prospectus of Gurdjieff's Institute, which he opened first in Tiflis in Georgia in 1919, offered as subjects for study 'gymnastics of all kinds (rhythmical, medicinal, and others); exercises for the development of will, memory, attention, hearing, thinking, emotion, instinct, and so on'. It made no mention, however, of the sacred dances or the breathing exercises that formed an essential part of Gurdjieff's system.

The memoirs of many of Gurdjieff's pupils suggest that they endured the rigorous discipline he imposed in the hope of achieving some kind of breakthrough into a state of higher consciousness that would bring with it the most extraordinary psychic powers. But it became clear to his more advanced pupils that Gurdjieff had not set up his working groups entirely out of altruism, to benefit

KNOW—TO UNDERSTAND—TO BE

The design, left, was for the 1923 programme of Gurdjieff's Institute for the Harmonious Development of Man, and shows the fruitful cooperation of opposing elements of life – art and music, science and technology – symbolised by an angel and a demon.

Everyone who met Gurdjieff, right, was aware of his personal magnetism and the immense vitality that he was able to impart to others. Some, however, found his appearance unprepossessing: Katherine Mansfield, for instance, described him as looking 'exactly like a carpet dealer from the Tottenham Court Road'.

Peter Ouspensky, below right, was Gurdjieff's chief Russian disciple. Ouspensky left Gurdjieff in 1924 to found a similar but distinct movement.

> GURDJIEFF MAINTAINED THAT THE DANCES EMBODIED ESOTERIC MEANINGS THAT WOULD BE APPARENT TO THE INITIATED... FOR THE INDIVIDUAL DANCERS, THE TASK OF MASTERING THE DIFFICULT MOVEMENTS WAS ITSELF A PHYSICAL DISCIPLINE THAT WAS TO ENABLE THEM TO ACQUIRE SUPERHUMAN CONTROL OVER THEIR FACULTIES.

Mankind, but to satisfy his own inner needs. In the course of his 20-year search, Gurdjieff had become convinced that esoteric knowledge was not enough. He needed also to increase his knowledge of practical psychology, and for this he needed a number of subjects to study at first hand. Early in his career, his healing work with drug and alcohol addicts gave him his opportunity; and in his book *The Herald of Coming Good,* he said that he became a healer of vices both to give 'conscientious aid to sufferers' and 'for the sake of my investigations'. His work with groups of his adherents in Russia and France gave him a continuing opportunity to develop his knowledge of the human psyche. C.S. Nott relates in his book *Further Teachings of Gurdjieff,* how he met Gurdjieff in Paris at the Café de la Paix, and complained bitterly that Gurdjieff had brought himself and another disciple, Orage, so far – and then left them 'seemingly in the air'. Gurdjieff listened quietly – and then said, with a sardonic grin: 'I needed rats for my experiments.'

THE SACRED DANCE

A large part of the system was taken up with practising and performing the sacred dances that Gurdjieff was understood to have learned within the confines of a Dervish monastery. Groups of otherwise inexperienced dancers were trained by Gurdjieff in these skills, and public performances were given on several occasions in Paris, London and New York. Gurdjieff maintained that the dances embodied esoteric meanings that would be apparent to the initiated: 'In the strictly defined movements and combinations of the dancers, certain laws are visually reproduced which are intelligible to those who know them.'

What was more, for the individual dancers, the task of mastering the difficult movements was itself a physical discipline that was to enable them to acquire superhuman control over their faculties.

To the uninitiated observer, however, the dances certainly did not come over as a language expressing knowledge of a higher order. At a public demonstration in New York in 1924, William Seabrook recorded his main impression of 'the amazing, brilliant, automaton-like, inhuman, almost incredible docility and robot-like obedience of the disciples... They were like a group of perfectly trained zombies.' Seabrook went on to write, in his book *Witchcraft, its Power in the World Today,* that the main purpose of the demonstration seemed to be to show how Gurdjieff had taught his pupils 'supernormal powers of physical control, coordination, relaxation', and so on, without which – when dancing in this way – they would certainly have broken limbs.

In spite of the scoffers, who described Gurdjieff variously as the 'Greek charlatan', 'the Armenian magic master' and the 'Caucasian wonder-worker', Gurdjieff's pupils remained convinced that he was a genuine mage, in possession of occult knowledge and special powers. Orage called him 'a kind of walking god', and he seems to have had some kind of psychic energy that he was able, on occasions, to transmit directly to his pupils in order to strengthen their physical and mental states. John Bennett reports, in his autobiography, *Witness,* an incident that happened while he was resident at the Prieuré

He woke one morning feeling ill; but nevertheless, driven by some 'superior will', he got up as usual and performed his day's programme of physical work, including Gurdjieff's strenuous dancing class in the afternoon. During the latter, Bennett felt himself growing weaker and weaker. He felt Gurdjieff's eyes upon him, willing him to continue. Suddenly, he felt 'an influx of immense power': his body seemed 'to have turned into light'.

Gurdjieff later told Bennett that what he called 'higher emotional energy' was necessary if one desired to develop oneself. Some rare people in the world, he said, are connected to what he regarded as a 'great accumulator' of this energy, and can transmit it to others. Gurdjieff implied that he himself was one of these people.

MYSTICAL STATES

Gurdjieff was also credited by many with telepathic powers. Ouspensky relates a curious experience, in 1916, when he was staying with Gurdjieff in a house in Finland. Ouspensky had been going through an intensive period of exercises that included fasting and special breathing sequences, and he claimed to have experienced mystical states – states that he was, however, unable to describe. While sitting in a small room with Gurdjieff and two other people, Ouspensky began to 'hear his thoughts'. Gurdjieff was talking to Ouspensky – but he was doing so telepathically:

'I heard his voice inside me as it were in the chest near the heart. He put a definite question to me. I looked at him; he was sitting and smiling. His question provoked in me a very strong emotion.'

Ouspensky went to bed. But the telepathic conversation continued during the night, with Ouspensky now able to send telepathic messages in return to Gurdjieff. This strange communication between them continued in this way, we are told, for several days.

Music also played an important part in Gurdjieff's system. Indeed, Gurdjieff himself wrote the music for his sacred dances, based on what he could remember of the music he had heard in the Dervish monastery. He played his own melodies on a small hand-organ, and several pupils testified to the psychic healing powers of the music. C. S. Nott recalled how he visited Gurdjieff in great distress after a severe and crippling accident to his young son. Gurdjieff led Nott into his sitting room, took up his hand-organ, 'and began to play a simple melody with strange harmonies, repeating and repeating, yet all the time with different combinations of notes'. Nott felt that Gurdjieff was conveying something to him through the music, and also through the 'telepathic means he knew so well'. A feeling of hope soon began to replace his 'dark depression'.

Gurdjieff died in Paris on 29 October 1949. His loyal and admiring pupils kept vigil over his body for several days while it lay in the chapel at the American hospital, and C.S. Nott reported that 'strong vibrations filled the place' and there seemed to be 'emanations or radiations from the corpse itself'. After Gurdjieff's death, some groups continued to follow his system in France, the United States and England. One of these was run by John Bennett at his house at Coombe Springs, outside London. Bennett claimed to have been close to Gurdjieff in the last months of his life, and recalls that Gurdjieff often referred 'to his own imminent departure from this world and to the coming of another who would complete the work he had started'. He also indicated that there was a teacher who was already preparing himself 'a long way from here', and he named that place as somewhere in the Far East.

In apparent fulfilment of this prediction, the Coombe Springs group abandoned the Gurdjieff system in 1957 and embraced a new philosophy – from Indonesia.

Prior to the interment of Gurdjieff at Fontainebleau in November 1949, below, his disciples stood vigil over his body for several days. One of them commented that 'strong vibrations filled the place', and there were apparently 'emanations or radiations from the corpse itself'.

HISTORY REVAMPED

Jesus was crucified in ancient Edinburgh; Bath was classical Athens... these were among the bizarre views of British patriot and journalist Comyns Beaumont

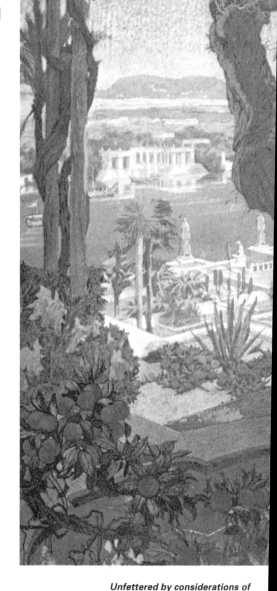

The Hanging Gardens of Babylon, right – a beautiful, if decadent, centre of ancient civilization – is placed by archaeologists in modern Iraq. Comyns Beaumont, however, believed that he knew better – they were, he said, in Rome, a city comparable in splendour and sin.

The mosaic in St Mark's, Venice, far right, shows scenes from the story of Noah and the Flood. Beaumont considered Mesopotamia an unlikely spot for the Deluge – the Atlantic, he claimed, was the real site.

Investigation into the mysteries of the ancient world can be a head-spinning task. So it is hardly surprising that not many authors feel they have hit upon the solution to age-old problems of history and religion, and have then pursued their flash of inspiration through thick and thin, disregarding all evidence to the contrary. Such an approach is definitely the hallmark of a crank – though this is, of course, a label to be applied with care. Nevertheless, Dr Immanuel Velikovsky, controversial author of *Worlds in Collision*, was accused in this way on the publication of his astounding and far-reaching claims, which flew in the face of the conventional view of world history.

But Velikovsky was not the first to attempt such a massive revision of the generally accepted view of world history. A previous, even more extreme stab at a grand rewriting of the past had been made in the 1940s by the eccentric English theorist Comyns Beaumont. Like Velikovsky, Beaumont was a catastrophist, who developed his own theory of a collision between the Earth and an enormous comet. Like Velikovsky, he also questioned the accepted dates for various geological ages, and even composed his own version of Egyptian history.

But whereas Velikovsky was satisfied with suggesting a 'revised chronology' for the ancient world, Beaumont went further still and beguiled his readers with the remarkable idea of a 'revised geography' for Man's history. In three volumes, he presented the case for one of the most fantastic assertions ever to reach the printed page – that all the events described in the *Bible*, and most of those in Greek myth and history, took place on the soil of the British Isles or closely neighbouring countries. The geography of the ancient world had been distorted, he argued, by the misunderstandings (or deliberate falsifications) of later Greek and Roman historians, and the 'truth' had been covered up. It was Beaumont's privilege to 'rediscover' the ancient centres of Israel, Judah, Greece and Egypt

Unfettered by considerations of logic or proof, Comyns Beaumont, left, developed a meticulous 'revised geography' to show that all the important classical and biblical sites were in Britain, as shown right. Many thousands of years ago, he said, Britain had also been Atlantis.

in the green and pleasant lands of England, Scotland and Wales. His theories even made the far-fetched claims of the 'British Israelites' – Victorian eccentrics, who believed the Anglo-Saxons were descended from the 'lost tribes of Israel' – seem restrained.

Strange though it may seem, there is no good reason to believe that Comyns Beaumont was actually insane. Born into a family of landed gentry claiming descent from the Normans, he worked for a while in the diplomatic service before becoming a journalist. He enjoyed a long and successful, albeit chequered, career as editor and writer for a host of English newspapers and popular magazines, playing an important part in publishing throughout the difficult years of two world wars. Yet, although he was extremely intelligent and erudite, Beaumont completely cast loose from the anchor of reason in a ruthless pursuit of his *idée fixe* – that Britain had been the motherland of world civilization, an idea epitomised in the title of his last book: *Britain: Key to World History*.

Although it is difficult to follow much of the reasoning behind Beaumont's extravagant proposals, one can trace out a fascinating, if disjointed, trail of wayward logic in his work, which began with some intriguing speculations but which led to confusion and, eventually, self-contradiction.

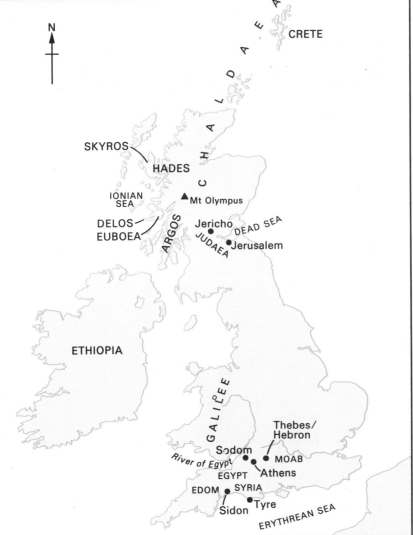

In the foreword to *The Middle of Prehistoric Britain*, Beaumont explained how he 'stumbled rather than deliberately walked into a recognition that the history of remote days as passed down was based on false premises in regard to the most famous of ancient peoples, both in regard to geography and chronology'. He was originally fascinated by the perennial problem of the location of Atlantis, the legendary lost continent and cradle of civilization, now supposedly submerged beneath the waves. Since the Greek philosopher Plato – to whom we owe the original Atlantis story – located the island in the Atlantic Ocean, Beaumont had little difficulty in following his patriotic inclinations and identifying it with the British Isles. Here, after all, are to be found the earliest traces of human habitation of any of the Atlantic islands. The story of Atlantis' destruction, he reasoned, concerned the break-up of an extended British land-mass that once stretched towards Scandinavia, resulting in the formation of the islands now known as the Shetlands, Hebrides and Orkneys.

PARALLEL ACCOUNTS

In Plato's account, the rich and powerful Atlanteans became corrupted by centuries of materialistic indulgence. Annoyed by their immorality, the gods destroyed their land with earthquake and flood. As Beaumont – and many others – noticed, this motif of a degenerate first race destroyed by natural catastrophe neatly parallels the biblical (and ancient Near Eastern) story of Noah's Flood, sent by God to obliterate the sinful.

Many have argued that a common origin for such myths, even the possibility of a real universal deluge, should be considered. But Beaumont had the temerity to turn the tables completely on the traditional view and insisted that the Flood had taken place in Britain rather than Mesopotamia. And if the Flood was an Atlantic event, then maybe Noah, and even the Hebrew patriarchs who followed him, were not really native to the Near East, but north-west Europe.

Beaumont mused on the antiquity of finds from the Atlantic coastal region, from the cave-paintings of the Dordogne to the profusion of megalithic remains found in the Orkneys. The Near East, at least at the time of Beaumont's writing, seemed to have comparatively little to offer in terms of prehistoric remains.

So, for Beaumont, it was logical to assume that north-west Europe was the real home of civilization and the cradle of Mankind, as described in so many mythologies.

He easily mustered support for this flash of inspiration with a hotch-potch of legends from many Old World cultures telling of a land of the gods, spirits or the dead that lay in the West. The widespread idea of a spirit land to the west is actually almost certainly due to the fact that this is the direction of the setting – or 'dying' – Sun. But Beaumont preferred a literal interpretation. Wringing every geographical clue he could from the myths, he fearlessly identified the Hades of Greek myth (the Amentet of the ancient Egyptians) with a group of islands off the coast of western Scotland. A feverish imagination led him to see, in the innocent Loch Carron and the nearby hamlet of Erbusaig, the hellish river Acheron and the Greek purgatory, Erebus. The famous burning river of Hades, the Styx, was seen in Loch Alsh and became the starting point for Beaumont's next extraordinary theoretical leap. The Greek hero Achilles was dipped in the river Styx by his mother to make him immortal, and then spent his childhood on the rocky island of Skyros. With great excitement, Beaumont believed he had found striking confirmation of his theory – at the mouth of Loch Alsh lay the island of Skye, 'unmistakably' Skyros!

After this revelation, there was no turning back. Skyros, unlike Erebus and Acheron, was not a mythical place but a historical location. To make things fit, Beaumont studiously shunted the various countries of classical Greece known to surround Skyros around the Scottish Highlands. He followed this up by scattering the peoples and places of the *Old Testament* around the map of Britain. Having taken the plunge, Beaumont dived deeper and deeper into the gulf of speculation and came up with what seemed to him to be pearls. Surely, he reasoned, the Ionian Greeks had lived in Iona, off the south-west coast of Mull, Scotland. The Scottish partiality for the name Alexander clearly reflected the days when Alexander the Great had lorded it over the

Achilles is seen left, being dipped into the Styx in the attempt to make him immortal. Beaumont believed that Loch Alsh, below, was the Styx and that Skyros, where Achilles was said to have grown up, was the Isle of Skye.

Bath, below left, is a city with a long history. But none of its records mentions that it was once commonly known as Athens, below right, as Beaumont claimed. But take away the B and add 'ens', and Bath becomes Athens, said Beaumont.

British Isles, he said. And weren't the Faeroe Islands so called because they were once ruled over by a pharaoh?

Site by site, all the important centres of the ancient world were whisked away by Beaumont from the Mediterranean and Near East, and arranged into a fantastic constellation around the North Sea. Wales became Galilee, Somerset became Egypt, and the river Severn became the

> THE INHABITANTS OF BRISTOL — HAD THEY KNOWN — WOULD HAVE BEEN SURPRISED TO LEARN THAT THEIR CITY WAS REALLY SODOM, RENOWNED IN THE BIBLE FOR ITS WICKEDNESS. BUT THE CROWNING GLORY OF BEAUMONT'S WORK WAS THE 'REAL' LOCATION OF THE HOLY CITY OF JERUSALEM... EDINBURGH.

In the scene, right, *Xerxes leads his army to attack Greece. Beaumont corrected what he said were the errors of centuries and relocated Greece in Britain. Xerxes, he said, had to march through Scotland to reach it.*

The Egyptian hieroglyphics, below left, *were on the wall of a tomb in Egypt – not Scotland as Beaumont believed. He used the Egyptian* Book of the Dead *in an attempt to 'prove' that the Egyptian Underworld was really Fingal's Cave on the Scottish Isle of Staffa,* below.

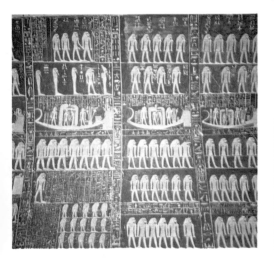

Nile. Hamburg in Germany, not Hissarlik in Turkey, had been the site of the Trojan War. Babylon was clearly Rome, not some insignificant mud-heap in Iraq. Snowy Ben Nevis was graced with the title of Olympus, home of the Greek gods. And the inhabitants of Bristol – had they known – would have been surprised to learn that their city was really Sodom, renowned in the *Bible* for its wickedness. But the crowning glory of Beaumont's work was to discover the 'real' location of the holy city of Jerusalem, and to trace the events leading to Christ's crucifixion through the streets of Edinburgh.

By now completely up a gum-tree, Beaumont's wild enthusiasm had led him into a world of inconsistent and facile methodology. While using the translation of the ancient Egyptian *Book of the Dead* to 'prove' that Fingal's Cave on the Scottish island of Staffa was the location of the Egyptian Underworld, he also had to deny that Egyptian hieroglyphics had been deciphered – he even asserted they were, in fact, untranslatable gibberish. And when we are asked by him to believe that Athens was really Bath – because one can ignore the B and add 'ens' – then it obviously becomes superfluous to subject Beaumont's work to any serious critique. One should simply enjoy it. Indeed, Beaumont's work became so undisciplined that any hope of scientific merit was left by the wayside. He must, however, take the prize for sheer extravagance of imagination.

According to Beaumont, Thucydides, below, *was one of the wayward Greek historians responsible for the widespread prejudice against an English Greece.*

It is to be regretted that Beaumont's promised further investigation of ancient history was never published. In this, he planned to show how geography had been distorted by the massive migrations of peoples from Britain and the deliberate falsification of Greek historians, such as Herodotus and Thucydides. We were also to be informed about how Xerxes' Persian army had marched through Scotland to attack a Greece relocated in England.

How a man of Beaumont's undoubted intelligence can have deluded himself to such a degree, it is difficult to imagine; but the *why* is clear. Beaumont was motivated by an intense patriotism, a force that coloured his career as an editor and journalist, as well as his view of ancient history. Basically liberal, but intensely nationalist, his greatest belief was in Britain as the mainstay of democracy, and he drifted from newspaper to newspaper in an endless quest for a publication that he felt really served the interests of the British people. The ups and downs of his career were described in his autobiography, *A Rebel in Fleet Street*.

Were he alive today, Beaumont would have been delighted to learn that ancient Europe's role in the rise of civilization has now been restored by a number of archaeological discoveries. But nothing – apart from an overwrought imagination – can transfer the scene of biblical stories and Greek myth to Beaumont's beloved homeland. Egypt remains in Egypt, and Greece remains in Greece, despite the earnest endeavours of Britain's greatest crank.

HEALING THROUGH HORROR

DEVOTEES OF A DECEASED DEACON OF PARIS UNDERWENT TORTURES THAT SHOULD HAVE BEEN MORE THAN FLESH COULD BEAR. YET THEY SURVIVED, AND WERE OFTEN HEALED

The strange events that took place in the little Paris churchyard of St Médard between 1727 and 1732 sound so incredible, and so preposterous, that the modern reader is tempted to dismiss them as pure invention. However, this would be a mistake, for an impressive mass of documents – including accounts by doctors, magistrates and other respectable public figures – attests to their genuineness. The miracles undoubtedly took place. But no doctor, philosopher or scientist

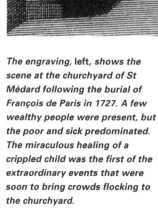

The engraving, left, shows the scene at the churchyard of St Médard following the burial of François de Paris in 1727. A few wealthy people were present, but the poor and sick predominated. The miraculous healing of a crippled child was the first of the extraordinary events that were soon to bring crowds flocking to the churchyard.

François de Paris, Deacon of Paris, left, gained the love of the poor and the enmity of the Church hierarchy during his short life. Uniquely among clerics of the time, he worked with his own hands. Here, he is seen weaving a tapestry; the proceeds of its sale were to go to the poor.

The prodigious feats performed by the devotees of François de Paris, as shown right, were all repulsive in some way. Women were beaten with clubs, pounded with rocks, and stabbed with spears and swords. Others plunged their heads into fire or licked the ulcers of the sick. Yet they emerged from their ordeals unharmed.

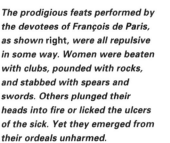

During his life, de Paris practised cruel self-mortifications. In the course of his devotions, he would whip himself with barbed flails, as in the illustration above. In a similar way, the miraculous activities of his devotees seemed to show that God could enable human beings to endure any torture – and even transform it into pleasure for the victim.

has even begun to explain how they could possibly have come about.

They began with the burial of François de Paris, the Deacon of Paris, in May 1727. François was only 37 years old, yet he was already widely revered as a holy man, with powers of healing. He was a follower of Bishop Cornelius Jansen, who taught that men can be saved only by divine grace, not by their own efforts. The Deacon had no doubt whatever that his own healing powers came from God.

INSTANT CURE

Great crowds followed his coffin, many weeping. It was laid in a tomb behind the high altar of St Médard. Then the congregation filed past, laying their flowers on the corpse. A father supported his son, a cripple, as he leaned over the coffin. Suddenly, the child went into convulsions; he seemed to be having a fit. Several people helped to drag him, writhing, to a quiet corner of the church. Suddenly, the convulsions stopped. The boy opened his eyes, looked around in bewilderment, and then slowly stood up. A look of incredulous joy crossed his face; then, to the astonishment of the spectators, he began to dance up and down, singing and laughing. His father found it impossible to believe, for the boy was using his withered right leg, which had virtually no muscles. Later, it was claimed that this leg had become as strong and normal as the other.

The news spread. Within hours, cripples, lepers, hunchbacks and blind men were rushing to the church. At first, few 'respectable' people believed the stories of these miraculous cures – the majority of the Deacon's followers were poor folk. The rich preferred to leave their spiritual affairs in the hands of the Jesuits, who were more cultivated and worldly. But it soon became clear that ignorance and credulity could not be used as a blanket explanation for all stories of such marvels. Deformed

limbs, it was said, were being straightened; hideous growths and cancers were disappearing without trace; and horrible sores and wounds were healing instantly.

The Jesuits declared that the miracles were either a fraud or the work of the Devil: the result was that most of the better-off in Paris flatly refused to believe that anything unusual was taking place in the churchyard of St Médard. But a few men of intellect were drawn by curiosity, and they invariably returned from the churchyard profoundly shaken. Sometimes, they recorded their testimony in print: some, such as Philippe Hecquet, attempted to explain the events by natural causes. Others, such as the Benedictine Bernard Louis de la Tasté, attacked those who performed the miracles on theological grounds, but were unable to expose any deception by them, or any error on the part of the witnesses. Indeed, the accumulation of written testimony was such that David Hume, one of the greatest of philosophers, wrote in *An Enquiry Concerning Human Understanding*:

'There surely never was a greater number of miracles ascribed to one person... But what is more extraordinary; many of the miracles were immediately proved upon the spot, before judges of unquestioned integrity, attested by witnesses of credit and distinction, in a learned age... Where shall we find such a number of circumstances, agreeing to the corroboration of one fact?'

One of those who investigated the happenings was a lawyer, Louis Adrien de Paige. When he told his friend, the magistrate Louis-Basile Carré de Montgeron, what he had seen, the magistrate assured him, patronisingly, that he had been taken in by conjuring tricks – the kind of 'miracles' performed by tricksters at fairgrounds. But he finally agreed to go with de Paige to the churchyard, if only for the pleasure of pointing out how the lawyer

Marie Anne Couronneau, left, was completely paralysed in her left leg. Two doctors pronounced the affliction 'absolutely incurable'. But she was allegedly healed by the convulsionnaires of St Médard – and celebrated by running up a flight of stairs and waving her crutches in the air.

The principal chronicler of the miracles of St Médard, Louis-Basile de Montgeron, presented the first volume of his account to King Louis XV, as shown below left – and was thrown into prison for his pains. The royal displeasure, prompted by the Jesuits' disapproval of de Paris and all his works, was eventually visited on the convulsionnaires: they, and many of their supporters, were dragged off to the Bastille, below.

had been deceived. They went there on the morning of 7 September 1731. De Montgeron left the churchyard a changed man – and even endured prison rather than deny what he had seen that day.

EXTRAORDINARY SPECTACLE

The first thing the magistrate saw when he entered the churchyard was a number of women writhing on the ground, twisting themselves into the most startling shapes, sometimes bending backwards until the backs of their heads touched their heels. These ladies were all wearing a long cloth undergarment that fastened around the ankles. De Paige explained that this was now obligatory for all women who wished to avail themselves of the Deacon's miraculous powers. In the early days, when women had stood on their heads or bent their bodies convulsively, prurient young men had begun to frequent the churchyard to view the spectacle .

However, in spite of this requirement, there was no lack of male devotees of the deceased Abbé to assist in the activities in the churchyard. De Montgeron was shocked to see that some of the women and girls were being sadistically beaten – at least, that is what at first appeared to be going on. Men were striking them with heavy pieces of wood and iron. Other women lay on the ground, apparently crushed under immensely heavy weights. One girl was naked to the waist: a man was gripping her nipples with a pair of iron tongs and twisting them violently. De Paige explained that none of these women felt any pain; on the contrary, many begged for more blows. And, most miraculous of all, an incredible number were cured of deformities or diseases by this violent treatment.

In another part of the churchyard, they saw an attractive, pink-cheeked girl of about 19, who was sitting at a trestle table and eating. That seemed normal enough, until de Montgeron looked more closely at the food on the plate, and realised from its appearance – as well as from the smell that reached him – that it was human excrement. In between mouthfuls of this sickening fare, she drank a yellow liquid which, de Paige explained, was

urine. This girl had come to the churchyard to be cured of what we would now call a neurosis: she had to wash her hands hundreds of times a day, and was so fastidious about her food that she would taste nothing that had been touched by another human hand. The Deacon had indeed cured her. Within days, she was eating excrement and drinking urine, and did so with every sign of enjoyment. Such cases might not be remarkable in asylums; but what was more extraordinary – even preposterous – was that after one of these meals, she opened her mouth as if to be sick, and milk came pouring out. De Paige collected a cupful; it was, apparently, perfectly ordinary cow's milk.

> *"* ONE GIRL WAS NAKED TO THE WAIST: A MAN WAS GRIPPING HER NIPPLES WITH A PAIR OF IRON TONGS AND TWISTING THEM VIOLENTLY. DE PAIGE EXPLAINED THAT NONE OF THESE WOMEN FELT ANY PAIN; ON THE CONTRARY, MANY BEGGED FOR MORE BLOWS. *"*

Long after the suppression of the activities at St Médard, bursts of religious zeal occasionally reappeared in Paris. One of the many crucifixions indulged in by a girl named Sister Françoise, for instance, was recorded by the scientist La Condamine. After more than three hours on the cross, as below right, she was taken down, exhausted but little the worse for the ordeal.

After staggering away from the eater of excrement, de Montgeron had to endure a worse ordeal. In another part of the churchyard, a number of women had volunteered to cleanse suppurating wounds and boils by sucking them clean. Trying hard to prevent himself vomiting, de Montgeron watched as someone unwound a dirty bandage from the leg of a small girl; the smell was horrible. The leg was a festering mass of sores, some so deep that bone was visible. The woman who had volunteered to clean it was one of the *convulsionnaires* – she had been miraculously cured and converted by her bodily contortions, and God had now chosen her to demonstrate how easily human beings' disgust can be overcome. Yet even she blenched as she saw and smelled the gangrenous leg. She cast her eyes up to heaven, prayed silently for a moment, then bent her head and began to lap, swallowing the septic matter. When she moved her face further down the child's leg, de Montgeron could see that the wound was now clean. De Paige assured him that the girl would almost certainly be cured when the treatment was complete.

What de Montgeron saw next finally shattered his resistance and convinced him that he was witnessing something of profound significance.

A 16-year-old girl named Gabrielle Moler had arrived, and the interest she excited made de Montgeron aware that, even among this crowd of miraculous freaks, she was a celebrity. She removed her cloak and lay on the ground, her skirt modestly round her ankles. Four men, each holding a pointed iron bar, stood over her. When the girl smiled at them, they lunged down at her, driving their rods into her stomach. De Montgeron had to be restrained from interfering as the rods went through the girl's dress and into her stomach. He

looked for signs of blood staining her dress. But none came, and the girl looked calm and serene. Next, the bars were jammed under her chin, forcing her head back. It seemed inevitable that they would penetrate through to her mouth; yet when the points were removed, the flesh was unbroken. The men took up sharp-edged shovels, placed them against a breast, and then pushed with all their might; but the girl went on smiling gently. The breast, trapped between shovels, should have been cut off but it seemed impervious to the assault. Then, the cutting edge of a shovel was placed against her throat, and the man wielding it did his best to cut off her head; but he did not seem able even to dent her neck.

Dazed, de Montgeron watched as the girl was beaten with a great iron truncheon that was shaped like a pestle. A stone weighing half-a-hundredweight (25 kilograms) was raised above her body and dropped repeatedly from a height of several feet. Finally, de Montgeron watched her kneel in front of a blazing fire, and plunge her head into it. He could feel the heat from where he stood; yet her hair and eyebrows were not even singed. When she picked up a blazing chunk of coal and proceeded to eat it, de Montgeron could stand no more and left.

Nevertheless, he went back repeatedly, until he had enough materials for the first volume of an amazing book. He presented it to the King, Louis XV, who was so shocked and indignant that he had de Montgeron thrown into prison. Yet de Montgeron felt he had to bear witness and was to publish two more volumes following his release, full of precise scientific testimony concerning the miracles.

MIND OVER MATTER

In the year following de Montgeron's imprisonment, 1732, the Paris authorities decided that the scandal was becoming unbearable and closed down the churchyard. But the *convulsionnaires* had discovered that they could perform their miracles anywhere, and continued for many years.

A hardened sceptic, the scientist La Condamine, was as startled as de Montgeron when, in 1759, he watched a girl named Sister Françoise crucified on a wooden cross, nailed by the hands and feet over a period of several hours, and stabbed in the side with a spear. He noticed that all this obviously hurt the girl, and that her wounds bled when the nails were removed; but she seemed none the worse for an ordeal that would have killed most people.

So how can we possibly explain these miracles from the standpoint of the late 20th century? Some writers believe they involved a kind of self-hypnosis. But while this could explain the excrement-eater and the woman who sucked festering wounds, it is less plausible in explaining Gabrielle Moler's feats of endurance. These remind us rather of descriptions of the practices of fakirs. For example, J.G. Bennett, in his autobiography *Witness*, describes watching a Dervish ritual in which a razor-sharp sword was placed across the belly of a naked man, after which two heavy men jumped up and down on it – all without even marking the flesh. What seems to be at work here is some form of 'mind over matter', far more effective than mere hypnosis, which is not yet understood but which certainly merits serious attention.

WHAT REALLY HAPPENED AT TUNGUSKA?

IN 1908, A VAST AREA OF SIBERIA WAS DEVASTATED BY AN EXPLOSION. WHAT CAUSED THIS INCIDENT? COULD IT HAVE BEEN THE BURN-UP OF A NUCLEAR-POWERED SPACECRAFT?

Willard F. Libby, below, was one of a team who thought they had found an increase in atmospheric radioactive carbon-14 following the Tunguska explosion.

On 30 June 1908, a brilliant fireball blazed through the Earth's atmosphere, exploding at a height of 5 miles (8 kilometres) above the valley of the Tunguska river, Siberia, with the force of a 12 megatonne nuclear bomb. According to one popular theory, the Tunguska explosion was a nuclear blast, caused by the burn-up of a nuclear-powered alien spacecraft. But another leading theory claimed the Tunguska object was the head of a small comet. What evidence is there to back up each of these rival theories? What really happened on that summer's night?

Important clues as to the nature of the Tunguska explosion were obtained on three expeditions to the site – in 1958, 1961 and 1962 – led by Soviet geochemist Kirill Florensky. His 1962 expedition used a helicopter to chart the disaster area. Instead of looking for large meteoritic fragments, as Leonid Kulik had done in the late 1920s, Florensky's team sifted the soil for microscopic particles that would have been scattered by the burn-up and disintegration of the Tunguska object. Their search proved fruitful. The scientists traced a narrow tongue of cosmic dust stretching for 150 miles (250 kilometres) north-west of the site. It was composed of magnetite (magnetic iron oxide) and glassy droplets of fused rock. The expedition found thousands of samples of metal and silicate particles fused together, indicating that the Tunguska object had not been of uniform composition. A low-density stony composition, containing flecks of iron, is believed to be typical of interplanetary debris, particularly meteors ('shooting stars'), which are themselves composed of dust from comets. The particles that spread north-west of the Tunguska blast were apparently the vaporised remains of a comet's head.

These actual samples of the Tunguska object should have been enough to settle the controversy once and for all. Florensky wrote about his expeditions in a 1963 article in the magazine *Sky & Telescope*. The article was entitled: 'Did a comet

Within a few hours of the explosion, Tunguska looked like this, with fresh green growth pushing up through the dead timber.

collide with the Earth in 1908?' Among astronomers, the comet theory had always been the front runner. In his article, Florensky said that this viewpoint 'was now confirmed'.

RADIATION CHECK

Florensky's expedition carefully checked for traces of radiation at the site. He reported that the only radioactivity in the trees from the Tunguska area was fall-out from atomic tests, which had been absorbed into the wood. His team also looked at the acceleration of forest growth in the devastated area, which some had put down to genetic damage from radiation. Biologists concluded that only the normal acceleration of growth after a fire, a well-known phenomenon, had taken place.

But what of the 'scabs' reported to have broken out on reindeer after the blast? In the absence of any veterinary report, one can only speculate, but it is most likely these were not caused by atomic radiation but occurred simply as a result of the great flash of heat given out by the blast, which also set fire to the trees. Humans near enough to have felt the heat of the fireball showed no signs of radiation sickness, and were found to be alive and healthy when Leonid Kulik visited the site over a dozen years later.

Believers in the nuclear explosion theory quote investigations in 1965 by three American physicists, Clyde Cowan, C.R. Atluri, and Willard Libby, who reported a 1 per cent increase in radiocarbon in tree rings following the Tunguska blast. A nuclear explosion releases a burst of neutrons, which turn atmospheric nitrogen into radioactive carbon-14 that is taken up by plants, along with ordinary carbon, during their normal photosynthesis. If the Tunguska blast were nuclear, excess radiocarbon would be expected in the plants growing at the time.

To test this prediction, the American scientists examined tree rings from a 300-year-old Douglas fir from the Catalina Mountains near Tucson, Arizona, and also from an ancient oak tree near Los Angeles. They found that the level of radiocarbon in the rings of both trees had jumped by 1 per cent from 1908 to 1909. But the picture is confused by erratic fluctuations of up to 2 per cent that exist in the levels of radiocarbon measured in the tree rings from year to year. Therefore, a 1 per cent radiocarbon increase is not outside the range of normal fluctuations caused by natural effects. An important double-check was made by three Dutch scientists on a tree from Trondheim, Norway – much nearer the blast, where the radiocarbon effects would be expected to be more noticeable. Instead of a radiocarbon rise in 1909, they found a steady decrease around that time. Therefore the increase in American trees found by Cowan, Atluri and Libby must have been due to local effects – and not to the Tunguska blast.

So what about the trees left standing at the centre of the Tunguska blast area, as were trees under the explosion point of the Hiroshima bomb, and the 'fiery pillar' seen after the explosion? Such effects are not unique to a nuclear blast. Any explosion is followed by an updraught of heated air and a puff of smoke. Brilliant exploding fireballs happen frequently as chunks of solar system debris plunge into the atmosphere. Fortunately for us, most of them are far smaller than the Tunguska object.

The healing processes of the Siberian forest have not yet obliterated the scars of the 1908 explosion. Within a few years, saplings had grown between the trunks strewn on the ground, top. But, even today, the fallen trees are still evident beneath a covering of moss and foliage, above.

A clump of standing trees would be left behind by an aerial explosion of any kind, as shown by the scale-model experiments of Igor Zotkin and Mikhail Tsikulin of the Soviet Academy of Sciences' meteorite committee. They set off small explosions over a field of model trees, and found they were able to reproduce the pattern of felled trees, including the central standing clump.

It therefore seems that all the 'evidence' adduced for a nuclear explosion at Tunguska is either misinterpretation or mischievous distortion.

METEORITE STRIKE?

Remarkably, the Tunguska event was repeated on a smaller scale over North America on the night of 31 March 1965. An area of nearly 390,000 square miles (1 million square kilometres) of the United States and Canada was lit up by the descent of a body that detonated over the towns of Revelstoke and Golden, 250 miles (400 kilometres) south-west of Edmonton, Alberta, Canada. Residents of those towns spoke of a 'thunderous roar' that rattled and broke windows. The energy released was equal to several kilotonnes of TNT.

Scientists predicted the meteorite's point of impact and set out to look for a crater, much as Leonid Kulik had done in Siberia half-a-century previously. Like him, they were unsuccessful. Scanning the snow-covered ground from the air, the scientists were unable to find traces of the meteorite, or of a crater. Only when investigators went into the area on foot did they find that a strange black dust coated the snow for miles around. Samples of this dirt were scraped up, and proved to have the composition of a particularly fragile type of stony meteorite known as a carbonaceous chondrite. The Revelstoke object fragmented in mid-air, raining

OUT OF THIS WORLD

thousands of tonnes of crumbly black dust upon the snow. Significantly, witnesses to the Tunguska blast described just such a 'black rain'.

Clinching evidence for the cometary nature of the Tunguska object comes from the results of Soviet expeditions to the site, reported in 1977. Microscopic rocky particles found in the 1908 peat layers have the same composition as cosmic particles collected from the upper atmosphere by rockets. Thousands of tonnes of this material are estimated to be scattered around the fall area. Along with these particles of rock from space were jagged particles of meteoric iron. The Soviet researchers concluded that the Tunguska object was of carbonaceous chondrite composition. This

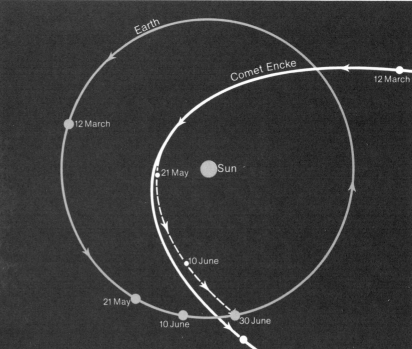

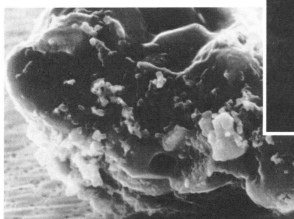

*The diagram, **top**, shows how the Tunguska explosion may have happened. The comet Encke could have shed a rock fragment that was captured by the Earth.*

*The dust grain, **above**, magnified 10,000 times, was collected in the stratosphere. It is thought to have come from a comet.*

*The rings of recent Tunguska trees, **top left**, are thicker than those of trees killed in the disaster, **bottom left**. Some scientists claim that radioactivity from the explosion caused a marked spurt in plant growth.*

comes as no surprise, for astronomers are finding that a carbonaceous chondrite composition is typical of interplanetary debris.

But if it was a comet, why was it not seen in the sky prior to impact? Perhaps it always stayed close to the Sun so that it was lost in glare; or, maybe, it was too small ever to have become bright enough to see even in a dark sky. Astronomers now believe that the Tunguska object was actually a fragment broken several thousand years ago from Comet Encke, an old and faint comet with the shortest known orbit of any comet around the Sun. A Czech astronomer, Lubor Kresak, pointed out, in 1976, that the orbit of the Tunguska object, deduced from the direction and angle at which it struck the Earth, was remarkably similar to that of Encke's comet. Dr Kresak estimates that the body had a diameter of only about 100 yards (100 metres) when in space, and a mass of up to a million tonnes. Dust from its disintegration in the atmosphere caused the bright nights experienced in the northern hemisphere in the period following the Tunguska event.

'The identification of the Tunguska object as an extinct cometary fragment appears to be the only plausible explanation of the event; and a common origin with Comet Encke appears very probable,' concludes Dr Kresak.

What is more, an event like Tunguska could well happen again. Astronomers have found a number of small asteroids with orbits that cross the path of the Earth. For instance, in 1976, a direct repetition of the Tunguska event was narrowly avoided as a previously unknown asteroid with a diameter of a few hundred yards swept past the Earth at a distance of 750,000 miles (1.2 million kilometres). Astronomers estimate that an object the size of the Tunguska comet hits the Earth once in about 2,000 years on average. So it is only a matter of time before we are hit again – and next time, of course, it could do a lot more damage if it comes anywhere near a built-up area.

A MEDIUM UNMASKED

FOR DECADES, THE FAMOUS
MEDIUM WILLIAM ROY
ASTOUNDED SITTERS AT
SEANCES WITH 'SPIRIT'
VOICES, MATERIALISATIONS
– AND INFORMATION THAT,
IT WAS BELIEVED, HE COULD
HAVE GAINED ONLY BY
PARANORMAL MEANS

When William Roy died in August 1977, the publication *Psychic News* said of him: 'In Spiritualism's long history there has never been a greater villain. He is now in a world where he cannot cheat.' Yet there were those who would not accept that verdict, for over the years Roy had so raised false hopes among his victims that a great many of them could never face the fact that he was a fraud. And the people he duped were not always simple, ill-educated types – far from it. They included prominent society figures, among them the late W. L. Mackenzie King.

Mackenzie King's involvement began during the Second World War, when he was Prime Minister of Canada. It was a post that he had held before, but war naturally brought with it many extra responsibilities, which included top-secret visits to London to confer with the War Cabinet. It was on one of these 'hush-hush' visits that he decided to

The 'medium' William Roy, above right, thrived on publicity, both good and bad. However, his early successes established his reputation among those who wanted to believe he was genuine. For example, during the Second World War, W. L. Mackenzie King, right, the Canadian Prime Minister, visited Roy under an assumed name – and was astonished to be given pertinent messages by an assortment of deceased statesmen. Yet Roy himself later confessed that this was all fraud, based on ingenious detective work that had established the identity of the sitter well in advance of the seance – enabling him to do his 'homework'.

consult William Roy – then famed as Britain's most outstanding medium.

Because of the nature of his visit to Britain, King thought it wise not to give his true name to Roy in advance of the consultation. So, on the surface, it looked as if Roy had no clue as to the real identity of his client. And yet Roy was able to give the Canadian Prime Minister a number of apparently convincing messages, and all from those who, in real life, would naturally and easily talk to a head of government. The grandest was Queen Victoria herself. Mackenzie King was thrilled as he chatted away to 'Her Majesty'.

More thrills came when Mr Gladstone 'came through' and gave a message of hope – just the kind of thing to cheer one up in the dark days of war. It was all very satisfying and comforting; so much so that the Canadian Prime Minister went back for further sessions and was overwhelmed when his dead brother and sister spoke to him.

Mackenzie King returned to Canada overjoyed and without any suspicions whatsoever about Roy – completely unaware that he had been thoroughly deceived by a scheming rogue. For Roy's 'psychic gifts' were non-existent. His sessions involved nothing more than play-acting, using fake voices and stage effects, while his 'revelations' or personal messages for the bereaved were, in fact, due to planning and trickery. So how did he do it?

His tricks were usually based on techniques that had been used at the height of the Spiritualist craze in the 19th century. He had added a few of his own but, in the main, he kept to stunts that had been well-tried by other tricksters before him. In fact, Roy had found most of his tricks carefully explained in a book called *Behind the Scenes with the Mediums*. This enlightening book was written by David Abbott in 1907 and published in the USA, although a few copies were sold in England by the Magical and Unique Novelty Company of London. Roy had the good fortune to find one of these copies and it set his mind reeling. In the pages of this obscure book was all the advice that Roy needed in order to set up a lucrative business. From then on, as far as he was concerned, Abbott's book was worth its weight in gold.

The equipment used by Roy and his accomplice in their bogus seances is shown below. The accomplice collected as much information as he could about the sitters and conveyed this to Roy from the next room by means of a cordless telephone. The connection was made by Roy placing his copper-soled shoes on metal tacks hidden in the carpet, which were wired to cables running through the wall. Wires that ran up Roy's trouser-leg, below right, ended in a miniature hearing aid – through which he could hear his accomplice, but the sitters could not.

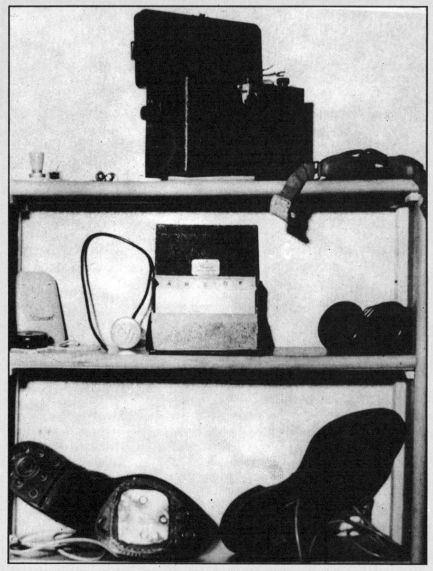

"
BUT ROY WAS FAMOUS FOR MORE THAN THE MESSAGES HE GAVE – IT WAS THE DRAMA WITH WHICH HE DELIVERED THEM THAT BROUGHT HIM RENOWN... SOMETIMES THERE WOULD EVEN BE TWO VOICES SPEAKING SIMULTANEOUSLY.
"

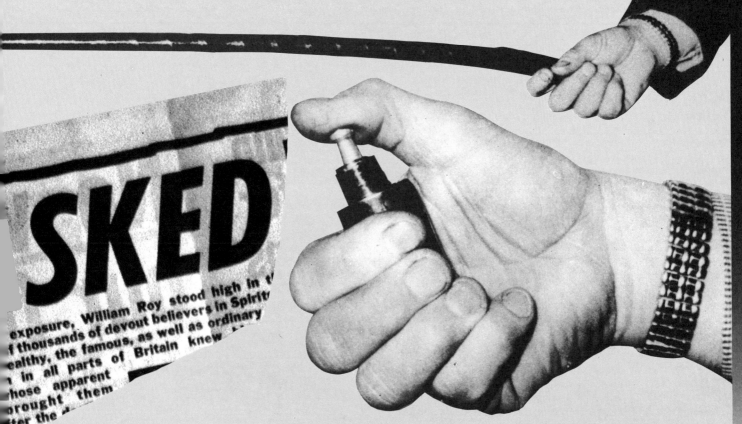

SKED

exposure, William Roy stood high in t'
f thousands of devout believers in Spirit
'ealthy, the famous, as well as ordinary
1 in all parts of Britain knew
hose apparent
`rought them
ter the

By the time Roy set himself up as a medium, he had mastered most of the tricks in the book. He even worked out a few refinements. His clients innocently walked into a trap every time they visited his home: they were expected to leave all coats and bags in a special cloakroom, and this gave Roy's accomplice a chance to search through their belongings for bits of useful information. Moreover, clients were kept waiting before each seance began. And as they chatted to pass the time away, hidden microphones picked up their words. By these means, Roy always knew more about his clients than they dreamed possible. Sometimes he would even overhear them name the dead relatives they hoped to contact. In this way, every sitting was neatly rigged beforehand. And when Roy ran out of authentic titbits, he was adroit enough to bluff his way out of trouble – which was partly done by calling on colourful 'spirit guides'. There was one called Joey, another called Dr Wilson and, best of the lot, a Red Indian called Tinka. Tinka was not only fashionable – Red Indians being 'in' as spirit guides – he was invaluable; for, if the questions became awkward, he would just sulk and grunt: 'No can answer... Me just simple Indian' – which would quickly smooth over any trickier parts of the evening.

The microphones and searches of coats and bags were not, however, the only preparations. Once Roy knew the names of his clients, he checked on their families at the registry in Somerset House, or looked up death notices and entries in *Who's Who*. He even contacted other fake mediums for extra information.

But his most masterly research involved his initial session with Mackenzie King. In that case, he had no opportunity to go through the Prime Minister's pockets and no chance to listen in to his conversation. All he knew in advance was that he was to have a sitting with a 'distinguished person'. And all he knew about the booking was that it was

Although the Spiritualist world knew of Roy's fraud as early as 1952, it was not until 1958 that the story made banner headlines in the **Sunday Pictorial, above left.** *Curiously, Roy seemed almost to delight in confessing, as well as in explaining how he accomplished his bogus effects. He revealed, among other tricks, how he used to make his 'spirit trumpet' fly around the darkened seance room: quite simply, it was attached to the end of a telescopic rod, which could be hidden in the hand, as above, or extended,* **top.**

made by a member of the Duke of Connaught's staff. That was little enough to go on, but Roy had to start somewhere – so he studied everything he could find about the Duke of Connaught. And he discovered that the Duke had been Governor General of Canada from 1911 to 1916. As soon as he read that, Roy made a brilliant deduction – this mysterious visitor could easily be a distinguished Canadian friend of the Duke. And the most distinguished Canadian known to embrace Spiritualism was their Prime Minister – Mackenzie King.

FAKE VOICES

Roy was so convinced that his deduction was right that he began practising passages in the voices of Gladstone and Queen Victoria, specifically tailored to King's character. The Queen's high-pitched voice was something of a strain; but by the time Mackenzie King turned up, it was good enough to fool him and make him want to know more about the communications.

But Roy was famous for more than the messages he gave – it was the drama with which he delivered them that brought him renown. He could make a luminous trumpet float throught the air in the darkened seance room and induce 'spirit voices' to speak through it. Sometimes there would even be two voices speaking simultaneously. And, remarkably enough, he could even produce extra voices in full light.

When he appeared at public meetings, he worked even more baffling stunts. In 1947, at Kingsway Hall, London, for instance, his hands were tied to the arms of a chair; his mouth was filled with coloured water and his lips were sealed with sticking plaster – yet he still produced 'spirit' voices. After the plaster was removed, his mouth was found to be still full of the coloured water – so fakery seemed ruled out. But Roy was responsible for all the voices, even when his mouth was filled

343

The system worked beautifully, especially as the earphone could double as a miniature loud-speaker. But it had its limits, so a second connection to the other room was called for. This was provided by a dummy power socket on the wall, which was wired not to the mains but to an amplifier. Thus, Roy was able to plug a cable into it and energize a miniature loudspeaker fixed on the tip of his telescopic rod. While his assistant's voice came through this speaker, Roy imitated one of his 'guides' and threw in occasional comments in his own voice. Small wonder that he was famed for his spellbinding sessions.

Roy's trickery was first exposed in 1952 when he fell out with his assistant – who promptly paid a visit to the offices of *Psychic News*. There, he opened a large suitcase and took out the apparatus used to fake the seances. It was all there, from telescopic rod to shoes fitted with copper plates. It looked like the end for Roy.

But there proved to be a problem, for the assistant did not want the matter to go any further. Following this, Roy promised to give up mediumship and leave the country, saying that he wanted to make a new start in South Africa. In fact, he did leave England and the whole sorry affair was silently laid to rest – or so it seemed.

SUPREME TRICKSTER

However, old habits die hard; and within a few years, Roy was organizing seances in South Africa. But then he had the supreme cheek to return to Britain and even started up his seances again. However, he had gone too far; this proved too much for the rest of the Spiritualist fraternity and one of their papers, *Two Worlds*, finally exposed him as a fraudulent medium.

Dramatic scenes followed this newspaper report. Roy's wife attacked the paper's editor with a riding crop, and Roy himself started a lawsuit against the editor. Roy's wife was fined £3 for the assault and Roy could afford to pay the fine with a smile – for he knew that, in effect, his lawsuit meant that he could go on milking his clients because his action had discouraged any further newspaper comment on the case until after the court hearing. Court actions, he knew, sometimes take years before they are heard – which is precisely what happened in Roy's case.

Roy carried on his fakery until February 1958. Then he dropped the lawsuit he knew he could never win and he agreed to pay costs to the editor of *Two Worlds*. Following that, he brazenly sold his story to the *Sunday Pictorial*. It was published in five instalments, and readers marvelled at how he had cheated his way to fame and fortune. At the end of the series, Roy wrote: 'I know that, even after this confession, I could fill the seance rooms again with people who find it a comfort to believe I am genuine.'

At the time that sounded like hot air or bravado, but Roy went on to make his boast come true. He set up shop under the name Bill Silver, and for years ran his old racket without challenge. Astonishingly, he numbered among his clients many who knew his real identity and who were fully aware of his history of cold-blooded fraud, cynical confessions and publicity-seeking.

and sealed. For him, that was just a minor inconvenience. In the darkness, it was easy for him to bend his head down and loosen the plaster with one tied hand – then the water was ejected through a rubber tube into a small container in his breast pocket. At the end of the evening, the water was sucked back up again, the plaster was smoothed back into place, and everyone was duly overawed at this astonishing display of Roy's psychic powers.

The private seances were a different matter. Most of the voices were produced by Roy but some were provided by his assistant, while others were tape-recordings. In that way, Roy was able to produce more than one voice at a time. And the methods he used – apart from the tape-recordings – were all drawn from that invaluable book by Abbott.

First, the trumpet flew through the air on the end of a telescopic rod – just as Abbott described. And the assistant in the next room passed information through to Roy by a telephone – again, exactly as in the book. Of course, the telephone connection was made without cords, for that would have given the game away. Instead, Roy wore copper plates on the soles of his shoes and these were soldered to thin wires that ran up the legs of his trousers and through his jacket to a small earphone on his wrist. To link up with his assistant, he had only to put his feet on to metal carpet tacks and he was connected – for the tacks were wired up to cables running through the wall.

Roy shows, above, *how to evade test conditions at a 'direct voice' seance, while one of his 'spirits' proves not to be so convincing when seen in a good light*, below.

WHO REALLY DISCOVERED AMERICA?

THE YEAR 1992 HAS SEEN WIDESPREAD CELEBRATIONS MARKING THE 500TH ANNIVERSARY OF THE ARRIVAL OF CHRISTOPHER COLUMBUS IN THE NEW WORLD. BUT WAS AMERICA DISCOVERED HUNDREDS OF YEARS EARLIER?

Christopher Columbus, as every schoolboy knows, discovered America. Columbus, who was born in Genoa, Italy, sailed his ships – *Pinta*, *Niña* and *Santa Maria* – to the New World under the Spanish flag, reaching the island of Guanahani, which the Spaniards renamed San Salvador, in the Bahamas, on 12 October 1492.

But Columbus may not have been the first to find America. 'Who discovered America?' was a question that sparked a heated, but often humorous, debate in the United Nations General Assembly in November 1982, after 36 nations – including Spain, Italy, South American and Caribbean countries – tabled an apparently uncontroversial motion calling for the UN to prepare for a dignified commemoration in 1992 to mark the five hundredth anniversary of Columbus' discovery.

Quick to enter the fray was Noel Dorr, the delegate from the Irish Republic to the UN, who asked: 'Is it not something of an exaggeration to speak so confidently of Columbus' landing as the discovery of America? For one thing, there were indigenous inhabitants.'

There were indeed 'native Americans'. They were thought to have arrived in America 30,000 years ago from Siberia via Alaska, across a land bridge that existed where the Bering Strait now is. The original band of Mongoloid people later split into different societies. They evolved, it is generally believed, without any outside influences.

But this, as the United Nations debate made clear, may be a much over-simplified picture of what really happened. It is highly possible that the native Americans were influenced by Irish monks who may have crossed the Atlantic in the sixth century – as Noel Dorr was eager to point out.

The Irish delegate was referring to St Brendan, though he conceded that it was not yet clear whether St Brendan actually made the journey.

The Aztec Emperor Montezuma welcomes Hernando Cortés in **The Conquistadors,** *a painting by Miguel Gonzales executed in 1698, reproduced on the previous page. Montezuma hailed Cortés as the reincarnation of the Aztecs' fair, bearded god Quetzalcoatl. It has been suggested that this legend reflects a memory of the visits of fair-skinned traders to the Americas.*

The map of the Atlantic Ocean by Bartolomeo Pareto, right, dates from 1455 – a few decades before Christopher Columbus' voyage to the Americas. The map shows the legendary island of Antilla – which, according to Portuguese tradition, was peopled by Christians who had fled the advancing Moors.

The 16th-century engraving, below right, shows Columbus' arrival in the Americas. Was he really the first European to discover the New World?

The Irish claim did not impress Spain's ambassador, Señor Jaime de Pinies, who declared: 'Up to this point, the only thing I have found [in the United States] from Ireland is the police force in New York City and distinguished Irishmen who belong to the American community.'

Joking apart, there were serious contenders in the battle for nations credited with the discovery of America. Hodur Helgason, Iceland's representative, was quick to bring to the UN's attention the achievement of Leif Ericsson, the Viking who, around the year AD 1000, discovered 'Vinland' at the end of a transatlantic voyage. It is now widely accepted that Vinland was, in fact, Newfoundland. Helgason complained: 'We feel that the historical fact of Leif Ericsson's discovery is so totally ignored in the wording of the draft resolution that we cannot give it our vote.'

VISITORS FROM THE ORIENT

There is plenty of evidence – some strong, some circumstantial – that America has been host to numerous foreign visitors in its past. If this is true, their arrival in North and South America must have influenced the development of the inhabitants.

The earliest visitors to America seem to have been Japanese and Chinese seafarers who landed on the west coast between 3000 BC and 2500 BC. The evidence for Japanese visitors is strong and comes in the form of a case of pottery, nearly 5,000 years old, that was found on the Valdivian coast of Ecuador. It is decorated in the same style as pottery from the Jomon area of Japan.

So how did it get there? One hypothesis is that a Japanese fishing vessel was caught in a storm and then drifted the 8,000 miles (13,000 kilometres) to the north-west coast of South America. The fishermen could have kept alive, through the seven months or more during which their boat would have drifted, by eating fish and drinking rainwater.

Evidence for the Chinese connection may not be as strong – but Robert von Heine-Geldern, an Austrian ethnologist, believes the Chinese exerted a very strong influence on the development of civilization in Central America and Peru. Indeed, there is a Chinese classic, the *Shan Hai King*, dated about 225 BC, which contains what appears to be an accurate description of the Grand Canyon

While seaborne explorers or lost fishermen may have been approaching the Americas across the Pacific, the Atlantic was almost certainly bringing visitors to the east coast. Indeed, the American archaeologist Alice B. Kehoe has drawn attention to 'oddities' in the north-east region of North America that strongly suggest the existence of early transatlantic trade routes.

The earliest specimens of woodworking tools and fishing gear are found in the Great Lakes area of Canada and the United States, and date from 2500 BC; ground slate knives, of a slightly later date and similar design, have been found in the Baltic countries. Dr Kehoe suggests that this may have been due to cod fishermen who strayed across the Atlantic and returned with the more efficient means of gutting their catch, learned from the original inhabitants of North America.

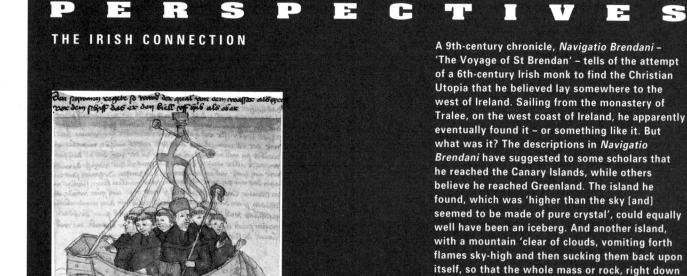

PERSPECTIVES

THE IRISH CONNECTION

A 9th-century chronicle, *Navigatio Brendani* – 'The Voyage of St Brendan' – tells of the attempt of a 6th-century Irish monk to find the Christian Utopia that he believed lay somewhere to the west of Ireland. Sailing from the monastery of Tralee, on the west coast of Ireland, he apparently eventually found it – or something like it. But what was it? The descriptions in *Navigatio Brendani* have suggested to some scholars that he reached the Canary Islands, while others believe he reached Greenland. The island he found, which was 'higher than the sky [and] seemed to be made of pure crystal', could equally well have been an iceberg. And another island, with a mountain 'clear of clouds, vomiting forth flames sky-high and then sucking them back upon itself, so that the whole mass or rock, right down to the sea level, glowed like a pyre', appears to have been a volcano. It seems quite possible that St Brendan crossed the Atlantic by way of volcanic Iceland, and travelled on to his Utopia – the New World – ten centuries before Columbus.

Whatever the truth of the matter, St Brendan's island appears in the western Atlantic on many 17th- and 18th-century maps. The Portuguese even claimed sovereignty over the island, and plots of land were sold to noble families. Despite attempts, financed in their embarrassment by the Portuguese, to find their mythical land, its exact location remains unknown.

In an illustration, left, from Navigatio Brendani, *St Brendan and his monks are encircled in their tiny, rudderless boat by a huge fish that holds its tail in its mouth.*

Further evidence of links between America and Europe are to be found in pottery in America dating from around 1000 BC. This closely matches Baltic pottery of the same age.

All too often, in assessing the likely influence of other civilizations on a country, the experts look for visits across land bridges. In fact, it is very probable that ancient mariners were capable of making long journeys and were familiar with navigation techniques that make trade and cultural links between continents seem far from impossible.

As Thor Heyerdahl's *Ra* expeditions showed, a combination of wind and current could take a papyrus raft from the African coast to America 'whether the crew wanted it or not'. Francis Hitching, in his book *World Atlas of Mysteries*, points out that some historians believe that an influx of Egyptian, Negro, Jewish and Chinese immigrants were together responsible for the sudden rise of the Olmec civilization in Mexico around 1200 BC. The seafaring Phoenicians are another group of people believed to have traded with America around 1000 BC, according to some interpretations of texts by Plato and Diodorus Siculus.

One puzzle that certainly suggests contact with other races is the existence in the Americas of sculpted heads dating from 1500 BC to AD 1500 that depict bearded men of Jewish appearance – American Indians are beardless.

Indeed, as Hitching points out, the conquistador Hernando Cortés was left in no doubt that someone had preceded him when he landed in Mexico in AD 1519. The Aztec Emperor Montezuma invited him

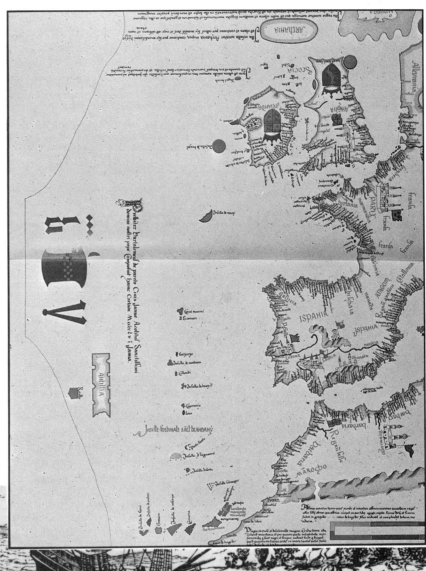

*In*Focus

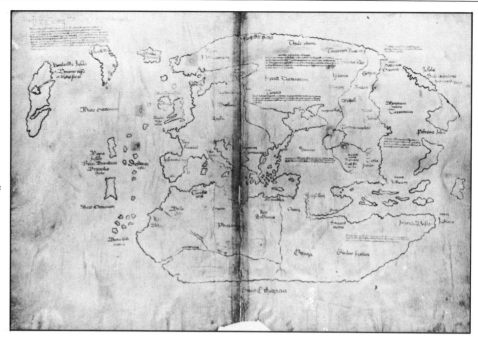

The Vinland map, right, is a medieval chart showing Iceland, Greenland – and Vinlanda Insula, in the top left corner. The mythical Fortunate Islands and St Brendan's Island are also marked.

THE LAND OF WINE

The History of the Archbishops of Hamburg-Bremen, by Adam of Bremen, which dates from 1075, describes the lands of the northern Atlantic known to the Scandinavians at the time. Writing of a conversation with their king, Adam recounts how a certain island got its name: 'He spoke also of yet another island of the many found in that ocean. It is called Vinland because vines producing excellent wines grow there.'

Vinland was the name given, probably by Leif Ericsson, to a new land he discovered in the North Atlantic around AD 1000. Ericsson's expedition was followed by a colonizing party who were excited by the prospect of such an abundant supply of 'wine berries', but it seems that they were to be disappointed; for, in the third year of the colonizing expedition, they complained that the wine banquets that had been promised to them had not taken place.

Final confirmation that Norsemen had indeed visited the New World came in 1963, when the ruins of what had clearly been a Norse settlement were discovered at the northernmost tip of Newfoundland.

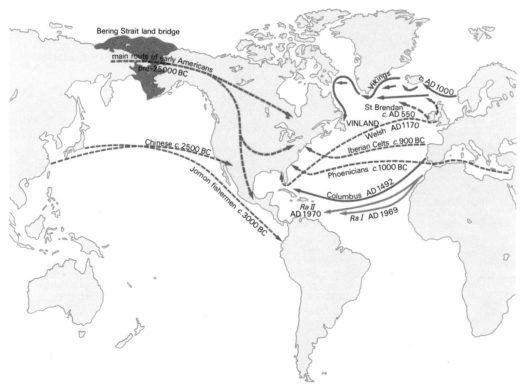

The map of the Americas, left, shows the route taken by Christopher Columbus in 1492, together with routes that may have been taken by other navigators. The routes taken by Thor Heyerdahl in 1969 and 1970 from Morocco to South America using raftships of papyrus reeds (Ra I and II) are also indicated. These expeditions were designed to test the theory that ancient people of the Mediterranean could have crossed the Atlantic and brought cultural influences to the natives of Mexico and Peru.

to court where he was greeted as the reincarnation of the Aztecs' fair, bearded god Quetzalcoatl, who had brought civilization 'from the sunrise', and then left, promising to return.

'Why,' Hitching asks, 'should a dark-skinned, beardless people worship a fair, bearded deity unless something of this sort had once been the living focus of their religious life?'

ARCHAEOLOGICAL MYSTERY

Quite apart from the folklore of the Americas and the archaeological finds that appear to have originated in other cultures, there are other archaeological mysteries of much greater proportions. There is, for instance, the evidence for the civilization that flourished along the Mississippi River – in the fertile area now known as American Bottom – about 1,200 years ago. Its capital was Cahokia, with a quarter of a million residents, and it flourished for 500 years. This civilization is believed to have equalled, if not surpassed, the great Indian cultures of Mexico and South America.

Writing about this civilization in *Fate* magazine in November 1982, Jim Miles observed:

A number of grass-covered mounds, such as those below, are all that is left of the city of Cahokia, close to Collinsville, in Illinois, USA. At its peak in the 13th century, the settlement covered an area of around 6 square miles (16 square kilometres), and some estimates have put its population as high as a quarter of a million. Archaeological investigations have revealed that the city appears to have been organized according to a formal plan, with ceremonial mounds, open squares, market places, workshop areas, burial grounds where the graves included those of human sacrifices, and segregated residential areas. When Cahokia was founded in the eighth century, its inhabitants were largely agricultural workers; but as the city flourished, labour became more specialized and trade developed. The finds at Cahokia indicate a level of culture unknown elsewhere in the United States. Among them are finely wrought arrow-heads, shown left, and the intricately carved stone tablet, below left.

'How it began and why the ancient civilization dispersed remain mysteries, but extensive ongoing study for the last quarter-century has uncovered the Cahokians' art, industry, massive mound construction and sophisticated astronomical knowledge.'

What has surprised the investigators is the Cahokians' extraordinary knowledge of mathematics at a level never before encountered in any so-called primitive society.

Among the remains of the Cahokians is the most extravagant ancient American grave ever discovered. The skeleton of someone believed to have been a ruler was unearthed in a grave together with the remains of six other people – who had probably been sacrificed to accompany him to the next world. The chief had been laid to rest on robes made of 20,000 pearls.

But to describe the Cahokians as a lost civilization would be wrong. They were visited in the 16th and 18th centuries by explorers who described their barbaric customs and the pyramid-style mounds that were a prominent feature of their settlements. What *is* lost is a satisfactory explanation of the influences that created the Cahokian culture. The truth is that the civilization of the so-called 'New World' may be far older than we suspect and – as the United Nations General Assembly discovered – many nations may be justified in claiming that they discovered the Americas .

" IS IT NOT SOMETHING OF AN EXAGGERATION TO SPEAK SO CONFIDENTLY OF COLUMBUS' LANDING AS THE DISCOVERY OF AMERICA? "

NOEL DORR

FEW PSYCHICS HAVE
BEEN AS RENOWNED
FOR THEIR WORLDLY
ACHIEVEMENTS IN THE ARTS
AND SCIENCES AS EMANUEL
SWEDENBORG. HE BECAME
INCREASINGLY FAMOUS
FOR HIS ODD ABILITY TO
LIVE IN BOTH THIS WORLD
AND THE NEXT, TOO

Of the rare breed of encyclopedic intellects who excel in every branch of knowledge they study, surely the Swede Emanuel Swedenborg (1688-1772) was the strangest. He was, for example, a scientist highly skilled in anatomy, chemistry, mathematics and physics. He was also a psychologist and psychoanalyst, a theologian, a linguist fluent in nine languages, a competent craftsman in seven arts, and the inventor of at least 11 contrivances that lacked only 20th-century technology to perfect them. He was a metallurgist and mining engineer, and prolific author of works that were translated into 30 languages. And not only was he a gardener, musician and poet, he was also a psychic of high quality and the inspiration for a new Christian denomination.

SWEDENBORG – MAN OF UNACCOUNTABLE TALENTS

Swedenborg's career as a scientist, however, came to an abrupt end in 1745 when he received a vocational 'call' to become a theologian. As the former, he had been a pioneer – anticipating, for instance, by inductive methods, some of the findings of modern nuclear physics. His theories about the workings of the brain have been confirmed by modern technology. Yet, long before 1745, he had shown a marked interest in religious matters and had mystical experiences that were harbingers of his future course. Swedenborg did not consider himself eccentric in looking for the seat of the soul in the 'spiritous fluid' that he believed to be the essence of blood; and he seems always to have been aware of the existence of his guardian angel.

His first recorded psychical-spiritual experience occurred in 1736. A state of profound meditation led to a lengthy 'swoon' that he said 'cleared his brain', giving him great powers of mental penetration – a process that was to be repeated at least once in his lifetime.

In the same year, he began to record his dreams. Again, he anticipated modern ideas – this time of dream symbolism – and saw a relationship between objects appearing in dreams and their counterparts on another plane. Light represented intelligence; heaps of rags, gross thoughts; and soldiers marching past his window, protection from harm. This was the beginning of his 'science of correspondences', which was related to poetic imagery but transcended it. An unpublished dream journal for the year 1744 depicts the struggle between Swedenborg's dependence on scientific methods and his growing interest in spiritual conceptions.

In April 1744, Swedenborg's first psychic crisis occurred. In bed, Swedenborg heard a noise as of many winds, was seized with trembling, flung on his face by an unseen power, felt a hand pressing his own – which were clasped in prayer – and beheld Jesus, with whom he talked for a short while.

A year later came his most important crisis. One day, after his typically indulgent midday meal, the room suddenly darkened, and the horrified Swedenborg saw the floor crawling with snakes and frogs. A man suddenly appeared in the corner, startling him by calling: 'Eat not so much!' Thereafter, Swedenborg's life became very much more abstemious. That night, the man reappeared, saying he was the Lord God who had chosen Swedenborg to declare to Mankind the spiritual content of the Scriptures which He would reveal to him in due course. That same night, the world of spirits, and heaven and hell, were opened to Swedenborg. From then on, he forsook the writing of worldly literature to deal only with spiritual matters.

From 1744 onwards, he produced a stream of theological works culminating, in 1771, in his great systematized theology *True Christian Religion*. From 1745, he claimed to be able to live simultaneously in this world and the world of spirits. His first awareness of spirits was 'by a sensation of obscure sight' and a consciousness of being surrounded by them. Later, he seems to have seen and chatted with them at will, and as easily and naturally as with living people, learning at first hand the conditions of the afterlife. The spirits themselves called him 'the unaccountable one', because he was the only human able to live at once in both worlds. He was a unique medium: it was not the spirits who entered his world, but he who entered theirs.

Emanuel Swedenborg (1688-1772), left, the great Swedish philosopher and theologian, had many talents including devising new ways of using metal in engineering works, shown below and bottom, as well as a host of other inventions that showed him to have one of the most enquiring and incisive of minds of post-Renaissance times. His gifts were not entirely academic, however, for he was also one of the most convinced – and convincing – psychics on record.

He developed a variety of psychic gifts, including precognition and prophecy. On one occasion, for instance, he predicted the death of a certain Olofsohn at 4.45 p.m. the following day, and, on a journey, that his ship would arrive at Stockholm 'this day week at 2 o'clock' – an incredibly short time for the voyage. Both these prophecies were fulfilled to the minute. He was also an automatic writer and 'direct voice' medium, taking dictation from spirits, although he destroyed his scripts because his mission was 'only to tell such things as flowed from God Messiah mediately [in due course] and immediately'. His powers of clairvoyance became legendary. He once told a mill-owner, with whom he was having dinner, that he should go at once to his mill, where the man found that a large piece of cloth had caught fire. On another occasion, he told a certain Dr Rosen, who had denied owning a particular book, its exact position on a shelf in Rosen's attic where the mystic had never been.

On Saturday, 19 July 1759, Swedenborg was one of 16 guests of William Castel at his home in Göteborg, 240 miles (385 kilometres) from

Stockholm. At 6 p.m., he left the company for a time, returning pale and greatly agitated. He announced that he 'knew' clairvoyantly that a great fire was raging in Stockholm, that a friend's house had been destroyed and that his own was threatened. Two hours later, he reported that the fire had been extinguished three doors from his home.

The following day, Swedenborg told the provisional governor how the fire had started, how long it had lasted and how it had been quenched. A messenger from Stockholm arrived on Monday evening and a royal courier on Tuesday – both confirmed Swedenborg's account in full.

There are many such stories about Swedenborg's remarkable powers. In 1760, M. de Marteville, Dutch ambassador to Stockholm, died. A year later, a goldsmith sent his widow a bill for a silver service he had sold the ambassador. Convinced that the payment had already been made, Madame de Marteville requested Swedenborg to ask her dead husband about it. This he did a few days later, when he met the ambassador in the spirit world. The latter promised Swedenborg that 'he would go

home that same evening and look after it.' It was only eight days after Madame de Marteville's interview with Swedenborg that her husband told her in a dream where the receipt lay.

SPIRIT CONTACT

Another famous incident occurred in October 1761. Augustus William of Prussia, brother of the Queen of Sweden, had died in 1758. The Queen, informed of Swedenborg's gifts, summoned him and asked him to undertake a mission to her dead brother. Three weeks later, the seer asked for a private audience with the Queen, whom he found playing cards. They retired into an apartment where Swedenborg told Her Majesty something confidential which he had sworn to keep private from everyone else. The Queen turned pale, tottered as if about to faint, and exclaimed: 'That is something which no one else could have told, except my brother!' When she emerged from her interview with Swedenborg, she was noticeably shaken.

On 17 July 1762, when Tsar Peter III of Russia was strangled in prison by conspirators, Swedenborg was at a party. A fellow guest noticed that, in the middle of the conversation, Swedenborg's expression changed and it was evident that 'his soul was no longer present in him and that something strange was taking place.' When Swedenborg came to himself, he described the Tsar's death at that very hour and urged the company to make notes of his pronouncements so that they might compare them with the announcement of the death when it appeared in the papers.

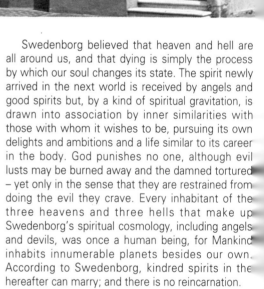

The Swedenborg Society headquarters in Bloomsbury, London, above right, *house a comprehensive library of Swedenborg's works, besides holding regular lectures on his extraordinary range of theories and beliefs pertaining to both this world and the next.*

The memorial plaques to Swedenborg, right, *are in the Swedish church in central London. In 1908, Swedenborg's body was removed from London to Uppsala at the request of the Swedish government.*

Swedenborg believed that heaven and hell are all around us, and that dying is simply the process by which our soul changes its state. The spirit newly arrived in the next world is received by angels and good spirits but, by a kind of spiritual gravitation, is drawn into association by inner similarities with those with whom it wishes to be, pursuing its own delights and ambitions and a life similar to its career in the body. God punishes no one, although evil lusts may be burned away and the damned tortured – yet only in the sense that they are restrained from doing the evil they crave. Every inhabitant of the three heavens and three hells that make up Swedenborg's spiritual cosmology, including angels and devils, was once a human being, for Mankind inhabits innumerable planets besides our own. According to Swedenborg, kindred spirits in the hereafter can marry; and there is no reincarnation.

What is to be made of a man with such convictions and eccentric claims? Contemporaries who knew him found him sane, sensible, of unimpeachable honesty, kind, generous, always agreeable, efficient in any work he undertook – but somewhat reserved. Jilted in his youth, he remained single though attracted by women, and this has led to the suggestion that his experiences were due to frustrated sexuality. All one can say is that many contemporaries who knew him well accepted him, and the phenomena, as genuine.